ANNOTATED EDITION

W9-AYG-507

Excel 2000

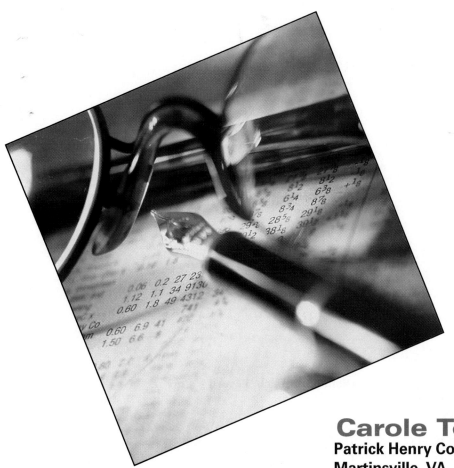

Carole Tobias
Patrick Henry Community College
Martinsville, VA

Glencoe
McGraw-Hill

New York, New York   Columbus, Ohio   Woodland Hills, California   Peoria, Illinois

This program has been prepared with the assistance of Gleason Group, Inc., Norwalk, CT.

Editorial Director: Pamela Ross

Developmental Editor: Michele Ruschhaupt, Thomas Cain

Copy Editor: Beth Conover

Composition: PDS Associates, Creative Ink, Inc.

Screens were captured using FullShot 97 For Windows from Inbit Incorporated, Mountain View, CA.

Glencoe/McGraw-Hill

A Division of The **McGraw-Hill** Companies

Excel 2000: A Professional Approach, Level 1 ("Core")
Teacher Edition
ISBN 0-02-805668-X

Copyright © 2000 by The McGraw-Hill Companies, Inc. All rights reserved. Printed in the United States of America. Except as permitted under the United States copyright Act of 1976, no part of this publication may be reproduced or distributed in any form or by any means, or stored in a data base or retrieval system, without the prior written permission of the publisher.

1   2   3   4   5   6   7   8   9   10   058/058   04   03   02   01   00   99

Microsoft, Microsoft Excel, and Windows are either registered trademarks or trademarks of Microsoft Corporation in the United States and/or other countries.

PostScript is a registered trademark of Adobe Systems, Inc.

Contents

If Your Students Aren't Familiar with Windows

If some of your students aren't familiar with Windows, suggest they review Appendix A: "Windows Tutorial." (Alternatively, if a large portion of your students is unfamiliar with Windows, you can review Appendix A in class.) For students who may need extra help, this Appendix refers students at appropriate points to Appendix B: "Using the Mouse" and Appendix C: "Using Menus and Dialog Boxes."

If Your Students Aren't Familiar with File Management

If some of your students aren't familiar with managing files in Windows, suggest they review Appendix D: "File Management." This Appendix covers files, folders, and paths, as well as the Windows Explorer. It explains how to perform eight of the most common file management tasks.

Teacher's Classroom Resources

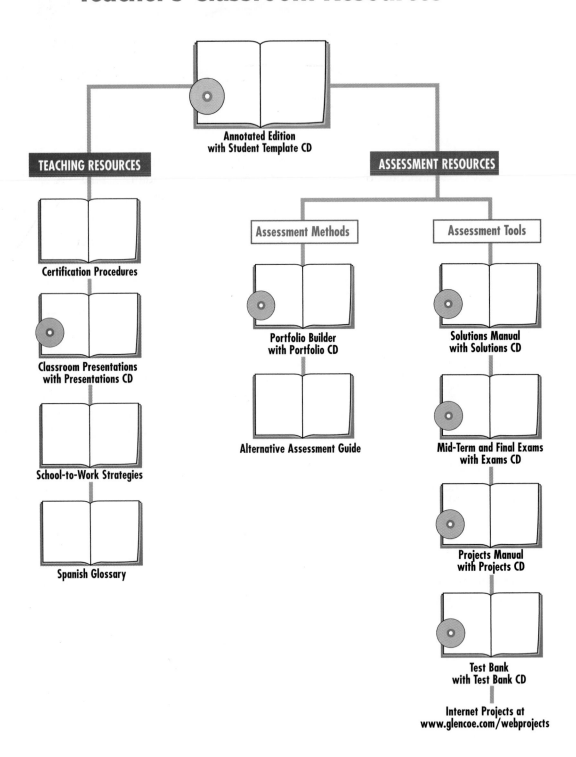

Annotated Edition
with Student Template CD

TEACHING RESOURCES

Certification Procedures

Classroom Presentations
with Presentations CD

School-to-Work Strategies

Spanish Glossary

ASSESSMENT RESOURCES

Assessment Methods

Portfolio Builder
with Portfolio CD

Alternative Assessment Guide

Assessment Tools

Solutions Manual
with Solutions CD

Mid-Term and Final Exams
with Exams CD

Projects Manual
with Projects CD

Test Bank
with Test Bank CD

Internet Projects at
www.glencoe.com/webprojects

Electronic Classroom Resources

Teacher's Classroom Resources

Annotated Edition

Your indispensable master guide. Exactly the same as your students' texts, plus teacher's notes in the margins that reference all the other Classroom Resources so you know when it's appropriate to use them. Includes a CD with all student files.

Certification Procedures

Describes the Microsoft Office User Specialist (MOUS) certification program in detail. MOUS Objectives are shown at the beginning of every lesson in the student text and are summarized in Appendix F of the student text. Now you can help your students gain this important certification.

Classroom Presentations

Meant for use in front of the class as you go through a lesson, each presentation lists the lesson's objectives and includes the screens encountered by students in the lesson. These PowerPoint presentations are included on a CD and provided with a booklet explaining how to integrate these presentations in your classroom.

School-To-Work Strategies

Outlines issues associated with the Federal Tech Prep/Applied Academics Reform Initiative. Describes programs and strategies for teaching students who will go directly into the workforce.

Spanish Glossary

Lists English computer terms followed by their Spanish translations and definitions.

Solutions Manual

Shows the solution worksheets for every exercise in the student's text and includes all the solution files on a CD.

Mid-Term and Final Exams

An exam is provided for every unit in the text. Exams feature both short-answer and applications components. Exams are provided in a reproducible form and on a CD, along with a key, solutions, Assessment Checklists, and a Certificate of Completion.

Projects Manual

A project is provided for every unit in the student text. Each project is provided in a reproducible form and on a CD, along with solutions and Assessment Checklists.

Test Bank

An easy-to-use test bank enables you to develop tailor-made lesson, unit, mid-term, or final exams. You can choose from an existing bank of questions, modify questions, or develop your own. Includes CD.

Internet Projects

Available on Glencoe's website.

Portfolio Builder

Provides help using the portfolio assessment method in your classroom.

Alternative Assessment Guide

Examines alternative assessment methods, including authentic assessment, rubrics, portfolios, and criteria-based evaluation.

The **Electronic Classroom Resources** includes all of the Classroom Resources on a CD for your convenience.

Using the Case Study

Many of your students won't have extensive business experience. They'll be learning a skill without a context in which to apply it. That's why the text includes a Case Study.

All the lessons relate to the clients of Kearny-Sansome Accounting, Inc., a fictional accounting company located in San Francisco, California. The worksheets and charts that students work with refer to clients of Kearny-Sansome.

The clients of Kearny-Sansome are also fictional. However, associating a specific company with a group of related worksheets heightens the students' sense of reality as they work in class. It also provides a rationale for some of the work they do on individual worksheets.

Review page 4 with students. This page establishes students as "interns" at Kearny-Sansome. Take time to discuss the three "foundation skills" and the five "competencies" identified by the Secretary of Labor (and introduced in the *SCANS Report for America 2000*.)

EXCEL CASE STUDY

EXCEL 2

Kearny-Sansome Accounting, Inc.

Kearny-Sansome Accounting, was formed in 1908 by a group San Francisco businesspeopl provide accounting services small San Francisco businesses tryin recover from the earthquake of 190 company has grown over the years, still focuses on smaller businesses.

CASE STUDY

There s more to learning a spreadsheet program like Microsoft Excel than simply keying data. You need to know how to use Excel in a real-world situation. That s why all the lessons in this book relate to everyday business tasks.

As you work through the lessons, imagine yourself working as an intern for Kearny-Sansome Accounting, a fictional accounting business located in San Francisco, California.

Kearny-Sansome Accounting, Inc.

Beginning a Lesson

Objectives
Key skills taught in the lesson. Each heading in the lesson corresponds to an Objective.

MOUS Activities
Lists the Microsoft Office User Specialist (MOUS) Activities that are covered by this lesson. The full listing of Activities for this important type of certification is provided in Appendix F.

Enhancing a Simple Worksheet

3

Estimated Time
Estimated time for a student to complete the lesson (up to the "Using Help" section, not including end-of-lesson Exercises). Especially useful in self-study and distance-learning situations.

OBJECTIVES

After completing this lesson, you will be able to:

Objective Note
A teacher's note indicates the number of the Objective corresponding to this section of the text.

M O U S
ACTIVI
In this lesso
XL2000 1.
XL2000 1.
XL2000 1.
XL2000 1.6
XL2000 1.7
XL2000 3.2
XL2000 3.5
XL2000 3.6
XL2000 3.8
XL2000 5.1

See Appendix F

e columns and rows.
lumns, and rows.
olumns, and rows.
and Redo commands.
enus.

7. Format numbers.
8. Apply to   d cell borders.

Heading
Each heading in the lesson cor-responds to an Objective.

🕐 Estimated Time: 1¼ hours

This lesson   ys to modify a w
cells, columns, and rows; changing th   deleting
played; and applying basic text, alignment a   ces dis-

Four-Part Teaching Plan
Teacher's notes in every lesson help you follow the teaching plan: PREPARE, TEACH, CLOSE, and ASSESS.

Objective 1

Selecting Multiple Columns a

As you learned in Lesson 2, clicking a row or
or column. You can also select several column   at row
                                                                 time.

PREPARE Point out to students that the learning objectives show what they will learn in the lesson. Each heading in the lesson correlates to a learning objective.
Required files:
USSales1.xls

TEACH Teaching Resources:
• Excel Classroom Presentations
• School-to-Work Strategies Manual
• Spanish Glossary
• Certification Procedures

77

Required Files
Files required in the lesson are listed, enabling you to make sure files are available for students in class.

Teaching Resources
Use this list to select among the Classroom Resources appropriate for the "TEACH" portion of the teaching plan.

Teaching a Lesson

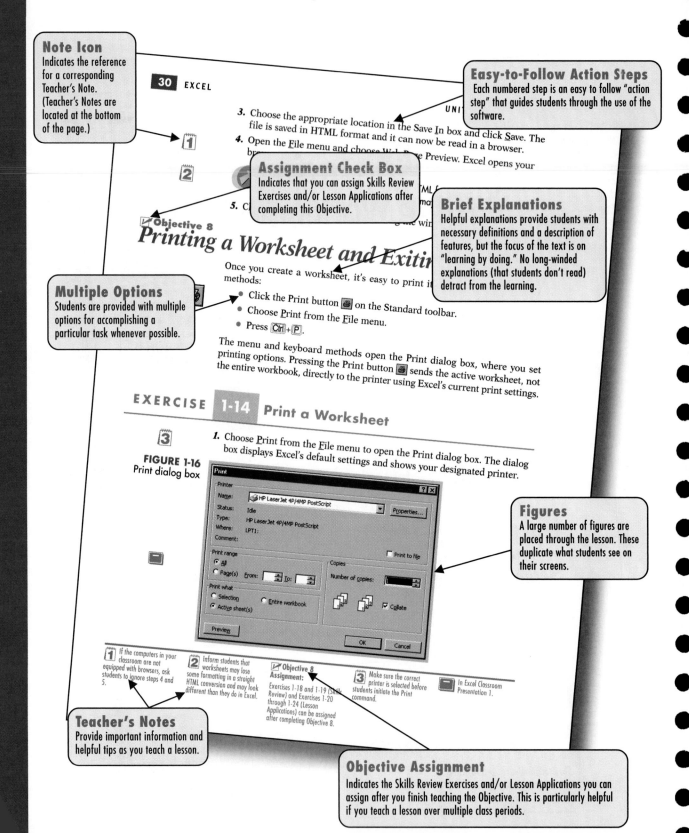

Note Icon
Indicates the reference for a corresponding Teacher's Note. (Teacher's Notes are located at the bottom of the page.)

Easy-to-Follow Action Steps
Each numbered step is an easy to follow "action step" that guides students through the use of the software.

Assignment Check Box
Indicates that you can assign Skills Review Exercises and/or Lesson Applications after completing this Objective.

Brief Explanations
Helpful explanations provide students with necessary definitions and a description of features, but the focus of the text is on "learning by doing." No long-winded explanations (that students don't read) detract from the learning.

Multiple Options
Students are provided with multiple options for accomplishing a particular task whenever possible.

Figures
A large number of figures are placed through the lesson. These duplicate what students see on their screens.

Teacher's Notes
Provide important information and helpful tips as you teach a lesson.

Objective Assignment
Indicates the Skills Review Exercises and/or Lesson Applications you can assign after you finish teaching the Objective. This is particularly helpful if you teach a lesson over multiple class periods.

---

30 EXCEL

3. Choose the appropriate location in the Save In box and click Save. The file is saved in HTML format and it can now be read in a browser.

4. Open the File menu and choose Web Page Preview. Excel opens your br...

5. C...

Objective 8
Printing a Worksheet and Exiti...

Once you create a worksheet, it's easy to print it... methods:

- Click the Print button on the Standard toolbar.
- Choose Print from the File menu.
- Press Ctrl + P.

The menu and keyboard methods open the Print dialog box, where you set printing options. Pressing the Print button sends the active worksheet, not the entire workbook, directly to the printer using Excel's current print settings.

EXERCISE 1-14 Print a Worksheet

1. Choose Print from the File menu to open the Print dialog box. The dialog box displays Excel's default settings and shows your designated printer.

FIGURE 1-16
Print dialog box

Teacher's Notes:

1. If the computers in your classroom are not equipped with browsers, ask students to ignore steps 4 and 5.

2. Inform students that worksheets may lose some formatting in a straight HTML conversion and may look different than they do in Excel.

Objective 8 Assignment: Exercises 1-18 and 1-19 (Skills Review) and Exercises 1-20 through 1-24 (Lesson Applications) can be assigned after completing Objective 8.

3. Make sure the correct printer is selected before students initiate the Print command.

In Excel Classroom Presentation 1.

Command Summary/Using Help

Command Summary
Reviews features taught in the lesson. Shows students three ways to accomplish a task: toolbar buttons, menu choices, and keyboard combinations.

Using Help
Teaches students how to use Excel's Help feature. Because software companies no longer provide extensive documentation (and because the documentation is often not available on the job), students must know how to use Help.

Class Presentation Icon
Indicates that a figure is included in a Classroom Presentation. Each Presentation lists the lesson's Objectives and includes all the screens encountered by the students in the lesson. Classroom Presentations are PowerPoint presentations intended for your use in the classroom.

LESSON 6 ■ RANGE NAMES AND SORTING

COMMAND
SUMMARY

EXCEL 195

FEATURE	BUTTON	MENU	KEYBOARD
Define Name		Insert, Name, Define	Ctrl + F3
Go To		Edit, Go To	F5 or Ctrl + G
Paste Name		Insert, Name, Paste	F3
Sort Ascending	↑↓	Date, Sort	
Sort Descending	↓↑	Date, Sort	

USING HELP

In this lesson you were given a tip on using the Label Ranges dialog box. To find out more about how and when to use this feature, ask the Office Assistant.

To find out how and when to use the Label Ranges dialog box:

1. Choose Show the Office Assistant from the Help menu. Click the Office Assistant to activate it.

2. Key **label ranges** in the text box and click Search.

3. Select "About labeling ranges using the Label Ranges dialog box." Maximize the Help window.

4. The Office Assistant displays information that shows you how to use the Label Ranges dialog box.

FIGURE 6-10
Labeling ranges using the Label Ranges dialog box

Microsoft Excel Help

About labeling ranges by using the Label Ranges dialog box

Specifying labels   When you select cells in labeled ranges to create formulas, Microsoft Excel can insert the labels in place of cell references in your formulas. Using labels can make it easier to see how a formula is constructed. You can use the **Label Ranges** dialog box (**Insert** menu, **Name** submenu, **Label** command) to specify the ranges that contain column and row labels on your worksheet.

Using dates as labels   When you label a range by using the **Label Ranges** dialog box and the range contains a year or date as a label, Excel defines the date as a label by placing single quotation marks around the label when you type the label in a formula. For example, suppose your worksheet contains the labels 1996 and 1997 and you have specified these labels by using the **Label Ranges** dialog box. When you type the formula =SUM(1997), Excel automatically updates the formula to =SUM('1997').

For more information about the options in the **Label Ranges** dialog box, click the question mark [?] and then click the option.

Tip   If you label a list by using the **Label** command and then zoom the view of the worksheet to 39 percent or less, Excel adds a blue border around the labels you have specified with the **Label Ranges** command on the worksheet. The blue border does not print and is not displayed when you zoom the worksheet view above 39 percent.

Additional resources

information and close the dialog box and the Office Assistant.

Encourage students to follow the steps in "Using Help" (with a blank workbook open). Software companies are increasingly using their Help programs—rather than documentation—to train users and assist in answering user questions.

 In Excel Classroom Presentation 6.

Concepts Review

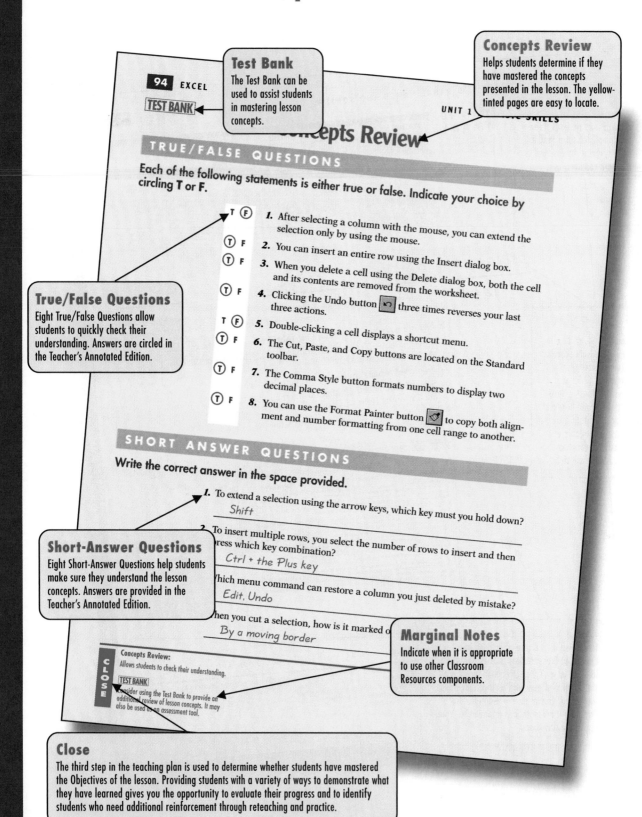

Test Bank
The Test Bank can be used to assist students in mastering lesson concepts.

Concepts Review
Helps students determine if they have mastered the concepts presented in the lesson. The yellow-tinted pages are easy to locate.

94 EXCEL

TEST BANK

UNIT 1

Concepts Review

TRUE/FALSE QUESTIONS

Each of the following statements is either true or false. Indicate your choice by circling T or F.

T **(F)** **1.** After selecting a column with the mouse, you can extend the selection only by using the mouse.

(T) F **2.** You can insert an entire row using the Insert dialog box.

(T) F **3.** When you delete a cell using the Delete dialog box, both the cell and its contents are removed from the worksheet.

(T) F **4.** Clicking the Undo button three times reverses your last three actions.

T **(F)** **5.** Double-clicking a cell displays a shortcut menu.

(T) F **6.** The Cut, Paste, and Copy buttons are located on the Standard toolbar.

(T) F **7.** The Comma Style button formats numbers to display two decimal places.

(T) F **8.** You can use the Format Painter button to copy both alignment and number formatting from one cell range to another.

True/False Questions
Eight True/False Questions allow students to quickly check their understanding. Answers are circled in the Teacher's Annotated Edition.

SHORT ANSWER QUESTIONS

Write the correct answer in the space provided.

1. To extend a selection using the arrow keys, which key must you hold down?
Shift

2. To insert multiple rows, you select the number of rows to insert and then press which key combination?
Ctrl + the Plus key

3. Which menu command can restore a column you just deleted by mistake?
Edit, Undo

4. When you cut a selection, how is it marked o...
By a moving border

Short-Answer Questions
Eight Short-Answer Questions help students make sure they understand the lesson concepts. Answers are provided in the Teacher's Annotated Edition.

Marginal Notes
Indicate when it is appropriate to use other Classroom Resources components.

CLOSE

Concepts Review:
Allows students to check their understanding.

TEST BANK

Consider using the Test Bank to provide an additional review of lesson concepts. It may also be used as an assessment tool.

Close
The third step in the teaching plan is used to determine whether students have mastered the Objectives of the lesson. Providing students with a variety of ways to demonstrate what they have learned gives you the opportunity to evaluate their progress and to identify students who need additional reinforcement through reteaching and practice.

Skills Review

LESSON 3 ■ ENHANCING A SIMPLE WORKSHEET   EXCEL 95

5. When you drag to insert cut cells, what symbol do you see while you drag
   to the new location?

   An I-beam

Critical Thinking Questions
Ask students to examine the way they work, to connect their learning with their experience, and to move outside the textbook into the real world for answers.

ow many decimal pl___
display?   mat numbers

   0 (zero

Skills Review Exercises
Provide guided practice for students, covering all of the Objectives in the lesson. Again, the yellow tinted pages make it easy for students to locate the pages they can use to review the lesson contents.

n which to
   Format

8. Which keyboa
   Shift + S

CRITICAL THINKING

Answer these questions on a separate piece of paper. There are no right or wrong answers. Support your answers with examples from your own experience, if possible.

CD Icon
Indicates that a file from the Student Template Disk is required for this Exercise.

ld a row of sales data for another product to an existing
ould you insert a row, or just selected cells? Why?
s formulas automatically after
ulas?

Exercise Overview
Indicates which lesson Objectives are reviewed in the Exercise.

Individualized Exercises
Exercises are "stand-alone," they do not require that students finish another Exercise in order to complete the current one. This means that you can assign Exercises individually, based on individual or class needs.

Skills Review

EXERCISE 3-18

Select multiple columns and rows; insert and delete cells, columns, and rows; and use the Undo command.

Guided Practice
When a new skill taught in the lesson is first encountered in the Skills Review Exercises, it is broken down into "a, b, c," action steps, ensuring that students practice the skill on their own.

1. Open the file **NWReps1.xls**.
2. Insert a cell to align the labels in column A with the data below by following these steps:
   a. Select cell A8.
   b. Choose Cells from the Insert menu.
   c. Choose Shift Cells Down in the Insert dialog box and click OK.
3. Insert a column by following these steps:
   a. Select any cell in column B.

' preferences,   Skills Review:
rch.   Provides guided practice for students. Objectives are   ◎ Exercise 3-18:
                                indicated for each Exercise.   Objectives 1–4
                                                                                         Required Files: NWReps1.xls
                                                                                         Solution Files: gl3-18.xls

Exercise Annotations
The CD icon appearing next to the Exercise number indicates that a file from the Student Template Disk is required. Each Exercise Annotation lists: Objectives taught in the Exercise, required files from the Student Template Disk, and Solution Files for the Exercise. Each solution worksheet is shown in the Solutions Manual. Solution files are provided on a Solution Disk included in the Solutions Manual.

Lesson Applications

Internet Projects
Projects related to the text are available on Glencoe's website.

Application Overview
Indicates which lesson Objectives are tested in the Application.

Lesson Applications
Provide independent practice for students and may be used for assessment. The Lesson Applications are arranged in order of their level of difficulty. The red-banded pages indicate to students that these are the more challenging Exercises used as out-of-class assignments.

28 EXCEL

UNIT 2 ■ DEVELOP

For Internet projects, go to
www.glencoe.com/webprojects

Lesson Applications

EXERCISE 7-13

Find and open a file, find and replace data, and spell-check a wo

Individualized Applications
Lesson Applications also do not "build." They do not require that students complete another Exercise or Application in order to work on this Application. You can assign individual Applications.

Correct and complete Beautiful Belle's cost of goods sol
second quarter.

1. Find and open **COGS2.xls.**
2. Key the values for fragrances as shown in Figure 7-11.

CD Icon
Indicates that a file from the Student Template Disk is required for this Application.

FIGURE 7-11

	A	B	C	D
15	Pacifica	6652	1665	9816
16	Taos	6654	4455	224
17	High Sierra	6698	4334	7358
18	Carmel	211	3669	10322
19	Santa Barbara	3983	1112	4983

Keying Text
Exercises often feature moderate text keying.

3. Use AutoSum and AutoFill to enter formulas that calculate monthly and product subtotals for the new data.
4. Replace the month labels "Jan," "Feb," and "Mar" with **Apr, May,** and **Jun,** respectively.
   Spell-check the entire worksheet, correcting any misspellings.
   Add the standard header with your name, filename, and date, and center the worksheet horizontally on the page.
   Save the workbook as *[your initials]7-13.xls* in your Lesson 7 folder and print the worksheet.
   Create a formula printout in landscape orientation with grids and row and column headings.
9. Close the workbook without saving it.

Challenging Steps
The Lesson Applications feature more challenging steps than the Skills Review Exercises. They do not provide "hand-holding" steps that tell a student how to perform specific operations.

Lesson Folders
Students save their work in Lesson Folders to teach good file management skills.

Lesson Applications:
Provide independent practice for students and may be used for assessment. Objectives are indicated for each Exercise.

○ Exercise 7-13·
Objectives 1, 3, 4
Required Files: COGS2.xls
Solution Files: gl7-13.xls in Solutions Manual or on Solutions Disk.

Becau
and o
file in a fold
other studen

Individualized Worksheets
Students save their work in an easy-to-use format that identifies the student and the Exercise. This allows students to retrace their steps if a they have a problem on a subsequent step. It also provides you with an "audit trail" to ensure that students actually work through the lesson.

Application Annotations
The CD icon appearing next to the Exercise number indicates that a file from the Student Template Disk is required. Each Exercise Annotation lists: Objectives taught in the Exercise, required files from the Student Template Disk, and solution files for the Exercise. Each solution worksheet is shown in the Solutions Manual. Solution files are provided on a Solution Disk included in the Solutions Manual.

Unit Applications

Application Overview
Provides students with an overview of what they will accomplish in the Application.

Unit Applications
Provide independent practice for students. Intended for use in student assessment. The Unit Applications are arranged in order of difficulty. The blue tinted, red-banded pages indicate that these are the most challenging Applications in the text, requiring students to know the content of the entire Unit. All the Applications (except for the last one) relate to the Case Study. The final Application, entitled "Making It Work for You," asks students to apply the skills learned in the Unit to their own lives.

CD Icon
Indicates that a file from the Student Template Disk is required for this Application.

UNIT 2

~~e workbook without saving~~
~~the workbook and save it as~~
~~the workbook.~~

UNIT APPLICATION 2-3

Use AutoSum and AutoFill. Create range names and
Sort data by salesperson's last name. Rename works
documentation, spell-check, navigate the worksheet u
headers, and print formulas.

Create a worksheet that calculates commissions for Beautif
west region and summarizes yearly sales, commissions, and
is, gross sales minus commissions.

Mini Case Study
Puts students' work in the context of the Case Study.

1. Open the file **SW.xls**.
2. In cell C15, use the AutoSum button to add the column.
3. Use AutoFill to copy the SUM formula
4. Create the name **rt** for th
   commissions due.

Portfolio Icon
Indicates that the completed document for this Application is suitable for use in the student's portfolio.

5. Create formulas using the
   calculate the commission
   columns, copy the formul

Individualized Applications
Lesson Applications also are "stand-alone," they do not "build." They do not require that students complete another Exercise or Application in order to work on this Application. You can assign individual Applications.

6. Create the names **sq1**, **sq2**
   quarter.
7. Create a formula in cell B17 that calculates the total sales for the year. Use names in the formula.
8. Create the names **com1**, **com2**, **com3**, and **com4** for the total commissions for each quarter.

Challenging Steps
The steps in the Unit Applications are the most challenging in the text.

9. Use the commission range names to create a formula in cell B18 that calculates the total commissions for the year.
10. Create a formula in cell B19 that calculates the annual net sales—that is, gross sales minus commissions—for the Southwest territory.
11. Select the range A5:J14. Sort data by last name, ascending.
12. Rename the Sheet1 tab **Commission**.
13. Rename the Sheet2 tab **User Information**.
14. Key the data from Figure U2-3 into the User Information sheet. Place the data in the worksheet so it is easy to read. Include formatting that might make it easy to read.

○ Unit Application 2-3:
Required Files: SW.xls
Solution Files: glu2-3.xls in Solutions Manual or on
Solutions Disk

The completed document for this application can be used in a student's portfolio.

Application Annotations
The CD icon appearing next to the Application number indicates that a file from the Student Template Disk is required. Each Application Annotation lists the required files from the Student Template Disk and solution files for the Application. Each solution worksheet is shown in the Solutions Manual. Solution files are provided on a Solution Disk included in the Solutions Manual.

Teaching Plan

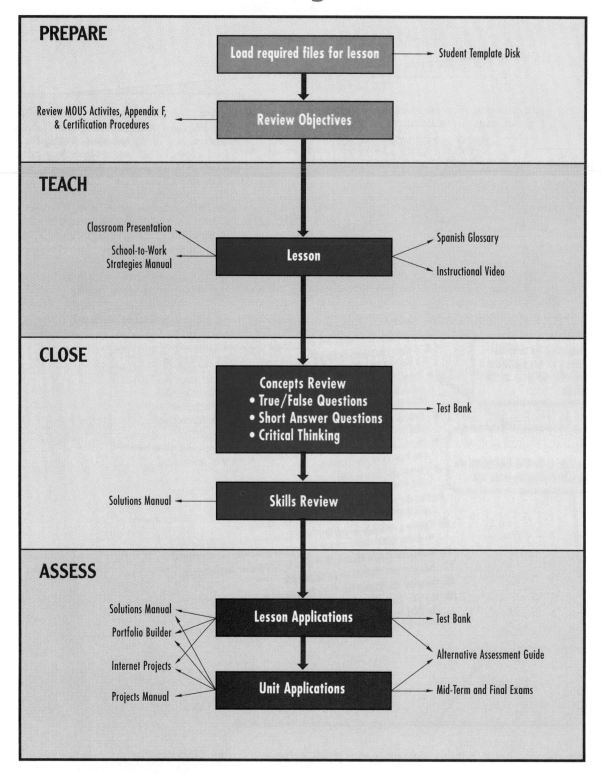

PREPARE

Load required files for lesson → Student Template Disk

Review MOUS Activites, Appendix F, & Certification Procedures ← Review Objectives

TEACH

Classroom Presentation
School-to-Work Strategies Manual → Lesson → Spanish Glossary
Instructional Video

CLOSE

Concepts Review
• True/False Questions
• Short Answer Questions
• Critical Thinking → Test Bank

Solutions Manual ← Skills Review

ASSESS

Solutions Manual
Portfolio Builder → Lesson Applications → Test Bank
Internet Projects
Projects Manual → Unit Applications → Alternative Assessment Guide
Mid-Term and Final Exams

One-Quarter Schedule

90-minute periods for 11 weeks, meeting 2 times a week, for 33 class-contact hours per quarter

UNITS	LESSONS	CLASS PERIODS
UNIT 1 **Basic Skills**	*1* What Is Excel?	2
	2 Creating a Simple Worksheet	1
	3 Enhancing a Simple Worksheet	2
	Unit 1 Applications	—
	Project 1	—
	**Exam 1*	1
UNIT 2 **Developing a Worksheet**	*4* Designing and Printing a Worksheet	2
	5 Copying Data and Using Toolbars	1
	6 Range Names and Sorting	1
	7 Spelling, Find/Replace, and File Management	1
	Unit 2 Applications	—
	Project 2	—
	**Exam 2*	1
UNIT 3 **Changing the Appearance of a Worksheet**	*8* Formatting Text and Numbers	2
	9 Changing Fonts, Patterns, Colors, and Formats	2
	Unit 3 Applications	—
	Project 3	—
	**Exam 3 (Mid-Term)*	1
UNIT 4 **Formulas and Advanced Printing**	*10* Using Functions	2
	11 Advanced Formulas	2
	12 Dates, Times, and Financial Functions	2
	13 Advanced Printing	1
	Unit 4 Applications	—
	Project 4	—
	**Exam 4*	1
UNIT 5 **Graphics**	*14* Creating Charts	2
	15 Enhancing Charts and Worksheets	1
	Unit 5 Applications	—
	Project 5	—
	**Exam 5*	1
UNIT 6 **Linking and Consolidating Worksheets**	*16* Working with Multiple Worksheets	1
	17 Linking and Consolidating Worksheets	2
	Unit 6 Applications	—
	Project 6	—
	**Exam 6 (Final)*	1
	Capstone Project: Portfolio Builder	—

*   Unit Applications, Projects, and the Capstone Project may be assigned for completion out of class.

**   A portion of the Exam may be assigned for completion out of class.

One-Semester Schedule

90-minute periods for 16 weeks, meeting 2 times a week, for 48 class-contact hours per semester

UNITS	LESSONS	CLASS PERIODS
UNIT 1 **Basic Skills**	1 What Is Excel?	2
	2 Creating a Simple Worksheet	2
	3 Enhancing a Simple Worksheet	3
	Unit 1 Applications	—
	Project 1	
	**Exam 1*	1
UNIT 2 **Developing a Worksheet**	4 Designing and Printing a Worksheet	4
	5 Copying Data and Using Toolbars	2
	6 Range Names and Sorting	2
	7 Spelling, Find/Replace, and File Management	1
	Unit 2 Applications	—
	Project 2	
	**Exam 2*	1
UNIT 3 **Changing the Appearance of a Worksheet**	8 Formatting Text and Numbers	3
	9 Changing Fonts, Patterns, Colors, and Formats	2
	Unit 3 Applications	—
	Project 3	
	**Exam 3 (Mid-Term)*	1
UNIT 4 **Formulas and Advanced Printing**	10 Using Functions	3
	11 Advanced Formulas	3
	12 Dates, Times, and Financial Functions	3
	13 Advanced Printing	2
	Unit 4 Applications	—
	Project 4	
	**Exam 4*	1
UNIT 5 **Graphics**	14 Creating Charts	3
	15 Enhancing Charts and Worksheets	2
	Unit 5 Applications	—
	Project 5	
	**Exam 5*	1
UNIT 6 **Linking and Consolidating Worksheets**	16 Working with Multiple Worksheets	2
	17 Linking and Consolidating Worksheets	3
	Unit 6 Applications	—
	Project 6	
	**Exam 6 (Final)*	1
	Capstone Project: Portfolio Builder	—

*   Unit Applications, Projects, and the Capstone Project may be assigned for completion out of class.

** A portion of the Exam may be assigned for completion out of class.

Excel 2000

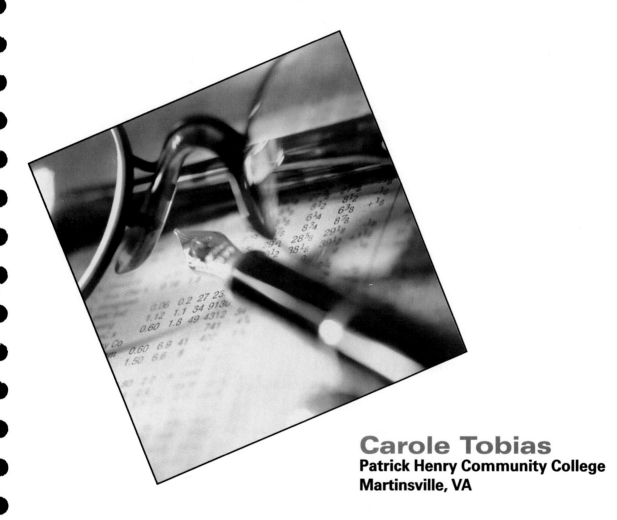

Carole Tobias
Patrick Henry Community College
Martinsville, VA

 **Glencoe**
McGraw-Hill

New York, New York   Columbus, Ohio   Woodland Hills, California   Peoria, Illinois

This program has been prepared with the assistance of Gleason Group, Inc., Norwalk, CT.

Editorial Director: Pamela Ross

Developmental Editor: Michele Ruschhaupt, Thomas Cain

Copy Editor: Beth Conover

Composition: PDS Associates, Creative Ink, Inc.

Screens were captured using FullShot 97 For Windows from Inbit Incorporated, Mountain View, CA.

Glencoe/McGraw-Hill

A Division of The **McGraw·Hill** Companies

Excel 2000: A Professional Approach, Level 1 ("Core")
Student Edition
ISBN 0-02-805587-X

Copyright © 2000 by The McGraw-Hill Companies, Inc. All rights reserved. Printed in the United States of America. Except as permitted under the United States copyright Act of 1976, no part of this publication may be reproduced or distributed in any form or by any means, or stored in a data base or retrieval system, without the prior written permission of the publisher.

1   2   3   4   5   6   7   8   9   10   058/058   04   03   02   01   00   99

Microsoft, Microsoft Excel, and Windows are either registered trademarks or trademarks of Microsoft Corporation in the United States and/or other countries.

PostScript is a registered trademark of Adobe Systems, Inc.

Contents

CASE STUDY

There's more to learning a spreadsheet program like Microsoft Excel than simply keying data. You need to know how to use Excel in a real-world situation. That's why all the lessons in this book relate to everyday business tasks.

As you work through the lessons, imagine yourself working as an intern for Kearny-Sansome Accounting, a fictional accounting business located in San Francisco, California.

Kearny-Sansome Accounting, Inc.

UNIT 2

Developing a Worksheet 113

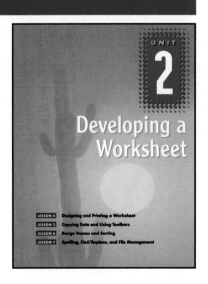

UNIT 2

Developing a Worksheet

LESSON 4   Designing and Printing a Worksheet
LESSON 5   Copying Data and Using Toolbars
LESSON 6   Range Names and Sorting
LESSON 7   Spelling, Find/Replace, and File Management

UNIT 3

Changing the Appearance of a Worksheet 241

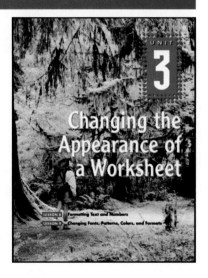

UNIT 4

Formulas and Advanced Printing   301

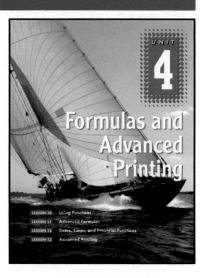

UNIT 5

Graphics   415

UNIT 6

Linking and Consolidating Worksheets

485

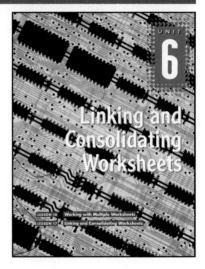

Portfolio Builder   P-1

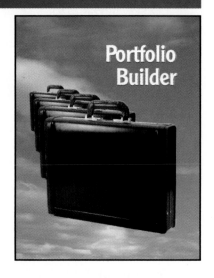

Preface

Excel 2000 is written to help you master Microsoft Excel for Windows. The text takes you step-by-step through the Excel features that you're likely to use in both your personal and business life.

Case Study

Learning about the features of Excel is one thing, but applying what you've learned is another. That's why a *Case Study* runs throughout the text. It offers you the opportunity to learn Excel within a realistic business context. Take the time to read the Case Study about Kearny-Sansome Accounting, Inc., a fictional business set in San Francisco. All the worksheets for this course deal with the clients of Kearny-Sansome.

Organization of the Text

The text includes six *units*. Each unit is divided into smaller *lessons*. There are seventeen lessons, each building on previously learned procedures. This building block approach, together with the Case Study and the features listed below, enable you to maximize the learning process.

Features of the Text

- ☑ *Objectives* are listed for each lesson
- ☑ Required skills for the *Microsoft Office User Specialist (MOUS) Certification Program* are listed for each lesson
- ☑ The *estimated time* required to complete each lesson (up to the "Concepts Review") is stated
- ☑ Within a lesson, each *heading* corresponds to an objective
- ☑ Easy-to-follow *Exercises* emphasize "learning by doing"
- ☑ *Key terms* are italicized and defined as they are encountered
- ☑ Extensive *graphics* display screen contents
- ☑ *Toolbar buttons* and *keyboard keys* are shown in the text when they are used
- ☑ *Large toolbar buttons in the margins* provide easy-to-see references
- ☑ Lessons contain important *Notes* and useful *Tips*
- ☑ A *Command Summary* lists the commands learned in the lesson
- ☑ *Using Help* introduces you to a Help topic related to lesson content
- ☑ *Concepts Review* includes true/false, short answer, and critical thinking questions that focus on lesson content

- ☑ *Skills Review* provides skill reinforcement for each lesson
- ☑ *Lesson Applications* ask you to apply your skills in a more challenging way
- ☑ *Unit Applications* give you the opportunity to use the skills you learn in a unit
- ☑ Appendices
- ☑ Glossary
- ☑ Index

MOUS Certification Program

The Microsoft Office User Specialist (MOUS) certification program offers certification at two skill levels—"Core" and "Expert." This certification can be a valuable asset in any job search. For more information about this Microsoft program, go to www.mous.net. For a complete listing of the MOUS skills for the Excel 2000 "Core" certification exam (and a correlation to the lessons in the text), see Appendix F: "MOUS Certification."

Conventions Used in the Text

This text uses a number of conventions to help you learn the program and save your work.

- Text that you're asked to key appears either in **boldface** or as a separate figure.
- Filenames appear in **boldface**.
- You're asked to save each document with your initials, followed by the Exercise name. For example, an Exercise may end with the instruction: "Save the workbook as *[your initials]*5-12.xls." Workbooks are saved in folders for each lesson after the first lesson.
- Menu letters you can key to activate a command are shown as they appear on screen, with the letter underlined (for example, "Choose Print from the File menu"). Dialog box options are also shown this way, and they appear in title case to increase readability (for example, in the Find dialog box, "Find What" rather than "Find what").

If You Are Unfamiliar with Windows

If you're unfamiliar with Windows 98, you'll want to work through *Appendix A: "Windows Tutorial"* before beginning Lesson 1. You may also need to review *Appendix B: "Using the Mouse," Appendix C: "Using Menus and Dialog Boxes,"* and *Appendix D: "File Management"* if you've never used a mouse or any version of Windows before.

Screen Differences

As you read about and practice each concept, illustrations of the screens help you follow the instructions. Don't worry if your screen is different from the illustration. These differences are due to variations in system and computer configurations.

Acknowledgments

We want to thank the reviewers of this text for their valuable assistance. We would particularly like to thank: Kathleen Anderson, Empire College, Santa Rosa, CA; Susan Olson, Northwest Technical College, East Grand Forks, MN; and John F. Walker, Dona Ana Community College (New Mexico State University), NM.

Installation Requirements

You'll need Microsoft Excel 2000 to work through this textbook. Excel needs to be installed on the computer's hard drive (or on a network). Use the following checklist to evaluate installation requirements.

Hardware

- ☑ Pentium computer with 32 MB or more of RAM
- ☑ 3.5-inch high-density disk drive and CD-ROM drive
- ☑ 200 MB or more of hard disk space for a "Typical" Office installation
- ☑ VGA or higher-resolution video monitor
- ☑ Printer (laser or ink-jet recommended)
- ☑ Mouse
- ☑ *Optional:* Modem

Software

- ☑ Excel 2000 (from Microsoft Office 2000)
- ☑ Windows 95 (or later) or Microsoft Windows NT Workstation 4.0 with Service Pack 3.0 installed
- ☑ *Optional:* Browser (and Internet Service Provider)

Installing New Features

While working in Excel, you may come across a file or a feature that requires installation. For example, some templates, wizards, add-in features, and Office Assistant characters must be installed from the Microsoft Office CD-ROM.

To install a feature:

1. Close all programs.

2. Click the Windows Start button, point to Settings, and click Control Panel.

3. Double-click the Add/Remove Programs icon.

4. Display the Install/Uninstall tab, if necessary.

5. If you installed Excel using the Office Setup program, choose Microsoft Office from the list of programs and click Add/Remove. If you installed Excel individually, choose Microsoft Excel from the list and click Add/Remove.

6. Click the plus sign to the left of an Office feature to expand the options. Click the down arrow to the right of a feature you want to add and choose Run All From My Computer. When you're done choosing features, click Update Now. Follow the onscreen instructions (which include loading the Office CD-ROM).

CASE STUDY

There's more to learning a spreadsheet program like Microsoft Excel than simply keying data. You need to know how to use Excel in a real-world situation. That's why all the lessons in this book relate to everyday business tasks.

As you work through the lessons, imagine yourself working as an intern for Kearny-Sansome Accounting, a fictional accounting business located in San Francisco, California.

Kearny-Sansome Accounting, Inc.

Kearny-Sansome Accounting, Inc.

Kearny-Sansome Accounting, Inc. was formed in 1908 by a group of San Francisco businesspeople to provide accounting services to small San Francisco businesses trying to recover from the earthquake of 1906. The company has grown over the years, but still focuses on smaller businesses.

Located in San Francisco's busy Financial District, Kearny-Sansome has clients from all across the nation, although the majority of clients are still from California. The company provides accounting, data processing, and consulting assistance to its clients.

Kearny-Sansome Accounting, Inc.
240 Montgomery St.,
San Francisco, CA 94101

Working As an Intern

You'll be working as an intern at Kearny-Sansome. This involves working with one client for a few weeks, then working with another client for a few weeks, and so on. Kearny-Sansome feels that it's important for new employees to gain experience working with a variety of clients before they begin working on their own.

Kearny-Sansome expects that any incoming employee will have a solid foundation of skills.*

• Basic Skills
Reading, writing, arithmetic/mathematics, listening, and speaking

• Thinking Skills
Creative thinking, decision making, problem solving, being able to visualize problems and solutions, knowing how to learn, and reasoning

• Personal Qualities
Responsibility, self-esteem, sociability, self-management, and integrity/honesty

In addition, Kearney-Sansome believes that the five competencies identified below are the keys to job-performance.

Keys to Successful Job-Performance*

1. **Resources: Identifies, organizes, plans, and allocates resources**
   A. *Time*—Selects goal-relevant activities, ranks them, allocates time, and prepares and follows schedules.
   B. *Money*—Uses or prepares budgets, makes forecasts, keeps records, and makes adjustments to meet objectives.
   C. *Material and Facilities*—Acquires, stores, allocates, and uses materials or space efficiently.
   D. *Human Resources*—Assesses skills and distributes work accordingly, evaluates performance and provides feedback.

2. **Interpersonal: Works with others**
   A. *Participates as a Member of a Team*—Contributes to the group effort.
   B. *Teaches Others New Skills*
   C. *Serves Clients/Customers*—Works to satisfy customers' expectations.
   D. *Exercises Leadership*—Communicates ideas to justify a position, persuades and convinces others, responsibly challenges existing procedures and policies.
   E. *Negotiates*—Works toward agreements involving exchanges of resources, resolves differing interests.
   F. *Works with Diversity*—Works well with men and women from diverse backgrounds.

3. **Information: Acquires and uses information**
   A. *Acquires and Evaluates Information*
   B. *Organizes and Maintains Information*
   C. *Interprets and Communicates Information*
   D. *Uses Computers to Process Information*

4. **Systems: Understands complex relationships**
   A. *Understands Systems*—knows how social, organizational, and technological systems work and operates effectively with them.
   B. *Monitors and Corrects Performance*—Distinguishes trends, predicts impacts on system operations, diagnoses systems' performance and corrects malfunctions.
   C. *Improves or Designs Systems*—Suggests modifications to existing systems and develops new or alternative systems to improve performance.

5. **Technology: Works with a variety of technologies**
   A. *Selects Technology*—Chooses procedures, tools or equipment including computers and related technologies
   B. *Applies Technology to Task*—Understands overall intent and proper procedures for setup and operation of equipment.
   C. *Maintains and Troubleshoots Equipment*—Prevents, identifies, or solves problems with equipment, including computers and other technologies.

* These skills and competencies were identified by the Secretary of Labor and the Secretary's Commission on Achieving Necessary Skills (SCANS). They are included in the report *What Work Requires of Schools: A SCANS Report for America 2000*, published in June, 1991, by the U.S. Department of Labor.

Your Clients During the Intern Period

ALPHA Pharmaceuticals

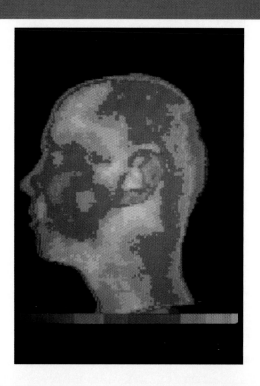

Alpha Pharmaceuticals

145 Bostwick Ave., NE
Grand Rapids, MI 49503
(616) 555-4698

Alpha Pharmaceuticals manufactures generic over-the-counter drugs, such as ibuprofen, acetaminophen, and aspirin, for large grocery and drug-store chains. You'll be helping Alpha Pharmaceuticals study historical data about pain relievers. Alpha's president, Mark Latzko, thinks that people are switching from aspirin to ibuprofen. Your worksheets will indicate if he's right.

Beautiful Belle Company

Beautiful Belle Company

103 Professional Center Drive
Santa Rosa, CA 95403
(707) 555-2398

The Beautiful Belle Company manufactures a moderately priced line of cosmetics. The company is currently promoting a product called "Sun Soft," a natural, hypo-allergenic lotion that has refined almond and sesame oils as main ingredients. Renata Santo, the Southwest regional sales manager, is test marketing Sun Soft in the Phoenix area. You'll be developing worksheets that track Sun Soft's sales performance against a competing product.

Clearey & Clayton

411 Fort Belknap Dr.
Roanoke, VA 24038
(703) 555-0371

C learey & Clayton got its start by producing scaled-down backpacks and camping gear for small people and children. They now produce camping gear such as backpacks, tents, and kayaks for people of all sizes. You'll be helping Bettina Clearey and John Clayton develop a promotional product list and an order blank for a mail-order catalog.

Dunkirk Canvas Company

7270 Mesa Drive
San Diego, CA 9211
(619) 555-8954

D unkirk Canvas Company used to make sails for boats. While they continue to make sails today, their fastest growing business is producing made-to-order canvas boat covers. In fact, the boat cover business has become so big, that the company now finds that it sometimes needs to use independent contractors to make some of their sails. You'll be helping Frank Bouchard and Mickey Finnegan computerize their business records and track independent contractors.

Harry Hascabar's Hand-Crafted Leather Goods

25529 Taylor St.
San Francisco, CA 94194
(415) 555-5895

Harry Hascabar has five shops in San Francisco that sell leather goods such as briefcases, shoes, and handbags. But Harry's first love is running. He's been making special running shoes for long-distance runners for over a decade—and now he wants to start a new company that will sell his shoes and other products for runners. You'll be helping Harry Hascabar create worksheets that present his unique experimental data in attractive charts.

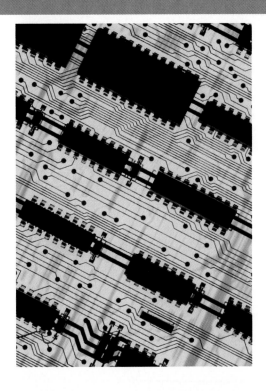

Feestone Electronics

17 New Rutherford Ave.
Boston, MA 02129
(617) 555-8700

Feestone Electronics is a nationwide distributor of business machines, such as cellular phones, fax machines, and copy machines. Each of its four regional offices writes its own invoices and keeps track of its own sales and inventory. They provide data to the central office each quarter. You'll be helping Craig Herman, the company's bookkeeper, put together a system that will use e-mail to consolidate data from all the regional offices in one worksheet.

Preview

As you learn Microsoft Excel, you'll produce professional worksheets similar to the ones shown below for the clients of Kearny-Sansome Accounting. By "working" as an intern at Kearny-Sansome Accounting, you'll gain experience that you can apply to a real-world situation.

ALPHA Pharmaceuticals

Drug Company Banks on Growing Pains

Alpha Pharmaceuticals manufactures generic over-the-counter drugs, such as ibuprofen and aspirin, for large grocery and drug-store chains. Because demographic studies are showing that the average age of the general population is trending upward, and since older people tend to have more minor aches and pains than younger people, Alpha anticipates that the pain-reliever business will grow steadily into the 21st century.

Alpha's president, Mark Latzko, has asked his market-research team to study the company's historical data to confirm his belief that people are switching from aspirin to ibuprofen as the pain reliever of choice.

Jean Brody, who heads up the market-research team, has requested the following information to fulfill Mark's request:

✔ A detailed worksheet showing sales of aspirin, acetaminophen, and ibuprofen for the past ten years in each of the four national sales regions, with a chart illustrating trends. **(Lesson 1)**

✔ A summary sheet showing Alpha's sales of each product for the last four years and projected sales for the current year. **(Lesson 2)**

✔ An attractively styled worksheet showing the five-year sales analyses developed in Lesson 2. **(Lesson 3)**

What Is Excel?

OBJECTIVES

After completing this lesson, you will be able to:

1. **Start Excel.**
2. **Change the active cell.**
3. **Navigate between worksheets.**
4. **Close and open workbooks.**
5. **Navigate within a worksheet.**
6. **Key data in a worksheet.**
7. **Save a workbook.**
8. **Print a worksheet and exit Excel.**

**MOUS
ACTIVITIES**

In this lesson:

XL2000 **1.5**
XL2000 **2.1**
XL2000 **2.2**
XL2000 **2.3**
XL2000 **2.6**
XL2000 **2.8**
XL2000 **4.1**
XL2000 **4.2**
XL2000 **5.5**

See Appendix F.

 Estimated Time: 1½ hours

Microsoft Excel is an electronic workbook that gives you the ability to perform business and scientific calculations effortlessly. It provides powerful charting, database management, and macro programming capabilities allowing you to produce professional worksheets and reports. Although Excel is powerful, it's very intuitive and easy to use. Once you learn a few basics, you'll become a productive Excel user very quickly.

Objective 1

Starting Excel

 There are several ways to start Excel, depending on your system setup and personal preferences. For example, you can use the Start button on the Windows

---

P R E P A R E
Point out to students that the learning objectives show what they will learn in the lesson. Each heading in the lesson correlates to a learning objective.

Required files:
Alpha1.xls

T E A C H
Teaching Resources:
• Excel Classroom Presentations
• School-to-Work Strategies Manual
• Spanish Glossary
• Certification Procedures

 Every computer in the classroom should access Excel the same way. You may want to give students a handout that describes how to access Excel. This is especially true in a networked environment.

FIGURE 1-1
Shortcut icon to
start Excel

taskbar or double-click an Excel shortcut icon that may
appear on your desktop.

 NOTE: Windows provides many ways to start
applications. If you have problems, ask your instructor
for help.

EXERCISE 1-1 Start Excel

1. Turn on your computer. Windows loads.

2. Click the Start button on the Windows taskbar and point to
Programs.

FIGURE 1-2
Starting Excel from
the Windows
taskbar

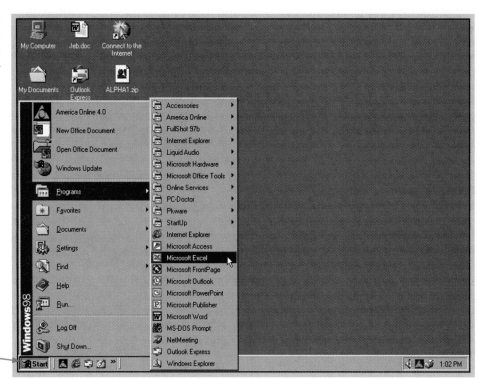

Start button

NOTE: Your screen may differ from the screen shown in Figure 1-2
depending on the programs installed on your computer.

3. On the Programs menu, click Microsoft Excel. The program is loaded in a
few seconds and the Excel window appears.

 Use Excel Classroom Presentation 1 to display
screens from the lesson in a slide-show format.

[1] You might ask students to create an Excel
shortcut icon for the desktop. To do this, right-
click a blank area of the desktop and select New,
Shortcut. In the Create Shortcut dialog box, use the
Browse button to locate Excel.exe. Look in the folder
Program Files/Microsoft Office/Office. Click the Open
button, the Next button, and the Finish button.

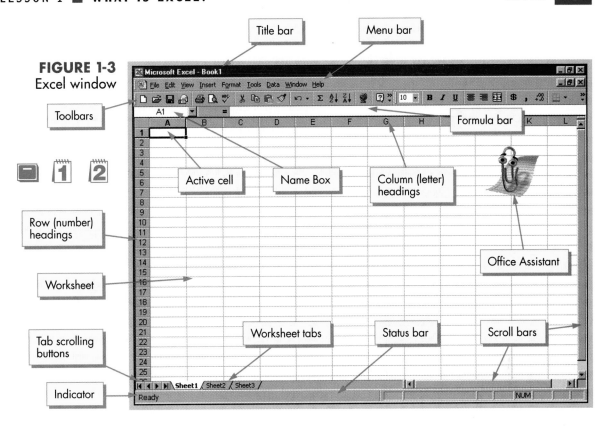

FIGURE 1-3
Excel window

TABLE 1-1   **Parts of the Excel Screen**

PART OF SCREEN	PURPOSE
Title bar	Displays the name of the workbook. The opening Excel window is always named "Book1."
Menu bar	Contains the menus you use to perform various tasks. You can open menus using the mouse or the keyboard.
Toolbars	Contain buttons you click to initiate commands. Each button is represented by an icon. Excel typically opens with the Standard and Formatting toolbars displayed in abbreviated form on one line.
Name Box	Indicates where data being keyed or edited appears on the worksheet.
Formula bar	Displays the formula in the current cell.
Worksheet	Area where you enter and work with data.

continues

 In Excel Classroom Presentation 1.

1 If students start Excel and the blank default workbook they see differs from the one shown here or does not open, instruct students to place Book.xlt into the XLStart folder on their computers. To learn more about this process, go to the following Help topic and subtopics: Default new workbook, Create a workbook template for new workbooks, and Default workbook template.

2 This book assumes that Excel was installed using the "Typical" installation and that it is running with default settings, including Arial set to 10 points and the Standard and Formatting toolbars displayed side by side. Your screen may look different than this and may show a different Office Assistant.

TABLE 1-1 **Parts of the Excel Screen** *continued*

PART OF SCREEN	PURPOSE
Column headings	Indicates columns on the worksheet. Columns are labeled with letters.
Row headings	Indicates rows on the worksheet. Rows are labeled with numbers.
Scroll bars	Used with the mouse to move right or left and up or down within the worksheet.
Tab scrolling buttons	Used to scroll between worksheet tabs.
Worksheet tabs	Used to move from one worksheet to another.
Status bar	Displays information about a selected command or an operation in progress.
Indicators	Displays modes of operation, such as NUM when the number keypad is on.
Active cell	Cell that is current—that is, ready to receive information.
Office Assistant	Provides tips as you work and suggests Help topics related to the work you're doing.

EXERCISE 1-2 Identify Toolbar Buttons

When you start Excel, the Standard and Formatting toolbars typically appear side by side below the menu bar. The Standard toolbar has a variety of buttons for controlling the file and manipulating data. The Formatting toolbar contains buttons for controlling your worksheet's appearance.

Only the basic buttons and those that were used most recently are displayed in the toolbars. To see more buttons for either toolbar, click the More Buttons button ⁞ at the end of each toolbar. To identify a toolbar button or any other onscreen button by name, point to it with the mouse.

FIGURE 1-4
Identifying a
toolbar button

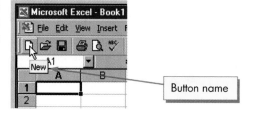

 The exercise assumes that Office Assistant is turned on. If not, you may want to point it out and turn it on now.

 Excel 2000 has adaptive menus and toolbars. The toolbars and menus contain basic buttons and commands, as well as the buttons or commands most recently used. The toolbars and menus change as students work in Excel. This can confuse students. Demonstrate this to the class.

 In Excel Classroom Presentation 1.

1. Position the pointer over the New icon on the Standard toolbar. This button opens a new workbook. The icon appears as a button when you point to it and a *ScreenTip* (a box with the button name) appears below the button. (See Figure 1-4.)

Standard toolbar

Formatting toolbar

FIGURE 1-5
Side by side
toolbars

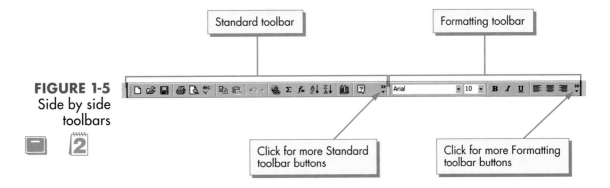

Click for more Standard toolbar buttons

Click for more Formatting toolbar buttons

NOTE: The buttons shown in Figure 1-5 and any other figure containing toolbar buttons may differ from the ones you see on your screen. Your computer may be set to display expanded Standard and Formatting toolbars on top of one another, rather than side by side.

2. Click the More Buttons button at the end of the Standard toolbar to see the rest of the toolbar's buttons. Move the mouse pointer over any button to identify it.

NOTE: Light gray icons are currently not available. Even if an icon is gray, you can identify it by positioning the mouse pointer over it.

3. Position the pointer over the Microsoft Excel Help button on the Standard toolbar. You may need to click the More Buttons button first to locate the button. Click the button to display the Office Assistant balloon. Notice that when you click (or "press") a button, its appearance changes.

TIP: Use the Office Assistant to discover quicker, easier ways to work. It provides Help topics and tips that can simplify and speed up your tasks. The Using Help section at the end of the lesson provides helpful information on using the Office Assistant.

---

1 You may want to have students move the Formatting toolbar below the Standard toolbar so they can see all the buttons. If you use this option, adapt this exercise to the expanded toolbars.

 In Excel Classroom Presentation 1.

2 Make sure students understand where the Standard toolbar ends and the Formatting toolbar begins. Also make sure they understand the need for the More Buttons button.

3 As students become familiar with Windows and moving among buttons, they may accidentally click the mouse button. They may also have this problem moving the pointer over menus. You may need to instruct students how to close a dialog box or stop a procedure.

4 Explain to tell students that the Office Assistant sometimes displays a small light bulb. This indicates the Assistant has a tip that may apply to their current worksheet activity.

4. Click the Microsoft Excel Help button 🔲 again to close the Office Assistant balloon. The Office Assistant remains on the screen.

5. Click the More Buttons button 🔳 on the Formatting toolbar. Identify the additional buttons, and then click in the worksheet area to hide them. Be careful not to click a menu option or toolbar button. If you do, click in the worksheet or ask your instructor for help.

EXERCISE ![1-3] **Identify Menus and Menu Commands**

Each item on the menu bar is an individual menu that contains a list of commands.

1. Move the pointer to <u>E</u>dit on the menu bar and click to open the menu. Excel displays a short version of the Edit menu with the most commonly used Edit menu commands.

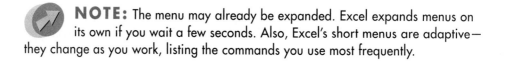

TIP: A menu shows commands with corresponding toolbar buttons and keyboard shortcuts. For example, you can save a workbook by choosing <u>S</u>ave from the <u>F</u>ile menu, by clicking the Save button 🔲 on the Standard toolbar, or by pressing [Ctrl]+[S].

2. Point to or click the arrows at the bottom of the menu to expand the Edit menu. Notice the additional commands on the expanded menu.

NOTE: The menu may already be expanded. Excel expands menus on its own if you wait a few seconds. Also, Excel's short menus are adaptive—they change as you work, listing the commands you use most frequently.

3. Without clicking the mouse button, move the pointer to <u>V</u>iew on the menu bar. Continue moving the pointer slowly across the menu bar until you display the <u>H</u>elp menu.

4. Click <u>H</u>elp on the menu bar to close the menu. You can also close a menu by clicking within the worksheet area of the screen or by pressing [Esc].

5. Click <u>V</u>iew to open the View menu. Without clicking the mouse button, move the pointer to the <u>T</u>oolbars command. The right-pointing arrow indicates a submenu that shows which toolbars are currently displayed. (See Figure 1-6 on the next page.)

6. Press [Esc] twice to close the submenu and then the menu.

1️⃣ Another way to expand a menu is to just wait a few seconds (with the pointer on the menu name).

2️⃣ Once a menu is expanded, all the menus are expanded until you choose a command or perform another action.

FIGURE 1-6
Displaying menu
options

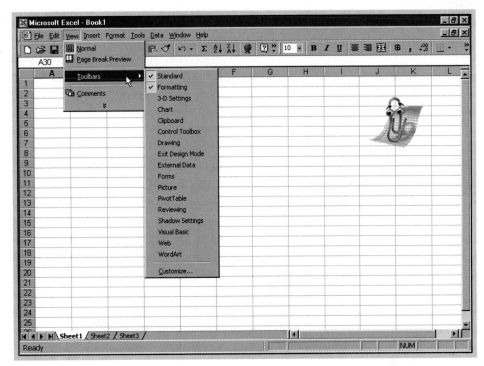

Objective 2
Changing the Active Cell

When you start Excel, a blank *workbook* named "Book1" appears, ready for you to create a new worksheet. The workbook contains three *worksheets* that you can visualize as pages bound in a notebook. You can add or remove worksheets from the workbook. A workbook can contain from 1 to 255 worksheets.

Each worksheet contains a grid that defines a series of rows and columns. A worksheet can use as many as 65,536 rows and 256 columns to store data. Rows are numbered. Columns are labeled A through Z, then AA through AZ, and so forth, up to column IV.

The intersection of a row and a column forms a rectangle called a *cell*. Each cell in a worksheet has a unique *cell address* that is determined by the column and row in which it is located. A cell address always indicates the column letter followed by the row number (for example, A1, C25, or AF14).

The cell that is current—that is, ready to receive information—is called the *active cell*. The active cell has a heavy border and its address is displayed in the Name Box.

In Excel Classroom Presentation 1.

1 The definitions of *workbook* and *worksheet* can confuse students. Make sure students understand the difference between these terms.

2 Point out that Excel numbers each new workbook in sequence with the current session. Students may discover their workbook is not "Book1."

EXERCISE 1-4 Change the Active Cell

1. Click in cell B3. It becomes the active cell. You can tell it's active because a heavy border surrounds it. The Name Box displays the address of the active cell, B3.

2. Press ⬇ twice. Notice that the active cell changes.

3. Hold down Ctrl and press Home. Cell A1 becomes active.

NOTE: Whenever keyboard combinations (such as Ctrl + Home) are indicated, hold down the first key while you press the second key. Release the second key and then release the first key. An example of the entire sequence is: Hold down Ctrl, press Home, release Home, and release Ctrl. With practice, you'll find it natural to execute this sequence.

FIGURE 1-7
The Name Box shows the address of the active cell.

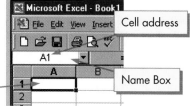

4. Notice that the pointer is a white cross. Point to cell A4 and click it. It becomes active.

5. Press ➡ five times. F4 is now the active cell.

6. Press Tab twice to make cell H4 active.

7. Press Ctrl + Home to return to cell A1.

Objective 3

Navigating Between Worksheets

To move between worksheets in a workbook, you can use:

- Keyboard commands
- Worksheet tabs, which also allow you to move to a specific worksheet in a workbook

EXERCISE 1-5 Navigate Between Worksheets

1. Press Ctrl + PgDn. The next worksheet appears in the window. The worksheet tab for Sheet2 is highlighted. The active cell is A1. (See Figure 1-8 on the next page.)

2. Using the white cross pointer, click cell B3.

---

1 Review keyboard combinations with students. Make sure they master this skill and understand how it is represented in this text.

In Excel Classroom Presentation 1.

FIGURE 1-8
Worksheet tab
Sheet2 is
highlighted.

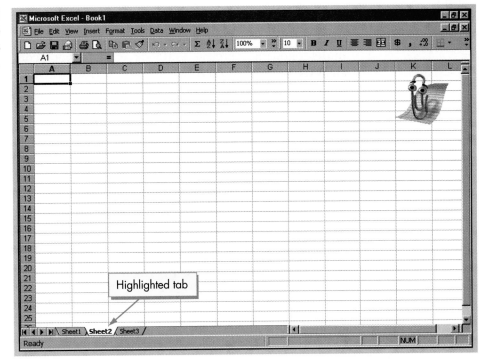

Highlighted tab

3. Press [Ctrl]+[PgUp] to return to Sheet1.
4. Click the worksheet tab for Sheet2. Worksheet 2 appears in the window again.
5. Click the worksheet tab for Sheet1 to return to worksheet 1.

FIGURE 1-9
Tab scrolling
buttons

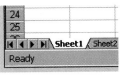

TIP: You can use the tab scrolling buttons to scroll between sheet tabs if there are so many worksheets that all of the tabs are not visible on the screen. For example, the First Tab Scrolling button ⏮ and the Last Tab Scrolling button ⏭ display the first and last tabs in the workbook. Note that the tab scrolling buttons only scroll the tabs. To open a worksheet, you can click the worksheet tab.

TABLE 1-2   **Keyboard Commands for Navigating Between Worksheets**

KEYSTROKE	ACTION
[Ctrl]+[PgDn]	Move to the next worksheet in the workbook.
[Ctrl]+[PgUp]	Move to the previous worksheet in the workbook.

 In Excel Classroom Presentation 1.

Closing and Opening Workbooks

☑ **Objective 4**

In the following exercises, you look at a workbook containing a 10-year sales analysis for Alpha Pharmaceuticals as you learn basic Excel skills. The worksheet is fairly large, showing historical data for Alpha's four sales regions and each of its products: aspirin, acetaminophen, and ibuprofen. Though it may seem confusing to you now, please keep in mind that this worksheet is an example of what you will be able to accomplish when you complete this course.

To open an existing workbook that's stored on a hard disk or floppy disk, you can:

● Choose <u>O</u>pen from the <u>F</u>ile menu.
● Click the Open button on the Standard toolbar.

In the next exercise, you use the Open button.

EXERCISE 1-6 Close and Open Workbooks

Before you open Alpha's workbook, you close "Book1," the workbook you were just examining. Normally, you would save the file before you close it, but since you didn't key any data in "Book1," it isn't worth saving. You learn how to save a file later in this lesson.

1. Click <u>F</u>ile to open the <u>F</u>ile menu. Click <u>C</u>lose to close the file.

NOTE: If no workbook is open, the workbook window is gray. You can open an existing workbook or start a new one.

2. Click the Open button on the Standard toolbar. You are going to open a file called **Alpha1.xls,** but first you must locate it.

3. Click the down arrow to the right of the Look <u>I</u>n box and choose the appropriate drive according to your instructor's directions. (See Figure 1-10 on the next page.)

TIP: The *Places bar* on the left side of the Open dialog box contains folders that provide easy access to files or folders that you placed in them or recently accessed. "My Documents" and "Web Folders" are folders created by Windows to help you organize your files. "History" lists the most recently opened files or folders. "Desktop" lists files or folders you want to open that are on your desktop. "Favorites" contains shortcuts to files or folders that you added.

☑ **Objective 4 Assignment:**
Exercise 1-16 (Skills Review) can be assigned after completing Objective 4.

[1] Make sure students know where files for this course are located. All files are included on the "Student CD-Rom." These files can be loaded on a hard disk or on a network. If it is not already done, all the files from the Student CD-Rom need to be loaded to a location where the student can access them.

[2] You can have students explore the folders in the Places bar, but guide them back to the directory containing the student files when they are finished.

FIGURE 1-10
Open
dialog box

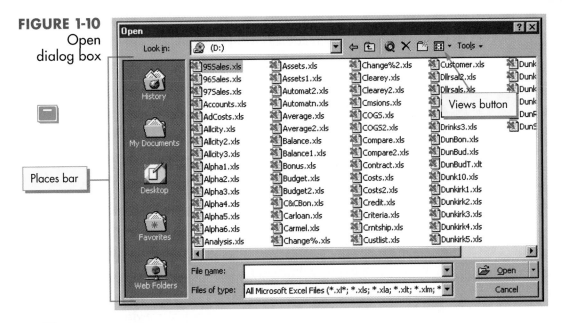

Places bar

NOTE: If file extensions are not visible in the Open dialog box, ask your instructor how to use Windows Explorer to change the View settings on your computer.

4. Once you locate the student files, click the arrow next to the Views button 🔳 in the Open dialog box to display a menu of view options.

5. Choose <u>L</u>ist to list all files by filename.

NOTE: Your files may already be shown in a list. You can click other views to see what they look like, but return to the List view before you proceed.

6. Locate the file **Alpha1.xls** and double-click it (you could also click it and then click <u>O</u>pen). Excel opens the Alpha Pharmaceuticals worksheet.

The Alpha Pharmaceuticals worksheet is formatted using shading, varying column widths, and several type sizes and number formats that will be discussed in later lessons. This worksheet provides an example of what you will be able to accomplish when you complete this course. This lesson provides an overview of Excel.

☑ **Objective 5**

Navigating within a Worksheet

As you learned when you changed the active cell, you can move to any location in the worksheet by pressing the Arrow keys. You can move to distant cells quickly using the scroll bar and keyboard commands.

In Excel Classroom Presentation 1.

1 Important: File extensions (".xls") are displayed in the figures throughout this course. If a computer doesn't show extensions, open Windows Explorer, choose Folder Options from the View menu, click the View tab, and make sure the following option is *not* selected: "Hide file extensions for known file types."

2 Stress to students that this worksheet is complex and provided here only as an example of what they will be able to accomplish upon course completion.

☑ **Objective 5 Assignment:**
Exercise 1-17 (Skills Review) can be assigned after completing Objective 5.

Notice that "Alpha Pharmaceuticals" appears in both the formula bar and the active cell. The cell address A1 appears in the Name Box.

EXERCISE 1-7 Navigate within a Worksheet Using Keyboard Commands

1. Press ⬇ four times. "National Sales Totals" appears in the formula bar and the cell address A5 appears in the Name Box.

2. Using ⬇ and ➡, move to cell C8. A formula that adds data in cells C17, C25, C34, and C43 appears in the formula bar. The formula result, 4.78, appears in the active cell.

3. Press Home. The active cell moves to column A in the current row.

4. Press PgDn to move down one screen.

 NOTE: The actual rows or columns that are visible vary from screen to screen, depending on the screen's size and settings.

5. Press PgUp to move up to the previous screen.

6. Press Alt + PgDn to move one screen to the right.

7. Press Alt + PgUp to move back to the original column.

8. Press Ctrl + ⬇ four times. Cell A17 is now the active cell. Each time you press Ctrl + ⬇, the active cell jumps to the edge of a group of cells containing data.

9. Press Ctrl + ⬆ three times. Cell A11 is now active.

10. Press Ctrl + ➡ once. The active cell jumps to cell K11, the last column in the table that starts at cell A5.

11. Press Ctrl + ➡ again. Column IV, the very last column in the worksheet, is displayed.

12. Press Ctrl + ⬇. Row 65536, the last row in the worksheet, appears. Move up or across the worksheet to get an idea of its huge size.

13. Press Ctrl + Home. Pressing this key combination always brings you back to cell A1.

14. Press Ctrl + End. The active cell moves to the cell in the last row in the last column that contains data or formatting instructions. (See Figure 1-11 on the next page.)

 NOTE: A chart showing Alpha Pharmaceuticals' sales figures appears at the bottom of the worksheet. Excel uses the numbers contained in the worksheet to create the chart.

---

1 Step 1 assumes that Cell A1 is active when the worksheet opens. If it isn't, tell students to press Ctrl+Home.

2 Students do not need to move all the way up or across the worksheet.

FIGURE 1-11
Cell K67 is
now active.

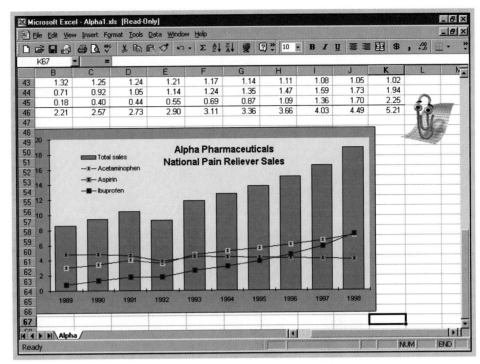

TABLE 1-3 Keyboard Commands for Navigating within a Worksheet

KEYSTROKE	ACTION
Arrow keys	Move one cell in the direction of the arrow.
Ctrl +Arrow keys	Move to the edge of a group of cells containing data.
Home	Move to the beginning of the row.
Ctrl + Home	Move to the beginning of the worksheet (cell A1).
Ctrl + End	Move to the lower right corner of the data in the worksheet.
PgDn	Move down one screen.
PgUp	Move up one screen.
Alt + PgDn	Move right one screen.
Alt + PgUp	Move left one screen.
Ctrl + Backspace	Move to the active cell if it is not visible on your screen.

In Excel Classroom Presentation 1.

EXERCISE **1-8** Navigate within a Worksheet Using Scroll Bars

You use the scroll bars to move through a worksheet using the mouse. When you use the scroll bars, the active cell does not move. You must click a cell to make it active.

1. Press [Ctrl]+[Home] to move back to cell A1.

2. Click the down arrow ▼ on the vertical scroll bar five times. The active cell scrolls out of view. The cell in the top left corner of the worksheet is A6. Notice that the Name Box still displays A1.

FIGURE 1-12
Scroll bars

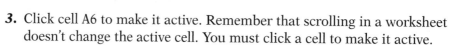
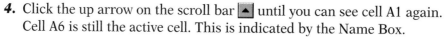

3. Click cell A6 to make it active. Remember that scrolling in a worksheet doesn't change the active cell. You must click a cell to make it active.

4. Click the up arrow on the scroll bar ▲ until you can see cell A1 again. Cell A6 is still the active cell. This is indicated by the Name Box.

5. Click the right arrow on the horizontal scroll bar ▶ six times to move to the right in the worksheet.

6. Drag the scroll box back to the left arrow ◀. Excel displays the column names that you pass over as you move to the left. Column A becomes visible.

▢ In Excel Classroom Presentation 1.

[1] Students may be unfamiliar with dragging. You might want to demonstrate how to drag and ask the students to practice.

TIP: To "drag" the scroll box, move the pointer to the box, hold down the left mouse button, and move the mouse.

7. On the vertical scroll bar, click between the scroll box and the down arrow ▼. Excel moves down the worksheet one screen (13 or more rows, depending on the size of your screen).

8. Click between the scroll box and the up arrow ▲ to move back up one screen in the worksheet.

9. In steps 4 through 8, cell A6 remained the active cell. Change the active cell back to cell A1 by clicking it.

TABLE 1-4　　　**Navigating with Scroll Bars**

ACTION	RESULT
Click up or down scroll arrow once	Scroll up or down one row.
Click left or right scroll arrow once	Scroll left or right one column.
Click between scroll arrow and scroll box	Scroll up, down, left, or right one screen (at least 9 columns or 13 rows).
Drag scroll box	Scroll a variable amount, depending on the distance you drag the scroll box.

EXERCISE　　**1-9**　　**Use the Go To Command**

You use the Go To command on the Edit menu to move to a specific cell address quickly.

1. Click Edit to open the Edit menu and choose Go To. (You may have to expand the menu.) The Go To dialog box appears.

FIGURE 1-13
Go To
dialog box

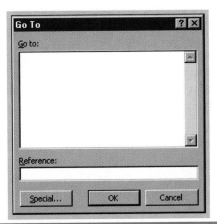

 In Excel Classroom Presentation 1.

2. Key **J17** in the Reference text box and click OK (or press Enter). The dialog box closes and cell J17 becomes the active cell.

 NOTE: Cell J17 displays the number 0.69, but notice that the formula bar displays the number 0.6869. The two differ because the number format for this cell is set for two decimal places. You learn about basic number formatting in Lesson 3.

3. Press F5, the shortcut key for the Go To command. (Ctrl+G also opens the Go To dialog box.)

4. Key **BX94** and press Enter. The active cell moves to column BX, row 94.

5. Press Ctrl+Home to return to cell A1.

 TIP: Go To maintains a list of the cells you moved to. You can select a cell from this list to return to it.

Objective 6
Keying Data in a Worksheet

In the following exercises you key data into the Alpha Pharmaceuticals worksheet.

EXERCISE 1-10 Key Data in a Worksheet

1. Click cell E17 to make it active.

2. Key **0.7023**. Notice that the Cancel button ☒ and the Enter button ☑ appear in the formula bar, indicating the formula bar is active. (See Figure 1-14 on the next page.)

 TIP: If you make a mistake while keying data, press Backspace to delete the error.

3. Press Enter. The numeric value 0.70 appears in cell E17 and cell E18 becomes active. Notice that the formula bar is no longer active because you have not keyed data in this cell.

4. Key **0.7193** in cell E18 and press ↓. The value 0.72 appears in cell E18 and cell E19 becomes active. Notice the change in cell E20.

 TIP: You can complete a cell entry by pressing Enter or an Arrow key.

Since this is the first time students are keying data, it may be helpful to review unique keys on the students' keyboard. For example, you might need to point out the Caps Lock indicator, the Num Lock key, or the number pad. Additionally, let students know that when they key cell references they do not need to capitalize the column letters. Excel understands lowercase letters and will substitute an uppercase letter for a lowercase one.

FIGURE 1-14
The formula bar becomes active when you key data.

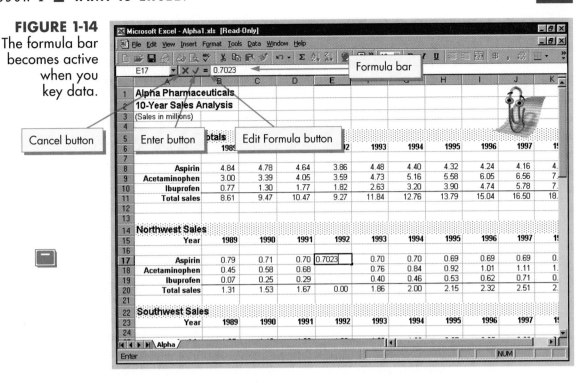

5. Key **3.941** in cell E19 and press Enter. Cell E20 reflects the new total, 5.36, which is the sum or total of the column of numbers entered.

EXERCISE 1-11 Change Data in a Worksheet

To change data in a worksheet, you move to the cell that contains the incorrect data, key the correct data, and press Enter or an Arrow key. The new data replaces the old data.

1. Press ↑ to move to cell E19.

2. Key **0.3941** and press Enter. The new corrected total is 1.82.

3. Press Ctrl + Home to move to cell A1.

Objective 7

Saving a Workbook

In Excel, workbooks are saved as files. When you create a new workbook or make changes to an existing one, you must save the workbook to make your changes permanent. Until you save your changes, they can be lost if you have a power failure or hardware problem. It is always a good idea to save your work frequently.

In Excel Classroom Presentation 1.

The first step in saving a workbook for future use is to give it a *filename*. In Windows, filenames can be up to 255 characters and are generally followed by a period and a three-character extension. Filename extensions are used to distinguish different types of files. For example, Excel workbooks have the extension .xls, and Word documents have the extension .doc.

 Throughout the exercises in this book, filenames consist of three parts:

- *[your initials]*, which may be your initials or the identifier your instructor asks you to use, such as **rst**
- The number of the exercise, such as **4-1**
- The **.xls** extension that Excel uses automatically for workbooks

An example of a filename is: **rst4-1.xls**

 NOTE: Filenames can include uppercase letters, lowercase letters, or a combination of both. They can also include spaces. For example, a file can be named "Business Plan.xls."

 You can use either the Save command or the Save As command to save a workbook. Use Save As when you name and save a workbook the first time or when you save an existing workbook under a new name. Use Save to resave an existing workbook as you key and edit.

Before you save a new workbook, decide where you want to save it. Excel saves workbooks in the current drive and folder unless you specify otherwise. For example, to save a workbook to a floppy disk, you need to change the drive to A: or B:, whichever is appropriate for your computer.

  NOTE: Your instructor will advise you on the proper drive and folder to use in this course.

EXERCISE 1-12 Name and Save a Workbook

1. Click <u>F</u>ile to open the <u>F</u>ile menu and choose Save <u>A</u>s. The Save As dialog box appears.

 2. In the File <u>N</u>ame text box, the suggested filename, **Alpha1.xls**, should be highlighted. Replace the filename by keying *[your initials]*1-12. You don't have to key the filename extension, .xls. Excel applies the extension automatically.

 NOTE: If file extensions are not visible in the Save As dialog box, ask your instructor how to use Windows Explorer to change the View settings on your computer.

1 In the text, students are told to save files using their initials and the exercise number. If using student initials presents a problem (if, for example, students with the same initials save files in a shared folder on a hard drive), assign a unique identifier to each student.

2 Emphasize the difference between Save and Save As. This concept is very important for students new to worksheet applications.

3 Tell students which drive to use when they save their files. Typically, students save their files on a formatted disk (the "student disk") that they use for all files in the class.

4 If the filename Alpha1.xls is not highlighted, you may need to instruct students how to highlight the filename by dragging over it.

3. At the top of the dialog box, click the down arrow in the Save In box and choose the appropriate drive for your data disk (3½ Floppy (A:), for example). Make sure a formatted disk is inserted in the drive.

4. Click Save. Your workbook is named and saved for future use.

FIGURE 1-15
Save As
dialog box

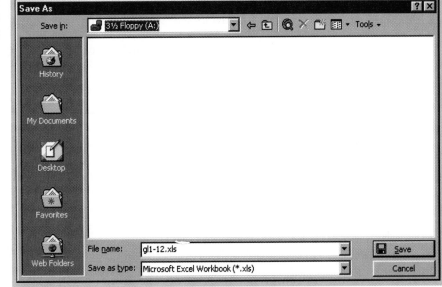

EXERCISE 1-13 Choose Another File Type

When you save a file with an .xls extension, you need to open and read the file using Excel. However, when you save a file using the HTML (*Hypertext Markup Language*) file format, anyone can open and read the workbook using a browser. This means that an Excel workbook saved using the HTML file format can be read by anyone with a browser, without opening Excel.

> **NOTE:** Workbooks saved in the HTML file format are often used to create Web pages.

1. Click File to open the File menu and choose Save as Web Page. At the bottom of the Save As dialog box, notice that Web Page is indicated as the file format in the Save As Type box. The file will have the extension .htm (which is short for HTML).

2. Key the filename *[your initials]*1-13 in the File Name text box.

> **TIP:** You can save only the active worksheet or the entire workbook as an HTML file by selecting either option beside Save in the Save As dialog box.

 In Excel Classroom Presentation 1.

 When it creates an HTML file, Excel saves all the files needed to view an HTML file within a folder. These are necessary for the worksheet to be viewed in its entirety in a browser or on the Internet. Make students aware that this folder will be present on their data disk.

3. Choose the appropriate location in the Save In box and click Save. The file is saved in HTML format and it can now be read in a browser.

4. Open the File menu and choose Web Page Preview. Excel opens your browser and displays the file.

NOTE: When you convert a file to HTML format and view it in a Web browser, be aware that some formatting may be lost.

5. Close the browser window by clicking the window's Close button ☒.

☑ Objective 8
Printing a Worksheet and Exiting Excel

Once you create a worksheet, it's easy to print it. You can use any of these methods:

- Click the Print button 🖨 on the Standard toolbar.
- Choose Print from the File menu.
- Press Ctrl + P.

The menu and keyboard methods open the Print dialog box, where you set printing options. Pressing the Print button 🖨 sends the active worksheet, not the entire workbook, directly to the printer using Excel's current print settings.

EXERCISE 1-14 Print a Worksheet

1. Choose Print from the File menu to open the Print dialog box. The dialog box displays Excel's default settings and shows your designated printer.

FIGURE 1-16
Print dialog box

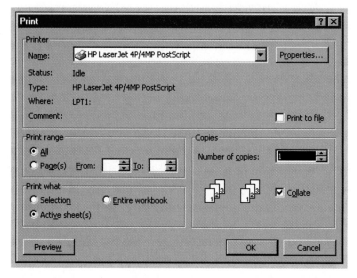

---

1 If the computers in your classroom are not equipped with browsers, ask students to ignore steps 4 and 5.

2 Inform students that worksheets may lose some formatting in a straight HTML conversion and may look different than they do in Excel.

☑ **Objective 8 Assignment:**
Exercises 1-18 and 1-19 (Skills Review) and Exercises 1-20 through 1-24 (Lesson Applications) can be assigned after completing Objective 8.

3 Make sure the correct printer is selected before students initiate the Print command.

In Excel Classroom Presentation 1.

2. Click OK or press Enter to accept the settings. A printer icon appears on the taskbar as the worksheet is sent to the printer.

 TIP: To print all worksheets in the workbook, you would click the Entire Workbook option in the Print dialog box under Print What.

EXERCISE 1-15 Close a Workbook and Exit Excel

When you finish working with a workbook and save it, you can close it and open another workbook or you can exit Excel.

The easiest ways to close a workbook and to exit Excel include using:

FIGURE 1-17
Close buttons

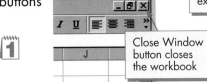

- The Close Window button ☒ in the upper right corner of the workbook window and the Close button ☒ in the upper right corner of the Excel window.

- The File menu. You already learned how to close a workbook using Close. To exit Excel, choose Exit. Closing Excel is the same thing as exiting Excel.

- Keyboard shortcuts. Ctrl+W closes a workbook and Alt+F4 exits Excel.

☒ **1.** Click the Close Window button ☒ to close the workbook.

2. Click the Close button ☒ to exit Excel and display the Windows desktop.

COMMAND SUMMARY

FEATURE	BUTTON	MENU	KEYBOARD
Save	🖫	File, Save	Ctrl+S
Print	🖨	File, Print	Ctrl+P
Go to a specified address		Edit, Go To	F5 or Ctrl+G
Close current workbook	☒	File, Close	Ctrl+W
Exit Excel	☒	File, Exit	Alt+F4

In Excel Classroom Presentation 1.

1 The Close buttons are the easiest way to close a document or exit the program. Emphasize to students that the top Close button closes Excel and the bottom button closes the workbook window.

2 Point out that the Command Summary lists a variety of ways to accomplish a specific task. Students can decide which method they prefer.

USING HELP

 The Office Assistant is your guide to Excel online Help. The Office Assistant provides tips based on the kind of work you're doing and directs you to relevant Help topics. It may also amuse you with its animated movements. If you find it annoying, you can hide it or choose another character.

Get acquainted with the Office Assistant:

1. Start Excel, if necessary.

2. Click the Office Assistant figure. If the Office Assistant is hidden, press F1. A balloon appears with the question "What would you like to do?"

3. Key **use office assistant** in the text box and click Search. The Office Assistant locates Help topics related to the text you keyed.

FIGURE 1-18
Using Office
Assistant

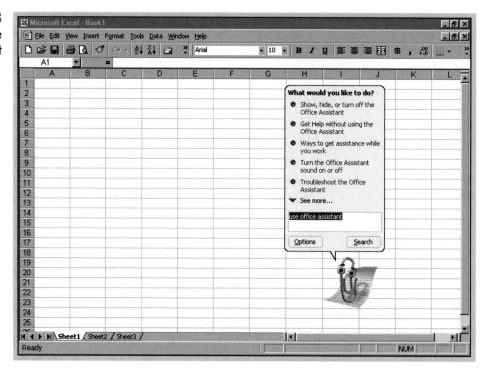

4. Review the displayed topics and click "See more" to display additional related topics.

5. Click "See previous" and then click the topic "Ways to get assistance while you work." A Microsoft Excel Help window with the same topic name is displayed beside the Excel window.

6. Scroll the Help window to review its contents.

7. Click the window's Close button to close Help.

Encourage students to follow the steps in "Using Help" (with a blank document open). Software companies are increasingly using their Help programs—rather than paper-based documentation—to train users and assist in answering questions.

Show students how to hide the Office Assistant by right-clicking it and choosing Hide from the shortcut menu. You might also show them how to choose another character: right-click the Office Assistant, click Choose Assistant, and then click the Gallery tab. Not all Office Assistant characters are installed with a Typical installation.

In Excel Classroom Presentation 1.

TEST BANK

Concepts Review

TRUE/FALSE QUESTIONS

Each of the following questions is either true or false. Indicate your choice by circling **T** or **F**.

T **(F)**   *1.* There is only one way to start Excel.

T **(F)**   *2.* The Standard toolbar indicates the location of data being keyed in the active cell.

(T) F   *3.* The default number of worksheets in a workbook is 3.

(T) F   *4.* PgDn moves one screen down.

T **(F)**   *5.* Columns are numbered and rows are labeled with letters.

(T) F   *6.* The address of the active cell is displayed in the Name Box.

(T) F   *7.* Scrolling with the scroll bar doesn't change the active cell.

T **(F)**   *8.* Moving to a cell using the Go To dialog box doesn't change the active cell.

SHORT ANSWER QUESTIONS

Write the correct answer in the space provided.

1. What is the name of the area on the screen that displays information about a selected command or an operation in progress?

Status bar

2. What is the name of the rectangle formed by the intersection of a row and a column?

Cell

3. What is the name of the area within a worksheet that is current, or ready to receive information?

Active cell

4. Which keyboard command moves you to the beginning of a row?

Home

5. Which keyboard command moves to the beginning of a worksheet (cell A1)?

Ctrl+Home

Concepts Review:
Allows students to check their understanding.

TEST BANK
Consider using the Test Bank to provide an additional review of lesson concepts. It may also be used as an assessment tool.

CLOSE

6. What command allows you to move to a specific cell address quickly?

Go To

7. Which filename extension is used for Excel workbooks?

.xls

8. Which filename extension is used for HTML files?

.htm

CRITICAL THINKING

Answer these questions on a separate piece of paper. There are no right or wrong answers. Support your answer with examples from your own experience, if possible.

1. What advantages would a worksheet program like Excel offer for a business compared with a noncomputerized pencil and paper worksheet? What advantages for an individual?

2. Excel allows great flexibility when naming files. Many businesses and individuals establish their own rules for naming files. What kinds of rules would you recommend for naming files in a business? For personal use?

Skills Review

EXERCISE 1-16

Start Excel, change the active cell, navigate between worksheets, and close the workbook without saving it.

1. Start Excel, if necessary, by following these steps:
   a. Click the Start button [Start] on the Windows taskbar.
   b. Point to Programs and click Microsoft Excel.

2. Use the Arrow keys to change the active cell to AB15 by following these steps:
   a. Press [↓] until the active cell is A15.
   b. Press [→] until the active cell is AB15.

3. Change to Sheet3 by pressing [Ctrl]+[PgDn] twice.

4. Make D5 the active cell.

Critical Thinking Questions:
Answers will vary based on students' preferences, observations, experiences, and research.

Skills Review:
Provides guided practice for students. Objectives are indicated for each Exercise.

Exercise 1-16:
Objectives 1–4
Required Files: None
Solution Files: No files saved.

5. Use the mouse to make Sheet1 the current worksheet by following these steps:

    a. Move the pointer over the Sheet1 tab.

    b. Click the worksheet tab for Sheet1.

6. Change the active cell to A1 by pressing Ctrl + Home .

7. Close the workbook by clicking the Close Window button ✖. (You don't save this workbook.)

EXERCISE 1-17

Open a file, change the active cell, and use keyboard commands to navigate within the worksheet.

1. Open the file **Alpha1.xls** by following these steps:

    a. Click the Open button 🖻 on the Standard toolbar.

    b. Locate the file in the Look In box.

    c. Double-click the file **Alpha1.xls**.

2. Use ↓ and → to move to cell K19.

3. Return to cell A1 by pressing Ctrl + Home .

4. Press PgDn three times to move down three screens.

5. Press PgUp twice to move up two screens.

6. Press Alt + PgDn two times to move two screens to the right.

7. Press Alt + PgUp once to move one screen to the left.

8. Use ↑ and ← to make cell I17 active.

9. Press Ctrl + → to move to the last column in this group of cells.

10. Press Ctrl + ↓ to move to the last row in this group of cells.

11. Press Ctrl + End to move to the last cell in the last row that contains data or formatting instructions.

12. Press Ctrl + ↑ . The active cell jumps to the edge of the previous group of cells containing data.

13. Press Ctrl + ↑ two more times. K41 becomes the active cell.

14. Return to cell A1.

15. Close the workbook without saving it.

EXERCISE 1-18

Open a file, change the active cell, use the scroll bars and the Go To Command to navigate within the worksheet, key data, print a worksheet, and save and close the workbook.

1. Open the file **Alpha1.xls**.

 Exercise 1-17:
Objectives 2, 4, 5
Required Files: Alpha1.xls
Solution Files: No files saved.

◉ Exercise 1-18:
Objectives 2, 4–8
Required Files: Alpha1.xls
Solution Files: gl1-18.xls in Solutions Manual or on Solutions Disk.

2. Make cell A1 active (if it isn't already).

3. Click the down arrow on the vertical scroll bar seven times to scroll down seven rows.

4. Click the right arrow on the horizontal scroll bar eight times to scroll eight columns to the right.

5. Drag the scroll box on the horizontal scroll bar to the left so the first column becomes visible again.

6. On the vertical scroll bar, click between the scroll box and the down arrow to move down one screen.

7. Use the Go To command by performing the following steps:
   a. Press F5.
   b. Key **E17** in the Reference box and click OK.

8. Key **0.59** and press Enter.

9. Key **0.55** in cell E18, press ↓, key **0.78** in cell E19, and press Enter.

10. Return to cell A1.

11. Save the file by following these steps:
   a. Choose Save As from the File menu.
   b. In the File Name box, key *[your initials]*1-18
   c. If necessary, change the drive to your data disk by clicking the down arrow in the Save In drop-down list and choosing the appropriate drive.
   d. Click Save.

12. Print your worksheet by following these steps:
   a. Choose Print from the File menu.
   b. Click OK.

13. Close the workbook.

EXERCISE 1-19

Change the active cell, open an existing file, navigate within a worksheet, change data, print a worksheet, save the workbook in different file formats, and close Excel.

1. Open the file **Alpha3.xls**.

2. Change the data as shown in Figure 1-19 by following these steps:
   a. Make the cell containing data you want to change active.
   b. Key the new data.
   c. Move to another cell or press Enter.

● Exercise 1-19:
Objectives 2, 4–8
Required Files: Alpha3.xls
Solution Files: gl1-19.xls and gl1-19.htm in Solutions
Manual or on Solutions Disk.

FIGURE 1-19

Salesperson	Qtr 1	Qtr 2	Qtr 3	Qtr 4	Total	% of Total
Robert Johnson	*65.3*	*62.7*	*58.6*	*52.9*		
Ewald Rhiner	61.0	65.5	70.1	75.3	271.9	10.0%
~~Ruth Seuratadot~~	~~81.7~~	~~60.7~~	~~54.0~~	~~47.3~~	243.7	9.0%
Buster Manatee	50.8	56.1	57.5	58.5	222.9	8.2%
Jose Garcia	75.2	77.9	72.4	73.8	299.3	11.0%
Colleen Masterhouse	65.3	70.9	54.6	74.5	265.3	9.8%
Anthony Chen	88.5	74.6	66.4	68.9	298.4	11.0%
Elouise Swift	66.7	73.9	64.7	69.9	275.2	10.1%
~~Lloyd Polaski~~	~~87.5~~	~~42.3~~	~~57.6~~	~~50.3~~	237.7	8.7%
Murray Diamond	61.0	65.8	74.6	74.2	275.6	10.1%
Barbara Bloomberg	70.0	87.7	82.3	90.2	330.2	12.1%
Richard Daniels	*53.1*	*51.1*	*56.7*	*72.8*		

These will change automatically

3. Press Ctrl+Home to return to cell A1.

4. Save the workbook as *[your initials]*1-19.xls.

5. Click the Print button 🖨 on the Standard toolbar to print the worksheet.

 NOTE: This worksheet should print with gridlines to give a different worksheet appearance.

6. Save the workbook as an HTML file by following these steps:

   a. Choose File, Save As Web Page. (You may have to extend the menu.)

   b. Verify that the filename is *[your initials]*1-19.htm in the File Name box.

   c. Choose the appropriate location in the Save In box, if necessary.

   d. Click Save.

7. Close the workbook and close Excel by following these steps:

   a. Choose Close from the File menu.

   b. Click the Close button ✖ in the upper right corner of the Excel Window.

---

1 This figure contains proofreading marks. You may want to review Appendix F: "Proofreaders' Marks" with students.

2 The worksheet prints with gridlines turned on. Emphasize that this is not a default setting, but is used here to show an alternate spreadsheet look.

ASSESS

Assessment Resources:
- Solutions Manual
- Test Bank
- Portfolio Builder
- Internet Projects
- Alternative Assessment Guide
- Certification Procedures

For Internet projects, go to
www.glencoe.com/webprojects

Lesson Applications

Start Excel, open an existing file, change the active cell, enter data, use the Save As command, print the worksheet, and close the workbook.

When proofing Alpha Pharmaceuticals' 10-year sales analysis worksheet, the marketing manager's administrative assistant found errors in some of the Northwest region's 1989 figures. You must correct them and add 1992 data to make the worksheet accurate.

1. Start Excel.

2. Open the file **Alpha1.xls.**

3. Make cell B17 active.

4. Change the data in cell B17 to **0.6314**

5. Change the data in cell B18 to **0.5563**

6. Add the following data for "Northwest Sales" in 1992:

Aspirin	**0.7233**
Acetaminophen	**0.7036**
Ibuprofen	**0.3179**

7. Return to cell A1.

8. Save the workbook as *[your initials]***1-20.xls**.

9. Print the worksheet and close the workbook.

Open a file, change the active cell, navigate within a worksheet, key data, save and print the worksheet, and close the workbook.

After reviewing the 10-year sales analysis numbers, the marketing manager found several mistakes in the data. You must correct these before the worksheet goes to the president.

1. Open the file **Alpha4.xls**.

2. Make K10 the active cell and change the data to **6.8431**

3. Use the Go To command to move to the following cells and change the data as shown:

Lesson Applications:

Provide independent practice for students and may be used for assessment. Objectives are indicated for each Exercise.

◉ **Exercise 1-20:**
Objectives 1, 2, 4, 6–8
Required Files: Alpha1.xls
Solution Files: gl1-20.xls in Solutions Manual or on Solutions Disk.

◉ **Exercise 1-21:**
Objectives 2, 4–8
Required Files: Alpha4.xls
Solution File: gl1-21.xls in Solutions Manual or on Solutions Disk.

Cell	Change Data to:
D18	**0.6219**
J19	**0.6891**
B25	**1.0618**
K27	**2.0662**
G34	**1.4817**
C36	**0.3993**
K43	**1.4216**
D45	**0.5225**

4. Go to cell A1.

5. Save the workbook as *[your initials]*1-21.xls.

6. Print the worksheet.

7. Close the workbook.

EXERCISE 1-22

Open a file, change the active cell, navigate in the worksheet, enter data, print a worksheet, save the workbook in different file formats, and close the workbook.

Because the sales volume in Alpha Pharmaceuticals' Northwest region is significantly lower than the other regions, the company president requested detailed figures for each salesperson. Complete the worksheet containing the sales data by entering the second- and fourth-quarter.

1. Open the file **Alpha5.xls**.

2. Move to cell C8 and key **66.4** (Ewald Rhiner's second-quarter sales).

3. Press [Enter] to enter the data and move down one cell.

 TIP: When entering data in more than one column, it's usually easier to press [Enter] and move down the column than to use the arrow keys to move across a row.

4. Continue keying the second-quarter data from Figure 1-20 (on the next page). When you finish entering it, enter the fourth-quarter data.

5. When you finish entering the data, verify that the total figure in cell F19 is 2,726.87. If it isn't, check the figures you keyed and correct them where necessary.

6. Go to cell A1 and save the workbook as *[your initials]*1-22.xls.

7. Print the worksheet.

8. Save the workbook as *[your initials]*1-22.htm.

9. Close the workbook.

○ Exercise 1-22:
Objectives 2, 4–8
Required Files: Alpha5.xls
Solution Files: gl1-22.xls and gl1-22.htm in Solutions
Manual or on Solutions Disk.

FIGURE 1-20

Salesperson	Qtr 2	Qtr 4
Ewald Rhiner	66.4	54.6
Ruth Seuratadot	82.2	86.0
Buster Manatee	73.8	74.1
Jose Garcia	50.3	81.6
Colleen Masterhouse	57.7	74.6
Anthony Chen	81.2	69.7
Elouise Swift	45.9	60.7
Lloyd Polaski	71.0	67.0
Murray Diamond	65.3	70.6
Barbara Bloomberg	79.8	52.4

EXERCISE 1-23

Open a file, navigate between worksheets, enter data, navigate in the worksheet, and save, print, and close the workbook.

The final sales figures for the Northwest and Southeast regions are now available. Complete the worksheets and print each region's worksheet for the marketing manager.

1. Open the file **Alpha2.xls**.
2. Go to cell B10 on the Northwest worksheet.
3. Key the following data in cells B10, C10, and D10:

   0.074

   0.071

   0.036
4. Go to cell B7 on the Southeast worksheet.
5. Key the following data in cells B7, C7, and D7:

   0.135

   0.097

   0.037
6. Go to cell A1 and save the workbook as *[your initials]***1-23.xls**.

● Exercise 1-23:
Objectives 2–8
Required Files: Alpha2.xls
Solution Files: gl1-23.xls in Solutions Manual or on Solutions Disk.

 The completed document for this Exercise may be used in a student's portfolio.

7. Print all the worksheets and close the workbook.

> **TIP:** To print all the worksheets in a workbook, click <u>E</u>ntire Workbook in the Print dialog box under Print What.

EXERCISE 1-24 *Challenge Yourself*

Open a file, change the active cell, key data in four worksheets within one workbook, and save, print, and close the workbook.

Alpha Pharmaceuticals' sales force is divided into four regions. Annual company sales are shown in a workbook that consists of four worksheets—one worksheet for each region. Some adjustments are needed in the Annual Sales figures for each region.

1. Open the file **Alpha6.xls**.

2. Add the following data for "May" to Sheet2:

Aspirin	**0.074**
Acetaminophen	**0.070**
Ibuprofen	**0.042**

3. Add the following data for "February" to Sheet3:

Aspirin	**0.126**
Acetaminophen	**0.080**
Ibuprofen	**0.030**

4. Change the amounts for "Ibuprofen" on Sheet4 as shown below:

October	**0.201**
November	**0.210**
December	**0.212**

5. Change the amounts for "September" on Sheet1 as shown below:

Aspirin	**0.132**
Acetaminophen	**0.202**
Ibuprofen	**0.207**

6. Save the workbook as *[your initials]***1-24.xls**.

7. Print the entire workbook, close the workbook, and close Excel.

⊙ **Exercise 1-24:**
Objectives 2–8
Required Files: Alpha6.xls
Solution Files: gl1-24.xls in Solutions Manual or on
Solutions Disk.

The completed document for this Exercise
may be used in a student's portfolio.

Creating a Simple Worksheet

OBJECTIVES

After completing this lesson, you will be able to:

1. Enter and edit data.
2. Use Pick From List and AutoComplete to enter labels.
3. Enter data in selected cells.
4. Construct basic formulas.
5. Use the SUM function.
6. Use AutoCalculate.

MOUS ACTIVITIES

In this lesson:

XL2000 **1.2**
XL2000 **1.3**
XL2000 **1.4**
XL2000 **2.4**
XL2000 **6.1**
XL2000 **6.2**
XL2000 **6.3**
XL2000 **6.5**
XL2000 **6.7**
XL2000 **6.8**

See Appendix F.

 Estimated Time: 1½ hours

In Lesson 1, you opened an existing worksheet, examined its contents, and keyed data. In this lesson, you create a simple worksheet from scratch—one that contains text, numeric values, and formulas.

Objective 1
Entering and Editing Data

Excel recognizes text and numbers automatically and formats them differently. For example:

- An entry that begins with a number or mathematical sign is recognized as a *value*. Values are aligned at the right margin of the cell by default and are included in calculations.

PREPARE

Point out to students that the learning objectives show what they will learn in the lesson. Each heading in the lesson correlates to a learning objective.

Required Files

None

TEACH

Teaching Resources:
- Excel Classroom Presentations
- School-to-Work Strategies Manual
- Spanish Glossary
- Certification Procedures

● An entry that begins with a letter is recognized automatically as a *label*. Labels are aligned at the left margin of the cell and are excluded from calculations.

TIP: You can format a number as a label if you begin the entry with an apostrophe (') or if the cell is formatted for text. The number is then excluded from calculations.

When you key data, the information appears in both the formula bar and the active cell. Before you complete the entry, you can use Backspace to edit the text or Esc to start over. To complete the entry, you can use one of several mouse or keyboard methods.

TABLE 2-1   **Methods for Completing an Entry**

ACTION	RESULT
Click another cell	Completes the entry and makes the selected cell active.
Click ☑	Completes the entry. The current cell remains active.
Press Enter	Completes the entry and the cell below becomes active.
Press Tab	Completes the entry and the cell to the right becomes active.
Press an Arrow key	Completes the entry and the cell above, below, to the right, or to the left becomes active.

EXERCISE **2-1** **Enter Labels and Values in a Worksheet**

1. Start Excel. The workbook Book1 appears and cell A1 on Sheet1 is the active cell.

2. Hide the Office Assistant, if necessary. (Choose Hide the Office Assistant from the Help menu.)

3. Key **Sales Analysis** in cell A1. (Do not press Enter yet.) Notice that the status bar indicates you are in Enter mode. The text appears in both the formula bar and the active cell. Notice also that the Enter button ☑ and the Cancel button ✕ appear on the formula bar in Enter mode. (See Figure 2-1 on the next page.)

4. Delete three of the characters you just keyed by pressing Backspace three times.

FIGURE 2-1
Text appears in the
formula bar in
Enter mode.

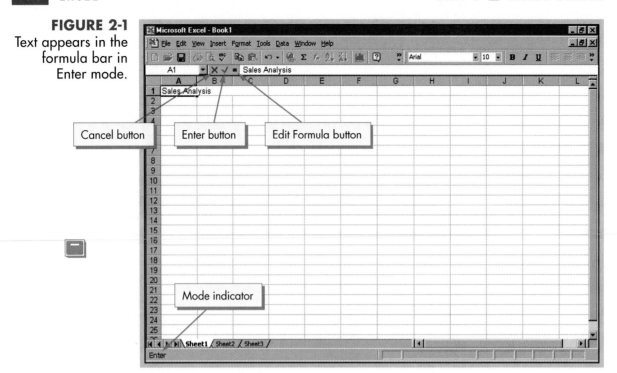

Cancel button   Enter button   Edit Formula button

Mode indicator

5. Key **sis** to complete the word "Analysis" and click the Enter button ☑ in the formula bar. A1 remains the active cell. Notice that the mode returns to Ready upon completion of the entry. The text appears in cell A1 and overlaps cell B1.

6. Key **Alpha Pharmaceuticals** and press ⏎Enter⏎. The new text replaces "Sales Analysis" in cell A1 and cell A2 becomes the active cell.

7. In cell A2, key **Regional Sales** and press ⏎Enter⏎ to complete the cell entry. Cell A3 becomes the active cell. Whenever you press ⏎Enter⏎, the active cell moves down one row.

8. In cell A3, key **Sales in $ millions** and press ⏎Enter⏎.

9. Press ⏎↑⏎ and key **1995** as a correction to cell A3, but do not press ⏎Enter⏎. Cell A3 now contains "1995." However, you actually want it to contain "Sales in $ millions."

10. Press ⏎Esc⏎. The correction is not made and the original cell content is restored.

TIP: If you overwrite a cell by mistake, do not press ⏎Enter⏎. Press ⏎Esc⏎ or click the Cancel button ☒ on the formula bar to restore the cell's previous contents.

11. Move to cell B7. Key an apostrophe ('), then key **1995**. The apostrophe tells Excel this entry is a label, not a value. Press ⏎Tab⏎, C7 is now the active cell, the apostrophe disappears from the 1995 label, and the year is left-aligned.

Use Excel Classroom Presentation 2 to display screens from this lesson, including this one, in a slide-show format.

[1] In all Microsoft Office applications, the status bar is an important work-in-progress indicator. Remind students to check the mode indicator on the status bar. Later in the lesson, students see how AutoCalculate is displayed in the status bar.

[2] The worksheet title, "Alpha Pharmaceuticals," and the two lines below it would normally be centered over the worksheet data. You may want to demonstrate how to center-align the title as a way of showing Excel's formatting capabilities.

[3] Explain to students the difference in starting the year labels with and without the apostrophe.

12. Key **'1996** in cell C7 (note the apostrophe) and press ⌨Tab⌨. The year is entered as a label and cell D7 becomes the active cell.

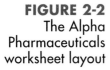

13. Key the remaining text as shown in Figure 2-2, entering all years as labels. The years all appear left-aligned.

FIGURE 2-2
The Alpha
Pharmaceuticals
worksheet layout

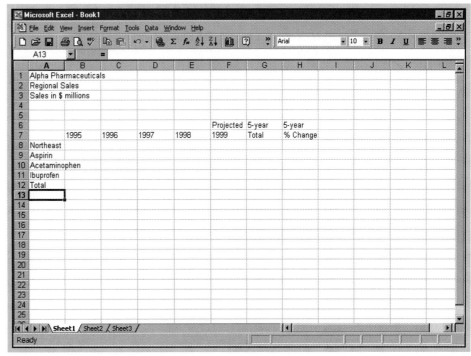

14. Widen column A to accommodate the column entry "Acetaminophen." To do this, click anywhere in column A, choose <u>C</u>olumn from the F<u>o</u>rmat menu, and choose <u>W</u>idth. Key **13** in the text box and click OK. (If the column is still not wide enough to accommodate the label, repeat the command, keying a larger value in the text box.)

EXERCISE ▌2-2▐ **Create a New Folder**

---

1. Choose Save <u>A</u>s from the <u>F</u>ile menu. You're going to save the document in a new folder that will contain all the files you create in this lesson.

2. Choose the folder location from the Save <u>I</u>n drop-down list. (For example, to save your files to a floppy disk, put a disk in the drive and make sure Save <u>I</u>n indicates drive A:.)

 NOTE: Check with your instructor about where to save the new folder.

 After keying the worksheet shown in Figure 2-2, students are instructed to adjust the width of column A to accommodate a long entry in the body of the worksheet. This step prevents creating a worksheet with a blank column and introduces the proper principles of worksheet design.

In Excel Classroom Presentation 2.

Students are asked to create a new folder into which they will place all Lesson 2 files. They create lesson folders from this point on in the course so they develop good file management habits. Tell students where to locate these folders (hard drive, network, or floppy disk). Make sure students know how to specify the location in the Save In box. Additionally, you may want students to create a Lesson 1 folder, and show them how to move their Lesson 1 files into this folder using Windows Explorer.

3. Click the Create New Folder button and key the folder name *[your initials]*Lesson 2.

4. Enter the filename *[your initials]*2-2 and click Save.

EXERCISE 2-3 Clear the Contents of a Cell

If you key incorrect data into a cell, you can clear the cell's contents by making the cell active and pressing Delete. Another way to clear a cell is to use the Clear option on the Edit menu.

1. In the current workbook, move to cell A8, which contains "Northeast."

FIGURE 2-3
Edit menu, Clear submenu

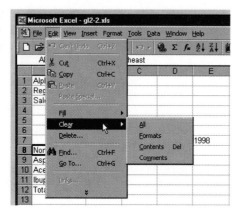

2. Choose Clear from the Edit menu. A submenu appears.

3. Choose Contents to clear cell A8.

4. Key **Southeast** in cell A8 and press Enter.

5. Press ↑ to reactivate cell A8 and press Delete to clear the cell.

6. Key **Northeast** in cell A8 and press Enter.

EXERCISE 2-4 Edit the Contents of a Cell

If a cell contains a long or complicated entry, you might want to edit the contents rather than rekey the entire entry.

To change to Edit mode you can:

- Double-click the cell.
- Click the cell to make it active and click the formula bar.
- Press F2.

1. Double-click cell A3. You are now in Edit mode, as indicated on the status bar. Notice that the pointer changes from a white cross to an I-beam and you can position the insertion point (the flashing vertical bar) to edit text.

2. Click the I-beam between "in" and "$" to position the insertion point.

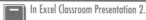

[1] You may want to explain briefly the difference between contents, formats, and comments.

■ In Excel Classroom Presentation 2.

[2] In step 5, you may want to mention that the Delete key only clears the content from a cell. If the cell contains formatting, the Delete key does not remove the formatting.

3. Press ⬅ and ➡ several times. The insertion point moves to the left or right, one character at a time.

4. Press [Home]. The insertion point moves to the left of "Sales." In Edit mode, keys such as [Home] and [End] operate within the cell, rather than within the entire worksheet as they do in Ready mode.

5. Press [Delete] nine times to delete "Sales in" and the space after "in."

6. Key **(** (open parenthesis) and press [End] to move to the end of the text in the cell.

7. Key **)** (close parenthesis) and press [Enter] to complete the entry and exit Edit mode. Cell A3 now contains "($ millions)."

TABLE 2-2   **Keystrokes in Edit Mode**

KEYSTROKE	RESULT
[Enter]	Completes the entry and returns to Ready mode.
[Esc]	Restores the previous cell contents and returns to Ready mode.
⬅ or ➡	Moves the insertion point left or right by one character.
[Home]	Moves to the beginning of the cell contents.
[End]	Moves to the end of the cell contents.
[Delete]	Deletes one character to the right of the insertion point.
[Ctrl] + [Delete]	Deletes text to the end of the line.
[Backspace]	Deletes one character to the left of the insertion point.
[Ctrl] + ⬅ or [Ctrl] + ➡	Moves left or right by one word.

✓ Objective 2
Using Pick From List and AutoComplete

Labels for rows are usually keyed in a single column and often are repeated. For instance, if your worksheet shows sales for three products in four regions, the product names appear four times, once in each region.

Excel provides two features that make it easier to enter labels:

- Pick From List
- AutoComplete

Both features use information that you already entered in the worksheet.

✓ **Objective 2 Assignment:**
Exercise 2-18 (Skills Review) can be assigned after completing Objective 2.

The AutoComplete feature can be enabled or disabled. Choose Options from the Tools menu and click the Edit tab. Clear the Enable AutoComplete For Cell Values check box to disable the feature or check the box to enable it.

EXERCISE 2-5 Use the Pick From List and AutoComplete Features

1. In cell A13, key **Southeast** and press Enter.

2. Right-click cell A14 (position the mouse pointer in cell A14 and click the right button). The shortcut menu appears.

FIGURE 2-4
Shortcut menu

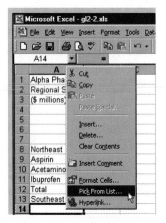

3. Choose Pick From List from the shortcut menu. The list contains the labels that you keyed in consecutive cells A8 through A13.

NOTE: The labels appearing in the Pick From List are from consecutive cells that appear above the current cell.

4. Click "Aspirin" in the list. (See Figure 2-5.) Excel automatically inserts this row label in cell A14.

5. Right-click cell A15, choose Pick From List, and click "Acetaminophen" in the list. Excel inserts this label in the active cell.

FIGURE 2-5
Using the Pick From List feature

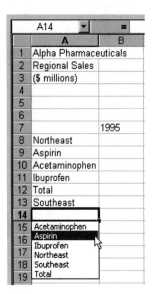

6. Move to cell A16 and key **I**. The AutoComplete feature highlights "buprofen" as a choice to complete the entry. AutoComplete chooses an item from the Pick From List when you key the first letters of that item. Because "Ibuprofen" is the only item that begins with an "I," you needed to key only one letter in this case. (See Figure 2-6.)

7. Press Enter to accept "Ibuprofen."

8. Key **As** in cell A17, but do not press Enter. AutoComplete suggests "Aspirin."

9. Press Esc to start over and key **T**. AutoComplete suggests "Total." Press Enter to complete the entry.

10. Complete the labels in column A as shown in Figure 2-7 (on the next page). Key text for the new entries. Use AutoComplete or the Pick From List feature to insert items that you already keyed.

FIGURE 2-6
AutoComplete suggests an item from the Pick From List.

 The worksheet created does not contain blank rows between sections (for example, to divide the Northeast and Southeast regions) so you can teach the Pick From list and AutoComplete features.

In Excel Classroom Presentation 2.

FIGURE 2-7

	A
18	Northwest
19	Aspirin
20	Acetaminophen
21	Ibuprofen
22	Total
23	Southwest
24	Aspirin
25	Acetaminophen
26	Ibuprofen
27	Total
28	Grand Total

Objective 3

Entering Data in Selected Cells

In many cases, you may find it convenient to work with a group of selected cells. One way to group selected cells is as a block. A *block* is a group of cells that are next to one another.

Excel provides three methods of selecting cells to form a block:

- Using the Keyboard
- Using the Mouse
- Using the Name Box

EXERCISE 2-6 Select a Block of Cells Using the Keyboard

When you make a cell active, you have actually selected it. To extend the selection using the keyboard, press [Shift] in combination with the navigation keys.

1. Make cell B9 active.

2. Hold down ⌈Shift⌋ and press → three times. A dark border surrounds the selected cells, B9 through E9. The first cell in the selection, B9, which is also the active cell, appears white. Cells C9 through E9 appear highlighted by transparent blue through which you can easily see data.

3. With ⌈Shift⌋ held down, press ↓ twice. The selected block now extends from B9 through E11.

FIGURE 2-8
Selected block of cells

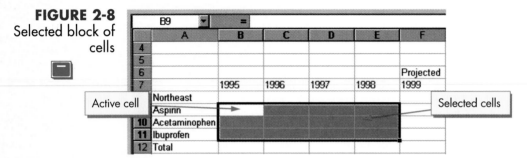

4. Key **1.112** and press ⌈Enter⌋. The value appears in cell B9 and B10 becomes active.

5. Key **1.465** and press ⌈Enter⌋. The value appears in cell B10 and B11 becomes active.

6. Key **1.085** and press ⌈Enter⌋. The value appears in cell B11. The next cell in the block, C9, becomes active.

TIP: Entering data in selected cells can be a very efficient technique, because ⌈Enter⌋ or ⌈Tab⌋ then moves only *within* the selected cells.

7. Key the remaining data for the selected block as shown in Figure 2-9.

FIGURE 2-9

	A	B	C	D	E
9	Aspirin	1.112	1.082	1.053	1.024
10	Acetaminophen	1.465	1.592	1.73	1.94
11	Ibuprofen	1.085	1.36	1.704	2.225

NOTE: Using the arrow keys or the mouse to position the active cell deselects the block.

In step 2, students may ask why the first cell in a selected group is white while the others are highlighted. Point out that the white cell is the active cell.

In Excel Classroom Presentation 2.

8. Press ⬇. The block is deselected.

9. Click cell F11 to make it active, hold down Shift, and press Home. The selection extends from F11 through A11.

10. Press Shift + Ctrl + Home. The selection extends from F11 through A1.

11. Press Shift + ⬇. The selection shrinks by one row.

12. Press any arrow key to deselect the block.

TABLE 2-3   **Navigation Key Combinations**

KEY COMBINATION	ACTION
Shift +Arrow key	Extend the selection one cell in the direction indicated by the Arrow key.
Shift + PgUp or Shift + PgDn	Extend the selection one screen up or down.
Shift + Ctrl + Home	Extend the selection to the beginning of the worksheet.
Shift + Home	Extend the selection to the beginning of the row.
Shift + Ctrl + End	Extend the selection to the end of the data in the worksheet.
Shift + Ctrl +Arrow key	Extend the selection to the edge of a block of data in the direction indicated by the Arrow key.
Ctrl + Spacebar	Select an entire column.
Shift + Spacebar	Select an entire row.
Ctrl + A or Ctrl + Shift + Spacebar	Select an entire worksheet.

EXERCISE   2-7   Select Cells Using the Mouse

Excel provides several ways to select cells in a block using the mouse:

- Click a column-heading letter to select an entire column or click a row-heading number to select an entire row.
- Click the Select All button to select the entire worksheet.
- Drag across adjacent cells to select a block.
- Hold down Shift and click a cell to select a block beginning with the active cell and ending at the new location.

You can also use the mouse to add a non-adjacent block of cells to an existing block of cells. Once the first block is selected, you can select additional

In addition to the keyboard selection methods taught in this Exercise, you may want to demonstrate using the F8 key. This method is less popular for most users, although those who have difficulty with the mouse may find it helpful. The F8 key turns Extend mode on and off. In Extend mode, the arrow keys (and other navigation keys) can be used to extend or reduce a selection. After selecting cells in Extend mode, you must press F8 again to turn the mode off.

blocks by holding down Ctrl and dragging across the cells in the additional block.

1. Click cell B14, hold down the mouse button, and then drag the pointer down and over to cell E16.

2. Release the mouse button. Cells B14 through E16 are selected and B14 is the active cell.

3. Click any cell to deselect the block.

4. Click column-heading A to select the entire column.

FIGURE 2-10
Selecting a column

Select All button

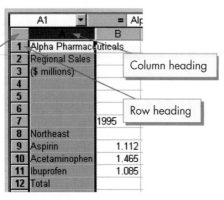

5. Click anywhere in the worksheet to deselect the column. Click row-heading 1 to select the entire row.

6. Click the Select All button (the gray square to the left of column heading A) to select the entire worksheet. (See Figure 2-10 for the location of the Select All button.)

7. Click cell B7 (containing "1995"), hold down Shift, and click cell E7. Cells B7 through E7 are selected.

8. Press Delete to clear the cells. The block is still selected and B7 is the active cell.

9. Rekey **1995**, **1996**, **1997**, and **1998** in cells B7, C7, D7, and E7, respectively, pressing Enter or Tab between each entry. Remember to enter the years as labels by beginning each entry with an apostrophe.

> **TIP:** Tab moves the active cell to the right. Shift+Tab moves the active cell to the left.

10. Press ↓ once to deselect the block of cells.

11. Drag from cell B14 to E16 to select this block.

12. Click the down arrow in the vertical scroll bar to display row 28 of the worksheet. To add a second block of cells to the range, hold down Ctrl and drag the mouse from cell B19 to E21.

13. Hold down Ctrl and drag the mouse from cell B24 to E26. A third block is added to the range.

14. Hold down Ctrl and click B14 to make it the active cell. (See Figure 2-11 on the next page.)

15. Key **1** and press Enter twice. B15 becomes the active cell.

16. Press Enter repeatedly to move through the range. Notice that the active cell moves from the end of one block to the beginning of the next block and from the end of the range to the beginning of the range.

In Excel Classroom Presentation 2.

FIGURE 2-11
Selected range of
non-adjacent
blocks

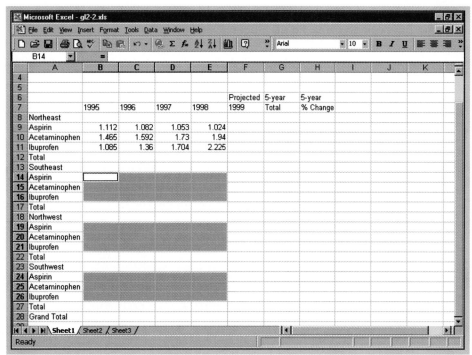

TIP: Enter moves the active cell down. Shift + Enter moves the active cell up.

17. Press Delete to clear the range contents.

18. Click anywhere in the worksheet to deselect the range.

NOTE: If you're using the Microsoft IntelliPoint Mouse, additional navigating options are available. For example, you can roll the wheel forward and backward instead of using the vertical scroll bars; hold down the wheel and drag in any direction to pan the document; or hold Ctrl and roll the wheel to change magnification.

EXERCISE   2-8   Select Cells Using the Name Box

You can select a range of cells by keying the first and last cells separated by a colon in the Name Box. For example, you can enter C9:E10 to select the block that includes cells C9, C10, D9, D10, E9, and E10.

FIGURE 2-12
Using the Name
Box to select cells

1. Click in the Name Box and key **b14:e16**. (Cell references are not case-sensitive, so you can key lowercase letters.)

 In Excel Classroom Presentation 2.

 Throughout the lesson, remind students that cell references and functions are not case-sensitive and can be keyed in lowercase letters.

2. Press ⌷Enter⌷. The cells in the specified range are selected.

3. Click any cell to deselect the block. Return to cell A1.

4. Save the worksheet as *[your initials]***2-8.xls** in your Lesson 2 folder.

✓Objective 4

Constructing Basic Formulas

Formulas are instructions that tell Excel how to perform calculations. Formulas can contain mathematical operators, values, cell references, cell ranges, and functions. Excel performs the operations indicated in the formula in a specific order.

TABLE 2-4	**Commonly Used Mathematical Operators**		
	OPERATOR	**PRECEDENCE**	**DESCRIPTION**
	^	1st	Exponentiate
	*	2nd	Multiply
	/	2nd	Divide
	+	3rd	Add
	-	3rd	Subtract
	( )		Used to control the order of mathematical operations

NOTE: The exponentiation operator (^) raises a value to a power. The expression 2^3 means "two to the third power," or 2^3, or 2x2x2.

Excel's *order of precedence* defines the order in which it performs formula operations. In a formula, Excel performs exponentiation operations first, multiplication and division next, and addition and subtraction last. Operations with equal precedence are performed from left to right. You can use parentheses () to override the order of precedence. Excel performs operations inside parentheses first. You can also "nest" expressions—that is, put parenthetical expressions within parentheses. The innermost operations are handled first. The following figure shows how parentheses change the order of precedence for operations.

✓**Objective 4 Assignment:**
Exercise 2-19 (Skills Review) can be assigned after completing Objective 4.

Although keying cell references in a formula is demonstrated, you may want to explain to students that this method is not always the best approach because it may result in errors. In the next Exercise, students learn to build a formula by pointing to a cell and clicking it.

FIGURE 2-13
These two formulas
include the same
numbers and
operators, but
parentheses
change the order
of operations.

$$\underset{2nd}{1} + \underset{1st}{2} * \underset{3rd}{3} - 1 =$$
$$1 + 6 - 1 \qquad = 6$$

$$(\,(\,\underset{1st}{1} + 2\,) * \underset{2nd}{3}\,) - \underset{3rd}{1} =$$
$$(\,(\,3\,) * 3\,) - 1 \qquad =$$
$$9 - 1 \qquad\qquad = 8$$

You can create formulas using the keyboard or by entering a combination of keystrokes and mouse clicks. As you key a formula, it appears in both the active cell and the formula bar. When you complete the entry, the result of the calculation appears in the active cell, but the formula bar displays the formula. Excel formulas begin with = (an equal sign). Because cell references in a formula are not case-sensitive, you can enter them in either uppercase or lowercase.

TABLE 2-5 Typical Excel Formulas

FORMULA	ACTION
=245+374	Adds the values 245 and 374.
=F4+F5	Adds the values in cells F4 and F5.
=c3+b3-d5	Adds the values in cells C3 and B3 and subtracts the value in cell D5 from the result.
=(A3+B3)/C9	Adds the values in cells A3 and B3 and divides the result by the value in cell C9.
=F5*1.02	Multiplies the contents of cell F5 by 1.02 (or 102%).
=F5*C10	Multiplies the contents of cell F5 by the contents of cell C10.

EXERCISE 2-9 Key an Addition Formula

1. In the current workbook, select and clear the contents of cells A13 through A28.

2. Move to cell B12, which will display the total of 1995 sales.

3. Key **=B9+B10+B11** and press Enter. The result, "3.662," appears in cell B12.

 TIP: Remember, cell references are not case-sensitive—you can enter them in either uppercase or lowercase.

4. Press ↑ to make B12 the active cell. The formula is displayed in the formula bar.

EXERCISE ## Build an Addition Formula with the Mouse

You can enter a cell reference in a formula by clicking the cell with the mouse. While building a formula, clicking another cell switches the worksheet into Point mode, which appears in the status bar. If you click the wrong cell or make another error, just press Backspace to delete the incorrect characters. You can then continue building the formula.

1. Move to cell C12 and click the Edit Formula button ≡. Excel changes to Edit mode, expands the formula bar, and enters an equal sign to start the formula. Notice the addition of the Function box.

FIGURE 2-14
The formula bar
expands when the
Edit Formula
button is clicked.

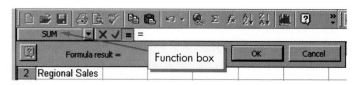

> **TIP:** You can drag the expanded formula bar out of the way to see cells it covers.

2. Click cell C9. Excel changes to Point mode and a moving dashed border surrounds cell C9. Notice that "=C9" appears in both the active cell and the formula bar.

3. Key **+** (the plus sign). The plus sign is added to the formula and the moving border disappears. Excel changes to Edit mode.

4. Click cell C10 and key **+** (the plus sign). The formula "=C9+C10+" appears.

5. Click cell C11 and then press Enter. The result, "4.034," appears in cell C12. C13 is now the active cell.

> **TIP:** You can also click the Enter button ✓ or OK on the formula bar to get the formula result. C12 would then remain the active cell.

EXERCISE **2-11** ## Build Multiplication Formulas

Alpha Pharmaceuticals' sales figures are available for the years 1995 through 1998, but a projection must be calculated for 1999. The company is predicting that aspirin sales will decrease by 5% in 1999 and acetaminophen and ibuprofen sales will increase by 2% and 3%, respectively.

1. In cell F9, key **=** (the equal sign) and click cell E9.

 In Excel Classroom Presentation 2.

2. Key * (the multiplication operator), key **.95**, and click the Enter button on the formula bar.

3. The formula "=E9*0.95" appears in the formula bar and "0.9728" appears in cell F9. This formula is equivalent to 5 percent less than E9, which is the projected decrease in aspirin sales for 1999.

4. Move to cell F10, key **=E10*1.02**, and press ⌊Enter⌋. The result, "1.9788," appears in cell F10. The formula "=E10*1.02" is equivalent to the formula "=E10+E10*0.02," which is the projected 2 percent increase in acetaminophen sales for 1999.

5. In cell F11, key the formula **=E11*1.03,** and click the Enter button . The result "2.29175" appears.

EXERCISE 2-12 Calculate a Percentage Change

The Alpha Pharmaceuticals worksheet needs calculations to determine the percentage change in each product over the five-year sales period. The general formula for a percentage change is (new-old)/old*100. The subtraction must be performed before division. The resulting decimal must be multiplied by 100 to convert it to a percentage.

1. Move to cell H9 and key **=(**

2. Click cell F9 and key **-** (the minus sign).

3. Click cell B9 and key **)**

4. Key **/** (the forward slash, which is the division operator).

5. Click cell B9, key ***,** key **100**, and press ⌊Enter⌋.

6. Move back to cell H9. The formula "=(F9-B9)/B9*100" appears in the formula bar and the result "-12.518" appears in cell H9.

7. In cell H10, enter the formula **=(F10-B10)/B10*100**. The result is 35.07167.

8. In cell H11, enter the formula **=(F11-B11)/B11*100**. The result shows that ibuprofen sales more than doubled over the five-year period, increasing 111.2212 percent.

FIGURE 2-15
Calculating percentage changes

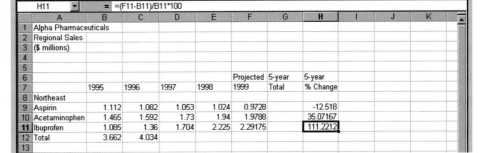

H11	▼	=	=(F11-B11)/B11*100							
	A	B	C	D	E	F	G	H	I	J	K
1	Alpha Pharmaceuticals										
2	Regional Sales										
3	($ millions)										
4											
5											
6						Projected	5-year	5-year			
7		1995	1996	1997	1998	1999	Total	% Change			
8	Northeast										
9	Aspirin	1.112	1.082	1.053	1.024	0.9728		-12.518			
10	Acetaminophen	1.465	1.592	1.73	1.94	1.9788		35.07167			
11	Ibuprofen	1.085	1.36	1.704	2.225	2.29175		111.2212			
12	Total	3.662	4.034								
13											

 In Excel Classroom Presentation 2.

Using the SUM Function

✓**Objective 5**

Keying individual cell references is a reasonable way to add two or three cells. It is not practical for adding a long column or row of values, however. Excel's SUM function greatly simplifies the process of adding many values.

In general, the formula for a function is constructed with an equal sign and the function name followed by a set of parentheses, with one or more cell references or values within the parentheses.

FIGURE 2-16
Structure of a
SUM formula

Parenthesis | Colon | Parenthesis

=SUM(E9:E11)

Equal sign | Function name | Cell references

In a SUM formula, the cell references can consist of a single cell or a block of cells. Excel refers to these references as a *range*. Technically, a range is any group of cells specified to be acted upon by a command. To identify a range, key the cell references for two diagonally opposite corners of a group of cells, separated by a colon.

TABLE 2-6

Examples of Ranges

RANGE	DEFINES
C4:C4	A single cell
B5:B10	A range of cells in column B
D3:G3	A range of cells in row 3
C5:F12	A rectangular range of cells in columns C through F, rows 5 through 12

EXERCISE **2-13** **Key a SUM Formula**

1. Move to cell D12.
2. Key **=SUM(D9:D11)** and press ⌨Enter⌨. The formula adds the contents of cells D9 through D11. The result, "4.487," appears in cell D12.

 NOTE: Like cell references, function names are not case-sensitive, so you can key them in lowercase letters.

✓**Objective 5 Assignment:**
Exercises 2-21 (Skills Review) and 2-22 (Lesson Applications) can be assigned after completing Objective 5.

1 Although SUM functions to be keyed are shown in uppercase letters, remind students again that they can use lowercase letters.

EXERCISE **2-14** **Enter a SUM Formula Using the Arrow Keys**

1. Move to cell E12.
2. Key **=SUM(**

 NOTE: Make sure you key the parenthesis.

3. Press ⬆️. A moving border surrounds cell E11 and "=SUM(E11" appears in the formula bar.
4. Key a colon (:) or a period to anchor the border. The formula "=SUM(E11:E11" appears in the formula bar.
5. Press ⬆️ twice. The border extends the range from cell E9 through cell E11.
6. Press Enter to complete the formula. Excel inserts the closing parenthesis for you automatically. The completed formula is "=SUM(E9:E11)" and the result is 5.189. In this case, you defined the cell range from the bottom to the top. Excel can add cell contents in either direction.

EXERCISE **2-15** **Use the Mouse to Enter a SUM Formula**

You can create SUM formulas using the mouse to drag across cells instead of using the Arrow keys. You can also use the buttons on the formula bar to build a SUM formula.

1. In cell G9, key **=SUM(**
2. Using the mouse, click cell B9.
3. Drag across the row from cell B9 to cell F9 and release the mouse button. A moving border surrounds the selected range and the formula "=SUM(B9:F9" appears in the formula bar.
4. Click the Enter button ✓ on the formula bar or press Enter. The formula is completed and the result, "5.2438," appears in cell G9.
5. Move to cell F12.
6. Click the Edit Forumula button ▣. An equal sign is entered in the cell to start the formula.
7. Click the Function box on the left of the formula bar. The SUM function and a suggested range are displayed in the formula bar and the Formula Palette pop-up window is displayed under the formula bar. (If the SUM function is not shown, click the drop-down arrow and choose SUM.)

FIGURE 2-17
Formula Palette
pop-up window

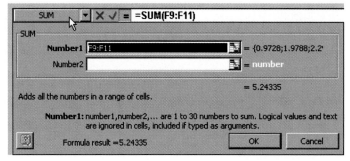

8. Click OK. The formula is completed and the result, "5.24335," appears in cell F12.

EXERCISE **2-16** | Use the AutoSum Button to Enter a SUM Formula

The AutoSum button is a shortcut for entering the SUM formula, similar to the Function box. It enters **=SUM(** and suggests a range to total. At the bottom of a column of values, AutoSum totals the column. At the right of a row of values, AutoSum totals the row.

1. Move to cell G10.

2. Click the AutoSum button Σ on the Standard toolbar. (You may need to click the More Buttons button to find it.) The formula "=SUM(B10:F10)" appears in the formula bar and in the cell and a moving border surrounds cells B10 through F10 on the worksheet.

TIP: You can also press Alt + = to use the AutoSum function.

3. Click the Enter button ✓ on the formula bar or press Enter. The result, "8.7058," appears in cell G10.

4. With cell G11 selected, double-click the AutoSum button Σ. The SUM formula is entered with the result "13.9496." Notice that the formula range is G9:G10 (for the column) rather than B11:F11 (for the row). The AutoSum feature automatically adds column numbers above a cell before adding row numbers to the left of the cell. Because two values appeared above cell G11, Excel assumed a column SUM formula.

5. To correct the range, click the AutoSum button Σ again. Notice the moving border surrounds the incorrect range.

6. Drag across cells B11 to F11 and press Enter. The correct result, "8.66575," appears in cell G11.

In Excel Classroom Presentation 2.

The AutoSum button is the easiest way to add a column or row. However, as step 4 demonstrates, it is sometimes necessary to correct the cell range suggested by AutoSum. Reinforce this concept to students.

7. Enter a SUM formula in cell G12, using any method. (Try double-clicking the AutoSum button Σ now, for instance.) Check that the formulas contain the correct ranges, then press Ctrl + Home to return to cell A1.

FIGURE 2-18
Completed
worksheet

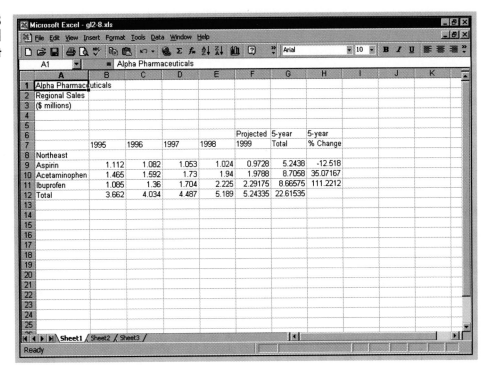

8. Save the workbook as *[your initials]*2-16.xls.

9. Print the worksheet.

NOTE: Cell H9 displays three decimal places on screen, but may print showing five.

☑ **Objective 6**

Using AutoCalculate

Excel includes an easy-to-use calculator. You can use this calculator, which is called AutoCalculate, to perform simple calculations without entering a formula. For example, if you select a range of cells, AutoCalculate displays the sum of the cells in the status bar.

NOTE: In addition to the SUM function, AutoCalculate can perform other functions, such as AVERAGE, MIN, and MAX. You can consult Excel's Help for more information on these functions.

 In Excel Classroom Presentation 2.

1 Although this lesson introduces formulas, students do not learn to display and print formulas until Lesson 4, where they also learn how to print column and row headings. You may want to have students display formulas by pressing Ctrl+' (left single quote). They also can use this key combination to restore numeric values.

2 You may want students to print worksheet pages with their filename as a header (the default is no header). To include a filename header, students can choose File, Page Setup, and then choose the Header/Footer tab, Custom Header, and click the File Name button (second from right). Adding headers is taught in Lesson 4.

☑ **Objective 6 Assignment:**
Exercises 2-20 (Skills Review) and 2-23 through 2-26 (Lesson Applications) can be assigned after completing Objective 6.

3 Make sure students understand that the AutoCalculate feature calculates and displays results in the status bar only—students must still enter the results in the worksheet.

EXERCISE 2-17 Use AutoCalculate to Find a Sum

1. Select cells D12 and E12, which contain the total sales for the years 1997 and 1998.

2. Right-click the status bar to display the AutoCalculate menu. Notice the various function names.

 NOTE: Functions are shown in uppercase letters in this text. When you key a function in Excel, it does not matter whether you use uppercase or lowercase.

FIGURE 2-19
Using
AutoCalculate

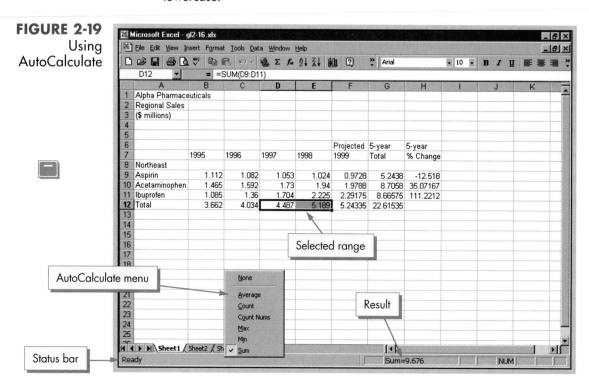

3. Choose SUM from the menu. The status bar displays "Sum=9.676."

 NOTE: AutoCalculate uses the last function chosen to calculate the current selection. If SUM was the last function chosen, for example, the sum of D12 and E12 is displayed as soon as the cells are selected.

4. Select another range of cells containing values. This time use the AVERAGE function. Notice the average displayed on the status bar.

5. Change back to the SUM function.

6. Close the workbook without saving it.

In Excel Classroom Presentation 2.

Tell students that the result in the status bar depends on the last function used. It may not be the same as the result in Figure 2-19. The result shown in Figure 2-19 is based on using the SUM function in AutoCalculate.

COMMAND SUMMARY

FEATURE	BUTTON	MENU	KEYBOARD
Delete cell contents		Edit, Clear, Contents	Delete
Cancel current entry	✕		Esc
Enter	✓		Enter
Edit Formula	=		
AutoSum	Σ		Alt + =

USING HELP

The previous lesson introduced you to the Office Assistant. You can also display ScreenTips without using the Office Assistant. Descriptive ScreenTips are available for menu commands, dialog box options, and parts of the Excel screen.

Display descriptive ScreenTips:

1. Open a new workbook. (Click the Open button on the Standard toolbar.)

2. Click Help to open the Help menu. Click the menu item What's This?

FIGURE 2-20
Help menu

(Notice that you can also press Shift + F1.) The pointer now has a question mark attached to it.

3. Click one of the tab scrolling buttons. Review the ScreenTip and click anywhere in the worksheet to close it.

4. Press Shift + F1 to display the question mark pointer again. Choose Save As from the File menu. Review the description of this command and click to close it.

5. Choose Properties from the File menu and click the Summary tab, if necessary. In the upper right corner of the dialog box, click the Help button  to display the question mark pointer. Click Subject (the word or the blank text box), review the description, and close it. You can repeat this process to see as many descriptions as you like.

6. Close the dialog box and close the workbook without saving it.

---

1 Point out that the Command Summary lists a variety of ways to accomplish a particular task. Students can decide which method they prefer to use for a specific purpose. The Command Summary contains comments not listed in the tables in the tables in this lesson.

2 Encourage students to follow the steps in "Using Help." Software companies are increasingly using their Help programs—rather than documentation—to train users and assist in answering user questions.

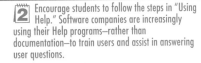 In Excel Classroom Presentation 2.

TEST BANK

Concepts Review

TRUE/FALSE QUESTIONS

Each of the following statements is either true or false. Indicate your choice by
circling **T** or **F**.

(T) F   **1.** The Delete key has the same effect as choosing Clear from the
Edit menu and then choosing Contents.

(T) F   **2.** If a cell containing a formula is included in another formula,
the value of the first formula is included in the calculation.

T **(F)**   **3.** In Excel, formulas begin with an asterisk (*).

(T) F   **4.** You can use parentheses () in a formula to control the order of
mathematical operations.

(T) F   **5.** The formula **=SUM(A6:D6)** adds the contents of the cells in row
6, from column A to column D.

T **(F)**   **6.** In formulas, function names must be entered in uppercase
letters only.

(T) F   **7.** You can use the AutoSum button $\boxed{\Sigma}$ to enter a SUM formula.

(T) F   **8.** You can use the SUM function to add the contents of both columns and rows.

SHORT ANSWER QUESTIONS

Write the correct answer in the space provided.

1. Which mode must be displayed in the status bar before you begin keying
information into a worksheet?

Ready

2. When you key information into a cell, where else does the information
appear on the screen?

Formula bar

3. In Edit mode, which key moves you to the beginning of selected cell
contents (as well as the first character in the formula bar)?

Home

4. Which mathematical operation is indicated by an asterisk (*)?

Multiplication

Concepts Review:
Allows students to check their understanding.

TEST BANK
Consider using the Test Bank to provide an
additional review of lesson concepts. It may
also be used as an assessment tool.

CLOSE

5. Which mathematical operations are given last priority in the order of precedence?

  Addition and subtraction

6. Which function adds columns or rows?

  SUM

7. What is the result given by the following formula =(10-4)/2?

  3

8. What is the result given by the following formula =10-4/2?

  8

CRITICAL THINKING

Answer these questions on a separate piece of paper. There are no right or wrong answers. Support your answers with examples from your own experience, if possible.

1. Your boss asks you to proofread a complex worksheet and its printed sources of data. How might AutoCalculate help you verify that data was entered accurately?

2. Last month's sales report worksheet lists products in rows and sales representatives in columns. Your boss asks you to update this report with new data. How can you select cells to speed your work? If your data came from the sales reports of individual sales representatives, would you press Enter or Tab after each entry? Why?

Skills Review

EXERCISE 2-18

Enter data, edit data, and enter labels using the Pick From List and AutoComplete features.

1. Click the New button ⬜ to start a new workbook, if necessary.
2. Key **Alpha Pharmaceuticals** in cell A1 and press Enter.
3. Key **1998 Sales - Northeast Region** in cell A2 and press Enter.
4. Key **(in thousands)** in cell A3 and press Enter.
5. Key **Region** in cell B5 and press Enter.

Critical Thinking Questions:
Answers will vary based on students' preferences, observations, experiences, and research.

Skills Review:
Provides guided practice for students. Objectives are indicated for each Exercise.

Exercise 2-18:
Objectives 1, 2
Required Files: None
Solution Files: gl2-18.xls in Solutions Manual or on Solutions Disk.

6. Label columns for regional data by following these steps:
   a. In cell B6, key **NE** and press [Tab].
   b. In cell C6, key **SE** and press [Tab].
   c. In cell D6, key **NW** and press [Tab].
   d. In cell E6, key **SW** and click the Enter button ☑ on the formula bar.

7. In cells A7 through A11, key the labels shown in Figure 2-21.

FIGURE 2-21

	A
7	Q1
8	Aspirin
9	Acetaminophen
10	Ibuprofen
11	Subtotal

8. In cell A12, enter **Q2** (for "second quarter").

9. In cell A13, use the Pick From List feature by following these steps:
   a. Right-click in cell A13 to display the shortcut menu.
   b. Choose Pick From List.
   c. Click "Aspirin" in the list.

10. Use AutoComplete to complete the labels for the second quarter by following these steps:
    a. In cell A14, key **Ac** and press [Enter] to enter "Acetaminophen."
    b. In cell A15, key **I** and press [Enter] to enter "Ibuprofen."
    c. In cell A16, key **S** and press [Enter] to enter "Subtotal."

11. To fit the 13-character row label "Acetaminophen," make sure any cell in column A is active and choose Column from the Format menu. Choose Width, key **13**, and click OK. (Enter a larger number if necessary.)

12. Edit cell A2 to read "1998 Sales" by following these steps:
    a. Double-click cell A2 to switch to Edit mode.
    b. Click the I-beam in the text to the right of "Sales" to position the insertion point.
    c. Press [Shift]+[End] to select the text to the end of the line.
    d. Press [Delete].
    e. Click the Enter button ☑ or press [Enter].

13. Enter the data shown in Figure 2-22.

FIGURE 2-22

	A	B	C	D	E
6		NE	SE	NW	SW
7	Q1				
8	Aspirin	250	175	150	200
9	Acetaminophen	500	485	390	450
10	Ibuprofen	600	500	480	510
11	Subtotal				
12	Q2				
13	Aspirin	240	180	160	210
14	Acetaminophen	520	470	400	460
15	Ibuprofen	610	640	490	520
16	Subtotal				

14. Clear the word "Subtotal" from cells A11 and A16 by selecting each cell and pressing [Delete].

 15. Make cell A1 active and save the workbook as *[your initials]*2-18.xls in your Lesson 2 folder.

16. Print the worksheet and close the workbook.

EXERCISE 2-19

Enter and edit data, enter data in selected cells, and construct basic formulas.

1. Start a new workbook.

2. Create a heading for the worksheet by keying **Alpha Pharmaceuticals** in cell A1 and **Quality Control Payroll** in cell A2.

3. Create column headings by keying the following text in cells A4 through D4, pressing [Tab] to move across columns:

Name   Salary   Years   Bonus

Students' headings and worksheets are not centered since these topics are not covered until later lessons. You may want to include a brief description of the steps for this.

Exercise 2-18:
Objectives 1, 3, 4
Required Files: None
Solution Files: gl2-18.xls in Solutions Manual or on Solutions Disk.

4. Practice selecting cell ranges by following these steps:

   a. Click column-heading B to select that column.
   b. Click row-heading 4 to select that row.
   c. Drag from cell A6 to cell A13 to select the range A6:A13.
   d. Click cell A6, hold down Shift, and click cell C13 to select the range A6:C13.
   e. Hold down Ctrl and drag across the range D6:D13 to add it to the selection.
   f. Click anywhere in the worksheet to deselect the block.

5. Select a cell range and then enter data for eight employees by following these steps:

   a. Select the range A6:C13.
   b. Enter the data shown in Figure 2-23, pressing Enter to move down each column. Begin with the name "Berenson."

FIGURE 2-23

	A	B	C
6	Berenson	28,000	2
7	Alvarez	33,000	6
8	Czerny	42,000	5
9	Teij	54,100	11
10	Silvers	22,200	3
11	Patino	57,000	9
12	Wang	35,300	2
13	Golden	41,000	6

6. Bonuses are calculated as 2% of salary multiplied by years of service (or $0.02 \times \text{Salary} \times \text{Years}$). Enter the appropriate bonus formulas by following these steps:

   a. In cell D6, key **=.02*B6*C6** and press Enter. Berenson's bonus is 1120, or 2% of 28,000 salary × 2 years of service.
   b. In cell D7, key **=.02***, click cell B7, key *, and click cell C7. Press Enter. Alvarez's bonus is 3960.
   c. Using either step a or step b as your entry method, enter bonus formulas for the rest of the employees.

Students are asked to type commas when they key salaries to make the numbers easier to read. You can ask them to omit the commas, as the column with formulas displays results without commas. Students learn basic number formatting to control commas and decimal places in Lesson 3.

7. Make cell A1 active and save the workbook as *[your initials]*2-19.xls in your Lesson 2 folder.

8. Print the worksheet and close the workbook.

Use the SUM function, construct formulas, and use AutoCalculate.

1. Open the file **QCBonus.xls**.

2. In cell A14, key **TOTALS**

3. Key a formula that uses the SUM function to calculate the Salary total by following these steps:

   a. Make B14 the active cell.

   b. Key **=SUM(B6:B13)** and press Tab.

4. Use the mouse to build a SUM formula that calculates the total years by following these steps:

   a. In cell C14, enter **=SUM(**

 NOTE: Don't forget the parenthesis.

   b. Click cell C6, hold down Shift, and click cell C13.

   c. Press Tab. The total years is 44.

5. Use the AutoSum button Σ to calculate the total of the bonuses by following these steps:

   a. In cell D14, click the AutoSum button Σ.

   b. Press Enter. The total for bonuses is 39,106.

6. Clear the contents of cell B14.

7. Use AutoCalculate to calculate the salary total by following these steps:

   a. Select cells B6 through B13.

   b. Jot down the number displayed in the status bar. (The number in the status bar should be preceded by "SUM=." If it is not, right-click the status bar and choose Sum from the AutoCalculate menu.)

   c. Select cell B14 and use the AutoSum button Σ to enter the total. This number should be the same as the number you just jotted down.

8. Make cell A1 active and save the workbook as *[your initials]*2-20.xls in your Lesson 2 folder.

9. Print the worksheet and close the workbook.

Students' headings and worksheets are not centered since these topics are not covered until later lessons. You may want to include a brief description of the steps for this.

○ Exercise 2-20:

Objectives 4, 5, 6
Required Files: QCBonus.xls
Solution Files: gl2-20.xls in Solutions Manual or on Solutions Disk.

EXERCISE 2-21

Create and interpret formulas.

1. Open the file **Stock.xls**.
2. In cell A21, key **Totals**
3. In cell B21, create a formula that totals years.
4. In cell C21, create a formula that totals shares of stock.
5. Save the workbook as *[your initials]*2-21.xls in your Lesson 2 folder.
6. Print the worksheet.
7. Examine the formulas in cells C6:C19 to see how shares of stock were calculated for each person. On the printout, write an explanation of how the number of shares is calculated. Do not just write the formula, but explain the logic behind the formula.
8. Close the workbook.

◉ Exercise 2-21:
Objective 4, 5
Required Files: Stock.xls
Solution Files: gl2-21.xls in Solutions Manual or on
Solutions Disk.

A
S
S
E
S
S

Assessment Resources:
• Solutions Manual
• Test Bank
• Portfolio Builder
• Internet Projects
• Alternative Assessment Guide
• Certification Procedures

Go ▼
For Internet projects, go to
www.glencoe.com/webprojects

Lesson Applications

EXERCISE 2-22

Enter data in selected cells and use the SUM function.

The Quality Control director at Alpha Pharmaceuticals asked you to create a
worksheet that calculates the weekly pay for Quality Control employees.

1. Open the file **QCPay1.xls**.
2. Select cells B6:C13 and delete their contents.
3. Key the data as shown in Figure 2-24, including the corrections.

FIGURE 2-24

	A	B	C	D
5	Name	Rate	Hours	Pay
6	Berenson	9.25 ~~2.95~~	40	
7	Alvarez	9.46	40	
8	Czerny	10.4⁵	38	
9	Teij	10.64	40	
10	Silvers	37.5	9.50	
11	Patino	10.00	40	
12	Wang	9.88 ~~2~~	40	
13	Golden	9.96	40	

NOTE: When you key 9.50 and 10.00, the zeros drop off after they
are entered. This is because the cells are not formatted to show decimal
places. You learn more about this in Lesson 3.

4. Create formulas that calculate the pay for each employee (rate × hours).
5. Key **Total** in cell A15.
6. In cell C15, use the SUM function to calculate the total hours.

Lesson Applications:
Provide independent practice for
students and may be used for
assessment. Objectives are indicated for
each Exercise.

◉ **Exercise 2-22:**
Objectives 1, 3, 5
Required Files: QCPay1.xls
Solution Files: gl2-22.xls in Solutions
Manual or on Solutions Disk.

1️⃣ You may want to explain to
students that entering the value
10.00 produces 10 in the worksheet,
because the cell is not formatted to
show decimal places.

2️⃣ This figure contains proofreading
marks. You may want to review
Appendix E: "Proofreaders' Marks" with
all students.

7. In cell D15, calculate the total pay using the AutoSum button Σ.

8. Make cell A1 active and save the workbook as *[your initials]*2-22.xls in your Lesson 2 folder.

9. Print the worksheet and close the workbook.

EXERCISE 2-23

Enter data, construct formulas, use the SUM function, and use AutoCalculate.

The Quality Control Director now needs to add overtime hours to the Quality Control employee payroll worksheet.

1. Open the file **QCPay2.xls**.

2. Key the headings and data shown in Figure 2-25.

FIGURE 2-25

	E	F
5	Overtime	O.T. Pay
6	2	
7	3	
8	0	
9	1.5	
10	0	
11	4.25	
12	2.5	
13	3	

3. Use AutoCalculate to total the hours in column C and enter this number in cell C15. Use the same method to enter the pay total in cell D15.

4. In cell E15, use the SUM function to calculate the total overtime hours.

 NOTE: If you use the AutoSum button Σ, remember to adjust the suggested cell range.

⊙ Exercise 2-23:
Objectives 1, 4–6
Required Files: QCPay2.xls
Solution Files: gl2-23.xls in Solutions Manual or on
Solutions Disk.

5. In cells F6:F13, create a formula for each employee to calculate his or her overtime pay. Use the formula "rate × overtime × 1.5." (Overtime pay is typically calculated as "time and a half"—that is, a rate of 1.5 hours.)

6. In cell F15, use the SUM function to calculate the total amount of overtime pay for all employees combined.

7. Make cell A1 active and save your workbook as *[your initials]*2-23.xls in your Lesson 2 folder.

8. Print the worksheet and close the workbook.

EXERCISE 2-24

Enter data, use AutoComplete and Pick From List, construct formulas, use the SUM function, and use AutoCalculate.

The Research and Development manager wants to see the vacation data of the R&D staff. She feels this department needs more vacation time and wants to show the worksheet to the president.

1. Open the file **R&DStaf.xls**.

2. Key the information shown in Figure 2-26, using AutoComplete and Pick From List where possible. Note that when cells are not consecutive, the features are not available.

FIGURE 2-26

	B	C	D	E	F
5	Clearance	Level	Years	Vacation Days	Manager
6					
7	None	D15	2		Tang
8	Mid	B23	2		Richards
9	Top	A43	3		Tang
10	Mid	B23	3		Tang
11	Top	A43	5		Stevens
12	Mid	B23	5		Stevens

continues

○ **Exercise 2-24:**
Objectives 1, 2, 4–6
Required Files: R&DStaf.xls
Solution Files: gl2-24.xls in Solutions Manual or on Solutions Disk.

The completed document for this Exercise may be used in a student's portfolio.

FIGURE 2-26 *continued*

	B	C	D	E	F
13					
14	Top	A43	6		Richards
15	Mid	B23	6		Stevens
16	None	D15	8		Tang
17					
18	None	B23	14		Stevens
19	None	C15	15		Richards
20	Mid	D15	19		Tang

3. Calculate the number of vacation days for each employee using the following information:

 TIP: Blank lines separate employees into the following categories.

- For 1 to 5 years: Years*0.1+5
- For 6 to 10 years: Years*0.1+10
- For more than 10 years: Years*0.15+15

4. Use AutoCalculate to calculate the total vacation days and enter this number in the appropriate cell.

5. Use the SUM function to calculate the total years.

6. Make cell A1 active and save your workbook as *[your initials]*2-24.xls in your Lesson 2 folder.

7. Print the worksheet and close the workbook.

EXERCISE 2-25

Enter data, construct formulas, and use AutoSum.

Alpha Pharmaceuticals' Marketing director wants to calculate the company's market share. You are to prepare a worksheet that shows market share as a percentage of national sales.

◉ **Exercise 2-25:**
Objectives 1, 4–6
Required Files: MktShare.xls
Solution Files: gl2-25.xls in Solutions Manual or on Solutions Disk

The completed document for this Exercise may be used in a student's portfolio.

1. Open the file **MktShare.xls**.
2. Key **1998 Market Share** in cell A2.
3. Select the cell range B8:C10 and key the data shown in Figure 2-27.

FIGURE 2-27

	B	C
8	19.671	4.085
9	25.093	7.314
10	29.384	7.457

4. In cell D8, calculate Alpha's market share for aspirin. Use the formula Alpha Sales/National Sales*100.
5. Create formulas to calculate the market share in cells D9 and D10.
6. Using either AutoCalculate or the SUM function, calculate the total pain reliever sales for National Sales and Alpha sales in cells B12 and C12, respectively.
7. Calculate Alpha's total market share for pain relievers in cell D12. (*Hint:* This is calculated the same way the market shares for cells D8:D10 are calculated.)
8. Make cell A1 active and save the workbook as *[your initials]*2-25.xls in your Lesson 2 folder.
9. Print the worksheet and close the workbook.

EXERCISE 2-26 *Challenge Yourself*

Enter data, construct formulas, and use AutoSum.

To prepare for an annual financial planning meeting, the Marketing director of Alpha Pharmaceuticals asked you to create a worksheet that calculates projected national sales for aspirin, acetaminophen, and ibuprofen for 1999 and 2000. These projected sales are based on 1998 sales information.

1. Open a new workbook and create an appropriate heading for the worksheet, with an indicator that the sales figures are expressed in millions.

Exercise 2-26:
Objectives 1, 4–6
Required Files: None
Solution Files: gl2-26.xls and gl2-26.htm in Solutions Manual or on Solutions Disk.

 The completed document for this Exercise may be used in a student's portfolio.

2. Enter the information in Figure 2-28 as 1998 data. Be sure to widen column A so the characters in "Acetaminophen" fit.

3. Make sure the text "1998" is entered as a label, so it is excluded from calculations. (This step also applies to other cells in the worksheet containing years.)

FIGURE 2-28

```
Product        1998

Aspirin        4.085

Acetaminophen  7.314

Ibuprofen      7.457
```

4. For 1999 and 2000 projected sales, show total sales that are a 2% increase over the previous year's sales for aspirin and acetaminophen, and a 3% increase each year for ibuprofen.

NOTE: Remember that a 2% increase over last year is 102% of last year's sales.)

5. Calculate total sales of pain relievers for each year. (Include a "Totals" label.)

6. Make cell A1 active and save the workbook as *[your initials]*2-26.xls in your Lesson 2 folder.

7. Print the worksheet and save the workbook as *[your initials]*2-26.htm in your Lesson 2 folder. (Remember to use Save As Web Page.)

8. Close the workbook.

Students' headings and worksheets are not centered since these topics are not covered until later lessons. You may want to include a brief description of the steps for this.

Enhancing a Simple Worksheet

LESSON 3

OBJECTIVES

After completing this lesson, you will be able to:

1. Select multiple columns and rows.
2. Insert cells, columns, and rows.
3. Delete cells, columns, and rows.
4. Use the Undo and Redo commands.
5. Use shortcut menus.
6. Move data.
7. Format numbers.
8. Apply text attributes and cell borders.

 Estimated Time: 1¼ hours

MOUS ACTIVITIES

In this lesson:

XL2000 **1.1**
XL2000 **1.3**
XL2000 **1.4**
XL2000 **1.6**
XL2000 **1.7**
XL2000 **3.2**
XL2000 **3.5**
XL2000 **3.6**
XL2000 **3.8**
XL2000 **5.1**

See Appendix F.

This lesson teaches easy ways to modify a worksheet by inserting and deleting cells, columns, and rows; changing the number of decimal places displayed; and applying basic text, alignment attributes, and cell borders.

Objective 1
Selecting Multiple Columns and Rows

As you learned in Lesson 2, clicking a row or column heading selects that row or column. You can also select several columns and rows at the same time.

PREPARE

Point out to students that the learning objectives show what they will learn in the lesson. Each heading in the lesson correlates to a learning objective.

Required files:
USSales1.xls

TEACH

Teaching Resources:
- Excel Classroom Presentations
- School-to-Work Strategies Manual
- Spanish Glossary
- Certification Procedures

EXERCISE 3-1 Select Multiple Columns and Rows with the Mouse

1. Open the file **USSales1.xls**.
2. Click column heading A to select the column.
3. Click and drag over the row headings for rows 2, 3, and 4. The column is deselected and the three rows are selected.
4. Click column heading B, hold down Shift, and click column heading E. Columns B through E are selected.
5. Drag over row headings 2 and 3 to select those rows.
6. Hold down Ctrl and click column heading B. Two rows and one column are selected.

FIGURE 3-1
Selecting columns and rows with the mouse

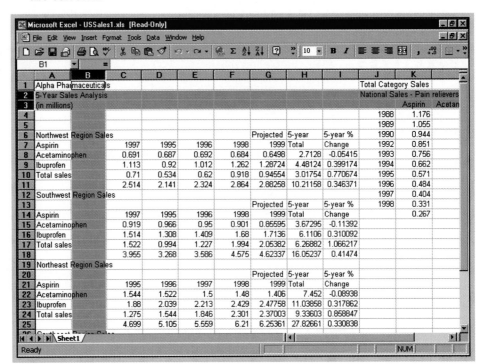

7. Click any cell in the worksheet to deselect the columns and rows.

EXERCISE 3-2 Select Multiple Columns and Rows with the Keyboard

1. In cell C7, press Shift+Spacebar to select row 7.
2. Select cell D5. Row 7 is now deselected.
3. Press Ctrl+Spacebar to select column D.

 This lesson expands the topic of selecting cells to selecting rows and columns. You might review selecting blocks of cells if considerable time has passed since students completed Lesson 2.

 Use Excel Classroom Presentation 3 to display screens from the lesson in a slide-show format.

4. While holding ⁅Shift⁆, press ⁅→⁆ three times. The selection is extended through column G.

5. Select cell B7.

6. Press ⁅Shift⁆+⁅→⁆ twice to select cells B7 through D7.

7. Press ⁅Ctrl⁆+⁅Spacebar⁆ to select columns B through D.

8. Use the keyboard to select cells C7 through E9 and then press ⁅Shift⁆+⁅Spacebar⁆. Rows 7 through 9 are selected.

9. Press any arrow key to deselect the rows.

TABLE 3-1   **Selecting Columns and Rows**

ACTION	RESULT
Click heading	Selects a column or row.
Drag across headings	Selects multiple columns or rows.
⁅Shift⁆+click heading	Extends the selection to include adjacent columns or rows.
⁅Ctrl⁆+click heading	Extends the selection to include nonadjacent columns or rows.
Click Select All button	Selects the entire worksheet.
⁅Shift⁆+⁅Spacebar⁆	Selects the current row.
⁅Ctrl⁆+⁅Spacebar⁆	Selects the current column.
⁅Shift⁆+Arrow keys, ⁅PgUp⁆ or ⁅PgDn⁆	Extends the row or column selection (first select a row or column).
⁅Shift⁆+Double-click	When the arrow pointer is displayed, selects the filled column or row in the direction of the vertical edge clicked.

Objective 2

Inserting Cells, Columns, and Rows

You can add cells, columns, and rows to a worksheet to make room for more data or to make the worksheet easier to read. You can do this using the Insert menu or the keyboard shortcut ⁅Ctrl⁆+⁅+⁆ (the plus key on the numeric keypad).

EXERCISE   3-3   Insert a Single Cell

A section of the **USSales1.xls** worksheet shows 10 years of national pain reliever sales, but contains some errors. When the row labels in column J were keyed, "1991" was skipped. You can insert a cell to correct this problem.

[1] The last action in Table 3-1 requires a Shift + double-click. To execute this action correctly, a drag and drop (arrow) pointer must be in view, not the selection (plus) pointer.

[2] The data in J1:N15 in this file is laid out in this manner for instructional purposes only, as will be seen in Exercise 3-5. Good worksheet design would place this data under columns A through E, starting at row 34, or on its own sheet.

1. Scroll to bring columns J through N into view.

2. Select cell J7. Notice that cell J6 contains "1990" and cell J7 contains "1992."

3. Choose Cells from the Insert menu. The Insert dialog box opens.

FIGURE 3-2
Insert dialog box

4. Click Cancel and press Ctrl + + on the numeric keypad. This is another way to open the Insert dialog box.

 NOTE: If you are using a laptop and do not have a numeric keypad, use Insert, Cells instead of Ctrl + + or press Ctrl + Shift + + on the regular keyboard.

5. Choose Shift Cells Down and click OK. An empty cell appears at cell J7. The labels below shift down one cell.

6. Key **1991** in cell J7 and press Enter.

EXERCISE 3-4 Insert an Entire Column and Row

You can insert an entire row or column in a worksheet at the position of the active cell. Use the Insert menu or the keyboard shortcut Ctrl + + on the numeric keypad.

1. Select cell A19.

 TIP: Remember, you can use the key combination Alt + PgUp to move one screen left.

2. Choose Rows from the Insert menu. A blank row appears at row 19 and all the information below this row moves down one row.

3. Select row 19 and press Ctrl + + or choose Rows from the Insert menu. Another row is inserted automatically. (You must select the entire row.)

4. Press F5 to open the Go To dialog box.

5. Key **J1** and click OK (or press Enter).

6. Click the column J heading to select the entire column.

7. Choose Columns from the Insert menu (or press Ctrl + +). A blank column appears at column J and all the information beyond column J moves right one column.

In Excel Classroom Presentation 3.

1 The year labels in this worksheet were not entered with an apostrophe to keep them out of automatic calculations such as AutoSum. Please make students aware that when this is the case, they should check formulas often when manipulating data.

2 You may want to review navigation keys throughout this lesson as students move through a large worksheet.

To insert several cells, columns, or rows in the same operation, select them before choosing a command. For example, if you select two rows, choosing Rows from the Insert menu (or pressing Ctrl + +) inserts two blank rows.

NOTE: When you insert rows or columns, be careful not to separate blocks of data by mistake. Rows and columns span the entire worksheet, not just the visible portion of your screen. Rows extend 256 cells across and columns stretch 65,536 cells down.

1. Select rows 28 and 29 and press Ctrl + + or choose Insert, Rows. Two blank rows are inserted to separate "Northeast Region Sales" from "Southeast Region Sales."

2. Select rows 12 and 13.

3. Scroll to the right so columns K through O are visible. Notice that inserting rows here would break up data inappropriately in columns K through O.

FIGURE 3-3
Selecting to insert
multiple rows

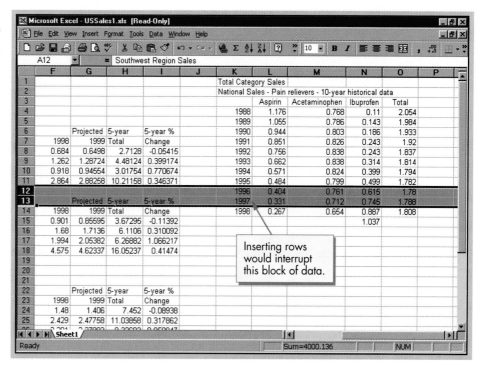

Inserting rows would interrupt this block of data.

4. Deselect the rows and scroll back to view column A.

5. Select cells A12 through I13 and press Ctrl + + or choose Insert, Cells.

⌐1 Warn students that inserting rows or columns may interrupt existing blocks of data that are not currently shown on the screen.

▭ In Excel Classroom Presentation 3.

6. In the Insert dialog box, choose Shift Cells <u>D</u>own and click OK. Blank cells appear at cells A12 through I13 and all the data from cells A12 through I13 moves down two cells.

7. Scroll to view the 10-year historical data. Notice that no blank cells interrupt the data.

Objective 3

Deleting Cells, Columns, and Rows

You can delete cells, columns, and rows in much the same way that you insert them. Choose <u>D</u>elete from the <u>E</u>dit menu or press Ctrl+- (the minus sign on the numeric keypad).

When you delete cells, those cells are removed from the worksheet and the surrounding cells move to fill the space. If the deleted cells contained data, the data is also removed from the worksheet. In contrast, *clearing the contents of cells* removes the information contained in those cells, but allows the cells to remain in the worksheet.

TIP: Never clear contents by keying a blank space in a cell. Although the cell appears blank, it actually contains a label. This label may ultimately affect calculations.

EXERCISE 3-6 Delete Cells, Columns, and Rows

1. Select cell N8. This cell contains the same entry as cell N7. The data in column N extends one row below the data in the other columns.

2. Choose <u>D</u>elete from the <u>E</u>dit menu. The Delete dialog box opens.

FIGURE 3-4
Delete dialog box

3. Choose Shift Cells <u>U</u>p and click OK. Cell N8 is deleted and the cells move up to fill the gap.

4. Select column B and choose <u>D</u>elete from the <u>E</u>dit menu. Column B is deleted.

5. Select column B, if necessary, and press Ctrl+[+] or choose <u>I</u>nsert, <u>C</u>olumns to insert the column.

6. Press Ctrl+- or choose <u>D</u>elete from the <u>E</u>dit menu to delete column B again.

7. Select column A.

8. Adjust the width of column A to accommodate the width of the label in cell A8 by choosing <u>C</u>olumn from the F<u>o</u>rmat menu, choosing <u>W</u>idth, and

---

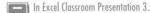

1 Students should get into the habit of using the keyboard's numeric keypad for the plus and minus sign in the keyboard shortcuts Ctrl+plus sign and Ctrl+minus sign. For students with laptops that do not have numeric keypads, the combination Ctrl+minus sign using the regular keyboard produces the correct result, but students have to press Ctrl+Shift+plus sign to insert.

In Excel Classroom Presentation 3.

2 Now that students learned about column headings, you may want to instruct them on how to change column width by dragging the right column border in the column heading.

then keying **18** in the text box. Click OK. (You may need to key a larger
number to fit the label.)

 TIP: Whenever possible remove blank columns and adjust column widths
to fit text.

☑ Objective 4

Using the Undo and Redo Commands

The Undo command reverses the last action you performed on the worksheet.
If you deleted a column, for example, Undo brings back the column and its
data. If you accidentally overwrite existing data in a cell, Undo restores the
original cell contents. To use the Undo command, it is best to choose it immediately after the action you want to undo. The Redo command reverses the action of the Undo command. (You can "undo" Undo.)

You can also use these commands to undo and redo multiple actions at
once. You can select Undo and Redo multiple times to step back through your
last actions. Undo and Redo reverse actions sequentially. That is, to reverse a
specific action, you must reverse any action that came after it first.

To use the Undo command, you can:

- Click the Undo button 🔄 on the Standard toolbar.
- Press Ctrl + Z.
- Choose Undo from the Edit menu.

To use the Redo command, you can:

- Click the Redo button 🔄 on the Standard toolbar.
- Press Ctrl + Y.
- Choose Redo from the Edit menu.

TIP: Undo and Redo are convenient tools, but their usefulness is limited. It
is always best to save your worksheet frequently. If you then make an
unrecoverable error, you can simply close the worksheet without saving it and
reopen the saved version.

EXERCISE 3-7 Use the Undo and Redo Commands

   1. Save the worksheet as *[your initials]***3-7.xls** in a new folder for Lesson 3.
Note that both the Undo 🔄 and Redo 🔄 buttons are shaded since there

---

☑ **Objective 4 Assignment:**
Exercise 3-18 (Skills Review) can be assigned after
completing Objective 4.

Remind students to save worksheets in a folder
for the Lesson. You may have to review the steps
involved in creating the folder and saving a file to it.

are no actions yet to undo or redo. (You may need to click the More Buttons button ⬚ on the Standard toolbar to find either of these buttons.)

2. Select column C by clicking its column heading.

3. Choose <u>D</u>elete from the <u>E</u>dit menu. The column is deleted. Notice that the shading on the Undo button ⬚ is gone.

4. Choose <u>U</u>ndo Delete from the <u>E</u>dit menu (or press Ctrl+Z). The column is restored. Notice that the shading on the Redo button ⬚ disappeared and the Undo button ⬚ is shaded. (If Undo did not work, close the workbook without saving it and open *[your initials]*3-7.xls again.)

5. Choose <u>R</u>edo Delete from the <u>E</u>dit menu (or press Ctrl+Y). The undo is reversed and the column is deleted again.

6. Select cell B11 and press Delete. The contents of B11 are cleared.

7. Click the down arrow on the Undo button ⬚ to see the drop-down list. Notice that the most recent action, which was clearing cell B11, is at the top of the list.

FIGURE 3-5
Undo drop-down list
⬚

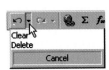

8. Click Delete on the drop-down list. The contents of cell B11 and column C are restored.

9. Click the Redo button ⬚. This reverses the last undo, which was the column C deletion, and column C is deleted again.

10. Click the Undo button ⬚ again. The column is restored.

11. Click any cell to deselect column C.

Objective 5

Using Shortcut Menus

Shortcut menus provide quick access to commands you use often, bypassing the menu bar. To display a shortcut menu, select a cell, a cell range, a row, or a column, and right-click the selection or press Shift+F10. The commands you are most likely to use are listed on the shortcut menu. To choose a command, click it with the left mouse button.

EXERCISE 3-8 Use Shortcut Menus

All the row labels in column A, starting in cell A7, are positioned one cell too high. To correct this problem, you can insert a cell at cell A7.

1. Make cell A7 the active cell.

2. While pointing inside cell A7, right-click. The shortcut menu appears.

FIGURE 3-6
Shortcut menu

3. Choose Insert from the shortcut menu.

4. In the Insert dialog box, choose Shift Cells Down and click OK. The row labels are positioned correctly.

☑ Objective 6

Moving Data to a New Location

You can easily move the contents of cells to another location without rekeying data. One way is to cut and paste the information, which is a two-step operation. First, you *cut* selected cells. You then move to a new location and *paste* the data in the cells at the new location. You can also copy a selection and paste a copy of it in a new location. You learn more about copying in Lesson 5.

To cut and paste selected data, you can use:

- The toolbar buttons Cut ✂ and Paste 📋
- Keyboard shortcuts Ctrl+X to cut and Ctrl+V to paste
- The shortcut menu

When you cut or copy data from selected cells, it is stored temporarily on the *Clipboard*, an area in the computer's active memory. The Paste command transfers the contents of the Clipboard to the location you choose.

EXERCISE   3-9   Move Data Using Cut and Paste

1. Right-click cell A3.

2. Choose Cut from the shortcut menu. A moving border surrounds cell A3.

3. Click cell A4 and click the Paste button 📋 on the Standard toolbar. Cell A3 is cleared, the moving border disappears, and the contents of cell A3 appear in cell A4.

4. Click the Undo button ↶ to undo the Paste command. The moving border marks cell A3 and cell A4 remains the active cell.

5. Press Enter. The text is moved. Pressing Enter has the same effect as the Paste command when the moving border marks a range of cut cells.

6. Click the Undo button ↶ to restore the text to cell A3. Press Esc to remove the moving border.

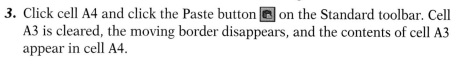

In Excel Classroom Presentation 3.

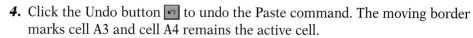

☑ **Objective 6 Assignment:**
Exercise 3-19 (Skills Review) can be assigned after completing Objective 6.

You might have students undo the Paste command and try other ways to cut and paste. Some students will prefer the keyboard methods, some may prefer the toolbar buttons, and others may prefer the shortcut menu.

EXERCISE 3-10 Move Data Using Insert Cut Cells

When you paste data into a cell range, any data contained in the range is overwritten by the new data. To insert data at a location that already contains data, use the Insert Cut Cells command. This command causes the existing cells to be shifted down or to the right when data is moved to that location.

1. Save the worksheet as *[your initials]*3-10.xls in your Lesson 3 folder.

2. Select cells B7 through B11.

3. Right-click the selection and choose Cut from the shortcut menu.

4. Select cell E7.

5. Press Ctrl+V, the keyboard shortcut for Paste. The "1998" data in cells E7 through E11 is overwritten by the "1997" data. Because the formulas in columns F, G, and H referenced the "1998" data, the notation #REF! appears in the cells that contain formulas, indicating a reference error.

6. Click the Undo button. The data is restored and the reference errors are no longer displayed.

7. With the moving border again surrounding cells B7 through B11, and cells E7 through E11 selected, choose Cut Cells from the Insert menu or choose Insert Cut Cells from the shortcut menu. The "1997" data is inserted between the "1996" and "1998" data.

FIGURE 3-7
Inserting cut cells

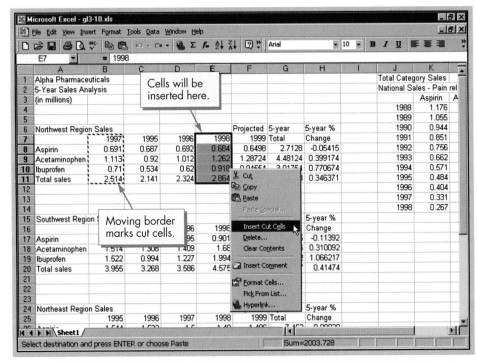

In Excel Classroom Presentation 3.

EXERCISE 3-11 Move Data Using Drag and Drop

When you move the white-cross pointer slowly across the border of an active cell or selected cells, it changes to an arrow. This arrow is the drag-and-drop pointer, which you use to move data to a new location. Old data is replaced with moved data when you release the mouse button.

1. Select cells A1 through A3.

2. Slowly move the white-cross pointer across the selection's border until the white cross changes into an arrow.

> **NOTE:** If the arrow pointer does not appear, choose Options from the Tools menu, click the Edit tab, and click the Allow Cell Drag and Drop check box to select the option.

3. Press and hold the left mouse button. Notice that the status bar indicates your options.

4. Move the arrow to cell D1. A light gray border surrounds cells D1 through D3.

FIGURE 3-8
Drag-and-drop to move data

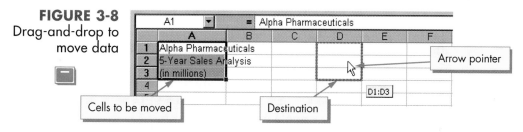

5. Release the mouse button. The data is moved and cells A1 through A3 are cleared.

6. Select cells B16 through B20.

7. Move the mouse pointer to the border of the selection until you see the arrow pointer.

8. Hold down Shift and begin to drag. An I-beam appears. Continue dragging and the I-beam alternates between vertical and horizontal. Drag it to the vertical gridline between columns D and E, with the top of the I-beam between rows 15 and 16.

FIGURE 3-9
Drag-and-drop to insert cut cells

9. Release the mouse button and then release Shift. You inserted the cut cells. The "1997" data is inserted between the "1996" and "1998" data.

1 You may want to warn students about dragging the AutoFill handle when they drag cell borders. The drag-and-drop pointer is an arrow that they use to move a selection. If the pointer is positioned over the AutoFill handle (a small black square), the pointer appears as a black cross.

2 In step 4, students are asked to move the worksheet title to a center column to practice moving data. The proper way to center a worksheet title is to center it across columns.

In Excel Classroom Presentation 3.

3 In step 8, emphasize that students must press the Shift key before dragging. Otherwise, Excel performs a replace and not an insert.

EXERCISE **3-12** **Check Cell References and Formulas after Moving Data**

When you move formulas, the cell references in the formulas remain the same, as do the calculations performed by those formulas. When you move cells that are referenced by formulas, Excel updates the formulas automatically so they reference the new location of the cells. For example, if a SUM function references the range C5:C10, and you move the contents of cell C10 to cell C12, the SUM function changes automatically to reference the range C5:C12. Always check formulas after moving data to ensure they are updated correctly.

1. Select cell G8. The correct formula, =SUM(B8:F8), appears on the formula bar.

2. Select cell H8. The correct formula, =(F8-B8)/B8, appears on the formula bar.

3. Check formulas throughout the worksheet.

Objective 7

Formatting Numbers: The Basics

You can format numbers to have a similar appearance without changing their mathematical values. For instance, the values resulting from division often have many decimal places, which may not be aligned. If you format cells to show only two decimal places, the results are neat and easy to read. Excel still stores all the undisplayed digits, however, and uses them in future computations. You can redisplay complete values at any time.

The Excel Formatting toolbar offers a convenient way to format numbers. An expanded Formatting toolbar showing all possible buttons on this toolbar appears in Figure 3-10.

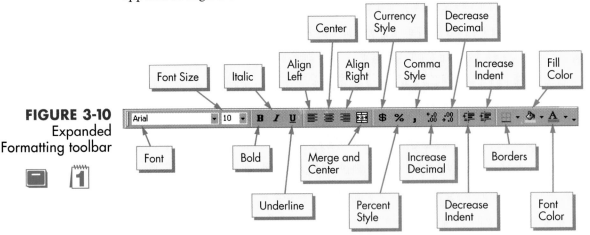

FIGURE 3-10
Expanded
Formatting toolbar

In Excel Classroom Presentation 3.

An expanded Formatting toolbar is shown here to give students a chance to get familiar with the most commonly used toolbar buttons.

EXERCISE 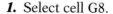 **3-13** **Format Numbers in Comma Style and Percent Style**

1. Select cell G8.
2. Click the Comma Style button ▪ on the toolbar (you may need to click the More Buttons button ▪ to locate it). Cell G8 is formatted with two decimal places. The Comma Style button ▪ inserts commas to separate thousands, if needed, and formats values to have two decimal places.
3. Select cells B8 through G11.
4. Click the Comma Style button ▪ again. All the selected cells are formatted with two decimal places and the decimals are aligned.
5. Select cells H8 through H11.

6. Click the Percent Style button ▪. The selected cells are formatted as percentages with no decimals.

EXERCISE **3-14** **Change the Number of Decimals Displayed**

You can use the Increase Decimal ▪ and Decrease Decimal ▪ buttons on the Formatting toolbar to control the number of decimal places displayed in cells.

1. Select cells B17 through G20.

2. Click the Decrease Decimal button ▪. The selected cells display two decimal places.

3. Click the Increase Decimal button ▪. The cells display three decimal places.
4. Select cells H17 through H20.
5. Click the Percent Style button ▪ and then click the Increase Decimal button ▪. The selected cells are displayed as percentages with one decimal place.

6. Using the Formatting toolbar, format all the sales region numbers to match the formatting of the "Southwest Region" numbers.

☑ **Objective 8**

Applying Text Attributes and Cell Borders

You can use the buttons on the Formatting toolbar to format text as well as numbers. You can control alignment in a cell, apply bold and italic, draw lines, and change the size of text. You can also use the Format Painter button ▪ on the Standard toolbar to copy these attributes from one cell or cell range to another.

⎡1⎤ Throughout this Lesson, remind students to click the More Buttons button, if necessary, to locate a button that does not appear on the Formatting or Standard toolbar.

⎡2⎤ Warn students that if they select the cell range B8:H11 and use the Increase Decimal button, the number formatting of cells H8:H11 changes to Comma Style.

☑ **Objective 8 Assignment:**
Exercises 3-20 and 3-21 (Skills Review) and Exercises 3-22 through 3-25 (Lesson Applications) can be assigned after completing Objective 8.

EXERCISE 3-15 Apply Text Attributes Using the Formatting Toolbar

1. Select cells D1 through D3.

2. Click the Center button ▤ on the Formatting toolbar. The text in cells D1 through D3 is centered in the cells, but spills over to cells in columns C and E.

3. Select cells D1 and D2.

4. Click the Bold button **B**. The selected text becomes bold.

5. Select cells F6 through H7.

6. Click the Align Right button ▤. The text is aligned with the numbers below it.

   TIP: Column titles should usually be aligned with their related data.

7. Select cells A6 through H7 and cells A11 through H11.

8. Click the Bold button **B** to make the selection bold.

FIGURE 3-11
Formatting the worksheet

	A	B	C	D	E	F	G	H	I	J	K
	A11 ▼	=	Total sales								
1			**Alpha Pharmaceuticals**							Total Category Sa	
2			**5-Year Sales Analysis**							National Sales - P	
3			(in millions)								Aspir
4										1988	1.
5										1989	1.l
6	**Northwest Region Sales**					**Projected**	**5-year**	**5-year %**		1990	0.!
7		**1995**	**1996**	**1997**	**1998**	**1999**	**Total**	**Change**		1991	0.l
8	Aspirin	0.687	0.692	0.691	0.684	0.650	3.404	-5.4%		1992	0.
9	Acetaminophen	0.920	1.012	1.113	1.262	1.287	5.594	39.9%		1993	0.l
10	Ibuprofen	0.534	0.620	0.710	0.918	0.946	3.728	77.1%		1994	0.!
11	**Total sales**	**2.141**	**2.324**	**2.514**	**2.864**	**2.883**	**12.726**	**34.6%**		1995	0.
12										1996	0..
13										1997	0.
14										1998	0.
15	Southwest Region Sales					Projected	5-year	5-year %			
16		1995	1996	1997	1998	1999	Total	Change			
17	Aspirin	0.966	0.950	0.919	0.901	0.856	4.592	-11.4%			
18	Acetaminophen	1.308	1.409	1.514	1.680	1.714	7.625	31.0%			
19	Ibuprofen	0.994	1.227	1.522	1.994	2.054	7.791	106.6%			
20	Total sales	3.268	3.586	3.955	4.575	4.623	20.007	41.5%			
21											
22											
23											
24	Northeast Region Sales					Projected	5-year	5-year %			
25		1995	1996	1997	1998	1999	Total	Change			

Sheet1

Ready   Sum=10010.79753

EXERCISE 3-16 Use Format Painter to Copy Attributes

Once you apply a variety of attributes to a cell range—such as bold and italic, alignment, and number styles—you can copy the attributes from one cell range to another using the Format Painter button ⬚ on the Standard toolbar.

It is best to center titles across the worksheet. However, the titles here are used to demonstrate drag and drop and center alignment.

In Excel Classroom Presentation 3.

1. Select cells A6 through H11.

2. Click the Format Painter button 🖌. A moving border surrounds the selection. You can now copy the formatting of this range to other sales region data in the worksheet.

3. Use the vertical scroll bar to display cells A15 through H20, if necessary.

NOTE: When you use the Format Painter, use the scroll bar to navigate around the screen instead of the arrow keys to prevent the cells between the source and destination cells from being painted.

4. Using the Format Painter pointer ✛🖌, select cells A15 through H20, the "Southwest Region Sales" data. The formatting is applied to the data.

FIGURE 3-12
Copying attributes with Format Painter

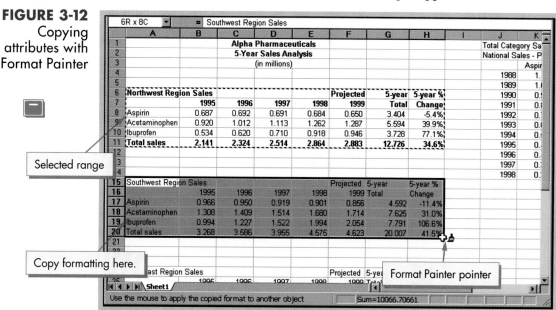

5. With the cell range A15 through H20 still selected, double-click the Format Painter button 🖌. Double-clicking this button allows you to apply attributes to more than one consecutive selection.

6. Use the Format Painter pointer to select cells A24 through H29 and then select cells A33 through H38. All the regions now have the same formatting.

7. Press ⎋ to restore the normal pointer.

EXERCISE 3-17 Apply Borders to the Bottoms of Cells

You can create a line to separate data by formatting cells with a bottom border. The easiest way to apply a border is by using the Borders button 🔲 on the Formatting toolbar.

 Be sure students understand that text must be selected before they use the Format Painter button to copy formatting.

In Excel Classroom Presentation 3.

1. Select cells A7 through H7.

2. Click the down arrow on the right side of the Borders button ▦. The Borders palette appears.

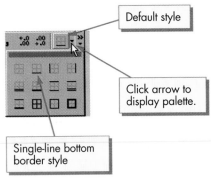

FIGURE 3-13
Borders palette

Default style

Click arrow to display palette.

Single-line bottom border style

3. Choose the single-line bottom border style (first row, second column) on the palette. The bottom borders of cells A7 through H7 are formatted as a single solid line. The Borders button default is now single-line bottom border.

4. Select cells A16:H16 and click the Borders button ▦. Remember, the Borders button ▦ uses the most recently applied border style as a default.

5. Apply the same border style to separate the headings from data in the other two regions.

6. Make cell A1 active and save the file as *[your initials]3-17.xls* in your Lesson 3 folder.

7. Print the worksheet and close the workbook.

COMMAND SUMMARY

FEATURE	BUTTON	MENU	KEYBOARD
Insert Cells		Insert, Cells, Rows, or Columns	Ctrl + +
Delete Cells		Edit, Delete	Ctrl + -
Cut	✂	Edit, Cut	Ctrl + X
Paste	📋	Edit, Paste	Ctrl + V
Undo	↶	Edit, Undo	Ctrl + Z
Redo	↷	Edit, Redo	Ctrl + Y

USING HELP

[?]

Excel's online Help is extremely comprehensive. The Office Assistant can direct you to Help topics related to the work you are doing, but you can also access Help directly by browsing through the Help Contents window or using the Help Index.

[1] Point out that the Borders button has two sides. Clicking the border icon shown on the left side applies that border format. Clicking the down arrow on the right side displays the Borders palette. After a border format is selected, it becomes the format displayed on the Borders button.

 In Excel Classroom Presentation 3.

[2] The Borders palette, once opened, can be dragged onto a worksheet by pointing to the small title bar at the top of the palette and dragging down to the desired position. Students can then pick any border style, as needed. You may want to demonstrate this. Close the palette by clicking its Close button.

[3] At this point, you may want to have students turn off gridlines (Tools menu, Options, deselect Gridlines) to see the effect of borders on the worksheet.

[4] Point out that the Command Summary lists a variety of ways to accomplish a particular task. Students can decide which method they prefer.

Explore the range of topics available in Help Contents:

1. Press ⌨F1 to start Help.

2. Under "What would you like to do," key **format cells** and click <u>S</u>earch.

3. Click the topic "Format cells quickly." Click the link <u>Copy formats from one cell or range to another</u>.

4. Click the Show button ⬅ to expand the Help window.

5. Click the Contents tab, if necessary. Scroll the list of topics, each of which is represented by a book icon ❧.

6. Click the plus sign to the left of the topic "Formatting Worksheets" to display subtopics.

7. Review the subtopics. Click any subtopic that interests you.

FIGURE 3-14
Exploring Help
Contents

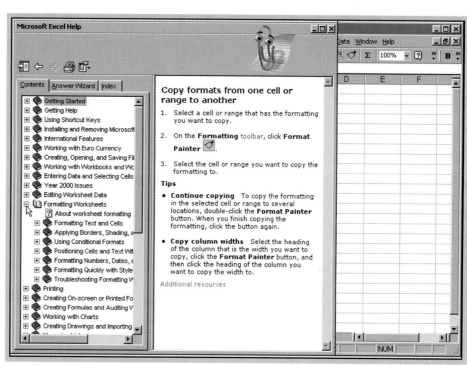

8. Click ❌ to close the Help window.

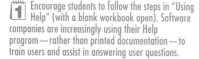

Encourage students to follow the steps in "Using Help" (with a blank workbook open). Software companies are increasingly using their Help program—rather than printed documentation—to train users and assist in answering user questions.

 In Excel Classroom Presentation 3.

TEST BANK

Concepts Review

TRUE/FALSE QUESTIONS

Each of the following statements is either true or false. Indicate your choice by circling **T** or **F**.

T (F) **1.** After selecting a column with the mouse, you can extend the selection only by using the mouse.

(T) F **2.** You can insert an entire row using the Insert dialog box.

(T) F **3.** When you delete a cell using the Delete dialog box, both the cell and its contents are removed from the worksheet.

(T) F **4.** Clicking the Undo button ↺ three times reverses your last three actions.

T (F) **5.** Double-clicking a cell displays a shortcut menu.

(T) F **6.** The Cut, Paste, and Copy buttons are located on the Standard toolbar.

(T) F **7.** The Comma Style button formats numbers to display two decimal places.

(T) F **8.** You can use the Format Painter button 🖌 to copy both alignment and number formatting from one cell range to another.

SHORT ANSWER QUESTIONS

Write the correct answer in the space provided.

1. To extend a selection using the arrow keys, which key must you hold down?

Shift

2. To insert multiple rows, you select the number of rows to insert and then press which key combination?

Ctrl + the Plus key

3. Which menu command can restore a column you just deleted by mistake?

Edit, Undo

4. When you cut a selection, how is it marked onscreen?

By a moving border

C L O S E

Concepts Review:
Allows students to check their understanding.

TEST BANK
Consider using the Test Bank to provide an additional review of lesson concepts. It may also be used as an assessment tool.

5. When you drag to insert cut cells, what symbol do you see while you drag
to the new location?

An I-beam

6. How many decimal places does the Percent Style button format numbers
to display?

0 (zero) or none

7. On which toolbar is the Bold button **B** located?

Formatting

8. Which keyboard combination selects the current row?

Shift + Spacebar

CRITICAL THINKING

Answer these questions on a separate piece of paper. There are no right or wrong answers. Support your answers with examples from your own experience, if possible.

1. You want to add a row of sales data for another product to an existing
worksheet. Should you insert a row, or just selected cells? Why?

2. If Excel updates formulas automatically after you move cells, why should
you check formulas?

Skills Review

EXERCISE 3-18

Select multiple columns and rows; insert and delete cells, columns, and rows; and use the Undo command.

1. Open the file **NWReps1.xls**.

2. Insert a cell to align the labels in column A with the data below by
following these steps:
   a. Select cell A8.
   b. Choose C**e**lls from the **I**nsert menu.
   c. Choose Shift Cells **D**own in the Insert dialog box and click OK.

3. Insert a column by following these steps:
   a. Select any cell in column B.

Critical Thinking Questions:
Answers will vary based on students' preferences,
observations, experiences, and research.

Skills Review:
Provides guided practice for students. Objectives are
indicated for each Exercise.

◉ **Exercise 3-18:**
Objectives 1–4
Required Files: NWReps1.xls
Solution Files: gl3-18.xls

   b. Choose <u>C</u>olumns from the <u>I</u>nsert menu.

4. Delete rows to close up the space between the worksheet heading and the data by following these steps:

   a. Drag over row headings 5 through 8 to select those rows.

   b. Press `Ctrl`+`-` (the minus key on the numeric keypad) or choose <u>D</u>elete from the <u>E</u>dit menu.

5. Choose <u>U</u>ndo Delete from the <u>E</u>dit menu to restore the four rows.

6. Delete three rows by following these steps:

   a. Click row heading 5 to select that row.

   b. Press and hold down `Shift` and click row heading 7.

   c. Press `Ctrl`+`-` or choose <u>D</u>elete from the <u>E</u>dit menu.

7. Select and delete column B.

8. Change the width of column A to 20.

9. Save the workbook as ***[your initials]*3-18.xls** in your Lesson 3 folder.

10. Print the worksheet and close the workbook.

EXERCISE 3-19

Insert cells, use the shortcut menu, and move data.

1. Open the file **NWReps2.xls**. Some data is missing and the quarterly information was keyed in the wrong order.

2. Insert cells to make room for new data by following these steps:

   a. Select cells A14:H14.

   b. Right-click the selection and choose <u>I</u>nsert from the shortcut menu.

   c. In the Insert dialog box, choose Shift Cells <u>D</u>own and click OK.

3. Key the data shown in Figure 3-15.

FIGURE 3-15

	Q4	Q3	Q2	Q1
Jose Garcia	73.8	72.4	77.912	75.1739

NOTE: Excel has a List AutoFill feature that is turned on by default. It automatically copies formatting and formulas to new rows when they are added to a list of data. It also updates totals in total columns. For the AutoFill feature to be turned on, there must be at least five rows in the list preceding the new row(s). Formats and formulas must also appear in at least three of those five rows.

● Exercise 3-19:
Objectives 2, 5–6
Required Files: NWReps2.xls
Solution Files: gl3-19.xls

The List AutoFill feature is new for Office 2000. It is turned on by default (Tools, Options, Edit tab, Extend List Formats and Formulas). Students should understand this feature because they will notice it when entering data in a long list.

4. Move the "Qtr 1" cells to column B by following these steps:
   a. Select cells F6:F19 and right-click the range.
   b. Choose Cut from the shortcut menu.
   c. Right-click cell B6 and choose Paste from the shortcut menu.

5. Move the "Qtr 4" cells to column F by following these steps:
   a. Select cells C6:C19.
   b. Move the mouse pointer to the border of the range until it becomes an arrow.
   c. Drag the selection to the range F6:F19 and release the mouse button.

6. Move the "Qtr 1" cells from column B to the blank column C.

7. Reverse the positions of the "Qtr 2" and "Qtr 3" information by following these steps:
   a. Select "Qtr 2" cells E6:E19.
   b. Press Ctrl + X to cut these cells.
   c. Select cell D6, which contains "Qtr 3."
   d. Choose Cut Cells from the Insert menu (or choose Insert Cut Cells from the shortcut menu).

8. Delete the blank column B.

9. Review the formulas in the "Total" column and correct them, if necessary. (They should add the sales in all four quarters for each salesperson.)

10. Review the formulas in the "% of Total" column. (They should divide the total sales for each salesperson by the total sales for all salespersons.)

11. Save the workbook as *[your initials]*3-19.xls in your Lesson 3 folder.

12. Print the worksheet and close the workbook.

EXERCISE 3-20

Move cells, format numbers, apply text attributes, and apply borders.

1. Open the file **NWReps3.xls**.

2. Format the dollar amounts in comma style and display only one decimal place by following these steps:
   a. Select cells C8:G17 and C19:G19.
   b. Click the Comma Style button on the Formatting toolbar.
   c. Click the Decrease Decimal button on the Formatting toolbar.

3. Format amounts in the "% of Total" column in percent style and displaying one decimal place by following these steps:
   a. Select cells H8:H19.
   b. Click the Percent Style button and then click the Increase Decimal button.

1 If the Clipboard toolbar appears after multiple cuts in this exercise or another exercise, tell students to click the toolbar's Close button. The Clipboard toolbar is taught in Lesson 5.

2 After students move columns, the Total column is incorrect. You might want to emphasize that cutting and pasting can change formulas.

3 Students may ask about the dollar signs in the % of Total column formulas (for example =F8/SF$19). You may want to give a brief explanation about relative and absolute cell references.

● Exercise 3-20:
Objectives 7–8
Required Files: NWReps3.xls
Solution Files: gl3-20.xls in Solutions Manual or on Solutions Disk.

4. Format and align the column labels by following these steps:

   a. Select cells A6:H6 and click the Bold button **B** to make the text bold.

   b. With the cells still selected, click the down arrow on the Borders button and choose the single-line bottom border.

   c. Select cells C6:G6 and click the Align Right button to right-align the text.

5. Format cells A1:A4 and A19:H19 as bold.

6. Delete the blank row 7.

7. In cells C18:H18, add a single-line top and a double-line bottom border (which is the last icon on the second row of the border palette) and delete the blank row 17.

TIP: Single-line borders under numbers indicate numbers above are to be calculated. Double-line borders under numbers indicate numbers immediately above are totals.

8. Delete column B and adjust the column width of column A to fit the longest salesperson's name in the column.

9. Save the workbook as *[your initials]*3-20.xls in your Lesson 3 folder.

10. Print the worksheet and close the workbook.

EXERCISE 3-21

Move cells and rows, format numbers, apply text attributes and borders, copy formats, and use shortcut menus.

1. Open the file **USSales2.xls**.

2. Under "Northwest Region Sales," move row 8 ("Acetaminophen") below row 9 ("Aspirin") to match the sequence in the other three regions. Follow these steps:

   a. Right-click row heading 8 and click Cut on the shortcut menu.

   b. Right-click row heading 10 and click Insert Cut Cells on the shortcut menu.

3. Move "Northeast Region Sales" before "Southwest Region Sales" by following these steps:

   a. Select rows 20 through 26 by dragging with the mouse.

   b. Press Ctrl+X to cut the selected rows.

   c. Right-click row heading 13 and click Insert Cut Cells on the shortcut menu.

4. Format the title in cells A1:A3 as bold.

● Exercise 3-21:
Objectives 5–8
Required Files: USSales2.xls
Solution Files: gl3-21.xls in Solutions Manual or on
Solutions Disk.

5. Format text in the "Northwest Region" by following these steps:

   a. Select the row and column labels and the totals (A6:H7, A8:A11, and B11:H11), and make them bold.

   b. Right-align cells G6:H7.

   c. Apply a heavy single-line bottom border to cells A7:H7.

   d. Apply a single-line top and double-line bottom border to cells B11:H11.

6. Format numbers in the "Northwest Region" by following these steps:

   a. To the dollar amounts in cells B8:G11, apply the comma style and add one decimal place. All numbers should have three decimal places.

   b. Apply the percent style to cells H8:H11 with one decimal place.

7. Copy the formats for the "Northwest Region" to the other three regions by following these steps:

   a. Select cells A6:H11 and double-click the Format Painter button ⬙.

   b. Using the Format Painter pointer, select the "Northeast Region Sales" range (A13:H18) to copy the formatting.

   c. Select the "Southwest Region" range, and then select the "Southeast Region" range.

   d. Press Esc to end the process and restore the normal pointer.

8. Make cell A1 active and save the workbook as *[your initials]*3-21.xls in your Lesson 3 folder.

9. Print the worksheet and close the workbook.

A
S
S
E
S
S

Assessment Resources:
• Solutions Manual
• Test Bank
• Portfolio Builder
• Internet Projects
• Alternative Assessment Guide
• Certification Procedures

For Internet projects, go to
www.glencoe.com/webprojects

Lesson Applications

Select rows and columns, move cells and columns, insert and delete rows, move data, format numbers, and apply text attributes and cell borders.

The marketing director needs an attractively formatted 1998 Market Share worksheet to show to the president. You must apply text and number formatting as well as rearrange some of the data.

1. Open the file **Share1.xls**.

2. Move the information in column E to column B.

3. Check the formulas now in column B to ensure they divide "Alpha Sales" by "National Sales."

4. Widen column A to accommodate the label in A8.

5. Insert two rows at row 4.

6. Format the title cells A1 and A2 as bold.

7. Delete the blank row 12.

8. Format the column labels as centered and bold, and apply a single-line bottom border to cells B7:D7.

9. Apply a single-line top and a double-line bottom border to cells B12:D12.

10. Format the row labels and total numbers as bold, and readjust the width of column A, if necessary.

11. Format the "Market Share" numbers in percent style displaying two decimal places.

12. Format the "National Sales" and "Alpha Sales" numbers in comma style displaying two decimal places.

13. Delete the blank row 8.

14. Make cell A1 active and save the workbook as *[your initials]***3-22.xls** in your Lesson 3 folder.

15. Print the worksheet and close the workbook.

Lesson Applications:
Provide independent practice for students and may be used for assessment. Objectives are indicated for each Exercise.

Exercise 3-22:
Objectives 1–3, 6–8
Required Files: Share1.xls
Solution Files: gl3-22.xls in Solutions Manual or on Solutions Disk.

EXERCISE 3-23

Select cells, insert rows, use shortcut menus, move data, format numbers and text, and apply cell borders.

Alpha Pharmaceuticals' auditor reviewed the worksheet that calculates gross pay for the company's Quality Control Division. He noticed that overtime hours were not entered and that employee Silvers is missing from the list. These errors must be corrected and the worksheet needs to be formatted to make it easier to read.

1. Open the file **QCPay3.xls**.

2. Insert three blank rows, starting at row 3.

3. Move all the data in the "Golden" row between the data for "Czerny" and "Patino."

4. Under "Patino," insert a new row with the data for employee Silvers as shown in Figure 3-16.

FIGURE 3-16

```
Name       Rate     Hours

Silvers    9.50     37.5
```

 NOTE: Excel copies the formulas to the new row automatically.

5. Check the formulas that were automatically entered by Excel in this row.

6. Format cell A1 as bold and cell A2 as bold and italic.

 TIP: The Italic button I is on the Formatting toolbar.

7. Right-align the text in rows 6 and 7 (except for "Name" in cell A7, which should be left-aligned).

8. Format rows 6, 7, and 16 as bold.

9. Apply a single-line bottom border to cells A7 through G7 and to cells C15 through G15.

10. Apply the comma style to numbers in rows 8 through 16 and display two decimal places.

◉ Exercise 3-23:
Objectives 1, 2, 5–8
Required Files: QCPay3.xls
Solution Files: gl3-23.xls in Solutions Manual or on
Solutions Disk.

11. Key the overtime hours for all employees as shown in Figure 3-17:

FIGURE 3-17

```
Berenson    2

Alvarez     3

Czerny      0

Golden      3

Patino      4.25

Silvers     0

Teij        1.5

Wang        2.5
```

12. Use AutoSum to total regular "Hours" and "Overtime" hours.

13. Make cell A1 active and save the workbook as *[your initials]***3-23.xls** in your Lesson 3 folder.

14. Print the worksheet and close the workbook.

EXERCISE 3-24

Select and insert rows and columns, move data, and format text and numbers.

  Alpha Pharmaceuticals' president needs to study U.S. population trends to make sales forecasts. He is especially interested in the over-40 age group, because this group uses more pain relievers than younger people. His population worksheet should be formatted and additional data must be inserted.

1. Open the file **PopData1.xls**.

2. Insert three blank rows at row 3.

3. Move the "1991" data so it is positioned above the "1992" data.

4. Insert three blank rows below the "1987" data to make room for the "1988," "1989," and "1990" data.

5. Key the missing and additional population figures, as shown in Figure 3-18 (on the next page). Key the years as labels using an apostrophe before each year.

● **Exercise 3-24:**
Objectives 1, 2, 6–8
Required Files: PopData1.xls
Solution Files: gl3-24.xls in Solutions Manual or on
Solutions Disk.

The completed document for this Exercise
may be used in a student's portfolio.

FIGURE 3-18

	Total	Over 40
1988	243.07	91.25
1989	245.35	92.61
1990	247.64	93.97
1996	263.87	105.30
1997	266.75	107.42
1998	269.65	109.55

NOTE: Excel did not update formulas in new rows 10-12 because there are not five rows in the list (A7:D20) preceding the new rows. For automatic updating, there must be at least five rows preceding the new rows, and three out of the five must contain formulas or formatting.

6. Create formulas in cells D10:D12 to calculate the percentage of the population over age 40. (Hint: Use one of the existing formulas as a model.)

7. Edit cell A1 to read **U.S. Population**

8. Format cells A1:A2 as bold.

9. Format the column headings in row 6 as right-aligned and bold.

10. Format the numbers in columns B and C to display one decimal place.

11. Format the numbers in column D to be displayed as percentages with one decimal place.

12. Make cell A1 active and save the workbook as *[your initials]***3-24.xls** in your Lesson 3 folder.

13. Print the worksheet and close the workbook.

E X E R C I S E 3-25   *Challenge Yourself*

Select multiple columns and rows, delete columns and rows, use the Undo command, move data, apply text attributes, and format numbers.

  Historical information on pain-reliever sales for the Northwest Region appears in three separate sections of a worksheet. The Marketing Director

◉ **Exercise 3-25:**
Objectives 1–8
Required Files: NWHist1.xls
Solution Files: gl3-25.xls and gl3-25.htm in Solutions Manual or on Solutions Disk.

The completed document for this Exercise may be used in a student's portfolio.

asked you to arrange the data in a single table that shows totals by year and by product.

1. Open the file **NWHist1.xls**.

2. Delete columns B and C simultaneously.

3. Delete rows 9 through 11.

4. Undo the row deletions.

5. Cut the data for "Aspirin" (B3:B14) and paste it beginning in cell D3 using the shortcut menu.

6. Cut the data for "Ibuprofen" (B29:B40) and paste it beginning in cell B3.

7. Cut the data for "Acetaminophen" (B16:B27) and paste it beginning in cell C3.

8. Clear the cells below row 15 in column A.

9. Key **Total** in E3 and create formulas in column E to total each year's sales. (*Hint:* Use AutoSum.)

10. In cell A15, key **Total**. When AutoComplete suggests "Total Category Sales," press ⌈Delete⌋ to restore "Total" and press ⌈Enter⌋.

11. Create formulas in row 15 that total individual and total product sales.

12. Clear cells A1:A2, which contain the title and key the title as shown in Figure 3-19. Insert enough rows to accommodate the title and to leave two blank lines below it.

FIGURE 3-19

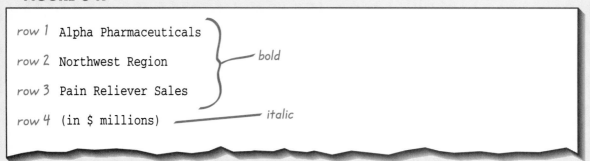

row 1 Alpha Pharmaceuticals
row 2 Northwest Region   — bold
row 3 Pain Reliever Sales
row 4 (in $ millions)   — italic

13. Insert the following data below "1998." (Be sure to enter "1999" as a label.)

   1999   0.209   0.133   0.054

 NOTE: Excel copies formulas to the new row automatically and updates the totals.

14. Check the formula in row 19 to make sure it does not include the year in the calculation.

15. Check the formulas in row 20 to make sure the data in row 19 is included in their calculations.

16. Delete the row containing the 1988 data, and check the formulas again.

17. Right-align the column labels and make row and column headings bold.

18. Apply a single-line heavy bottom border to the column labels (B7:E7).

19. Apply a single-line bottom border to the sales data for "1999" (B18:E18) and a double-line bottom border to the totals in cells B19:E19.

20. Format all figures in comma style displaying two decimal places.

21. Make all totals bold.

22. Make cell A1 active and save the workbook as *[your initials]*3-25.xls in your Lesson 3 folder.

23. Print the worksheet and save the workbook as *[your initials]*3-25.htm in your Lesson 3 folder.

24. Close the workbook.

For Internet projects, go to
www.glencoe.com/webprojects

Unit 1 Applications

UNIT APPLICATION 1-1

Enter and edit data, use AutoSum, create formulas, move data, and format text and numbers.

You have been asked to prepare a statement of assets for Alpha Pharmaceuticals, listing the things of value that the company owned at the end of 1998. The statement will become part of Alpha's balance sheet and be included in Alpha's annual report.

1. Open the file **Assets1.xls**.

2. Change the width of column A to accommodate the label in A6 and the width of column B to accommodate the label in B13.

3. In the cell range C7:C10, key the following data:

   2600
   5960
   4710
   600

4. In cell C11, use AutoSum to create a formula for "Total current assets."

5. In cell C13, key **4980**. In cell C14, key **1520**

6. Cut the text in cell C15 and paste it into cell B15.

7. In cell C15, create a formula that subtracts "Depreciation" from "Property, plant, and equipment."

8. In cell C16, key **1390** for "Other Assets."

9. Italicize the amounts for "Total current assets," "Net fixed assets," and "Other Assets." Create a formula in cell C17 that totals these three amounts. Make that total bold.

10. Right-align the labels "Total current assets" and "Net fixed assets." Make both labels italic.

11. Format cells A1 and A2 as bold.

12. Format the values in column C in comma style with no decimals.

13. Apply a single-line bottom border to cells C10, C14, and C16.

14. Apply a double-line bottom border to cell C17.

15. Edit the label "(Depreciation)" so it reads **(Less depreciation)**

16. Edit cells so only the first letter of the first word of each label is capitalized. (Do not edit the title, however.)

17. Make cell A1 active and save the workbook as *[your initials]***u1-1.xls** in a new folder for Unit 1 Applications.

ASSESS

Assessment Resources:
• Solutions Manual • Test Bank
• Portfolio Builder
• Alternative Assessment Guide
• Certification Procedures
• Projects Manual
• Mid-Term and Final Exams

Unit Applications:
Provide independent practice of the skills acquired from each lesson in the Unit.

Exam:
You can now assign Exam 1 from the Mid-Term and Final Exams booklet.

Project:
You can now assign Project 1 from the Projects Manual.

○ Unit Application 1-1:
Required Files: Assets1.xls
Solution Files: glu1-1.xls in Solutions Manual or on Solutions disk.

18. Print the worksheet and close the workbook.

UNIT APPLICATION 1-2

Enter data, construct formulas, use the Sum function, and format text and numbers.

A statement of liabilities and shareholders' equity shows who has claims on the assets of a company. For instance, you can see the amounts owed to outsiders (long-term debt, current debt, accounts payable) and the amounts claimed by the owners (shareholders' equity). You have been asked to prepare such a statement for Alpha Pharmaceuticals. It will later become part of the company's balance sheet.

1. Open the file **Liablts1.xls**.

2. Change the width of column B so the label in A15 does not extend beyond the right border of column B.

3. Move the label in cell C13 to cell B13.

4. Enter the data in column C as shown in Figure U1-1, including Sum formulas in cells C8 and C13.

FIGURE U1-1

	A	B	C
5	Long-term liabilities		
6		Long-term debt	690
7		Other long-term liabilities	510
8		Total long-term liabilities	(SUM)
9	Current liabilities		
10		Debt due for repayment	1090
11		Accounts payable	1350
12		Other current liabilities	1760
13		Total current liabilities	(SUM)
14	Shareholders' equity		13320
15	Total liabilities and shareholders' equity		

○ **Unit Application 1-2:**
Required Files: Liablts1.xls
Solution Files: glu1-2.xls in Solutions Manual or on
Solutions disk.

5. Format cells C8, C13, and C14 as italic, add a single-line bottom border to cells C7, C12, and C14, and add a double-line bottom border to cell C15.

6. Move the current liabilities (rows 9 through 13) before the long-term liabilities (rows 5 through 8). (Hint: Cut the cells and use Cut Cells from the Insert menu to insert them in the new location.)

7. Check to make sure the formulas are still correct.

8. Create a formula in cell C15 that adds "Total current liabilities," "Total long-term liabilities," and "Shareholders' equity." Format the cell as bold.

9. Insert a new row at row 1. Make the first two lines of the title read:
   Alpha Pharmaceuticals
   Liabilities and Shareholders' Equity

10. Format the first three lines of the title as bold.

11. Format all the values in comma style with no decimals.

12. Make cell A1 active and save the workbook as *[your initials]***u1-2.xls** in your Unit 1 Applications folder.

13. Print the worksheet and close the workbook.

UNIT APPLICATION 1-3

Edit data, move data, insert and delete rows, construct formulas, use AutoCalculate, and use Save As Web Page.

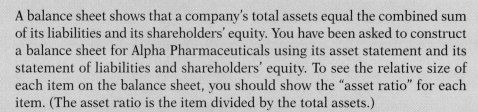

A balance sheet shows that a company's total assets equal the combined sum of its liabilities and its shareholders' equity. You have been asked to construct a balance sheet for Alpha Pharmaceuticals using its asset statement and its statement of liabilities and shareholders' equity. To see the relative size of each item on the balance sheet, you should show the "asset ratio" for each item. (The asset ratio is the item divided by the total assets.)

1. Open the file **Balance1.xls**.

2. Cut the liabilities and owner's equity information in cells D6:F15.

3. Paste the material below the asset information, beginning in cell A19.

4. Edit cell A1 to read **Balance Sheet for Alpha Pharmaceuticals**

5. Insert a row at row 19, format blank cell A19 as bold, and key
   Liabilities and Owners' Equity

6. Format cell A5 (which contains the label "Assets") as bold.

7. Insert a new row at row 5.

8. Key $ (dollar sign) in cell C5 and key **% Assets** in cell D5. Format both cells as bold and centered.

◉ **Unit Application 1-3:**
Required Files: Balance1.xls
Solution Files: glu1-3.xls and glu1-3.htm in Solutions Manual or on Solutions disk.

9. In cell D8, enter the formula **=C8/C18**. (Cell C18 contains the value for total assets. The formula gives the percentage of total assets represented by the value in cell C8—that is, the asset ratio.)

10. In column D, create asset ratio formulas for all the remaining assets in the balance sheet including total assets. Be sure to divide by total assets (C18).

11. Format the values in column D in percent style to display one decimal place.

12. Format the values in column C in comma style to display no decimals.

13. Use AutoCalculate to verify the subtotals.

14. Make cell A1 active and save your workbook as *[your initials]***u1-3.xls** in your Unit 1 Applications folder.

15. Print the worksheet and save the workbook as *[your initials]***u1-3.htm** in your Unit 1 Applications folder.

16. Close the workbook.

UNIT APPLICATION 1-4

Enter data in a selected range, construct formulas, use AutoSum, format text and numbers, and insert columns and rows.

In addition to a balance sheet, Alpha Pharmaceuticals' annual report will include an income statement. An income statement shows the revenues, expenses, and net income for a company over a period of time. You have been asked to prepare this statement and to format it attractively.

1. Open a new workbook.
2. In the cell range A1:B10, key the data shown in Figure U1-2.

FIGURE U1-2

	A	B
1	Revenue	34050
2	Cost of goods sold	20410
3	Sales expenses	2400
4	Administrative expense	5210
5	Depreciation	480

continues

Unit Application 1-4:
Required Files: None
Solution Files: Sample glu1-4.xls in Solutions Manual
or on Solutions disk.

 The completed document for this
Application may be used in a student's
portfolio.

FIGURE U1-2   *continued*

	A	B
6	Other expenses	200
7	Earnings before interest and taxes	
8	Interest expense	310
9	Income taxes	1930
10	Net income	

3. Change the width of column A to accommodate the label in A7.

4. Move the entire block of labels and numbers so "Revenue" appears in cell A7.

5. Starting in cell A1, key the following title:

   Income Statement
   Alpha Pharmaceuticals
   1998
   (Dollars in thousands)

6. Left-align the label in A3 if it was entered as a value.

7. Format the first three lines of the title as bold.

8. In cell B13, create a formula that subtracts cells B8:B12 (which are expenses and cost of goods sold) from "Revenue" (cell B7).

9. In cell B16, create a formula that subtracts both interest and taxes (cells B14:B15) from "Earnings before interest and taxes" (cell B13).

10. Key $ in cell B6 and % in cell C6. Format both cells as bold and centered.

11. In column C, create formulas that divide each item in column B by "Revenue" (B7). (Hint: The first three formulas are **=B7/B7**, **=B8/B7**, and **=B9/B7**.)

12. Format the values in column C in percent style to display one decimal place.

13. Format the values in column B in comma style to display no decimals.

14. Apply single-line bottom borders to cells B12:C12 and B15:C15. Apply double-line bottom borders to cells B16:C16.

15. Proofread the worksheet.

16. Make cell A1 active and save the workbook as *[your initials]*u1-4.xls in your Unit 1 Applications folder.

17. Print the worksheet and close the workbook.

UNIT APPLICATION 1-5

Enter data; construct formulas; use AutoSum; format text and numbers; and insert and delete cells, columns, and rows, as needed.

  Prepare an income statement for yourself, your household, or another individual.

1. In a new workbook, enter the income categories and data. Figure U1-3 lists suggested categories to include. (You **must** include the categories shown in bold.)

FIGURE U1-3

 Income (include at least two subcategories)

Job1

Job2

Investments

Interest

Total income

Expenses (include at least three subcategories)

Food

Housing

Utilities

Transportation

Clothing

Insurance

Medical

Loan payments

Entertainment

Total expenses

Earnings before taxes

Taxes

Net income

Unit Application 1-5:
Required Files: None
Solution Files: Sample
glu1-5.xls in Solutions Manual
or on Solutions disk.

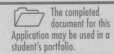 The completed document for this Application may be used in a student's portfolio.

[1] In this Application, students are asked to create an income statement. Solutions will vary. A sample file is shown in the Solution Manual and on the Solutions disk.

[2] Figure U1-3 lists *suggested* categories for students. The categories used by individual students will differ. Some students may prefer not to enter data about themselves or their families. These students could be encouraged to either make up data or, for extra credit, to research a typical family's income and expenses for the area and reflect the researched data in their worksheet.

2. Complete the worksheet by including the following information and formatting:

- A title identifying the name of the statement and the period of time it covers.
- Column labels for dollar amounts and for percentage of total income (not net income).
- Bottom borders on cells before subtotals and totals.
- Numbers and text formatted appropriately.
- Attractive and clear layout.

3. Save your workbook as *[your initials]***u1-5.xls** in your Unit 1 Applications folder.

4. Print the worksheet and close the workbook.

UNIT APPLICATION 1-6 *Making It Work for You*

Enter data, use Pick From List or AutoComplete, construct formulas, move data, format text and numbers, use Format Painter, and use Save As Web Page.

Now that you know how to create income statements, you can use a spreadsheet to create a future-look at your "dream" income for the years 2005, 2006, and 2007. Use labels and totals for Income, Expenses, and Net Income (no subcategories necessary), and calculate your percent of Income. Remember, this is your "dream" income; be optimistic, but realistic, too. Enter labels so you can use Pick From List and AutoComplete when possible, then use cut and paste to position data on the worksheet. Make the worksheet attractive with a meaningful title and good formatting using Format Painter when possible. Save the workbook as *[your initials]***u1-6.xls** in your Unit 1 Applications folder and print the worksheet. Then save the file as a Web page, *[your initials]***u1-6.htm** in your Unit 1 Applications folder.

Unit Application 1-6:

Required Files: None
Solution Files: Samples glu1-6.xls and glu1-6.htm in Solutions Manual or on Solutions disk.

In this Application, students are asked create a future income statement. Solutions will vary. A sample file is shown in the Solution Manual and on the Solutions disk.

Developing a Worksheet

Beautiful BelleCompany

Sun Soft Heats Up Skin Care Market

The Beautiful Belle Company, also known as BBC, manufactures a moderately priced line of cosmetics. BBC is currently promoting a product named "Sun Soft." It's a 100%-natural hypo-allergenic lotion that has refined almond and sesame oils as its main ingredients. Although it's not proven, and can't be used in advertising, researchers have recently claimed that these oils are beneficial in protecting against skin cancer.

BBC is test-marketing Sun Soft in its Southwest region. Renata Santo, BBC's Southwest regional-sales manager, has decided to concentrate her efforts in the Phoenix area. However, Phoenix is a challenging market for Soft Sun, because a competing product, Corn Silk Cream, has a significant market share of skin care products there.

For the test marketing, Renata will need the following:

✔ A worksheet to keep track of weekly sales of Sun Soft and the competing product, Corn Silk Cream, over a two-month period. **(Lesson 4)**

✔ Once the test is complete, a worksheet that tracks Sun Soft sales in relation to Corn Silk Cream sales for three months. **(Lesson 5)**

✔ A worksheet that shows sales of selected creams for four quarters, with sales broken down by months and by product. **(Lesson 6)**

✔ A worksheet that compares Sun Soft sales by quarter for the last three years. **(Lesson 7)**

Designing and Printing a Worksheet

OBJECTIVES

MOUS
ACTIVITIES
In this lesson:
XL2000 **4.1**
XL2000 **4.3**
XL2000 **4.4**
XL2000 **4.5**
XL2000 **4.7**
XL2000 **4.8**
XL2000 **4.9**
XL2000 **5.3**
XL2000 **5.4**
XL2000 **5.7**
XL2000 **E.10.9**
XL2000 **E.12.2**

See Appendix F.

After completing this lesson, you will be able to:

1. **Plan a worksheet on paper.**
2. **Put a worksheet plan on screen.**
3. **Keep row and column labels in view.**
4. **Select display options.**
5. **Create user documentation.**
6. **Protect files.**
7. **Print workbooks and print areas.**
8. **Print formulas.**

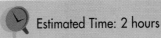
Estimated Time: 2 hours

Creating a worksheet requires careful planning. A well-designed worksheet is easy to read, the data is arranged in a logical order, and the results are readily apparent. Decide what you want to accomplish with the worksheet before you create it. Designing the worksheet with a specific purpose in mind will help you decide what you want Excel to do with the data you enter. You can then choose from a variety of print settings so the final, printed worksheet has the appearance you intended.

PREPARE
Point out to students that the learning objectives show what they will learn in the lesson. Each heading in the lesson correlates to a learning objective.

Required files:
TextMkt.xls

TEACH
Teaching Resources:
• Excel Classroom Presentations
• School-to-Work Strategies Manual
• Spanish Glossary
• Certification Procedures

Planning a Worksheet on Paper

Objective 1

To design a worksheet that meets your goals, start your planning using pencil and paper. Even experienced users often sketch a worksheet before they key data. Your plan should include:

- Titles that indicate who the worksheet is for and what it is about
- An entry area, if necessary, for single input items that provide additional information about the worksheet in general, such as a date, or a department title
- The worksheet body, the input and output area that contains multiple entries, labels, and formulas

The procedures in this lesson generate a worksheet to help the sales manager of a small manufacturing company analyze the results of a two-month test-marketing program. The purpose of the worksheet is to compare test-market sales with those of a competing product.

EXERCISE **4-1** Sketch the Planned Worksheet

1. Write the worksheet heading **Sun Soft vs. Corn Silk Sales** at the top left corner of a blank piece of paper. The heading of the worksheet must clearly state the purpose of the worksheet and provide a concise overview of its contents. In this case, the heading names the products and promises a competitive analysis based on sales.

2. Write the subtitles **April through May, 1999** and **(Broken down by gender)** on two separate rows under the heading.

 NOTE: You do not use an entry area in this worksheet.

3. Now consider the *purpose* of your worksheet. What do you want it to do? You want it to store weekly sales information over a two-month period and make calculations that provide useful competitive information.

 TIP: Although there are no hard-and-fast rules for worksheet design, it is generally a good idea to put items that are being compared in columns and repetitive items in rows. An analysis that compares two categories usually looks better when the categories are placed side by side. This makes it easy for a user to glance back and forth to evaluate information quickly.

4. Plan the *structure* of your worksheet body by determining the placement of data in columns and rows. The first column of the body holds the date labels. The next two columns hold Sun Soft data broken down by gender. The last two columns hold Corn Silk data broken down by gender.

---

1 Some students may not see the benefit of using paper and pencil to plan and design a worksheet. You may want to talk about how much time planning can save once students begin entering data.

2 Students need a blank sheet and pen or pencil for this Exercise. You may want to provide ruled accountant's paper with at least 8 columns and 20 rows for your students.

3 Discuss good worksheet design with the class. Specifically, you should address such issues as: blank columns, rules for what labels should be used for a column vs. a row, and the types of acceptable abbreviations for labels. This can form the beginning of a "Worksheet Design Guide" that you can create as the class proceeds.

5. Define the labels that identify the rows of the worksheet. For your worksheet, the labels are the weekly dates for the two-month analysis. So, skip two rows to allow for column labels, and write the following labels in a column along the left side of the page.

April 9
April 16
April 23
April 30
Subtotal
May 7
May 14
May 21
May 28
Subtotal
Grand total

6. Consider the column headings. Remember, you are comparing products based on gender, so first you need to identify the products, then you have to identify the gender. You will need two levels of column headings.

7. Move approximately two rows above the row labels. Write **Sun Soft Lotion.** On the same row but further to the right, write **Corn Silk Cream**. This is your first-level column heading.

8. In the row beneath the column heading **Sun Soft Lotion,** write the labels **Men**, **Women**, and **Total**. In the same row beneath the heading **Corn Silk Cream,** repeat the same three labels. This is your second-level column heading. Now the preliminary design of your worksheet is complete.

FIGURE 4-1
Preliminary
worksheet design

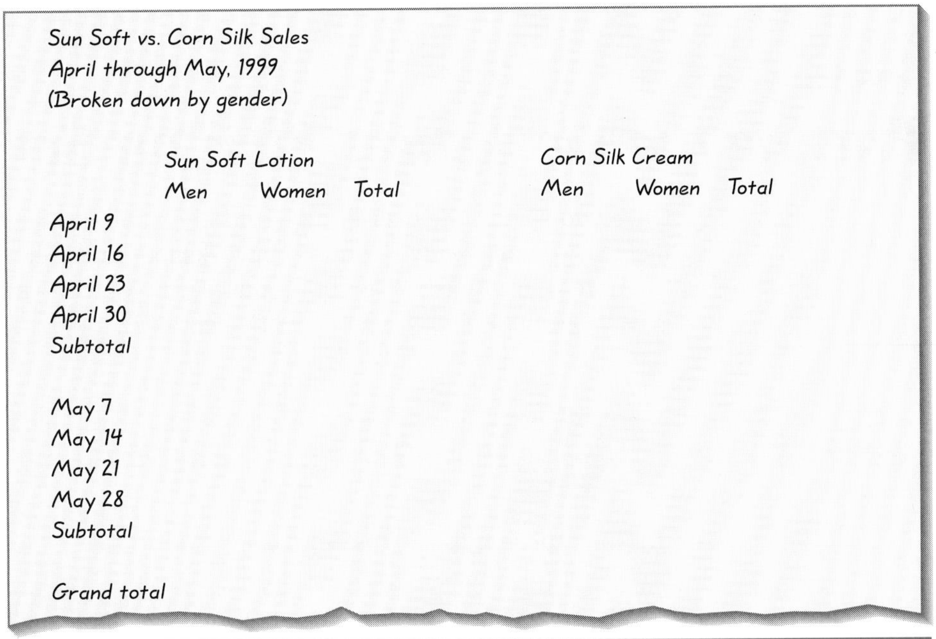

Sun Soft vs. Corn Silk Sales
April through May, 1999
(Broken down by gender)

	Sun Soft Lotion			Corn Silk Cream		
	Men	Women	Total	Men	Women	Total
April 9						
April 16						
April 23						
April 30						
Subtotal						
May 7						
May 14						
May 21						
May 28						
Subtotal						
Grand total						

9. Decide which formulas to use and where to put them on the worksheet. Your worksheet calculates monthly subtotals and a grand total of sales for both months. It also calculates total sales to men and women for both the test product and the competing product. Write an "F" (for "Formula") in all the locations where you will need to write a formula to make a calculation. (You'll use the SUM function to calculate these values.)

FIGURE 4-2
Final worksheet
design

Sun Soft vs. Corn Silk Sales
April through May, 1999
(Broken down by gender)

	Sun Soft Lotion			Corn Silk Cream		
	Men	Women	Total	Men	Women	Total
April 9			F			F
April 16			F			F
April 23			F			F
April 30			F			F
Subtotal	F	F	F	F	F	F
May 7			F			F
May 14			F			F
May 21			F			F
May 28			F			F
Subtotal	F	F	F	F	F	F
Grand total	F	F	F	F	F	F

☑ Objective 2

Putting the Worksheet Plan on Screen

Once you sketch the overall plan and know what data and formulas you will include, you are ready to build the worksheet in Excel.

After your worksheet is set up onscreen, you can validate the data, choose cells by content, and name the worksheet tabs.

EXERCISE ⬛4-2⬛ Enter Row and Column Labels

1. Open the workbook **TestMkt.xls**.

⬛1⬛ Point out that sums in the "Subtotal" and "Grand total" rows of the "Total" column sum either the column amounts or the row amounts.

☑ **Objective 2 Assignment:**
Exercise 4-24 (Skills Review) can be assigned after completing Objective 2.

⬛2⬛ Students open an existing file to enter a worksheet plan. For convenience, the column widths of Sheet2 of this workbook are already adjusted.

NOTE: Usually you create a new workbook when you implement a sketch in Excel. To save class time, however, you start with an existing workbook.

2. In cell A1, edit the title to read **Sun Soft vs. Corn Silk Sales**

3. In cell A2, edit the subtitle to read **April through May, 1999**

4. In cell A3, edit the second subtitle to read **(Broken down by gender)**. This subtitle should remain bold italic.

 TIP: A worksheet title should not be longer than three lines and there should be some visible difference from one line of the title to the next.

5. In cell B5, key **Sun Soft Lotion**

6. In cell E5, key **Corn Silk Cream**

7. In cells B6, C6, and D6, key the following labels and center-align:

   Men   Women   Total

 8. In cells E6, F6, and G6, key the same labels a second time. Center-align these labels.

9. In cell A7, key **April 9**. Notice that the date appears in the cell as "9-Apr." The date is displayed on the formula bar in the date format mm/dd/yyyy and reflects the current year.

 TIP: You can change the date format of selected cells. Choose C**e**lls from the F**o**rmat menu and click the Number tab. Choose Date in the **C**ategory list, select the **T**ype of format, and click OK.

10. In cells A8 through A10, key the following dates:

    April 16

    April 23

    April 30

11. In cells A13 through A16, key the following dates:

    May 7

    May 14

    May 21

    May 28

12. To complete the worksheet design, key **Subtotal** in cells A11 and A17, and **Grand total** in cell A19. You use these rows to summarize the data. (See Figure 4-3 on the next page.)

---

1 Students are asked to center-align column labels. Have students use their best judgment when aligning column labels. In some cases, labels are best right-aligned or left-aligned.

2 The Exercise assumes the default date format. The Tip explains how to change the date format. Remind students to select column A before changing the format, if necessary.

FIGURE 4-3
Worksheet plan
with labels entered

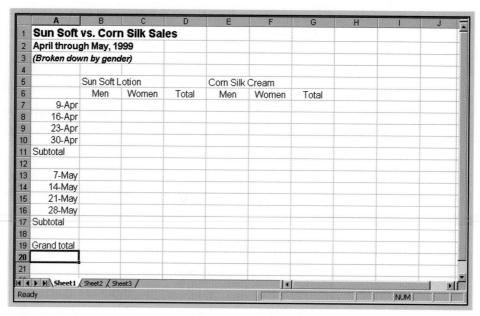

	A	B	C	D	E	F	G	H	I	J
1	**Sun Soft vs. Corn Silk Sales**									
2	**April through May, 1999**									
3	**(Broken down by gender)**									
4										
5		Sun Soft Lotion			Corn Silk Cream					
6		Men	Women	Total	Men	Women	Total			
7	9-Apr									
8	16-Apr									
9	23-Apr									
10	30-Apr									
11	Subtotal									
12										
13	7-May									
14	14-May									
15	21-May									
16	28-May									
17	Subtotal									
18										
19	Grand total									
20										
21										

Sheet1 / Sheet2 / Sheet3 /

Ready   NUM

EXERCISE 4-3 **Enter Test Data**

The body of the worksheet consists of data. You can enter test data into the worksheet to test formula calculations. *Test data* should consist of numbers that are easy to calculate in your head so you can tell at a glance whether your formulas are correct.

1. Key the following test data for Sun Soft in columns B and C. Start with
    1000 in cell B7.

April 9	**1000**	**2000**
April 16	**1000**	**2000**
April 23	**1000**	**2000**
April 30	**1000**	**2000**
May 7	**1000**	**2000**
May 14	**1000**	**2000**
May 21	**1000**	**2000**
May 28	**1000**	**2000**

2. Key the following test data for Corn Silk in columns E and F. Start with
    1000 in cell E7.

April 9	**1000**	**2000**
April 16	**1000**	**2000**
April 23	**1000**	**2000**

Use Excel Classroom Presentation 4 to display
screens from the lesson in a slide-show format.

Point out that test data should be simple enough
to calculate in their heads.

April 30	1000	2000
May 7	1000	2000
May 14	1000	2000
May 21	1000	2000
May 28	1000	2000

3. Select all the numbers and format them for commas and no decimal places. (Remember to press [Ctrl] when you click to select nonadjacent cells.) Click the Comma Style button [,] on the Formatting toolbar, then click the Decrease Decimal button [.%] until you can see the numbers and no decimal places remain.

> **NOTE:** When there is not enough room in a cell for data, Excel inserts ### to alert you to reformat the data or widen the column.

FIGURE 4-4
Worksheet plan
with data entered

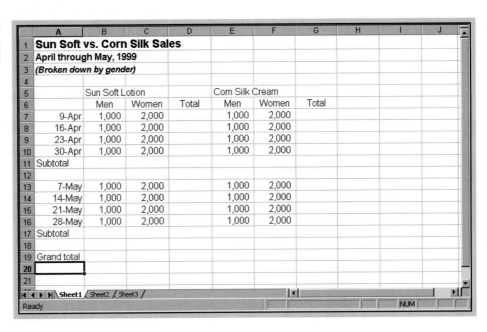

EXERCISE 4-4 Enter Formulas

Once the worksheet data is entered, you can enter formulas to automate the calculations. Since you are adding rows and columns, this is a good time to use the SUM function or the AutoSum button [Σ].

1. Select cells D7 through D10 and click the AutoSum button [Σ] on the Standard toolbar. The SUM function is entered in each cell and the total

 In Excel Classroom Presentation 4.

values are displayed. Add the totals in your head to check the values as you go through the remaining steps.

2. Select cells B11 through D11 and click the AutoSum button ∑. This totals the three separate ranges in the same step.

3. Select cells B13 through D17 (the data cells and the cells for their totals).

4. Click the AutoSum button ∑. Excel automatically sums the rows and columns of selected data.

5. Select cells E7 through G11, hold down Ctrl, and select cells E13 through G17.

6. Release Ctrl and click the AutoSum button ∑ to enter the totals for the two cell ranges at the same time. All the totals and subtotals for Corn Silk are now entered.

7. Move to cell B19 and click the AutoSum button ∑. Excel suggests cell B17, the second subtotal to be included in the formula.

8. Hold down Ctrl and click cell B11, the first subtotal to include it in the formula.

9. Release Ctrl and press Enter. Excel totals the two subtotals. The formula =SUM(B17,B11) appears in the formula bar for cell B19.

FIGURE 4-5
Worksheet with formulas

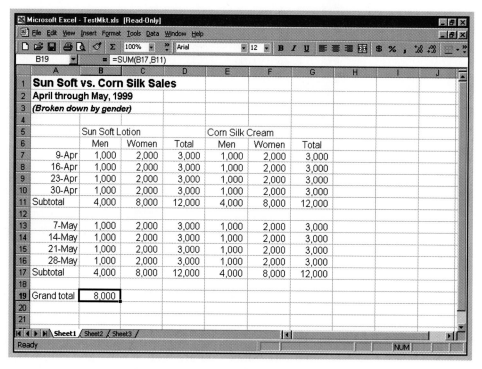

10. Select cells C7 through C19 and click the AutoSum button ∑. The formula in cell C20 adds the two subtotals in column C.

11. Do the same for column D.

12. Select cells E7 through G19 and click the AutoSum button ☒. Examine the formula in cell G19. Notice that it adds the grand totals of columns E and F instead of summing the subtotals of column G (which would produce the same result).

EXERCISE 4-5 Validate Data

You can control the type of data entered in cells, such as whole numbers, date, time, and text length. If you or someone else tries to enter data into a cell that is validated, you can have Excel display a prompt specifying the type of data to enter. Excel returns an error message if incorrect data is keyed.

1. Select all the cells containing **1,000**. (Remember to press ⌃Ctrl and click the mouse to select nonadjacent cells.)

2. Choose Validation from the Data menu to open the Data Validation dialog box.

FIGURE 4-6
Data Validation
dialog box

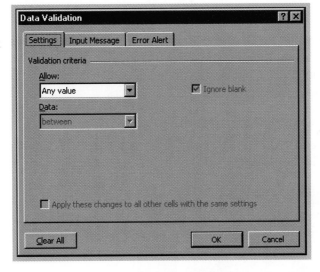

3. Click the Settings tab, if necessary, and choose "Whole number" from the Allow drop-down list.

4. Choose "greater than or equal to" from the Data drop-down list and key **0** in the Minimum text box.

5. Click the Input Message tab.

6. Under Title, key **Sales**

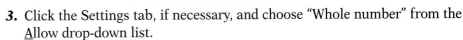

In this Exercise, students learn data validation. For teaching purposes they validate test data. Normally, test data would not be validated. Remind students that the validation process works the same for any data they validate.

In Excel Classroom Presentation 4.

7. In the Input Message text box, key **Enter sales for men** and click OK. Notice the message box that appears over the last set of cells selected with the input message you created.

8. Select any cell containing **1,000**. Notice that the same message box appears.

 NOTE: The message reminds users what to key in that cell. If the validation message box hampers your selection, drag the box to another location on the worksheet.

9. Change the number in a cell containing 1,000 to **1,000.75**. When you try to enter the number in the cell, a message indicates the value you entered is not valid. Click Cancel.

 TIP: To turn off data validation, click the Clear All button at the bottom of the Data Validation dialog box. (See Figure 4-6 on the previous page.) This also clears any messages you created.

EXERCISE 4-6 Select Cells by Content

Once your worksheet is set up, you may find it useful to select cells by content. You can use this method to select a cell or group of cells that have common characteristics (such as validated data or formulas), whether they are adjacent on the worksheet or not.

1. Press Ctrl + Home to return to cell A1.

2. Choose Go To from the Edit menu. When the Go To dialog box opens, click Special to open the Go To Special dialog box.

FIGURE 4-7
Go To Special
dialog box

 In Excel Classroom Presentation 4.

TIP: You can also press Ctrl+G to open the Go To dialog box and then click Special to open the Go To Special dialog box.

3. Click Data Validation and click OK. All the cells with validated data are selected. Press Ctrl+Home.

4. Try this for the cells with formulas by choosing Formulas in the Go To Special dialog box. Choose Numbers under the Formulas option and deselect the others. When you are finished, press Ctrl+Home to return to cell A1.

EXERCISE 4-7 Name Worksheet Tabs

 As you learned in Lesson 1, each new Excel workbook opens with three sheets that are named "Sheet1" through "Sheet3" by default. When you work with more than one worksheet, it's a good idea to name worksheet tabs so their purposes are obvious.

1. Double-click the Sheet1 tab. The tab name is highlighted.

2. Key **Sales Comparison** over the Sheet1 tab name.

3. Double-click the Sheet2 tab. Sheet2 becomes active and the tab name is highlighted.

4. Key **User Information** over Sheet2. (You use this sheet later in the lesson.)

 5. Click the Sales Comparison tab to make the Sales Comparison worksheet active again.

 TIP: Sheet names should describe what the sheet includes using only a word or two. Sheet names can be up to 31 characters long, including spaces.

Objective 3

Keeping Row and Column Labels in View

Frequently, the rows and columns of a worksheet extend beyond the display screen. You can split the worksheet into multiple *panes* so you can see row and column labels as you key data or formulas. Using multiple panes you can also scroll through data to locate and select cells to be included in calculations. You do this using *split bars*. For example, when you create a grand total, you might need to scroll to the top of a large worksheet to include one or more subtotals.

---

1 Ideally, a workbook should not contain a blank worksheet. If you come across a workbook that contains a blank worksheet, you may want to show students how to delete the worksheet. Select the worksheet to be deleted and choose Delete Sheet from the Edit menu. Warn students that deleted sheets cannot be restored. If they delete a sheet by mistake, they should close the file without saving it and reopen the file. Also, remind students to delete worksheets right before saving or when they complete work in the workbook.

2 At this point in the lesson, you may want to have students save their work as *[your initials]*4-7.xls in a new folder for Lesson 4 files.

EXERCISE 4-8 Split a Worksheet into Panes

1. Select cell A7 on the Sales Comparison worksheet.

2. Choose Split from the Window menu. The screen is split into two horizontal panes by a split bar. Each pane has its own vertical scroll bar, permitting it to be scrolled on its own.

> **TIP:** You can also split a worksheet horizontally by selecting an entire row first.

3. Click the down vertical scroll arrow for the bottom pane to move row 13 directly under the column labels. Splitting the screen under the column labels makes it easier to enter formulas for the May subtotal and the grand total.

FIGURE 4-8
Screen split horizontally

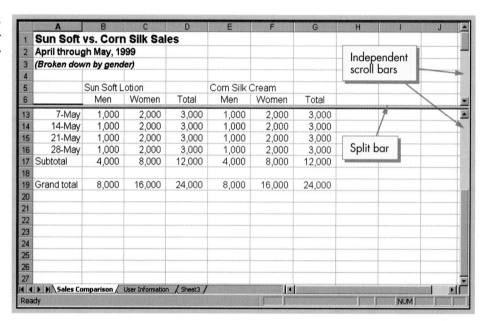

4. Experiment with the scroll buttons in both panes.

5. Choose Remove Split from the Window menu. The original view of the worksheet is restored.

> **NOTE:** The Split option on the Window menu changes to Remove Split when a worksheet is split into panes.

6. Select cell B7. (*Hint*: You may need to drag the Validation Input Message box out of the way.)

 You may want to emphasize that splitting worksheets is most useful when working with very large worksheets.

 In Excel Classroom Presentation 4.

7. Choose Split from the Window menu. The window splits above and to the left of the active cell. In four panes, you can see both row and column labels at the same time. Scroll to move row 13 just below column labels and select cell A1 by clicking it.

TIP: To create a vertical split only, select a column other than column A (or select a cell in row 1 other than cell A1) before choosing Split from the Window menu.

FIGURE 4-9
Screen split horizontally and vertically

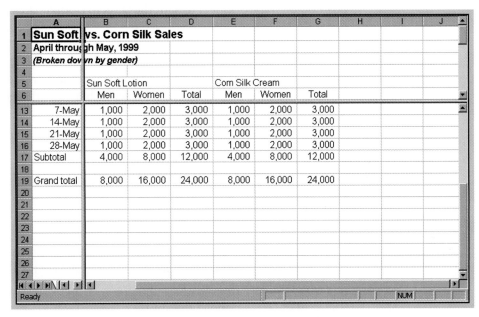

	A	B	C	D	E	F	G	H	I	J
1	**Sun Soft vs. Corn Silk Sales**									
2	**April through May, 1999**									
3	*(Broken down by gender)*									
4										
5		Sun Soft Lotion			Corn Silk Cream					
6		Men	Women	Total	Men	Women	Total			
13	7-May	1,000	2,000	3,000	1,000	2,000	3,000			
14	14-May	1,000	2,000	3,000	1,000	2,000	3,000			
15	21-May	1,000	2,000	3,000	1,000	2,000	3,000			
16	28-May	1,000	2,000	3,000	1,000	2,000	3,000			
17	Subtotal	4,000	8,000	12,000	4,000	8,000	12,000			
18										
19	Grand total	8,000	16,000	24,000	8,000	16,000	24,000			
20										
21										
22										
23										
24										
25										
26										
27										

Ready   NUM

EXERCISE 4-9 Freeze Panes

You use the Freeze Panes command on the Window menu to freeze row labels, column labels, or both. A single set of scroll arrows and buttons moves data only, but leaves labels in place.

1. Choose Remove Split from the Window menu.

2. Select cell B7.

3. Choose Freeze Panes from the Window menu. Single lines divide the worksheet, marking frozen areas.

4. Experiment with the scroll buttons and the arrow keys.

5. Choose Unfreeze Panes from the Window menu to restore the original view of the worksheet.

Watch for students who lose their place in worksheet panes. It can be confusing to have multiple copies of the same worksheet labels, information, and formulas onscreen.

In Excel Classroom Presentation 4.

You may want to emphasize that freezing worksheets is most useful when working with very large worksheets.

EXERCISE 4-10 Use Split Boxes and Split Bars

Another way to split a screen into multiple panes is to use the horizontal and vertical *split boxes*. The horizontal split box appears in the upper right corner of the document window; it is the gray, rectangular box located above the vertical scroll arrow. The vertical split box is found at the far right of the horizontal scroll bar at the bottom of the document window.

Clicking a split box produces a split bar, which you can drag to the desired position on the worksheet to split the screen. Double-click a split box to position the split bar automatically.

1. Select cell B7, if necessary.

FIGURE 4-10
Split boxes

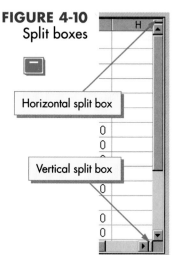

2. Move the mouse pointer to the horizontal split box at the top of the vertical scroll bar. The mouse pointer changes to a split pointer ♦.

3. Double-click the split box. A split bar appears above the active cell.

4. Move the mouse pointer to the vertical split box at the right of the horizontal scroll bar.

5. Double-click the split box and the split bar appears between column A and B.

6. Move the mouse pointer to the intersection of the two split bars. The pointer becomes a four-headed arrow ✛.

7. Double-click the intersection of the two split bars to remove the split.

8. Press Ctrl + Home.

⭐ **TIP:** To adjust horizontal or vertical splits, drag the split bar to the new location. You can also change the location of a four-pane split by dragging its intersection.

☑ Objective 4

Selecting Display Options

You can change how a worksheet is displayed on the screen so it is easier to work with. *Zoom* options change the magnification of the display. You can enlarge it to see more detail or reduce it to show more of the worksheet at one time.

You can also choose to display gridlines and row and column headings.

The box at the *right* of the horizontal scroll bar is the vertical split box. The box on the *left* of the horizontal scroll bar lengthens or shortens the scroll bar.

 In Excel Classroom Presentation 4.

The drag and drop feature for creating multiple panes using split boxes is deliberately not taught. This is because Excel often duplicates the column label row and row label column when students try to drag and drop a split bar beneath column labels or to the right of row labels. If you want to teach this, and students have problems, they can double-click the split boxes to automatically position split bars and reposition them using the intersection of the two points, if necessary.

☑ **Objective 4**
Assignment:

Exercise 4-25 (Skills Review) can be assigned after completing Objective 4.

EXERCISE | **4-11** | ## Zoom to Magnify and Reduce the Display

Zoom acts like a magnifying glass. The size of the characters displayed on the screen is expressed in terms of percentages. Higher percentages display larger characters, but less of the worksheet. Lower percentages display smaller characters, but show more of the worksheet. Zoom does not affect the size of the printed worksheet.

Excel provides two ways to use zoom:

FIGURE 4-11
Zoom dialog box

- Choose <u>Z</u>oom from the <u>V</u>iew menu.
- Use the Zoom box 100% ▾ on the Standard toolbar.

1. Choose <u>Z</u>oom from the <u>V</u>iew menu and the Zoom dialog box opens.

2. In the Zoom dialog box, click 75% and click OK. The displayed text becomes smaller and you can see more of the worksheet. The Zoom box 75% ▾ now displays "75%."

3. Select cell D7.

4. Choose <u>Z</u>oom from the <u>V</u>iew menu.

FIGURE 4-12
Zoom box and
Zoom button

Zoom box

5. Click Custom, key **400**, and click OK. 400% is the largest display type you can specify.

6. Click the Zoom button (the arrow at the right of the Zoom box on the Standard toolbar) to open the drop-down list box, and click 75%.

EXERCISE | **4-12** | ## Remove Gridlines and Headers from the Screen

You can use other Excel options to vary the onscreen appearance of the worksheet. For example, you can choose to display cell gridlines or row and column headings.

1. Press [Ctrl]+[Home] and choose <u>O</u>ptions from the <u>T</u>ools menu. The Options dialog box appears.

2. Click the View tab, if necessary.

FIGURE 4-13
Options dialog
box, View tab

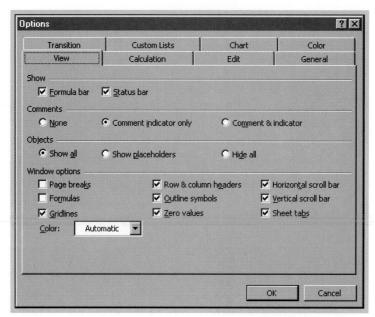

3. Under Window Options, click the Gridlines check box and the Row & Column Headers check box to clear them. Click OK. You removed gridlines and row and column headings from the worksheet display.

4. Move about the worksheet using the Arrow keys. Note that even though the gridlines are not visible, each cell is outlined when active. In addition, although the row and column headers are not visible, the address of the active cell appears in the reference area of the formula bar.

5. Select cell D19, which contains a formula. Note that the contents of the cell appear in the entry area of the formula bar.

6. Reset the options in the Options dialog box so both gridlines and row and column headings are displayed on the worksheet.

7. Press Ctrl + Home.

Objective 5
Creating User Documentation

Once you create a worksheet, you may want others to be able to use it. You can provide users with basic information about this worksheet or an entire workbook on a separate worksheet in the workbook. You might label this worksheet User Information or something similar. This sheet should include file information, the purpose of the worksheet, and instructions to the user. It should be easy to read.

In Excel Classroom Presentation 4.

EXERCISE 4-13 Create User Documentation

1. Click the **User Information** tab to move to the second worksheet, and change the view to 75% using the Zoom box. The varying column widths in the worksheet are already adjusted to create an easy-to-read final worksheet.

2. In cell A1, key **User Information** in bold.

3. Key the following labels as bold and right-aligned in column B, beginning in cell B3. Leave a row space between **Date created:** and **Date revised:** and a row space between **Revised by:** and **Contact for help:**

   Created by:
   Date created:
   Date revised:
   Revised by:
   Contact for help:

4. Key the following labels in bold in cells A11 and A14.

   Purpose
   User Instructions

5. In column C, starting in cell C3, key the information requested using Figure 4-14 as a reference. For example, key your name beside "Created by:" and so on down column C. Make these items left-aligned.

FIGURE 4-14
Worksheet
documentation

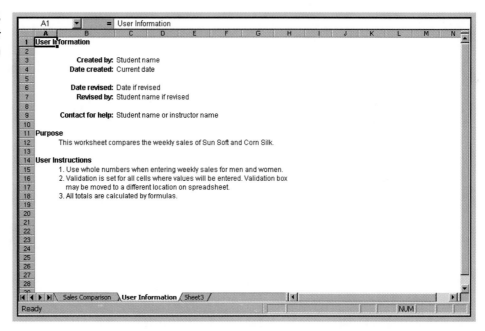

6. Using the information in Figure 4-14, in cell B12, key the purpose of this worksheet under the label **Purpose**. Below this, key user instructions for

Documentation is for the current user and future users of a worksheet. It should tell the user what the worksheet is, does, and how to use it. You can also provide further information about a workbook by choosing Properties from the File menu. Although this information cannot be printed, it is attached to the file and available to anyone using the file. You may want to explore and require this dialog box as an additional documentation tool.

In Excel Classroom Presentation 4.

another user or for yourself beginning in cell B15. It's a good idea to number these instructions for clarity. Put each numbered item in a separate cell. Also, put the second line of item 2 in its own cell directly below the first line of item 2.

7. Turn off gridlines for viewing using the Window Options in the Options dialog box (View tab) and return to cell A1.

8. Unused worksheets should be deleted once the workbook is complete. Right-click on Sheet3 tab. Click <u>D</u>elete and then click OK. Another way to delete a sheet is to make the sheet to be deleted active, then select De<u>l</u>ete Sheet from the <u>E</u>dit menu, and click OK.

☑ **Objective 6**

Protecting Files

Workbooks often include formats and formulas that you don't want changed. You can protect a file so users can key only in the areas you leave unlocked.

Protecting a file is a two-step process:

- Unlock areas for data entry
- Protect the file

EXERCISE 4-14 Unlock Data Entry Areas

1. Click the Sales Comparison tab and select the cells that contain test data. Do not select cells containing formulas.

2. Choose C<u>e</u>lls from the F<u>o</u>rmat menu and click the Protection tab in the Format Cells dialog box.

3. Clear the <u>L</u>ocked check box and click OK. The selected cells are unlocked. When you protect the workbook, they remain available to users.

4. Press Ctrl + Home to return to cell A1.

 NOTE: By default, all cells are locked in a workbook. Locked cells become inaccessible only after you protect the worksheet.

EXERCISE 4-15 Protect a Worksheet

The <u>P</u>rotection command on the <u>T</u>ools menu offers two options:

☑ **Objective 6 Assignment:**
Exercise 4-26 (Skills Review) can be assigned after completing Objective 6.

- Protect <u>W</u>orkbook prevents a user from adding, deleting, renaming, or moving worksheets and from resizing or moving windows.
- <u>P</u>rotect Sheet prevents a user from changing data in a worksheet.

1. Point to <u>P</u>rotection on the <u>T</u>ools menu and choose <u>P</u>rotect Sheet from the submenu. The Protect Sheet dialog box appears.

FIGURE 4-15
Protect Sheet
dialog box

2. In the <u>P</u>assword text box, key *[your initials]*. The text box displays asterisks instead of the characters you key to ensure the secrecy of your password. A password can be up to 255 characters long and include any combination of letters, numerals, and symbols. Passwords are case-sensitive, so you must remember whether you use uppercase or lowercase characters.

3. Click OK and the Confirm Password dialog box appears.

4. Rekey *[your initials]* in this dialog box and click OK.

5. Press Tab repeatedly to move to the cells that are available for data entry.

6. Go to cell A7 and try to key your name. The Microsoft Excel dialog box opens reminding you that the cell is protected.

Objective 7
Printing Workbooks and Print Areas

In Excel, you can control how your work is printed. You can:

- Preview a worksheet or an entire workbook before printing.
- Change page orientation.
- Position the print area on the page.
- Create headers and footers.
- Print with or without gridlines or row and column headings.
- Print all or part of a worksheet or workbook.

EXERCISE 4-16 Preview the Workbook before Printing

Preview a worksheet before you print it so you can see the page layout, headers and footers, print formatting, and page breaks. Although it is always a good idea to preview a worksheet, it makes particular sense if it contains graphics, drawings, or charts. After all, it takes less time to preview a complex worksheet than to print it.

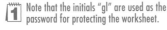 Note that the initials "gl" are used as the password for protecting the worksheet.

 In Excel Classroom Presentation 4.

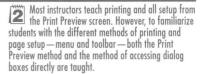 Most instructors teach printing and all setup from the Print Preview screen. However, to familiarize students with the different methods of printing and page setup—menu and toolbar—both the Print Preview method and the method of accessing dialog boxes directly are taught.

1. With the Sales Comparison worksheet displayed, choose Print Pre_view_ from the _F_ile menu or click the Print Preview button ⧉ on the Standard toolbar. At the top of the Print Preview screen, the _N_ext button is dimmed. The current worksheet fits on one page and the second worksheet is not available.

FIGURE 4-16
Print Preview
display

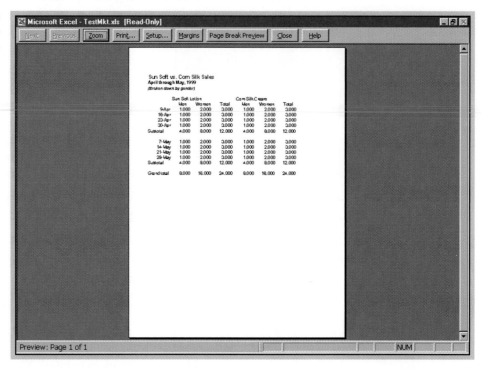

2. Click the Prin_t_ button to open the Print dialog box, select _E_ntire workbook under Print What, and click the Previe_w_ button. Preview: Page 1 of 2 appears in the Print Preview status bar, and the _N_ext button becomes available.

3. Click _N_ext. The User Information sheet ("Preview: Page 2 of 2") is displayed.

4. Click _Z_oom at the top of the preview screen (or click the reduced document). The worksheet is displayed in actual size.

> **TIP:** Click the magnifier pointer ⊕ on the full-page document to Zoom to actual size. Click the arrow pointer ⬚ on the enlarged document to Zoom to the reduced display.

5. Use the scroll arrows to view other parts of the worksheet in actual size.

6. Click _P_revious to display page 1 again.

7. Click _C_lose to close the Preview window.

EXERCISE 4-17 Choose a Page Orientation

One of the most useful print functions offered by Excel is *page orientation*, which you use to print worksheets in either *portrait* or *landscape* orientation. In portrait orientation, the page is vertical, 8½ inches by 11 inches. In landscape orientation, the page is horizontal, 11 inches by 8½ inches. You print worksheets with relatively few columns in portrait orientation. Wide worksheets require landscape orientation.

1. Choose Page Setup from the File menu to open the Page Setup dialog box.

 NOTE: The Setup button at the top of the Print Preview screen also opens the Page Setup dialog box.

2. Click the Page tab, if necessary.

FIGURE 4-17
Choosing page orientation

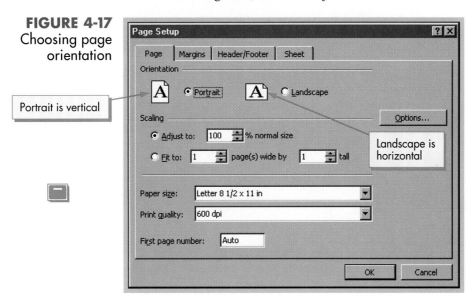

3. Click Landscape and click OK. The worksheet might look better in landscape orientation, especially if its width exceeds its length.
4. Click the Print Preview button 🔍.

 NOTE: Page Setup options apply only to the current worksheet.

EXERCISE 4-18 Center the Print Area on a Page

You can center worksheets on a page to improve the page layout. This is especially useful when worksheets are relatively small or all the pages are the same size.

1. Click <u>S</u>etup and click the Margins tab.
2. Click the Hori<u>z</u>ontally check box under the Center On Page section. The Preview area in the dialog box displays the centered settings.

 NOTE: Normally a worksheet is centered horizontally, but not vertically. You might consider vertically centering a worksheet if it contains a chart or other graphics.

FIGURE 4-18
Page Setup
dialog box,
Margins tab

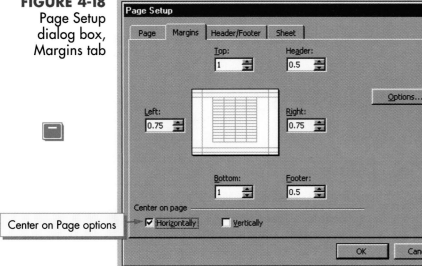

Center on Page options

EXERCISE 4-19 Enter a Header and a Footer

Headers and footers provide helpful information about a printed document. You can format these features in Excel using the Page Setup dialog box or the <u>S</u>etup button on the Print Preview screen.

You may want to ask students to horizontally center all worksheets they produce for class. This can be added to the "Worksheet Design Guide" you generate as the class proceeds.

In Excel Classroom Presentation 4.

From this point forward, a standard header is established that includes the student's name, filename, and date. A standard footer can also be established that includes the page number if there are multiple pages in a worksheet (this worksheet does not contain multiple pages). Some professionals consider it bad form to show a footer with the page number on a one-page worksheet. This can also be added to the "Worksheet Design Guide."

1. Click the Header/Footer tab.

2. Click <u>C</u>ustom Header. The insertion point is automatically positioned in the Left Section box so you can change the header.

3. Key your name in the Left Section box. This portion of the header appears in the upper left corner of the printed page.

4. Press Tab. The insertion point moves to the Center Section box.

 5. Click the File Name button to show the filename in the Center Section header. The ampersand (&) and the word "File" in brackets indicate the worksheet filename will appear in the header.

 6. Press Tab and click the Date button to include the current date in the <u>R</u>ight Section header.

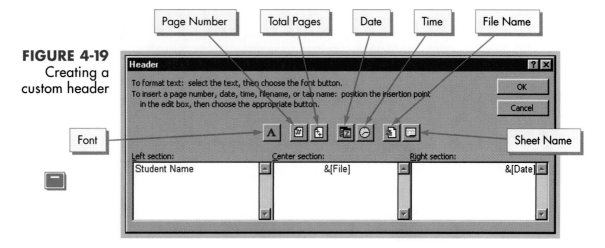

FIGURE 4-19
Creating a
custom header

7. Click OK. Your changes appear in the Header text box.

8. Open the drop-down list under <u>F</u>ooter and choose Page 1 of ?. This is a good footer to use when a worksheet spans more than one page.

9. Open the drop-down list again under <u>F</u>ooter and choose (none) to remove the footer.

> **TIP:** You can remove a header by choosing (none) from the drop-down list under <u>H</u>eader.

10. Click <u>C</u>ustom Footer and press Tab. The insertion point moves to the <u>C</u>enter Section box of the Footer dialog box.

 11. Click the Sheet Name button to include the current sheet name in the footer, which is represented by &[Tab].

12. Click OK. Your changes appear in the Footer text box.

 In Excel Classroom Presentation 4.

FIGURE 4-20
New header and
footer

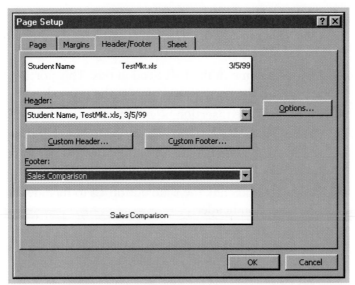

13. Click OK to close the Page Setup dialog box and notice the header and footer positioned on the page.

14. Close the Print Preview window.

15. Move to the User Information sheet. Use Page Setup to center the worksheet and to make the same changes to the header and footer of this sheet.

EXERCISE 4-20 Print a Workbook

Now that you set up the worksheet, it's time to print. You can print single sheets or multiple sheets of a workbook.

1. Move to the Sales Comparison worksheet and save the workbook as *[your initials]*4-20.xls in a new Lesson folder for Lesson 4.

TIP: Save a workbook immediately before or after printing to preserve the current print settings.

2. Choose Print from the File menu or press Ctrl+P to open the Print dialog box. The dialog box displays Excel's default settings and identifies the designated printer. (See Figure 4-21 on the next page.)

TIP: You can click the Print button 🖨 on the Standard Toolbar to print the current worksheet automatically or choose Print from the Print Preview screen to open the Print dialog box.

 In Excel Classroom Presentation 4.

 You may want to point out that it is usually the best policy to save before printing. This preserves the workbook even if a mishap occurs during printing that causes your computer to crash. If the student does not save, the correct filename will not appear in the header.

FIGURE 4-21
Print dialog box

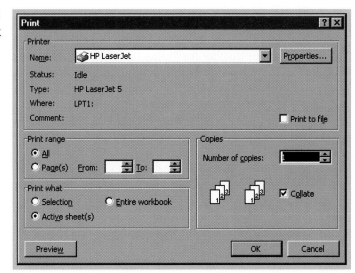

3. Click Entire Workbook and click OK to print both sheets of your workbook. The Printing dialog box appears as your workbook is sent to the printer.

EXERCISE 4-21 Change the Print Area

Excel automatically prints the entire worksheet unless you specify otherwise. Sometimes you may want to print a specific range of cells—called a *print area*. If you select multiple print areas, each area begins printing on a separate page. Headers and footers also appear when you print a print area.

1. On the Sales Comparison sheet, select cells A5 through D11.

2. Choose Print from the File menu.

3. Click Selection.

4. Click OK. Excel prints the selected portion of the worksheet.

TIP: You can also define a print area by selecting a range of cells, choosing Print Area from the File menu, and choosing Set Print Area. Clicking the Print button 🖨 on the Standard toolbar prints the current print area. To deselect the print area, choose File, Print Area, and then Clear Print Area.

5. Select cells A6 through D11.

6. Hold down Ctrl, select cells A13 through D17, and release Ctrl. Two areas are selected.

7. Choose Print from the File menu.

8. Click Selection and click OK. Excel prints the selected portions of the worksheet on two separate pages.

 In Excel Classroom Presentation 4.

Printing Formulas

 **Objective 8**

You may want to display formulas onscreen or in your printed worksheet for documentation purposes or to find and correct problems. You can either check the Formulas box on the View tab of the Options dialog box or use the keyboard shortcut Ctrl+⌐.

EXERCISE **4-22** Set View for Formulas

1. Press Ctrl+Home and choose Options from the Tools menu.

2. Select the View tab, if necessary.

> **NOTE:** View options affect the onscreen appearance of your worksheet. The Formulas option, however, also affects the printed worksheet. You must control most print options—such as row and column headings and gridlines—through the Page Setup dialog box.

3. Click the Formulas check box and click OK. Excel displays all formulas entered in their appropriate worksheet cells. Note that the column widths change to accommodate the wider formulas. As a result, only a portion of the worksheet fits onscreen. Also, the dates change to serial dates and the title is not fully visible.

> **NOTE:** Column widths may not always be automatically widened enough to accommodate extremely wide formulas. In this case you will need to manually widen the columns so you can see the formulas onscreen and on the printed worksheet.

FIGURE 4-22
Formulas displayed
in worksheet

	A	B	C	D	E	F	G
1	Sun Soft vs. Corn						
2	April through May, 199!						
3	(Broken down by gende						
4							
5		Sun Soft Lotion			Corn Silk Cream		
6		Men	Women	Total	Men	Women	To
7	36259	1000	2000	=SUM(B7:C7)	1000	2000	=SUM(E7:
8	36266	1000	2000	=SUM(B8:C8)	1000	2000	=SUM(E8:
9	36273	1000	2000	=SUM(B9:C9)	1000	2000	=SUM(E9:
10	36280	1000	2000	=SUM(B10:C10)	1000	2000	=SUM(E1(
11	Subtotal	=SUM(B7:B10)	=SUM(C7:C10)	=SUM(D7:D10)	=SUM(E7:E10)	=SUM(F7:F10)	=SUM(E11
12							
13	36287	1000	2000	=SUM(B13:C13)	1000	2000	=SUM(E1:
14	36294	1000	2000	=SUM(B14:C14)	1000	2000	=SUM(E1‹
15	36301	1000	2000	=SUM(B15:C15)	1000	2000	=SUM(E1!
16	36308	1000	2000	=SUM(B16:C16)	1000	2000	=SUM(E1€
17	Subtotal	=SUM(B13:B16)	=SUM(C13:C16)	=SUM(B17:C17)	=SUM(E13:E16)	=SUM(F13:F16)	=SUM(E17
18							
19	Grand total	=SUM(B17,B11)	=SUM(C17,C11)	=SUM(D17,D11)	=SUM(E17,E11)	=SUM(F17,F11)	=SUM(E19
20							
21							

4. Press Ctrl+⌐. The worksheet is displayed normally. (The ⌐ key is found to the left of the ① key.)

5. Press Ctrl+⌐ to display formulas once again.

 **Objective 8**
Assignment:

Exercise 4-27 (Skills Review) and Exercises 4-28 through 4-31 (Lesson Applications) can be assigned after completing Objective 8.

1 The View tab in the Options dialog box does not generally control print options. Most print options are controlled from the Page Setup dialog box. Printing formulas is an exception—you choose Formulas on the Options View tab. The Gridlines and the Row & column headers View options, however, affect the screen display only.

2 Students should be reminded never to save in Formula view. Printing formulas is part of documentation and it aids in rebuilding a worksheet if it becomes corrupted.

 In Excel Classroom Presentation 4.

EXERCISE 4-23 Print with Grids and Headings

You can add gridlines and row and column headings to your worksheet printout using Page Setup. Printing a formula view with gridlines and row and column headings will help you rebuild your worksheet if needed.

1. Choose Page Setup from the File menu and click the Sheet tab, if necessary.
2. Click Gridlines and Row and Column Headings in the Print area of the dialog box.
3. Click the Print Preview command button to view the worksheet before printing. Click Next to look at the second page of the formula printout.

 NOTE: You can fit the formula printout on one page by clicking Fit on the Page tab in Page Setup. However, in some worksheets this makes the text too small to read.

4. Click the Print button at the top of the Print Preview window to open the Print dialog box and click OK.
5. Close the workbook. Don't save the changes.

 TIP: If you save settings that print formulas, you have to change settings the next time you want to print the normal worksheet.

COMMAND SUMMARY

FEATURE	BUTTON	MENU	KEYBOARD
Go To Special		Edit, Go To, Special	Ctrl + G
Split		Window, Split	
Freeze Panes		Window, Freeze Panes	
Zoom	100% ▾	View, Zoom	
Print Preview	🔍	File, Print Preview	
Page Setup		File, Page Setup	
Protect Workbook		Tools, Protection, Protect Workbook	
Protect Worksheet		Tools, Protection, Protect Worksheet	
Print	🖨	File, Print	Ctrl + P
Display Formulas		Tools, Options	Ctrl + `
Set View		Tools, Options	

1 Tell students that gridlines and headings are usually only added to printouts when formulas are printed.

2 Point out that the Command Summary lists a variety of ways to accomplish a particular task. Students can decide which method they prefer.

USING HELP

Another way to get help on an Excel function is to use the Help Index, where all Help topics are listed alphabetically. Simply key a subject and choose from the list of related topics. Often, one topic will lead you to several related subtopics. Some topics may provide useful information that you can print for future reference.

Use the Help Index to explore topics about troubleshooting printing:

1. Press [F1] and key **use the help index**. Click Search.
2. Click the topic "Get Help without using the Office Assistant."
3. Review the explanation in the Help window, then click the Show button 🔲.
4. Click the Index tab, if necessary.
5. In the Type Keywords text box, key **print**.
6. Click Search. The Help Index displays a list of related topics.
7. Review the list of topics. Click the topic "Troubleshoot printing."

FIGURE 4-23
Using the
Help Index

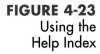

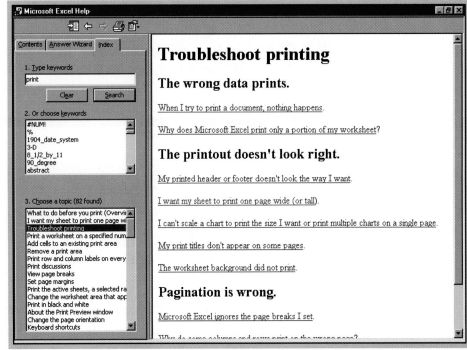

8. Review the list of topics on the right side of the Help Window, scrolling as needed. To learn more about a topic, click it. To print a topic, click the Print button 🖨 in the Help Window.
9. Close the Help Window when you're done.

Encourage students to follow the steps in "Using Help" (with a blank workbook open). Software companies are increasingly using their Help program—rather than printed documentation—to train users and assist in answering user questions.

In Excel Classroom Presentation 4.

TEST BANK

Concepts Review

TRUE/FALSE QUESTIONS

Each of the following statements is either true or false. Indicate your choice by circling **T** or **F**.

T **(F)** **1.** It's best to begin entering data in Excel before you design a worksheet with pencil and paper.

T **(F)** **2.** You should place comparative information in rows.

(T) F **3.** The formula bar displays the current cell's contents and the name box displays the cell address.

(T) F **4.** It's possible to select cells based on their contents, such as all cells containing formulas.

T **(F)** **5.** You use Zoom to speed up the printing process.

T **(F)** **6.** You can only validate data that is made up of whole numbers.

(T) F **7.** You can select page orientation from the Page Setup dialog box.

(T) F **8.** You can validate data using Validation on the Data menu.

SHORT ANSWER QUESTIONS

Write the correct answer in the space provided.

1. What name is given to simple numbers you can add in your head that are used to verify the accuracy of formulas?

Test data

2. Which function would you use to keep other users from changing formulas in a worksheet?

Protect Sheet

3. Which command enables you to divide a worksheet into two parts?

Split

4. Which command enables you to keep row and column labels in one place while you scroll data?

Freeze Panes

Concepts Review:
Allows students to check their understanding.

**C
L
O
S
E**

TEST BANK
Consider using the Test Bank to provide an additional review of lesson concepts. It may also be used as an assessment tool.

5. What do you call a range of cells to be printed?

Print area

6. Which part of the screen identifies each worksheet of an Excel workbook?

Worksheet tabs

7. Which dialog box enables you to enter a custom header and footer?

Page Setup

8. Which page orientation displays the worksheet horizontally?

Landscape

CRITICAL THINKING

Answer these questions on a separate piece of paper. There are no right or wrong answers. Support your answer with examples from your own experience, if possible.

1. Planning and sketching a worksheet with pencil and paper might seem like a waste of time in the "computer age." What might happen if you skip the planning stage? In what types of situations would it be especially important to plan and sketch the worksheet before entering data in Excel?

2. Describe a project or work situation in which you would have liked to have documentation available. What problem were you trying to solve? How would good documentation of the project have helped you?

Skills Review

EXERCISE 4-24

Plan a worksheet in pencil, enter labels, data validation, test data, and formulas onscreen, select cells by content, name the worksheet tab, and delete unused worksheets.

1. Plan and sketch a worksheet showing sales for each month of the first quarter for five sales representatives by following these steps:

   a. Write the worksheet heading **First Quarter Sales** at the top of a blank page.

   b. Write the entry area item **Report date: [current date]** two rows below the heading in the first column and use the current date.

   c. Write the following labels in a column along the left side of your page two rows below the entry area item:

Critical Thinking Questions:
Answers will vary based on students' preferences, observations, experiences, and research.

Skills Review:
Provides guided practice for students. Objectives are indicated for each Exercise.

Exercise 4-24:
Objectives 1, 2
Required Files: None
Solution Files: gl4-24.xls

The worksheet plan for this Exercise is located in the solutions file on the worksheet labeled Plan4-24.

Sales Rep
Davis
Jackson
Miller
Pierce
Brown
Total

d. Write the labels **January**, **February**, **March**, and **Total** in the row to the right of the label **Sales Rep.**

e. Write **F**'s in the cells that contain row and column totals.

2. Enter row and column labels onscreen by following these steps:

   a. Open a new Excel workbook.

   b. Key the heading **First Quarter Sales** in cell A1 in bold.

   c. Key **Report Date:** in cell B3 in bold and aligned right. Key the current date in cell C3.

   d. Key the row labels from your paper sketch in cells A5 through A11.

   e. Key the column labels from your paper sketch center-aligned in cells B5 through E5.

3. Enter data validation in the test data cells by following these steps:

   a. Select cells B6 through D10.

   b. Open the Data Validation dialog box (Data menu, Validation) and click the Settings tab, if necessary.

   c. Allow for whole numbers greater than or equal to 0.

   d. Click the Input Message tab and key **Monthly sales amount** as the input message with no title.

   e. Click OK.

4. Enter the test data shown in Figure 4-24 in the worksheet and format it for comma style and no decimals using the Comma Style button 🔲 and the Decrease Decimal button 🔲.

FIGURE 4-24

	B	C	D
6	1000	2000	3000
7	1000	2000	3000
8	1000	2000	3000
9	1000	2000	3000
10	1000	2000	3000

In this Exercise, students validate test data. Stress that validation is normally applied to entry cells only. Validation is used to inform users what needs to be entered in a cell or cells.

5. Enter formulas onscreen using the following steps:

   a. Select cells E6 through E10 and click the AutoSum button Σ.

   b. Select cells B11 through E11 and click the AutoSum button Σ.

6. Select the monthly sales test data by content by following these steps:

   a. Press Ctrl+Home.

   b. Press Ctrl+G.

   c. Click Special.

   d. Click Data Validation.

   e. Click OK.

7. Name the worksheet tab by following these steps:

   a. Double-click the Sheet1 tab.

   b. Key **Quarter 1**.

   c. Press Enter.

8. Delete the unused worksheets by following these steps:

   a. Right-click on Sheet2 tab.

   b. Select Delete and click OK.

   c. Repeat the above steps for Sheet3.

9. Save the workbook as ***[your initials]*4-24.xls** in your Lesson 4 folder.

10. Print the worksheet and close the workbook.

EXERCISE 4-25

Split a worksheet into panes, freeze panes, use Zoom, remove gridlines and headers from the screen, remove the split, and unfreeze the panes.

1. Open the file **Expense1.xls**.

2. Split the worksheet into panes by following these steps:

   a. Select cell B10.

   b. Choose Split from the Window menu.

   c. If necessary, click the down vertical scroll arrow for the bottom pane until the Total row for the Phoenix office becomes visible.

3. Freeze the worksheet panes by following these steps:

   a. Choose Freeze Panes from the Window menu.

   b. If necessary, click the horizontal scroll bar to compare data for the two offices.

4. Change the size of the worksheet onscreen by following these steps:

   a. Choose Zoom from the View menu.

   b. Choose 75%.

   c. Click OK.

5. Remove gridlines and headers from the screen by following these steps:

   a. Choose Options from the Tools menu.

● Exercise 4-25:
Objectives 3, 4
Required Files: Expense1.xls
Solution Files: gl4-25.xls

Students make changes to the worksheet that do not affect the appearance of the printed final version. However, students are asked to print their version regardless of this to make sure no mistakes were made.

       b. When the Options dialog box appears, click the View tab, if necessary.

       c. Clear the <u>G</u>ridlines and Row & Column H<u>e</u>aders check boxes and click OK.

  6. Remove splits and unfreeze panes by following these steps:

       a. Choose Un<u>f</u>reeze Panes from the <u>W</u>indow menu.

       b. Choose Remove <u>S</u>plit from the <u>W</u>indow menu.

  7. Press Ctrl+Home and save the workbook as *[your initials]*4-25.xls in your Lesson 4 folder.

  8. Print the worksheet and close the workbook.

EXERCISE 4-26

Create user documentation, unlock data entry areas, turn off gridlines for viewing, and protect a worksheet.

  1. Open the file **Expense2.xls**. Look at the first two sheets.

  2. Create documentation for the worksheet by following these steps:

       a. Click the Documentation tab and key **User Information** in cell A1 in bold. (Column widths are already adjusted for easy reading.)

       b. Key the labels and data in Figure 4-25. Key the labels in Column B in bold and right-align them. Key the information left-aligned in column C.

FIGURE 4-25

	B	C
3	**Created by:**	Jaime Santo
4	**Date created:**	29-Jun
5		
6	**Date revised:**	Current date
7	**Revised by:**	Student name
8		
9	**Contact for help:**	Jaime Santo

  3. Key the labels and information in Figure 4-26 in the appropriate columns and rows. Make the labels bold.

● **Exercise 4-26:**

Objectives 5, 6
Required Files: Expense2.xls
Solution Files: gl4-26.xls in Solutions Manual or on
Solutions Disk.

FIGURE 4-26

	A	B
11	Purpose	
12		This worksheet shows projected increases in Q1 expenses.
13		
14	User Instructions	
15		1. Use whole numbers when keying expense amounts.
16		2. Formulas are used to calculate percentages and totals.

4. Turn off gridlines for viewing by following these steps:
   a. Choose Options under the Tools menu.
   b. Click the View tab, if necessary.
   c. Clear the Gridlines check box and click OK.

5. Unlock data entry for the Quarter cells in the San Francisco Increase sheet by following these steps:
   a. Click the San Francisco Increase worksheet tab.
   b. Select cells B4 through C9.
   c. Choose Cells from the Format menu.
   d. Click the Protection tab on the Format Cells dialog box.
   e. Clear the Locked check box and click OK.
   f. Press Ctrl+Home.

6. Protect the worksheet by following these steps:
   a. Choose Protection from the Tools menu.
   b. Choose Protect Sheet.
   c. Enter *[your initials]* in the password section of the Protect Sheet dialog box and click OK.
   d. Enter *[your initials]* again in the Confirm Password dialog box and click OK.
   e. Test the protection by pressing Tab. (*Hint:* Only the cells available for data entry should be accessible.)

7. Press Ctrl+Home and save the workbook as *[your initials]***4-26.xls** in your Lesson 4 folder.

8. Print the entire workbook by following these steps:
   a. Press Ctrl+P.
   b. Select Entire Workbook in the Print dialog box and click OK.

9. Close the workbook.

EXERCISE 4-27

Choose page orientation, change the print area, change headers and footers, and print with and without gridlines, headings, and formulas.

1. Open the file **Revenue.xls**.
2. Choose landscape orientation by following these steps:
   a. Choose Page Set<u>u</u>p from the <u>F</u>ile menu.
   b. Click the Page tab, if necessary.
   c. Click <u>L</u>andscape.
   d. Click Print Previe<u>w</u> to view the entire worksheet on one page.
3. Center the print area on the page by following these steps:
   a. While still in Print Preview, click <u>S</u>etup.
   b. Click the Margins tab.
   c. Click the Hori<u>z</u>ontally check box under the Center on Page section.
4. Change the headers and footers by following these steps:
   a. Click the Header/Footer tab in the Page Setup dialog box and click <u>C</u>ustom Header.
   b. Key your name in the <u>L</u>eft section box and press `Tab`.
   c. Click the File Name button 🔳 in the <u>C</u>enter section of the header and press `Tab`.
   d. Click the Date button 🔳 in the <u>R</u>ight section of the header and click OK.
   e. Click C<u>u</u>stom Footer and press `Tab`.
   f. Click the Sheet Name button 🔳 and click OK.
   g. Click OK and then click <u>C</u>lose.
   h. Save the workbook as *[your initials]***4-27.xls** in your Lesson 4 folder.
5. Print the worksheet without gridlines by following these steps. (*Hint:* The default is that gridlines are turned off for printing. In this worksheet they are on.)
   a. Choose Page Set<u>u</u>p from the <u>F</u>ile menu and then click the Sheet tab in the Page Setup dialog box.
   b. Clear the <u>G</u>ridlines check box and click Print Previe<u>w</u> to view the worksheet in Print Preview.
   c. Click Prin<u>t</u> to open the Print dialog box and click OK to print the worksheet.
6. Change the print area and print the worksheet with headings and formulas by following these steps:
   a. Select the range A1 through D18, choose Prin<u>t</u> Area from the <u>F</u>ile menu, and choose <u>S</u>et Print Area.
   b. Press `Ctrl`+`` ` ``.
   c. Choose Page Set<u>u</u>p from the <u>F</u>ile menu and click the Sheet tab, if necessary.

⊙ **Exercise 4-27:**
Objectives 7, 8
Required Files: Revenue.xls
Solution Files: gl4-27.xls in Solutions Manual or on
Solutions Disk.

      d. Check the Gridlines and Row and column headings boxes.

      e. Click Print Preview to view the worksheet before printing. Click Zoom to take a closer look.

      f. Click Print to open the Print dialog box and click OK to print.

7. Close the workbook without saving it.

A S S E S S

Assessment Resources:
- Solutions Manual
- Test Bank
- Portfolio Builder
- Internet Projects
- Alternative Assessment Guide
- Certification Procedures

For Internet projects, go to
www.glencoe.com/webprojects

Lesson Applications

EXERCISE 4-28

Enter a label and data, add formulas, change headers and footers, and print horizontally centered with and without formulas, grids, and row and column headings.

Nate Rosario, the controller for the Beautiful Belle Company, needs to prepare a forecast of profits (or net income) for the next five years.

1. Open the file **NetInc1.xls**. Gridlines for viewing are turned off in this worksheet, which is not the default setting.

2. Insert a row between the "Administration" and "Marketing" labels.

3. Label the new row **Salaries** and insert the data below.

   550   650   780   870   900

4. Insert Total Expenses formulas that sum Administration, Salaries, Marketing, and Research expenses for each year.

5. Insert Net Income formulas for each year. Calculate net income by subtracting Total Expenses from Sales.

6. Apply a single-line top border and a double-line bottom border to the Net Income values (below the total expense cells).

7. Format the labels "Sales," "Expenses," and "Net Income" in bold.

8. Center the worksheet horizontally on the page.

9. Create a new header that includes your name on the left, the filename in the center, and the date on the right.

10. Save the workbook as *[your initials]***4-28.xls** in your Lesson 4 folder and print the worksheet.

11. Create a formula printout that shows all formulas with gridlines and row and column headings in landscape orientation. In Page Setup add a Page 1 of ? footer. (*Hint:* Open the drop-down list under Footer and choose Page 1 of ?)

12. Close the workbook without saving it.

EXERCISE 4-29

Enter data and labels, create and enter formulas, select cells by content, set up the worksheet to print in portrait orientation, and print it with gridlines, row and column headings, and formulas.

Lesson Applications:

Provide independent practice for students and may be used for assessment. Objectives are indicated for each Exercise.

◉ **Exercise 4-28:**

Objectives 2, 7, 8
Required Files: NetInc1.xls
Solution Files: gl4-28.xls in Solutions Manual or on Solutions Disk.

The executives at Beautiful Belle want to examine third-quarter sales data by comparing the differences in male and female purchasers of Sun Soft and Corn Silk products.

1. Open the file **Totals.xls**.

2. Insert two rows between the July and Subtotals rows in the Men and Women sections shown in Figure 4-27. Then enter the data for the months of August and September making the appropriate corrections.

FIGURE 4-27

		Sun Soft	Corn Silk
Men	July	11,685	9,350
	AUGUST *(lower case)*	12,550	9,800
	September	8,794	12,810
	Subtotal	11,685	9,350
Women	July	24,030	49,400
	Augst	22,104	38,465
	September	24,366	18,700
	Subtotal	24,030	49,400

3. Check and correct the Men and Women subtotal formulas, if necessary.

4. Insert two rows above the Grand Total row and key the labels **August** and **September** under "July" in the Total section.

5. Create formulas that calculate the August and September totals.

6. Check and correct the Grand Total formula, if necessary.

7. Select cells with formulas using select by content (Go To Special dialog box) and make them all italic.

8. Set up the worksheet to print in portrait orientation. (The default orientation is portrait; however, this worksheet's orientation is landscape.)

9. Center the worksheet horizontally on the page.

10. Create a standard header that includes your name on the left, the filename in the center, and the date on the right.

11. Make cell A1 active and save the workbook as *[your initials]*4-29.xls in your Lesson 4 folder and print the worksheet.

12. Create a formula printout that shows all formulas with gridlines and row and column headings.

13. Close the workbook without saving it.

◉ Exercise 4-29:
Objectives 2, 7, 8
Required Files: Totals.xls
Solution Files: gl4-29.xls in Solutions Manual or on Solutions Disk.

[1] This figure contains proofreading marks. You may want to review Appendix E: "Proofreaders' Marks" with students.

EXERCISE 4-30

Freeze panes, enter data and formulas, use Zoom, use set-up options, preview the worksheet, protect and unprotect the worksheet, and print it without and with formulas.

The Beautiful Belle Company wants to extend the comparative-sales worksheet to include test-marketing data for Sun Soft and Corn Silk through July.

1. Open the file **MktTest.xls**.
2. Edit the title in cell A2 to read **April through July, 1999**.
3. Add new rows to the Sales Comparison worksheet by selecting cells A20 through A32 and choosing <u>R</u>ows from the <u>I</u>nsert menu.
4. Freeze panes in cell A8 so column headings remain visible.
5. Enter the data shown in Figure 4-28 beginning in row 20. Make sure the numbers are formatted to match the others.

FIGURE 4-28

	A	B	C	D	E	F	G
		Sun Soft			Corn Silk		
		Men	Women	Total	Men	Women	Total
20	4-Jun	2,300	3,400		1,250	1,050	
21	11-Jun	2,200	5,200		1,370	1,100	
22	18-Jun	1,950	4,300		1,290	1,000	
23	25-Jun	2,700	5,800		1,400	950	
24	Subtotal						
25							
26	2-Jul	2,500	4,500		1,500	1,100	
27	9-Jul	2,735	6,900		1,550	1,300	
28	16-Jul	2,800	5,430		1,650	1,550	
29	23-Jul	3,200	5,700		1,780	1,760	
30	30-Jul	3,300	5,820		1,910	1,880	
31	Subtotal						

● **Exercise 4-30:**
Objectives 2–4, 6–8
Required Files: MktTest.xls
Solution Files: gl4-30.xls in Solutions Manual or on
Solutions Disk.

The completed document for this Exercise
may be used in a student's portfolio.

6. Unfreeze panes and enter or revise formulas to calculate totals, subtotals, and grand totals. (Grand totals must include the two new months' data.)

7. Reduce the size of the worksheet to 50%.

8. View the worksheet in Print Preview.

9. Set the worksheet to print in landscape orientation without gridlines or row and column headings.

10. Center the worksheet horizontally on the page and create a standard header that includes your name on the left, filename in the center, and date on the right.

11. Close Print Preview. Change the display to 75% using the Zoom box on the Standard toolbar.

12. Protect the worksheet leaving only the cells containing weekly sales numbers available for entry. Make any cells containing formulas unavailable. Use your three initials as your password.

13. Make cell A1 active if it is not, save the workbook as *[your initials]*4-30.xls in your Lesson 4 folder, and print the worksheet.

14. Unprotect the worksheet.

15. Create a formula printout that shows all formulas with gridlines and row and column headings in landscape orientation. Choose the Page 1 of ? footer. Widen columns to show formulas if necessary.

16. Close the workbook without saving it.

EXERCISE 4-31 *Challenge Yourself*

Sketch a worksheet plan, enter the plan in a worksheet, validate data, select all formula cells, create documentation, name sheet tabs, use print preview and page set-up options, print the workbook, and print formulas.

  The Beautiful Belle Company wants a worksheet that calculates the difference between monthly sales of Sun Soft and Corn Silk products to men and women for their Northeast division. The worksheet should also calculate the difference in total sales by gender to both groups.

1. Sketch a worksheet to calculate these values. Title the worksheet **Sun Soft vs. Corn Silk Sales.** Two rows below the title enter **Division:** and in the row below Division: enter **Year:.** The report is to be divided into two sections, **Men** and **Women.** Place these section headings in column A. Each section should have the following row labels: **April**, **May**, **June**, and **July**, which should begin below "Men" and below "Women" in

---

Students design a worksheet from a written description, so the layout may vary. Students submit four pages: the plan, the two worksheets, and the formula printout of the first worksheet.

The completed document for this Exercise may be used in a student's portfolio.

Exercise 4-31:
Objectives 1, 2, 5, 7, 8
Required Files: None
Solution Files: Sample gl4-31.xls in Solutions Manual or on Solutions Disk.

column B. The last row of each section should be a **Subtotal** row and the last row in the worksheet should be a **Total** row. There should be three columns of data labeled **Sun Soft**, **Corn Silk**, and **Difference**.

2. Include formulas in this worksheet plan in the subtotal and total rows. Abbreviate using an F.

3. Key the title and labels in a new Excel worksheet. Use text formatting to distinguish the title and labels from other worksheet data.

4. Validate entry cells that contain sales data for men and women. Validate for whole numbers greater than 500.

5. Key the sales data for men from Figure 4-29 formatted in Comma style with no decimals:

FIGURE 4-29

		Sun Soft	Corn Silk	Difference
Men				
	April	3,300	6,600	
	May	6,450	8,150	
	June	9,150	5,310	
	July	11,235	6,480	

6. Key the following sales data for women formatted in Comma style with no decimals:

FIGURE 4-30

		Sun Soft	Corn Silk	Difference
Women				
	April	3,300	6,600	
	May	6,800	8,000	
	June	18,700	4,100	
	July	22,530	5,710	

7. Create the formulas to calculate the men's and women's subtotals.

8. Create the formulas to calculate differences between Sun Soft and Corn Silk subtotals only. (Subtract Corn Silk data from Sun Soft data.) Format the figures in Comma style, no decimals.

9. Create the formulas to calculate the totals for each section. Format the figures in Comma style, no decimals, if necessary.

10. Create the formula for the difference between product totals.

11. Select all cells containing formulas and make them italic.

12. Rename the Sheet1 tab **Sales by Gender** and delete Sheet3.

13. Rename the Sheet2 tab **User Information**.

14. Create user information as follows using the basic layout you learned in the lesson to place the documentation elements. (Don't worry about column width when placing these elements, but follow the basic design you learned in the lesson.) Use the information from Figure 4-31.

FIGURE 4-31

```
User Information

Created by:          Jane Doe

Date created:        8/13/99

Date revised:        [current date]

Revised by:          [your name]

Contact for Help:    Jane Doe

Purpose              This worksheet compares Sun Soft and Corn Silk
                     sales data by gender.

User Instructions    1. The worksheet is protected. To move to
                     unprotected entry cells, press the Tab key.

                     2. All totals, subtotals, and differences are
                     calculated by formulas.
```

15. Turn off gridlines for viewing.

16. Center the Sales by Gender sheet horizontally.

17. Create the standard header that shows your name on the left, the filename in the center, and the date at the right on both sheets.

18. Preview the workbook.

19. Save the workbook as *[your initials]***4-31.xls** in your Lesson 4 folder and print the entire workbook.

20. Create a formula printout of the Sales by Gender worksheet. Print the sheet in landscape orientation, showing gridlines and row and column headings. Use a Page 1 of ? footer, if there is more than one page of formulas to print. If not, use the Sheet tab as the footer center at the bottom.

21. Close the workbook without saving it. Submit the plan, the Sales by Gender worksheet, the User Information worksheet, and the Formula view.

 The worksheet plan for this Exercise is in the
solutions file on the worksheet labeled Plan4-31.

Copying Data and Using Toolbars

OBJECTIVES

MOUS
ACTIVITIES
In this lesson:
XL2000 **1.7**
XL2000 **1.10**
XL2000 **E.7.1**
XL2000 **E.7.2**

See Appendix F.

After completing this lesson, you will be able to:

1. Build a worksheet with copy and paste.
2. Copy using drag and drop.
3. Copy using Fill and AutoFill.
4. Use Excel's toolbars.

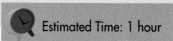 Estimated Time: 1 hour

Designing and developing worksheets in Excel often involves repeating basic elements, including cells, formulas, and formatting. You can copy these elements to build a worksheet quickly and easily. This lesson also demonstrates the versatility of Excel's toolbars and different ways to display them.

☑**Objective 1**

Building a Worksheet with Copy and Paste

You can copy, move, and cut cell contents in Excel. A copy is an exact duplicate of the element you select. The copy can be pasted or inserted into other locations of a worksheet or the document area of other Windows applications. Unlike moving or cutting, you don't affect the original element when you copy it. The data remains in the original location, but is also on the Clipboard (which is a temporary computer memory location). Information is erased from the Clipboard when you initiate a new Copy or Cut command.

P R E P A R E
Point out to students that the learning objectives show what they will learn in the lesson. Each heading in the lesson correlates to a learning objective.

158

Required files:
Compare.xls

T E A C H
Teaching Resources:
• Excel Classroom Presentations
• School-to-Work Strategies Manual
• Spanish Glossary
• Certification Procedures

☑**Objective 1 Assignment:**
Exercise 5-10 (Skills Review) can be assigned after completing Objective 1.

You can choose the Copy and Paste commands three ways:

- Use the <u>E</u>dit menu.
- Use the keyboard shortcuts [Ctrl]+[C] for Copy and [Ctrl]+[V] for Paste.
- Click the Copy 📋 and Paste 📋 buttons on the Standard toolbar.

EXERCISE ▐ **5-1** ▐ **Copy and Paste Using the Edit Menu**

In this Exercise you construct a worksheet with both detail and summary comparisons of 1999 second-quarter sales for the test product, Sun Soft Lotion, and its competing product, Corn Silk Cream.

1. Open the file **Compare.xls**.

2. Select cells A6 through B9 as the *source range*. The source range is the area of the worksheet from which you copy or remove data.

3. Choose <u>C</u>opy from the <u>E</u>dit menu. A moving border surrounds the selected cells. The contents of the cells you just copied are now on the Clipboard. (The clipboard's contents don't appear on the screen.)

FIGURE 5-1
Source range
selected

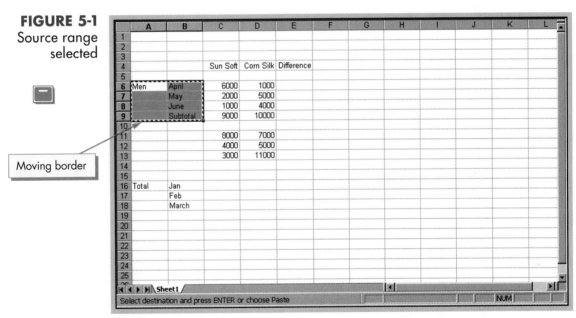

Moving border

4. Select cell A11. This cell is in the upper left corner of the *target range*. The target range is the new location for the data you want to copy or move.

5. Choose <u>P</u>aste from the <u>E</u>dit menu. A copy of the data from the source range appears in the target range. A copy of the data also remains on the Clipboard. To show this, Excel still displays a moving border around the source range.

📝 The terms *target range* and *source range* are introduced in this lesson with Copy and Paste operations.

 Use Excel Classroom Presentation 5 to display screens from the lesson in a slide-show format.

FIGURE 5-2
Source range
copied to
target range

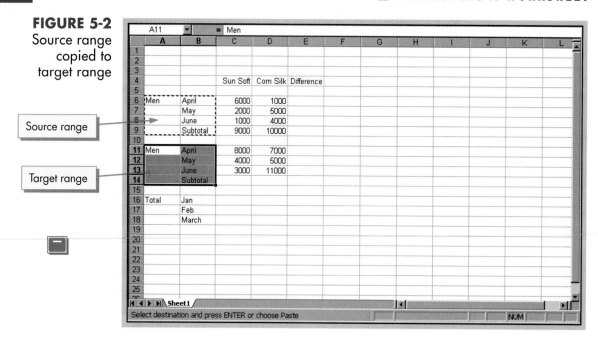

Source range

Target range

 TIP: Copy and Paste are available from the shortcut menu. To see this, right-click the selected source or target, but don't choose a command. Press Esc to close the shortcut menu.

6. Press Esc to remove the moving border around the source range.

NOTE: When the moving border is no longer displayed, you cannot paste the data from the Clipboard.

7. Edit cell A11 to read **Women**.

EXERCISE **5-2** Overwrite and Insert with Copy and Paste

The Copy and Paste commands overwrite existing cell data. You can also use Copy to insert new cells and data between existing cells.

1. Select cells B11 to B13 and press Ctrl+C (the Copy keyboard shortcut).

2. Select cells B16 to B18 and press Ctrl+V (the Paste keyboard shortcut). The months "Jan" through "March" are replaced by "April" through "June."

3. Press Esc to exit Copy mode.

In Excel Classroom Presentation 5.

 You may want to mention that using shortcut menus to copy and paste is one of the most convenient ways to build a worksheet.

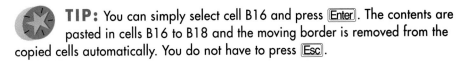

TIP: You can simply select cell B16 and press Enter. The contents are pasted in cells B16 to B18 and the moving border is removed from the copied cells automatically. You do not have to press Esc.

4. Select cell A16 and choose Copy from the Edit menu.

5. Select cell E4 and choose Copied Cells from the Insert menu. The Insert Paste dialog box opens.

FIGURE 5-3
Insert Paste
dialog box

6. Select Shift Cells Right and click OK. The copy of "Total" appears in cell E4 and the word "Difference" shifts one cell to the right.

7. Press Esc to exit Copy mode.

8. Delete the label "Difference" in cell F4.

EXERCISE 5-3 Copy and Paste Using the Toolbar

Like the Copy and Paste commands on the Edit menu, you can use the Copy button 🖹 and the Paste button 🖺 to copy cell values, formulas, and formatting.

1. Select all cells with numbers and format them for Comma style with no decimals.

2. Use the AutoSum button Σ to total April sales for Sun Soft and Corn Silk in cell E6.

3. With cell E6 selected, click the Copy button 🖹.

4. Select cell E7 and click the Paste button 🖺. Excel copies the formula and the formatting; it also adjusts the cell references so the formula is =SUM(C7:D7). This change in cells is called a *relative cell reference*. With relative referencing, Excel knows that if you copy a formula to a new row, you intend to add the numbers in the new row rather than the numbers in the original row. This type of referencing occurs with any method of copying and pasting formulas.

5. Select cell E8 and click the Paste button 🖺.

6. Select cell E9 and press Enter. Excel pastes the contents and completes the copy action, erasing the Clipboard. All the copied formulas are adjusted with relative cell references and the cell formatting is also copied.

TIP: You can use the Paste Special command on the Edit menu to paste certain aspects of a cell's contents, including its formatting, values only, validation, or everything except borders. This is a handy tool if you need to be specific about what you are pasting.

 In Excel Classroom Presentation 5.

1 Office 2000 offers a new clipboard called Office Clipboard. Office Clipboard (View, Toolbars, Clipboard) and Windows Clipboard (Start, Program, Accessories, Clipboard viewer) are separate. Up to 12 copies can be placed on the Office Clipboard. When you copy multiple copies to the Office Clipboard only the last copy is placed on the Windows Clipboard.

2 In step 6, "erasing the Clipboard" refers to the Windows Clipboard and not the Office Clipboard. The Office Clipboard will maintain a maximum of 12 copies until cleared by the user.

Copying Using Drag and Drop

 Objective 2

You can also copy data and formulas using drag-and-drop. This is an easy way to copy information using the mouse. You can make only a single copy using this method, however.

EXERCISE 5-4 Copy Using Drag and Drop

1. Select cells E6 through E8.

2. Move the mouse pointer across the border of the selection until it becomes an arrow.

 TIP: Avoid the lower right corner of the selection.

3. Press and hold down Ctrl. The pointer becomes the drag-and-drop pointer, with a tiny cross appearing to the right of the arrow. When the cross is present, you're copying data, not moving it.

4. Drag the selected cells to cells E11 through E13. Note the gray outline in the shape of the source range and the yellow message box containing the cell addresses as you move the mouse. When the selected cells are positioned at the target range, release the mouse button and the Ctrl key.

 TIP: You must hold down the Ctrl key to copy while dragging. Notice the + sign that appears to the right of the arrow pointer.

5. Select cells C9 to E9.

6. Drag and drop this information into cells C14 to E14. Excel copies both the formula and its formatting, and adjusts the cell references accordingly.

FIGURE 5-4
Copying using the drag-and-drop method

	A	B	C	D	E	F	G	H	I	J	K	L
1												
2												
3												
4			Sun Soft	Corn Silk	Total							
5												
6	Men	April	6,000	1,000	7,000							
7		May	2,000	5,000	7,000							
8		June	1,000	4,000	5,000							
9		Subtotal	9,000	10,000	19,000							
10												
11	Women	April	8,000	7,000	15,000							
12		May	4,000	5,000	9,000							
13		June	3,000	11,000	14,000							
14		Subtotal										
15												
16	Total	April										
17		May										
18		June										
19												
20												
21												

C14:E14

Objective 2 Assignment:
Exercise 5-11 (Skills Review) can be assigned after completing Objective 2.

 Warn students in advance that using the mouse to drag and drop and AutoFill can be tricky. It may take students some time to get the hang of it. Drag and drop is especially sensitive and students may end up moving data instead of copying it.

In Excel Classroom Presentation 5.

7. Verify that the formulas are correct for the new location.

☑**Objective 3**

Copying Using Fill and AutoFill

Worksheets frequently contain repetitive formulas. Instead of copying each formula using Copy and Paste, the Fill and AutoFill commands are often a quicker technique.

EXERCISE **5-5** **Copy Using the Fill Command**

---

1. Enter the formula **=C6+C11** in cell C16.

2. Select cells C16 through C18. Be sure to select the cell that contains the desired formula and all cells to which that formula is to be copied. These cells must be adjacent to one another to use the Fill command.

3. Choose the F̲ill command from the E̲dit menu and choose D̲own from the submenu (or press ⌐Ctrl⌐+⌐D⌐). Excel copies the formula to the selected cells and adjusts the cell references.

FIGURE 5-5
Using Fill to copy formulas (with formulas displayed)

	C16	▼	=	=C6+C11								
	A	B	C	D	E	F	G	H	I	J	K	L
1												
2												
3												
4			Sun Soft	Corn Silk	Total							
5												
6	Men	April	6,000	1,000	7,000							
7		May	2,000	5,000	7,000							
8		June	1,000	4,000	5,000							
9		Subtotal	9,000	10,000	19,000							
10												
11	Women	April	8,000	7,000	15,000							
12		May	4,000	5,000	9,000							
13		June	3,000	11,000	14,000							
14		Subtotal	15,000	23,000	38,000							
15												
16	Total	April	14,000									
17		May	6,000									
18		June	4,000									
19												
20												
21												
22												
23												
24												
25												

|◄ ◄ ► ►|\ Sheet1 /　　　　　　　　　　　|◄|　　　　　►|
Ready　　　　　　　　　　　　　　　　　Sum= 　　24,000　　　　NUM

4. Click outside the selection.

5. Select cells C16 through E16.

6. Choose F̲ill from the E̲dit menu and choose R̲ight from the submenu (or press ⌐Ctrl⌐+⌐R⌐).

☑**Objective 3 Assignment:**
Exercise 5-12 (Skills Review) and Exercises 5-14 through 5-16 (Lesson Applications) can be assigned after completing Objective 3.

 In Excel Classroom Presentation 5.

7. Click outside the selection.

8. To view the formulas you copied, press [Ctrl]+[ ] (or choose <u>O</u>ptions from the <u>T</u>ools menu, click Formulas, and click OK).

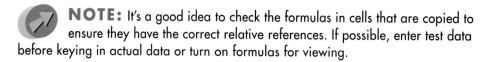

NOTE: It's a good idea to check the formulas in cells that are copied to ensure they have the correct relative references. If possible, enter test data before keying in actual data or turn on formulas for viewing.

EXERCISE 5-6 Copy Using the AutoFill Command

Using AutoFill, you can copy a formula in a single cell to multiple cells in a single step. Drag and drop is a good way to copy when the source area and the target area are not adjacent but both are the same size. AutoFill, on the other hand, should be used for copying to adjacent cells.

1. Press [Ctrl]+[ ] to clear the formulas from the screen.

TIP: You can also choose <u>O</u>ptions from the <u>T</u>ools menu and click to clear the Formulas checkbox.

2. Select cell D16 and position the mouse pointer on the *fill handle*, which is the small box in the lower right corner of the cell. The mouse pointer changes to a black cross.

FIGURE 5-6
Using AutoFill to copy formulas

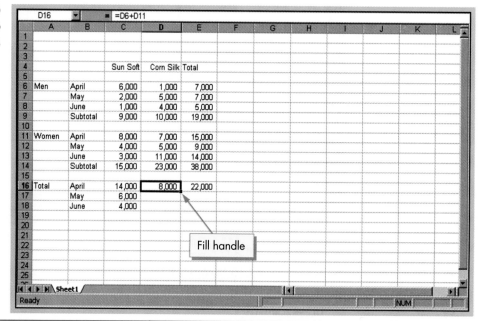

D16		▼	= =D6+D11								
	A	B	C	D	E	F	G	H	I	J	K
4			Sun Soft	Corn Silk	Total						
6	Men	April	6,000	1,000	7,000						
7		May	2,000	5,000	7,000						
8		June	1,000	4,000	5,000						
9		Subtotal	9,000	10,000	19,000						
11	Women	April	8,000	7,000	15,000						
12		May	4,000	5,000	9,000						
13		June	3,000	11,000	14,000						
14		Subtotal	15,000	23,000	38,000						
16	Total	April	14,000	8,000	22,000						
17		May	6,000								
18		June	4,000								

Fill handle

Sheet1

Ready NUM

In Excel Classroom Presentation 5.

3. Drag the fill handle until cells D17 and D18 are both selected. The cells are bordered in gray.

4. Release the mouse button. Excel copies the formula from cell D16 to cells D17 and D18.

5. Copy the formula in cell E16 to cells E17 and E18 using the same method.

6. In cells A1 and A2, key the following title in bold:

    Sun Soft/Corn Silk Sales Comparison
    Quarter 2, 1999

7. Create a header that includes your name in the left section, the filename in the center section, and the date in the right section.

8. Center the worksheet horizontally on the page.

9. Save the workbook as *[your initials]*5-6.xls in a new folder for Lesson 5 and print the worksheet.

10. Create a formula printout with gridlines and row and column headings in landscape orientation.

11. Turn off formulas for viewing.

✓ Objective 4

Using Toolbars in Excel

To this point, you used Excel's predefined Standard and Formatting toolbars to make your work easier. Excel provides many other predefined toolbars that make chart construction, drawing, accessing the World Wide Web, moving and copying text, and other functions faster and more convenient. You can control how toolbars appear on the screen and what functions they perform.

TABLE 5-1 | **Predefined Toolbars in Excel**

TOOLBAR NAME	FUNCTION
PivotTable	Retrieve and analyze data from databases.
Chart	Create and modify charts. It automatically displays when you work on a chart.
Reviewing	Create and edit comments in files that can be sent as e-mail.
Forms	Create custom forms.
Clipboard	Keep track of copies, cut and paste in any Office program.
Stop Recording	Stop recording a macro.

continues

Students are asked to create a header with their name, the filename, and the date. They are also asked to create a formula printout. These two tasks and creating footers for a multiple page spreadsheet are standard from this point forward. Students should know how to accomplish these tasks from Lesson 4.

✓**Objective 4 Assignment:**

Exercise 5-13 (Skills Review) and Exercise 5-17 (Lesson Applications) can be assigned after completing Objective 4.

You may want explain how to customize Excel's predefined toolbars: Choose View, Toolbars to open the Toolbars submenu. Click Customize and select the toolbar you want to modify. Choose the category that contains the button you want to add. Drag and drop the desired button to the toolbar you're customizing. If students aren't sure what a particular button does, they can click it and read the description at the bottom of the dialog box. To return a toolbar to its original installed settings, select it in the Customize dialog box and click Reset.

TABLE 5-1   **Predefined Toolbars in Excel**   *continued*

TOOLBAR NAME	FUNCTION
External Data	Work with data imported from an external database.
Auditing	Trace precedents, dependents, and errors within formulas.
Full Screen	Return to Normal view after displaying the full screen.
Circular Reference	Identify circular references in cells.
Visual Basic	Work with macros.
Web	Access the World Wide Web.
Control Toolbox	Create controls to run macros.
Drawing	Create graphic objects. It contains standard drawing tools such as line, arc, and rectangle.
WordArt	Create attractive text.
Picture	Control the look of images imported into Excel.
Shadow Settings	Place shadows behind graphics.
3-D Settings	Create a 3-D effect with graphics.

EXERCISE   5-7   Display Multiple Toolbars

FIGURE 5-7
Toolbars submenu

Sometimes it's useful to display several toolbars simultaneously. For example, your worksheet may contain multiple formulas and be targeted to someone outside your company. In that case, the Auditing toolbar helps you trace multiple calculations and the Clipboard toolbar is handy to collect and store up to 12 separate cut or copied items without erasing previous items. This toolbar acts as up to 12 separate Clipboards.

 NOTE: Remember, a Clipboard is a temporary storage space.

1. Choose <u>T</u>oolbars from the <u>V</u>iew menu. The Toolbars submenu opens.

 Opened toolbars may appear in different locations than the locations indicated in this section. You may need to assist students if their toolbar locations differ.

In Excel Classroom Presentation 5.

2. Choose <u>C</u>ustomize. In the Customize dialog box, click Tool<u>b</u>ars, if necessary, to see the complete list of existing toolbars. The Office Assistant may open to see if you want help. If it does, it closes when you close the dialog box.

FIGURE 5-8
Customize dialog box

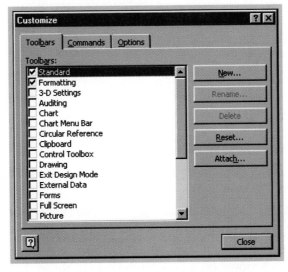

3. Click next to Auditing to display the Auditing toolbar. Click Close in the Customize dialog box.

4. Move the pointer across each button on the Auditing toolbar to identify its name and function.

TIP: Remember, to identify a toolbar button, point to the button and pause for a few seconds. A small box containing the name of the button appears under the button.

5. Change the view of the document to 75%, select cell C14, and click the Trace Precedents button . An arrow appears onscreen, tracing the precedents for cell C14 (the cells to which the formula in cell C14 refers).

NOTE: If the toolbar is in the way, click and hold the left mouse button in the toolbar title bar and drag it over slightly.

6. With the same cell selected, click the Trace Dependents button . An arrow appears onscreen tracing the cells that are dependent upon the value in cell C14. (See Figure 5-9 on the next page.)

NOTE: Audit arrows are removed automatically when you save a workbook, but you can redisplay them at any time.

In Excel Classroom Presentation 5.

FIGURE 5-9
Using the
Auditing toolbar

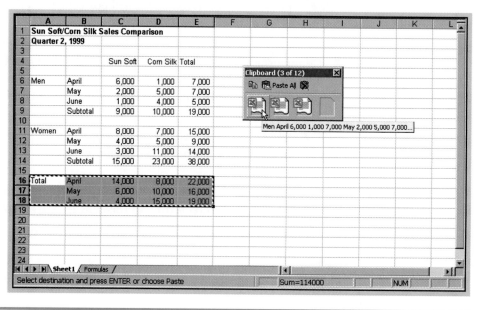

FIGURE 5-9
Using the
Auditing toolbar

7. Click the Remove All Arrows button ⌖.

8. Position the mouse on any toolbar and right-click. The Toolbar shortcut menu appears. It looks just like the Toolbars submenu.

9. Click next to Clipboard on the Toolbars submenu. The Clipboard toolbar appears.

10. If the Clear Clipboard button ▨ is visible (not grayed out) on the toolbar, click it now to clear any Clipboards. If not, move to the next step.

11. Select cells A6:E9 and click the Copy button ▤ on the Clipboard toolbar. The data is stored on a new Clipboard visible on the toolbar.

12. Select cells A11:E14 and press Ctrl + C to copy the data. The data is stored on a new Clipboard.

13. Select cells A16:E18 and press Ctrl + X to cut the data. The data is stored on a new Clipboard. Notice that the Clipboard toolbar title bar reflects the number of items available for pasting from the Clipboard.

14. Point to the first Clipboard to display its contents.

FIGURE 5-10
Clipboard toolbar
with three
Clipboards filled

In Excel Classroom Presentation 5.

15. Select cell G6 and click the third Clipboard. The cut data is pasted in cells G6:K8.

16. Select cell G11 and click the Paste All button on the Clipboard toolbar.

17. Click the Undo button 🔄 four times to remove each pasted Clipboard.

18. Click the Clear Clipboard button 🗙 to clear all the Clipboards.

19. Press Ctrl + Home to return to cell A1.

> **NOTE:** You can customize toolbars in the Customize dialog box. Just click the Commands to add buttons to other toolbars. Let the Office Assistant help you learn how to customize toolbars.

EXERCISE 5-8 Move and Reshape Toolbars

Toolbars can appear either "docked" or "floating." A *docked toolbar* appears in a fixed position outside the work area (like the Standard and Formatting toolbars). A *floating toolbar* appears over the work area. You can dock a floating toolbar by dragging it out of the work area. You can float a docked toolbar by dragging it into the work area. You can also reshape a floating toolbar.

> **NOTE:** This section contains instructions for moving toolbars to different areas in the Excel window. This can be tricky. If you have problems positioning the mouse correctly, ask your instructor for help.

1. Position the pointer on the thick horizontal separator line between the Standard toolbar and the Formatting toolbar. The pointer changes to a four-headed arrow ✛.

2. Click the left mouse button, and with the four-headed arrow ✛, drag the Formatting toolbar just below the Standard toolbar. Release the mouse button. If the Formatting toolbar is not flush left under the Standard toolbar, drag it to the left using the four-headed arrow on the thick horizontal line.

> **NOTE:** Moving the Formatting toolbar below the Standard toolbar expands both toolbars.

3. Position the pointer on the title bar of the Auditing toolbar (not on a toolbar button), click the left mouse button, and drag the toolbar to a

---

1 From this point forward, this text expands the Formatting toolbar and places it below the expanded Standard toolbar. It is left in this configuration for the remainder of the course as a convenience for students. If students have already changed to this configuration, they can ignore steps 1 and 2 of this Exercise.

2 Make sure students drag the Auditing toolbar on the Formula bar. If they drag it above the Formula bar, the toolbar docks beside the Formatting toolbar and only one button is visible.

position on the formula bar. The Auditing toolbar is now docked below the Standard and Formatting toolbars.

4. Position the pointer on a thin separator line between two buttons on the docked Auditing toolbar (not on a button) and hold down the left mouse button.

5. Drag the toolbar into the work area and release the left mouse button. The Auditing toolbar is now floating.

6. Drag the Clipboard toolbar to the far right side of the screen, until it is vertically positioned over the scroll bar. Excel docks the toolbar on this side of the screen and the worksheet window is resized to accommodate it.

FIGURE 5-11
Docked and floating toolbars

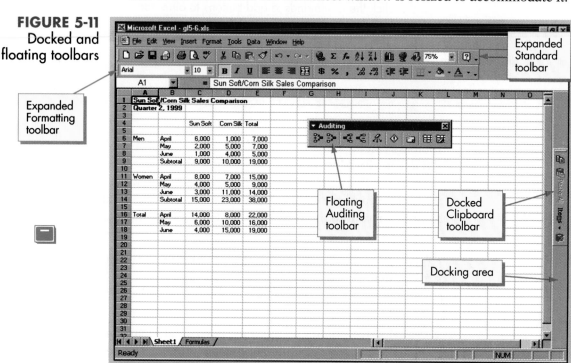

NOTE: Double-clicking a docking area displays the Customize dialog box.

7. Double-click the title bar on the Auditing toolbar (not a button) to dock it again. Notice that it docks where you previously docked it.

8. Double-click a thin separator line (between two buttons) in the gray area of the docked Auditing toolbar to undock it.

9. Position the pointer on the left side of the bottom border of the Auditing toolbar, so the pointer changes to a double-headed arrow.

10. Drag the bottom border down about half an inch and release the mouse button. The toolbar buttons are grouped in rows.

 In Excel Classroom Presentation 5.

11. Drag the bottom border down even further, until the toolbar becomes a column of buttons. Reshape it again into a more rectangular arrangement and then back to its original shape, a single row of buttons.

12. Using the four-headed arrow ✛, float the Clipboard toolbar. (Remember to point to the thick gray line at the top of the toolbar and drag the toolbar to the work area.)

EXERCISE 5-9 Close Toolbars

There's no restriction on the number of toolbars you can display in Excel, but it may be hard to read the worksheet if too many are open.

1. Position the mouse on a toolbar and click the right mouse button. The Toolbar shortcut menu appears. Notice the check mark located next to the open Clipboard toolbar. (Remember, the Auditing toolbar is listed in the Customize dialog box.)

2. Click Clipboard to deselect it. Excel closes the Clipboard toolbar. Be sure the Standard and Formatting toolbars remain checked.

3. Click the Close button ⊠ in the upper right corner of the Auditing toolbar to close it.

4. Close the workbook without saving it.

COMMAND SUMMARY

FEATURE	BUTTON	MENU	KEYBOARD
Copy	📋	Edit, Copy	Ctrl + C
Fill right		Edit, Fill	Ctrl + R
Fill down		Edit, Fill	Ctrl + D
Trace Precedents	📲		
Trace Dependents	📭		
Remove All Arrows	🔏		

USING HELP

This lesson showed you how to use Excel's AutoFill feature to copy data into adjacent cells. AutoFill is a powerful tool you can also use to create a data series such as numbers, dates, or text.

📝 Point out that the Command Summary lists a
1 variety of ways to accomplish a particular task.
Students can decide which method they prefer.

For example, you can start with the month Jan-97 in a cell and build a series that places Feb-97, Mar-97, and so on in adjacent cells. You can also create custom AutoFill series to build complex worksheets quickly.

To find out how AutoFill can create a series of data, use the Office Assistant:

1. Choose Show the <u>O</u>ffice Assistant from the <u>H</u>elp menu.

2. Click the Office Assistant, key **autofill** in the Office Assistant text box, and click <u>S</u>earch.

3. Select "Automatically fill in data based on adjacent cells." Notice that a Microsoft Excel Help window opens with the same title.

FIGURE 5-12
Using AutoFill to fill in data

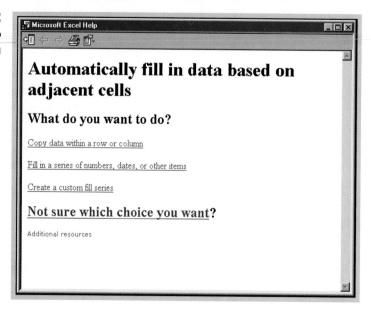

4. Select "Fill in a series of numbers, dates, or other items" and read the information, paying attention to the Fill Months series that you can generate.

5. Close the dialog box when you finish and close the Office Assistant.

Encourage students to follow the steps in "Using Help" (with a blank workbook open). Software companies are increasingly using their Help program—rather than printed documentation—to train users and assist in answering user questions.

In Excel Classroom Presentation 5.

TEST BANK

Concepts Review

TRUE/FALSE QUESTIONS

Each of the following statements is either true or false. Indicate your choice by circling T or F.

T **(F)** **1.** Copying a cell moves its data to a new location in the worksheet.

(T) F **2.** You can paste cells using keyboard shortcuts, menu commands, or toolbar buttons.

(T) F **3.** When you copy cells, you must first indicate the source range.

(T) F **4.** The target range is the new location for data that you copy, cut, or move.

(T) F **5.** A relative cell reference is automatically adjusted in any formula you copy.

T **(F)** **6.** To copy cells using the drag-and-drop method, use the mouse pointer and the [Alt] key.

(T) F **7.** You should use AutoFill to copy only to adjacent cells.

(T) F **8.** A docked toolbar appears in a position outside the work area.

SHORT ANSWER QUESTIONS

Write the correct answer in the space provided.

1. Which keyboard command copies the active cell?

Ctrl+C

2. Which button copies the active cell?

Copy

3. When you copy data, the information remains in the original location and is also copied to what location? (*Hint:* It's not in the worksheet.)

Clipboard

4. What appears around selected cells to highlight them after you choose the Copy command?

Moving border

Concepts Review:
Allows students to check their understanding.

C L O S E

TEST BANK
Consider using the Test Bank to provide an additional review of lesson concepts. It may also be used as an assessment tool.

5. Which key do you use with the mouse to copy data when using the drag-and-drop method?

   Ctrl

6. Which keyboard shortcut copies and fills cells to the right?

   Ctrl+R

7. Which part of the cell do you drag to copy data using AutoFill?

   Fill handle

8. Name the two predefined toolbars that appear on screen by default when you first open Excel.

   Standard and Formatting

CRITICAL THINKING

Answer these questions on a separate piece of paper. There are no right or wrong answers. Support your answer with examples from your own experience, if possible.

1. What are some of the potential dangers posed by relative cell references when you build a worksheet? What are the advantages? How can you effectively manage this feature?

2. Think of some other ways you might be able to use the Copy, Fill, and AutoFill features. Name at least one new way that you might use these powerful tools.

Skills Review

EXERCISE 5-10

Copy and paste using the Edit menu and the toolbar.

1. Open the file **Bonus.xls**.

2. Key the following data in cells B7 through B10:

   1500

   1800

   1800

   1500

3. Format cells B7 through B10 in Comma style with no decimal places.

Critical Thinking Questions:
Answers will vary based on students' preferences, observations, experiences, and research.

Skills Review:
Provides guided practice for students. Objectives are indicated for each Exercise.

Students should mention the danger of cell references in copied formulas not matching the cells they want in the calculation. Carefully checking copied formulas is a way to manage this feature.

◉ **Exercise 5-10:**
Objective 1
Required Files: Bonus.xls
Solution Files: gl5-10.xls

4. Enter the formula **=B7*C7** in cell D7.

5. Copy and paste the formula in cell D7 using the <u>C</u>opy and <u>P</u>aste commands from the <u>E</u>dit menu by following these steps:

    a. Select cell D7.

    b. Choose <u>C</u>opy from the <u>E</u>dit menu.

    c. Select cells D8 through D10 and choose <u>P</u>aste from the <u>E</u>dit menu.

    d. Press Esc to remove the moving border from the source range.

6. Select cells B11 and D11 and click the AutoSum button Σ.

7. Copy and paste data and formulas using the toolbar by following these steps:

    a. Select cells B7 through D7 as the source range.

    b. Click the Copy button.

    c. Select cell B12 as the first cell of the target range.

    d. Click the Paste button.

    e. Press Esc to remove the moving border from the source range.

8. Copy data and formulas using a variety of methods by following these steps:

    a. Select cells B8 through D8 and choose <u>C</u>opy from the <u>E</u>dit menu.

    b. Select cell B13 and press Ctrl+V.

    c. Select cell B14 and click the Paste button.

    d. Select cells B15 through D16 and press Enter.

9. Key the following data in cells B12 through B16, overwriting the data you previously copied:

2800

1800

1700

2750

4200

10. Use AutoSum to total the May revenues in cell B17 and the May commissions in cell D17.

11. Key **Total** in cell A18 in bold and use AutoSum to total all revenues in cell B18 and all commissions in cell D18.

12. Format the unlabeled subtotals (cells B11, B17, D11, and D17) as italic.

13. Format the totals (cells B18 and D18) as bold.

14. Add a header with your name in the left section, the filename in the center section, and the date in the right section.

15. Save the workbook as *[your initials]***5-10.xls** in your Lesson 5 folder and print the worksheet.

16. Create a formula printout with gridlines and row and column headings, and close the workbook without saving it.

EXERCISE 5-11

Copy and paste using the menus, the toolbar, keyboard shortcuts, and drag and drop.

1. Open the file **SalesUp.xls**.

2. In cell C7, enter the formula **=B7*1.015**.

3. Copy this formula into cells C8 through C16 using <u>C</u>opy and <u>P</u>aste from the <u>E</u>dit menu by following these steps:

   a. Select cell C7 and choose <u>C</u>opy from the <u>E</u>dit menu.
   b. Select cells C8 through C16 and choose <u>P</u>aste from the <u>E</u>dit menu.
   c. Press Esc to remove the moving border from the source range.
   d. Format cells C7 through C16 in Comma style with no decimal places.

4. Copy formulas using drag and drop by following these steps:

   a. Select cells C7 through C16.
   b. Move the mouse pointer across the border of the selection until it becomes an arrow.
   c. Press and hold down Ctrl to change the pointer to the drag-and-drop pointer.
   d. Drag the source range to the target range, cells D7 through D16, and release the mouse button and Ctrl.

5. In cell E7, enter the formula **=B7*1.22**.

6. Copy this formula into cells E8 through E16 using a keyboard shortcut by following these steps:

   a. Select cell E7 and press Ctrl + C.
   b. Select cells E8 through E16 and press Enter.
   c. Format cells E7 through E16 in Comma style with no decimal places.

7. Copy formulas using the toolbar by following these steps:

   a. Select cells C7 through D16 as the source range.
   b. Click the Copy button 🖺.
   c. Select cell F7.
   d. Click the Paste button 🖺.
   e. Press Esc.

8. Create a "Total" row by following these steps:

   a. Key **Total** in cell A17. Format the text as bold.
   b. Select cells B17:G17 and click the AutoSum button Σ.
   c. Format the totals as bold and currency style with no decimal places.

9. Add a header with your name in the left section, the filename in the center section, and the date in the right section.

10. Save the workbook as *[your initials]***5-11.xls** in your Lesson 5 folder and print the worksheet.

◉ Exercise 5-11:
Objectives 1, 2
Required Files: SalesUp.xls
Solution Files: gl5-11.xls

11. Create a formula printout in landscape orientation with gridlines and row and column headings. Use a Page 1 of ? footer if the printout exceeds more than one page.

12. Close the workbook without saving it

EXERCISE 5-12

Copy formulas using the Fill command and AutoFill.

1. Open the file **NetInc2.xls**.

2. Enter the following formulas in cells B9 through B11:

   =B6*0.2

   =B6*0.35

   =B6*0.3

3. Format cells B9 through B11 in Comma style with no decimal places.

4. Select cell B12, click the AutoSum button Σ, and press Enter.

5. Select cells B9 through F12.

6. Choose the Fill command from the Edit menu and choose Right from the submenu.

7. Enter the formula **=B6-B12** in cell B14 to calculate the net income for the year 1997 ("Sales" - "Total Expenses"). The cell is already formatted.

8. Use AutoFill to copy the formula in cell B14 to cells C14 through F14 by following these steps:

   a. With cell B14 selected, position the mouse pointer on the fill handle.
   b. Drag the fill handle to select cells C14 through F14.
   c. Release the mouse button.

9. Add bold formatting to the Total Expenses and Net Income figures.

10. Add a header with your name in the left section, the filename in the center section, and the date in the right section.

11. Save the workbook as *[your initials]*5-12.xls in your Lesson 5 folder and print the worksheet.

12. Create a formula printout in landscape orientation with gridlines and row and column headings. Use a Page 1 of ? footer if the printout exceeds one page.

13. Close the workbook without saving it.

EXERCISE 5-13

Open multiple toolbars, move and reshape toolbars, and use the Audit toolbar.

1. Open the file **Q4.xls**.

◉ **Exercise 5-12:**
Objective 3
Required Files: NetInc2.xls
Solution Files: gl5-12.xls in Solutions Manual or on Solutions Disk.

◉ **Exercise 5-13:**
Objective 4
Required Files: Q4.xls
Solution Files: gl5-13.xls in Solutions Manual or on Solutions Disk.

2. Open multiple toolbars using the following steps:

   a. Choose Toolbars from the View menu to open the Toolbars submenu.

   b. Select the Chart toolbar. Repeat the steps to select the Picture toolbar.

   c. If necessary, drag one toolbar down or up to reveal the hidden toolbar.

   d. Right-click the title bar of the Chart toolbar. Select the Forms toolbar from the shortcut menu.

   e. Right-click a thin separator line between two buttons of the Forms toolbar and select Customize from the shortcut menu.

   f. Select Auditing and click Close.

3. Move and reshape toolbars by following these steps:

   a. Double-click the title bar of the Chart toolbar to dock it.

   b. Drag the Auditing toolbar onto the formula bar to dock it.

   c. Drag the Forms toolbar to the left side of the screen over the row heading to dock it.

   d. Drag the bottom border of the Picture border down until it becomes square. The toolbar should contain five rows of buttons. Drag it back to its original shape. (This toolbar may already be a square. If so, practice resizing it and return it to a long rectangular shape.)

   e. Float all the toolbars you opened in step 2, except the Auditing toolbar, by double-clicking a thin separator line between two buttons in the toolbar.

4. Close the Chart toolbar by right-clicking the Chart title bar and deselecting Chart on the Toolbar shortcut menu. Do the same for the Forms toolbar.

5. Close the Picture toolbar by clicking the Close button ☒ in the upper right corner of the title bar.

6. Add a header with your name in the left section, the filename in the center section, and the date in the right section

7. Center the worksheet horizontally.

8. Save the workbook as *[your initials]*5-13.xls in your Lesson 5 folder.

9. Use the Auditing toolbar to trace formula paths by following these steps:

   a. Select cell D14 and click the Trace Precedents button ▣.

   b. Select cell D9 and click the Trace Dependents button ▣.

10. Float the Auditing toolbar by double-clicking a thin separator line between two buttons in the toolbar and close it by clicking the Close button ☒.

11. Print the worksheet, including the tracing arrows.

12. Create a formula printout in landscape orientation with gridlines and row and column headings.

13. Close the workbook without saving it.

A S S E S S

Assessment Resources:
• Solutions Manual
• Test Bank
• Portfolio Builder
• Internet Projects
• Alternative Assessment Guide
• Certification Procedures

For Internet projects, go to
www.glencoe.com/webprojects

Lesson Applications

EXERCISE 5-14

Use the Copy and Paste commands, copy using drag and drop, and copy using Fill and AutoFill.

The Beautiful Belle Company needs to break down its revenues by product line and by region. The worksheet must also show product totals and subtotals, regional totals, and the grand total.

1. Open the file **Product.xls.**
2. Create a formula that totals revenues for the Monterey product line.
3. Copy the formula to cell D16 using the Copy button and the Paste button .
4. Copy the formula from cell D16 to cells D17 through D20 using the Fi̱ll, Ḏown command.
5. Select cells D17 through D20. Copy this range to cells D9 through D12 using the drag-and-drop method.
6. Create a formula that finds the subtotal for Creams sold in the Northwest territory.
7. Copy this formula to cells C13 and D13 using AutoFill.
8. Copy cells B13 through D13. Paste them in cells B21 through D21 using Ctrl+C and Ctrl+V.
9. Enter a formula to add the subtotals for Creams and Fragrances in cell B23.
10. Copy this formula to cells C23 and D23 using AutoFill.
11. Change the view to 100% and format the numbers in the subtotal and total rows as bold.
12. Add a header with your name in the left section, the filename in the center section, and the date in the right section.
13. Save the workbook as *[your initials]***5-14.xls** in your Lesson 5 folder and print the worksheet.
14. Create a formula printout in landscape orientation with gridlines and row and column headings.
15. Close the workbook without saving it.

Lesson Applications:
Provide independent practice for students and may be used for assessment. Objectives are indicated for each Exercise.

◉ **Exercise 5-14:**
Objectives 1–3
Required Files: Product.xls
Solution Files: gl5-14.xls in Solutions Manual or on Solutions Disk.

EXERCISE 5-15

Copy using the Fill command, toolbar buttons, drag and drop, and AutoFill.

1. Open the file **Frgrnce.xls.**
2. Copy the labels as shown in Figure 5-13 to cells A15 through A21. (Copy the labels only. Don't copy the values.)

FIGURE 5-13

	A
6	**Fragrances**
7	Pacifica
8	Taos
9	High Sierra
10	Carmel
11	Santa Barbara
12	Total

3. Create a formula that finds the 1997 total revenues for the Pacifica product line (cell D7).
4. Copy this formula to cells D8 through D11 using the F<u>i</u>ll, <u>D</u>own command.
5. Enter the formula **=B7*1.1** in cell B16 (Pacifica 1998 sales in the Northwest).
6. Copy and paste this formula to cell C16 using the toolbar buttons.
7. Select cells B16 through C20 and copy the formulas using the F<u>i</u>ll, <u>D</u>own command.
8. Copy the formulas from cells D7 through D11 to cells D16 through D20 using drag and drop.
9. Format all the numbers in row 16 in Currency style with no decimals. Format numbers in cells B17 through D20 and B8 through D11 in Comma style with no decimals.
10. Create a formula in cell B21 that finds the projected total revenues for the Northwest territory in 1998.

● Exercise 5-15:
Objectives 1–3
Required Files: Frgrnce.xls
Solution Files: gl5-15.xls in Solutions Manual or on
Solutions Disk.

11. Copy this formula to cells C21 and D21 using AutoFill.

12. Copy cells B21 through D21 and create total formulas for 1997 using the drag-and-drop method.

13. Format the numbers in the total rows in bold.

14. Add a header with your name in the left section, the filename in the center section, and the date in the right section.

15. Save the workbook as *[your initials]*5-15.xls in your Lesson 5 folder and print the worksheet.

16. Create a formula printout in landscape orientation with gridlines and row and column headings.

17. Close the workbook without saving it.

EXERCISE 5-16

Copy using Fill, AutoFill, and drag and drop.

Build a worksheet to compare sales by quarter for Sun Soft for the years 1996 through 1998. Create formulas that calculate total sales for each year. Include a percentage change for 1996 to 1997 and 1997 to 1998.

1. Open the file **Change%.xls**.

2. Make corrections and entries as shown in Figure 5-14. Format the numbers as Comma style with no decimals as shown in the figure.

FIGURE 5-14

	A	B	C	D
4		1996	1997	1998
5	Qtr 3¹	64,955	96,500	80,530	(tr)
6	Qtr 2 ~~Quarter 3~~	70,130	90,130	100,540
7	Qtr 3	110,140	*150,350*	180,020
8	Qtr 3⁴	95,600	120,040	135,060

3. Create a formula that totals the four quarters for 1996 in cell B10.

4. Copy the formula to total 1997 and 1998 sales using AutoFill.

○ Exercise 5-16:
Objectives 2, 3
Required Files: Change%.xls
Solution Files: gl5-16.xls in Solutions Manual or on Solutions Disk.

[1] This figure contains proofreading marks. You may want to review Appendix E: "Proofreaders' Marks" with students.

5. In cell E5, enter a formula that calculates the 1996 to 1997 change in sales as a percentage of 1996 sales. (*Hint:* Subtract 1996 sales from 1997 sales and divide the difference by 1996 sales.)

 NOTE: Cell E5 and the cells used in the next few steps are already formatted for Percent with one decimal place.

6. Copy the formula to Qtr2 through Qtr4 for 1997 using the Fi̱ll, Do̱wn command.

7. Copy the formula to Qtr1 through Qtr4 for 1998 using the Fi̱ll, Ri̱ght command.

8. Create totals for the 1997 and 1998 percentage changes by copying the Qtr4 formulas (cells E8 and F8) to row 10 using drag and drop.

9. Key the row label **Total** in row 10 in bold.

10. Change the page orientation to portrait. (This worksheet's default orientation was previously changed to landscape.) Center the page horizontally.

11. Add a header with your name in the left section, the filename in the center section, and the date in the right section.

12. Save the workbook as *[your initials]***5-16.xls** in your Lesson 5 folder and print the worksheet.

13. Create a formula printout in landscape orientation with gridlines and row and column headings. Use a Page 1 of ? footer if the printout extends past one page.

14. Close the workbook without saving it.

EXERCISE 5-17 *Challenge Yourself*

Copy and paste formulas, use Fill or AutoFill, copy using drag and drop, and use toolbars.

Construct a worksheet comparing second-quarter sales for Sun Soft and Corn Silk for 1997, 1998, and 1999.

1. Plan the worksheet on a sheet of paper in landscape orientation. Create a two-line title that explains the worksheet, and in the body of the worksheet include labels for Sun Soft and Corn Silk sales comparisons for 1997, 1998, and 1999. Also include labels for a calculated percentage of Sun Soft as a Percent of Corn Silk for 1997, 1998, and 1999. (These should be the column labels, nine columns altogether.)

Exercise 5-17:
Objectives 1–4
Required Files: None
Solution Files: Sample gl5-17.xls in Solutions Manual or on Solutions Disk.

The completed document for this Exercise may be used in a student's portfolio.

Solutions for this Exercise will vary from student to student.

2. Include labels for the second quarter months plus a total line with a blank row before the total line. (These should be the row labels, four rows altogether.)

3. Use F for formula locations.

4. Transfer the design to the computer by keying titles and labels. Format them attractively.

5. Input test data in the Sun Soft months for 1997, 1998, and 1999. Format the data for commas with no decimals.

6. Copy and paste the test data to the Corn Silk months for 1997, 1998, and 1999.

7. Calculate the three-month total for Sun Soft in 1997. Copy that formula to the appropriate cells for Sun Soft and Corn Silk.

8. Calculate Sun Soft's sales as a percentage of Corn Silk sales for April 1997. (*Hint:* Divide Sun Soft sales by Corn Silk sales.)

9. Format the percentage formula in percent style with no decimal places.

10. Use Fill or AutoFill to copy the percentage change to the rest of the months for 1997 through 1999.

11. Use drag and drop to copy the formula to the Percent Total.

12. Check your formulas for accuracy and enter the data in Figure 5-15 into the monthly quarter cells for 1997, 1998, and 1999.

FIGURE 5-15

	Sun Soft			Corn Silk		
	1997	1998	1999	1997	1998	1999
April	19,650	24,800	36,540	33,550	28,150	26,540
May	22,630	31,300	24,000	23,260	18,440	16,500
June	27,850	34,030	31,250	29,360	25,040	21,350

13. Reduce the view to 75% and set up the worksheet to print in landscape orientation centered horizontally on one page.

14. Name the worksheet tab **Comparison**.

15. Name the Sheet2 tab **User Information** and create documentation that includes the following: File Information (Created by, Date created, Date revised, Revised by, Contact for help); Purpose of worksheet (paragraph form); and Instructions to User (special instructions needed by user to enter data correctly). Style the documentation for easy reading.

16. Add the standard header to both sheets including your name, filename, and date.

17. Delete Sheet3.

18. Save the workbook as *[your initials]***5-17.xls** in your Lesson 5 folder.

19. Use the Auditing toolbar to trace the precedents for the April 1998 percentage change formula in the Comparison worksheet.

20. Print the workbook, including the precedent arrows. Remove the precedent arrows, and then close the Auditing toolbar.

21. Create a formula printout of the Comparison sheet in landscape orientation with grids and row and column headings. Add a Page 1 of ? footer for multiple pages, if necessary.

22. Close the workbook without saving it. Submit your plan, worksheet, user documentation, and formula printout.

Range Names and Sorting

OBJECTIVES

MOUS
ACTIVITIES
In this lesson:
XL2000 **E.6.1**
XL2000 **E.6.2**

See Appendix F.

After completing this lesson, you will be able to:

1. **Name ranges and constants.**
2. **Use names in formulas.**
3. **Change and delete range names.**
4. **Navigate in the worksheet using range names.**
5. **Paste names into worksheets.**
6. **Sort data in the worksheet.**

 Estimated Time: 1¼ hours

Instead of trying to remember a particular cell address, such as E17, or a cell range, such as I7:J43, you can use a name to designate a location. For example, you could name a cell that contains a formula "total," and use the name "total" to refer to the cell when you create other formulas. In addition to naming cells, you can also assign names to constants. For example, you could assign the name "rate" to the constant 0.07. Naming cells also makes it easier to find a particular location in a large worksheet.

At times, you will find it necessary to rearrange the information in your worksheet. You can use the Data Sort command to sort selected information in ascending or descending order according to the contents of a key column within the worksheet.

PREPARE
Point out to students that the learning objectives show what they will learn in the lesson. Each heading in the lesson correlates to a learning objective.
Required Files
98Sales.xls

TEACH
Teaching Resources:
• Excel Classroom Presentations
• School-to-Work Strategies Manual
• Spanish Glossary
• Certification Procedures

185

Naming Ranges and Constants

Objective 1

A *range name*—the name you give to a cell or range of cells—must begin with a letter. Although range names can be from 1 to 255 characters long, it is best to keep them short, but still recognizable. Range names must *not*:

- Have the form of a cell reference, such as q1 or A13.
- Use "R" or "C" as a single-letter name.
- Contain spaces.
- Contain hyphens (-) or special characters ($, %, &, #).

To separate parts of a name such as "saleseast," you can use capital letters, a period, or an underline (for example, "SalesEast," "sales.east," or "sales_east").

TABLE 6-1 | **Examples of Valid and Invalid Range Names**

VALID NAMES	INVALID NAMES
Total.Sales	Total Sales
East_sales	east-sales
EntertainPct	Entertain%
qt1	q1
X	R

EXERCISE 6-1 Name an Individual Cell

You can name ranges using the Define Name dialog box or by keying the name in the Name Box at the left of the formula bar.

1. Open the file **98Sales.xls**.
2. Move to cell E9.
3. Choose <u>N</u>ame from the <u>I</u>nsert menu.
4. Choose <u>D</u>efine from the submenu. The Define Name dialog box appears. (See Figure 6-1 on the next page.)
5. Key **qt1** in the Names In <u>W</u>orkbook text box and click OK. The name appears in the Name Box at the left of the formula bar.
6. Move to cell E18 and click in the Name Box at the left of the formula bar. The cell address is selected.

 1 Point out to students that a one-word name is easier to use in formulas and when navigating the worksheet. If possible, use a one-word name that clearly identifies the cell, range, or constant.

2 You may want to point out the convenience of using the keyboard shortcut for naming at the beginning of the lesson. Students save time as they work through the Exercises if they use the keyboard shortcuts rather than clicking the menus.

FIGURE 6-1
Define Name
dialog box

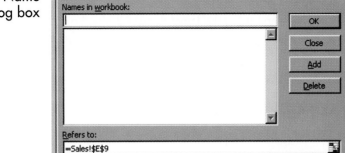

7. Key **qt2** and press Enter. The name appears in the Name Box.

8. Name cell E27 **qt3** using the Define Name dialog box.

9. Name cell E36 **qt4** by keying the text directly into the Name Box at the left of the formula bar.

EXERCISE 6-2 Name a Group of Cells

You can name any group of cells. Excel suggests a name for the range based on the title of the selected column or row. If you don't want the suggested name, you can assign a different name to the range.

1. Select all the totals for "New Century," which appear in cells E5, E14, E23, and E32.

> ⭐ **TIP:** Remember, to select nonadjacent cells, press Ctrl while selecting the cells.

2. Choose <u>N</u>ame from the <u>I</u>nsert menu.

3. Choose <u>D</u>efine. The Define Name dialog box opens. Notice that Excel suggests the name Total.

4. Key **New_Century** in the Names In <u>W</u>orkbook text box and click OK.

5. Select cells E6, E15, E24, and E33.

6. Click in the Name Box at the left of the formula bar.

7. Key **Golden** and press Enter.

8. Name cells E7, E16, E25, and E34 **Monterey**, and name cells E8, E17, E26, and E35 **Herbal**.

Use Excel Classroom Presentation 6 to display screens from this lesson in a slide-show format.

Emphasize that when students use the Name Box on the formula bar they must press the Enter key for the name to be created. This is the most typical error made by students when using this feature.

TIP: You can use the Label Ranges dialog box (<u>I</u>nsert, <u>N</u>ame, <u>L</u>abel) to specify ranges that contain column and row labels on your worksheet. When you label a range using the Label Ranges dialog box, and the range contains a year or a date as a label, Excel defines the date as a label by placing single quotation marks around the label when you type the label in a formula.

EXERCISE 6-3 Name a Constant

In addition to assigning names to cells or ranges of cells, you can assign names to *constants*. Constants are unchanging values used in formulas. Named constants don't appear in the worksheet. For example, if you assign the name "rate" to the constant .075, you could then use the name "rate" in formulas instead of the value. When you change the constant value assigned to "rate," any formula that contains "rate" automatically changes to include the new value.

1. Press Ctrl+F3 to open the Define Name dialog box.
2. Key **pro** in the Names In <u>W</u>orkbook text box.
3. Edit the text to read **=.12** in the <u>R</u>efers To text box.
4. Click OK. The value 0.12 is assigned the name "pro." This name is used later in this lesson to increase the sales figures by 12%.

NOTE: You cannot name a constant in the Name Box.

 Objective 2

Using Names in Formulas

Once you create names for cell references or constants, you can use these names in formulas. You key the formula in the normal way, but key the name instead of the cell reference. To use constants, key the name for the constant wherever you would key the constant in the formula.

EXERCISE 6-4 Create Formulas Including Names

1. In cell B41, key **=sum(new_century)** and press Enter. Once you enter the formula in the cell, Excel converts the name to include uppercase letters as you created it.

TIP: You can use F3 to place a name in a formula. For instance, key **=sum(** Then, press F3, select the name from the list, click OK, and finish the formula.

Objective 2 Assignment:
Exercise 6-9 (Skills Review) can be assigned after completing Objective 2.

1 Mention that using names in formulas is not always the fastest and most convenient method for building a worksheet, but knowing how to use names is an important skill to complement copying and pasting and the Fill and AutoFill features.

2 Formulas have the same length limit as names, which can include as many as 255 characters. Because you can key cell and range names in formulas, they should be recognizable, but short. Point out that most scroll boxes display approximately 15 characters.

3 The Tip introduces using the F3 key. The biggest errors students make when using range names are using incorrect names and misspellings. Encourage students to use the F3 key whenever possible because it reduces these errors.

2. In cell B42, key **=sum(golden)**

3. In cell B43, key **=sum(monterey)**

4. In cell B44, key **=sum(herbal)**

5. In cell C41, calculate a 12% projected sales increase for 1999 by keying **=B41*(1+pro)**. (B41 is the 1998 total and "1+pro" equals 1.12, since you earlier defined "pro" to be 0.12.)

6. Copy this formula to cells C42, C43, C44, and C45. Format cell C45 as bold; it equals zero for now.

7. In cell B45, use the cell names you created by keying **=qt1+qt2+qt3+qt4**

FIGURE 6-2
Total projected
1999 sales, so far

B45	▼	= =qt1+qt2+qt3+qt4		
	A	B	C	D
40		**1998**	**1999**	
41	New Century	474,015	530,897	
42	Golden Gate	328,731	368,179	
43	Monterey	353,950	396,424	
44	Herbal Essence	627,284	702,558	
45	TOTAL:	1,783,980	1,998,058	
46				

8. In cells D32 through D35, enter the data as shown below. When you finish, the total for 1999 in cell C45 should be 2,199,716.

	Dec
New Century	**79,658**
Golden Gate	**22,457**
Monterey	**32,568**
Herbal Essence	**45,369**

☑**Objective 3**

Changing and Deleting Range Names

You can change a name or delete one that you no longer need. When you change a name, Excel does not replace the old name with the new name in relevant formulas. The old formulas remain valid, however, unless you delete the old name.

EXERCISE 6-5 **Change and Delete Range Names**

1. Press ⌈Ctrl⌋+⌈F3⌋ to open the Define Name dialog box.

2. Choose **New_Century** from the Names In Workbook list box.

3. Highlight "New_" in the Names In Workbook text box and press ⌈Delete⌋. "Century" remains in the text box.

4. Click OK.

In Excel Classroom Presentation 6.

☑**Objective 3 Assignment:**
Exercise 6-10 (Skills Review) can be assigned after completing Objective 3.

5. Move to cell B41. The name New_Century is not changed in the formula bar.

6. Choose <u>N</u>ame from the <u>I</u>nsert menu and then choose <u>D</u>efine.

7. Choose "New_Century" from the Names In <u>W</u>orkbook list box.

8. Click <u>D</u>elete and click OK. The formulas that refer to New_Century display the #NAME? error message.

 NOTE: You can use the Undo command to reverse the deletion of a name.

9. In cell B41, double-click New_Century in the formula bar to select it and key **century** to change the formula to reflect the new range name.

 NOTE: You can also edit the cell by highlighting New_ and then pressing Delete, or you can use F3 to paste Century into the formula.

10. Click the check box in the formula bar. The #NAME? error message is no longer displayed in cell B41 or cell C41 and the formulas calculate correctly.

Objective 4

Navigating Using Range Names

 Named ranges not only make calculations easier, but also enable you to move around a worksheet more quickly. For example, you can assign a name to a cell and then locate the cell by choosing <u>G</u>o To from the <u>E</u>dit menu (or pressing F5). Excel opens the Go To dialog box, which lists all named cells in the worksheet. It also lists the last four cell addresses the <u>G</u>o To command located. You can also use the Name Box drop-down list to move to named ranges.

EXERCISE 6-6 **Move to Named Ranges**

1. Select cells B4 through E9.

2. Choose <u>N</u>ame from the <u>I</u>nsert menu and choose <u>D</u>efine.

3. Key **one** in the Names In <u>W</u>orkbook text box and click OK.

4. Select cells B13 through E18.

5. Click in the Name Box, key **two**, and press Enter.

6. Name cells B22 through E27 **three**, cells B31 through E36 **four**, and cells B40 through C45 **grandtot**.

Point out the convenience of using the F5 keyboard shortcut for the Go To command. When students are building and using worksheets, under the time pressures of work in the "real world," keyboard shortcuts and navigating tools (such as using names with Go To) help to complete work quickly. Students can also use the Name Box drop-down list to select a name and go to a cell or range of cells.

7. Choose <u>G</u>o To from the <u>E</u>dit menu or press F5 . The Go To dialog box appears.

FIGURE 6-3
Go To dialog box

8. Double-click the named range "two." Excel moves to the selected range. (You may have to scroll down the list.)

FIGURE 6-4
Name Box
drop-down list

9. Press Ctrl + Home to move to cell A1. Click the Name Box arrow. The drop-down list appears. (See Figure 6-4.)

10. Click the named range "one." Excel moves to the selected range.

11. Practice moving to named ranges using both the <u>G</u>o To command and the Name Box drop-down list.

☑ **Objective 5**

Pasting Names into Worksheets

You can use the Define Name dialog box to display a list of named ranges and constants to see how a worksheet is set up. Using the Paste Name dialog box, you can paste a list of range names and references into a worksheet as documentation. You can also use this dialog box to paste range names and constants into formulas.

EXERCISE 6-7 **Paste Range Names into Worksheets**

Before pasting a list of range names, move to a clear area of your worksheet. Make sure the area is large enough so the paste does not overwrite existing data.

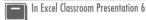 In Excel Classroom Presentation 6.

 ☑ **Objective 5 Assignment:**
Exercise 6-12 (Skills Review) and Exercises 6-13, 6-14, and 6-16 (Lesson Applications) can be assigned after completing Objective 5.

1. Move to cell A18 in the sheet named User Information.

2. Key the label **Range Names** in bold and press Enter.

3. Move to cell B19 and key **The following range names have been created in the Sales worksheet.**

4. Move to cell B21 and key **Name** in bold. In cell C21, key **Location** in bold.

5. Move to cell B22, choose <u>N</u>ame from the <u>I</u>nsert menu, and choose <u>P</u>aste.

FIGURE 6-5
Paste Name
dialog box

The Paste Name dialog box appears.

6. Click the Paste <u>L</u>ist button. (See Figure 6-6.) The list of named ranges is pasted into the Documentation worksheet. You can key descriptions of the named ranges into the worksheet as necessary.

7. If necessary, change the view to 75% so you can see all the range names.

8. In the documentation worksheet, key today's date for "Date revised" and key your name for "Revised by." Turn off gridlines for viewing.

FIGURE 6-6
Names pasted into
a worksheet

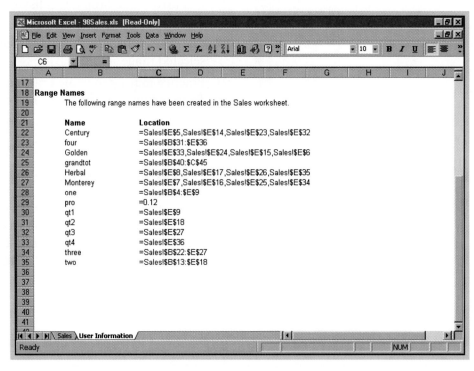

9. Save the workbook as *[your initials]*6-7.xls in a new folder for Lesson 6.

In Excel Classroom Presentation 6.   Students are asked to save in this Exercise, but not to print. Students will sort in Exercise 6-8. If students have problems in Exercise 6-8, they can close and retrieve Exercise 6-7 or click the Undo button.

Sorting Information in a Worksheet

☑Objective 6

You can use the <u>S</u>ort command from the <u>D</u>ata menu to rearrange information in the worksheet. You sort information by first selecting the range to be sorted. Then you choose the <u>S</u>ort command and specify the column the information will be sorted by and the sort order.

EXERCISE 6-8 Sort Information in a Worksheet

1. Move to cell A5 in the sheet named Sales.

2. Highlight the range A5:E8.

FIGURE 6-7
Highlighted
sort range

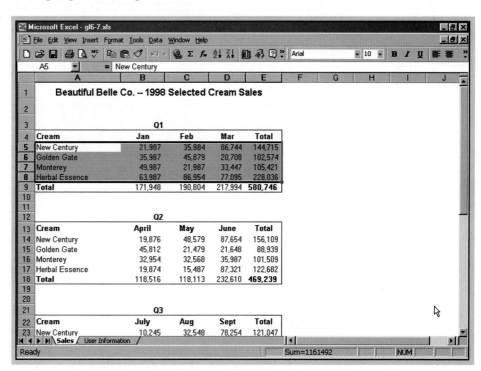

3. Choose <u>S</u>ort from the <u>D</u>ata menu. The Sort dialog box appears (see Figure 6-8 on the next page.) Notice that the Sort By text box automatically matches the column label of the active cell, A5. The list will, therefore, be arranged in alphabetical order by Cream. The Ascending order of arrangement is also selected. This orders the list from smallest to largest (if they are numbers) or A to Z (if they are labels). The Descending order arranges items largest to smallest (if numbers) or Z to A (if labels).

☑Objective 6 Assignment:

Exercise 6-11 (Skills Review) and Exercise 6-15 (Lesson Applications) can be assigned after completing Objective 6.

Encourage students to save before sorting. Also, students should omit the Total formulas in the highlight.

 In Excel Classroom Presentation 6.

FIGURE 6-8
Sort dialog box

NOTE: You can also use the Sort Ascending 🔼 and Sort Descending 🔽 buttons on the Standard toolbar to sort a selected range.

4. Click the OK button. The highlighted information is rearranged in alphabetical order by Creams.

FIGURE 6-9
Sorted information

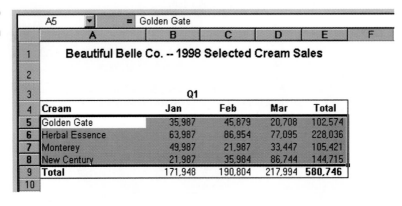

	A	B	C	D	E	F
	A5		=	Golden Gate		
1	Beautiful Belle Co. -- 1998 Selected Cream Sales					
2						
3			Q1			
4	Cream	Jan	Feb	Mar	Total	
5	Golden Gate	35,987	45,879	20,708	102,574	
6	Herbal Essence	63,987	86,954	77,095	228,036	
7	Monterey	49,987	21,987	33,447	105,421	
8	New Century	21,987	35,984	86,744	144,715	
9	Total	171,948	190,804	217,994	**580,746**	
10						

5. Move to cell A14 and highlight the range A14:E17. Click the Sort Descending button 🔽 to sort the information in descending order.

6. Click the Undo button 🔙.

7. Click the Sort Ascending button 🔼 to sort the information in ascending order.

8. Sort the ranges A23:E26, A32:E35, and A41:C44 in ascending order.

9. Add the standard header containing your name, filename, and date to both sheets.

10. Save the workbook as *[your initials]*6-8.xls in your Lesson 6 folder.

11. Print the entire workbook, and then create the standard formula printout for the Sales sheet with grids and row and column headings. Add a Page 1 of ? footer to the formula printout if it exceeds one page.

12. Close the workbook without saving it.

COMMAND SUMMARY

FEATURE	BUTTON	MENU	KEYBOARD
Define Name		Insert, Name, Define	Ctrl + F3
Go To		Edit, Go To	F5 or Ctrl + G
Paste Name		Insert, Name, Paste	F3
Sort Ascending	↕	Data, Sort	
Sort Descending	↕	Data, Sort	

USING HELP

In this lesson you were given a tip on using the Label Ranges dialog box. To find out more about how and when to use this feature, ask the Office Assistant.

To find out how and when to use the Label Ranges dialog box:

1. Choose Show the Office Assistant from the Help menu. Click the Office Assistant to activate it.

2. Key **label ranges** in the text box and click Search.

3. Select "About labeling ranges using the Label Ranges dialog box." Maximize the Help window.

4. The Office Assistant displays information that shows you how to use the Label Ranges dialog box.

FIGURE 6-10
Labeling ranges using the Label Ranges dialog box

5. Read the information and close the dialog box and the Office Assistant.

---

1 Point out that the Command Summary lists a variety of ways to accomplish a particular task. Students can decide which method they prefer to use for a specific purpose.

2 Encourage students to follow the steps in "Using Help" (with a blank workbook open). Software companies are increasingly using their Help programs—rather than documentation—to train users and assist in answering user questions.

 In Excel Classroom Presentation 6.

TEST BANK

Concepts Review

TRUE/FALSE QUESTIONS

Each of the following statements is either true or false. Indicate your choice by circling **T** or **F**.

T (F)   *1.* A range name can include spaces and hyphens.

(T) F   *2.* A cell or range name can include as many as 255 characters.

T (F)   *3.* Named cells can contain only formulas.

T (F)   *4.* Range names can include special characters like $, &, and #.

(T) F   *5.* Names applied to constants can later be used in formulas.

(T) F   *6.* You can use range names to replace cell references in formulas.

T (F)   *7.* When you change a name, Excel automatically replaces the old name with the new name in the appropriate formulas.

(T) F   *8.* The Go To dialog box lists all named cells in the worksheet.

SHORT ANSWER QUESTIONS

Write the correct answer in the space provided.

1. Which command enables you to move to the location of a named cell in the worksheet?

Go To

2. What do you call an unchanging value in a formula?

Constant

3. Which keyboard combination do you use for the Define Name command?

Ctrl+F3

4. Which keyboard combination do you use for the Paste Name command?

F3

5. Which menu commands do you use to name a range?

Insert, Name, Define

6. Which dialog box is opened by pressing F5?

Go To dialog box

C L O S E

Concepts Review:
Allows students to check their understanding.

TEST BANK

Consider using the Test Bank to provide an additional review of lesson concepts. It may also be used as an assessment tool.

7. Which menu commands do you use to paste a range name?

Insert, Name, Paste

8. Which menu commands do you use to sort a list?

Data, Sort

CRITICAL THINKING

Answer these questions on a separate piece of paper. There are no right or wrong answers. Support your answer with examples from your own experience, if possible.

1. What are some of the possible disadvantages related to using range names and cell names in formulas? How can you avoid these potential drawbacks?

2. Describe potential uses for range names in Excel other than those described in this lesson. Explain how you would apply each use in a worksheet.

Skills Review

EXERCISE 6-9

Create names for cell ranges and constants, and use names in formulas.

1. Open the file **Lotions.xls**.
2. Create names for cell ranges by following these steps:
   a. Select cells B7 through D7.
   b. Choose Name from the Insert menu and choose Define.
   c. Excel suggests the name "Cypress" in the Names In Workbook text box. Click OK.
   d. Select cells B8 through D8.
   e. Choose Name from the Insert menu and then choose Define.
   f. Excel suggests the name "Jojoba" in the Names In Workbook text box. Click OK.
   g. Select cells B9 through D9.
   h. Press Ctrl+F3.
   i. Excel suggests the name "Sesame" in the Names In Workbook text box. Click OK.
   j. Select cells B10 through D10.
   k. Choose Insert, Name, and then choose Define.

Critical Thinking Questions:
Answers will vary based on students' preferences, observations, experiences, and research.

Skills Review:
Provides guided practice for students. Objectives are indicated for each Exercise.

● **Exercise 6-9:**
Objectives 1, 2
Required Files: Lotions.xls
Solution Files: gl6-9.xls in Solutions Manual or on Solutions Disk.

  l. Edit the suggested name "Joshua_Tree" in the Names In <u>W</u>orkbook text to **Joshua** and click OK.

 3. Create names for constants by following these steps:

  a. Choose <u>I</u>nsert, <u>N</u>ame, and then choose <u>D</u>efine.

  b. Key **slow** in the Names In <u>W</u>orkbook text box.

  c. Edit the text to read **=1.05** in the <u>R</u>efers To text box. Click <u>A</u>dd.

  d. Edit the text in the Names In <u>W</u>orkbook text box to read **moderate**

  e. Edit the text to read **=1.1** in the <u>R</u>efers To text box. Click <u>A</u>dd.

  f. Edit the text in the Names In <u>W</u>orkbook text box to read **fast**

  g. Edit the text to read **=1.15** in the <u>R</u>efers To text box. Click OK.

 4. Use names in formulas by following these steps:

  a. Key **=sum(cypress)** in cell E7.

  b. Key **=sum(jojoba)** in cell E8.

  c. Key **=sum(sesame)** in cell E9.

  d. Key **=sum(joshua)** in cell E10.

 5. Build formulas with range names and constant names by following these steps:

  a. Key **=cypress*slow** in cell B17.

  b. Use AutoFill to copy this formula to cells C17 and D17.

  c. Key **=jojoba*moderate** in cell B18.

  d. Use AutoFill to copy this formula to cells C18 and D18.

  e. Key **=sesame*fast** in cell B19.

  f. Use AutoFill to copy this formula to cells C19 and D19.

  g. Key **=joshua*slow** in cell B20.

  h. Key **=joshua*moderate** in cell C20.

  i. Key **=joshua*fast** in cell D20.

  j. Use AutoSum and AutoFill to enter formulas for the totals of each type of lotion in cells E17 through E20.

 6. Add the standard header including your name, filename, and date.

 7. Save the workbook as *[your initials]***6-9.xls** in your Lesson 6 folder and print the worksheet.

 8. Create a standard formula printout in landscape orientation with grids and row and column headings and close the workbook without saving it.

EXERCISE 6-10

Use names in formulas, change range names, and delete range names.

 1. Open the file **Powders.xls**.

 2. Use names in formulas by following these steps:

  a. Key **=sum(sahara)** in cell E6.

  b. Key **=sum(marin)** in cell E7.

◉ Exercise 6-10:
Objectives 2, 3
Required Files: Powders.xls
Solution Files: gl6-10.xls in Solutions Manual or on
Solutions Disk.

    c. Key **=sum(mohave)** in cell E8.

    d. Key **=sum(april_fresh)** in cell E9.

    e. Key **=sum(spring_day)** in cell E10.

    f. Key **=april_fresh+spring_day** in cell B12.

3. Use AutoFill to copy the formula from cell B12 to cells C12 and D12.

4. Use AutoSum to enter a formula that totals the new products in cell E12.

5. Change range names by following these steps:

    a. Choose Insert, Name and then choose Define.

    b. Choose "april_fresh" from the Names In Workbook list box.

    c. Delete "_fresh" from the name. Click Add.

    d. Choose "spring_day" from the Names In Workbook list box, change the name to **spring**, and click OK.

6. Delete range names by following these steps:

    a. Press Ctrl+F3.

    b. Choose "april_fresh" from the Names In Workbook list box and click Delete.

    c. Choose "spring_day" from the Names In Workbook list box, click Delete, and click OK.

7. Use the new range names in formulas by following these steps:

    a. Move to cell E9.

    b. Double-click "april_fresh" in the formula to select it and key **april**.

    c. Press Enter.

    d. In cell E10, change the name "spring_day" in the formula to **spring**.

    e. Change the formula in cell B12 to **=april+spring**.

    f. Copy the new formula in cell B12 to cells C12 and D12.

8. In cell A13, key **Grand Total**. In cells B13 through E13, calculate the totals for each month and for the three-month period. Do not include the "New Product Totals" in the "Grand Totals."

9. Add the standard header including your name, filename, and date, and center the worksheet horizontally on the page.

10. Save the workbook as *[your initials]***6-10.xls** in your Lesson 6 folder and print the worksheet.

11. Create a standard formula printout with grids and row and column headings. Use a Page 1 of ? footer.

12. Close the workbook without saving it.

EXERCISE 6-11

Name a range of cells and navigate in the worksheet using range names.

    1. Open the file **Credit.xls**.

◉ Exercise 6-11:
Objectives 1, 4, 6
Required Files: Credit.xls
Solution Files: gl6-11.xls in Solutions Manual or on Solutions Disk.

2. Add the following data for each customer into the worksheet:

Hall, Martha	**240**	**9%**
Spencer, Jon	**150**	**10%**
May, Violet	**23**	**7%**
Bernard, Frank	**542**	**13%**
Brown, JoAnne	**500**	**11%**

3. Name a range of cells by following these steps:
  a. Select cells A24 through C24.
  b. Choose Insert, Name, and then choose Define.
  c. Excel suggests the name "Hall_Martha" in the Names In Workbook text box. Click OK.

4. Use the Go To command to navigate with names in the worksheet by following these steps:
  a. Choose Go To from the Edit menu.
  b. Double-click the range "Ferrara_Joseph."
  c. Press F5.
  d. Double-click the range "fifteen." All new customers with credit at the 15% interest rate are selected.

5. Sort the list of customers by customer name in ascending order.
  a. Select cells A6 through C28.
  b. Choose Sort from the Data menu. Notice how Excel recognized the bold row as column headings and omitted them from the sort highlight. Click OK.

6. Add the standard header including your name, filename, and date.

7. Save the workbook as *[your initials]***6-11.xls** in your Lesson 6 folder and print the worksheet.

8. Create a standard formula printout in landscape orientation with grids and row and column headings and close the workbook without saving it.

EXERCISE 6-12

Name constants, paste names into a formula, and paste names into a worksheet.

1. Open the file **Freight1.xls**.

2. Name constants using the following steps:
  a. Choose Insert, Name, then choose Define.
  b. Key **mileage** in the Names In Workbook text box.
  c. Edit the text to read **=4** in the Refers To text box.
  d. Click Add.
  e. Key **weight** in the Names In Workbook text box.

    f. Edit the text to read **=.0015** in the <u>R</u>efers To text box.

    g. Click OK.

3. Change a formula by inserting the newly named constants using these steps:

    a. Select and delete the contents of cell D7.

    b. Key **=b7/mileage*c7*weight** and press ⌷Enter⌷.

4. Using AutoFill, copy the new formula in cell D7 to cells D8 through D16.

5. Paste names into a worksheet by following these steps:

    a. Move to cell A18 in the sheet labeled **User Information**.

    b. Key the label **Constant names** in bold and press ⌷Enter⌷.

    c. In cell B19, key **These are the constant names used in the worksheet.**

    d. In cell B21, key **Name** in bold and in cell C21 key **Refers to** in bold.

    e. In cell B22, choose <u>N</u>ame from the <u>I</u>nsert menu and choose <u>P</u>aste. The Paste Name dialog box appears.

    f. Click the Paste <u>L</u>ist button.

    g. Change the "Date revised" to today's date and key your name for "Revised by."

    h. Turn off gridlines for viewing.

6. Add the standard header including your name, filename, and date to both worksheets, and center the first worksheet horizontally on the page.

7. Save the workbook as *[your initials]***6-12.xls** in your Lesson 6 folder and print it.

8. Create a standard formula printout in landscape orientation with grids and row and column headings, and close the workbook without saving it.

A S S E S S

Assessment Resources:
• Solutions Manual
• Test Bank
• Portfolio Builder
• Internet Projects
• Alternative Assessment Guide
• Certification Procedures

For Internet projects, go to
www.glencoe.com/webprojects

Lesson Applications

Name constants, use names in formulas, define range names, change range names, and paste range names into the worksheet.

Complete and revise Beautiful Belle's fuel estimation worksheet so managers can better control the costs associated with product shipments.

1. Open the file **Freight2.xls**.

2. Enter the data shown in Figure 6-11 (making the corrections shown).

FIGURE 6-11

Seattle	*827*	Van	524
Denver	1270	Light truck	1642
Portland	652	Semi	2159
Albuquerque	11⁷2	Van	312
Los Angeles	403	semi	4⁸42493
Phoenix	800	Semi	2200
Dallas	1806	semi	3200
SaltLake City	759	Semi	3200
Mexico City	2419	Semi	2047
Topeka	1811	Van	750

3. Name the following constants:

Van = 16

Truck = 10

Semi = 6

4. Substitute the appropriate names (**Van, Truck,** or **Semi**) for the name "mileage" in the Fuel Estimate formulas in column E.

Lesson Applications:
Provide independent practice for students and may be used for assessment. Objectives are indicated for each Exercise.

◉ **Exercise 6-13:**
Objectives 1–5
Required Files: Freight2.xls
Solution Files: gl6-13.xls in Solutions Manual or on Solutions Disk.

⬚1 This figure contains proofreading marks, you may want to review Appendix E: "Proofreaders' Marks," with students.

5. Enter the following labels in cells A18 through A21. Make "Territories" bold.

   Territories

   Northwest

   Southwest

   Midwest

6. Key **Total Fuel** in cell B18 in bold.

7. Define the range name "Northwest" to include the values in the Fuel Estimate column for the following cities: Seattle, Portland, and Salt Lake City.

8. Define the range name "Southwest" to include Fuel Estimates for the following cities: Albuquerque, Los Angeles, Phoenix, and Mexico City.

9. Define the range name "Midwest" to include Fuel Estimates for the following cities: Denver, Dallas, and Topeka.

10. Create a formula using range names to calculate the total estimated fuel for each territory: "Northwest," "Southwest," and "Midwest."

11. Format cells containing formulas (Total Fuel, Fuel Estimates) as Comma style with two decimal places and all other cells containing values as Comma style, no decimals.

12. Paste the range names somewhere at the bottom of the worksheet so your instructor can check your work.

13. Add the standard header including your name, filename, and date, and center the worksheet horizontally on the page.

14. Save the workbook as *[your initials]***6-13.xls** in your Lesson 6 folder and print the worksheet.

15. Create a standard formula printout with gridlines and row and column headings in landscape orientation. (The printout may cut off range name locations. Disregard this for now.) Use a Page 1 of ? footer if the printout exceeds one page.

16. Close the workbook without saving it.

EXERCISE 6-14

Define range names, build formulas using range names, change and delete range names, navigate in a worksheet using range names, and paste range names into the worksheet.

  Develop a worksheet that audits selected Beautiful Belle product sales by store.

1. Open the file **Stores.xls**.

◉ Exercise 6-14:
Objectives 1–5
Required Files: Stores.xls
Solution Files: gl6-14.xls in Solutions Manual or on Solutions Disk.

The completed document for this Exercise can be used in a student's portfolio.

2. Define range names for each city in the worksheet by highlighting the corresponding cells in the Amount column.

3. In cells A27 through A33, enter the labels shown below. Format the labels in bold.

Store Totals
Dallas
New York
Chicago
San Francisco
Boston
Indianapolis

4. Use these range names to build formulas that calculate the total sales for each store. Enter the formulas in column B beside the appropriate label and format the results in Comma style with two decimals.

5. Change the range name "Dallas" to **Denver**.

6. Delete the range name "Dallas."

7. Change the name "Dallas" to **Denver** in the formula that calculates the store total.

8. Change the labels in the Store column and Store Totals column from "Dallas" to **Denver**.

9. Use the Go To command to highlight the Denver sales amounts.

10. Paste the range names somewhere at the bottom of the worksheet so your instructor can check your work.

11. Add the standard header including your name, filename, and date.

12. Save the workbook as *[your initials]*6-14.xls in your Lesson 6 folder and print the worksheet.

13. Create a standard formula printout with grids and row and column headings and a Page 1 of ? footer.

14. Close the workbook without saving it.

 NOTE: The formula printout may cut off range name locations. You can disregard this for now.

EXERCISE 6-15

Create range names, build formulas using range names, paste names into the worksheet, and use the Go To command to navigate in the worksheet.

 Construct a worksheet for the Beautiful Belle Company that calculates the total sales and commissions paid over four quarters.

1. Open the file **Cmsions.xls**.

 Exercise 6-15:
Objectives 1, 2, 4–6
Required Files: Cmsions.xls
Solution Files: gl6-15.xls in Solutions Manual or on Solutions Disk.

 The completed document for this Exercise can be used in a student's portfolio.

2. In cell C16, use the AutoSum button Σ to add the column.

3. Use Autofill to copy the SUM formula to cells D16 through J16.

4. Create the name **rt** for the constant **.07** (7%).

5. Create formulas using the constant name "rt" in cells D4, F4, H4, and J4 that calculate the commission due for each quarter. Copy the formulas using AutoFill to complete the columns.

6. Create the names **sq1**, **sq2**, **sq3**, and **sq4** for the total sales for each quarter.

7. Create a formula in cell B17 that uses names to calculate the total sales for the year.

8. Create the names **com1**, **com2**, **com3**, and **com4** for the total commissions for each quarter.

9. Use the commission range names to create a formula in cell B18 that calculates the total commissions for the year.

10. In cell B21, paste all the names you created on the worksheet.

11. Key the following information in cells A21, A25, and A26 and make all labels bold.

commission q1

commsn rate

sales q1

12. Use the <u>G</u>o To command to locate the cell named "sq4."

13. Sort the data in rows 4 through 15 in ascending order.

14. Add the standard header including your name, filename, and date and center the worksheet horizontally on the page.

15. Set up the worksheet to print without gridlines in landscape orientation on a single page.

 TIP: On the Page tab in the Page Setup dialog box, activate <u>F</u>it To under Scaling and make sure the number of pages is 1 to have the worksheet fit on one page.

16. Save the workbook as *[your initials]*6-15.xls in your Lesson 6 folder.

17. Create a standard formula printout with grids and row and column headings and a Page 1 of ? footer.

 TIP: On the Page tab in the Page Setup dialog box, activate <u>A</u>djust To under Scaling and make sure the percentage is 100 so the printout does not fit on one page.

18. Close the workbook without saving it.

EXERCISE 6-16   *Challenge Yourself*

Name cells, create formulas using named cells, and paste range names into the user documentation.

 In an effort to understand its expenses by region, the Beautiful Belle Company needs to calculate quarterly, biannual, and yearly total expenses based on its 1999 expense information.

1. Create a worksheet sketch that includes a title, row and column labels, and an area for data and formulas. The worksheet should include January through December expense information (columns) for the Southeast, Northeast, and Northwest regions (rows). (*Hint:* Use abbreviations and start a new section for the second half of the year below the first section.) There should also be row labels for monthly totals, totals for each quarter, and half-year totals for each section. Use F for formula locations.

2. Transfer the sketch into Excel by keying and formatting the labels including the title. Key the data from Figure 6-12 in the worksheet formatted in Comma style, no decimals.

FIGURE 6-12

	Jan	Feb	Mar	Apr	May	Jun
S.E.	32,098	189,074	156,976	82,514	188,365	174,958
N.E.	11,098	294,651	192,634	99,254	201,648	89,254
N.W.	132,098	486,277	326,584	135,698	543,958	142,360

	Jul	Aug	Sept	Oct	Nov	Dec
S.E.	124,725	93,581	54,321	42,587	748,512	154,879
N.E.	124,521	84,516	68,954	859,641	365,894	254,369
N.W.	123,695	99,365	67,987	102,587	411,758	254,879

3. Include calculations for monthly total expenses.

4. Name each cell containing a monthly total.

5. Below the monthly data, use your range names to calculate quarterly expenses based on the monthly totals for all regions.

6. Below the quarterly totals, use cell names to calculate half-year expenses.

Exercise 6-16:
Objectives 1, 2, 5
Required Files: None
Solution Files: gl6-16.xls in Solutions Manual or on Solutions Disk.

 The completed document for this Exercise can be used in a student's portfolio.

7. Format all the cells containing values in Comma style with no decimal places.

8. Format the cells above monthly totals with bottom borders.

9. Rename Sheet1 **Regions,** Sheet 2 **User Information**, and delete Sheet 3.

10. On the User Information worksheet, create the following:

    File Information (with the following subheads: **Created by**, **Date created**, **Date revised**, **Revised by**, **Contact for help**)

    Purpose/Description of Worksheet *[Use a paragraph form]*

    Instructions to User *[Add special instructions needed by the user to enter data correctly]*

    Range Names *[Provide the names used in the worksheet and their location]*

11. Style the documentation for easy reading.

12. Add the standard header including your name, filename, and date to both worksheets, and center the Regions worksheet horizontally on the page.

13. Save the workbook as *[your initials]***6-16.xls** in your Lesson 6 folder.

14. Print the entire workbook, then create a standard formula printout in landscape orientation with grids and row and column headings. Use the Page 1 of ? footer for multiple pages. Do not fit the formula printout on one page.

15. Close the workbook without saving it.

1 The worksheet and user documentation are created by the student, so final versions may differ.

Spelling, Find/ Replace, and File Management

OBJECTIVES

MOUS ACTIVITIES

In this lesson:
XL2000 **1.8**
XL2000 **2.7**
XL2000 **5.6**

See Appendix F.

After completing this lesson, you will be able to:

1. **Check spelling.**
2. **Use AutoCorrect.**
3. **Find and replace data.**
4. **Find files.**
5. **Rename, copy, and delete files.**

 Estimated Time: 1 hour

C reating and building a workbook is only the beginning of effective data management and analysis. You must make your workbooks accurate and easy to use, and Excel can help. Excel provides automated dictionaries to check your spelling. It also provides a Find and Replace function you can use to make global changes and revisions.

Excel's Open dialog box lets you find files easily and offers many file management functions.

Objective 1
Checking Spelling

Excel's spell-checker scans the active worksheet and highlights words not found in any of its dictionaries. It also finds repeated words. A Spelling dialog

---

P R E P A R E

Point out to students that the learning objectives show what they will learn in the lesson. Each heading in the lesson correlates to a learning objective.

208

Required files:
Change%2.xls

T E A C H

Teaching Resources:
• Excel Classroom Presentations
• School-to-Work Strategies Manual
• Spanish Glossary
• Certification Procedures

box provides a choice of options for handling the highlighted word, as shown in Table 7-1.

TABLE 7-1   **Spell-Checking Options**

BUTTON	ACTION
Ignore	Do not take any action; do not change the spelling. If it is a repeated word, do not delete or change it.
Ignore All	Do not take any action for all occurrences of this word in the worksheet.
Change	Change the current spelling of this word to the spelling highlighted in the Change To box.
Delete	Delete a repeated word.
Change All	Change all occurrences of this word to the spelling highlighted in the Change To box.
Add	Add this word to the dictionary. Once added, Excel no longer highlights this word as "Not in Dictionary."
Suggest	Display a list of proposed suggestions.
Undo Last	Reverse the last action.
Cancel/Close	End spell-checking.
AutoCorrect	Add to the list of corrections that AutoCorrect makes as you key text in a worksheet.

You can customize the spell-checker so it works smarter for you. Adding words to a dictionary is especially useful for worksheets that contain data from specific fields, such as law, real estate, or science. You can also turn off the Suggestions list box choice and ignore words that contain numbers or all uppercase letters.

EXERCISE   7-1   Spell-Check the Entire Worksheet

Excel begins spell-checking at the active cell. If you begin spell-checking in the middle of the worksheet, a dialog box appears when the spell-checker reaches the end. You can continue spell-checking at the beginning of the worksheet.

1. Open the file **Change%2.xls**.

2. Select cell A1 to begin spell-checking from the beginning of the worksheet.

1 Point out that spell-check is shared by other Microsoft applications. So, for example, if you add terms in Excel, they will be recognized as correctly spelled in Word.

3. Choose <u>S</u>pelling from the <u>T</u>ools menu or press F7. Excel locates the first word not found in its dictionary, "Introducsion." The correct spelling appears in both the Change <u>T</u>o text box and the Suggestio<u>n</u>s drop-down list box.

FIGURE 7-1
Spelling dialog
box

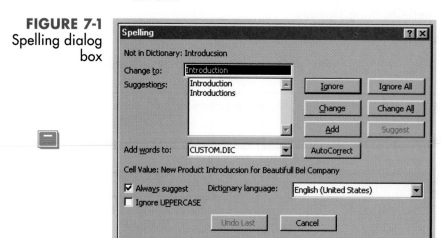

4. Click <u>C</u>hange. Excel changes the word to "Introduction" and locates the next word not found in its dictionary.

> ★ **TIP:** You may want to view a word in the worksheet before you change its spelling. To move the Spelling dialog box, drag its title bar.

5. Continue spell-checking until you reach the end of the worksheet. Click <u>I</u>gnore if no change is required. If the correct spelling appears in the Suggestio<u>n</u>s drop-down list box but not in the Change <u>T</u>o text box, select the correct word from the list and click <u>C</u>hange.

> ⊘ **NOTE:** If the correct word does not appear in the drop-down list, key it directly into the Change <u>T</u>o text box and click <u>C</u>hange.

6. When the spell-check is completed, click OK in the dialog box.

EXERCISE   7-2   Spell-Check a Range in the Worksheet

To spell-check a range in a worksheet, highlight the range to be checked and choose <u>S</u>pelling from the <u>T</u>ools menu (or press F7, or click the Spelling button on the Standard toolbar). Excel checks only the highlighted range.

1. Move to the User Information sheet and select cells A1 through D7.

2. Click the Spelling button on the Standard toolbar. The Spelling dialog box appears. Excel locates "Creted," the first word in the selected range not found in its dictionary.

3. Click "Created" in the Suggestions drop-down list box, if necessary, and click <u>C</u>hange to change the misspelled word to "Created." Excel locates "Dat," the next word not found in its dictionary.

4. Click "Date" in the Suggestions drop-down list box, if necessary, and click <u>C</u>hange.

5. Click <u>C</u>hange to correct "Revisd" to "Revised."

6. Click "by" in the Suggestions drop-down list and click <u>C</u>hange. A dialog box appears when the spell-check of the range is complete.

7. Click OK and deselect the range.

☑ **Objective 2**

Using AutoCorrect

The AutoCorrect feature automatically corrects your spelling as you key text. You can customize AutoCorrect by adding words you commonly misspell to Excel's list. You can also turn off AutoCorrect, if desired.

EXERCISE 7-3 **Use AutoCorrect to Correct Typos**

---

1. Choose <u>A</u>utoCorrect from the <u>T</u>ools menu. (Remember, you may have to expand the menu.) The AutoCorrect dialog box appears.

FIGURE 7-2
AutoCorrect
dialog box

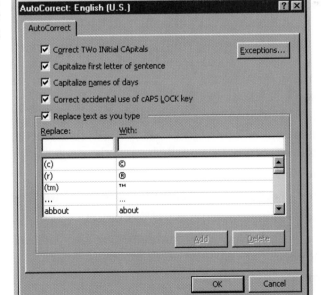

Point out to students that spell-checking and AutoCorrect can find and correct many spelling errors, but they miss usage errors. These tools *augment* the user's spelling and grammar skills—but they cannot *replace* good spelling and writing skills.

 In Excel Classroom Presentation 7.

2. Clear the Replace <u>T</u>ext As You Type check box and click OK. The AutoCorrect feature is deselected and Excel will not correct spelling automatically.

3. Key **Purpse** in bold in cell A9 and press ⌷Enter⌷. Remember to key the word exactly as shown. With AutoCorrect deselected, the spelling error is not corrected.

4. Choose <u>A</u>utoCorrect from the <u>T</u>ools menu.

5. Click the Replace <u>T</u>ext As You Type check box to select it and click OK. AutoCorrect becomes active again, but does not correct existing text.

6. Key the following text in cell B10 exactly as shown to see AutoCorrect at work:

Analyze teh sale groth of new product line

AutoCorrect changes the word "teh" to "the" as you type. Note, however, that the misspelled word "groth" was not corrected. In addition, errors in sentence syntax, such as the word "sale" in this entry, are not corrected by AutoCorrect or the spell-checker.

EXERCISE 7-4   ## Add AutoCorrect Entries for Your Common Typos

You can have AutoCorrect automatically correct a word you misspell often. Simply add the misspelling and its correction to AutoCorrect's list of words.

1. Select cells A9 through B10.

2. Click the Spelling button . Excel suggests "Purpose" to correct the first word in the range that does not match its dictionary.

3. Double-click "Purpose" in the Suggestio<u>n</u>s drop-down list box (another way to select a word). Excel finds "groth," the next word in the range not found in its dictionary. Select "growth" in the Suggestio<u>n</u>s drop-down list box.

4. Click AutoCo<u>r</u>rect. Excel changes the spelling of the word and adds this correction to AutoCorrect's list of words to correct as you type. A dialog box appears when the spell-check of the range is complete.

5. Click OK.

6. Move to cell B10 and change the word "sale" to **sales.**

7. Choose <u>A</u>utoCorrect from the <u>T</u>ools menu.

8. Key the following words in the <u>R</u>eplace and <u>W</u>ith text boxes and click <u>A</u>dd. Be sure to type the words exactly as shown.

produtc   product

 Warn students to watch for corrections that AutoCorrect makes automatically that may not be what the user wants. In such a case, the user might consider changing the listing in AutoCorrect. If it happens frequently, the user may decide to deselect AutoCorrect.

 If the misspelled words are not found by spell-check, go to the custom dictionary on the hard drive and check the contents for that misspelled word. To locate the custom dictionary, use the Find tool in Windows Explorer. Look for the file **custom.dic**. Use Word or Notepad to open the file.

FIGURE 7-3
Adding a new
AutoCorrect listing

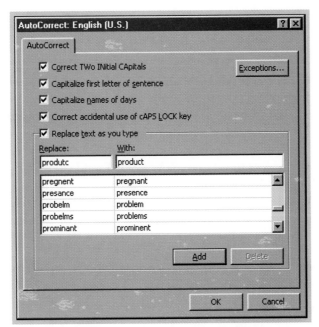

9. Scroll up the Replace and With text boxes to confirm that the word "groth" was added to the AutoCorrect list.

10. Choose "groth," and click Delete to remove it from the list.

11. Click OK, return to cell A1, and turn off gridlines for viewing.

TIP: You can also use AutoCorrect to create abbreviations that speed data entry. For example, assume that you type the phrase "Pending Release" frequently in your worksheets. Just add the abbreviation "pr" to the Replace text box and the full phrase "Pending Release" to the With text box in the AutoCorrect dialog box.

☑ **Objective 3**

Finding and Replacing Data

Find and Replace are handy tools for updating worksheets. Find locates occurrences of a *character string*—a sequence of characters in a formula or text. You can use Find to return to a particular location in a worksheet, to verify that text is consistent, or to check that a formula appears in all intended locations.

Replace locates occurrences of a character string and replaces them, either one at a time or globally. As a result, it can change a formula that occurs in multiple cells. You can also use Replace to change repeated labels, such as a category or product name.

In Excel Classroom Presentation 7.

☑ **Objective 3 Assignment:**
Exercise 7-10 (Skills Review) can be assigned after completing Objective 3.

EXERCISE 7-5 Find Data in a Worksheet

You can use the Find command in relatively long worksheets that contain too many formulas and values to check individually. Find is especially useful in locating all instances of a formula or error in a worksheet. Excel uses the asterisk (*) as a *wildcard* symbol, which instructs Excel to allow any combination of letters or numbers to replace it. If, for example, Excel was searching for 7-*, it would locate 7-1, 7-2, 7-A, 7-SOFT, and so on.

All error values begin with # (the number sign), so you can key **#** in the Find What text box to locate error values in a worksheet. You can also look for specific error values, such as #DIV/0!, the error value produced if you try to divide by zero.

1. Move to the Sun Soft worksheet and choose <u>F</u>ind from the <u>E</u>dit menu or press Ctrl + F. The Find dialog box appears.

FIGURE 7-4
Find dialog box

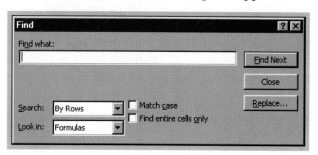

2. Key **=SUM(C7:C10)** in the Fi<u>n</u>d What text box.

3. Choose Formulas from the <u>L</u>ook In drop-down list box, if necessary. Make sure the Match <u>C</u>ase box is not checked so Excel does not try to match the case (upper or lower) of the word you keyed.

4. Click <u>F</u>ind Next. Excel finds the formula in cell C12 and displays the cell reference in the Name box and the formula in the Formula bar.

 TIP: Drag the Find dialog box out of the way so you can see the selected cell in the worksheet.

5. Edit the text in the Fi<u>n</u>d What text box to read **=SUM(*7:*10)** and click <u>F</u>ind Next. Excel selects cell D12.

6. Click <u>F</u>ind Next to find the next occurrence of the formula. Excel selects cell B12.

 NOTE: You cannot edit the worksheet when the Find dialog box is open. If you close the Find dialog box, however, you can repeat the last search by pressing F4.

7. Click Find Next. Excel selects cell C12 again.

8. Choose Values from the Look In drop-down list.

9. Key **#** in the Find What text box (replacing the formula) and click Find Next. Excel finds cell E7, which contains a formula that attempts to perform division by zero. (The formula "C7/B7" is a division by zero, because cell B7 is empty.)

10. Close the Find dialog box.

11. In cell B7, key **57,809** to correct the error.

EXERCISE 7-6 Replace Data in a Worksheet

You can replace character strings globally or one at a time.

1. Select cell A6 and choose Replace from the Edit menu (or press Ctrl+H). The Replace dialog box appears. The Find What text box contains # (the number sign), which is the last entry in the Find dialog box.

FIGURE 7-5
Replace dialog box

Most recent
Find string

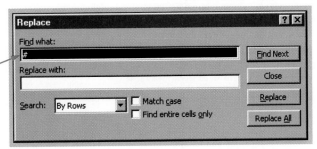

2. Key **1997** in the Find What text box (replacing #), press Tab, and key **Year 1** in the Replace With text box.

3. Click Find Next.

 TIP: Drag the Replace dialog box out of the way so you can see the selected cell in the worksheet.

4. Click Replace. The worksheet displays "Year 1" in cell B6.

5. Close the Replace dialog box. Select cell B6 and right-align the label.

6. Choose Find from the Edit menu, edit the date in the Find What text box to read **1998**, and click Find Next. Cell C6 is selected.

7. Click Replace to expand the Find dialog box to the Replace dialog box.

8. Make the Replace With text box read **Year 2** and choose Replace All. Both occurrences of "1998" are replaced with "Year 2."

 Caution students about using wildcards and the Replace All button in the Replace dialog box. Replace All should not be used unless the user is absolutely sure of the results of the action. Otherwise, using the Find Next button together with the Replace button is a safer bet.

 In Excel Classroom Presentation 7.

9. Choose R̲eplace from the E̲dit menu. Edit the Fi̲nd What box to read **1999** and edit the Replace With box to read **Year 3**.

10. Click F̲ind Next. Excel moves to cell D6.

11. Click R̲eplace and Excel moves to cell F6.

12. Click R̲eplace.

13. Close the Replace dialog box and right-align the rest of the column labels on row 6.

14. Change the title text in cell A3 to **Year 1-Year 3** and the text in cell A15 to reflect the same.

FIGURE 7-6
Revised worksheet

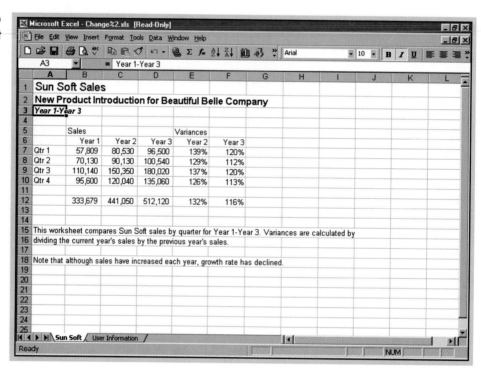

15. Add the standard header with your name, filename, and date to both worksheets and make the Sun Soft worksheet active if it is not already.

16. Save the workbook as *[your initials]***7-6.xls** in a new folder for Lesson 7.

17. Print the entire workbook and then close it.

☑ **Objective 4**

Finding Files

You can use Excel's Open dialog box to find a file, even if you do not remember its exact name. You can also display different types of details about files to determine which file to open.

In Excel Classroom Presentation 7.

☑ **Objective 4 Assignment:**
Exercise 7-11 (Skills Review) and Exercises 7-13, 7-15, and 7-16 (Lesson Applications) can be assigned after completing Objective 4.

TABLE 7-2   Open Dialog Box Buttons

BUTTON	BUTTON NAME/ACTION
⬅	*Back* changes the current location in the Look In text box to the last folder viewed.
🖿	*Up One Level* moves up the file tree shown in the Look In drop-down list.
🔍	*Search the Web* accesses the World Wide Web.
✕	*Delete* removes the selected file or files.
🗀	*Create New Folder* adds a new folder to the current location.
▦	*Views* offers a menu of viewing options for displaying filenames and folders.
Tools	*Tools* offers a menu of options.

If you choose <u>F</u>ind from the Too<u>l</u>s menu and check the Searc<u>h</u> Subfolders checkbox, Excel searches in the current folder and any subfolders.

You can also have Excel search for files that contain specific words or phrases. To take this approach, choose <u>F</u>ind from the Too<u>l</u>s menu, select "Contents" from the <u>P</u>roperty drop-down list, select "includes words" from the <u>C</u>ondition drop-down list, key the text in the Val<u>u</u>e text box, and click <u>A</u>dd to List before you start your search.

EXERCISE 7-7 Find a Workbook

Excel can search for specific filenames or for filenames containing a certain pattern. For example, you can search for all filenames with a specific prefix or extension.

1. Click the Open button 🖿 or choose <u>O</u>pen from the <u>F</u>ile menu or press Ctrl + O. The Open dialog box appears.

2. Specify the location of your student files in the Look <u>I</u>n drop-down list.

 NOTE: If you are unsure of the location to use in the above step, ask your instructor.

3. Choose All Microsoft Excel Files from the Files of <u>T</u>ype drop-down list, if necessary.

 Students are asked to go to the folder in which their Student Template Files are located. If these files are located on a network, explain how to specify their location in the Look <u>I</u>n drop-down list. You may want to review using the Up One Level, Favorites, and Add to Favorites buttons.

4. Choose <u>F</u>ind from the Too<u>l</u>s drop-down list to open the Find dialog box that is used specifically to find files.

5. Key **Sales*** in the Val<u>u</u>e text box. Click <u>A</u>dd to List.

> **TIP:** The asterisk * is the wildcard character, so Sales* means any filename beginning with "Sales". You could key *[your initials]*6* to search for all your answer files in Lesson 6, for example.

FIGURE 7-7
Finding files

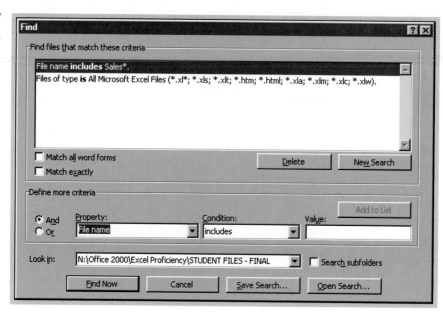

6. Click <u>F</u>ind Now. The Open dialog box appears with a list of all Excel-type filenames that begin with "Sales."

7. Click Cancel.

> **TIP:** When you double-click the Find Fast icon in the Windows Control Panel, you open the Find Fast utility. Find Fast creates indexes to speed up file searches by content, properties, or both. For information about using Find Fast, refer to Help in the Find Fast dialog box.

Objective 5

Renaming, Copying, and Deleting Files

You can open, copy, print, rename, or delete files directly from the Open dialog box. However, when a file is already open, you cannot rename it.

In Excel Classroom Presentation 7.

Find Fast is not installed as part of the Typical Installation. Click the Start button, choose Settings, Control Panel, double-click the Find Fast icon, and then follow instructions to load the Microsoft Office CD-ROM.

Objective 5 Assignment:
Exercises 7-12 (Skills Review) and 7-14 (Lesson Applications) can be assigned after completing Objective 5.

 File management tasks can be accomplished many different ways in Excel and Windows 98. You may want to describe Windows Explorer for students who seek a more robust file management tool. In addition, encourage students to experiment with Find on the Windows 98 Start menu and Find Fast in the Control Panel (if it is installed).

EXERCISE 7-8 Rename, Copy, and Delete a File Using the Open Dialog Box

1. Click the Open button . In the Open dialog box, locate the file *[your initials]***7-6.xls**, which you saved earlier in this lesson. Click the file once to select it, but do not open it.

2. Choose the <u>P</u>review option from the Views drop-down list ▦. The upper left corner of the selected file appears in the Preview box.

FIGURE 7-8
File preview in the Open dialog box

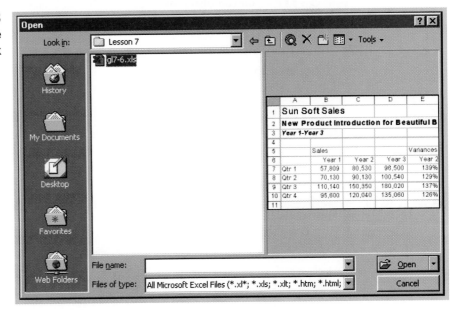

3. With the file *[your initials]***7-6.xls** still selected, press Ctrl+C. The file is copied to the Clipboard (there is no change on the screen, however).

4. Press Ctrl+V to paste a copy of the file into the current folder.

5. Click the file **Copy of** *[your initials]***7-6.xls** to select it, if necessary, and choose <u>P</u>rint from the Too<u>l</u>s drop-down list.

6. Excel opens the file, prints the active worksheet in the workbook, and then closes the file and the Open dialog box.

TIP: You can also right-click a filename and choose <u>P</u>rint from the shortcut menu.

7. Click the Open button to open the Open dialog box again.

8. Right-click the file **Copy of** *[your initials]***7-6.xls** to open the shortcut menu.

9. Choose Rena<u>m</u>e, key *[your initials]***7-8.xls** (making sure to key the ".xls"), and press Enter. Excel changes the filename.

 In Excel Classroom Presentation 7.

NOTE: Be sure to key the file extension (.xls) when you rename a file. Otherwise, that file cannot be recognized as a file of its type.

10. Select the file *[your initials]*7-8.xls, if necessary.

11. Click the Delete button ☒. A dialog box appears asking if you're sure you want to delete the file.

12. Click Yes. The file is deleted.

 TIP: You can also press Delete or choose Delete from the shortcut menu.

13. Open the Views drop-down list 🔳 and choose List.

14. Close the Open dialog box.

TIP: You may want to access other information about your files. Explore the other options available in the Tools drop-down list.

COMMAND SUMMARY

FEATURE	BUTTON	MENU	KEYBOARD
Spell-check	🔤	Tools, Spelling	F7
Find		Edit, Find	Ctrl + F
Replace		Edit, Replace	Ctrl + H
Repeat (last) Find			F4
AutoCorrect		Tools, AutoCorrect	
Find and Manage files	🖼	File, Open	Ctrl + O

USING HELP

Suppose you need to get data from an Excel worksheet to someone in another city quickly. One way to accomplish this is to send the worksheet via e-mail. To find out more about using the e-mail feature (including the system requirements for mailing workbooks and worksheets), search "e-mail" in Help. Locate the topic "Distribute workbooks and worksheets to other people."

 File extensions must be typed only when extensions are displayed.

Point out that the Command Summary lists a variety of ways to accomplish a particular task. Students can decide which method they prefer.

This portion of Using Help directs students to the Help topic that contains information about e-mailing workbooks. The following Exercise shows students how to do it. If you assign this practice Exercise, make sure students have an appropriate e-mail address.

NOTE: Before you send e-mail, consult your instructor to make sure your computer is correctly set up and that you have an appropriate e-mail address to use. Individual configurations may cause the E-Mail feature to work differently than described below.

To send a workbook via e-mail:

1. With an Excel worksheet open, click the E-Mail button  on the Standard toolbar. The E-Mail toolbar appears.

FIGURE 7-9
E-Mail toolbar

2. In the "To" box, enter the recipient's name. (If there is more than one, separate them by commas). Do the same for the "Cc" box.

TIP: To select a recipient (for either the "To" box or the "Cc" box), click the icon next the "To" box or the "Cc" box. You could also use the Address button 📖 to review names in your Address book.

3. Key a Subject for the e-mail. (In some configurations, the title of the Workbook may appear on the "Subject" line. In others, the last "Subject" may appear.)

4. Set the options you want for this message. For example, you can specify the urgency of the e-mail using the Set Priority button 🔽.

NOTE: You could also attach an entire Workbook to an e-mail using the Attach File button 📎.

5. Click Send this Sheet 🖳. Your e-mail is sent and the E-Mail toolbar closes.

6. Close the worksheet.

In Excel Classroom Presentation 7.

TEST BANK

Concepts Review

TRUE/FALSE QUESTIONS

Each of the following statements is either true or false. Indicate your choice by circling T or F.

T **(F)** **1.** Excel's spell-checker automatically deletes repeated words.

T **(F)** **2.** You access the <u>F</u>ind and <u>O</u>pen commands from the same menu.

(T) F **3.** You can add words to customize Excel's spell-checking dictionaries.

(T) F **4.** A character string is a sequence of characters in a formula or worksheet text.

(T) F **5.** All error values in Excel begin with the number sign (#).

(T) F **6.** You can use a wildcard to find and replace data or to find files.

(T) F **7.** AutoCorrect identifies common typos and automatically changes them to the correct spelling.

T **(F)** **8.** Using the Open dialog box, you can copy worksheets, but you can't print them.

SHORT ANSWER QUESTIONS

Write the correct answer in the space provided.

1. Which key starts Excel's spell-checker?

F7

2. Which menu commands do you use to open the Replace dialog box?

Edit, Replace

3. Which keystroke combination do you use to open the Find dialog box?

Ctrl+F

4. Which Excel dialog box offers file-management tools?

Open

Concepts Review:
Allows students to check their understanding.

C L O S E

TEST BANK
Consider using the Test Bank to provide an additional review of lesson concepts. It may also be used as an assessment tool.

5. Which keystroke combination do you use to access the Open dialog box?

Ctrl+O

6. How do you instruct Excel to allow any combination of letters or numbers to replace a symbol in a search?

Asterisk wildcard

7. How do you look at a worksheet without opening it?

In Open dialog box, Views, Preview

8. How do you print from the Open dialog box?

Tools, Print (or use Print from shortcut menu)

CRITICAL THINKING

Answer these questions on a separate piece of paper. There are no right or wrong answers. Support your answer with examples from your own experience, if possible.

1. Describe a work situation in which Excel's Replace feature would be useful. Can Replace <u>All</u> be too much of a good thing?

2. What are the implications of features such as AutoCorrect that seem to do the thinking for you?

Skills Review

EXERCISE 7-9

Spell-check a worksheet, spell-check a range, and correct typos with AutoCorrect.

1. Open the file **MktExp.xls.**

2. Spell-check the worksheet by following these steps:
   a. Move to cell A1, if necessary, and click the Spelling button 📝.
   b. Select or key appropriate spellings in the Change <u>T</u>o text box and click <u>C</u>hange. Remember Excel's suggested replacement may not be the correct word for your worksheet.
   c. Click OK when the spell-check is finished.

3. Key the text as shown in Figure 7-10 on the next page, starting at cell A16.

Critical Thinking Questions:	**Skills Review:**	⊙ **Exercise 7-9:**
Answers will vary based on students' preferences, observations, experiences, and research.	Provides guided practice for students. Objectives are indicated for each Exercise.	Objectives 1, 2 Required Files: MktExp.xls Solution Files: gl7-9.xls

FIGURE 7-10

	A	B	C	D	E
16	Pacifica	9200	9800	10000	12000
17	Taos	5000	5000	7500	8500
18	High Sierra	3000	4000	6000	7500
19	Carmel	9550	9550	12500	12500
20	Santa Barbara	2300	2500	6000	9000

4. Key **Total** in cell F15.

5. Spell-check the range you just entered using these steps:
   a. Select cells A16 through E20.
   b. Choose Spelling from the Tools menu (or press F7).
   c. Change any misspelled words. If you're a good typist, the range may not include any misspelled words. Remember, Excel's suggested replacement may not be the correct word for your worksheet.
   d. Click OK when the spell-check is finished.

6. Enter formulas to find the product and quarterly totals by following these steps:
   a. Select cell F7. Click the AutoSum button Σ twice.
   b. Copy this formula to cells F8 through F12 using AutoFill.
   c. Select cell B12. Click the AutoSum button Σ twice.
   d. Copy this formula to cells C12 through E12 using AutoFill.
   e. Copy the range F7 through F12 to cells F16 through F21 by dragging the range.
   f. Use the AutoSum button Σ to calculate totals in cells B21 through E21.

7. Key **Subtotal** in cell A21.

8. Use AutoCorrect to correct typos by keying the following text, exactly as shown, in cell A24:

   Acn we acheive any ohter cost savings in teh third quater?

9. Format the individual product expenses in Comma style with no decimal places.

10. Format the totals in Currency style with no decimal places.

11. Add the standard header with your name, filename, and date, and center the worksheet horizontally on the page.

12. Save the workbook as *[your initials]*7-9.xls in your Lesson 7 folder and print the worksheet.

13. Create a formula printout that fits on one page in landscape orientation with grids and row and column headings. (*Hint:* Use the Fit To feature in the Page Setup dialog box.)

14. Close the workbook without saving it.

EXERCISE 7-10

Use AutoCorrect to correct common typos, and find and replace values in a formula.

1. Open the workbook **AdCosts.xls**.

2. Use AutoCorrect for common typos by following these steps:

   a. Choose AutoCorrect from the Tools menu.

   b. Key the following words in the Replace and With text boxes and click Add. Be sure to type the words exactly as shown.

   diretc   direct

   mial   mail

   c. Click OK.

3. Key the following misspelling in cell A10 and watch AutoCorrect at work:

   Diretc Mial

4. Key the following amounts in the cells indicated:

   B10: **1000**   D10: **1500**   E10: **2000**

5. Copy the formula from cell F9 to cells F10 and F11 using AutoFill.

6. Find and replace data in the worksheet using these steps:

   a. Select cell A1 and choose Find from the Edit menu.

   b. Key **=SUM(*7:*9)** in the Find What text box.

   c. Choose Formulas from the Look in drop-down list box, if necessary. Make sure the Match Case box is not checked.

   d. Click Find Next. Excel finds the formula in cell C11.

   e. Click Replace.

   f. In the Replace With text box key **=SUM(C7:C10)** and then click Replace.

   g. Click Close.

7. Format all values in Comma style with no decimal places.

8. Delete the AutoCorrect entries you made in this exercise by following these steps:

   a. Choose AutoCorrect from the Tools menu.

   b. Select "diretc" in the scroll box and click Delete.

 Exercise 7-10:

Objectives 2, 3
Required Files: AdCosts.xls
Solution Files: gl7-10.xls

 If students are sharing Excel installations, be sure they delete the AutoCorrect entries they make.

    c. Select "mial" in the scroll box and click <u>D</u>elete.

    d. Click OK.

9. Add the standard header with your name, filename, and date, and center the worksheet horizontally on the page.

10. Save the workbook as *[your initials]***7-10.xls** in your Lesson 7 folder and print the worksheet.

11. Create a formula printout in landscape orientation with grids and row and column headings that fits on one page. (*Hint:* Use the Fit <u>T</u>o feature in the Page Setup dialog box.)

12. Close the workbook without saving it.

EXERCISE 7-11

Find and open a file, and find and replace data.

1. Find a file containing the word "inventory" and open it by following these steps:

    a. Click the Open button 🖻.

    b. Choose the drive containing your student files (if necessary) from the Look <u>i</u>n drop-down list box or key the location directly in the text box.

    c. Click Too<u>l</u>s and click <u>F</u>ind.

    d. Key **Inv** in the Val<u>u</u>e text box and click <u>A</u>dd to List. Click <u>F</u>ind Now.

    e. Open the file **InvntyQ1.xls**.

2. Find and replace data in the worksheet using these steps:

    a. In cell A1, choose <u>R</u>eplace from the <u>E</u>dit menu.

    b. Key **subtotal** in the Fi<u>n</u>d What text box.

    c. Key **Monthly subtotal** in the Re<u>p</u>lace With text box.

    d. Select By Columns from the <u>S</u>earch drop-down list box.

    e. Click <u>F</u>ind Next. Excel selects cell A13.

    f. Click <u>R</u>eplace. Excel selects cell A22.

    g. Move the Replace dialog box out of the way to see the selected cell, if necessary.

    h. Click <u>R</u>eplace again. Excel selects cell E6.

3. Change the text to be replaced by following these steps:

    a. Key **Product subtotal** in the Re<u>p</u>lace With text box.

    b. With cell E6 selected, click <u>R</u>eplace. Excel selects cell E16.

    c. Click <u>R</u>eplace again.

    d. Click Close.

4. Add the standard header with your name, filename, and date.

5. Save the workbook as *[your initials]***7-11.xls** in your Lesson 7 folder and print the worksheet.

◉ **Exercise 7-11:**
Objectives 3, 4
Required Files: InvntyQ1.xls
Solution Files: gl7-11.xls in Solutions Manual or on
Solutions Disk.

6. Create a formula printout in landscape orientation with grids and row and column headings.

7. Close the workbook without saving it.

EXERCISE 7-12

Use the Open dialog box to copy, rename, and delete a file; use the Open dialog box to print a file.

1. Open the file **COGS.xls** and save it as *[your initials]***7-cogs.xls** in your Lesson 7 folder. Close the workbook.

2. Copy a file using the Open dialog box by following these steps:
   a. Open the Open dialog box.
   b. Open the Views drop-down list 🔲 and choose List, if necessary.
   c. Click the icon for the file *[your initials]***7-cogs.xls** to select it and press Ctrl + C.
   d. Press Ctrl + V to paste a copy of the file into the same drive or folder.

3. Rename a file using the Open dialog box by following these steps:
   a. Right-click the file **Copy of *[your initials]***7-cogs.xls** to open the shortcut menu.
   b. Choose Rename, key *[your initials]***7-12.xls**, and press Enter.

4. Copy this file, *[your initials]***7-12.xls**, into its current folder (see steps 1c and 1d).

5. Print the copy of your file using the Open dialog box by following these steps:
   a. Click the file **Copy of *[your initials]***7-12.xls** to select it, if necessary.
   b. Choose Print from the Tools drop-down list.

6. Delete the copy of your file by following these steps:
   a. Open the Open dialog box and click the file **Copy of *[your initials]***7-12.xls** to select it.
   b. Press Delete. A dialog box appears asking if you're sure you want to delete the file.
   c. Click Yes.
   d. Perform these steps again to delete the file *[your initials]***7-cogs.xls**.
   e. Close the Open dialog box.

● Exercise 7-12:
Objective 5
Required Files: COGS.xls
Solution Files: gl7-12.xls in Solutions Manual or on
Solutions Disk.

ASSESS

Assessment Resources:
• Solutions Manual
• Test Bank
• Portfolio Builder
• Internet Projects
• Alternative Assessment Guide
• Certification Procedures

For Internet projects, go to
www.glencoe.com/webprojects

Lesson Applications

EXERCISE 7-13

Find and open a file, find and replace data, and spell-check a worksheet.

Correct and complete Beautiful Belle's cost of goods sold worksheet for the second quarter.

1. Find and open **COGS2.xls**.

2. Key the values for fragrances as shown in Figure 7-11.

FIGURE 7-11

	A	B	C	D
15	Pacifica	6652	1665	9816
16	Taos	6654	4455	224
17	High Sierra	6698	4334	7358
18	Carmel	211	3669	10322
19	Santa Barbara	3983	1112	4983

3. Use AutoSum and AutoFill to enter formulas that calculate monthly and product subtotals for the new data.

4. Replace the month labels "Jan," "Feb," and "Mar" with **Apr**, **May**, and **Jun**, respectively.

5. Spell-check the entire worksheet, correcting any misspellings.

6. Add the standard header with your name, filename, and date, and center the worksheet horizontally on the page.

7. Save the workbook as *[your initials]***7-13.xls** in your Lesson 7 folder and print the worksheet.

8. Create a formula printout in landscape orientation with grids and row and column headings.

9. Close the workbook without saving it.

Lesson Applications:
Provide independent practice for students and may be used for assessment. Objectives are indicated for each Exercise.

◉ **Exercise 7-13:**
Objectives 1, 3, 4
Required Files: COGS2.xls
Solution Files: gl7-13.xls in Solutions Manual or on Solutions Disk.

 Because one objective of this Exercise is to find and open a file, you might want to "hide" the file in a folder that is different from the folder where other student template files are located.

EXERCISE 7-14

Find and open a file, use AutoCorrect to convert abbreviations into words, and use the Open dialog box to rename and print a file.

   Create a worksheet showing the sales history for the Carmel product line.

1. Find and open the file **Carmel.xls**.

2. Use AutoCorrect to convert the following abbreviations into complete words:

Abbreviation	Complete word
Qtr	**Quarter**
Tot	**Total**

3. Key the data as shown in Figure 7-12. Bold and center-align the column labels.

FIGURE 7-12

	A	B	C	D	E	F
5		Qtr 1	Qtr 2	Qtr 3	Qtr 4	Tot
6	1997	26544	25799	30124	35666	
7	1998	30118	69765	45625	50217	
8	1999	54339	26001	35612	58378	

4. Enter formulas to find the annual and quarterly totals.

5. Format the values in Comma style with no decimal places.

6. Spell-check the worksheet.

7. Delete the AutoCorrect entries you made in this exercise (Qtr and Tot).

8. Add the standard header with your name, filename, and date, and center the worksheet horizontally on the page.

9. Save the workbook as *[your initials]*7-sales.xls in your Lesson 7 folder and close it.

10. Use the Open dialog box to rename the file *[your initials]*7-sales.xls as *[your initials]*7-14.xls.

11. Print the worksheet from the Open dialog box.

● **Exercise 7-14:**
Objectives 2, 3, 5
Required Files: Carmel.xls
Solution Files: gl7-14.xls in Solutions Manual or on Solutions Disk.

 Because one objective of this Exercise is to find and open a file, you might want to "hide" the file in a folder that is different from the folder where other student template files are located.

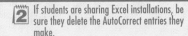 If students are sharing Excel installations, be sure they delete the AutoCorrect entries they make.

EXERCISE 7-15

Find and open a file, find and replace data, spell-check a worksheet, and print a workbook from the Open dialog box.

The Beautiful Belle Company's product sales analysis should be for the year 1999, not 1998. In addition, the company president wants to change the terms "Men" and "Women" in the worksheet to "Males" and "Females."

1. Find and open the file **Compare2.xls**.

2. Replace the column label **Men** with **Males**.

3. Replace the column label **Women** with **Females**.

4. Replace all occurrences of **1998** with **1999** (including the weekly dates where the year is not displayed).

5. Spell-check the worksheet.

6. Check the dates in cell A23 to verify the change in year.

7. Add the standard header with your name, filename, and date.

8. Save the workbook as *[your initials]***7-15.xls** in your Lesson 7 folder and close it.

9. Print the worksheet from the Open dialog box.

10. Open the file *[your initials]***7-15.xls** and save it as *[your initials]***7-15.htm**.

11. Close the workbook.

EXERCISE 7-16   *Challenge Yourself*

Find and open a file, replace labels, spell-check a worksheet, and use the Open dialog box to rename and print a worksheet.

In this exercise, you create a six-month sales comparison for Sun Soft sales based on men and women. Unfortunately, you key in an incorrect six-month period and several spelling errors. So you enter the correct six-month period and correct your spelling errors. In addition, you use the Open dialog box to copy, rename, and print the worksheet.

1. Sketch on paper a worksheet for a six-month sales comparison for Sun Soft sales based on men and women. Create a title, column labels for comparison, and monthly row labels with the months Jun., Jul., Aug., Sept., Oct., and Nov. Include a place for totals for the months and for gender.

◉ Exercise 7-15:
Objectives 1, 3, 4
Required Files: Compare2.xls
Solution Files: gl7-15.xls and
gl7-15.htm in Solutions Manual or on
Solutions Disk.

 Because one objective of this Exercise is to find and open a file, you might want to "hide" the file in a folder that is different from the folder where other student template files are located.

The completed document for this Exercise may be used in a student's portfolio.

Exercise 7-16:
Objectives 1, 3, 4
Required Files: None
Solution Files: gl7-16.xls in Solutions
Manual or on Solutions Disk.

2. Transfer your sketch to Excel and format the title and labels accordingly.

3. Insert the data in Figure 7-13 and format the numbers in Comma style, no decimals. Correct the row labels as shown.

FIGURE 7-13

	Women	Men
Jul. ~~Jun~~	2500	4200
Aug. ~~Jul~~	5000	4000
Sep. ~~Aug~~	6500	2000
Oct. ~~Aug~~	5500	2000
Nov. ~~Sept~~	6000	2800
Dec. ~~Nov~~	5600	4000

4. Create formulas that calculate month totals and gender totals.

5. Key **Results indcate that theer is moer brand loyelty among wemen than men** two rows below the last row of data. (You correct the misspellings in the next step.)

6. Spell-check the worksheet. Make the necessary corrections.

7. Create the standard header with your name, filename, and date, and center the worksheet horizontally.

8. Rename Sheet1 **Compare** and rename Sheet 2 **User Information**.

9. In the User Information worksheet, create documentation, which includes the following:

    File Information (With the following subheads: **Created by**, **Date created**, **Date revised**, **Revised by**, **Contact for help**)

    Purpose/Description of Worksheet *[Use a paragraph form]*

    Instructions to User *[Add special instructions needed by the user to enter data correctly]*

10. Style the documentation for easy reading and spell-check your work.

11. Add the standard header to the documentation worksheet and print it. Make the Compare worksheet active.

12. Save the workbook as *[your initials]***7-compare** in your Lesson 7 folder and close it.

13. Use the Open dialog box to rename the file *[your initials]***7-16.xls**.

14. Print the worksheet *[your initials]***7-16.xls** from the Open dialog box.

15. Open the file again and create a formula printout with grids and row and column headings.

16. Close the workbook without saving it.

 NOTE: When you turn on formulas for printing the data you keyed, the results of the comparison get cut off as well as the title, which has been standard up to this point.

Go ▾
For Internet projects, go to www.glencoe.com/webprojects

Unit 2 Applications

UNIT APPLICATION 2-1

Sketch a worksheet. Enter labels in a new Excel worksheet, create and enter formulas, center and print the worksheet. Display formulas and create a custom header. Print in landscape orientation showing column and row labels with gridlines.

The Beautiful Belle Company wants to construct a worksheet that calculates the difference between first quarter monthly sales for men and women for two of its products: Pacifica and Taos. The worksheet should also calculate the difference in total sales.

1. Sketch the worksheet giving it a title (**Pacifica vs. Taos Sales**), column labels (**Pacifica**, **Taos**, and **Difference**), and row labels (see Figure U2-1). Use F for formulas, but note that differences should only be figured in the two subtotal rows and the total row.
2. Open a new workbook.
3. Key the title and labels into the worksheet. Format the labels using bold or italic and center-alignment where necessary.
4. Key the data as shown in Figure U2-1 in appropriate rows and columns.

FIGURE U2-1

		Pacifica	Taos	Difference
Men	January	7,985	16,544	
	February	2,697	9,800	
	March	10,655	9,402	
	Subtotal			
Women	January	9,557	20,550	
	February	10,665	14,675	
	March	9,418	16,550	
	Subtotal			
Total	January			
	February			
	March			
	Total			

ASSESS

Assessment Resources:
- Solutions Manual
- Test Bank
- Portfolio Builder
- Alternative Assessment Guide
- Certification Procedures
- Projects Manual
- Mid-Term and Final Exams

Unit Applications: Provide independent practice of the skills acquired from each lesson in the Unit.

Project: You can now assign Project 2 from the Projects Manual.

Exam: You can now assign Exam 2 from the Mid-Term and Finals booklet.

Unit Application 2-1: Required Files: None. Solution Files: glu2-1.xls in Solutions Manual or on Solutions Disk

5. Create formulas that calculate the men's subtotal for "Pacifica" and "Taos." Calculate the subtotal difference for the two products in this section.

6. Create formulas that calculate the women's subtotal for "Pacifica" and "Taos." Calculate the subtotal difference for the two products in this section.

7. Create formulas that calculate the totals for January, February, and March. Calculate the total subtotal difference for the two products in this section.

8. Format all values in Comma style, no decimals.

9. Preview the worksheet.

10. Add a standard header including your name, filename, and date. Center the page horizontally.

11. Delete the blank worksheets.

12. Save the workbook as *[your initials]***u2-1.xls** in a new folder for Unit 2.

13. Print the worksheet.

14. Create a formula printout with grids, row and column headings, and a landscape orientation.

15. Close the workbook without saving it. Submit the worksheet sketch, the normal worksheet, and the formula printout.

UNIT APPLICATION 2-2

Copy using drag and drop, the toolbar, the Fill command, AutoFill, and keyboard shortcuts. Freeze column titles and insert data. Create a custom header. Open and dock the Auditing toolbar and trace precedents for a cell.

Complete a worksheet that compares Pacifica and Taos product sales in the second quarter for two consecutive years.

1. Open the file **PacTaos.xls**.

2. Copy cells B8 through B20 to cells G8 through G20 using the drag-and-drop method.

3. Key the 1999 product data as shown in Figure U2-2 (on the next page).

4. Freeze column titles.

5. Copy the formula in cell E8 to cell J8 using the Copy button and the Paste button.

6. Using the Fill command, copy the formula to cells J9 through J11.

7. Use the drag-and-drop method to copy the formulas in cells J8 through J11 to cells J13 through J16.

Worksheet layouts may vary as students follow the instructions to create worksheet sketches and worksheets.

● Unit Application 2-2:
Required Files: PacTaos.xls
Solution Files: glu2-2.xls in Solutions Manual or on Solutions Disk

This worksheet design is not practical for business use; however, for teaching purposes we have included a blank column and duplicated row labels.

FIGURE U2-2

	G	H	I
		Pacifica	Taos
8	April	11,600	10,650
9	May	13,500	8,401
10	June	14,877	11,650
13	April	15,400	19,680
14	May	19,102	12,120
15	June	21,241	15,611

8. Create a formula that subtotals men's 1999 "Pacifica" sales.

9. Copy the formula in cell H11 to cell I11 using AutoFill.

10. Copy both of these formulas to subtotal women's sales using the Copy and Paste commands.

11. Using drag and drop, copy the formulas for calculating the monthly totals for April 1998 to April 1999.

12. Select cells H18 through H20 and calculate the totals for the remaining months using Fill, Down.

13. Select cells H18:I20 and Fill, Right.

14. Create a grand total for 1999 "Pacifica" sales for the second quarter and copy it to cell I22 using AutoFill.

15. Copy the difference formula from cell J16 to J18 and then to J19, J20, and J22 in the "Second-Quarter Total" row using the Copy button 📋 and the Paste button 📋.

16. Add a standard header including your name, filename, and date.

17. Save the workbook as *[your initials]*u2-2.xls in your Unit 2 folder.

18. Activate the Auditing toolbar and dock it. Trace the precedents for cell D22.

19. Undock the Auditing toolbar and close it.

20. Print the worksheet, including the tracing arrow.

21. Create a formula printout in landscape orientation with gridlines, row and column headings, and a Page 1 of ? footer. (The tracing arrow is still present.)

22. Close the workbook without saving it.

23. Reopen the workbook and save it as *[your initials]*u2-2.htm, then close the workbook.

UNIT APPLICATION 2-3

Use AutoSum and AutoFill. Create range names and build formulas using names. Sort data by salesperson's last name. Rename worksheet tabs. Create documentation, spell-check, navigate the worksheet using names, create custom headers, and print formulas.

Create a worksheet that calculates commissions for Beautiful Belle's Southwest region and summarizes yearly sales, commissions, and net sales—that is, gross sales minus commissions.

1. Open the file **SW.xls**.

2. In cell C15, use the AutoSum button to add the column.

3. Use AutoFill to copy the SUM formula to cells D15 through J15.

4. Create the name **rt** for the constant **.07** to calculate quarterly commissions due.

5. Create formulas using the constant name in cells D5, F5, H5, and J5 to calculate the commission due for each quarter. To complete the columns, copy the formula using AutoFill.

6. Create the names **sq1**, **sq2**, **sq3**, and **sq4** for the total sales for each quarter.

7. Create a formula in cell B17 that calculates the total sales for the year. Use names in the formula.

8. Create the names **com1**, **com2**, **com3**, and **com4** for the total commissions for each quarter.

9. Use the commission range names to create a formula in cell B18 that calculates the total commissions for the year.

10. Create a formula in cell B19 that calculates the annual net sales—that is, gross sales minus commissions—for the Southwest territory.

11. Select the range A5:J14. Sort data by last name, ascending.

12. Rename the Sheet1 tab **Commission**.

13. Rename the Sheet2 tab **User Information**.

14. Key the data from Figure U2-3 into the User Information sheet. Place the data in the worksheet so it is easy to read. Include formatting that might make it easy to read.

○ **Unit Application 2-3:**

Required Files: SW.xls
Solution Files: glu2-3.xls in Solutions Manual or on Solutions Disk

The completed document for this application can be used in a student's portfolio.

FIGURE U2-3

```
User Information

Created by:          Your name

Date created:        Current date

Date revised:

Revised by:

Purpose              Calculate commission for SW territory based on
                     sales by quarter.

User Instructions    1. Note the range and constant names below.
                     2. The constant name rt is used for the commission
                     rate of .07.
```

15. After the last line of text from Figure U2-3, skip a row and paste all the names you created into the worksheet.

16. Spell-check the User Information worksheet.

17. In the Commission worksheet, use the Go To command to locate the cell named "sq4."

18. Add the standard header including your name, filename, and date to both worksheets.

19. Save the workbook as *[your initials]***u2-3.xls** in your Unit 2 folder.

20. Print the entire workbook.

21. Create a formula printout in landscape orientation of the Commissions worksheet. Use gridlines, row and column headings, and a Page 1 of ? footer. Do not fit this on one page. (*Hint:* Change the Adjust To under Scaling in the Page Setup dialog box to 100%.)

22. Close the workbook without saving it.

UNIT APPLICATION 2-4

Find and open a file. Replace labels, spell-check, and train AutoCorrect to recognize typos. Use AutoSum and AutoFill to enter formulas. Create a custom header and change print settings. Use the Open dialog box to copy a file and print a worksheet.

  Find and adapt a workbook to total fourth quarter cream and fragrance sales for Beautiful Belle.

1. Open the file **Prdcts.xls**.

Unit Application 2-4:
Required Files: Prdcts.xls
Solution Files: glu2-4.xls in Solutions Manual or on Solutions Disk

The completed document for this application can be used in a student's portfolio.

2. Spell-check the worksheet.

3. Train AutoCorrect to recognize the misspelled word **Otcober**

4. Edit "July" with **Otcober** in both cells where July appears.

5. Delete the AutoCorrect entry.

6. Use the Replace command to replace all occurrences of "August" and "September" with **November** and **December**, respectively.

7. Use AutoSum and AutoFill to enter formulas for the "Totals" rows and columns.

8. Replace "Third Quarter" with **Fourth Quarter**.

9. Add the standard header including your name, filename, and date.

10. Save the workbook as *[your initials]*u2-4.xls in your Unit 2 folder.

11. Create a formula printout with grids and row and column headings in landscape orientation. Fit the printout to one page using the Fit To option under Scaling in the Page Setup dialog box.

12. Close the workbook without saving it.

13. Use the Open dialog box to create a copy of *[your initials]*u2-4.xls in your Unit 2 folder.

14. Print the worksheet from the Open dialog box.

15. Delete the copy of your file.

UNIT APPLICATION 2-5

Design a worksheet. Check spelling. Copy and paste data and formulas. Create range names and create formulas using range names. Use AutoSum and AutoFill. Find and replace data. Create documentation and paste range names into a worksheet. Create custom headers, change print settings, and use the Open dialog box to copy and print a worksheet.

 Imagine you are a product manager for the Beautiful Belle Company charged with projecting revenue for three new lines of shampoo being launched in the third quarter of the current year. You need to create an initial worksheet design for the third quarter and enter data. After you transfer the design to Excel, your boss needs to add information to the worksheet for fourth quarter projections; this information is not included in your initial design.

1. Sketch a worksheet that contains:

- An appropriate title
- A single-entry area "Quarter:" (remember, this is a label below the worksheet title and above the row headings, usually with a blank row above and below it)
- Column labels for three types of shampoo

Unit Application 2-5:
Required Files: None
Solution: Sample file glu2-5.xls in Solutions Manual or on Solutions Disk

 The completed document for this application can be used in a student's portfolio.

- Row labels for the third quarter (abbreviate these)
- A column and a row for product and month totals (Use F for formulas.)

2. Transfer the title and labels to Excel, formatting them as necessary. Key **Third** in the cell to the right of "Quarter:" in the single-entry area and enter the data in Figure U2-4.

FIGURE U2-4

```
              Jaz       Britely  Frezia   Total
    Jul       5800      6800     6000
    Aug       3200      7200     4500
    Sept      2800      8400     3800
    Total
```

3. Spell-check the worksheet and make necessary corrections.
4. Use AutoSum and AutoFill to create formulas that calculate the monthly totals.
5. Use AutoSum and AutoFill to create formulas that calculate the product line totals for the third quarter.
6. Create a formula that calculates the total projected sales for the three new products in the third quarter.
7. Format all numbers in Comma style, no decimals.
8. Copy the range that contains labels and data including the single-entry item and paste it into the worksheet beneath the third-quarter data.
9. In the pasted text, replace "Third" with **Fourth** and replace "Jul," "Aug," and "Sept," with **Oct**, **Nov**, and **Dec**, respectively.
10. Create the name **rt** for the constant **1.1** that you will use to calculate projected sales growth for the fourth quarter.
11. Create an appropriate range name for the first product value for "Jul."
12. Create an appropriate range name for the first product value for "Aug."
13. Create an appropriate range name for the first product value for "Sept."
14. Create formulas that use the range names for the first product in the third quarter and the constant name **rt** to calculate projected sales growth for the fourth quarter.
15. Create similar range names and formulas for the other two products.
16. Rename the worksheet tab **Projections** and name the Sheet2 tab **User Information**. Delete Sheet3.
17. Create user documentation on the User Information sheet and include a pasted list of named ranges.

18. Add the standard header with your name, filename, and date to both worksheets. Horizontally center the Projections worksheet on the page.

19. Save the workbook *[your initials]*u2-5.xls in your Unit 2 folder. Print the User Information worksheet only.

20. In the Projections sheet trace the dependents to the first shampoo sales projection for October.

21. Create a formula printout in landscape orientation with grids and row and column headings.

22. Turn off the formula display and close the Auditing toolbar.

23. Use Page Setup to change the print settings to print in portrait orientation without gridlines and row and column headings.

24. Save and close the workbook.

25. Use the Open dialog box to create a copy of the file.

26. Print the file **Copy of *[your initials]*u2-5.xls** from the Open dialog box.

27. Delete the file **Copy of *[your initials]*u2-5.xls**.

28. Submit the worksheet sketch, the normal worksheet, and the formula printout.

UNIT APPLICATION 2-6 *Making It Work for You*

Design a worksheet. Create formulas and copy and paste. Check spelling. Create custom headers and documentation. Print worksheet and formulas.

You have been hired for your first job and you have opened a checking account to deposit your weekly paycheck and maintain a record of your expenses. Create a worksheet that you will use to double-check the current balance in your checking account. Your worksheet should have, but is not limited to, columns for the date of your checking transaction, check number, payee, description, deposit amount, check amount, and current balance. Be sure to title the worksheet.

Create a preliminary sketch before you key the information. Next, build your formulas and supply a minimum of 10 checking transactions in addition to an opening balance. Typical checking transactions would be a paycheck deposit and checks issued for rent, utilities, food, and other living expenses. Use numbers that are easy to calculate. Format numbers in Comma style, two decimals. Create User Information. Add the standard headers to both worksheets and delete Sheet3. Center the check register horizontally on the page. Save the workbook as *[your initials]*u2-6.xls in your Unit 2 folder. Create a formula printout with grids and row and column headings in landscape orientation. Use a Page 1 of ? footer, if needed. Close the worksheet without saving it.

1 Student answers will vary as to product names and exact User Information sheets. Range names will also vary. Calculations may vary if students use a constant other than the suggested "1.1."

Unit Application 2-6:
Required Files: None
Solution: Sample file glu2-6.xls in Solutions Manual or on Solutions Disk

 The completed document for this application can be used in a student's portfolio.

2 Worksheet layouts may vary as students follow the instructions to create worksheet sketches and worksheets.

Changing the Appearance of a Worksheet

Short-Camper Gear Stands Tall in Sales

Clearey & Clayton produces camping gear for backpacking, boating, skiing, and other wilderness activities. The business got its start when Bettina Clearey, a former fashion designer, sewed her own backpack to accommodate her petite 5-foot frame. She soon found there was a huge demand for scaled-down camping equipment. John Clayton, an advertising executive, became her partner and Clearey & Clayton was formed.

Clearey & Clayton's products were so well designed that it wasn't long before the company become one of the largest suppliers of camping gear in the country. Their best-selling products are their backpacks, sunglasses, camping chairs, kayaks, duffel bags, and mountaineering tents.

To increase their market share, Clearey & Clayton need to create the following worksheets to use as promotional material.

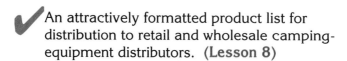

An attractively formatted product list for distribution to retail and wholesale camping-equipment distributors. **(Lesson 8)**

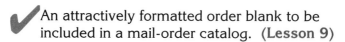

An attractively formatted order blank to be included in a mail-order catalog. **(Lesson 9)**

Formatting Text and Numbers

OBJECTIVES

After completing this lesson, you will be able to:

1. Format numbers.
2. Suppress the display of zero values.
3. Work with stored numbers.
4. Align text.
5. Change column width and row height.
6. Hide columns and rows.

 Estimated Time: 1¼ hours

MOUS
ACTIVITIES

In this lesson:

XL2000 **3.2**
XL2000 **3.3**
XL2000 **3.4**
XL2000 **3.5**
XL2000 **3.6**
XL2000 **3.9**
XL2000 **3.10**
XL2000 **5.2**

See Appendix F.

You can change the appearance of a worksheet by formatting numbers and text in different ways. Number formats include commas, dollar signs, and decimal places. Text formats include alignment in a cell, alignment over a group of cells, and text wrap within a cell. You can also change column width and row height.

☑ **Objective 1**

Formatting Numbers

The default *format*—that is, the attributes of text or numbers, such as font style, underlining, bold, number of decimal places, and alignment—is called the Normal style. For numbers, the General format code is used. With this format, numbers are right-aligned; decimals, commas, and dollar signs are not displayed unless keyed; and the font is 10-point Arial.

P
R
E
P
A
R
E

Point out to students that the learning objectives show what they will learn in the lesson. Each heading in the lesson correlates to a learning objective.

Required files:

TWOut.xls

T
E
A
C
H

Teaching Resources:
• Excel Classroom Presentations
• School-to-Work Strategies Manual
• Spanish Glossary
• Certification Procedures

☑ **Objective 1 Assignment:**
Exercise 8-15 (Skills Review) can be assigned after completing Objective 1.

NOTE: The default format for text in the Normal style is left-aligned, 10-point Arial.

In Lesson 3, you used the Formatting toolbar to perform basic number formatting. In this lesson, you use the Format Cells dialog box, choosing from additional standard formats, as well as creating custom formats. You can apply number formats to entire columns, rows, worksheets, or individual cells.

EXERCISE **8-1** **Choose a Number Format**

1. Open the file **TWOut.xls**.
2. Select cells D8 through E10 and cells D13 through E14. (*Hint:* Press Ctrl to select the second set of cells.)
3. Choose Cells from the Format menu.
4. In the Format Cells dialog box, click the Number tab, if necessary. The Number options appear.
5. Choose Currency from the Category list box.

⭐ **TIP:** The Currency format is used for general monetary values. The Accounting format aligns currency symbols and decimal points in a column.

6. Choose the third format code ($1,234.10) in the Negative numbers list box. Notice that the default Symbol is the $. With this option, a dollar sign appears beside each number in the selected cells.

  NOTE: The options in the Negative numbers list box indicate how Excel handles negative numbers. For example, if you are "in the red" and want to show a loss in 1999, Quarter 4, the second or last options in red are good choices. If you don't have a color printer and plan to print the worksheet, avoid the red options.

7. Key 0 in the Decimal places box to have numbers appear without decimal places. (See Figure 8-1 on the next page.)
8. Click OK. The numbers in cells E13 and E14 now contain commas that separate thousands from hundreds, and all selected cells have dollar signs next to the values.

📝 Spend time differentiating these two formats. You can also discuss when students should use currency symbols in a column (at the top and the total).

FIGURE 8-1
Number options in
the Format Cells
dialog box

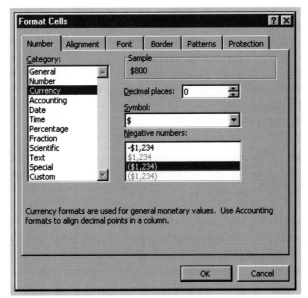

EXERCISE 8-2 Create a Custom Format

You can create custom format codes to meet special needs. For example, you can insert dashes within Social Security numbers or parentheses and dashes to indicate area codes and phone numbers. You can include text in a code by surrounding it with quotation marks. You can even hide numbers so they are used in calculations but do not appear in the worksheet cells.

TABLE 8-1 Examples of Custom Format Codes

FORMAT CODE	NUMBER	DISPLAY
000-00-0000	123456789	123-45-6789
(000) 000-0000	2035551234	(203) 555-1234
"Purchase No." 0000	1234	Purchase No. 1234
#.##	0.7	.7
#.##	5211.129	5211.13
#.0#	15	15.0
#.0#	1234.568	1234.57

continues

 Use Excel Classroom Presentation 8 to display screens from the lesson in a slide-show format.

Table 8-1 can be difficult for some students to understand. Make sure you discuss the Note following the table in class. Explain that the ;; (two semicolon) format is used to suppress the display of a value in the selected cell. Note that the value still appears in the Formula Bar.

TABLE 8-1

Examples of Custom Format Codes *continued*

FORMAT CODE	NUMBER	DISPLAY
0.0%	.7889	78.9%
00000	06477 (ZIP code)	06477
#,##0;#,##0-	-1234	1,234-
#.#0	18.1	18.10
;;	1234	No value displayed

NOTE: A # symbol in a format code represents a single digit, a zero represents leading or trailing zeros that fall immediately before or after the decimal position, and a semicolon separates format codes for positive and negative numbers. The ;; format suppresses the display of a number in a cell, but the value still appears in the Formula Bar.

In this Exercise, you insert dashes and create item numbers.

1. Select cells B8 through B10 and cells B13 through B14.

2. With the white cross over one of the highlighted cells, click the right mouse button and choose <u>F</u>ormat Cells from the shortcut menu. The Format Cells dialog box appears.

FIGURE 8-2
Shortcut menu with
Format Cells
highlighted

TIP: You can also press Ctrl + 1 to open the Format Cells dialog box.

3. Click the Number tab, if necessary, and choose Custom from the <u>C</u>ategory list box.

4. Choose the format code 0.00 from the <u>T</u>ype list box. The format code 0.00 appears in the <u>T</u>ype text box.

5. Position the insertion point in the <u>T</u>ype text box and delete the period from the code. After the three zeros, key **0-000**. The new code should read 0000-000.

6. Click OK. Dashes appear in cells B8 through B10 along with the numbers.

7. Key the following data in cells B13 and B14:

5217988

5218088

Notice that the new format now applies to these numbers.

When students select cells to be formatted and want to use the shortcut menu to get to the Format Cells dialog box, they must make sure the white cross appears in one of the selected cells before clicking the right mouse button.

In Excel Classroom Presentation 8.

In step 4, encourage students to browse through the different number formats available in the Format Cells dialog box. Students may find them useful. For instance, although students create custom formats for Social Security numbers and phone numbers in some of the Exercises, these options are available under Special in the Category list.

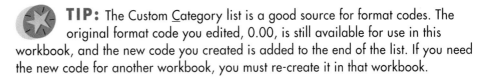

TIP: The Custom Category list is a good source for format codes. The original format code you edited, 0.00, is still available for use in this workbook, and the new code you created is added to the end of the list. If you need the new code for another workbook, you must re-create it in that workbook.

Objective 2

Suppressing the Display of Zero Values

When a large worksheet contains many zero entries, it can be hard to read. You can suppress the zero values in the worksheet to make it more readable.

EXERCISE **8-3** **Suppress the Display of Zero Values**

---

1. Scroll down to rows 17 through 19. Notice the zero values in columns D and E.
2. To hide these zeros, choose Options from the Tools menu.
3. In the Options dialog box, click the View tab, if necessary. The View options appear.
4. Click the Zero Values check box to clear it.

FIGURE 8-3
View options
in the Options
dialog box

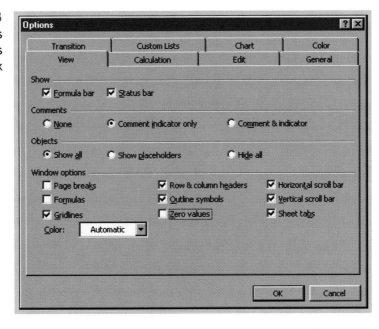

5. Click OK. The zeros in cells D17 through E19 disappear.

NOTE: The Zero values setting works for only the active worksheet—not the entire workbook. You can restore the zeros by clicking the Zero Values check box a second time.

 In Excel Classroom Presentation 8.

Working with Stored Numbers

✓**Objective 3**

When you key a number, Excel rounds it according to the cell's format. For instance, if you key **30** and the cell is formatted for two decimal places, Excel displays 30.00. Similarly, if the cell is formatted for no decimal places and you key **9.9**, Excel displays 10. Excel stores the number that you key (9.9) internally and uses that number in calculations. This characteristic is called *Full Precision*.

Sometimes, if you change numbers in a worksheet column after the column is totaled, and Excel rounds the new numbers up or down, the total may appear to be incorrectly calculated. To avoid this, you can store numbers as the rounded values that appear onscreen (10). This option is called *Precision as Displayed*.

EXERCISE | **8-4** | **Calculate Using the Precision as Displayed Option**

1. Key the following data to replace the numbers in cells D13 and D14:
   1000.45   2000.35
   Notice that the total for column D now appears to be incorrect (although, of course, it is actually correct to an undesired level of precision). The numbers stored internally in full precision are used in the arithmetic rather than the displayed numbers.

2. Choose Options from the Tools menu.

3. In the Options dialog box, click the Calculation tab.

FIGURE 8-4
Calculation options
in the Options
dialog box

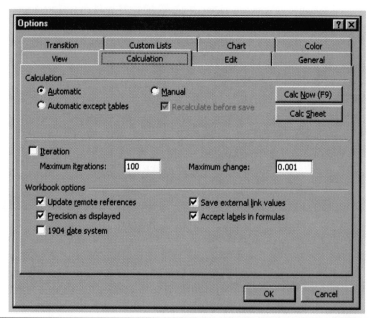

✓**Objective 3 Assignment:**
Exercise 8-16 (Skills Review) can be assigned after completing Objective 3.

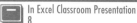 Discuss how numbers stored in Full Precision could cause confusion in a worksheet. Discuss the difference between what is displayed on the screen and what is actually stored in the cell.

The functions ROUND and INT can also be used to control precision, which allow more flexibility since values can be restored to their original precision. This topic is discussed in Lesson 10: "Using Functions."

In Excel Classroom Presentation 8.

4. Click the Precision as Displayed check box to turn on this option and click OK.

5. Click OK at the prompt that says data will permanently lose accuracy. The sum in Column D now appears to be correct.

NOTE: Once you calculate with the Precision as Displayed option, you cannot restore values to full precision. In addition, this choice affects the entire workbook, not just the worksheet in which you change the setting.

Objective 4
Aligning Text

You can change the Normal style for text alignment (left-aligned) several ways. You can realign text within a cell or across cells. You can also rotate text or wrap it on several lines in a cell.

EXERCISE **8-5** **Align Text in a Cell**

You use the Alignment command to align text to the left, right, or center of a cell. You can also align text vertically with the top, bottom, or center of the cell. In addition, wrapped text can be justified to fill the entire width of a cell, with even margins appearing on each side of the cell contents.

1. Select cells A4 through E4 and cells A7 and A12.

2. To center the text horizontally in these cells, click the Center button ▤ on the Formatting toolbar.

3. Select cells A8 through A10 and cells A13 through A14.

4. Click the Align Right button ▤ on the Formatting toolbar. All the text is now horizontally right-aligned.

5. Next, you center the text vertically. Select cells A4 through E4.

6. Press Ctrl + 1 to open the Format Cells dialog box.

7. Click the Alignment tab, if necessary. The Alignment options appear. (See Figure 8-5 on the next page.)

8. Choose Center from the Vertical drop-down list. (Center under Horizontal is already selected because you applied this formatting in step 2 using the Center button ▤.)

9. Click OK. Although you cannot see it on the screen, the text is centered vertically in the cells. (You see the effects of this alignment in a later Exercise.)

Stress that if students don't know how a value will be used in a worksheet, it is best to have the value at Full Precision. Point out that you could always make a copy of the worksheet and change the values in the copy to Precision as Displayed. This way you can recover the value at Full Precision.

FIGURE 8-5
Alignment options
in the Format Cells
dialog box

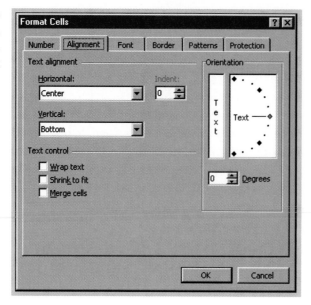

 TIP: Both text and numbers can also be left-aligned. In addition, you can align titles over lists of data to make reading easier. If a list is left-, right-, or center-aligned, the title should have the same alignment as the list. If a list is extremely wide and left- or right-aligned, the title can be centered.

EXERCISE 8-6 Center Text Over a Range of Columns

If you want to center the title of a worksheet over all its columns or center other text over a range of columns, you can use one of two methods. You can use the Merge and Center button ▦ on the Formatting toolbar to merge a selected range of cells and center a title within the merged cell. You can also center a title across a range of cells, without merging the cells, using the Alignment tab in the Format Cells dialog box.

1. Position the mouse pointer in cell A1 and key **Clearey & Clayton** and make it bold.

NOTE: Always enter the title in the column farthest to the left of the range of columns over which you want to center it.

2. Select cells A1 through E1.

3. Press Ctrl+1 to open the Format Cells dialog box.

In Excel Classroom Presentation 8.

You may want to tell students to follow the worksheet design suggestions in the Tip for all the worksheets they prepare in class. This suggestion also could be added to a "Worksheet Design Guide" generated as the class proceeds.

4. Click the Alignment tab, if necessary.

5. Choose Center Across Selection from the Horizontal drop-down list.

6. Click OK. The text in A1 is centered across cells A1 through E1. If the screen gridlines are turned on, they do not display between the columns that contain the centered title. If you click the pointer across the row, notice that there are still separate cells within this range.

7. Now, you'll merge selected cells into a single cell. To begin, in cell A2, key **Product List** and make it bold.

8. Select cells A2 through E2. These selected cells include the range of cells in which you center the subtitle.

9. Click the Merge and Center button . The text becomes a subtitle for the worksheet. Again, notice that if the screen gridlines are turned on, they don't display between the columns that contain the centered title. Also notice that the cell pointer shows that the range is now a single cell.

10. To remove the formatting, click the Undo button. Notice that the individual cells in the range are redisplayed.

11. Press Ctrl+1 to open the Format Cells dialog box.

12. Choose Center Across Selection from the Horizontal drop-down list.

13. Click OK. The subtitle is now centered across A2 through E2. The cells in the range are not merged.

> **TIP:** You can also open the Alignment dialog box by choosing Format Cells from the shortcut menu after you select the text to be aligned. (Remember to position the white cross in a highlighted cell when you click the right mouse button.) You can then select Center Across Selection from the Horizontal drop-down list. You can also click the Merge cells check box to merge selected cells.

EXERCISE 8-7 Wrap Text on Several Lines Within a Cell

When you key a line of text that is too wide for a column, the text extends into the next column if it's blank. If the next column is not blank, the text that doesn't fit in the column is hidden from view. You can widen the column to view the text. If you don't want to widen the column, you can wrap the text on several lines within the cell.

1. Key the text shown in Figure 8-6 (on the next page) in cell C8. Do not press Enter at the end of each line.

Have students click on and off the merged cells so they can clearly see that the range is now a single cell. Point out that the Merge and Center button is best used in the body of the worksheet. For aligning titles across the worksheet, use Format, Cells, Alignment, and choose Center Across Section from the Horizontal drop-down list.

FIGURE 8-6

This tent is designed for spring, summer, and fall. It has a separate rain
fly and fiberglass poles. Packed size is 18" x 5.5". Weight: 4.5 lbs.

2. Press Enter. The next column hides the text.

3. To make the text wrap in the cell, select cell C8 and open the Format Cells dialog box.

4. Click the Alignment tab, if necessary.

5. Click the Wrap text check box to select it and click OK. The text wraps in the cell and the height of the other cells in the row is adjusted.

 NOTE: When you wrap text on several lines within a cell, the height of the row adjusts to accommodate the font size. If you change the font size or column width after wrapping the text, the row height does not change.

EXERCISE   8-8   **Change Indents and Rotate Text within a Cell**

 You may find you can improve the appearance of a worksheet by indenting specific text from the left edge of the cell. You may also find it useful to rotate text within a cell, so you can narrow the column containing the text.

1. Select cell C8, if necessary.

2. Click the Increase Indent button ▣ on the Formatting toolbar. The text is indented from the left edge of the cell.

3. Click the Increase Indent button ▣ once again. The text is indented even more.

4. Click the Decrease Indent button ▣ on the Formatting toolbar. The indentation is reduced. This is an appropriate amount of indentation for this text. Centering the text vertically will improve the appearance further.

 NOTE: You can also control indentation using the Format Cells dialog box. In the Alignment tab, under Text Alignment, you can enter a specific Indent value.

5. Open the Format Cells dialog box. Click the Alignment tab, if necessary.

 Discuss when text might be rotated in a worksheet. Some examples might be printing a line vertically if it applies to a number of rows and printing an identifier such as "Sold Out" or "Sale Item" in a product catalog.

6. Choose Center from the <u>V</u>ertical drop-down list and click OK. The text is now indented and vertically aligned in the cell.

7. To rotate text within a cell, select cell A7.

8. Open the Format Cells dialog box. Click the Alignment tab, if necessary.

9. Under Orientation, drag the indicator in the right window up to a 45-degree position and click OK. "Tents" rotates upward.

10. Press Ctrl+Z to undo the formatting.

EXERCISE 8-9 Create Line Breaks within a Cell

Text wraps to the next line when it reaches the end of the column. If you want it to go to the next line before this point, you must create a *line break*, or a forced movement of the cursor to the next line within the cell. Line breaks are also useful for making a wide column narrower.

1. Select cells D4 and E4.

2. Open the Format Cells dialog box using the shortcut menu.

3. Click the Alignment tab, if necessary.

4. Click the <u>W</u>rap Text check box and click OK.

5. To create a line break in cell D4, key **Wholesale**, and press Alt+Enter.

6. Key **Price** and press Enter. A line break appears after "Wholesale."

7. Repeat these steps for cell E4. In this cell, key **Suggested**, press Alt+Enter to create a line break, key **Retail Price**, and press Enter. Notice how the text in the other cells in row 4 is vertically centered (you did this in Exercise 8-5).

✍ Objective 5

Changing Column Width and Row Height

You can increase column width to display text that won't fit in the current column or to make a worksheet more readable. You can also decrease column width to make room for other columns. Additionally, you can adjust row height to create proper spacing between rows or to adjust to a new font size when working with wrapped text.

Excel provides three ways to change column width and row height:

- Using the mouse
- Using the Column Width and Row Height dialog boxes
- Using the AutoFit option to maximize the columns visible on the screen and those that print on each page

---

You reached a midway point in the lesson. You may want students to save their files if you are going to divide the lesson into two periods. Ask them to save the worksheet as *[your initials]*8-9.xls in a new folder for Lesson 8.

✍ **Objective 5 Assignment:**
Exercise 8-17 (Skills Review) can be assigned after completing Objective 5.

EXERCISE 8-10 Change Column Width and Row Height with the Mouse

1. Scroll the worksheet to display columns C and D, if necessary.

2. To increase column width, move the pointer to the divider line between column C and column D in the lettered gray area that frames the worksheet (see Figure 8-7).

3. When the pointer becomes a two-headed arrow ↔, drag until the column width increases about 0.5 inch or to approximately 17.00. (The column size displays in a ScreenTip immediately above the pointer.)

FIGURE 8-7
Changing
column width

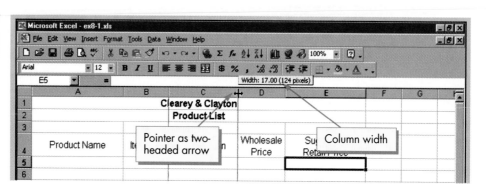

NOTE: The column-size number refers to the average number of characters of the default text font that fit in a cell. Your numbers may vary if your default text font is different from the standard.

4. Change the document view to 75%. Position the pointer along the divider line between row 8 and row 9 in the numbered gray area.

5. When the pointer becomes a two-headed arrow, drag up until the row height decreases to about 189.00.

6. Change the document view back to 100%.

7. Position the pointer along the divider line between row 4 and row 5 and with the two-headed arrow, drag down until the row height increases about 0.5 inch to 45.00.

8. To change multiple columns at the same time, click the letter C and drag to the letter E.

9. Position the pointer at the top right border of any selected column until the pointer becomes a two-headed arrow. Drag to decrease the column width about 0.5 inch. The width of all selected columns decreases by the same amount.

In Excel Classroom Presentation 8.

> **NOTE:** When a column is not sufficiently wide to accommodate the number of characters in a cell, values (numbers) are displayed with the # symbol. This does not affect the actual content of the cell. To remove the # characters, simply widen the column.

10. With the columns still selected, increase the width by the same amount, to approximately 17.00. The columns are now all the same width.

EXERCISE 8-11 Use the Column Width and Row Height Dialog Boxes

---

1. Select column B.

2. Choose <u>C</u>olumn from the F<u>o</u>rmat menu. The Column submenu appears.

FIGURE 8-8
Column submenu

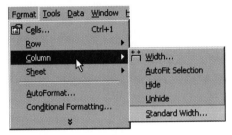

3. Choose <u>W</u>idth. The Column Width dialog box appears.

FIGURE 8-9
Column Width
dialog box

4. Key **15** in the <u>C</u>olumn Width text box and click OK or press Enter. The column width increases.

5. Select rows 7 and 12.

> **TIP:** To select nonadjacent rows or columns, press Ctrl when you select subsequent rows or columns.

6. Choose <u>R</u>ow from the F<u>o</u>rmat menu. The Row submenu appears.

7. Choose H<u>e</u>ight. The Row Height dialog box appears.

8. Key **30** in the <u>R</u>ow Height text box and click OK. The row height increases.

Point out to students that since they now know how to widen columns, they should not leave blank columns in their worksheets unless the blank column serves a design function. Discuss when blank columns are appropriate.

 In Excel Classroom Presentation 8.

EXERCISE 8-12 Use AutoFit and Shrink to Fit

The AutoFit option is a fast way to adjust the column width so the longest item fits exactly in the column. This feature helps maximize the number of columns you can see on your screen and print on a page. You can also adjust row height using the AutoFit option. If you prefer not to change the size of a row or a column, you can use the Shrink to Fit alignment option.

1. Position the pointer on the right border of column B until it turns into a two-headed arrow and double-click. The column width adjusts to fit the items in the cells.

2. To change the height of row 4 to fit the items in the cells, position the pointer on the bottom border of row 4 until the pointer turns into a two-headed arrow and double-click. The row height adjusts to fit the items in the cells.

3. To change columns C and D at the same time, select both columns.

4. Choose Column from the Format menu. The Column submenu opens.

5. Choose AutoFit Selection. The column widths of both columns are adjusted.

 NOTE: You can also double-click with the two-headed arrow positioned on the right border of column C or D to change the column widths to fit the items in the cells.

6. Delete row 6.

7. Select cell C18 and key **Model Discontinued**. The text is too large to fit in the cell. Instead of changing the column width or row height, you can use the Shrink to Fit feature.

8. With cell C18 selected, choose Cells from the Format menu and click the Alignment tab, if necessary.

9. Click the Shrink to Fit check box and click OK. The contents of C18 shrink to fit the size of the cell.

EXERCISE 8-13 Reset Column Width and Row Height

You may sometimes need to return column widths or row heights to their original settings.

1. To return column B to its standard size, select column B.

2. Choose Column from the Format menu. The Column submenu appears.

3. Choose Standard Width. The Standard Width dialog box appears and a number appears next to Standard Column Width. This value is the default standard width for all columns that are not set individually. (The standard width varies for different computers.)

4. Make note of the value in the Standard Width dialog box, and then click OK.

5. Choose Column from the Format menu and choose Width. The Column Width dialog box appears.

6. Enter the default width in the text box (the value you noted in step 4) and click OK. The column is sized down to the standard width.

7. Press Ctrl + Z to undo the column size change.

8. Select rows 6 and 11.

9. Choose Row from the Format menu. The Row submenu appears.

10. Choose Height and key **15**, the standard row height, in the Row Height dialog box. (The standard row height may vary depending on your computer. Use 15 for this Exercise.)

11. Click OK. The row height is resized.

12. Press Ctrl + Z to undo the row height size change.

☑ **Objective 6**

Hiding Columns and Rows

You can hide rows or columns temporarily so they do not print or appear on the screen. You may want to hide the salaries column when you print a payroll worksheet, for example, or you may want nonconsecutive rows to appear consecutively when you view them on your screen.

EXERCISE **8-14** **Hide Columns and Rows**

1. Select column D and choose Column from the Format menu.

2. Click Hide. Column D is hidden from view.

3. Select columns C through E, which appear on either side of the hidden column. (Select the columns by clicking and dragging so column D is included in the range.)

4. Choose Column from the Format menu and click Unhide. Column D reappears.

☑ **Objective 6 Assignment:**
Exercise 8-18 (Skills Review) and Exercises 8-19 through 8-22 (Lesson Applications) can be assigned after completing Objective 6.

📝 Discuss when it would be a good idea to hide columns and rows in a work environment. Point out that often people work on sensitive material in an open area or a cubicle. It might be a good idea to hide sensitive data from people who might be passing your desk.

5. Select row 4 and choose Row from the Format menu

6. Click Hide. The row is hidden from view.

7. Select rows 3 through 5, which are on either side of the hidden row.

8. Choose Row from the Format menu and click Unhide. The row becomes visible again.

9. Make sure gridlines are turned on for printing and add the standard header to the worksheet with your name, the filename, and the date.

10. Save the workbook as *[your initials]*8-14.xls in a new folder for Lesson 8.

11. Print the worksheet and close the workbook.

COMMAND SUMMARY

FEATURE	BUTTON	MENU	KEYBOARD
Format cells		Format, Cells	Ctrl + 1
Right-align	▤	Format, Cells	
Center	▥	Format, Cells	
Left-align	▤		
Center across columns	▦	Format, Cells, Center across selection	
Increase indent	▥	Format, Cells	
Decrease indent	▥	Format, Cells	
Hide rows		Format, Row, Hide	Ctrl + 9
Unhide rows		Format, Row, Unhide	Ctrl + Shift + (
Hide columns		Format, Columns, Hide	Ctrl + 0
Unhide columns		Format, Columns, Unhide	Ctrl + Shift +)

USING HELP

You learned how to create custom number formats. Excel can give you more information about their makeup.

Use Microsoft Excel Help to learn more about custom number formats:

1. Press F1 to activate the Office Assistant.

2. In the text box, key **custom number formatting**

---

1 Point out that the Command Summary lists a variety of ways to accomplish a particular task. Students can decide which method they prefer.

2 Encourage students to follow the steps in "Using Help." Software companies are increasingly using their Help program—rather than printed documentation—to train users and assist in answering user questions.

3. Click Search.

4. Click the topic "Create a custom number format." Review the information about creating custom number formats.

FIGURE 8-10
Help for creating custom number formats

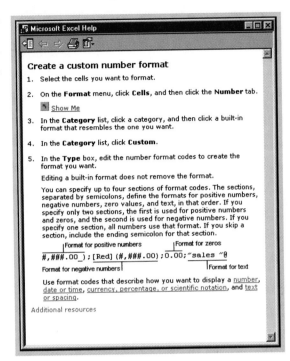

5. Close the Help window and hide the Office Assistant.

TEST BANK

Concepts Review

TRUE/FALSE QUESTIONS

Each of the following statements is either true or false. Indicate your choice by circling **T** or **F**.

T **(F)**   **1.** The default format for numbers is left-aligned, 12-point Palatino.

T **(F)**   **2.** You cannot insert dashes in custom number formats.

(T) F   **3.** A pound sign in a number format code represents an integer (a whole number).

T **(F)**   **4.** When you use the Suppress the Display of Zeros option, you can see zeros in an onscreen worksheet, but cannot print them.

T **(F)**   **5.** To center the title of a worksheet over all its columns, you use the Center button ▤.

(T) F   **6.** A forced movement of the cursor to the next line within the cell is called a line break.

(T) F   **7.** You can use the mouse to increase column width to display text that doesn't fit in the current column.

(T) F   **8.** You can hide rows or columns temporarily so they do not print or appear on the screen.

SHORT ANSWER QUESTIONS

Write the correct answer in the space provided.

1. What are the keystrokes used to open the Format Cells dialog box?

Ctrl+1

2. What do you call Excel's ability to store internally the number you key in a cell and then use this number in calculations?

Full Precision

3. Under what menu do you access the Columns submenu?

Format menu

4. If you want to align text to the right in a cell, which button do you use?

Align Right button

CLOSE

Concepts Review:
Allows students to check their understanding.

TEST BANK
Consider using the Test Bank to provide an additional review of lesson concepts. It may also be used as an assessment tool.

5. What are the keystrokes used to create a line break in a cell?

Alt+Enter

6. Which check box do you click to suppress the display of zero values?

Zero values

7. On which toolbar is the Merge and Center button located?

Formatting toolbar

8. To rotate text in a cell, which dialog box do you open?

Format Cells dialog box

CRITICAL THINKING

Answer these questions on a separate piece of paper. There are no right or wrong answers. Support your answer with examples from your own experience, if possible.

1. If you had to present your company's projected quarterly report of revenues in 2008, what row headings might you include? How might you align the various accounts in the report (using indents, etc.)?

2. You can change the column width and row height in Excel three different ways—using the mouse, with dialog boxes, or using the AutoFit option. Which approach do you prefer? Describe instances of using each option in the same worksheet.

Skills Review

EXERCISE 8-15

Format numbers.

1. Open the file **Employee.xls**.

2. Apply the first currency number format to column D by performing the following steps:

    a. Select the values in column D.

    b. Press Ctrl + 1.

    c. Click the Number tab, if necessary.

    d. Select Currency from the Category list box.

    e. Select None for Symbol.

    f. Click OK.

Critical Thinking Questions:
Answers will vary based on students' preferences, observations, experiences, and research.

Skills Review:
Provides guided practice for students. Objectives are indicated for each Exercise.

⊙ Exercise 8-15:
Objective 1
Required Files: Employee.xls
Solution Files: gl8-15.xls in Solutions Manual or on Solutions Disk.

3. Precede the numbers in column B with the abbreviation "No." (for "Number") by completing the following steps:

   a. Select the values in column B.

   b. Press `Ctrl`+`1`.

   c. Select Custom from the Category list box.

   d. Choose the 0.00 format code from the Type list box.

   e. Delete the period in the format code in the Type text box.

   f. Add three zeros to the format code. In front of the six zeros, key a quotation mark, then **No.** and a space, and another quotation mark (**"No. "**).

   g. Click OK.

4. Format the numbers in column C to appear as Social Security numbers by completing the following steps:

   a. Select the values in column C.

   b. Open the Format Cells dialog box.

   c. Select Special from the Category list box.

   d. Select Social Security Number.

   e. Click OK.

5. Delete row 2.

6. Add the standard header to the worksheet with your name, the filename, and the date.

7. Horizontally center the worksheet.

8. Save the workbook as *[your initials]***8-15.xls** in your Lesson 8 folder.

9. Print the worksheet and close the workbook.

EXERCISE 8-16

Suppress the display of zero values and work with stored numbers.

1. Open the file **Sales.xls**.

2. Suppress zeros in the worksheet by completing the following steps:

   a. Choose Options from the Tools menu.

   b. Click the View tab.

   c. Click Zero values to deselect it.

   d. Click OK.

3. Change the total in column C to reflect the correct total for the column. (It is now being calculated using full precision.) Use the Precision as Displayed option by completing the following steps:

   a. Choose Options from the Tools menu.

   b. Click the Calculation tab.

   c. Click Precision as Displayed to select it.

   d. Click OK.

   e. Click OK when the prompt appears that describes how the data will permanently lose its accuracy.

● Exercise 8-16:
Objectives 2, 3
Required Files: Sales.xls
Solution Files: gl8-16.xls in Solutions Manual or on
Solutions Disk.

4. Add the standard header to the worksheet with your name, the filename, and the date.

5. Save the workbook as *[your initials]*8-16.xls in your Lesson 8 folder.

6. Print the worksheet and close the workbook.

EXERCISE 8-17

Align text and change column width and row height.

1. Open the file **States.xls**.

2. Center "Clearey & Clayton Sales Comparison" over columns A through F by completing the following steps:

    a. Select cells A1 through F1.

    b. Click the Merge and Center button ▦.

3. Key text in cell A12 and make it wrap in the cell by completing the following steps:

    a. In cell A12, key **Please note that this is for the sale of tents only** and press ⏎Enter.

    b. Select cell A12.

    c. Press ⌃Ctrl+1 to open the Format Cells dialog box.

    d. Click the Alignment tab.

    e. Click Wrap text.

    f. Click OK.

4. Change the width of column F using the AutoFit option by following these steps:

    a. Position the mouse pointer on the divider line between columns F and G in the lettered gray area that frames the worksheet.

    b. Double-click when the two-headed arrow is displayed.

5. Change the width of column A using the mouse by completing the following steps:

    a. With the two-headed arrow, drag the right border of column A just past the "o" in "Mexico."

    b. Release the mouse button.

6. Change the height of row 12 by dragging the bottom border of the row up with the two-headed arrow to approximately 60.75.

7. Add the standard header to the worksheet with your name, the filename, and the date.

8. Horizontally center the worksheet.

9. Save the workbook as *[your initials]*8-17.xls in your Lesson 8 folder.

10. Print the worksheet and close the workbook.

⊙ Exercise 8-17:
Objectives 4, 5
Required Files: States.xls
Solution Files: gl8-17.xls in Solutions Manual or on
Solutions Disk.

EXERCISE 8-18

Hide and unhide columns and rows.

1. Open the file **Clearey.xls**.

2. Hide column C by performing the following steps:
   a. Select column C.
   b. Choose <u>C</u>olumn from the F<u>o</u>rmat menu to open the Column submenu.
   c. Choose <u>H</u>ide.

3. Hide row 5 by completing the following steps:
   a. Select row 5.
   b. Choose <u>R</u>ow from the F<u>o</u>rmat menu to open the Row submenu.
   c. Choose <u>H</u>ide.

4. Hide row 4.

5. Insert five rows after the entry "Hankle, Michele" and key the information shown in Figure 8-11 in columns A and B.

FIGURE 8-11

Jenkins, Ross	125,950
Latham, Mary	256,857
Norton, Marie	301,205
Peters, Joanne	187,500
Ravin, Mike	99,500

6. Hide rows 11 and 12.

7. Unhide rows 4 and 5 by completing the following steps:
   a. Select rows 3 through 6 using [Shift].
   b. Choose <u>R</u>ow from the F<u>o</u>rmat menu.
   c. Choose <u>U</u>nhide from the Row submenu.

8. Add the standard header to the worksheet with your name, the filename, and the date.

9. Horizontally center the worksheet on the page.

10. Save the workbook as **[your initials]8-18.xls** in your Lesson 8 folder.

11. Print the worksheet and close the workbook.

● **Exercise 8-18:**
Objective 6
Required Files: Clearey.xls
Solution Files: gl8-18.xls in Solutions Manual or on
Solutions Disk.

A S S E S S

Assessment Resources:
• Solutions Manual
• Test Bank
• Portfolio Builder
• Internet Projects
• Alternative Assessment Guide
• Certification Procedures

For Internet projects, go to
www.glencoe.com/webprojects

Lesson Applications

EXERCISE 8-19

Hide a column, format numbers, and change column width and row height.

Clearey & Clayton likes to keep the phone numbers and Social Security numbers of its employees in a separate list. Format the following worksheet for readability and apply phone number and Social Security formatting.

1. Open the file **Employee.xls**.
2. Hide column B.
3. Clear column D and key the text shown in Figure 8-12, including the corrections, beginning in cell D3.

FIGURE 8-12

```
Phone (bf)

9085515532   (tr)

9085553474

9085551234

9085559002   (tr)

9085556453

9085550984
        5 4
908558934

9085559342

9085550902

9085550221

9085555555
    9 8
809555124 5

908555 6486
```

Lesson Applications:
Provide independent practice for students and may be used for assessment. Objectives are indicated for each Exercise.

⊙ Exercise 8-19:
Objectives 1, 5, 6
Required Files: Employee.xls
Solution Files: gl8-19.xls in Solutions Manual or on Solutions Disk.

1 This figure contains proofreading marks. You may want to review Appendix E: "Proofreaders' Marks" with students.

4. Format the numbers in column C as Social Security numbers and the numbers in column D as phone numbers with the area code enclosed in parentheses.

5. Use the AutoFit option to change the width of columns C and D as necessary.

6. Increase the height of rows 4 through 13 to 18 points.

7. Center the headings in cells C3 and D3.

8. Add the standard header to the worksheet with your name, the filename, and the date.

9. Horizontally center the worksheet.

10. Save the workbook as *[your initials]*8-19.xls in your Lesson 8 folder.

11. Print the worksheet and close the workbook.

EXERCISE 8-20

Suppress the display of zero values, format numbers, hide rows, work with stored numbers, and align text.

Bettina Clearey would like a printout of sales amounts for tents and kayaks for the first four months of the year. Format the worksheet to remove the extra months and have the numbers represent sales amounts with rounded-off column totals.

1. Open the file **Kayaks.xls**.

2. Suppress the zeros found in column E and hide rows 8 through 17.

3. Format cells B4 through E7 to have no dollar signs.

4. Format the Totals row as accounting, with a leading dollar sign but no decimal places.

5. Change the amount in cell B5 to **30,056.95**, the amount in cell B6 to **34,677.55**, and the amount in cell B7 to **458.65**.

6. Correct the total for column B. (Use the P̲recision as Displayed option.)

7. Right-align the column headings in B3 through E3.

8. Key the title **Tents and Kayaks** in cell A1, make it bold, and center it over the worksheet columns.

9. Add the standard header to the worksheet with your name, the filename, and the date.

10. Horizontally center the worksheet.

11. Save the workbook as *[your initials]*8-20.xls in your Lesson 8 folder.

12. Print the worksheet and close the workbook.

● **Exercise 8-20:**

Objectives 1–4, 6
Required Files: Kayaks.xls
Solution Files: gl8-20.xls in Solutions Manual or on
Solutions Disk.

EXERCISE 8-21

Align text, format numbers, change column width and row height, suppress the display of zero values, and hide rows.

Clearey & Clayton also sells chairs for camping. Format the worksheet to show the sales figures and totals for January through April for their five best-selling chairs. Resize rows and columns. Add a worksheet title and column headings for readability.

1. Open the file **Monthly.xls**.
2. Key the titles **Clearey & Clayton** in cell A1 and **Monthly Sales of Camp Chairs** in cell A2. Center these titles over the entire worksheet without merging the cells and make them bold.

> **TIP:** Put each line of the title in its own row in the first cell of the row, and align the entire title at the same time.

3. Enter the following data as column headings in row 4, over columns B through E:
   Ultimate   Rester Chair   Travel Chair   Crazy Chair
4. Format the headings in columns B through F for word wrap and center-align them vertically and horizontally.
5. Vertically center-align the column A heading.
6. Format B5:F16 as currency without dollar signs or decimals.
7. Use the AutoFit feature to adjust the width of the Totals column.
8. Adjust the height of row 5 to put additional space between the column headings and the data that follows them.
9. Suppress the display of zeros for months that have no data.
10. Hide the rows for months that have no data and the blank row above the totals.
11. Add the standard header to the worksheet with your name, the filename, and the date.
12. Save the workbook as **[your initials]8-21.xls** in your Lesson 8 folder.
13. Print the worksheet.
14. Save the workbook **[your initials]8-21.htm** in your Lesson 8 folder, and then close the workbook.

◉ Exercise 8-21:
Objectives 1, 2, 4–6
Required Files: Monthly.xls
Solution Files: gl8-21.xls and gl8-21.htm in Solutions
Manual or on Solutions Disk.

 The completed document for this Exercise may be used in a student's portfolio.

EXERCISE 8-22 *Challenge Yourself*

Change column width and row height, hide columns and rows, format numbers, suppress the display of zero values, and align text.

  At the beginning of each quarter, Bettina Clearey likes to see comparisons of the present year's first quarter versus the same quarter for the previous year for each member of the sales force. She also wants to see bonus amounts included in the sales figures.

1. Create a worksheet sketch that includes a worksheet title, row and column labels, and an area for data and formulas. The worksheet should include each member of the sales force (rows). The information for each sales person (columns) should include First Quarter 1998 sales, First Quarter 1999 sales, the Change between the two quarters, their 1998 Bonus, and a cell for Notes. (*Hint:* Use abbreviations for the quarterly headings.) Use a formula to compute the difference between the most recent quarter and the previous quarter.

2. Transfer the sketch into Excel by keying the label titles. Format the headings and titles for bold, apply a 12-point font to the titles, and center them across the worksheet. Then key the data from Figure 8-13 in the worksheet.

FIGURE 8-13

	Title	Q1-1998	Q1-1999	Bonus
Adams, John	Marketing Rep	78,655	80,066	0
Christian, Susan	Sales Mgr	46,098	45,001	500
Clayton, John	Marketing Rep	22,099	23,046	0
Clearey, Bettina	Sales Mgr	77,988	77,649	0
Delaney, George	Sales Mgr	79,988	78,098	900
Gilbertson, Sam	Sales Mgr	91,434	91,938	900
Hankie, Michele	Marketing Rep	56,987	55,875	0
Walker, Jim	Marketing Rep	45,324	44,654	0
Williamson, Lee	Sales Mgr	76,909	77,988	900

Exercise 8-22:

Objectives 1, 2, 4–6
Required Files: None
Solution Files: gl8-22.xls in Solutions Manual or on Solutions Disk.

 The worksheet and user documentation are created by the student, so final versions may differ.

 The completed document for this Exercise may be used in a student's portfolio.

3. Use AutoFit to adjust all the columns in a single step, and then decrease the width of column A so it's just wide enough to display the longest name, if necessary.

4. Hide the "Title" column.

5. Set the height of the rows containing the names of the salespeople to approximately 20 points.

6. Adjust the row height of the column headings to approximately 30 points and center their contents vertically.

7. Using the mouse, widen each column individually to make it easier to read, as needed.

8. Format all values as Number style with commas, no decimal places displayed, and negative numbers displayed in red within parentheses.

9. Format the values in the "Bonus" column as currency with dollar signs and no decimal places, using the shortcut menu.

10. Suppress the zeros in the worksheet. Set the cells in the "Notes" column for Wrap Text.

11. In the "Notes" cell for John Adams, key **Best improvement over last year**. Adjust row height and column width so the note wraps to three lines.

12. Right-align the column headings for all columns containing numeric data. Center the titles over the worksheet.

13. Rename Sheet1 **Sales** and rename Sheet2 **User Information**. Delete Sheet 3.

14. In the User Information worksheet, create documentation that includes the following: File Information (Created by, Date created, Date revised, Revised by, Contact for help); Purpose of worksheet (paragraph form); Instructions to User (special instructions needed by user to enter data correctly). Style the documentation for easy reading.

15. Apply protection to the worksheet. (Be sure to first unlock the areas for data entry before protecting the worksheet.)

16. Add the standard header including your name, the filename, and the date to both worksheets, center the worksheets horizontally on the page, and turn on the gridlines for the Sales worksheet.

17. Save the workbook as *[your initials]*8-22.xls in your Lesson 8 folder.

18. Print the workbook and create a standard formula printout using landscape orientation with gridlines and row and column headings. Use the Shrink to Fit option or adjust the column widths so the printout fits on a single page.

19. Close the workbook without saving.

Changing Fonts, Patterns, Colors, and Formats

OBJECTIVES

MOUS ACTIVITIES

In this lesson:
XL2000 **1.7**
XL2000 **1.9**
XL2000 **1.11**
XL2000 **2.5**
XL2000 **3.1**
XL2000 **3.7**
XL2000 **3.8**
XL2000 **3.11**

See Appendix F.

After completing this lesson, you will be able to:

1. **Work with fonts.**
2. **Add borders.**
3. **Use patterns and colors.**
4. **Color borders.**
5. **Copy cell formatting.**
6. **Work with styles and autoformats.**
7. **Create a hyperlink.**

 Estimated Time: 1½ hours

Y ou can enhance the appearance of a worksheet by changing the types and sizes of fonts, adding borders and shading to cells, and even coloring cell borders. After you make these changes to one cell, you can copy the format to other cells. In fact, you can create a unique set of formatting instructions, give this set of instructions a name, and easily apply the formatting to other cells.

☑**Objective 1**

Working with Fonts

A *font* is a type design applied to an entire set of characters, including all the letters of the alphabet, numerals, punctuation marks, and other keyboard symbols. Fonts can be plain like Arial (Excel's default font) or more ornate like Times New Roman.

PREPARE

Point out to students that the learning objectives show what they will learn in the lesson. Each heading in the lesson correlates to a learning objective.

270

Required files:
Order.xls

TEACH

Teaching Resources:
• Excel Classroom Presentations
• School-to-Work Strategies Manual
• Spanish Glossary
• Certification Procedures

☑**Objective 1 Assignment:**
Exercise 9-14 (Skills Review) can be assigned after completing Objective 1.

FIGURE 9-1
Examples of fonts

ABCDEFGHIJKLMNOPQRSTUVWXYZ
abcdefghijklmnopqrstuvwxyz
1234567890!@#$%

> Arial

ABCDEFGHIJKLMNOPQRSTUVWXYZ
abcdefghijklmnopqrstuvwxyz
1234567890!@#$%

> Times New Roman

ABCDEFGHIJKLMNOPQRSTUVWXYZ
abcdefghijklmnopqrstuvwxyz
1234567890!@#$%

> Courier New

TIP: There are two types of fonts available: TrueType fonts and PostScript fonts. For PostScript fonts to print correctly, you must have a PostScript printer. If you don't have one or are unsure of your printer set-up, select TrueType fonts so your workbook prints as it appears on your screen. (TrueType fonts have TT beside them in the Font drop-down list box that you use in the next Exercise.)

Fonts are also available in a variety of sizes, which are measured in *points*. There are 72 points to an inch. Like other character formatting, you can use different fonts and font sizes in the same document.

FIGURE 9-2
Examples of different point sizes

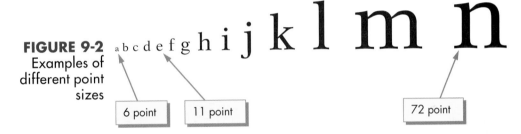

abcdefghijklmn

6 point   11 point   72 point

Excel provides two ways to choose fonts and font size:

- Formatting toolbar
- Font dialog box

EXERCISE **9-1** ## Choose Fonts and Font Size Using the Formatting Toolbar

The easiest way to choose fonts and font sizes is with the Formatting toolbar. You can also apply bold, italic, and underlining to worksheet data from the Formatting toolbar.

1. Open the file **Order.xls**.
2. Select cells A1 through A2.

1 Suggest that students look in magazines, newspapers, and annual reports (available at many public libraries) for examples of fonts used in worksheets. Discuss the types and sizes of fonts used in the material.

3. Click the down arrow in the Font box on the Formatting toolbar to open the drop-down list box. Scroll up and choose the font Arial.

FIGURE 9-3
Font drop-down
list box on the
Formatting toolbar

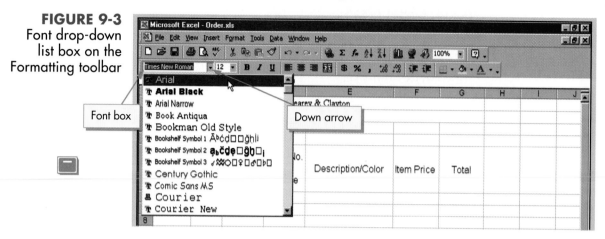

Font box

Down arrow

NOTE: This lesson assumes that both the Standard and Formatting toolbars are fully displayed, with the Standard toolbar on top of the Formatting toolbar. If your toolbar configuration is different, you may have to click the More Buttons button 🛗 to see some of the requested buttons.

B

4. To apply bold formatting to the worksheet title, click the Bold button 🅱 on the Formatting toolbar while cells A1 and A2 are still selected. The title becomes boldface Arial.

I **U**

TIP: You can apply italic with the Italic button 🅸 and underlining with the Underline button 🆄. You can also use the keystrokes Ctrl+B for bold, Ctrl+I for italic, and Ctrl+U for underlining.

5. To change the font size, with cells A1 and A2 still selected, click the down arrow to open the Font Size drop-down list box and choose 14 point. With the increased size, the first two rows now stand out as worksheet titles.

FIGURE 9-4
Changing font size
from the Font Size
drop-down list box

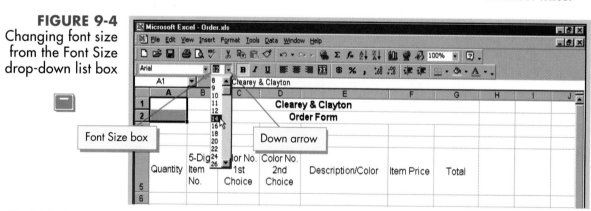

Font Size box

Down arrow

 Use Excel Classroom Presentation 9 to display
screens from the lesson in a slide-show format.

Make sure students understand that if they have
the Standard and Formatting toolbars on one
line, they may have to click More Buttons to see some
of the buttons used in this lesson.

TIP: It's a good idea to use plain fonts such as Arial and Helvetica (if it is available). Good worksheet design uses the same font throughout, changing the font size or adding italic only when needed.

EXERCISE 9-2 ## Choose a Font and Font Size Using the Format Cells Dialog Box

The Font options in the Format Cells dialog box give you a wider variety of options than are available on the Formatting toolbar. You can also preview the options as you choose them. You can even apply formatting to selected text within a cell.

1. Select rows 5 through 17.
2. Open the Format Cells dialog box. (Press [Ctrl]+[1] or choose C**e**lls from the F**o**rmat menu.)
3. Click the Font tab, if necessary.
4. Use the arrow to scroll down the list under the F**o**nt box.
5. Choose Times New Roman.

6. Choose Regular from the list under the F**o**nt Style box. (The font appears without formatting such as bold or italic.) The Preview box displays the font size and style you select. For this worksheet, leave the font size at 12 points.

NOTE: You can change the font size by selecting a different point size from the list under the S**i**ze box.

FIGURE 9-5
Changing the font with the Font options in the Format Cells dialog box

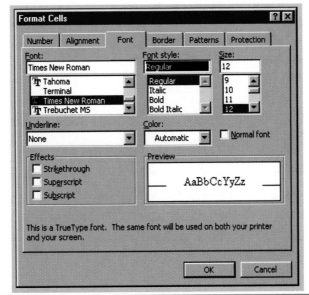

---

[1] Although it is good worksheet design to use the same font throughout the worksheet, different fonts are used here to emphasize styling.

[2] You can ask students to browse through other options in the Font options in the Format Cells dialog box. They can try underlining and coloring text, and creating character effects.

 In Excel Classroom Presentation 9.

7. Click OK. The rows are formatted for 12-point Times New Roman. Next, you change the font of selected characters in a cell.

8. Select cell C5.

9. Select the text "1st Choice" in the formula bar by dragging across it with the mouse. (You can also double-click on cell C5 and select the text within the cell.)

10. Choose C<u>e</u>lls from the F<u>o</u>rmat menu. The Format Cells dialog box is displayed.

11. Choose a F<u>o</u>nt style of Bold Italic and click OK. The selected text in C5 changes. Select any cell in the worksheet to show the new formatting in the cell. Note that you can also format selected characters in a cell as you enter them by choosing Format, Cells from the menu.

12. Use the Undo button to restore the selected text to its previous format.

Objective 2
Adding Borders

You can add borders to the right, left, top, or bottom of a cell, to each cell in a range of cells, or around any group of cells for an outline effect. Borders can add emphasis and make a worksheet easier to read or understand. Cells share borders, so adding a border to the bottom of cell A1 has the same effect as adding a border to the top of cell A2.

Excel provides two ways to add borders to a selected cell or cells:

- Use the Format Cells dialog box.
- Use the Borders button 🔲.

In Lesson 3, you learned how to apply simple bottom borders using the Borders button 🔲. Using the Border options in the Format Cells dialog box, you have additional options, such as a wider variety of border line weights and border colors.

EXERCISE 9-3 Add Borders to Cells

1. Select cells A15 through G15 and choose C<u>e</u>lls from the F<u>o</u>rmat menu.

2. Click the Border tab, if necessary. The Border options appear.

3. Under Line <u>S</u>tyle, click the fifth option on the right, which is the second darkest single-line border style.

⬚1 Discuss the use of borders in worksheets. If you have any design requirements in relation to borders (for example, if colors are permitted, whether all worksheets need borders, etc.), discuss them with students at this time

FIGURE 9-6
Border options in
the Format Cells
dialog box

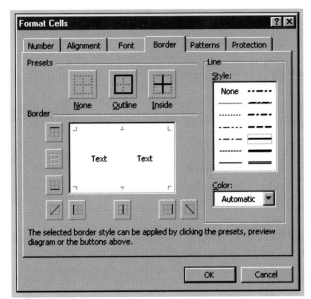

4. Under Border, click the top Border box. Then click OK.

5. Click anywhere in the worksheet to deselect the selection. Notice the rule that appears above row 15.

6. Now you add a border using the Borders button . Start by selecting cells A15 through B15.

7. Click the arrow to the right of the Borders button ▦ on the Formatting toolbar.

8. Click the Thick Bottom Border option, which is in the middle row, second from the left.

9. Select cell E15.

> ✸ **TIP:** The last border used is displayed on the button. You can select that border by clicking the button rather than the arrow.

10. Click the arrow to the right of the Borders button ▦ and select the No Border option (the top left choice). Select any other cell and notice that the top border disappears in cell E15.

> ➤ **NOTE:** When you select None from the border options, the border tool removes all borders from selected cells.

EXERCISE ▮ **9-4** ▮ **Add Gridline Borders to Cells**

Gridlines are lines displayed on every border of a range of cells. The default is for gridlines to be displayed on the entire worksheet. You can turn this option

▭ In Excel Classroom Presentation 9.

 When creating borders, it is often helpful to turn off the gridlines, since gridlines and borders tend to obscure one another on the screen. You may want to have students turn off gridlines when borders are used in the future.

off and display borders for a range of selected cells. By removing gridlines around every cell and using them on only cells that need them, a short worksheet sometimes looks cleaner and is easier to read.

1. Choose Options from the Tools menu.
2. Click the View tab, if necessary. The View options in the Options dialog box appear.
3. Click Gridlines to turn off gridlines.
4. Click OK. No gridlines appear in the worksheet.
5. Select cells A5 through G13.
6. Press Ctrl+1 to open the Format Cells dialog box.
7. Click the Border tab, if necessary.
8. To apply gridline borders to the cells, click Outline and Inside. Then click OK, and select any cell to see the gridline borders.

FIGURE 9-7
Cells with gridline borders

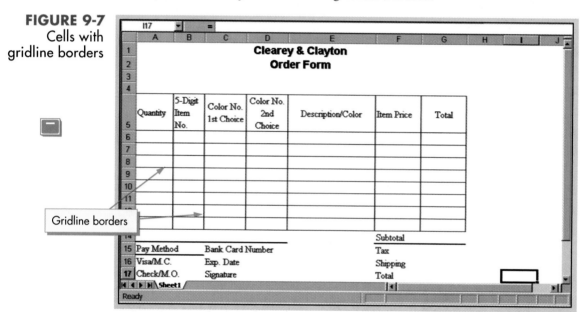

9. Select cells F14 through G17.
10. Click the arrow to the right of the Borders button .
11. Click the All Borders option (last row, second from the left). Gridline borders are added to the cells.

TIP: You can drag the Borders button ▣ drop-down palette to any location on the worksheet for easy access when styling with borders.

---

[1] You may want to have a "before" and "after" presentation prepared to demonstrate the point that removing gridlines can make the worksheet easier to read. It also might be useful to discuss situations in which removing gridlines is not helpful.

▣ In Excel Classroom Presentation 9.

EXERCISE 9-5   Outline Cells

You can outline any group of selected cells, placing a border on their outer edges.

1. Select cells A15 through B17.
2. Open the Format Cells dialog box.
3. Click the Border tab, if necessary.
4. Click <u>O</u>utline under Presets and click OK. The cells are outlined.

☑ Objective 3

Using Patterns and Colors

You can shade cells with a variety of gray or colored patterns or with solid colors. Patterns and colors can improve the appearance of a worksheet and make the data easier to read.

EXERCISE 9-6   Add a Shading Pattern

1. Select cells A5 through G5.
2. Press Ctrl + 1 to open the Format Cells dialog box.
3. Click the Patterns tab, if necessary. The Patterns options appear.
4. Click the arrow in the <u>P</u>attern box. A palette of patterns and colors appears.

FIGURE 9-8
Pattern options in the Format Cells dialog box

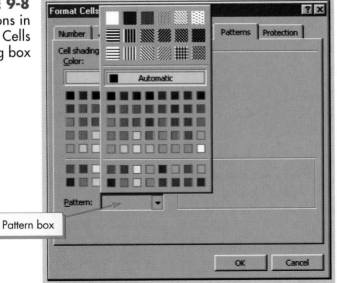

Pattern box

 Discuss when it would be helpful to outline a group of cells. You may want to demonstrate that too many design features used together can make a worksheet difficult to read.

☑**Objective 3 Assignment:**
Exercises 9-15 (Skills Review) and 9-19 (Lesson Applications) can be assigned after completing Objective 3.

 If your class is not using color monitors, you may want to skip this objective or focus only on patterns that can be easily viewed on your students' monitors. Additionally, keep in mind the printers that your students are using.

 In Excel Classroom Presentation 9.

5. Choose the 12.5% Gray dotted pattern in the top row, the second cell from the right, and click OK. The cells contain a dotted pattern.

6. Open the Pattern options again. Click the arrow in the Pattern box to apply a color to the dotted pattern. (Cells A5 through G5 should still be selected.)

7. Choose Light Green (fifth row of colors, fourth cell from the left) and click OK. The pattern is made up of green dots.

8. Click the Bold button ☐. Text usually looks better in bold against a shaded background. Click anywhere in the worksheet to observe the changes.

EXERCISE 9-7 Add Background Colors

You can choose background colors for plain cells or cells with patterns. If you choose colors for cells with patterns, the color appears behind the pattern.

NOTE: Background colors and colored patterns print as shades of gray on a black-and-white printer. If you do not want them to print this way, choose the Sheet options in the Page Setup dialog box and click the Black and White check box.

1. Select cells A1 through G2.

2. Click the arrow next to the Fill Color button ☐ on the Formatting toolbar.

3. Choose Turquoise (fourth row, fifth cell from the left). Select any other cell to see that the cells have a solid turquoise background.

4. Select cells F17 through G17.

5. Open the Format Cells dialog box.

6. Click the Patterns tab, if necessary.

7. Choose Yellow (fourth row, third cell from the left) from the Color box and click OK. Select any other cell to see that these cells are yellow.

TIP: When you use dark colors or heavy shading patterns in cells, it can be hard to read the text. Increase the font size, make text bold, or change the font to a light color or white with the Font Color button ☐ on the Formatting toolbar. Click the arrow next to the button to see the available font colors. Note, however, that some printers have trouble printing white text on black backgrounds.

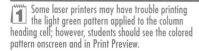
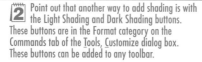

1 Some laser printers may have trouble printing the light green pattern applied to the column heading cell; however, students should see the colored pattern onscreen and in Print Preview.

2 Point out that another way to add shading is with the Light Shading and Dark Shading buttons. These buttons are in the Format category on the Commands tab of the Tools, Customize dialog box. These buttons can be added to any toolbar.

3 Students are introduced to the Font Color button in this Tip. You could ask them apply font color using the Font Color button to some of the text in the worksheet.

Coloring Borders

☑Objective 4

Borders can also be colored. Colored gridlines draw attention to important areas of a worksheet.

EXERCISE 9-8 Color Cell Borders

1. Select cells C15 through D15.
2. Open the Format Cells dialog box.
3. Click the Border tab, if necessary.
4. Click the thickest border style.
5. Click the arrow under the Color box. The color palette opens.
6. Choose red from the color palette.
7. Click Outline to apply an outline around the cells, and click OK. Select any other cell to see that the cells have a thick red outline.
8. Repeat this process for cells C16 through D16 and cells C17 through D17.

☑Objective 5

Copying Cell Formatting

You can copy the formatting of a cell, like its shading or color. Excel provides two ways to copy these characteristics:

- Use the Format Painter button 🖌 on the Standard toolbar.
- Use the Copy and Paste Special options from the Edit menu.

EXERCISE 9-9 Use Copy and Paste Special

1. Select cells C15 through D17.
2. Choose Copy from the Edit menu or press Ctrl + C.
3. Select cells A15 through B17.
4. Choose Paste Special from the Edit menu. The Paste Special dialog box opens.
5. Click the Formats option button and click OK. Press Esc to turn off Paste Special. Select any other cell and notice that the cells A15 through B17 have a thick red outline.

TIP: You can also use Paste Special to copy formulas, values, notes, everything in the cell, or everything except the borders, as well as the formatting of a selected cell or cells.

☑Objective 4 Assignment:
Exercise 9-18 (Lesson Applications) can be assigned after completing Objective 4.

If your class is not using color monitors, you may want to skip this objective. Again, keep in mind the printers that your students are using.

☑Objective 5 Assignment:
Exercises 9-16 (Skills Review) and 9-20 (Lesson Applications) can be assigned after completing Objective 5.

EXERCISE 9-10 **Clear Cell Formats and Use the Repeat Command**

Once a cell is formatted, you can clear all cell formatting using the command Edit, Clear, Formats. You can use the Repeat command on the Edit menu to apply the same format to another cell or range of cells.

1. Select cell A5.
2. Choose Edit, Clear, Formats. All formatting is removed from the cell.
3. Click the Undo button 🔄. The formatting is restored to cell A5.
4. Select cells F14 through G14.
5. Apply the same yellow background color to these cells as the color in cell F17. (Use the Fill Color button 🔽 on the Formatting toolbar and select the yellow in the fourth row.)
6. Select cells F15 through G16.
7. Choose Edit, Repeat Format Cells from the menu to repeat the formatting. Select any other cell and notice that cells F14 through G17 have a yellow background.

☑ **Objective 6**

Working with Styles and Autoformats

A *style* is a set of formatting instructions that you can apply to the cells of a worksheet. Styles make it easier to apply formatting and ensure consistency of formatting throughout the worksheet.

In every workbook, Excel maintains a list of style names and their formatting specifications. Every workbook contains six predefined styles for numbers and text: Comma, Comma [0], Currency, Currency [0], Normal, and Percent. You can apply these styles as they are, modify them, or create your own styles.

An *autoformat* is a built-in set of formatting instructions that apply fonts, borders, colors, and other formatting features to a range of cells, usually a list or a table. When you click AutoFormat under the Format menu, you have 16 different autoformats from which to choose.

EXERCISE 9-11 **Define, Apply, and Remove Styles**

1. Key the items shown in Figure 9-9 in rows 6 through 8.

☑ **Objective 6 Assignment:**
Exercises 9-17 (Skills Review) and 9-21 (Lesson Applications) can be assigned after completing Objective 6.

📝 **1** If students are familiar with Microsoft Word, they will probably understand Excel styles, since they are very similar conceptually to Word's styles.

FIGURE 9-9

2	34521	Blue	Red	Sierra backpack	25
1	24375	Green	Brown	Round top	250
2	12432	Black	Blue	Kiowe	400

2. Select cells A6 through E6.

3. Choose Style from the Format menu. The Style dialog box opens.

FIGURE 9-10
Style dialog box

 NOTE: The default style for a workbook is called *Normal style* .

4. Key **INVOICE** in all caps in the Style Name text box. The settings change to reflect the formatting of selected cells.

5. Click Modify to open the Format Cells dialog box.

6. Click the Font tab and change the Font to Regular, 12-point Arial. Do not click OK yet.

7. Click the Alignment tab and choose Left (Indent) Horizontal alignment.

8. Click OK. The settings beside the check boxes change.

9. Click Add to add the style to the style list and click OK. Notice that the cells are now left-aligned, 12-point Arial.

TIP: To create a style based on an example cell, select the cell that has the formatting you want in the style, open the Style dialog box, and key a new style name. You don't have to add it to the list. Just close the dialog box by clicking OK and the style becomes available for use in the workbook.

In Excel Classroom Presentation 9.

An interesting class project would be to develop a specific "class style" for use in worksheets produced for the class. Encourage class participation in defining style elements.

10. To apply the INVOICE style, select cells A7 through E8.

11. Choose Style from the Format menu to open the Style dialog box.

12. Choose INVOICE from the Style Name drop-down list box.

13. Click OK. The style is applied to these cells.

14. You can also delete unnecessary styles from the style list. Open the Style dialog box and choose Comma from the list of styles.

15. Click Delete and the style is removed from the list. Repeat this process for Comma [0], Currency, Currency [0], and Percent. The Normal and INVOICE styles remain in the list. (Make sure that INVOICE is shown as the Style name before you click Close or OK.)

16. Add the standard header to the worksheet with your name, the filename, and the date.

17. Save the workbook as *[your initials]*9-11.xls in a new folder for Lesson 9.

18. Print the worksheet.

EXERCISE 9-12 Apply an Autoformat

1. Select cell A5.

2. Chose AutoFormat from the Format menu. The AutoFormat dialog box is displayed. Notice that the order form (excluding the titles) is automatically selected.

FIGURE 9-11
AutoFormat
dialog box

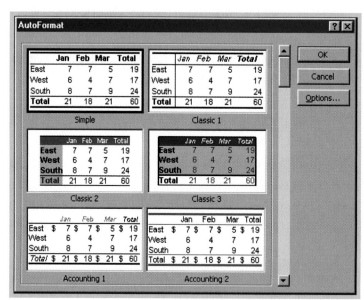

3. Scroll through the autoformat options.

4. Choose List 2 and click OK. The autoformat is applied to the order form.

 TIP: Use the Options button on the AutoFormat dialog box to control the formatting options you want to apply to the range of cells.

5. Remove the fill color from A1:G2.

6. You can change any element of the formatting that has been applied to the range of cells by the autoformat. For example, select cells A5:G5 and use the Font Color button [A] on the Formatting toolbar to change the font color from white to black.

7. With cells A5:G5 still selected, remove the background pattern and color, and add a top and bottom border to the cells.

Objective 7
Creating Hyperlinks

A *hyperlink* is colored and underlined text or graphic in a worksheet that links to another file or to a location on the Internet. When you click a hyperlink, the file or Web address specified by the hyperlink automatically opens. You can use hyperlinks to link your worksheet to charts, documents, Web sites, or other worksheets. Hyperlinks can be created for new or existing files. The link may refer to a specific location within the files. A hyperlink can be created that allows users to create an e-mail message with the correct e-mail address. You can even create a hyperlink that links to a specific location within the current worksheet.

There are several ways to add Hyperlinks to your worksheet:

- The Insert Hyperlink button 🖳 on the Standard toolbar
- The Hyperlink command on the shortcut menu.
- The Hyperlink command on the Insert menu.

EXERCISE 9-13   Add a Hyperlink

A hyperlink appears as a specially formatted cell in a worksheet.

1. Select cell B19.

2. Key **Visit us on the World Wide Web:**

3. Select cell E19 and key **clearey&clayton.com**

4. With cell E19 still selected, click the Insert Hyperlink button on the Standard toolbar or choose Insert, Hyperlink from the menu. The Insert Hyperlink dialog box is displayed. Notice under Text To Display, the contents of cell E19 were entered automatically.

FIGURE 9-12
Insert Hyperlink
dialog box

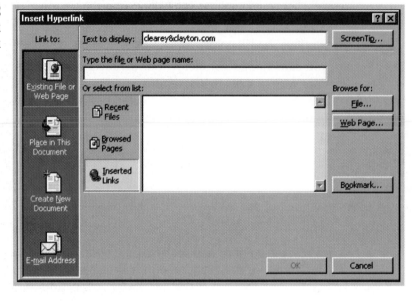

5. Under Link To, click Existing File or Web Page, if necessary.

6. In the Type the File or Web Page Name text box, key **http://www.clearey&clayton.com**. This is the Internet address of the Web page to which the hyperlink connects.

7. Click OK. Excel adds the hyperlink to cell E19.

8. Move the pointer over the hyperlink. The pointer changes to a hand, and a ScreenTip displays the Internet address of the hyperlink.

> **NOTE:** Since this is a fictitious Web address, don't click the hyperlink unless your instructor tells you to do so. If you click the hyperlink, Excel will attempt to connect to the link.

9. Save the workbook as *[your initials]*9-13.xls in your Lesson 9 folder.

10. Print the worksheet and close the workbook.

In Excel Classroom Presentation 9.

1 The Insert Hyperlink dialog box may display a history of recently visited Web sites under the "Or Select from List" text box.

2 Caution students not to click the fictional hyperlink. However, if an Internet connection is available, you might want to use a legitimate Web address and demonstrate how hyperlinks actually work.

COMMAND SUMMARY

FEATURE	BUTTON	MENU	KEYBOARD
Bold	**B**	Format, Cells	Ctrl + B
Italic	*I*	Format, Cells	Ctrl + I
Underline	U	Format, Cells	Ctrl + U
Add borders	⊞	Format, Cells	
Add outline border	⊞	Format, Cells	Ctrl + Shift + &
Remove all borders	⊞	Format, Cells	Ctrl + Shift + _
Add background color	🎨	Format, Cells,	
Copy cell formatting	🖌	Edit, Copy, Paste Special	
Repeat formatting		Edit, Repeat	Ctrl + Y
Add or edit hyperlink	🔗	Insert, Hyperlink	Ctrl + K
Change font color	A	Format, Cells	

USING HELP

If you created a worksheet with a significant amount of formatting, and you want to use the formatting in other similar worksheets, you can create a template from the worksheet. A *template* is a workbook that can be used as the basis for other workbooks or worksheets. You can create your own templates or you can use existing templates provided by Excel.

Use Microsoft Excel Help to learn more about templates:

1. Press F1 to activate the Office Assistant.

2. In the text box, key **templates**

3. Click Search.

4. Click the topic "Create a sheet template for new worksheets." The Microsoft Excel Help dialog box displays information about the procedures for creating your own template. (See Figure 9-13 on the next page.)

5. Read through the information about creating a template.

6. Click See More in the Office Assistant balloon. Click the topic "Ready-to-use forms and templates included with Microsoft Excel." Read through the information about Excel's built-in templates.

1️⃣ Point out that the Command Summary lists a variety of ways to accomplish a particular task. Students can decide which method they prefer.

2️⃣ Encourage students to follow the steps in "Using Help." Software companies are increasingly using their Help program—rather than printed documentation—to train users and assist in answering user questions.

FIGURE 9-13
Information on
creating a template

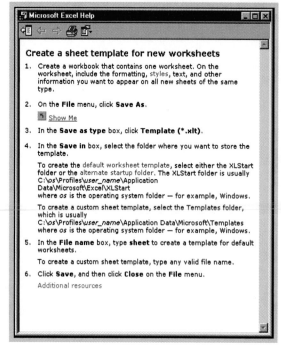

Microsoft Excel Help

Create a sheet template for new worksheets

1. Create a workbook that contains one worksheet. On the worksheet, include the formatting, styles, text, and other information you want to appear on all new sheets of the same type.

2. On the **File** menu, click **Save As**.

   Show Me

3. In the **Save as type** box, click **Template (*.xlt)**.

4. In the **Save in** box, select the folder where you want to store the template.

   To create the default worksheet template, select either the XLStart folder or the alternate startup folder. The XLStart folder is usually C:\os\Profiles\user_name\Application Data\Microsoft\Excel\XLStart where os is the operating system folder — for example, Windows.

   To create a custom sheet template, select the Templates folder, which is usually C:\os\Profiles\user_name\Application Data\Microsoft\Templates where os is the operating system folder — for example, Windows.

5. In the **File name** box, type **sheet** to create a template for default worksheets.

   To create a custom sheet template, type any valid file name.

6. Click **Save**, and then click **Close** on the **File** menu.

   Additional resources

7. Close the Help window and hide the Office Assistant.

Concepts Review

TRUE/FALSE QUESTIONS

Each of the following statements is either true or false. Indicate your choice by circling **T** or **F**.

T (F) **1.** A font is a type design applied to an entire set of characters, excluding punctuation marks.

(T) F **2.** The easiest way to choose fonts is with the Formatting toolbar.

T (F) **3.** You can add borders to only the right and left sides of a cell.

(T) F **4.** You can copy cell formatting using Copy and Paste Special options.

T (F) **5.** You cannot outline any group of selected cells.

T (F) **6.** You cannot choose colors for cells with patterns.

(T) F **7.** You can add color to Borders.

(T) F **8.** A style is a set of formatting instructions that you can apply to text.

SHORT ANSWER QUESTIONS

Write the correct answer in the space provided.

1. What do you call a list of style names and their formatting specifications?
Style sheet

2. Which command do you use to repeat a command?
Edit, Repeat

3. Where are Font options located?
Format Cells dialog box

4. What do you call lines on every border of a range of cells?
Gridlines

5. Where is the Fill color button located?
Formatting toolbar

6. What is the default font in Excel?
Arial

Concepts Review:
Allows students to check their understanding.

TEST BANK
Consider using the Test Bank to provide an additional review of lesson concepts. It may also be used as an assessment tool.

CLOSE

7. How many points are there in an inch?

72

8. Which button do you use to apply bold formatting to items in cells?

Bold button

CRITICAL THINKING

Answer these questions on a separate piece of paper. There are no right or wrong answers. Support your answer with examples from your own experience, if possible.

1. You were just given a worksheet that lists sales of all products made by the water ski company for which you work. You need to make certain areas of the worksheet stand out. The list needs to be printed and you do not have a color printer. How might you enhance these areas of the worksheet?

2. Excel provides many ways to use color in worksheets. Do you find that using color is helpful in drawing attention to a specific area? What colors look best to you? When do they become overwhelming?

Skills Review

EXERCISE 9-14

Work with fonts.

1. Open the file **Market.xls**.

2. Using the Formatting toolbar, change the title in cells A1 through A2 to 16-point, bold Arial by following these steps:

   a. Select cells A1 through A2.

   b. Click the arrow beside the Font box on the Formatting toolbar.

   c. Choose Arial from the drop-down list box.

   d. Click the arrow beside the Font Size box.

   e. Choose 16.

   f. Click the Bold button **B**.

3. Using the Format Cells dialog box, change the column headings to 14-point, italic Times New Roman by following these steps:

   a. Select cells A4 through C4.

   b. Open the Format Cells dialog box. (Press Ctrl + 1 .)

Critical Thinking Questions:
Answers will vary based on students' preferences, observations, experiences, and research.

Skills Review:
Provides guided practice for students. Objectives are indicated for each Exercise.

○ Exercise 9-14:
Objective 1
Required Files: Market.xls
Solution Files: gl9-14.xls in Solutions Manual or on Solutions Disk.

    c. Click the Font tab, if necessary.

    d. Choose Times New Roman under Font, Italic under Font style, and 14 under Size.

    e. Click OK.

4. Change the font in rows 5 through 13 to Times New Roman.

5. Add the standard header to the worksheet with your name, the filename, and the date.

6. Save the workbook as *[your initials]***9-14.xls** in your Lesson 9 folder.

7. Print the worksheet and close the workbook.

EXERCISE 9-15

Add borders and use patterns.

1. Open the file **Market2.xls**.

2. Turn off the display of gridlines. (Open the Options dialog box under the Tools menu, click the View tab, and deselect Gridlines.)

3. Add gridline borders using the Borders button 🔲 by following these steps:

    a. Select cells A5 through C14.

    b. Click the arrow next to the Borders button 🔲.

    c. Choose All Borders (third row, second from left).

4. Outline the worksheet title with a double-line border using the Format Cells dialog box by following these steps:

    a. Select cells A1 through C3.

    b. Open the Format Cells dialog box by pressing Ctrl + 1.

    c. Click the Border tab, if necessary.

    d. Choose the double-line border.

    e. Choose Outline.

    f. Click OK.

5. Add a dotted yellow pattern to the title box by following these steps:

    a. Select cells A1 through C3, if necessary.

    b. Open the Format Cells dialog box.

    c. Click the Patterns tab.

    d. Click the arrow in the Pattern box to open the Pattern palette.

    e. Choose the 25% Gray pattern (the fourth dotted pattern from the left in the top row).

    f. Click the arrow in the Pattern box to open the Pattern palette again.

    g. Choose yellow in the fourth row of colors.

    h. Click OK.

6. Make the titles in A1 through A3 bold.

⊙ **Exercise 9-15:**
Objectives 2, 3
Required Files: Market2.xls
Solution Files: gl9-15.xls in Solutions Manual or on
Solutions Disk.

1️⃣ If your class is not using color monitors, you may want to modify this Exercise.

7. Add the standard header to the worksheet with your name, the filename, and the date.

8. Horizontally center the worksheet.

9. Save the workbook as *[your initials]*9-15.xls in your Lesson 9 folder.

10. Print the worksheet and close the workbook.

EXERCISE 9-16

Color borders and copy cell formatting.

1. Open the file **Clearey2.xls**.

2. Color the border around the worksheet title blue by following these steps:
   a. Select cells A1 through C1.
   b. Open the Format Cells dialog box.
   c. Click the Border tab, if necessary.
   d. Select the thickest single-line border.
   e. Click the arrow next to the Color box.
   f. Choose the blue in the second row.
   g. Choose Outline and click OK.

3. Copy the outline border color from the title to the column headings using Copy and Paste Special by following these steps:
   a. Select cells A1 through C1, if necessary.
   b. Click the Copy button .
   c. Select cells A3 through C3.
   d. Choose Paste Special from the Edit menu.
   e. Select Formats and click OK.

4. Color the outline border around the rest of the worksheet, cells A4 through C13, using the same border format as in step 2.

5. Format the worksheet, except for the title, as left-aligned.

6. Add the standard header to the worksheet with your name, the filename, and the date.

7. Save the workbook as *[your initials]*9-16.xls in your Lesson 9 folder.

8. Print the worksheet and close the workbook.

EXERCISE 9-17

Work with styles.

1. Open the file **Months.xls**.

2. Key the text shown in Figure 9-14 in rows 13 through 15.

◉ **Exercise 9-16:**
Objectives 4, 5
Required Files: Clearey2.xls
Solution Files: gl9-16.xls in Solutions
Manual or on Solutions Disk.

1 If your class is not using color monitors, you may want to modify this Exercise.

2 Students are shown that Paste Special copies all cell formatting from one cell to another, not just the most recently applied formatting.

◉ **Exercise 9-17:**
Objective 6
Required Files: Months.xls
Solution Files: gl9-17.xls in Solutions
Manual or on Solutions Disk.

FIGURE 9-14

Oct	745	456	677
Nov	345	7465	3532
Dec	2456	5678	867

3. Create a style named "months" that is 12-point Times New Roman, center-aligned vertically, with a currency number format containing no "$" and no decimals by following these steps:

 a. Choose Style from the Format menu.

 b. Key **months** for Style Name.

 c. Click Modify and click the Number tab.

 d. Choose Currency. Under Symbol, replace $ with None and key **0** for Decimal Places.

 e. Click the Alignment tab.

 f. Select General under Horizontal, if necessary, and Center under Vertical.

 g. Click the Font tab.

 h. Choose Times New Roman, Regular, 12 point, and click OK.

 i. Click Add and click OK.

4. Apply the style to rows 4 through 15 by following these steps:

 a. Select rows 4 through 15.

 b. Open the Style dialog box.

 c. Under Style Name, choose months.

 d. Click OK.

5. Delete rows 1 and 2.

6. Vertically center all the column headings. Right-align the headings for columns B, C, and D.

7. Use AutoFit to adjust the widths of the columns.

8. Insert three blank rows at the top of the worksheet. In cell A1 key the title **Clearey & Clayton** and in cell A2 key **Top-selling Products**. Center the titles across the worksheet and format them in 14-point bold.

9. Add the standard header to the worksheet with your name, the filename, and the date.

10. Save the workbook as *[your initials]*9-17.xls in your Lesson 9 folder.

11. Print the worksheet and close the workbook.

A
S
S
E
S
S

Assessment Resources:
• Solutions Manual
• Test Bank
• Portfolio Builder
• Internet Projects
• Alternative Assessment Guide
• Certification Procedures

Go ▾

For Internet projects, go to
www.glencoe.com/webprojects

Lesson Applications

EXERCISE 9-18

Work with fonts, add borders, and use colored borders.

A worksheet providing a sales comparison for the years 1997, 1998, and 1999 in seven of Clearey & Clayton's biggest states is needed for a sales meeting. Format the worksheet so the printout of the comparison is attractive and easy-to-read.

1. Open the file **States.xls**.
2. Use the formatting toolbar to make the title 16-point, bold italic Arial.
3. Center the title over the columns and place a blue outline around it.
4. Increase column F using AutoFit, so the text fits in the column.
5. Apply a gridline border around cells A3 through F10 using the Borders button 🔲.
6. Delete column B and increase the size of column A using AutoFit.
7. Horizontally center the worksheet on the page and add the standard header to the worksheet with your name, the filename, and the date.
8. Save the workbook as *[your initials]*9-18.xls in your Lesson 9 folder.
9. Print the worksheet and close the workbook.

EXERCISE 9-19

Work with fonts, add borders, and use patterns and colors.

Clearey & Clayton monitor the performance of their top sales people. Format this comparison of 1998 and 1999 sales in an easy-to-read worksheet for the Board of Directors meeting.

1. Open the file **Perform.xls**.
2. Change the title in the first row to 14-point, bold Arial.
3. Make the rest of the worksheet title 12-point, bold Arial.
4. Change the text in cells A5 through F14 to 12-point Times New Roman.
5. Place borders on the left, right, top, and bottom sides of cells A5 through F5, and make the column headings bold.
6. Apply a gray pattern to these cells. (Make sure the pattern is light enough so you can see the text. Do not add a color background.)

Lesson Applications:
Provide independent practice for students and may be used for assessment. Objectives are indicated for each Exercise.

◉ **Exercise 9-18:**
Objectives 1, 2, 4
Required Files: States.xls
Solution Files: gl9-18.xls in Solutions Manual or on Solutions Disk.

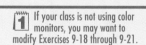 If your class is not using color monitors, you may want to modify Exercises 9-18 through 9-21.

◉ **Exercise 9-19:**
Objectives 1–3
Required Files: Perform.xls
Solution Files: gl9-19.xls in Solutions Manual or on Solutions Disk.

7. Apply the same gray pattern to the worksheet title (cells A1 through F3), then apply light green as the pattern color.

8. Give the column headings a yellow background using the Fill Color button . (The colored pattern should remain in place.)

9. Increase the height of row 5 and center the text vertically.

10. Increase the width of column B so the worksheet title appears more evenly centered in the patterned area. Make sure the "Difference" column fits on page 1.

11. Add the standard header to the worksheet with your name, the filename, and the date.

12. Save the workbook as *[your initials]*9-19.xls in your Lesson 9 folder.

13. Print the worksheet and close the workbook.

EXERCISE 9-20

Work with fonts, add borders, copy cell formatting, and use patterns and colors.

The New York and San Diego stores are the company's largest. The head office maintains a worksheet for each quarter's budget for the two stores. In the past, the format of the worksheet was dreary and hard to review. You need to change the worksheet to make the information easier to read.

1. Open the file **Budget.xls**.

2. Turn off the display of gridlines on the screen.

3. Change the font for the entire worksheet to 12-point Times New Roman.

4. Change the font in cells A1 and A2 to 14-point Times New Roman bold.

5. Add top and bottom borders to cells C4 through G4 and cells C6 through G6.

6. Copy the formatting of cells C6 through G6 using the Format Painter button or Copy and Paste Special to the rows for "Equipment" and "Advertising" under the "New York, NY" section only.

7. Add a light shading pattern to cells C6 through G6, C8 through G8, and C10 through G10.

8. Enclose cells C4 through G18 in an outline.

9. Copy the format of cells C5 through G10 to cells C12 through G17.

10. Change cells C4 through G4 to bold with a turquoise background and right-align the headings over the columns.

11. Increase the width of the "Total" column so it appears somewhat larger than columns D, E, and F.

12. Move the worksheet titles in cells A1 and A2 to cells C1 and C2.

 Exercise 9-20:
Objectives 1–3, 5
Required Files: Budget.xls
Solution Files: gl9-20.xls and gl9-20.htm in Solutions
Manual or on Solutions Disk.

The completed document for this Exercise may be used in a student's portfolio.

13. Delete row 11 and increase the height of the new row 11 to slightly more than twice its current height.

14. Add the standard header to the worksheet with your name, the filename, and the date.

15. Save the workbook as *[your initials]*9-20.xls in your Lesson 9 folder.

16. Print the worksheet.

17. Save the workbook as *[your initials]*9-20.htm in your Lesson 9 folder and then close the workbook.

EXERCISE 9-21   *Challenge Yourself*

Work with fonts, use patterns and colors, add borders, and work with styles.

     An important item to track is employee birthdays, especially since the company owners at Clearey & Clayton often do something special for employees on their birthdays. Format the following worksheet so the birthdays are easier to read.

1. Create a worksheet sketch that includes a title, column labels, and an area for data. The worksheet should include each employee's name (rows) and a column for his or her birth date.

2. Transfer the sketch into Excel by keying the labels and formatting them. Then key the data from Figure 9-15 in the worksheet.

FIGURE 9-15

```
Bilton, Angela        12/23/52

Delaney, George       6/19/65

Gilbertson, Sammie    11/30/70

Hankle, Michele       8/12/63

Williamson, Lobella   6/23/71

Adams, John           6/22/58

Rishi, Joanie         3/10/59

Christian, Susan      4/28/58

Robertson, Bill       9/15/64

Walker, Idgi          7/19/70
```

Exercise 9-21:
Objectives 1–3, 6
Required Files: None
Solution Files: gl9-21.xls in Solutions Manual or on Solutions Disk.

 The completed document for this Exercise may be used in a student's portfolio.

 This Exercise includes features from Lesson 4 (designing a worksheet and user documentation), Lesson 6 (sorting), and Lesson 7 (formatting text and numbers).

3. Adjust the width of the columns to an appropriate size.

4. Turn off the default display of gridlines. Change the font of the worksheet title, make it bold, and center the title across the worksheet.

5. Give the titles a simple patterned background and a light background color.

6. Insert a blank row after the title. Make sure you clear the pattern and colors from the inserted row.

7. Place a left, right, and top border around the cells containing the column headings.

8. Create a style called "employee." Choose whatever font you like, but keep it 12-point, Regular. Make the text left-aligned with borders on the left, right, top, and bottom. Set the Number format for Date, using the Type 03/14/98.

9. Left-align the column headings, if necessary, and make them bold.

10. Apply the "employee" style to the cells containing the employee names and their birth dates.

11. If necessary, change the font of the worksheet title to the same font as the "employee" style. Change the font size of the title to 14-point.

12. Add an outline border around the entire worksheet, including the titles. Adjust the column widths, if necessary, to make the data easier to read. Sort the list by employee name in ascending order.

13. Rename Sheet1 **Birthdays** and rename Sheet2 **User Information**. Delete Sheet3.

14. In the User Information worksheet, create documentation that includes the following: File Information (Created by, Date created, Date revised, Revised by, Contact for help); Purpose of worksheet (paragraph form); Instructions to User (special instructions needed by user to enter data correctly). Style the documentation for easy reading.

15. Center the worksheets horizontally and add the standard header to both worksheets with your name, the filename, and the date.

16. Save the workbook as *[your initials]***9-21.xls** in your Lesson 9 folder.

17. Print both worksheets and close the workbook.

For Internet projects, go to
www.glencoe.com/webprojects

Unit 3 Applications

UNIT APPLICATION 3-1

Format numbers, suppress the display of zero values, align text, change column width, and add a border.

John Clayton needs to construct a worksheet for the bank showing employee bonuses. He asked you to make the worksheet attractive.

1. Open the file **C&CBon.xls**.

2. Choose a currency format for columns B through E that does not have dollar signs, but does have two decimal places.

3. Suppress zeros in the worksheet.

4. Left-align the text in cells A4 through A13 and center the worksheet title over the columns. Make the title bold.

5. Make the column headings bold and right-align the headings in columns B through E.

6. Use AutoFit to adjust all columns that need widening.

7. Delete row 2 and add a gridline border around the cells that contain data in the worksheet, including the title.

8. Turn off the default gridlines for viewing.

9. Add the standard header to the worksheet with your name, the filename, and the date.

10. Save the workbook as *[your initials]*u3-1.xls in a new Unit 3 Applications folder.

11. Print the worksheet and close the workbook.

UNIT APPLICATION 3-2

Hide a column, use color borders, use patterns and color shading, change row height, and work with fonts.

John Clayton must include the first-quarter budget in a report he is presenting. He wants you to make the worksheet attractive.

1. Open the file **Budget2.xls**.

2. Hide column G.

3. Add a background color to the title area of the worksheet. Make sure the title text is readable.

A S S E S S

Assessment Resources:
• Solutions Manual • Test Bank
• Portfolio Builder
• Alternative Assessment Guide
• Certification Procedures
• Projects Manual
• Mid-Term and Final Exams

Unit Applications:
Provide independent practice of the skills acquired from each lesson in the Unit.

Project:
You can now assign Project 3 from the Projects Manual.

Exam:
You can now assign Exam 3 from the Mid-Term and Finals booklet.

◉ Unit Application 3-1:
Required Files: C&CBon.xls
Solution Files: glu3-1.xls in Solutions Manual or on Solutions Disk

◉ Unit Application 3-2:
Required Files: Budget2.xls
Solution Files: glu3-2.xls in Solutions Manual or on Solutions Disk

4. Add thick, red top and bottom borders to the column headings, cells A4 through H4. (Be sure to change the color and thickness before adding the borders.)

5. Make the cell background a shaded blue pattern in cells A4 through H4.

6. Make the background color in cells A5 through H18 the lightest green possible.

7. Change the font size for the entire worksheet to 12 point.

8. Increase the height of row 4 and row 12 by about 50% of their current height.

9. Turn off default gridlines for viewing.

10. Right-align the column headings and make them bold.

11. Add the standard header to the worksheet with your name, the filename, and the date.

12. Save the workbook as *[your initials]*u3-2.xls in your Unit 3 Applications folder.

13. Print the worksheet and close the workbook.

UNIT APPLICATION 3-3

Work with fonts, add borders, use color borders, format numbers, change column width and row height, and change alignment.

  Bettina Clearey is meeting with an insurance salesperson. She wants to provide the agent with an attractive list of employee insurance plans.

1. Open the file **Insure.xls**.

2. Create a worksheet title and center it over the columns. Make it 16-point, bold Arial.

3. Add a thick, blue outline around the title.

4. Format the policy numbers to have dashes after the first two numbers and after the next three numbers.

5. Increase the row height by slightly less than twice the current height for the rows containing the employee names and insurance information.

6. Make the column titles wrap to the next line, and adjust the row height if you cannot read them after wrapping.

7. Left-align the employee names.

8. Increase the width of column D so the column heading fits on one line, and left-align the text in the column.

9. Vertically center the column headings.

◉ Unit Application 3-3:
Required Files: Insure.xls
Solution Files: glu3-3.xls in Solutions Manual or on Solutions Disk

The completed document for this application can be used in a student's portfolio.

10. Make sure a blank row appears between the title and the body of the worksheet.

11. Turn off gridlines for viewing.

12. Add the standard header to the worksheet with your name, the filename, and the date.

13. Save the workbook as *[your initials]*u3-3.xls in your Unit 3 Applications folder.

14. Print the worksheet and close the workbook.

UNIT APPLICATION 3-4

Work with fonts, copy cell formatting, work with styles, hide rows, and work with stored numbers.

John Clayton wants to show the sales force the monthly camp chair sales in an attractive worksheet format.

1. Open the file **Monthly2.xls**.

2. Create a worksheet title in the first two rows, using 14-point, bold Arial. Center it over the columns.

3. Enter the following data as headings over columns B through E:

   Ultimate   Rester Chair   Travel Chair   Crazy Chair

4. Copy the formatting in cell A5 to the rest of the month cells in column A, excluding the "Totals" cell.

5. Create a style named "new" based on cell B5. Change the number format to currency with no dollar signs and no decimal places. Change the alignment to right-aligned and create a green border similar to the one in cell A5. (Examine the Format Cells dialog box for cell A5 to determine the precise color and thickness of the border.)

6. Apply the "new" style to cells B5 through F16.

7. Hide rows 9 through 16.

8. Turn on the Precision as Displayed option to correct the total in column B.

9. Copy the formatting in row 4 to the totals row.

10. Delete row 17. Turn off the default display of gridlines.

11. Adjust the widths of columns B through E so all the headings display appropriately and right-align the column headings.

12. Add the standard header to the worksheet with your name, the filename, and the date.

◉ **Unit Application 3-4:**
Required Files: Monthly2.xls
Solution Files: glu3-4.xls in Solutions Manual or on Solutions Disk

 The completed document for this application can be used in a student's portfolio.

13. Save the workbook as *[your initials]***u3-4.xls** in your Unit 3 Applications folder.

14. Print the worksheet and close the workbook.

UNIT APPLICATION 3-5

Create a worksheet title; create column heads; choose fonts, font size, and font style; and use color backgrounds, borders, and shading.

Bettina Clearey needs to see the projections for the year 2000 for Clearey and Clayton's nine top-selling tents. Create a worksheet sketch that includes a worksheet title, column labels, and an area for data. The worksheet should list each tent (rows) and sales amounts (columns) for the years 1998, 1999, and 2000.

Transfer the sketch into Excel by keying in the labels and formatting them. Key the data in Figure U3-1 with corrections, in order from 1 to 9, as the body of the worksheet (do not key the numbers before the tent name). The number columns are for years 1998, 1999, and 2000.

FIGURE U3-1

	1998	1999	2000
1. Boston blue *(not bold)*	25380	37870	02500
3. Yllelow rover	16920	14320	15000
9. lockerZip Gray	58760	48760	550000
4. Purple ptite	7870	15130	49500
7. brown baskin	8320	9380	10000
6. S mall round	9960	178870	12000
2. Green mountain	108920	78560	85000
8. Hikers night	55850	77420	65000
5. Snow bound	78520	65900	60000

Be creative in your use of fonts, colors, borders, and cell backgrounds. Make the worksheet as colorful and attractive as possible. Be sure to use colors that do not hide text. Make sure the worksheet is horizontally centered and add the standard header to the worksheet with your name, the filename, and the date.

Unit Application 3-5:
Required Files: None
Solution Files: Sample glu3-5.xls in Solutions Manual or on Solutions Disk

The completed document for this application can be used in a student's portfolio.

1 Some students may need extra help with this type of Application in which there are no numbered step procedures.

2 This figure contains proofreading marks. You may want to review Appendix E: "Proofreaders' Marks," with students.

3 In this Application, students are asked to make formatting decisions. Consequently, the solution worksheets will vary. A sample file is shown in the Solutions Manual and on the Solutions Disk.

Rename Sheet1 appropriately and rename Sheet2 User Information. In the User Information worksheet, create documentation that includes the following: File Information (Created by, Date created, Date revised, Revised by, Contact for help); Purpose of worksheet (paragraph form); Instructions to User (special instructions needed by user to enter data correctly). Style the documentation for easy reading. Save the workbook as *[your initials]*u3-5.xls in your Unit 3 Applications folder. Print and close the workbook.

UNIT APPLICATION 3-6 *Making It Work for You*

Create a worksheet title; create column heads; choose fonts, font size, and font style; format numbers; align text; and use color backgrounds, borders, and shading.

Set up a worksheet for taxable deductions, showing itemized deductions in various categories. The categories might include charitable giving, business expenses, or medical expenses. You can use your own information, someone in your family, or you can make up tax deductions for a famous person.

Be creative in your use of fonts, colors, borders, and cell backgrounds. Be sure to include formulas showing subtotals and grand totals, if applicable.

Add the standard header, including your name, the filename and the date. Save the workbook as *[your initials]*u3-6.xls in your Unit 3 Applications folder. Print the workbook and create a standard formula printout using landscape orientation with gridlines and row and column headings. Close the workbook without saving.

Unit Application 3-6:

Required Files: None
Solution Files: Sample glu3-6.xls in
Solutions Manual or on Solutions Disk

 The completed document for this application can be used in a student's portfolio.

⌐1⌐ Some students may need extra help with this type of Application in which there are no numbered step procedures.

⌐2⌐ In this Application, students are asked to make content and formatting decisions. Consequently, the solution worksheets will vary. A sample file is shown in the Solutions Manual and on the Solutions Disk.

Formulas and Advanced Printing

Dunkirk Canvas Company

Custom Boat Covers Keep Business Afloat

For over 40 years, the Dunkirk Canvas Company manufactured sails for boats. Facing increased competition, the company recently began making boat covers. Each boat cover is custom made, using a special computerized cloth-cutting machine that stores patterns and data about the amount of cloth used in a particular customer's boat cover.

Dunkirk was founded by Frank Bouchard and Mickey Finnegan. The company spent a considerable amount of money buying the cutting machine and is just beginning to see a profit on its boat cover operation. Sales volume has increased so much, however, that the company needs to use independent contractors to make some of its sails. This has caused the company to focus on automating some of its everyday business tasks.

In order to start automating the business records, the Dunkirk Canvas Company needs to produce:

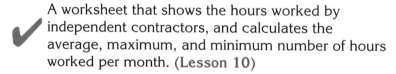

✔ A worksheet that shows the hours worked by independent contractors, and calculates the average, maximum, and minimum number of hours worked per month. **(Lesson 10)**

✔ Worksheets calculating commissions and markup for canvas goods, bonuses for sales reps, and the costs and prices of some of Dunkirk's products. **(Lesson 11)**

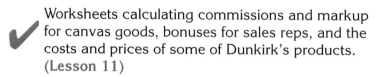

✔ Worksheets maintaining employee information and analyzing the present value of a business loan. **(Lesson 12)**

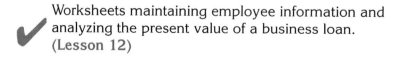

✔ Print a worksheet in an attractive, multi-page format that shows sales over a twelve-month period. **(Lesson 13)**

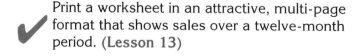

Using Functions

OBJECTIVES

After completing this lesson, you will be able to:

1. Enter functions.
2. Use the AVERAGE function.
3. Use the MIN and MAX functions.
4. Use the COUNT function.
5. Use the COUNTA function.
6. Use the INT and ROUND functions.
7. Use nested functions.

MOUS ACTIVITIES

In this lesson:
XL2000 **6.6**
XL2000 **6.7**

See Appendix F.

 Estimated Time: 1¾ hours

Functions are built-in formulas. Excel provides many functions besides the SUM function introduced in Lesson 2. The SUM function is a mathematical function. This lesson covers the statistical functions AVERAGE, MIN, MAX, COUNT, and COUNTA, as well as two additional mathematical functions, INT and ROUND.

Objective 1

Entering Functions

There are two ways to enter functions in your worksheets. You can key the formulas or use Paste Function. Using Paste Function is easier, but keying formulas helps you learn formula construction.

PREPARE

Point out to students that the learning objectives show what they will learn in the lesson. Each heading in the lesson correlates to a learning objective.

Required files:
Dunkirk1.xls Dunkirk2.xls Dunkirk3.xls

TEACH

Teaching Resources:
• Excel Classroom Presentations
• School-to-Work Strategies Manual
• Spanish Glossary
• Certification Procedures

The values that a function operates on are called *arguments,* which are placed inside parentheses after the function name. A function's arguments can consist of:

- Constants (a number keyed directly in a formula)
- Cell references (individual cells or cell ranges)
- Additional functions
- Defined names

NOTE: To use a cell range as an argument, you separate the beginning and ending cell references with a colon.

If the function takes more than one argument, commas separate the arguments. The value that the function returns is called the *result.*

Objective 2

Using the AVERAGE Function

You use the AVERAGE function to calculate an average mean. The arguments for this function can be cell references, defined names, or constants. For example, the Dunkirk Canvas Company tracks the hours that contractors work. You could use the AVERAGE function to calculate the average hours worked per month by all contractors.

Use the format =AVERAGE(arguments). The arguments can be one or more cell ranges or constants for which you want to find the average. The AVERAGE function ignores:

- Text
- Blank cells (but not zeros)
- Error values
- Logical values (*logical values* are the values TRUE and FALSE, which are the result of formulas that use comparison operators such as = or >. You learn more about this type of value later in this course.)

TABLE 10-1

Examples of the AVERAGE Function

FUNCTION	CELL DATA	RESULT
=AVERAGE(A1:A3)	A1=10, A2=20, A3=30	20
=AVERAGE(50,60)	(none)	55
=AVERAGE(A1,100)	A1=50	75
=AVERAGE(A1, B2, C1:C2)	A1=2, B2=2, C1=4, C2=4	3

1 Review the structure of a function: the equal (=) symbol, function name, left parenthesis, value to be operated on, and the right parenthesis. Mention that some functions do not have anything between the parentheses, such as =NOW().

2 Point out that the argument in the last example calculates the average in nonadjacent ranges, with each range separated by a comma.

EXERCISE 10-1 Use the AVERAGE Function

1. Open the file **Dunkirk1.xls**.

2. Select cell A15 and key **Average Hours:**

3. Select cell C15 and enter **=AVERAGE(C4:C13)**. Excel displays the error value #DIV/0!. Error values always start with the # symbol and indicate the formula contains some sort of problem. This error indicates there is no data in the specified range to calculate or that division by zero was attempted.

 TIP: You can key formulas in lowercase letters for convenience. Excel automatically converts the text to uppercase in the formula bar.

4. Key the following data in column C, starting with cell C4:

    10
    N/A
    20
    10
    10
    20
    20
    0
    0
    0

    The result, 10.00, is displayed in cell C15. The cells with zeros are counted in the Average, while the cell containing "N/A" does not affect the average.

5. Compare your result to the result found with AutoCalculate by highlighting the range C4:C13. If the AutoCalculate area at the bottom of the screen does not show Average, right-click the AutoCalculate area and choose Average. The AutoCalculate value and the number in C15 should both be 10.00.

6. Copy the formula in cell C15 to cells D15 through F15.

☑ **Objective 3**

Using the MIN and MAX Functions

You use the MIN and MAX functions to find the minimum and maximum values in a range of values. For example, in the Dunkirk1 worksheet, you can use the MIN and MAX functions to return the lowest and highest number of hours worked.

The MIN and MAX functions ignore:

- Text
- Blank cells (but not zeros)

☑ **Objective 3 Assignment:**
Exercise 10-9 (Skills Review) can be assigned after completing Objective 3.

- Error values
- Logical values (such as TRUE and FALSE)

Use the format =MIN(arguments) or =MAX(arguments). The arguments represent the values for which you want to find a minimum or maximum.

TABLE 10-2

Examples of the MIN and MAX Functions

FUNCTION	CELL DATA	RESULT
=MAX(A1:A3)	A1=10, A2=20, A3=30	30
=MAX(A1,B2,C3)	A1=3, B2=6, C3=10	10
=MIN(A1:A3)	A1=2, A2=20, A3=30	2
=MIN(-50,60)	(none)	-50
=MIN(A1,0)	A1=50	0

EXERCISE 10-2 Use the MIN Function

1. Select cell A16 and key **Least Hours Worked:**
2. Select C16 and key **=MIN(C4:C13)**
3. Copy the formula in cell C16 to cells D16 through F16.
4. Key the following data in column D, starting with cell D4 and leaving the second-to-last cell blank, as indicated:

   22
   19
   20
   N/A
   21
   20
   15
   30
   (Leave blank)
   10

   The results, 0.00 and 10.00, are displayed in cells C16 and D16, respectively. The MIN function ignores the blank cell, D12, and the cells with text, C5 and D7.

5. Select cell D12, key **0** and press ⏎ Enter . The zero is counted as the minimum value in the column and the result becomes 0.00.

Review the results in Table 10-2. Ask students to write their own functions and ask classmates to provide the result. Also, point out the functions that calculate the MAX and MIN in nonadjacent ranges, with each range separated by a comma.

EXERCISE **10-3** Use the MAX Function with Paste Function

In the previous Exercises, you keyed the specified formulas. In this Exercise you use Paste Function to write the function for you.

1. Select cell A17 and key **Most Hours Worked:**
2. Select cell C17.

3. Click the Paste Function button or press the keys Shift + F3. The Paste Function dialog box appears.

FIGURE 10-1
Paste Function dialog box

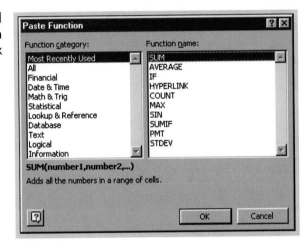

4. Choose Statistical from the Function Category list box.
5. Choose MAX from the Function Name list box.
6. Click OK. The MAX function is displayed in the formula bar and the Formula Palette pop-up window is displayed under the formula bar. Notice that the Formula Palette provides a text box for each MAX function argument. You can key a cell reference, defined name, or constant in an argument text box.

FIGURE 10-2
Formula Palette for the MAX function

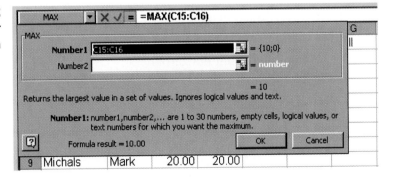

  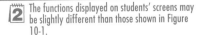

Some instructors believe that students learn syntax better by entering functions manually. If you prefer not to have students use Paste Function, instruct them to enter the functions manually as they did in previous Exercises.

Use Excel Classroom Presentation 10 to display screens from the lesson in a slide-show format.

The functions displayed on students' screens may be slightly different than those shown in Figure 10-1.

7. Key **C4:C13** in the Number1 argument box. As you key arguments, the cell range is entered in the formula bar, the values of the cells are displayed in the text box to the right of the argument box, and the result of the function is displayed in the lower left corner of the Formula Palette.

 TIP: Rather than keying a cell range, you can move the pointer out of the dialog box and select a cell range in the worksheet by clicking and/or dragging.

8. Click OK.

9. Copy the formula in cell C17 to cells D17 through F17.

10. Key the following data in column E, starting with cell E4 and leaving the second-to-last cell blank, as indicated:

N/A
18
20
N/A
21
23
19
10
(Leave blank)
10

The results are displayed in cells C17, D17, and E17. The MAX function ignores the blank cell and the cells that contain text.

✓**Objective 4**

Using the COUNT Function

You use the COUNT function to count how many cells contain numbers within a specified range of cells.

The COUNT function ignores:

- Text
- Blank cells (but not zeros)
- Error values
- Logical values (such as TRUE and FALSE)

Use the format =COUNT(arguments), where the arguments refer to the values you want to count.

✓Objective 4 Assignment:
Exercise 10-15 (Lesson Applications) can be assigned after completing Objective 4.

TABLE 10-3 **Examples of the COUNT Function**

FUNCTION	CELL DATA	RESULT
=COUNT(A1:A3)	A1 is blank, A2=40, A3=30	2
=COUNT(A1:A3)	A1=31, A2 is blank, A3=N/A	1
=COUNT(A1:A3)	A1=0, A2 is blank, A3=N/A	1
=COUNT(13,21,111)	(none)	3
=COUNT(A1, B2, C1:C2)	A1=2, B2 is blank, C1=4, C2=4	3

EXERCISE **10-4** **Use the COUNT Function with Paste Function**

1. Select cell A18 and key **Available Contractors:**
2. Select cell C18.
3. Click the Paste Function button [fx] or choose Function from the Insert menu. The Paste Function dialog box appears.
4. Choose Statistical from the Function Category list box.
5. Choose COUNT from the Function Name list box.
6. Click OK. The Formula Palette pop-up window appears.
7. Key **C4:C13** in the Number1 argument box. The cell range is displayed in the formula bar. The values of the cells and the result of the function are displayed in the Formula Palette window.
8. Click OK.
9. Copy the formula in cell C18 to cells D18 through F18.
10. Key the following data in column F, starting with cell F4 and leaving the second-to-last cell blank, as indicated:

   20
   15
   15
   20
   N/A
   22
   N/A
   10
   (Leave blank)
   N/A

   The result, 6, is displayed in cell F18. The COUNT function does not count the blank cell or the cells that contain text.

[1] Review the results in Table 10-3. Ask students to write their own functions and ask classmates to provide the result. Also, point out that the argument in the last example calculates the count in nonadjacent ranges, with each range separated by a comma.

[2] Instead of using Paste Function, you may prefer to have students enter functions manually.

[3] If your students used Paste Function, suggest they try completing a text box in the Formula Palette by moving the pointer out of the pop-up window and selecting the cell range on the worksheet.

12. Highlight the range F4:F13 and use AutoCalculate, selecting Count Nums. The result should agree with the value in F18.

☑ **Objective 5**

Using the COUNTA Function

You use the COUNTA function to count how many items are found in a range of cells. Unlike the COUNT function, COUNTA counts cells that contain text as well as cells that contain numbers.

The COUNTA function ignores:

- Blank cells (but not zeros)
- Error values
- Logical values (such as TRUE and FALSE)

Use the format =COUNTA(arguments), where the arguments refer to the values you want to count.

TABLE 10-4

Examples of the COUNTA Function

FUNCTION	CELL DATA	RESULT
=COUNTA(A1:A3)	A1 is blank, A2=40, A3=30	2
=COUNTA(A1:A3)	A1=31, A2=40, A3=N/A	3
=COUNTA(A1:A3)	A1=0, A2 is blank, A3=N/A	2
=COUNTA(A1, B2, C1:C2)	A1=2, B2 is blank, C1=N/A, C2=4	3

NOTE: Count in AutoCalculate generates the same result as the COUNTA function. Count Nums in AutoCalculate produces the same result as the COUNT Function.

EXERCISE 10-5 **Use the COUNTA Function**

1. Select cell A19 and key **Total Contractors:**

2. Widen column A to accommodate row headings in rows 15 through 19. Do not use Best Fit.

3. Select cell B19 and enter **=COUNTA(B4:B13)**. The COUNTA function counts all the cells that contain text. The result is 10.

☑ **Objective 5 Assignment:**
Exercise 10-10 (Skills Review) can be assigned after completing Objective 5.

1 Review the results in Table 10-4. Ask students to write their own functions and ask classmates to provide the result. Also, point out that the argument in the last example calculates the count in nonadjacent ranges, with each range separated by a comma.

4. Copy the formula in cell B19 to cells C19 through F19. The COUNTA function counts text and numbers, but not blank cells.

5. Center the worksheet and add the standard header to the worksheet with your name, the filename, and the date.

6. Save the workbook as *[your initials]*10-5.xls in a new folder for Lesson 10.

7. Print the worksheet and close the workbook.

FIGURE 10-3
Worksheet with
functions entered

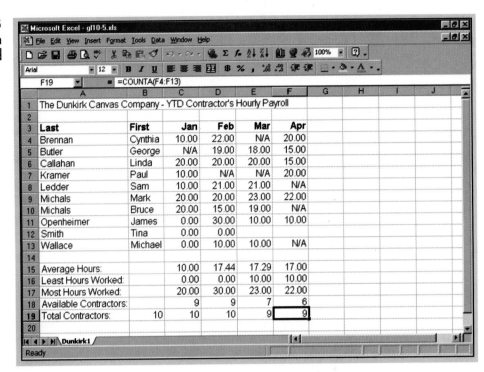

Objective 6
Using the INT and ROUND Functions

Sometimes the numbers that Excel uses in its calculations do not match the numbers displayed. This discrepancy occurs because Excel stores the full number of decimals keyed or calculated for a cell, even if the cell is formatted for rounded values. For example, if you key 3.569 in a cell formatted for two decimal places, the cell displays 3.57. In calculations, however, Excel uses the full precision, 3.569. You can use the INT (integer) and ROUND functions to control the amount of precision that Excel uses in calculations.

You use the INT function to round a number down to the nearest integer. For example, the INT function rounds 2.99 to 2. Use the format =INT(number), where (number) is the value you want to round down to the nearest integer.

In Excel Classroom Presentation 10.

Objective 6 Assignment:
Exercises 10-11 (Skills Review) and 10-13 (Lesson Applications) can be assigned after completing Objective 6.

TABLE 10-5

Examples of the INT Function

FUNCTION	CELL DATA	RESULT
=INT(9.7)	(none)	9
=INT(B20)	B20 = -9.7	-10
=INT(A1)	A1 = 100.55	100

Use the ROUND function to round a number to a specified number of decimal places.

Use the format =ROUND(number, num_digits), where number is the number you want to round and num_digits is the number of decimal places to which you want to round the number.

- If num_digits is greater than 0, the number rounds to the specified number of decimal places.
- If num_digits is 0, the number rounds to the nearest integer.
- If num_digits is less than 0, the number rounds to the specified number of places to the left of the decimal point.

TABLE 10-6   **Examples of the ROUND Function**

FUNCTION	CELL DATA	RESULT
=ROUND(1.55,1)	(none)	1.6
=ROUND(A1,0)	A1=1.55	2
=ROUND(100.55,-1)	(none)	100
=ROUND(-1.555,B10)	B10 = -2	0

EXERCISE 10-6 Use the INT Function

1. Open the file **Dunkirk2.xls**.
2. Select cell E4 and enter **=INT(B4)**. The result is 0.
3. Go to the formula bar and edit the formula by adding ***D4** after the ending formula parenthesis. The result is still 0.
4. Key the following data in column B, beginning in cell B4:

Review the results in Tables 10-5 and 10-6. Ask students to write their own functions and ask classmates to provide the result.

5.22
5.52
6.23
6.42
6.86

5. Copy the formula in cell E4 to cells E5 through E8. The INT function in the formula rounds down the column B values to the nearest integer, providing a whole number in column E. The result in E4 is 135.

EXERCISE 10-7 Use the ROUND Function

1. Select cell F4 and enter **=ROUND(C4*D4,0)**. The result is 0.

TIP: A quick way to ensure that you include all required arguments and parentheses when you enter a function manually is to press Ctrl + Shift + A after you type the equal sign and function name. This automatically inserts the argument names and parentheses.

2. Key the following data in column C, beginning with cell C4:

5.09
5.45
6.14
6.23
6.51

Excel rounds the total in F4 to the nearest integer.

4. Copy the formula in cell F4 to cells F5 through F8. Format cells F4:F8 in Accounting style with the $ symbol and no decimal places. Format cells D4:E8 in Comma style with no decimal places.

FIGURE 10-4
Results of the ROUND function

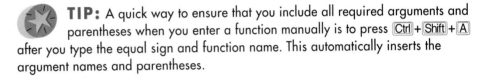

	A	B	C	D	E	F	G	H	I
	F8		=ROUND(C8*D8,0)						
1			Dunkirk Canvas Co. - Material Order List						
2									
3	Material	Weight in Lbs. Per Yard	Cost Per Yard	Quantity	Total Lbs.	Total Cost			
4	Canvas 101	5.22	5.09	27	135	$ 137			
5	Canvas 102	5.52	5.45	120	600	$ 654			
6	Canvas 103	6.23	6.14	320	1,920	$ 1,965			
7	Canvas 104	6.42	6.23	220	1,320	$ 1,371			
8	Canvas 105	6.86	6.51	550	3,300	$ 3,581			
9									
10									

5. Center the worksheet and add the standard header to the worksheet with your name, the filename, and the date.

6. Save the workbook as *[your initials]*10-7.xls in your Lesson 10 folder.

7. Print the worksheet and close the workbook.

 In Excel Classroom Presentation 10.

Using Nested Functions

☑ Objective 7

A function used as an argument inside another function is called a *nested function*. Paste Function and the Formula Palette are especially useful for inserting nested functions. In the following Exercise, you use nested functions to sum separate groups of items and then take an average of the two sums.

EXERCISE 10-8 Use Nested Functions

1. Open the file **Dunkirk3.xls**.
2. Select cell C8 and click the Paste Function button 🔲.
3. Choose Most Recently Used from the Function <u>C</u>ategory list box.
4. Choose AVERAGE from the Function <u>N</u>ame list box. (If AVERAGE does not appear in the list, select the Statistical category first.)
5. Click OK. The Formula Palette is displayed.
6. To insert a function as an argument, click the down arrow next to the Function box on the formula bar. A drop-down list is displayed. (The names displayed in the drop-down list may be different than the ones shown in Figure 10-5.)

FIGURE 10-5
Function box
drop-down list

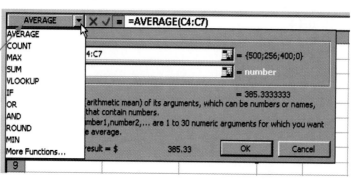

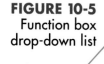

7. Choose SUM. The formula bar now shows the argument of the AVERAGE function as a nested SUM function.
8. Key B4:B6 in the Number1 argument box.
9. Click the word AVERAGE in the formula in the formula bar so you can continue entering arguments for the AVERAGE function. Notice that as you click a function name in the formula bar, Excel displays the function's arguments in the argument boxes on the Formula Palette.

 NOTE: When a formula contains nested functions, the argument boxes displayed on the Formula Palette change to show which function is currently selected in the formula bar.

☑ Objective 7 Assignment:

Exercise 10-12 (Skills Review) and Exercises 10-14 and 10-16 (Lesson Applications) can be assigned after completing Objective 7.

1 Instead of using Paste Function, you may prefer to have students enter functions manually.

2 For every left parenthesis in a function, there must be a matching right parenthesis. You must correct these errors before Excel accepts the formula. If your students used Paste Function, point out that it adds the parentheses for you.

 In Excel Classroom Presentation 10.

3 You might want to point out that students are clicking the word "AVERAGE" in the formula displayed in the Formula Bar. Some students may find this confusing at first since they have not encountered this procedure before in Excel.

10. Click the Number2 argument box to insert another argument for the AVERAGE function.

11. Click the Function box, which now displays SUM. The formula bar now shows a second argument for the AVERAGE function, which is another nested SUM function. Notice that you did not need to use the drop-down list to select the SUM function because the Function box automatically inserts the most recently used function.

12. Key **C4:C6** in the Number1 argument box and click OK.

FIGURE 10-6
Worksheet with nested functions

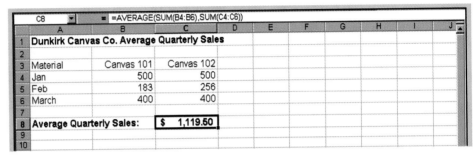

	A	B	C	D	E	F	G	H	I	J
	C8		= =AVERAGE(SUM(B4:B6),SUM(C4:C6))							
1	Dunkirk Canvas Co. Average Quarterly Sales									
2										
3	Material	Canvas 101	Canvas 102							
4	Jan	500	500							
5	Feb	183	256							
6	March	400	400							
7										
8	Average Quarterly Sales:		$ 1,119.50							
9										
10										

13. Add the standard header to the worksheet with your name, the filename, and the date.

14. Save the workbook as *[your initials]***10-8.xls** in your Lesson 10 folder.

15. Print the worksheet and close the workbook.

TIP: You can use Paste Function to create and edit formulas that contain functions. To edit an existing formula containing a function, select the desired cell and click the Paste Function button ⓕ. Excel opens the Formula Palette. As you click each function name in the formula bar, the function's arguments appear in the argument boxes. Click OK to enter additional changes and to close the Formula Palette.

COMMAND SUMMARY

FEATURE	BUTTON	MENU	KEYBOARD
Paste Function	ⓕ	Insert, Function	Shift + F3
Insert Arguments			Ctrl + Shift + A

In Excel Classroom Presentation 10.

☐1 Point out that the Command Summary lists a variety of ways to accomplish a particular task. Students can decide which method they prefer.

USING HELP

This lesson introduced you to seven of Excel's built-in functions and Paste Function, which assists you in entering them. You can use Excel Help to learn more about specific functions and how to use them.

Use Help to view detailed information about an individual function:

1. Press [F1] to activate the Office Assistant.
2. Key **count function** and click Search.
3. Click the topic "COUNT worksheet function." The Microsoft Excel Help dialog box displays information about the COUNT function.
4. Review the information, which includes an explanation of the function, its syntax, and examples of its use.

FIGURE 10-7
COUNT function
Help screen

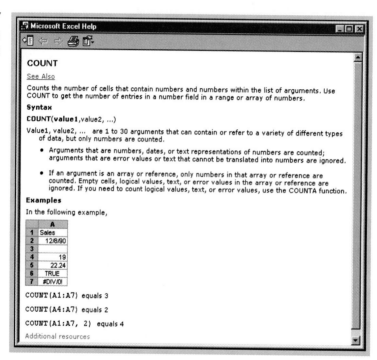

5. Click the link See Also. Choose another function and click Display.
6. Review the information, and then close the Help window and hide the Office Assistant.

Encourage students to follow the steps in "Using Help." Software companies are increasingly using their Help program—rather than printed documentation—to train users and assist in answering user questions.

In Excel Classroom Presentation 10.

TEST BANK

Concepts Review

TRUE/FALSE QUESTIONS

Each of the following statements is either true or false. Indicate your choice by circling **T** or **F**.

T **(F)** *1.* Using Paste Function is the only way to enter functions in a worksheet.

(T) F *2.* The arguments for an Excel function are enclosed in parentheses following the function name.

T **(F)** *3.* The arguments for an Excel function can consist of only constants or cell references.

T **(F)** *4.* When using Paste Function, all argument boxes shown in the Formula Palette must be completed.

(T) F *5.* The value returned by a function is called the result.

T **(F)** *6.* The MAX function can be found in the Math & Trig Function Category in the Paste Function dialog box.

(T) F *7.* The COUNTA function counts cells containing text as well as cells containing numbers.

T **(F)** *8.* The AVERAGE function ignores zeros.

SHORT ANSWER QUESTIONS

Write the correct answer in the space provided.

1. Which menu command do you use to access Paste Function?

   Insert, Function

2. What is the value operated on by a function called?

   Argument

3. If a function takes more than one argument, which keyboard character do you use to separate the arguments?

   Comma

4. What name is given to a function that is, itself, the argument of another function?

   Nested function

CLOSE

Concepts Review:
Allows students to check their understanding.

TEST BANK
Consider using the Test Bank to provide an additional review of lesson concepts. It may also be used as an assessment tool.

5. Which category of functions in the Paste Function dialog box contains the AVERAGE, MIN, and MAX functions?

   Statistical category

6. Which function do you use to find the highest number in a range of values?

   MAX

7. Which function do you use to round a number down to the nearest integer?

   INT

8. Which function do you use to round a number to a specific number of decimal places?

   ROUND

CRITICAL THINKING

Answer these questions on a separate piece of paper. There are no right or wrong answers. Support your answers with examples from your own experience, if possible.

1. What advantages and disadvantages do you see in using Excel's Paste Function when developing formulas in your worksheets?

2. When can nested functions be especially useful?

Skills Review

EXERCISE 10-9

Enter formulas using the AVERAGE, MIN, and MAX functions.

1. Open the file **Dunkirk4.xls**.

2. Enter a formula that calculates the average cost per yard by following these steps:

   a. Select cell B16.

   b. Key **=AVERAGE(B4:B14)**

3. Enter a formula that calculates the minimum stock by following these steps:

   a. Select cell F17 and click the Paste Function button **fx**.

   b. Choose Statistical from the Function Category list box.

Critical Thinking Questions:
Answers will vary based on students' preferences, observations, experiences, and research.

Skills Review:
Provides guided practice for students. Objectives are indicated for each Exercise.

⊙ Exercise 10-9:
Objectives 1–3
Required Files: Dunkirk4.xls
Solution Files: gl10-9.xls in Solutions Manual or on Solutions Disk.

⌐1⌐ Students use Paste Function in this Exercise. You may prefer that they enter the functions manually.

       c. Choose MIN from the Function Name list box.

       d. Click OK to display the Formula Palette.

       e. Key **F4:F14** in the Number1 argument box.

       f. Click OK.

4. Enter a formula that calculates the maximum stock by following these steps:

       a. Select cell F18 and click the Paste Function button ☑.

       b. Choose Statistical from the Function Category list box.

       c. Choose MAX from the Function Name list box.

       d. Click OK.

       e. Key **F4:F14** in the Number1 argument box.

       f. Click OK.

5. Add the standard header to the worksheet with your name, the filename, and the date.

6. Save the workbook as *[your initials]***10-9.xls** in your Lesson 10 folder.

7. Print the worksheet.

8. Create a formula printout in landscape orientation with grids and row and column headings. Use the Fit To option to make the printout fit on a single page.

9. Close the workbook without saving.

E X E R C I S E 10-10

Enter formulas using the COUNT and COUNTA functions.

1. Open the file **Dunkirk5.xls**. Key the data shown in Figure 10-8 beginning in cell C4 (leave cells blank where indicated.)

FIGURE 10-8

	C	D
4	yes	1
5		n/a
6	yes	3
7	yes	2
8		n/a

◉ Exercise 10-10:
Objectives 1, 4, 5
Required Files: Dunkirk5.xls
Solution Files: gl10-10.xls in Solutions Manual or on Solutions Disk.

Students use Paste Function in this Exercise. You may prefer that they enter the functions manually.

2. Enter a formula that counts the number of employees whose insurance covers dependents by following these steps:

   a. Select cell D10 and click the Paste Function button .

   b. Choose Statistical from the Function Category list box.

   c. Choose COUNT from the Function Name list box.

   d. Click OK.

   e. Key **D4:D8** in the Value1 argument box.

   f. Click OK.

3. Enter a formula that counts the employees with hospitalization coverage by following these steps:

   a. Select cell C11.

   b. Key the COUNTA function, specifying the range for the argument as C4:C8.

4. Add the standard header to the worksheet with your name, the filename, and the date.

5. Save the workbook as ***[your initials]*10-10.xls** in your Lesson 10 folder.

6. Print the worksheet.

7. Create a formula printout with grids and row and column headings. Use the Fit To option so the printout fits on a single page.

8. Close the workbook without saving.

EXERCISE 10-11

Create a formula using the INT and ROUND functions.

1. Open the file **Dunkirk6.xls**.

2. Enter a formula that rounds a 10% price increase by following these steps:

   a. Select cell E4 and click the Paste Function button .

   b. Choose Math & Trig from the Function Category list box.

   c. Choose ROUND from the Function Name list box.

   d. Click OK.

   e. Key **B4*1.1** in the Number argument box.

   f. Key **2** in the Num_Digits argument box.

   g. Click OK.

3. Copy this formula from cell E4 to cells E5 through E8.

4. Enter a formula that totals the New Total Cost, rounding the total down to the nearest integer by following these steps:

   a. Select cell F4.

   b. Key **=INT(C4*E4)**

5. Copy this formula from cell F4 to cells F5 through F8.

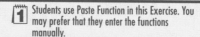

Students use Paste Function in this Exercise. You may prefer that they enter the functions manually.

This function includes a constant in the formula. Some instructors feel this technique is not good practice. Ways to avoid it are described in Lesson 11, but you may want to discuss the topic briefly here.

6. Add the standard header to the worksheet with your name, the filename, and the date.

7. Save the workbook as *[your initials]***10-11.xls** in your Lesson 10 folder.

8. Print the worksheet.

9. Create a formula printout in landscape orientation with grids and row and column headings. Use the Fit To option so the printout fits on one page.

10. Close the workbook without saving.

EXERCISE 10-12

Create a formula using nested functions.

1. Open the file **Dunkirk7.xls**.

2. Select cell B8 and key **5126**

3. Select cell C8 and key **6295**

4. Enter a formula using a nested function that finds average annual sales by following these steps:

   a. Select cell B10 and click the Paste Function button.

   b. Choose Statistical from the Function Category list box.

   c. Choose AVERAGE from the Function Name list box.

   d. Click OK.

   e. Click the arrow next to the Function box and choose SUM from the drop-down list.

   f. Key **B5:B8** in the Number1 argument box.

   g. Click the word AVERGE in the formula bar.

   h. Click the Number2 argument box.

   i. Click the Function box to select a SUM function as a second argument for the AVERAGE function.

   j. Key **C5:C8** in the Number1 argument box.

   k. Click OK.

5. Add the standard header to the worksheet with your name, the filename, and the date.

6. Save the workbook as *[your initials]***10-12.xls** in your Lesson 10 folder.

7. Print the worksheet.

8. Create a formula printout with grids and row and column headings. Make sure column B is wide enough to display formulas. Adjust the width of columns A and C so the printout fits on one page.

9. Close the workbook without saving.

◎ **Exercise 10-12:**
Objectives 1, 2, 7
Required Files: Dunkirk7.xls
Solution Files: gl10-12.xls in Solutions Manual or on Solutions Disk.

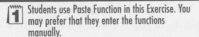 Students use Paste Function in this Exercise. You may prefer that they enter the functions manually.

Assessment Resources:
• Solutions Manual
• Test Bank
• Portfolio Builder
• Internet Projects
• Alternative Assessment Guide
• Certification Procedures

Go ▾

For Internet projects, go to
www.glencoe.com/webprojects

Lesson Applications

Create a worksheet that includes formulas using the AVERAGE, MIN, MAX, COUNT, and COUNTA functions.

Create a worksheet that calculates weekly commissions for salespeople. It should also include average sales earned, the minimum and maximum sales earned, the number of salespeople selling that week, and the total number of salespeople on the regular sales force.

1. Open the file **Dunkirk8.xls**.

2. Key the data shown in Figure 10-9, beginning in cell B4.

FIGURE 10-9

Callahan	23,098.00	.045
Davis	32,427.00	.055
Jefferson	vacation	.040
Lerner	12,835.44	.056
Matthews	10,098.53	.060
Nicholson	42,098.65	.030
Peters	56,987.54	.050
Stuart	vacation	.065
Vaughn	5,098.87	.133

3. To calculate the commissions, rounding the number to two decimal places, select cell D4 and key **=ROUND(B4*C4,2)**

4. Copy the formula in cell D4 to cells D5 through D12.

5. Key **0** in cells D6 and D11.

6. Select cell A14 and key **AVERAGE:**

7. To calculate the weekly average, select cell B14 and key **=AVERAGE(B4:B12)**

8. Select cell A15 and key **MAX:**

Lesson Applications:
Provide independent practice for students and may be used for assessment. Objectives are indicated for each Exercise.

● **Exercise 10-13:**
Objectives 1–6
Required Files: Dunkirk8.xls
Solution Files: gl10-13.xls in Solutions Manual or on Solutions Disk.

9. To calculate the maximum sales earned by a salesperson, select cell B15 and key **=MAX(B4:B12)**

10. Select cell A16 and key **MIN:**

11. To calculate the minimum sales earned by a salesperson, select cell B16 and key **=MIN(B4:B12)**

12. Select cell A18 and key **Active Salespersons:**

13. To calculate the number of salespersons working that week, select cell B18 and key **=COUNT(B4:B12)**

14. Select cell A19 and key **Total Salespersons:**

15. To calculate the number of salespeople on the regular sales force, select cell B19 and key **=COUNTA(B4:B12)**

16. Format cells B18 and B19 with no decimal places.

17. Select cell A20 and key **% Active:**

18. To calculate the percentage of salespeople working this week, select cell B20 and key **=B18/B19**

19. Format cell B20 for percent with no decimal places.

20. Format the range D4:D12 in comma style with two decimal places.

21. Add the standard header to the worksheet with your name, the filename, and the date.

22. Save the workbook as *[your initials]***10-13.xls** in your Lesson 10 folder.

23. Print the worksheet.

24. Create a formula printout with grids and row and column headings. Make columns narrower so the printout fits on one page.

25. Close the workbook without saving.

EXERCISE 10-14

Construct a worksheet that includes formulas using nested AVERAGE, MIN, MAX, INT, or ROUND functions.

  Construct a worksheet that analyzes monthly sales by product. For each product, calculate the most units sold and the least units sold by any region. In addition, calculate the average revenue and the total revenue for all regions, rounded to the nearest dollar.

1. Open the file **Dunkirk9.xls**. Key the data shown below, beginning in cell C5:

Units Sold
320
254

○ Exercise 10-14:
Objectives 1–3, 6, 7
Required Files: Dunkirk9.xls
Solution Files: gl10-14.xls in Solutions Manual or on
Solutions Disk.

 The completed document for this Exercise
may be used in a student's portfolio.

634
300
720
310
540
230

2. Center the region text in the range B4:B12.

3. In cell A16, key **Most Units**

4. In cell B16, calculate the most units sold for Cover C-9087.

5. In cell C16, calculate the most units sold for Cover C-9088.

6. In cell A17, key **Least Units**

7. In cell B17, calculate the least units sold for Cover C-9087.

8. In cell C17, calculate the least units sold for Cover C-9088.

9. In cell A18, key **Average Units**

10. In cell B18, calculate the average number sold for Cover C-9087.

11. In cell C18, calculate the average number sold for Cover C-9088.

12. In cell A19, key **Total Revenue**

13. In cell B19, calculate the total revenue rounded to the nearest dollar for Cover C-9087. Use 11.5 as the price of each unit.

14. In cell C19, calculate the total revenue rounded to the nearest dollar for Cover C-9088. Use 13.11 as the price of each unit.

15. Format cells B19 and C19 for currency with no decimal places and a dollar sign. Use the Format Cells dialog box, not the toolbar, to add the currency formatting.

16. Add the standard header to the worksheet with your name, the filename, and the date.

17. Save the workbook as *[your initials]***10-14.xls** in your Lesson 10 folder.

18. Print the worksheet.

19. Create a formula printout in landscape orientation with grids and row and column headings.

20. Close the workbook without saving.

EXERCISE 10-15

Create a worksheet that includes formulas using the MIN, MAX, and COUNT functions.

Create a worksheet that shows employees, their salaries, and their job performance ratings.

1. Open the file **Dunk10.xls**. Key the data shown in Figure 10-10.

Students are instructed to use the Format Cells dialog box to format cells for currency, since using the Currency Style button on the toolbar produces the accounting format.

⊙ Exercise 10-15:
Objectives 1–4
Required Files: Dunk10.xls
Solution Files: gl10-15.xls and gl10-15.htm in Solutions Manual or on Solutions Disk.

FIGURE 10-10

Name	Full-time	Part-time Hourly	Performance Rating
Anderson	50,000		3
Boyd		18.00	4
Carlson	35,000		3
Dugan	28,000		4
Evans	45,000		4
Jenkins		10.00	2

2. In cell A11, key **Count:**
3. In cell B11, enter a function that counts the number of full-time employees.
4. In cell C11, enter a function that counts the number of part-time employees.
5. In cell A12, key **Max:**
6. In cell A13, key **Min:**
7. In cells B12 and C12, enter functions that show the highest salary for full-time employees and the highest hourly rate for part-time employees, respectively.
8. In cells B13 and C13, enter functions that show the lowest salary for full-time employees and the lowest hourly rate for part-time employees, respectively.
9. Format column B in accounting style, with dollar signs and no decimal places.
10. Format column C in accounting style, with dollar signs and two decimal places.
11. Format cells B11 and C11 in number style with no decimal places.
12. Add the standard header to the worksheet with your name, the filename, and the date.
13. Save the workbook as *[your initials]***10-15.xls** in your Lesson 10 folder.
14. Print the worksheet.
15. Save the workbook as *[your initials]***10-15.htm** in your Lesson 10 folder.

16. Create a formula printout in landscape orientation with grids and row and column headings.

17. Close the workbook without saving.

EXERCISE 10-16   *Challenge Yourself*

Construct a worksheet using the AVERAGE, INT, COUNTA, and ROUND functions.

  The Dunkirk Canvas Company needs a worksheet that shows transportation charges for the month of May for each of its carriers.

1. Create a worksheet sketch that includes a worksheet title, column labels, and an area for data. The worksheet should include each carrier (rows), and columns showing the mileage for each carrier, the charge per mile, and formulas computing the total mileage charges for each carrier. Below the area for data, there should be formulas showing the total number of carriers, the average mileage and total mileage for all carriers, and the total transportation charges for the month. Leave a few blank lines before entering these formulas.

2. Using a 12-point font for all data, transfer the sketch into Excel by keying and formatting the labels. Then key the following data:

Carrier	Miles	Charge Per Mile
Allied Trans.	5636.5	0.75
United Freight	4397.6	0.47
Eastern Trans.	5107.1	0.95
Coastal Trans.	7130.4	0.49

3. Create formulas to show the total charges for each carrier.

4. Show the total transportation charges for all carriers rounded to the nearest dollar. Use Paste Function to create a formula with a nested function.

5. Use the COUNTA function to show the total number of carriers.

6. Use the INT function to round the total mileage and the average mileage.

7. Format all cells that show the number of miles in the number style with a comma separator and one decimal place, except for the total and average mileage cells, which should have no decimal places.

8. Format all dollar amounts in the currency style with no decimal places and a dollar sign, except for the "Charge Per Mile" cells, which should have two decimal places. Use the Format Cells dialog box, not the toolbar, to apply the formatting.

Exercise 10-16:

Objectives 1, 2, 4, 6, 7
Required Files: None
Solution Files: gl10-16.xls in Solutions Manual or on Solutions Disk.

The completed document for this Exercise may be used in a student's portfolio.

1 This Exercise includes features from Lesson 4 (designing a worksheet and user documentation), Lesson 8 (formatting numbers), and Lesson 9 (using borders and colors).

2 Students are instructed to use the Format Cells dialog box to format cells for currency, since using the Currency Style button on the toolbar produces the accounting format.

9. Center the titles over the worksheet, and add light blue shading to the title area. Make the column labels bold, widen the columns where necessary, and right-align the column labels in columns B through D. Add a thick outline border around the entire worksheet.

10. Rename Sheet1 "Charges" and rename Sheet2 "User Information." Delete Sheet3.

11. In the User Information worksheet, create documentation, which includes the following: File Information (Created by, Date created, Date revised, Revised by, Contact for help); Purpose of worksheet (paragraph form); Instructions to User (special instructions needed by user to enter data correctly). Style the documentation for easy reading.

12. Center the worksheets horizontally and add the standard header to the worksheets with your name, the filename, and the date.

13. Save the workbook as *[your initials]***10-16.xls** in your Lesson 10 folder.

14. Print the workbook.

15. Create a formula printout of the Charges worksheet in landscape orientation on one page with grids and row and column headings and close the workbook without saving.

Advanced Formulas

OBJECTIVES

After completing this lesson, you will be able to:

1. **Use absolute and mixed cell references.**
2. **Create an IF function.**
3. **Create an IF function with multiple conditions.**
4. **Insert text with the IF function.**
5. **Use the VLOOKUP and HLOOKUP functions.**
6. **Use comments to annotate a formula.**
7. **Correct circular references.**

MOUS ACTIVITIES

In this lesson:
XL2000 **6.4**
XL2000 **6.8**
XL2000 **6.11**
XL2000 **E.6.3**

See Appendix F.

 Estimated Time: 1¾ hours

Understanding differences in the types of cell references is the key to making the most of Excel's formula capabilities. As this lesson demonstrates, using the right type of cell reference is important when you copy formulas between cells. This lesson also explains how to use the IF function to create more powerful formulas, how to create lookup tables to automate data-entry tasks, and how to document complicated formulas by attaching comments to cells. Finally, circular cell references—a common error in creating formulas—are explained.

PREPARE

Point out to students that the learning objectives show what they will learn in the lesson. Each heading in the lesson correlates to a learning objective.

Required files:
Cost2.xls   DunBon.xls   Rates.xls

TEACH

Teaching Resources:
- Excel Classroom Presentations
- School-to-Work Strategies Manual
- Spanish Glossary
- Certification Procedures

Using Absolute and Mixed Cell References

 Objective 1

So far, you have worked primarily with *relative cell references* in formulas. In relative cell references, the cell's address is relative to the address of the cell containing the formula. Excel automatically adjusts relative cell addresses when you copy a formula from one cell to another.

Sometimes, you do not want Excel to adjust the cell references when you copy a formula. In those instances, use *absolute cell references* or *mixed cell references*. In absolute cell references, the addresses of cells remain unchanged when a formula is copied from one cell to another. With mixed cell references, either the row or the column portion of the address is absolute, and the other portion of the address is relative.

> **NOTE:** Cell references of named cells are absolute.

EXERCISE **11-1** **Use an Absolute Cell Reference in a Formula**

You create absolute cell references by placing dollar signs in front of the column letter and row number (for example, $A$3, $A$4).

> **TIP:** With the insertion point within a cell reference in the formula bar, pressing F4 provides a shortcut method for cycling among relative, absolute, and mixed cell references.

1. Open the file **Rates.xls**.
2. Select cell C6.
3. Key **=B6+(B6*G4)**. This formula calculates a 50% markup price for the first yardage item—the markup amount is in cell G4. The result is 37.5.

> **NOTE:** The parentheses in the above formula are not needed since order of precedence dictates that the multiplication is performed before the addition. However, the parentheses are included for clarity.

4. Use AutoFill to copy the formula to cells C7 and C8. The formulas in cells C7 and C8 are incorrect because of the relative reference to cell G4.
5. Double-click cell C6, move the insertion point after the "G" in the formula, and press F4. Dollar signs appear before the "G" and the "4," indicating that both column G and row 4 are absolute references.

 Objective 1 Assignment:
Exercise 11-13 (Skills Review) can be assigned after completing Objective 1.

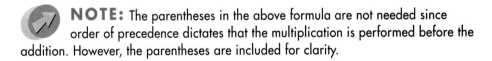 Ask students if they know why cell G4 did not remain as the reference cell after the AutoFill.

FIGURE 11-1
Changing a cell
address to absolute

	A	B	C	D	E	F	G	H	I	J	K
1	Dunkirk Canvas Commission Table										
2											
3				Commission Rate			Markup				
4	Yardage Item No.	Cost	Price	10%	15%	20%	0.5				
5							0.6				
6	1015	25.00	=B6+(B6*$G$4)								
7	1016	50.00	80								
8	1019	75.00	75								
9											

SUM ▼ X ✓ ■ =B6+(B6*$G$4)

Absolute cell reference

NOTE: Pressing F4 doesn't work if the insertion point is positioned in front of the equal sign in the formula. Always move the insertion point within the cell reference that requires the $ signs.

6. Enter the formula and use AutoFill to copy it to cells C7 and C8. The results are 75 and 112.5, respectively. The formulas are now correct, because the absolute cell reference $G$4 does not adjust in its copied locations.

EXERCISE 11-2 View a Named Cell as an Absolute Reference in a Formula

When you use named cells in formulas, Excel makes the reference to the named cell absolute.

1. Select cell G5.

2. Give this cell a name by choosing <u>I</u>nsert, <u>N</u>ame, <u>D</u>efine. The Define Name dialog box is displayed.

3. Key **sixty**. At the bottom of the box, the cell reference is absolute: Rates!$G$5. (The Rates! portion of the address is added automatically, and specifies the current workbook: "Rates.xls.")

4. Click OK.

5. Select cell C6 and change the formula to **=B6+(B6*sixty)**

6. Copy the formula to cells C7 and C8. The name "sixty," which always refers to cell $G$5, is copied to each cell, as references to named cells are absolute.

TIP: It is good practice to use named cells for constant values in formulas whenever possible. Names make formulas easier to understand and changing the value of the constant doesn't necessitate changing the formula.

Use Excel Classroom Presentation 11 to display screens from the lesson in a slide-show format.

Discuss the undesirability of using an absolute value (as opposed to a named cell) as a constant in a formula.

EXERCISE 11-3 Use a Mixed Cell Reference

To create a mixed cell reference, place a dollar sign ($) in front of the part of the cell reference (the row number or column letter) that you want to be absolute.

1. Select cell D6 and key **=C6*D4**. This formula is intended to multiply the price in column C by the commission rate in D4. The result should be 4.00.

2. Copy this formula to cells D6 through F8.

3. Select cell F8. The cell references in the formula are incorrect. The formula should refer to column C, the "Price" column, but now it refers to column E. Similarly, the formula should refer to row 4, which contains the commission rates. Instead, it refers to row 6.

4. Double-click cell D6.

5. Position the insertion point in the cell reference C6 (after the equal sign).

6. Press F4 three times to make the reference to column C absolute. The cell reference changes to $C6. This keeps this portion of the formula fixed on the "Price " column when it is copied across columns.

7. Position the insertion point in the cell reference D4.

8. Press F4 twice to change the cell reference to D$4, making row 4 absolute. This keeps this portion of the formula fixed on row 4 (the location of the commission values) when the formula is copied down rows.

9. Press Enter and copy the formula to cells D6 through F8.

FIGURE 11-2
Copying a formula with mixed cell references

D6		=	=$C6*D$4								
	A	B	C	D	E	F	G	H	I	J	K
1		Dunkirk Canvas Commission Table									
2											
3				Commission Rate			Markup				
4	Yardage Item No.	Cost	Price	10%	15%	20%	0.5				
							0.6				
	Mixed cell references		40	4.00	6.00	8.00					
7	1016	50.00	80	8.00	12.00	16.00					
8	1019	75.00	120	12.00	18.00	24.00					
9											

10. Compare the formula in D6 (=$C6*D$4) with the formula in cell F8 (=$C8*F$4). Notice that the formula in cell F8 now refers to the "Price" column and the commission value in row 4 because you used mixed cell references in the original formula.

TIP: You can quickly scan your formulas in the worksheet using Ctrl+` (left single quote) to toggle between displaying the values in your worksheet and displaying the formulas. This is the same as choosing Tools, Options and choosing Formulas from the View tab.

In Excel Classroom Presentation 11.

11. Add the standard header to the worksheet with your name, the filename, and the date.

12. Save the workbook as *[your initials]***11-3.xls** in a new folder for Lesson 11.

13. Print the worksheet and close the workbook.

☑**Objective 2**

Creating an IF Function

You use the IF function to create conditional expressions—formulas of the form "If X, then Y." For example, "If the bill is past 30 days late, then you will pay a late fee of 2%."

The IF function in Excel takes the form, "If X, then Y, otherwise Z." The IF function evaluates whether X is true or false. It returns the value Y if the conditional expression is true and the value Z if it is false. An example is "If cell C5 is greater than 50, then charge a late fee; otherwise, state 'Thank you for your payment.'"

The IF function takes three arguments in this format:

=IF(logical_test, value_if_true, value_if_false)

- Logical_test is the expression that evaluates to true or false. For example, the expression C5>50 is either true or false.

- Value_if_true is the value that is returned if logical_test is true. Value_if_true can be a constant, a formula, text, or a cell reference.

- Value_if_false is the value that is returned if logical_test is false. Value_if_false can be a constant, a formula, text, or a cell reference.

Table 11-1 shows the operators you can use to construct the logical_test portion of the function.

TABLE 11-1 **Operators to Use in Functions**

OPERATOR	MEANING
=	Equal to
<>	Not equal to
>	Greater than
<	Less than
>=	Greater than or equal to
<=	Less than or equal to

☑**Objective 2 Assignment:**

Exercise 11-14 (Skills Review) can be assigned after completing Objective 2.

EXERCISE 11-4 Use the IF Function in a Formula

1. Open the file **DunBon.xls**.
2. Select cell D4 and key **=IF(B4>20000,500,0)**. The formula returns a bonus of 500 if the value in B4 is greater than $20,000; otherwise, it returns a zero. Since Jack Bell's sales are greater than $20,000, he receives a $500 bonus.
3. Copy the formula in cell D4 to cells D5 through D8.

FIGURE 11-3
IF function determining who receives bonuses

	D4		=	=IF(B4>20000,500,0)						
	A	B	C	D	E	F	G	H	I	J
1				Dunkirk Canvas Bonus Table						
2										
3	Name	Sales	Rate	Bonus 1	Bonus 2	Bonus 3	Bonus 4			
4	Bell, Jack	21,000	10%	500						
5	Sue	0	15%	0						
6	z	18,000	10%	0						
7	om	20,000	20%	0						
8	Summers, Lynn	21,305	20%	500						
9										

(Formula using IF function)

NOTE: No comma or dollar punctuation can be used with numbers inside the IF function

Objective 3

Using IF Functions with Multiple Conditions

You can use logical functions such as AND, OR, and NOT for the logical_test part of a conditional expression. When you use functions for the logical_test argument, the functions are enclosed in parentheses. Excel then evaluates the conditional formula, starting with the innermost parentheses that enclose the nested arguments.

The AND expression can be summed up as "All conditions must be met." It returns "TRUE" if all of its conditions test true, and "FALSE" if one or more of its conditions test false. Use the format AND(logical_1,logical_2,...), where you can test as many as 30 conditions, beginning with logical_1.

TABLE 11-2 Examples of the AND Function

EXPRESSION	EXCEL RETURNS
AND(1+2=3, 3+3=6)	TRUE
AND(2+2=4, 1+1=3)	FALSE
AND(C2>1, C2<100)	TRUE if cell C2 contains a number greater than 1 and less than 100; otherwise FALSE

In Excel Classroom Presentation 11.

The OR expression can be summed up as "At least one condition must be met." It returns "TRUE" if at least one of its conditions tests true, and "FALSE" if none of its conditions tests true. Use the format OR(logical_1,logical_2,...), where as many as 30 conditions, beginning with logical_1, can be true or false.

TABLE 11-3   **Examples of the OR Function**

EXPRESSION	EXCEL RETURNS
OR(1+1=3, 3+3=6)	TRUE
OR(2+0=4, 1+1=1)	FALSE
OR(A1:A3)	TRUE only if the cells in A1:A3 contain at least one formula or expression that evaluates true; otherwise FALSE

When using the AND and OR functions, keep the following points in mind:

- AND and OR ignore empty cells and cells with text.
- If the references in AND or OR contain no logical values, Excel returns the #VALUE! error message.

The NOT expression can be summed up as "The reverse of the condition must be met." It returns "TRUE" if its conditions test false and "FALSE" if its conditions test true. Use the format NOT(logical), where logical is an expression or value that can be true or false.

TABLE 11-4   **Examples of the NOT Expression**

EXPRESSION	EXCEL RETURNS
NOT(A3=0)	TRUE if cell A3 contains any number other than 0; FALSE if cell A3 contains 0
NOT(2+2=4)	FALSE

EXERCISE 11-5   Use AND in a Formula

1. Select cell E4.

2. Click the Paste Function button [fx] or choose Function from the Insert menu. The Paste Function dialog box appears.

---

[1] The NOT logical function may confuse students because it reverses the value of the argument. Remind students to use NOT when the value in the argument is not equal to a particular value.

[2] If you prefer not to have students use Paste Function, instruct them to enter the functions manually.

3. Choose Logical from the Function <u>C</u>ategory list box.

4. Choose IF from the Function <u>N</u>ame list box.

5. Click OK. The Formula Palette appears.

6. Click the down arrow next to the Function box. Choose More Functions from the drop-down list. The Paste Function dialog box is displayed once again.

7. Choose Logical from the Function <u>C</u>ategory list box, if necessary.

8. Choose AND from the Function <u>N</u>ame list box.

9. Click OK. The Formula Palette is redisplayed. Notice that the AND function is in bold in the formula bar, which indicates you enter the arguments for the AND function in the argument boxes on the Formula Palette.

FIGURE 11-4
Formula Palette for the AND function

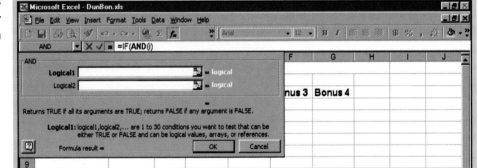

10. Key **B4>20000** in the Logical1 argument box.

11. Key **C4=.2** in the Logical2 argument box. Notice in the formula bar that the AND function was inserted as the "X" part of the "If X, then Y, otherwise Z" conditional expression.

12. Click the IF function name in the formula displayed in the formula bar. The Formula Palette now displays the argument boxes for the remaining arguments in the IF function. Notice that the AND function serves as the Logical_test argument.

FIGURE 11-5
Formula Palette for the rest of the IF function

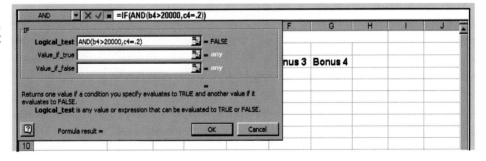

 In Excel Classroom Presentation 11.

13. Key **500** in the Value_if_true argument box. It becomes the "Y" part of the conditional expression.

14. Key **0** in the Value_if_false argument box. It becomes the "Z" part of the conditional expression.

> **NOTE:** If you forget to key 0 in the Value_if_false argument box, Excel displays the value FALSE in the worksheet instead of the value 0. To complete the formula, you can edit it manually in the formula bar. Key **0** preceded by a comma where the Value_if_false argument belongs.

15. Click OK. Because cell B4 is greater than 20,000, but cell C4 is not 20%, the formula calculates 0 (no bonus).

16. Copy the formula to cells E5 through E8.

EXERCISE 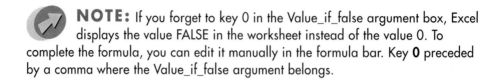 **11-6** **Use OR in a Formula**

1. Select cell F4 and click the Paste Function button **f_***.

2. In the Paste Function dialog box, choose Logical from the Function <u>C</u>ategory list box and IF from the Function <u>N</u>ame list box.

3. Click OK. The Formula Palette is displayed.

4. Click the down arrow next to the Function box and choose More Functions from the drop-down list. The Paste Function dialog box is displayed again.

5. Choose Logical from the Function <u>C</u>ategory list box and OR from the Function <u>N</u>ame list box.

6. Click OK. The Formula Palette is redisplayed.

7. Key **B4>20000** in the Logical1 argument box.

8. Key **C4=.2** in the Logical2 argument box.

9. Click the IF function name in the formula displayed in the formula bar. The remaining arguments for the IF function are displayed in the Formula Palette.

10. Key 500 in the Value_if_true argument box.

11. Key 0 in the Value_if_false argument box and click OK. Because one condition was met, the formula calculates a $500 bonus.

12. Copy the formula to cells F5 through F8. Notice the difference in bonus amounts using OR versus AND.

If you prefer not to have students use Paste Function, instruct them to enter the functions manually

EXERCISE 11-7 Use NOT in a Formula

1. Select cell G4.

2. Key **=IF(NOT(B4=0),500,0)**

3. Copy the formula to cells G5 through G8. Using NOT in the IF formula, all salespeople receive $500 commissions under Bonus Plan 4 unless they have zero sales.

FIGURE 11-6
Using the NOT expression in an IF formula

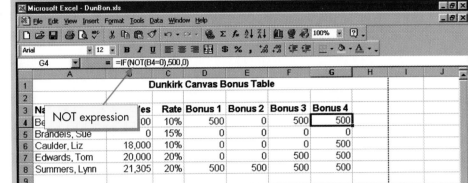

4. Add the standard header to the worksheet with your name, the filename, and the date.

5. Save the workbook as *[your initials]***11-7.xls** in your Lesson 11 folder.

6. Print the worksheet and close the workbook.

☑ Objective 4

Using IF Functions to Insert Text

You can create a formula using the IF function that displays text based on whether a condition is true or false. For example, you could display the text "Delinquent Account" if the value in the "Days Overdue" column of a worksheet is greater than 30. To add text in an IF function, you enclose the text in quotes. For example, you could use the following IF statement to display "Current Account" if an account is less than or equal to 30 days late, and "Past Due" if the account is more than 30 days late: IF(G3<=30,"Current Account","Past Due").

You also can replace Excel's error messages with easier-to-understand messages. For example, if a cell contains a formula for division, and the number is divided by zero, the #DIV/0! error message appears. To replace this error message, you can create a formula, such as IF(B2=0,"You cannot divide by zero.",B1/B2). If a user keys 0, the text you defined appears; otherwise, Excel performs the division.

In Excel Classroom Presentation 11.

☑ **Objective 4 Assignment:**
Exercise 11-15 (Skills Review) can be assigned after completing Objective 4.

EXERCISE 11-8   Insert Text with an IF Function

1. Open the file **Costs2.xls**.

2. In cell E4, enter the formula **=IF(D4>40,"Yes","No")**. Because the value in cell D4 is greater than 40, Excel displays "Yes."

FIGURE 11-7
Using text in
an IF formula

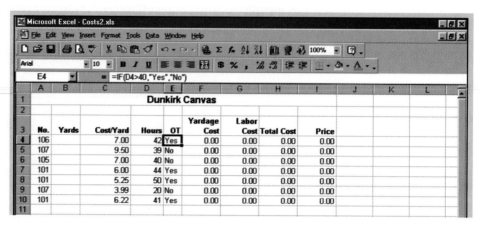

3. Copy the formula to cells E5 through E10.

TIP: You can insert a blank as either the true or false statement by using double quotation marks ("") with no space in between.

☑ Objective 5

Using VLOOKUP and HLOOKUP

You can create a "lookup table" in one area of a worksheet that is used to retrieve values for another area of the worksheet. You can also create a separate worksheet (or even a separate workbook) that is used to retrieve values for another worksheet (or workbook). This operation involves using the VLOOKUP and HLOOKUP functions. For example, you could create a table that lists item numbers and prices in one area of an invoice worksheet. When you key the item number in the item column of the worksheet, Excel "looks up" the price for the item in the "lookup table" and automatically places it in the price column. Besides saving work, these functions help prevent data-entry errors.

Excel can look up values in the far left column of a "lookup table" within the worksheet using the function VLOOKUP. (Think of VLOOKUP as representing a "Vertical Lookup.") Use the following format:

=VLOOKUP(lookup_value,table_array,col_index_num,range_lookup)

 In Excel Classroom Presentation 11.

☑ **Objective 5 Assignment:**

Exercise 11-19 (Lesson Applications) can be assigned after completing Objective 5.

📝 Inform students that if a table used by a VLOOKUP function is deleted, the formula cells referencing the table display the error message: #N/A. Adding a Comment (which they learn about in the next Exercise) to the formula cell can be especially useful in such a case.

- Lookup_value is the value for which VLOOKUP searches. It can be a value, text string, or cell reference.
- Table_array is the range of cells through which Excel searches for the lookup_value. It is a good idea to use a range name for this table. VLOOKUP searches down the far left column in the table for a match to the lookup_value. Table_array can contain numbers, text, or logical values. The values in the first column must appear in ascending order (1,2,3...; A-Z...; FALSE, TRUE) unless an exact match is desired.
- Col_index_num is the column number in the table_array from which the matching value should be returned. A col_index_num of 1 returns the value in the first column in table_array; a col_index_num of 2 returns the value in the second column in table_array; and so on.
- Range_lookup is an optional argument. It is a logical value (TRUE or FALSE) that specifies whether you want VLOOKUP to find an exact match or an approximate match. When it is TRUE or omitted, VLOOKUP finds the largest value that is less than the lookup_value. If you want VLOOKUP to find an exact match for the lookup_value, the range_lookup should be FALSE.

HLOOKUP works just like VLOOKUP, except it searches the top row of the "lookup table" for the lookup_value, and it uses a row_index_num to indicate the row number in the table from which the matching value is returned. (Think of HLOOKUP as a "Horizontal Lookup".) Use the following format:

=HLOOKUP(lookup_value,table_array,row_index_num,range_lookup)

Note the following characteristics of VLOOKUP and HLOOKUP:

- If VLOOKUP and HLOOKUP cannot find lookup_value, and range_lookup is TRUE, they use the largest value that is less than the lookup_value.
- If lookup_value is less than the least value in the first column of the table_array, VLOOKUP returns the #N/A error value. The same applies to HLOOKUP and the first row of the table_array.

EXERCISE 11-9 Use the VLOOKUP Function

1. Go to the Table worksheet by clicking the Table tab.
2. Select cells A2:B8 and name the range **T_Yardage**.

TIP: Give range names to your tables and use these names in your VLOOKUP and HLOOKUP functions instead of cell addresses. It is also a good idea to establish a naming convention for table range names to distinguish them from other range names, as in the "**T_**" portion of the above range name.

3. Return to the Costs worksheet, select cell B4, and key
=VLOOKUP(A4,T_Yardage,2)

 TIP: When entering a formula that uses a named range, you can use F3 to paste the range name into the formula.

4. Copy the formula in cell B4 to cells B5 through B10. Because lookup_value is relative, Excel adjusts the formula and looks up all the corresponding yardage items in the table.

FIGURE 11-8
VLOOKUP function
used in the
worksheet

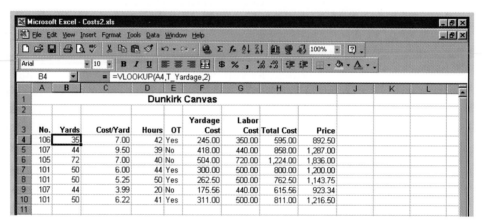

 Objective 6

Using Comments to Annotate Formulas

 You can attach a comment that contains descriptive text to a cell. This is help-ful to explain complicated formulas or to warn other users not to key data in a cell containing a formula.

To create and view the comments in a worksheet, use the Comment option on the Insert menu. You can also use the New Comment button 🗒 and the Show All Comments button 🗒, which are on the Auditing and Reviewing toolbars. In addition, you can use the keyboard shortcut Shift + < to create and edit comments.

Cells with comments have a small, red triangle in their upper-right corner. You can print the comments when you print the worksheet by selecting File, Page Setup, and selecting Comments from the Sheet tab. You can print com-ments as displayed on the worksheet or on a separate page at the end of the worksheet.

EXERCISE **11-10** **Use a Comment to Annotate a Formula**

1. Select cell B4.

 In Excel Classroom Presentation 11.

Objective 6 Assignment:
Exercises 11-17 and 11-20 (Lesson Applications) can be assigned after completing Objective 6.

As an example, describe what happens when a table used by a VLOOKUP function is deleted. The formula cells referencing the table display the error message: #N/A. This is a good example of a situation in which adding a note to the formula cell can be useful.

2. Choose Comment from the Insert menu or press `Shift`+`<`. A new Comment box appears.

FIGURE 11-9
A new Comment box

Comment 1 ▼	=												
	A	B	C	D	E	F	G	H	I	J	K	L	
1					Dunkirk Canvas								
2													
3	No.	Yards	Student:		OT	Yardage Cost	Labor Cost	Total Cost	Price				
4	106	35			Yes	245.00	350.00	595.00	892.50				
5	107	44			No	418.00	440.00	858.00	1,287.00				
6	105	72			No	504.00	720.00	1,224.00	1,836.00				
7	101	50			Yes	300.00	500.00	800.00	1,200.00				
8	101	50	5.25	50	Yes	262.50	500.00	762.50	1,143.75				
9	107	44	3.99	20	No	175.56	440.00	615.56	923.34				
10	101	50	6.22	41	Yes	311.00	500.00	811.00	1,216.50				
11													

NOTE: The name that appears at the top of a new Comment box is the default user name. Although you can change this name in the Comment box when you add your comments, the status bar continues to show the default user name.

3. Use `Backspace` to delete the default user name.

4. Key *[your initials]*: and press `Enter`.

5. Key the following text:

Do not key data in this column. Change data only in the Yardage Lookup Table on the Table worksheet.

6. Expand the size of the Comment box to display the entire message by using the bottom resize handle on the Comment box.

7. Select any cell in the worksheet. The small, red triangle in cell B4 indicates the presence of a comment.

EXERCISE 11-11 View and Edit the Contents of a Comment

1. Move the pointer over cell B4 without selecting it. The Comment box appears when the pointer is placed over a cell that contains a comment. Notice that the message in the status bar indicates the presence of a comment.

2. Select cell B4 and choose Edit Comment from the Insert menu or press `Shift`+`<`. The Comment box appears.

3. At the beginning of the comment, key **IMPORTANT!**

4. Select any cell in the worksheet. The edited comment is applied to cell B4.

 In Excel Classroom Presentation 11.

The user name appearing in the comment box is a system default. This varies depending on the setup of the computers in your classroom. The user name can be changed on the General tab of the Tools, Options command. Excel then must be exited and reloaded for the change to take effect.

Correcting Circular References

☑**Objective 7**

A formula cannot contain a reference to its own cell address. For example, the formula =A1+A2+A3 is incorrect if it appears in cell A3. Such a reference in a formula, called a *circular reference*, is a fairly common mistake. If you try to enter a formula with a circular reference, Excel produces an error message to let you know you need to correct the formula.

EXERCISE 11-12 Enter and Correct a Circular Reference and Print Comments on a Sheet

1. Select cell E4.

2. In the formula bar, change "D4" to **E4** and enter the formula. Excel displays an error message that describes the presence of a circular reference in the formula.

3. Click Cancel. (Click OK if the Cancel button is not present; Excel displays a slightly different error message if you have already seen the circular reference message and Help screens during your current session.)

4. Change "E4" back to **D4** to correct the formula, if necessary.

5. Select File, Page Setup from the menu. Click the Sheet tab if it is not already displayed. Click the down arrow next to Comments and choose At End of Sheet. The comments are printed on a separate page after the worksheet.

6. Add the standard header to the Costs worksheet with your name, the filename, and the date. Use a Page 1 of ? footer.

7. Save the workbook as *[your initials]***11-12.xls** in your Lesson 11 folder.

8. Print the worksheet and close the workbook.

COMMAND SUMMARY

FEATURE	BUTTON	MENU	KEYBOARD
Create a cell comment	🖼	Insert,Comment	Shift + <
Switch between displaying formulas and values		Tools, Options, View	Ctrl + ` (left single quote)

☑**Objective 7 Assignment:**

Exercises 11-16 (Skills Review) and 11-18 (Lesson Applications) can be assigned after completing Objective 7.

📝 Point out that the Command Summary lists a variety of ways to accomplish a particular task. Students can decide which method they prefer.

USING HELP

This lesson introduced you to the VLOOKUP function, and showed you how you can use it in formulas. The HLOOKUP function is similar to VLOOKUP, except the table data is oriented in rows rather than columns. You can use Excel's online Help to learn more about the HLOOKUP function and how it differs from VLOOKUP.

Use Help to view detailed information about the HLOOKUP function:

1. Press F1 to activate the Office Assistant.

2. Key **HLOOKUP function** and click <u>S</u>earch.

3. Click the first topic, "HLOOKUP worksheet function." The Microsoft Excel Help dialog box displays information about the HLOOKUP function.

4. Scroll through the Help information provided, which includes an explanation of the function and its syntax. Read the examples of its use.

FIGURE 11-10
HLOOKUP function
Help screen

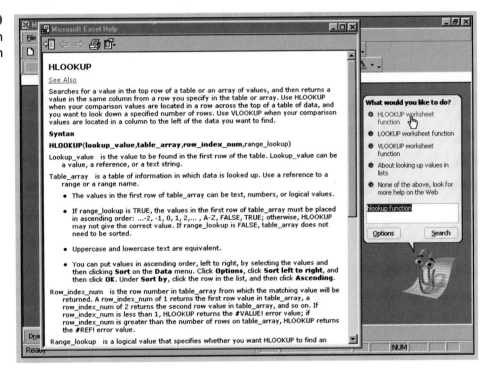

5. Click the <u>See Also</u> link at the top of the dialog box to read about other lookup and reference functions.

6. Close the <u>H</u>elp window and hide the Office Assistant.

 Encourage students to follow the steps in "Using Help." Software companies are increasingly using their Help program—rather than printed documentation—to train users and assist in answering user questions.

 In Excel Classroom Presentation 11.

TEST BANK

Concepts Review

TRUE/FALSE QUESTIONS

Each of the following statements is either true or false. Indicate your choice by circling **T** or **F**.

(T) F **1.** Excel automatically adjusts relative cell references in a formula when the formula is copied from one cell to another.

T (F) **2.** $A$3 is an example of a relative cell address.

T (F) **3.** Two types of cell references exist in Excel: relative and absolute.

(T) F **4.** When creating or editing a formula, you press F4 to move through the cell reference types.

(T) F **5.** Cell references of named cells are considered absolute.

T (F) **6.** An IF function takes two arguments.

(T) F **7.** An IF function can use logical functions such as AND, OR, and NOT for the logical_test part of the conditional expression.

(T) F **8.** Excel automatically displays an error message when a circular reference is used in a formula.

SHORT ANSWER QUESTIONS

Write the correct answer in the space provided.

1. Which type of cell reference combines absolute and relative cell addresses?

Mixed cell reference

2. Which keyboard character is added to a cell address in a formula when you press F4?

_$_

3. Which type of cell reference do you use in a formula when you want to copy a formula, but do not want the cell reference to change?

Absolute cell reference or mixed cell reference

4. Which function evaluates a condition and provides one answer if the condition is true and another answer if the condition is false?

IF function

C L O S E

Concepts Review:
Allows students to check their understanding.

TEST BANK
Consider using the Test Bank to provide an additional review of lesson concepts. It may also be used as an assessment tool.

5. Which keyboard character do you use to surround text in an IF function?

Quotations marks

6. Which functions retrieve a value from a table in another area of the worksheet and place it in the formula cell?

VLOOKUP and HLOOKUP

7. Which command from the Insert menu do you use to annotate a worksheet cell?

Comment

8. What type of marker is displayed in a cell that contains a comment?

Red triangle

CRITICAL THINKING

Answer these questions on a separate piece of paper. There are no right or wrong answers. Support your answers with examples from your own experience, if possible.

1. Why might you set up a table in a separate workbook that is referenced in a VLOOKUP function? How might this option prove useful in a company?

2. How might the Comment feature be beneficial to you as an employee taking over someone else's work?

Skills Review

EXERCISE 11-13

Use relative, mixed, and absolute cell references.

1. Open the file **DunRev.xls**.

2. Select cell C7.

3. Key **=$B7*C$4+$B7**. This formula contains mixed cell addresses. Each quarterly projection is based on the percentage indicated in row 4 multiplied by the fourth quarter's actual numbers in column B. The fourth-quarter number is then added to the increase.

4. Copy the formula to cells C7 through F8. Because you used mixed cell references, you can key the formula once and copy it to the cell range.

5. Copy the formula from cell B10 to cells C10 through F10.

Critical Thinking Questions:
Answers will vary based on students' preferences, observations, experiences, and research.

Skills Review:
Provides guided practice for students. Objectives are indicated for each Exercise.

◉ **Exercise 11-13:**
Objective 1
Required Files: DunRev.xls
Solution Files: gl11-13.xls in Solutions Manual or on Solutions Disk.

6. Select cell C15.

7. Key **=B15*F13+B15**. The projections for expenses for each quarter are based on the percentage in cell F13 multiplied by the previous quarter's expenses.

8. Edit the formula in cell C15. Use F4 to make cell reference F13 the absolute cell address, $F$13. The formula should now be: =B15*$F$13+B15.

9. Copy the formula from cell C15 to cells C15 through F16.

10. Copy the formula from cell B18 to cells C18 through F18.

11. In cell F4, key **7%**

12. In cell F13, key **4%**. Changes appear in affected worksheet cells.

13. Add the standard header to the worksheet with your name, the filename, and the date.

14. Save the workbook as *[your initials]***11-13.xls** in your Lesson 11 folder.

15. Print the worksheet.

16. Create a formula printout in landscape orientation on one page with grids and row and column headings.

17. Close the workbook without saving.

EXERCISE 11-14

Use relative and absolute cell references with an IF function with a single condition.

1. Open the file **Salaries.xls**.

2. In cell F5, key **4%**

3. In cell F6, key **5%**

4. Select cell D5.

5. Key **=IF(C5>3,$F$6,$F$5)**

6. Copy the formula from cell D5 to cells D6 through D8.

7. Format column D in percentage style with no decimal places.

8. Select cell E5.

9. Key **=B5*D5+B5**

10. Copy the formula from cell E5 to cells E6 through E8.

11. Add the standard header to the worksheet with your name, the filename, and the date.

12. Save the workbook as *[your initials]***11-14.xls** in your Lesson 11 folder.

13. Print the worksheet.

● **Exercise 11-14:**
Objectives 1, 2
Required Files: Salaries.xls
Solution Files: gl11-14.xls in Solutions Manual or on Solutions Disk.

1 Some teachers feel that money should be rounded to the nearest integer. They would use ROUND to 0 decimal places.

14. Create a formula printout in landscape orientation on one page with grids and row and column headings.

15. Close the workbook without saving.

EXERCISE 11-15

Create an IF function with multiple conditions, one of which inserts text.

1. Open the file **Reorder.xls**.

2. Select cell G4 and click the Paste Function button .

3. Choose Logical from the Function Category list box, choose IF from the Function Name list box, and click OK.

4. Click the down arrow next to the Function box and choose OR from the drop-down list.

5. Key **F4<=D4*.10** in the Logical1 argument text box.

6. Key **F4<5** in the Logical2 argument text box and click the IF function name in the formula displayed in the formula bar.

7. Key **YES** in the Value_if_true argument text box.

8. Key **""** (double quotation marks) in the Value_if_false argument text box. The cell is left blank if the answer is false.

9. Click OK. Copy the formula from cell G4 to cells G5 through G8. The cells in column G that meet either condition contain the answer "YES;" otherwise, they are left blank.

10. Change the value in cell E4 to 23. Cell G4 is updated with the answer "YES."

11. Add the standard header to the worksheet with your name, the filename, and the date.

12. Save the workbook as *[your initials]***11-15.xls** in your Lesson 11 folder.

13. Print the worksheet.

14. Create a formula printout in landscape orientation on one page with grids and row and column headings. Make sure column G is wide enough to display the formulas.

15. Close the workbook without saving.

EXERCISE 11-16

Use relative, absolute, and mixed cell references with the VLOOKUP function. Use comments to annotate the formula, and correct a circular reference.

1. Open the file **Vacation.xls**.

⊚ Exercise 11-15:
Objectives 2–4
Required Files: Reorder.xls
Solution Files: gl11-15.xls in Solutions Manual or on Solutions Disk.

⊚ Exercise 11-16:
Objectives 1, 5–7
Required Files: Vacation.xls
Solution Files: gl11-16.xls in Solutions Manual or on Solutions Disk.

2. Key the data by following these steps:
   a. In cell B5, key **8/10/94**
   b. In cell B6, key **2/3/95**
   c. In cell B7, key **5/5/95**
   d. In cell B8, key **6/1/95**
   e. In cell B9, key **10/10/98**
   f. In cell B10, key **4/2/93**

3. Select cell C5 and key **=ROUND((F$1-B5)/365.25,1)**. This formula subtracts the employment date in cell B5 from the current date in cell F1; it then divides by 365.25 to convert the days to years.

4. Copy the formula from cell C5 to cells C6 through C10.

5. Format column C in number style, with one decimal place.

6. Insert a new worksheet, placing it after the Vacation worksheet. Rename the new sheet **Table**.

7. Key the table as shown in Figure 11-11, beginning in cell A1 on the Table sheet.

FIGURE 11-11

	A	B
1	Years of Service	Vacation Days Due
2	1	5
3	5	10
4	10	15

8. Make the titles in row 1 bold and format them so the text wraps.

9. Name the range A2 through B11 **T_Days**.

10. On the Vacation sheet, select cell D5 and key **=VLOOKUP(C5,T_Days,2)**

11. Copy the formula from cell D5 to cells D6 through D10.

12. Select cell D4 and choose Comment from the Insert menu.

13. Replace the default user name in the Comment box with *[your initials]*: and press Enter.

14. Key **Maximum vacation is 15 days.** and then select any cell.

15. Select cell B11 and key **Employees with vacation due:**

16. Select cell D11, key **=COUNT(D5:D11)**, and press Enter.

17. Click Cancel to remove the circular reference error message. (Click OK if the Cancel button is not present.)

18. Edit the formula in cell D11. Change "D11" to **D10**.

19. Add the standard header to both worksheets with your name, the filename, and the date. Use a Page 1 of ? footer.

20. Save the workbook as *[your initials]***11-16.xls** in your Lesson 11 folder.

21. Print the entire workbook and the comment at the end of the sheet.

22. Create a formula printout in landscape orientation on one page with grids and row and column headings. Make sure the formula is displayed in columns C and D. Do not include the comments with this printout.

23. Close the workbook without saving

A S S E S S

Assessment Resources:
• Solutions Manual
• Test Bank
• Portfolio Builder
• Internet Projects
• Alternative Assessment Guide
• Certification Procedures

For Internet projects, go to
www.glencoe.com/webprojects

Lesson Applications

Use relative, absolute, and mixed cell references, and use comments to annotate a formula.

Create a worksheet that determines quantity-based discounts received from a supplier. Create formulas with relative and absolute cell addresses that calculate the discount prices.

1. Open a new workbook.
2. Construct the worksheet as shown in Figure 11-12.

FIGURE 11-12

	A	B	C	D	E	F
1	Dunkirk Canvas Company					
2	Material Order List					
3			2%	3%	4%	5%
4	Part No.	Cost Per Yard		Quantity Ordered		
5			50	100	200	Over 200
6	Canvas 101	5.09				
7	Canvas 102	5.45				
8	Canvas 103	6.14				
9	Canvas 104	6.23				
10	Canvas 105	6.51				

3. Format the range B6:F10 in number style, with two decimal places.
4. Right-align the heading for cell F5.

Lesson Applications:
Provide independent practice for students and may be used for assessment. Objectives are indicated for each Exercise.

Exercise 11-17:
Objectives 1, 6
Required Files: None
Solution Files: gl11-17.xls in Solutions Manual or on Solutions Disk.

5. Center the titles in A1:A2 across the worksheet and make them bold.

6. Widen columns A and B to accommodate the data and headings.

7. Center the "Quantity Ordered" heading over the four columns below it.

8. Select cell C6 and key **=B6-(B6*C3)**. The formula calculates the new price for a quantity of 50, based on a 2% discount.

9. Edit the formula in cell C6. Change cell reference C3 to the mixed cell reference that adjusts the column, but not the row, when the formula is copied.

10. Change both B6 cell references in the formula to the mixed cell reference that adjusts the row, but not the column, when the formula is copied.

11. Copy the formula from cell C6 to cells C6 through F10.

12. Widen columns to display the values, if necessary.

13. Create a comment in cell A1. Change the default user name to *[your initials]:* and key the following text for the comment:

    Call supplier on a monthly basis to review discounts received.

14. Insert a row between the titles and the column headings.

15. Rename the Sheet1 tab Discounts and delete the unused sheets.

16. Add the standard header to the worksheet with your name, the filename, and the date. Use a Page 1 of ? footer. Horizontally center the worksheet on the page, and set the comments to print at the end of the sheet.

17. Save the workbook as *[your initials]***11-17.xls** in your Lesson 11 folder.

18. Print the worksheet and the comment at the end of the sheet.

19. Create a formula printout in landscape orientation on one page with grids and row and column headings. Do not include the comments with the printout. Remove the footer.

20. Close the workbook without saving.

EXERCISE 11-18

Create an IF function with a single condition and correct a circular reference.

 Construct a worksheet for analyzing overtime. Use formulas that include IF functions that track hours worked and overtime pay.

1. Open a new workbook.

2. Key the worksheet as shown in Figure 11-13 on the next page.

Exercise 11-18:
Objectives 2, 7
Required Files: None
Solution Files: gl11-18.xls in Solutions Manual or on Solutions Disk.

The completed document for this Exercise may be used in a student's portfolio.

FIGURE 11-13
Worksheet
to be keyed.

	A	B	C	D	E	F	G	H
1	Dunkirk Canvas Company - Part-time Payroll							
2								
3	Week of January 6							
4	Employee	Pay Rate	Hours Worked	Regular Hours	OT Hours	Regular Pay	OT Pay	Total Pay
5	Boyd	18.00						
6	Jenkins	10.00						
7								
8	Total Pay							
9								

3. Format the text in cells B4 through F4 to wrap and make the necessary cell format and column format changes as shown in the figure.

4. Select cell D5.

5. Key **=IF(C5>=40,40,C5)**. The result is 0. This formula tests the value in cell C5. If the value is greater than or equal to 40, the number 40 is entered in cell D5 as regular hours worked. If the value is less than 40, the value in cell C5 is entered in cell D5 as regular hours.

6. Copy the formula in cell D5 to cell D6.

7. Select cell E5 and enter a subtraction formula that determines the overtime hours. Copy the formula from cell E5 to cell E6.

8. Select cell F5 and enter a multiplication formula that determines the regular pay. The result is 0.

9. Copy the formula from cell F5 to cell F6.

10. Select cell G5 and enter a multiplication formula that determines the overtime pay. Overtime hours are paid at 1.5 times the regular pay rate.

11. Copy the formula in cell G5 to cell G6.

12. Select cell H5 and enter a formula that adds regular pay to overtime pay. Copy the formula to cell H6.

13. To test the formulas, select cell C5 and enter **43**

14. In cell C6, enter **50**

15. Select cell F8 and key **=SUM(F5:F8)**. Click Cancel to remove the circular reference error message. (Click OK if the Cancel button is not present.)

16. Correct the circular reference error in cell F8. Copy the corrected formula to cells G8:H8.

17. Format the cells H5:H6 and F8:H8 in accounting style with dollar signs and two decimal places. Format F5:G6 in the same style without the dollar sign.

18. Rename the Sheet1 tab to **Part-time payroll** and delete the unused sheets.

19. Add the standard header to the worksheet with your name, the filename, and the date. Horizontally center the worksheet on the page.

20. Save the workbook as *[your initials]***11-18.xls** in your Lesson 11 folder.

21. Print the worksheet.

22. Create a formula printout in landscape orientation on one page with grids and row and column headings.

23. Close the workbook without saving.

EXERCISE 11-19

Create an IF function that inserts text and use the VLOOKUP function.

  Construct a worksheet that shows the status of delinquent accounts and calculates a 2% late fee using the IF function. Use a lookup table to insert the company name next to the corresponding company number.

1. Open the file **Accounts.xls**.

 2. Use the information shown in Figure 11-14 for the following steps.

FIGURE 11-14

Co. No.	Invoice Date	Amount
1014	6/28/99	24,369.00
1011	7/30/99	13,254.21
1015	8/20/99	34,547.33
1013	4/22/99	6,241.01
1016	9/14/99	27,362.00
1012	7/9/99	14,925.08

3. Enter the data in Figure 11-14, starting in cells A4, C4, and D4.

4. Select cell E4. This cell contains a formula that calculates the number of days late. The named range Current_Date is the date located in cell H2. Create a better formula that hides the numbers appearing in the "Days Late" column if the invoice date is blank and that calculates days late when an invoice date exists: Key **=IF(C4=0,"",Current_Date-C4)**. The value_if_false argument calculates the days late when an invoice date exists.

⊙ Exercise 11-19:

Objectives 2, 4, 5
Required Files: Accounts.xls
Solution Files: gl11-19.xls and gl11-19.htm in
Solutions Manual or on Solutions Disk.

The completed document for this Exercise may be used in a student's portfolio.

You may want to have students change the "As Of" date in cell H2 to the actual current date. Because the results of the IF functions depend on the date in this cell, students should also change the entries under "Invoice Date" as well to make the results more meaningful. You may want to specify which dates they choose so all students have the same results.

5. Copy the formula in cell E4 to cells E5 through E9.

6. Select cell F4.

7. Click the Paste Function button 🔧 to begin entering a formula that displays "Over 30" for accounts 30 days past due, "Over 60" for accounts 60 days past due, and "Collection" for accounts 90 days past due.

8. Choose Logical from the Function Category list box.

9. Choose IF from the Function Name list box. Click OK.

10. Key **E4>90** in the Logical_test argument box.

11. Key **"Collection"** in the Value_if_true argument box.

12. Click the Value_if_false argument box, then click the down arrow on the Function box to insert another IF function as a nested argument.

13. Choose IF from the drop-down list.

14. Key **E4>60** in the Logical_test argument box.

15. Key **"Over 60"** in the Value_if_true argument box.

16. Click the Value_if_false argument box, then click the down arrow on the Function box to insert another IF function as a nested argument. Choose IF from the drop-down list.

17. Key **E4>30** in the Logical_test argument box.

18. Key **"Over 30"** in the Value_if_true argument box.

19. Key **0** in the Value_if_false argument box. Click OK.

20. Copy the formula in cell F4 to cells F5 through F9.

21. Place a comment in cell F4 explaining how the formula works. Select cell F4 and choose Comment from the Insert menu.

22. Replace the default user name with *[your initials]:* then key the following text in the Comment box:

Logical tests are for 90, 60, and 30 days past due.

23. Select any cell. Create a name for the constant .02 called **late_fee**.

24. Select cell G4. Create a formula that charges a 2% late fee for accounts more than 60 days past due by keying **=IF(E4>60,D4*late_fee,0)**

25. Copy the formula in cell G4 to cells G5 through G9.

26. Select cells A2:B7 in the Table sheet and name this range **T_Company**. It serves as the table_array in a VLOOKUP function.

27. Select cell B4 in the Accounts sheet. To create a formula that inserts the company name next to the corresponding company number, key **=VLOOKUP(A4,T_Company,2)**

28. Copy the formula in cell B4 to cells B5 through B9.

29. Adjust the column widths so all text shows and the worksheet can print on one page. Format the values in columns D, G, and H in number style

with two decimal places and commas. Left-align the values in column A, and right-align the results of the formulas in column F.

30. Add the standard header to both worksheets with your name, the filename, and the date. Use a Page 1 of ? footer, and set comments to print at the end of the sheet.

31. Save the workbook as *[your initials]***11-19.xls** in your Lesson 11 folder.

32. Print the entire workbook and the comment at the end of the sheet.

33. Save the workbook as *[your initials]***11-19.htm** in your Lesson 11 folder.

34. Create a formula printout in landscape orientation with grids and row and column headings. Do not include the comment with this printout. Be sure to adjust column widths so all formulas are displayed.

35. Close the workbook without saving.

EXERCISE 11-20 *Challenge Yourself*

Create an IF function that inserts text and use the VLOOKUP function.

  Create a worksheet that lists debits and credits against specific accounts for a monthly journal for the Dunkirk Canvas Company.

1. Create a worksheet sketch that includes a title, column labels, and an area for data. The worksheet should include each account number (rows) and columns showing the account description, its category, debit, and credit. The description and category should be computed with formulas that use a lookup table. The last row of the data area should include a row that will show totals for the debits and credits. Sketch the lookup table on a separate page. The table should have columns for the account number, description, and category.

2. Using a 12-point font for all data, transfer the sketch into Excel by keying and formatting the labels. Then key the information shown in Figure 11-15. (This portion of the worksheet resembles a "monthly journal" in accounting terms.)

FIGURE 11-15

Acc#	Description	Category	Debit	Credit
100			100.00	85.00
201			300.00	325.00
101			142.00	

Exercise 11-20:
Objectives 4–6
Required Files: None
Solution Files: gl11-20.xls in Solutions Manual or on Solutions Disk.

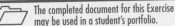 The completed document for this Exercise may be used in a student's portfolio.

This Exercise includes features from Lesson 4 (designing a worksheet and user documentation), Lesson 6 (using names in formulas), Lesson 8 (formatting numbers, changing row height, and aligning text), and Lesson 9 (using borders and colors).

3. Rename the Sheet1 tab "Journal," rename Sheet2 "Table," and rename Sheet3 "User Information."

4. Transfer the sketch of the lookup table to the Table sheet, using a 12-point font and formatting the headings. Then key the information shown in Figure 11-16.

FIGURE 11-16

Acc#	Description	Category
100	Cash	Asset
101	Securities	Asset
102	Notes Receivable	Asset
200	Notes Payable	Liability
201	Taxes Payable	Liability
202	Wages Payable	Liability

5. Name the table "T_Description." Do not include the column headings in the range.

6. In the "Description" column on the Journal sheet, create a formula to enter the description automatically when the account number is keyed. Construct the formula so no #N/A messages appear if the "Account Number" column is blank. (Hint: Use IF and VLOOKUP with nesting.)

7. In the "Category" column, create another formula to enter the category automatically when the account number is keyed. Construct the formula so no #N/A messages appear if the "Account Number" column is blank.

8. Widen columns B and C to accommodate the results of the formulas.

9. Assume that nine additional rows of data will be entered. Extend the formulas through these rows.

10. Add a row to total the debits and credits.

11. Below the total, enter a formula that displays the message, "Debits do not equal credits," when the total debits do not match the total credits.

12. Enhance the worksheet by adding formatting such as bold and borders. Format the total values appropriately. Make the titles a larger font than the rest of the worksheet and add a colored pattern to the background in the title area. Increase the row height of the column labels and

1 In this Exercise, students copy formulas down 9 extra rows below the last entry on the top of the monthly journal. Because these 9 extra rows are accommodated on the worksheet for the journal entries, the Total formulas should be keyed below those extra rows.

vertically center them within the row. Align labels appropriately with text and values. Add appropriate comments to a cell in each column containing the VLOOKUP formulas.

13. In the User Information worksheet, create documentation that includes the following: File Information (Created by, Date created, Date revised, Revised by, Contact for help); Purpose of workbook (paragraph form); Instructions to User (special instructions needed by user to enter data correctly); and Range Names. Style the documentation for easy reading.

14. Add the standard header to all worksheets with your name, the filename, and the date. Horizontally center the worksheets. Use a Page 1 of ? footer, and set the comments to print at the end of the sheet.

15. Save the workbook as *[your initials]*11-20.xls in your Lesson 11 folder.

16. Print the entire workbook.

17. Create a formula printout of the Journal worksheet in landscape orientation with grids and row and column headings. Do not include comments with this printout.

18. Close the workbook without saving.

Dates, Times, and Financial Functions

OBJECTIVES

MOUS
ACTIVITIES
In this lesson:
XL2000 **6.9**
XL2000 **6.10**

See Appendix F.

After completing this lesson, you will be able to:

1. **Use automatic date formats.**
2. **Work with date functions.**
3. **Use date math.**
4. **Work with time functions.**
5. **Work with financial functions.**

Estimated Time: 1¾ hours

This lesson covers several Excel date and time functions and introduces calculations involving dates and times. In addition, you see how financial functions assist in evaluating and analyzing loan and investment terms. You can calculate present and future values of investments, interest rates and amounts, the number of payment periods in an annuity, and payment amounts. Once you become familiar with Excel's financial functions, you can evaluate an investment and even choose the best loan terms.

Objective 1
Working with Dates

In Excel, dates are stored as numbers. Excel uses as a default the 1900 Date System, which uses *serial numbers* from 1 to 2,958,525 to store dates in cells with the date format. Each serial number represents a date: 1 stands for January 1, 1900, while the last number, 2,958,525, represents December 31, 9999. Storing dates as numbers enables Excel to perform calculations with dates.

PREPARE

Point out to students that the learning objectives show what they will learn in the lesson. Each heading in the lesson correlates to a learning objective.

Required files:

Employ1.xls Employ2.xls Finance.xls

TEACH

Teaching Resources:
• Excel Classroom Presentations
• School-to-Work Strategies Manual
• Spanish Glossary
• Certification Procedures

You can key dates in a variety of ways. As with numbers, Excel assigns the closest matching date format to the date you key. The date format displayed onscreen may not exactly match the one you keyed, depending on whether your date format matches one of Excel's built-in date formats.

TABLE 12-1   **Excel's Date Formats**

KEYED CHARACTERS	DATE CODE	SCREEN DISPLAY
12-1-99	m/d/yy	12/1/99
12/1/99	m/d/yy	12/1/99
1-Jan-99	d-mmm-yy	1-Jan-99
1-January-1999	d-mmm-yy	1-Jan-99
March-99	mmm-yy	Mar-99
3-99	mmm-yy	Mar-99

When you enter a date in a cell and you only use two digits for the year, Excel interprets the year as follows:

- 00 through 29 are interpreted as the years 2000 through 2029
- 30 through 99 are interpreted as the years 1930 through 1999.

For example, if you type 4/28/19, Excel assumes the date is April 28, 2019. You can have Excel interpret the date as 1919 in this example by entering four digits for the year.

EXERCISE 12-1 Use Automatic Date Formats

Excel formats the cells for dates when you enter them.

1. Open a new workbook.
2. In cells A6:E6, key the following dates:
   12/1/99 12-1-99 1-Dec-99 1-December-1999 12/99
3. Select cell D6 and choose Cells from the Format menu. Click the Number tab, if necessary. In the Format Cells dialog box, Excel chooses the date format code that most closely matches the date you keyed.
4. Click Cancel.

NOTE: When you see a number in a cell where you keyed a date, the cell is formatted for a number and the date's serial number is displayed. Conversely, when you see a date in a cell where you keyed a number, the cell is formatted for the date. When this type of formatting error occurs, change the cell's format to the appropriate option.

☑ **Objective 2**

Working with Date Functions

Excel's built-in date functions make it possible to use dates in calculations. You can enter functions into your worksheet in the following ways:

- Key the function directly
- Use the <u>F</u>unction command on the <u>I</u>nsert menu
- Use the Paste Function button 🔲 to select from several types of date and time functions.

TABLE 12-2

Excel's Date Functions

FUNCTION	DESCRIPTION OF FUNCTION
=DATE()	Returns the serial number of a specified date
=NOW()	Returns the current system date and time
=TODAY()	Returns the current system date
=YEAR()	Returns the year, given a serial number or a date enclosed in quotes
=MONTH()	Returns the month number (for example, "3" for March), given a serial number or a date
=DAY()	Returns the day number of the month, given a serial number or a date
=WEEKDAY()	Returns the day of the week (for example, "2" for Monday), given a serial number or a date

EXERCISE **12-2** **View the Serial Number of a Date**

The DATE function returns the serial number of a particular date. You must enter the arguments of the DATE function in the order of year, month, and then day. For example, "99,8,27" are the correct arguments for August 27, 1999.

☑ **Objective 2 Assignment:**
Exercises 12-18 (Skills Review) and 12-21 (Lesson Applications) can be assigned after completing Objective 2.

📝 You may want to discuss the date functions listed in Table 12-2 before students begin Exercise 12-2.

1. In cell A1, enter **=DATE(99,8,27)**

2. Select cell A1 and choose C̲ells from the F̲ormat menu. Click the Number tab, if necessary, and choose General in the C̲ategory list box. The Sample box displays the serial number for the date.

3. Click OK. The serial number appears on the screen. The result is 36399.

4. To display the date again, choose C̲ells from the F̲ormat menu.

5. From the C̲ategory list, choose Date. Then, choose the format "3/14/98" and click OK. The date is displayed as "8/27/99."

> **TIP:** You can also click the right mouse button and choose F̲ormat Cells from the shortcut menu to open the Format Cells dialog box. To generate the d-mmm-yy format, you can use the keyboard shortcut Ctrl + Shift + # .

6. Add the standard header to the worksheet with your name, the filename, and the date.

7. Save the workbook as *[your initials]*12-2.xls in a new folder for Lesson 12 and print the worksheet.

8. Close the workbook.

EXERCISE 12-3 Enter the Current Date

The TODAY function displays the current date stored in your computer. This date is updated each time you recalculate your worksheet. TODAY uses the format TODAY(). Note that the TODAY function (and the NOW function) produce different results as the day or time changes.

1. Open the file **Employ1.xls**.

2. In cell F1, enter **=TODAY()**

> **TIP:** You can also generate the current day by pressing Ctrl + ; . Note that, unlike TODAY(), the current date generated by this keystroke combination is not updated when the system clock changes.

☑ Objective 3
Using Date Math

You can use addition, subtraction, multiplication, and division to perform calculations with dates. For example, the formula =TODAY()+30 displays the date 30 days from today. To calculate with a cell formatted for date, simply key the

---

1 Reinforce the practice of right-clicking the mouse and using the shortcut menu to open the Format Cells dialog box.

☑ **Objective 3 Assignment:**
Exercises 12-17 (Skills Review) and 12-22 (Lesson Applications) can be assigned after completing Objective 3.

2 Although TODAY() is used in the following Exercises as a way to teach date math, some instructors do not use TODAY() in calculations because it can produce errors if the system date is incorrect. After checking that the system date is correct, you may want to instruct students to convert the results of TODAY() to a constant.

cell reference in the formula. To enter a date directly in a formula, key quotation marks around the date. This format instructs Excel to use the serial number for the date. For example, to calculate the number of days between April 15, 1997, and March 1, 1999, you could use the formula ="3-1-99"-"4-15-97".

When you calculate dates, make sure the dates in the cell are formatted appropriately. Excel uses the stored serial number to calculate no matter how the date is formatted on the screen.

EXERCISE **12-4** **Calculate Elapsed Days**

1. Select cell E5 and key **=TODAY()-D5**
2. Copy the formula from cell E5 to cells E6 through E10.
3. Open the Format Cells dialog box and apply the General number format to the cells E5:E10. The values in cells E5 through E10 show the length of service in days. (Your values will differ from those in Figure 12-1 because the TODAY() date is different.)

FIGURE 12-1
Calculating differences in dates

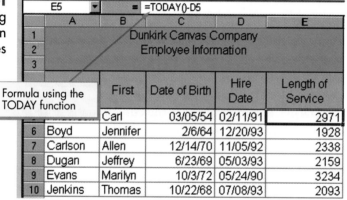

TIP: If you want to use the serial number for the current date in a calculation, but you don't want the number to change (as is the case when you use the TODAY() function), a quick way to get the serial value of the current date is to key =TODAY() and press F9 before you enter the function.

EXERCISE **12-5** **Convert Days to Years**

After the length of service is calculated, you can make the result more meaningful if you convert the days to years.

In Exercises 12-4 through 12-6, remind students that the results in cells E5:E10 will be updated daily because the TODAY function is used in the formula to determine the employees' length of service as of the current date. The accompanying figures reflect different values than those shown.

Use Excel Classroom Presentation 12 to display screens from the lesson in a slide-show format

1. Double-click cell E5 to edit its contents.

2. Enclose the existing formula in parentheses by placing a left parenthesis before the "T" in "Today" and a right parenthesis at the end of the formula.

3. At the end of the formula, key **/365.25** Press Enter.

 NOTE: 365.25 is the average number of days in a year, taking into account leap years.

4. Copy the formula from cell E5 to cells E6 through E10. (Remember, your values will differ from those in the figure because the date is different.)

FIGURE 12-2
Converting number of days into years

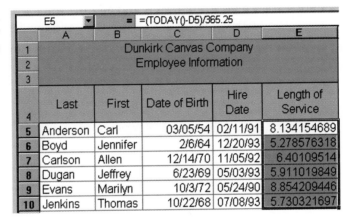

E5	▼	=	=(TODAY()-D5)/365.25	
	A	B	C	D	E
1	Dunkirk Canvas Company				
2	Employee Information				
3					
4	Last	First	Date of Birth	Hire Date	Length of Service
5	Anderson	Carl	03/05/54	02/11/91	8.134154689
6	Boyd	Jennifer	2/6/64	12/20/93	5.278576318
7	Carlson	Allen	12/14/70	11/05/92	6.40109514
8	Dugan	Jeffrey	6/23/69	05/03/93	5.911019849
9	Evans	Marilyn	10/3/72	05/24/90	8.854209446
10	Jenkins	Thomas	10/22/68	07/08/93	5.730321697

EXERCISE 12-6 Use the Integer Part of a Year

You may want to show only the whole number of years elapsed. Use the INT(Number) function to round down to the integer.

1. Select cell E5. The result of the formula is displayed in the General format.

2. Double-click cell E5 to edit the contents of the cell.

3. Position the insertion point after the = symbol and key **INT(**

4. Position the insertion point at the end of the formula and key a closed parenthesis **)**

5. Press Enter. The number of years elapsed is rounded down to the integer.

6. Copy the formula from cell E5 to cells E6 through E10.

In Excel Classroom Presentation 12.

1 Remind students that they always need the same number of right and left parentheses in a formula. When you use the Arrow keys to move through a formula as you are editing it, Excel highlights the paired parentheses.

FIGURE 12-3
Rounding down
number of years to
an integer

	A	B	C	D	E
	E5 ▼ = =INT((TODAY()-D5)/365.25)				
1	Dunkirk Canvas Company				
2	Employee Information				
3					
	Last	First	Date of Birth	Hire Date	Length of Service
		Carl	03/05/54	02/11/91	8
6	Boyd	Jennifer	2/6/64	12/20/93	5
7	Carlson	Allen	12/14/70	11/05/92	6
8	Dugan	Jeffrey	6/23/69	05/03/93	5
9	Evans	Marilyn	10/3/72	05/24/90	8
10	Jenkins	Thomas	10/22/68	07/08/93	5

Formula using the INT function

7. Center the values in column E and add the standard header to the worksheet with your name, the filename, and the date.

8. Save the workbook as *[your initials]***12-6.xls** in your Lesson 12 folder.

9. Print the worksheet and close the workbook.

EXERCISE 12-7 Calculate a Future Date

You may need to use the serial number of a specific date in a calculation. You can use the DATE function to calculate the serial number for a given date. The function uses the format DATE(year,month,day).

1. Open a new workbook. Use Excel to calculate the maturity date of a loan based on the issue date of June 6, 1994, and a term of 20 years.

2. Select cell A1 and key **Dunkirk Canvas Company**

3. Select cell A3 and key **Loan**

4. Select cell B3 and key **Maturity Date**

5. Select cell A4 and key **No. 100**

6. Make the title and column headings bold and widen column B to accommodate the heading. Right-align the heading in B3.

7. Select cell B4 and key **=DATE(94,6,6)+20*365.25**

8. Format cell B4 in the date format of March 14, 1998. The calculation determines the loan matures on June 6, 2014.

EXERCISE 12-8 Calculate the Day of the Week

The WEEKDAY function calculates a date's day number of the week. Sunday is 1, Monday is 2, and so on. The WEEKDAY function uses the form

1 The WEEKDAY function calculates the day number of the week (shown as an integer from 1 to 7), not to be confused with the function DAY, which calculates the day number of the month (shown as an integer from 1 to 31).

WEEKDAY(serial_ number,return_type), where the serial_number is a date or the cell address of a date.

1. Select cell C3 and key **Weekday**

2. Make the text bold, widen the column to accommodate the heading, and right-align the heading.

3. Select cell C4 and enter **=WEEKDAY(B4)**. The result is 6, which represents Friday. In the next steps, you use a lookup table to convert this value to text.

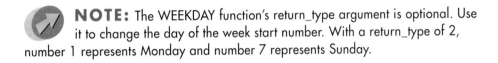 **NOTE:** The WEEKDAY function's return_type argument is optional. Use it to change the day of the week start number. With a return_type of 2, number 1 represents Monday and number 7 represents Sunday.

4. Build the lookup table by keying the following data in columns A and B, starting in cell A8:

Number	Day
1	Sunday
2	Monday
3	Tuesday
4	Wednesday
5	Thursday
6	Friday
7	Saturday

5. Name this table T_Days.

6. Edit the formula in cell C4 to read **=VLOOKUP(WEEKDAY(B4),T_Days,2)** The formula now returns the text "Friday."

7. Right-align cell C4 and add the standard header to the worksheet with your name, the filename, and the date.

8. Save the workbook as *[your initials]***12-8.xls** in your Lesson 12 folder.

9. Print the worksheet and close the workbook.

☑ **Objective 4**

Working with Time Functions

Excel's time functions operate much like its date functions. Time is stored as a number and is displayed according to the format you select. A time number is stored as a decimal number. For example, the time number for 12:00 noon is 0.5, because it is half of the day.

---

1 You may want to remind students that it is good practice to place lookup tables on separate worksheets. It is placed on this worksheet for simplicity in instruction.

☑ **Objective 4 Assignment:**
Exercises 12-19 (Skills Review) and 12-23 (Lesson Applications) can be assigned after completing Objective 4.

You can calculate with time numbers, and Excel provides several useful time functions. Note that the time functions, like TODAY(), are dynamic, changing as the system day or time changes. This will happen every time the worksheet is updated or retrieved.

TABLE 12-3

Excel's TIME Functions

FUNCTION	DESCRIPTION OF FUNCTION
=NOW()	Returns the current system date and time
=TIME()	Returns the serial number of the specified time
=TIMEVALUE()	Returns the serial number of a time written as text and enclosed in quotation marks
=HOUR()	Returns the hour portion of a given serial number
=MINUTE()	Returns the minute portion of a given serial number
=SECOND()	Returns the second portion of a given serial number

EXERCISE 12-9 Use Automatic Time Formats

The TIME function returns the serial number of a particular time. It uses the format TIME(hour,minute,second).

1. Open the file **Employ2.xls**.

2. Select cell E1 and key **=TIME(7,30,25)**. The arguments represent hour, minute, and second.

3. Format cell E1 in number format with two decimal places. Notice how the time number is stored as a fraction of a 24-hour day, which is calculated by taking the number of hours passed in the day and dividing it by 24.

FIGURE 12-4
Time in number format, displayed as a decimal

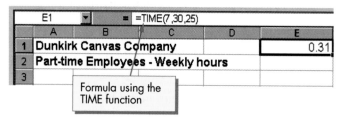

4. Format cell E1 in time format, using the 13:30:55 format. The time displays as 7:30:25.

TIP: You can use the keyboard shortcut Ctrl + Shift + @ to format a cell in the h:mm AM/PM time format.

EXERCISE 12-10 Use Time Math

You can calculate with time numbers as well as date numbers. Remember to multiply a time number by 24 to convert it to hours.

1. In the range A6:F6, key the following data, skipping cell E6 and using a space between the time and am/pm:

1/7/99 7:00 am 11:30 am 12:00 pm 4:00 pm

 NOTE: You can key "am" or "pm" in lowercase letters and Excel automatically converts them to uppercase.

2. In cells A7:F7, key the following data, skipping cell E7:

1/8/99 7:30 am 12:00 pm 12:45 pm 5:00 pm

 TIP: You can generate the current time from the computer's clock by pressing Ctrl + Shift + ; .

3. Select cell E6 and key **=(D6-C6)*24**. This formula converts the time number difference between Lunch Out and Lunch In to show Lunch Time as a fraction of an hour, rather than as a fraction of a day.

4. Format cell E6 in number format with two decimal places. The date format is replaced by a number format that shows the Lunch Time as a fraction of an hour.

5. Copy the formula from cell E6 to cell E7.

6. Select cell G6 and key **=(F6-B6)*24**

7. Format cell G6 in number format with two decimal places.

8. To edit the formula so it subtracts the lunch time, double-click G6, and then position the insertion point at the end of the formula. Key **-E6** and press Enter.

9. Copy the formula from cell G6 to cell G7.

10. Add the standard header to the worksheet with your name, the filename, and the date.

11. Save the workbook as *[your initials]***12-10.xls** in your Lesson 12 folder.

12. Print the worksheet and close the workbook.

FIGURE 12-5
Completed
worksheet with
formula converting
time number into
hours

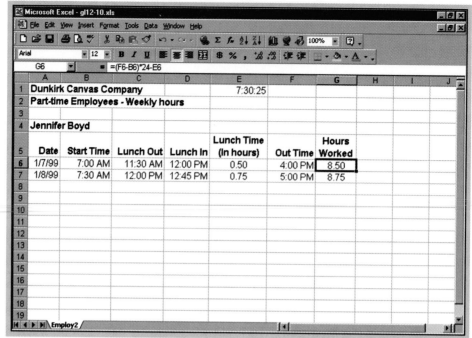

📝Objective 5

Working with Financial Functions

You can use Excel's financial functions to evaluate and analyze various loan and investment terms. This lesson focuses on the financial functions PMT, PV, RATE, NPER, FV, IPMT, and PPMT. In all financial functions, amounts of payments are represented by negative values if the payments are to be paid out and by positive values if they are to be received.

Many of the above functions take the same arguments, so the arguments are described below.

NOTE: Note that some of the argument names are the same as the function names. For clarity, the argument names are shown in lowercase letters within parentheses. Function names are shown in uppercase letters.

- (rate)
  The interest rate per period. To reflect the rate period in which the payments are made, you must enter the annual rate as a fraction that indicates how many payments per year are made. For example, a loan at an 8% annual rate for which the payments are made monthly is shown as 8%/12.

In Excel Classroom Presentation 12.

📝**Objective 5 Assignment:**
Exercises 12-20 (Skills Review) and 12-24 (Lesson Applications) can be assigned after completing Objective 5.

As students work with financial functions, make sure they do not confuse the function names with the argument names. Point out that arguments are shown in lowercase and function names appear in uppercase.

- (nper)
  The number of payment periods in an annuity. For a five-year loan with monthly payments, nper is shown as 5*12.

- (pv)
  The present value of an annuity. It is the total current value of the future payments.

- (fv)
  The future value of an annuity or the balance remaining after the last payment is made. In the case of loans, the future value should be 0 (and, in that instance, it is omitted).

- (type)
  Specifies whether payments are to be made at the beginning of the period (type 1) or at the end of the period (type 0 or omitted from function).

EXERCISE 12-11 Use the PMT Function

The PMT function calculates the amount of each payment for an *annuity*, which is a constant periodic payment paid over a fixed time period. The PMT function uses the format PMT(rate,nper,pv,fv,type).

1. Open the file **Finance.xls** and display the PMT worksheet. You'll use different worksheets in this workbook for Exercises 12-11 through 12-16.

2. In cell B4, key **10**

3. To calculate the (nper), select cell B5 and key **=B4*12**

4. In cell B6, key **150000** for the present value of the loan.

5. In cell B7, key **13%**

6. In cell B9, enter **=PMT(B7/12,B5,B6)**. The arguments represent the rate (the annual rate divided by 12 to show the monthly rate), the nper, and the pv. The fv argument is omitted because this is a loan, and the type argument can be omitted when its value is 0, which means payments are made at the end of the period.

7. Adjust the column width, if necessary. The result ($2,239.66) is negative because it represents a value that is owed and negative numbers in this format are displayed in red. When the type argument is omitted, Excel makes the calculation based on a monthly payment made at the end of each month.

8. In cell B10, enter **=PMT(B7/12,B5,B6,0,1)**. The fv and type arguments are included here. The fv (future value) is 0. You can omit this argument as you did in the previous formula, except you want to use the type

---

1 Remind students that in the financial functions, payment amounts are shown as negative values when payments are to be paid out, and positive values when payments are to be received. Since the PMT function returns an amount to be paid out, its results are negative.

2 Students can find out how different loan terms affect the amount of the payments by changing the values for the length of the loan in cell B3 and the interest rate in cell B6.

argument of 1, which specifies payments made at the beginning of each month. It is clear from the two formulas that payments are lower when they are made at the beginning of the month.

FIGURE 12-6
Using the
PMT function

	B10	▼	=	=PMT(B7/12,B5,B6,0,1)

	A	B	C
1	Dunkirk Canvas Company		
2	Business Loan Payments		
3			
4	Length of loan in years	10	
5	Number of periods	120	
6	Present value	150,000	
7	Annual rate	13%	
8			
9	**Type 0 payment**	($2,239.66)	
10	**Type 1 payment**	($2,215.66)	

9. Add the standard header to the worksheet with your name, the filename, and the date. Add a Page 1 of ? footer.

10. Save the workbook as *[your initials]***12-11.xls** in your Lesson 12 folder but do not close the workbook.

EXERCISE 12-12 Use the PV Function

You use the PV function to determine the value of an annuity at the present time. It uses the format PV(rate,nper,pmt,fv,type). The pmt argument is the payment made each period. It must be entered as a negative value. If both fv and type are 0, you can omit them.

1. Display the PV worksheet by clicking the PV tab of the workbook you saved in the last exercise.

2. Select cell B4 and key **9.7%**

3. Select cell B5 and key **10**

4. Select cell B6. The formula in this cell calculates the nper argument.

5. Because the bond pays semi-annually, key **=B5*2**

6. In cell B7, key **-7900**

7. In cell B8, key **100000**

8. Format cells B5:B8 in comma style and no decimal places. Adjust the column width, if necessary.

9. In cell B9, enter **=PV(B4/2,B6,B7)**. The result returned is $99,715.76. The fv and type arguments are omitted because both are 0. The rate argument is the annual interest rate divided by 2, since there are semi-annual payments.

10. In cell B11, enter **=B9-B8**. The difference between the cost and the actual value of the bond is ($284.24). Because the asking price is higher than the present value of the bond, it is not a good investment.

FIGURE 12-7
Using the
PV function

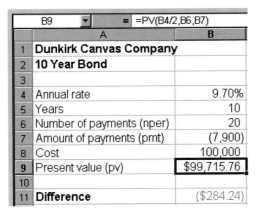

	A	B
	B9 ▼ = =PV(B4/2,B6,B7)	
1	**Dunkirk Canvas Company**	
2	**10 Year Bond**	
3		
4	Annual rate	9.70%
5	Years	10
6	Number of payments (nper)	20
7	Amount of payments (pmt)	(7,900)
8	Cost	100,000
9	Present value (pv)	$99,715.76
10		
11	**Difference**	($284.24)

11. Add the standard header to the worksheet with your name, the filename, and the date. Add a Page 1 of ? footer. Do not close the workbook.

EXERCISE 12-13 Use the RATE Function

You use Excel's RATE function to calculate the interest rate per period of an annuity. The RATE function has the format RATE(nper,pmt,pv,fv,type,guess). The guess argument is your estimate of the rate. If you omit it, Excel assumes the rate is 10% annually. If the result is not at least 0.0000001 (or 0.00001%), RATE does not find a result, and the #NUM error value is displayed. You can then try entering different values as a guess.

1. Display the RATE worksheet by clicking the RATE tab.

2. Beginning in cell B4, key the following data in column B:

> 4
> =B4*12
> -100
> 3500
> 350

3. Format the range B4:B8 in comma style with no decimal places.

4. In cell B9, enter the formula with the "guess" argument omitted:
=RATE(B5,B6,B7,B8)

5. Change the format to show the percentage with two decimal places.

6. In cell B11, enter **=B9*12**

7. Format the cell in percent style with two decimal places.

In Excel Classroom Presentation 12.

The solutions for Exercises 12-12 through 12-16 are all included in gl12-16.xls in the Solutions Manual and on the Solutions Disk.

You may want to use a simple, everyday example to help students understand this function.

FIGURE 12-8
Using the RATE
function

	B9 ▼	= =RATE(B5,B6,B7,B8)
	A	**B**
1	**Dunkirk Canvas Company**	
2	**Equipment Lease**	
3		
4	Length of lease in years	4
5	Number of payment periods	48
6	Amount of payments	(100)
7	Present value	3,500
8	Future value of balance	350
9	Monthly rate of lease	1.11%
10		
11	**Yearly rate of lease**	13.31%

8. Add the standard header to the worksheet with your name, the filename, and the date. Add a Page 1 of ? footer.

9. Save the workbook as *[your initials]***12-13.xls** in your Lesson 12 folder, but do not close the workbook.

EXERCISE 12-14 Use the FV Function

The FV function calculates the future value of an annuity. It provides the value of an investment or loan after all payments are made over a given period of time at a given interest rate. The FV function uses the format FV(rate,nper,pmt,pv,type).

The pmt argument is the amount of each periodic payment for the annuity and is represented by a negative number because it is paid to the lender.

1. Display the FV worksheet.

2. Beginning in cell B4, key the following data:

    4.5%

    12

    -250

    -500

3. In cell B9, enter **=FV(B4/12,B5,B6,B7,1)**

4. Increase the column width to display the future value of $3,597.11, if necessary. (See Figure 12-9 on the next page.)

5. Add the standard header to the worksheet with your name, the filename, and the date. Add a Page 1 of ? footer.

6. Save the worksheet as *[your initials]***12-14.xls** in your Lesson 12 folder but do not close the workbook.

In Excel Classroom Presentation 12. |1| See gl12-16.xls for the solution. |2| See gl12-16.xls for the solution.

FIGURE 12-9
Using the
FV function

	A	B	C
	B9 ▼ = =FV(B4/12,B5,B6,B7,1)		
1	**Dunkirk Canvas Company**		
2	**One-Year Savings Plan**		
3			
4	Rate	4.50%	
5	Number of payments	12	
6	Amount of payment	(250)	
7	Present value	(500)	
8			
9	**Future value**	$3,597.11	
10			

EXERCISE 12-15 Use the IPMT Function

When payments are made to reduce a loan, each payment includes both an interest amount and a portion of the principal. The *principal* is the amount borrowed, or the present value. *Interest* is the amount paid to the lender as the lender's profit; it accrues at a set rate.

The IPMT function calculates the amount of the interest payment for a period of an annuity. It uses the format IPMT(rate,per,nper,pv,fv,type).

The per argument is the period for which you want to calculate the interest amount. It must be a whole number ranging from 1 to the number of payments (nper).

1. Display the PMT worksheet by clicking the PMT tab of the workbook you saved in the previous exercise.

2. Beginning in cell A12, key the following data:

   Type 0 Payments

   Interest for the first month

   Principal payment for the first month

3. Increase the width of column A.

4. In cell B13, enter **=IPMT(B7/12,1,B5,B6)**. The result is ($1,625.00), which is the amount of the interest payment for the first month.

EXERCISE 12-16 Use the PPMT Function

The PPMT function calculates the amount of the principal payment for a period of an annuity. It uses the format PPMT(rate,per,nper,pv,fv,type).

1. In cell B14, enter **=PPMT(B7/12,1,B5,B6)**. The result is ($614.66), which is the principal payment for the first month. The result from cell B13 and the result from cell B14 add together to make up the periodic payment.

FIGURE 12-10
Using the IPMT
and PPMT
functions

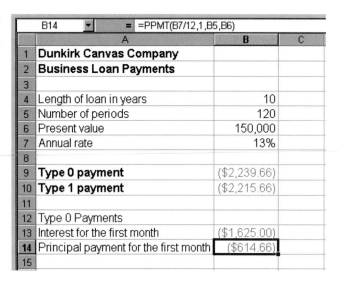

	A	B	C
	B14	= =PPMT(B7/12,1,B5,B6)	
1	**Dunkirk Canvas Company**		
2	**Business Loan Payments**		
3			
4	Length of loan in years	10	
5	Number of periods	120	
6	Present value	150,000	
7	Annual rate	13%	
8			
9	**Type 0 payment**	($2,239.66)	
10	**Type 1 payment**	($2,215.66)	
11			
12	Type 0 Payments		
13	Interest for the first month	($1,625.00)	
14	Principal payment for the first month	($614.66)	
15			

2. Save the workbook as *[your initials]***12-16.xls** in your Lesson 12 folder and print the entire workbook.

3. Close the workbook.

**COMMAND
SUMMARY**

FEATURE	BUTTON	MENU	KEYBOARD
d-mmm-yy date format		Format, Cells	Ctrl + Shift + #
h:mm AM/PM time format		Format, Cells	Ctrl + Shift + @

USING HELP   [?]

This lesson introduced you to several Excel date functions and showed you how to use them to perform date arithmetic. Excel contains a number of other useful date functions. For example, the WORKDAY function allows you to calculate the number of working days before or after a given date. You can use this function to exclude weekends and holidays when computing a completion date for a project, or invoice due dates.

In Excel Classroom Presentation 12.

[1] Point out that the Command Summary lists a variety of ways to accomplish a particular task. Students can decide which method they prefer.

[2] Encourage students to follow the steps in "Using Help." Software companies are increasingly using their Help program—rather than printed documentation—to train users and assist in answering user questions.

Use Help to view detailed information about the WORKDAY function:

1. Press [F1] to activate the Office Assistant.

2. Key **workday function** and click <u>S</u>earch.

3. Click the topic "WORKDAY worksheet function." The Microsoft Excel Help dialog box displays information about the WORKDAY function.

4. Scroll through the Help information provided, which includes an explanation of the function, its syntax, and examples of its use.

 NOTE: You must have the Analysis Toolpak installed on your system to use this function.

FIGURE 12-11
WORKDAY
function Help
screen

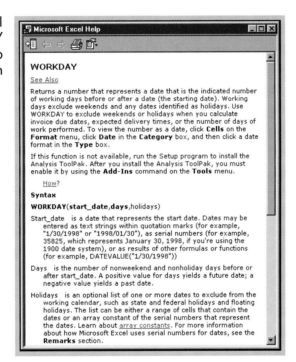

5. Close the Help window and hide the Office Assistant.

TEST BANK

Concepts Review

Each of the following statements is either true or false. Indicate your choice by circling **T** or **F**.

(T) F   **1.** When you key a date in a cell, it is sometimes displayed differently on the screen.

T (F)   **2.** The TODAY function displays the current system date and time.

(T) F   **3.** Because Excel stores dates as numbers, date calculations are possible.

T (F)   **4.** In all financial functions, amounts of payments are represented by positive values if the payments are to be paid out.

T (F)   **5.** The function TIMEVALUE() returns the current date and time.

(T) F   **6.** When using the PV(rate,nper,pmt,fv,type) function, you can omit the fv and type arguments if their values are both 0.

(T) F   **7.** When you type a time in a cell, it is stored as a time number and is displayed according to the format you select.

T (F)   **8.** The RATE function, which is used to calculate the interest rate per period of an annuity, always returns a result.

SHORT ANSWER QUESTIONS

Write the correct answer in the space provided.

1. Which function would you use to determine the serial number of a specific date?

DATE

2. Which function would you use to calculate the amount of each payment for an annuity over a certain period of time at a given interest rate?

PMT

3. Dates are stored as what type of number so they can be used in calculations?

Serial number

Concepts Review:
Allows students to check their understanding.

C L O S E

TEST BANK
Consider using the Test Bank to provide an additional review of lesson concepts. It may also be used as an assessment tool.

4. Given a serial number or a date, which function would you use to calculate the day of the week?

WEEKDAY

5. If you want to enter a date directly in a formula, you surround the date with which keyboard symbol?

Quotes

6. How is a time number recorded in a cell?

Decimal number

7. When payments are to be made at the beginning of the period, is the type argument in a financial function specified as 1 or 0?

1

8. The PPMT function is used to calculate the amount of which type of payment for a period of an annuity?

Principal

CRITICAL THINKING

Answer these questions on a separate piece of paper. There are no right or wrong answers. Support your answers with examples from your own experience, if possible.

1. When might a business need to calculate elapsed workdays and exclude weekends and holidays? Is there a date and time function that performs this calculation?

2. Can you use financial functions to evaluate an adjustable rate mortgage? Why or why not?

Skills Review

EXERCISE 12-17

Use date and time functions and date math.

1. Open the file **Employ3.xls**.

2. Select cell F1 and key the formula for the current date: **=TODAY()**

3. Select cell E5 and key the formula to calculate the years to retirement based on age 65: **=65-INT(($F$1-C5)/365.25)**

Critical Thinking Questions:
Answers will vary based on students' preferences, observations, experiences, and research.

Skills Review:
Provides guided practice for students. Objectives are indicated for each Exercise.

⊙ **Exercise 12-17:**
Objectives 1–3
Required Files: Employ3.xls
Solution Files: gl12-17.xls in Solutions Manual or on Solutions Disk.

4. Copy the formula from cell E5 to the range E6:E8.

5. Center-align the values in column E and add the standard header to the worksheet with your name, the filename, and the date.

6. Save the workbook as *[your initials]***12-17.xls** in your Lesson 12 folder and print the worksheet.

7. Create a formula printout in landscape orientation on one page with grids and row and column headings. Make sure the entire the entire formula in column E is visible.

8. Close the workbook without saving.

EXERCISE 12-18

Use functions that calculate the day of the week and create formulas that place the day of the week in worksheet cells.

1. Open the file **Schedule.xls**.

2. Select cell G5 and key the formula **=WEEKDAY(F5)**

3. Copy the formula from cell G5 to the range G6:G12, using Paste Special to copy only the formulas. (This leaves the bottom border intact.)

4. On the Table worksheet, name the lookup table that starts in cell A2 T_Days. Do not include the column headings.

5. On the Schedule worksheet, select cell H5 and enter a formula using a VLOOKUP function to look up the number of the weekday in the T_Days table and return the day of the week to the formula cell.

6. Copy the formula from cell H5 to the range H6:H12, using Paste Special to copy only the formulas.

7. Center-align the values in column G.

8. Add the standard header to the worksheet with your name, the filename, and the date.

9. Save the workbook as *[your initials]***12-18.xls** in your Lesson 12 folder and print the Schedule worksheet.

10. Create a formula printout of the Schedule worksheet on one page in landscape orientation with grids and row and column headings.

11. Close the workbook without saving.

EXERCISE 12-19

Use automatic time formats and time math to compute the total number of hours worked in a day.

1. Open the file **Contract.xls**.

---

1 Answers may vary from the Solution file depending on the current year returned by the TODAY function.

○ **Exercise 12-18:**
Objective 2
Required Files: Schedule.xls
Solution Files: gl12-18.xls in Solutions Manual or on Solutions Disk.

○ **Exercise 12-19:**
Objective 4
Required Files: Contract.xls
Solution Files: gl12-19.xls in Solutions Manual or on Solutions Disk.

2. Select cell A8 and key **Wallace, M.**

3. In cells D8 and E8, key the following data:

   6:00 am 5:45 pm

4. Select cell L5 and key the formula:

   =SUM((C5-B5),(E5-D5),(G5-F5),(I5-H5),(K5-J5))

5. Copy the formula from cell L5 to the range L6:L8, using Paste Special and copying only the formulas.

6. Add the standard header to the worksheet with your name, the filename, and the date.

7. Save the workbook as *[your initials]***12-19.xls** in your Lesson 12 folder and print the worksheet.

8. Create a formula printout in landscape orientation on one page with grids and row and column headings. Make sure the entire the entire formula in column L is visible.

9. Close the workbook without saving.

EXERCISE 12-20

Use financial functions to analyze different payment plans for a loan and calculate the future value of the loan amount.

1. Open the file **Analysis.xls**.

2. In cells B5:B8, key the following data:

   1 =B5*12 10,000 10%

3. Select cell B10 and key **=PMT(B8/12,B6,B7)**

4. Select cell B11 and key **=PMT(B8/12,B6,B7,0,1)**

5. In the range E5:E8, key the following data:

   6% 12 1,000 1,000

6. Select cell E10 and key **=FV(E5/12,E6,E7,E8,1)**

7. Add the standard header to the worksheet with your name, the filename, and the date.

8. Save the workbook as *[your initials]***12-20.xls** in your Lesson 12 folder and print the worksheet.

9. Create a formula printout in landscape orientation on one page with grids and row and column headings.

10. Close the workbook without saving.

◉ **Exercise 12-20:**
Objective 5
Required Files: Analysis.xls
Solution Files: gl12-20.xls in Solutions Manual or on
Solutions Disk.

**A
S
S
E
S
S**

Assessment Resources:
• Solutions Manual
• Test Bank
• Portfolio Builder
• Internet Projects
• Alternative Assessment Guide
• Certification Procedures

For Internet projects, go to
www.glencoe.com/webprojects

Lesson Applications

EXERCISE 12-21

Use automatic date formats and date functions to compute days late based on the current date.

One of Dunkirk Canvas Company's largest clients is overdue on its accounts. Set up an accounts receivable worksheet for overdue accounts.

1. Open the file **Smith1.xls**.

2. Key the following data in columns B and C, beginning in cell B3:

1,009.65	6/10/99
2,376.23	6/10/99
34,987.22	6/12/99
203,979.00	6/19/99
542.18	7/12/99
1,409.67	7/14/99
311.98	7/18/99
2,906.12	8/14/99
4,032.86	8/15/99
22,091.48	8/18/99

3. Create a formula in D3 that adds 30 days to the invoice date.

4. Copy the formula through cell D12 by dragging the fill handle.

5. Create a formula in E3 that subtracts the due date from the current date.

6. Copy the formula to cells E4 through E12.

7. Format the values in column E for number style with no decimal places, and center the values.

8. In the range F3:F12, use the IF function to enter a formula that displays "Yes" if the invoice is more than thirty days late and "No" if it is not. Center the results in the column.

9. Add the standard header to the worksheet with your name, the filename, and the date.

10. Save the workbook as *[your initials]***12-21.xls** in your Lesson 12 folder and print the worksheet.

11. Create a formula printout in landscape orientation on one page with grids and row and column headings.

12. Close the workbook without saving.

Lesson Applications:
Provide independent practice for students and may be used for assessment. Objectives are indicated for each Exercise.

◉ **Exercise 12-21:**
Objectives 1, 2
Required Files: Smith1.xls
Solution Files: gl12-21.xls in Solutions Manual or on Solutions Disk.

As the results in the "Days Late" and "2nd Notice" columns depend on the current date from the system clock, you may want students to input more recent dates than those shown. As an alternative, students can use a specific date and the DATE function in the formula instead of the TODAY function. All students would then have the same results. The solution shown in the Solutions Manual assumes a date of September 23, 1999.

EXERCISE 12-22

Use automatic date formats and date math to compute the number of days between dates.

  In an effort to improve customer service, Dunkirk Canvas Company is re-searching the number of days it took to ship a product after it was ordered.

1. Open the file **DunShip.xls**.
2. Beginning in cell C5, key the following data:

   5/5/99

   5/5/99

   5/6/99

   5/6/99

   5/6/99

   5/9/99

   5/9/99

   5/10/99

   5/11/99

   5/11/99

   5/11/99

3. Select cell D5 and key a formula that subtracts the date the order was received from the date the order was shipped.
4. Copy the formula from cell D5 to the range D6:D15.
5. Format the values in column D for number style with no decimal places.
6. Select cell A17 and key **Average**
7. Select cell D17 and key a formula using the AVERAGE function to calculate the average turnaround days. Format the cell to display one decimal place.
8. Add the standard header to the worksheet with your name, the filename, and the date.
9. Save the workbook as *[your initials]***12-22.xls** in your Lesson 12 folder and print the worksheet.
10. Create a formula printout in landscape orientation on one page with grids and row and column headings.
11. Close the workbook without saving.

◉ Exercise 12-22:
Objectives 1, 3
Required Files: DunShip.xls
Solution Files: gl12-22.xls in Solutions Manual or on Solutions Disk.

The completed document for this Exercise may be used in a student's portfolio.

EXERCISE 12-23

Use automatic date and time format, and date and time math, to compute elapsed times.

Dunkirk Canvas Company needs a worksheet to track customer phone inquiries. It wants to know when the phone call was returned and whether the problem was resolved, using sample phone data collected by the Customer Service Department.

1. Open the file **Customer.xls**.

2. Key the following data in columns C and D, beginning in cell C6:

Column C	Column D
9-16-99 3:00 pm	**Yes**
9-17-99 9:00 am	**Yes**
9-17-99 12:30 pm	**No**
9-18-99 9:30 am	**Yes**
9-18-99 10:00 am	**No**
9-19-99 8:00 am	**Yes**

3. In cell E6, key a formula to determine the turnaround time. The first part of the formula should subtract the dates and times of the two phone calls (make sure you place parentheses around this part of the formula); the second part should multiply this value by 24.

4. Copy the formula from cell E6 to cells E7:E11.

5. Format the range A5:E11 with an outline border, choosing the third line from the bottom, on the right side of Style list box.

6. Format column E using the number format with one decimal place.

7. Using the same line style, add a border between each column and row in the A5:E11 range.

8. Vertically center the column headings and center align the data in cells D6:E11.

9. Add the standard header to the worksheet with your name, the filename, and the date.

10. Save the workbook as *[your initials]***12-23.xls** in your Lesson 12 folder and print the worksheet.

11. Save the workbook as *[your initials]***12-23.htm** in your Lesson 12 folder.

12. Create a formula printout in landscape orientation on one page with grids and row and column headings.

13. Close the workbook without saving.

● Exercise 12-23:
Objectives 1, 4
Required Files: Customer.xls
Solution Files: gl12-23.xls and gl12-23.htm in
Solutions Manual or on Solutions Disk.

Students should key the data in column C exactly as shown in the Exercise, with one space between the date and the time.

EXERCISE 12-24 *Challenge Yourself*

Use a financial function to calculate mortgage payments at different interest rates.

   Dunkirk Canvas Company is in the process of choosing a mortgage loan to finance its expansion. Information was obtained from four banks about their interest rates. A mortgage loan analysis worksheet is needed to calculate the monthly payments based on the following: All loans are 15-year mortgages with payments due at the end of each month, so there will be 180 monthly payments. All loans have a present value of $200,000.

1. Create a worksheet sketch that includes a worksheet title, column and row labels, and an area for data. The data area consists of two columns that include labels and data for the following information: the annual rate, the number of periods (nper), and the amount of the loan (pv). In the adjacent columns are column headings for the interest rates of four different banks, labeled Bank 1, Bank 2, and so on. Under the data area is a row containing the formulas that compute payments for each of the four banks.

2. Using a 12-point font for all data, transfer the loan analysis sketch into Excel by keying and formatting the labels.

3. Rename Sheet1 **Payments** and rename Sheet2 **User Information**.

4. Key the following information in the data area of the Payments worksheet:

	Bank1	Bank2	Bank3	Bank4
Annual Rate:	11%	10.5%	9.7%	11.3%
No. of periods (nper): 180				
Amount of Loan (pv): 200000				
Payments:				

5. In the Payment row under each bank, enter formulas using the PMT function to compute the monthly payments. Remember that the annual rate argument must be divided by 12. You can omit the fv and type arguments. Use absolute and mixed cell addresses in the formula for Bank1 and copy it to the remaining three banks. (*Hint:* Use a mixed cell address for the rate and absolute cell addresses for the nper and pv arguments.)

6. Format the worksheet attractively, using the percent style with one decimal place for the rates and currency style with two decimal places for the payment amounts. Format Amount of Loan for currency with no decimal places. Use the negative number format that displays values in parentheses.

Exercise 12-24:
Objective 5
Required Files: None
Solution Files: gl12-24.xls in Solutions Manual or on Solutions Disk.

 This Exercise includes features from Lesson 4 (designing a worksheet and user documentation), Lesson 8 (formatting numbers and aligning text), and Lesson 9 (using borders and colors).

The completed document for this Exercise may be used in a student's portfolio.

7. Right-align the labels in column A. Make the Bank headings bold and right-aligned. Left-align the data in column B. Make "Payments" in cell A8 bold.

8. Center the title across the worksheet. Add a light blue patterned background to the title area. Be sure the titles display clearly over the pattern. Enclose the title area with a thick, red outline border.

9. Delete any blank lines between the title and column headings. Add thin, black, left and right borders to the Bank columns. Enclose the entire worksheet with a thick, red outline border.

10. In the User Information worksheet, create documentation that includes the following: File Information (Created by, Date created, Date revised, Revised by, Contact for help); Purpose of worksheet (paragraph form); and Instructions to User (special instructions needed by user to enter data correctly).

11. Add the standard header to the worksheets with your name, the filename, and the date. Horizontally center the worksheets.

12. Save the workbook as *[your initials]*12-24.xls in your Lesson 12 folder and print the entire workbook.

13. Create a formula printout of the Payments worksheet in landscape orientation on one page with grids and row and column headings. Make sure all formulas are visible before printing.

14. Close the workbook without saving.

Advanced Printing

OBJECTIVES

After completing this lesson, you will be able to:

1. Insert and remove page breaks.
2. Scale a worksheet.
3. Add print titles.
4. Change margins in Print Preview.
5. Change column widths in Print Preview.
6. Modify preset headers and footers.
7. Change page order and print page ranges.
8. Print named ranges.

MOUS
ACTIVITIES

In this lesson:

XL2000 **4.1**
XL2000 **4.4**
XL2000 **4.5**
XL2000 **4.6**
XL2000 **4.8**
XL2000 **4.9**

See Appendix F.

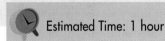 Estimated Time: 1 hour

Excel provides many features that can make printed worksheets more readable. You can create a logical, attractive layout and automate repetitive data-entry tasks.

Objective 1

Inserting and Removing Page Breaks

You can insert page breaks to control what appears on each printed page. Onscreen, inserted page breaks appear as long dashed lines. Automatic page breaks appear as short dashed lines. You can also view page breaks in Page Break Preview mode.

PREPARE
Point out to students that the learning objectives show what they will learn in the lesson. Each heading in the lesson correlates to a learning objective.

Required files:

Salesyr.xls   Salesyr2.xls

TEACH
Teaching Resources:
• Excel Classroom Presentations
• School-to-Work Strategies Manual
• Spanish Glossary
• Certification Procedures

In Lesson 4, you learned to split windows. Page breaks are inserted and removed in much the same way—above, and to the left, of the active cell. You choose Page Break (or Remove Page Break) from the Insert menu.

EXERCISE 13-1 Insert and Remove Page Breaks

1. Open the file **Salesyr.xls** and zoom to 50% to see more of the worksheet.

2. Choose Options from the Tools menu, click the View tab, check Page Breaks in the Windows options group, and click OK. Automatic page breaks are displayed between columns G and H, and columns M and N.

3. View the worksheet in Print Preview, click Next or the scroll bar to see all three pages, and close Print Preview.

TIP: To navigate in Print Preview, you can also use PgUp, PgDn, ↑, ↓, Ctrl+↑, and Ctrl+↓.

4. Select cell F1 and choose Page Break from the Insert menu. Excel inserts a vertical page break to the left of the active cell. A new automatic page break appears between columns K and L. All the first quarter (Q1) information now appears on a separate page.

FIGURE 13-1
Page breaks

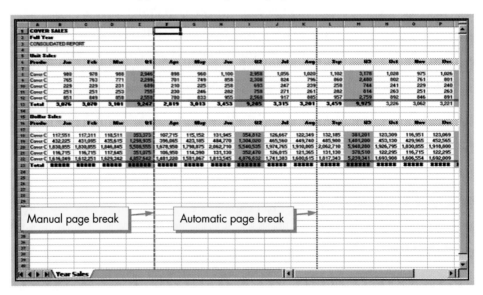

Manual page break   Automatic page break

5. Select cell J1 and choose Page Break from the Insert menu. All the second quarter (Q2) information now appears on a separate page.

6. Insert a page break between columns K and L and between columns R and S. (You'll change some of these breaks in the next Exercise.)

 Page breaks are more visible when gridlines are turned off. You may want students to turn them off when they open the Options dialog box.

 Students may wonder why a page break is applied between columns K and L instead of columns M and N. Tell them this is corrected in Exercise 13-2.

 Use Excel Classroom Presentation 13 to display screens from the lesson in a slide-show format.

7. Select cell A15 and insert a page break. This page break appears above the active cell.

8. View the worksheet in Print Preview. It now covers 12 pages (one is blank).

9. Close Print Preview.

10. Select cell F15. This cell is below one page break and to the right of another.

11. Choose <u>I</u>nsert, Remove Page <u>B</u>reak from the menu bar. The page breaks between columns E and F and above row 15 are removed.

EXERCISE 13-2 Adjust Page Breaks in Page Break Preview Mode

1. Choose <u>P</u>age Break Preview from the <u>V</u>iew menu. The Welcome to Page Break Preview dialog box appears.

2. Click OK. The automatic page break appears as a long dashed blue line. The manual breaks appear as solid blue lines.

FIGURE 13-2
Page Break
Preview mode

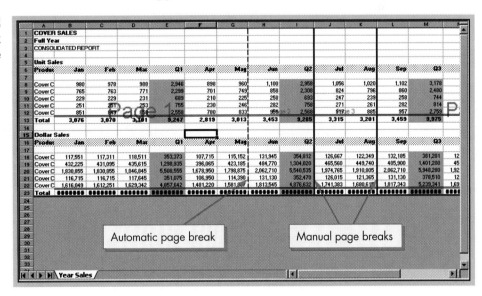

3. Position the pointer over the manual break between columns K and L until the pointer becomes a two-headed arrow ↔.

4. Drag the page break between columns M and N. Page 3 now contains all the third quarter data.

5. Choose <u>N</u>ormal from the <u>V</u>iew menu to return to Normal view and remove the page break between columns M and N.

The Welcome to Print Preview dialog box may not appear if it is turned off.

In Excel Classroom Presentation 13.

Scaling a Worksheet

☑ **Objective 2**

Scaling is enlarging or reducing the size of a worksheet's contents. As you learned in Lesson 4, you can fit a worksheet onto a specified number of pages. You can also enlarge or reduce worksheet contents by a specified percentage. The Page tab of the Page Setup dialog box offers scaling options.

EXERCISE **13-3** **Scale a Worksheet by a Percentage**

---

1. Open the Print Preview window and click <u>S</u>etup.
2. Click the Page tab, if necessary.

FIGURE 13-3
Page tab of the
Page Setup
dialog box

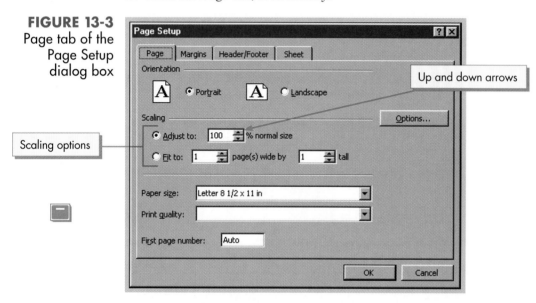

3. Click the <u>L</u>andscape option button.

4. Select the <u>A</u>djust To option, if necessary, and key **80** in the % Normal Size box (or click the down arrow to change the value to "80").
5. Click OK. The worksheet now spans three pages.
6. Move to page 2 in Print Preview. The data on page 2 almost fills the landscape page.

Objective 3

Adding Print Titles

You can generate consistent titles and column or row headings across multiple pages. You specify which rows or columns to use in the Print Titles section of

---

☑ **Objective 2 Assignment:**
Exercise 13-10 (Skills Review) can be assigned after completing Objective 2.

Using the Fit to option can create awkward page breaks. Point out that it's a good way to get an idea of how to adjust the layout using other methods to make it fit on a specific number of pages.

 In Excel Classroom Presentation 13.

It's not a good idea to scale the font size up or down by too large a percentage because the print quality becomes poor. Explain that if you need to scale by a large percentage, you should change the actual font size used in the worksheet, rather than scaling the worksheet.

the Sheet tab in the Page Setup dialog box. Print titles can be in multiple rows or columns, but they must be adjacent.

EXERCISE 13-4 Set Print Titles for Each Printed Page

1. Click <u>P</u>revious to return to page 1. Only page 1 of the worksheet has the print title beginning "Cover Sales" and the labels in column A.
2. Close Print Preview.
3. Choose Page Set<u>u</u>p from the <u>F</u>ile menu.

 NOTE: You cannot set print titles by clicking <u>S</u>etup from the Print Preview window.

4. Click the Sheet tab.

FIGURE 13-4
Sheet tab of the
Page Setup
dialog box

Print area section

Print titles section

Page order section

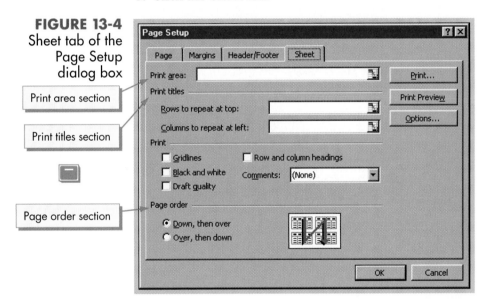

5. Key **A:A** in the <u>C</u>olumns to Repeat at Left text box. You must key a range of columns (like A:A or B:D), even if you want to print titles from only one column.
6. Click Print Previe<u>w</u> and page through the worksheet. All the pages now have the titles and labels from column A on page 1. (The titles are truncated on pages 2 and 3.)

 NOTE: You can generate consistent row headings across multiple pages just as you can set column titles. Use the <u>R</u>ow to Repeat at Top option on the Sheet tab of the Page Setup dialog box, specifying the row numbers to repeat.

[1] Explain to students that when you set print titles, any formatting of the titles, columns, or rows in their original position affects their appearance on the rest of the pages. Also, make sure they understand that no matter what print range is set, the print titles always print.

In Excel Classroom Presentation 13.

Changing Margins in Print Preview

☑**Objective 4**

You can change margins in the Page Setup dialog box or in Print Preview. To change margins in Print Preview, you drag margin lines to the desired position. An advantage of changing margins in Print Preview is that you see the results immediately.

EXERCISE 13-5 **Change Margins in Print Preview**

1. Return to page 1. If margin lines do not appear in Print Preview, click Margins at the top of the Print Preview window. Dotted lines delineate the header and footer areas and the margins and column handles appear at the top of the page.

FIGURE 13-5
Changing margins
in Print Preview

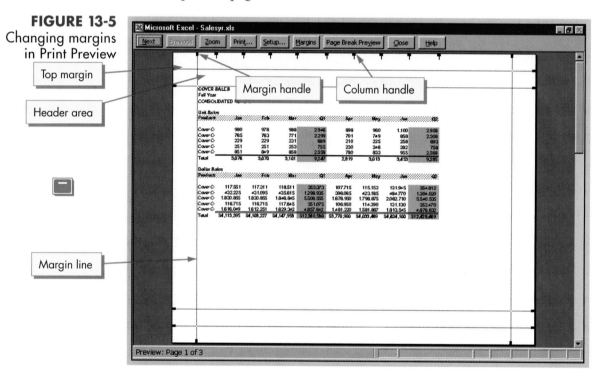

2. Click Setup and click the Margins tab.

3. Double-click in the Top text box and key **2** to set the top margin to 2 inches.

4. Click OK. Print Preview displays the new margin setting. View the other pages and notice that the margins changed on all three pages. Return to page 1.

☑**Objective 4 Assignment:**

Exercise 13-11 (Skills Review) can be assigned after completing Objective 4.

In Excel Classroom Presentation 13.

5. Position the pointer on the top margin, either on the margin handle or on the dotted line itself. (It is the second dotted line from the top.) The pointer changes to the sizing pointer, like the one used to size rows in a worksheet.

6. Drag the line up to the one-inch line. Watch the indicator in the Status bar.

 NOTE: You may not be able to move a margin to an exact position by dragging.

Objective 5

Changing Column Widths in Print Preview

 You can change column widths in Print Preview by dragging the column handles (the square boxes at the top of the page).

EXERCISE **13-6** **Change Column Widths in Print Preview**

---

1. In Print Preview, with the Margins showing, display page 2.

2. Zoom in, and adjust the screen so you can see the furthest left column handles. Position the pointer on the first column handle, which controls the width of the Print title column (column A). The pointer changes to the sizing pointer.

3. Drag the first column handle to the right until you see all the titles. The Status bar shows a measurement of about 27.

4. Move to page 1, and notice that column A is widened there, too. Adjust the remaining column widths on page 1, so the data fills the page and columns B through I are evenly spaced (each about 15 characters wide).

FIGURE 13-6
Page 1 in Print
Preview after
resizing columns

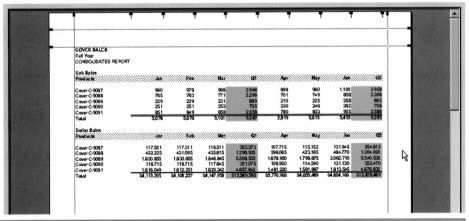

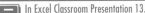 Remind students that they know how to adjust column widths in Normal view. You may want them to compare the two methods.

In Excel Classroom Presentation 13.

5. Click <u>N</u>ext. The columns on page 2 already fill the page and need no adjustment.

6. Click <u>N</u>ext. Only the Print titles and current prices appear on page 3.

7. Move to page 1.

☑ Objective 6
Modifying Preset Headers and Footers

Headers print repetitive information about the worksheet across the top of the page. *Footers* print repetitive information across the bottom of the page. Headers are positioned just below the top margin on the printed page. Footers are placed just above the bottom margin.

You can key information in a header or footer; insert codes for the page number, total number of pages, date, time, filename, or sheet name; and format header and footer text. Excel also offers several preset headers and footers that you can use or edit.

FIGURE 13-7
Buttons in the
Header dialog box

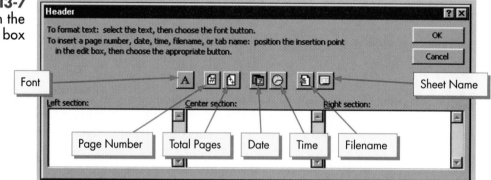

EXERCISE 13-7 Use and Customize Preset Headers and Footers

1. Click <u>S</u>etup in Print Preview and click the Header/Footer tab.

2. Click the He<u>a</u>der drop-down arrow. The Header drop-down list displays preset headers. (See Figure 13-8 on the next page.)

3. Choose the preset header: Prepared by *[a name] [today's date]*, Page 1. The list closes.

4. Click <u>C</u>ustom Header to edit the header.

5. In the Header dialog box, delete the name after "Prepared by," and key *[your name].*

6. Select the text, excluding the date in the <u>C</u>enter section (Prepared by *[your name]*), and click the Font button.

☑ **Objective 6 Assignment:**
Exercises 13-12 (Skills Review) and 13-15 (Lesson Applications) can be assigned after completing Objective 6.

In Excel Classroom Presentation 13.

FIGURE 13-8
Header/Footer tab
in Page Setup
dialog box

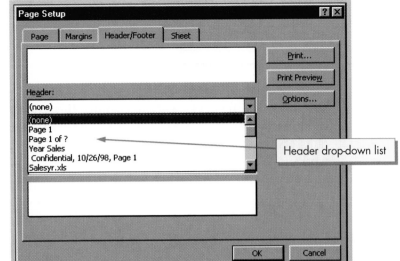

7. In the Font dialog box, choose Bold from the Font style list and click OK.

8. In the Right section delete all the page number information and click the Filename button to insert the filename.

9. Click OK to close the Header dialog box.

10. Click the Footer drop-down arrow and choose the preset footer: Year Sales, Confidential, Page 1. (The computer's user name may appear before "Confidential.")

11. Click Custom Footer to edit the footer.

12. Key **Dunkirk Canvas Company** before Confidential.

13. Click OK to close the Footer dialog box and click OK to close Page Setup. Examine the headers and footers in Print Preview.

14. Close Print Preview.

15. Press Ctrl + Home.

16. Save the workbook as *[your initials]***13-7.xls** in a new folder for Lesson 13.

17. Print the worksheet and close the workbook.

Objective 7

Changing Page Order and Printing

When data is on more than one page, Excel prints by default from the first page down and then across. If you want the pages to print across and then down, you can specify this in the Page Setup dialog box.

You can also print a specified range of pages. In the Print dialog box, choose Pages in the Print Range section and specify the beginning and ending pages in the From and To boxes.

In Excel Classroom Presentation 13.

The options on the Header drop-down list may be somewhat different than the ones shown in the figure.

Remind students that they must apply font changes to each section of a header or footer using the Font dialog box.

EXERCISE 13-8 Print a Range of Pages Across and Then Down

1. Open the file **Salesyr2.xls**.

2. Move around the worksheet. The data for the first quarter is in the top left portion of the worksheet, the data for the second quarter is to the right of the first-quarter data, and the data for the third and fourth quarters is below the first and second quarters. It is clear that this worksheet is meant to be read across and then down, rather than down and then across.

3. Press Ctrl + Home to move to the top of the worksheet and open Print Preview. The data on page 1 is the first-quarter data.

4. Click Next to move to page 2. The third-quarter data is on page 2.

5. Click Next. Page 3 contains the prices used in the formulas that calculate Dollar Sales.

6. Page through the rest of the worksheet. The second-quarter data is on page 4 and the fourth-quarter data is on page 5. Excel is reading down the worksheet then across, which is not the intended order.

 NOTE: Page 6 is blank because there is no data in the area to the right of the price data and below the fourth-quarter data.

7. Click the Previous button until you return to page 1.

8. Click the Setup button and click the Sheet tab.

9. In the Page Order section, choose Over, Then Down. Then click OK.

10. Page through the worksheet in Print Preview to see the corrected page order. The second-quarter data is on page 2, the third-quarter data is on page 3, and the fourth-quarter data is on page 4.

11. Insert the standard header with your name, filename, and date. Also insert a Page 1 of ? footer.

12. Close Print Preview.

13. Save the workbook as *[your initials]***13-8.xls** in your Lesson 13 folder.

14. Press Ctrl + P, choose Pages in the Print dialog box, key **1** in the From box and **2** in the To box, and click OK.

✔ **Objective 8**

Printing Named Ranges

As you know, you can select an area and print it or you can define the print area for a worksheet. You can also name ranges that you expect to print frequently so you can quickly select the named range and print it.

✔ **Objective 8 Assignment:**

Exercise 13-13 (Skills Review) and Exercises 13-14, 13-16, and 13-17 (Lesson Applications) can be assigned after completing Objective 8.

1 Explain that naming ranges in large workbooks with many sections and many worksheets makes it much easier to quickly find and print a specific section.

EXERCISE 13-9 Print a Named Range

1. Select cells A1 through G24.

2. Click in the Name Box, key **Qtr1**, and press Enter.

TIP: To name a range, you can also choose Name from the Insert menu and click Define.

3. Assign the name **Qtr2** to the range H1:N24, **Qtr3** to the range A26:G49, and **Qtr4** to the range H26:N49.

4. Press Ctrl + Home and save the workbook as *[your initials]***13-9.xls** in your Lesson 13 folder.

5. Remove the footer. Select Qtr3 from the Name drop-down list or the Go To dialog box.

6. Choose Print from the File menu, choose the Selection option, and click OK. Excel prints the selected cells.

TIP: You can also specify a named range to print in the Page Setup dialog box. Key the named range in the Print Area text box in the Sheet options.

7. Close the workbook without saving it.

USING HELP

There are times when you may want to print multiple copies of a worksheet. If the worksheet has several pages, you can have Excel collate the copies for you as it is printed.

Use Help to view detailed information about how to print multiple copies of a worksheet:

1. Press F1 to activate the Office Assistant.

2. Key **print multiple copies** and click Search.

3. Click the topic "Print more than one copy of a sheet or workbook." The Microsoft Excel Help dialog box displays information about printing more than one copy.

4. Read the Help information provided, which includes a description of how to print multiple copies, as well as information about collating pages.

5. Close the Help window and hide the Office Assistant.

---

1. An extra-credit topic related to printing, in which students could use Help as a research tool, is printing to a file.

2. Encourage students to follow the steps in "Using Help." Software companies are increasingly using their Help program—rather than printed documentation—to train users and assist in answering user questions.

TEST BANK

Concepts Review

TRUE/FALSE QUESTIONS

Each of the following statements is either true or false. Indicate your choice by circling **T** or **F**.

T **(F)** **1.** You can delete manual and automatic page breaks.

(T) F **2.** When you scale a worksheet, you change the size of the worksheet contents.

(T) F **3.** An advantage of changing the margins and column widths in Print Preview is that you can see the results immediately.

T **(F)** **4.** To change column widths in Print Preview, you double-click the column handles.

T **(F)** **5.** Although Excel has many preset headers and footers you can apply to worksheets, you cannot change or add to any of the preset information.

T **(F)** **6.** Excel can only print going down the worksheet first, then across.

T **(F)** **7.** You must use the mouse to move around in Print Preview.

(T) F **8.** Printing a named range is like printing a selection.

SHORT ANSWER QUESTIONS

Write the correct answer in the space provided.

1. What do you call enlarging or reducing the view of data on a physical page?

Scaling

2. Which option on the Page tab of the Page Setup dialog box do you use to make the worksheet automatically fit on a specific number of pages?

Fit To Option

3. Which area on the Sheet tab of the Page Setup dialog box do you use to generate identical titles on each printed page?

Print titles

4. What do you drag to adjust column widths in Print Preview?

Column handles

C L O S E

Concepts Review:
Allows students to check their understanding.

TEST BANK
Consider using the Test Bank to provide an additional review of lesson concepts. It may also be used as an assessment tool.

5. What is the information positioned at the top of the page just below the margin called?

Header

6. If the preset headers and footers do not provide the information you need, what option can you use to modify them?

Custom Headers and Custom Footers

7. In what default direction does Excel begin to read a multiple page worksheet?

Down, then over

8. Which print option must you select to print a selected named range?

Selection option

CRITICAL THINKING

Answer these questions on a separate piece of paper. There are no right or wrong answers. Support your answers with examples from your own experience, if possible.

1. You know how to adjust column widths several ways, in both the worksheet and in Print Preview. Which would you recommend to an inexperienced user? Why?

2. People are growing more conscious of the environmental impact of trash. The "paperless office" has long been a goal of the corporate world. Many people think, however, that the use of computers has actually caused people to use *more* paper than ever. Can you think of any alternatives to printing worksheets? What are some other ways to share relevant information without using paper?

Skills Review

EXERCISE 13-10

Add manual page breaks and scale the worksheet.

1. Open the file **Halfyr1.xls**.

2. Key the second-quarter information in the range F8:I13 as shown in Figure 13-9 on the next page, entering SUM formulas in the "Q2" column and "Total" row.

Critical Thinking Questions:
Answers will vary based on students' preferences, observations, experiences, and research.

Skills Review:
Provides guided practice for students. Objectives are indicated for each Exercise.

⊙ Exercise 13-10:
Objectives 1, 2
Required Files: Halfyr1.xls
Solution Files: gl13-10.xls in Solutions Manual or on Solutions Disk.

FIGURE 13-9

April	May	June	Q2
341	365	418	
266	285	326	
80	86	98	
87	93	107	
296	317	363	

3. Apply formatting in the Quarter 1 and Quarter 2 Unit Sales data so it matches the formatting of the Dollar Sales data. In the Total row, use the Accounting format without the currency symbols. AutoFit columns F through I.

4. Add and remove page breaks in the worksheet by following these steps:
   a. Choose Options from the Tools menu and click the View tab, if necessary.
   b. Check Page Breaks and click OK.
   c. Select cell F15.
   d. Choose Page Break from the Insert menu.
   e. Select cell A15.
   f. Choose Remove Page Break from the Insert menu.

5. Use Page Break Preview mode to manipulate page breaks by following these steps:
   a. Choose Page Break Preview from the View menu.
   b. Click OK if the Welcome to Page Break Preview dialog box appears.
   c. Move the pointer over the middle, solid-blue page break until it becomes a two-headed arrow.
   d. Drag the line between columns B and C to move the manual page break.
   e. Drag the line back between columns E and F.
   f. Choose Normal from the View menu.

6. Scale the data to fill the page by following these steps:
   a. Click the Print Preview button.
   b. Click Setup and click the Page tab.
   c. Choose Adjust To and key **125** in the % Normal Size box (or use the up arrow).
   d. Select Landscape.

e. Click the Margins tab and center the pages horizontally.

f. Insert the standard header in the worksheet and a Page 1 of ? footer. Click OK.

g. Page through the worksheet and close Print Preview.

h. Press Ctrl + Home.

7. Save the workbook as *[your initials]***13-10.xls** in your Lesson 13 folder and print the worksheet.

8. Create a formula printout with grids and row and column headings. Adjust to 100% in the <u>A</u>djust To option of the Page in the Page Setup dialog box. Remove the page break between columns E and F. Adjust the right column widths so the printout fits on three pages.

9. Close the workbook without saving it.

EXERCISE 13-11

Add print titles and change margins in Print Preview.

1. Open the file **Halfyr2.xls**.

2. Add print titles as indicated by following these steps:

a. Choose Page Set<u>u</u>p from the <u>F</u>ile menu.

b. Click the Sheet tab.

c. Key **A:A** in the <u>C</u>olumns To Repeat at Left text box.

TIP: Instead of keying a range, you can click in the <u>C</u>olumns To Repeat at Left text box and select columns in the worksheet.

d. Click Print Previe<u>w</u>. Make sure the small view is displayed.

3. If margin lines are not displayed, click <u>M</u>argins.

4. Drag the left margin line to the right, to the 2.0-inch mark.

5. Drag the right margin line to the left, to the 1-inch mark.

6. Add the standard header and a Page 1 of ? footer using the Setup button.

7. Close Print Preview.

8. Save the workbook as *[your initials]***13-11.xls** in your Lesson 13 folder and print the worksheet.

9. Close the workbook.

EXERCISE 13-12

Change column widths in Print Preview and create headers and footers.

1. Open the file **Halfyr3.xls**.

◉ Exercise 13-11:
Objectives 3, 4
Required Files: Halfyr2.xls
Solution Files: gl13-11.xls in Solutions Manual or on Solutions Disk.

◉ Exercise 13-12:
Objectives 5, 6
Required Files: Halfyr3.xls
Solution Files: gl13-12.xls in Solutions Manual or on Solutions Disk.

2. Open Print Preview. If margin lines are not displayed, click <u>M</u>argins.

3. Adjust the column widths by following these steps:

    a. Drag the first column handle to the right until column A is about 22 characters wide.

    b. Drag the rest of the column handles to the right so each column is about 14 characters wide and the data roughly fills the page (margin to margin).

    c. Click <u>N</u>ext.

    d. Starting with the second column handle, drag each column handle to the right so each column is about 14 characters wide and the last column moves onto page 3.

4. Choose a preset header and modify it by following these steps:

    a. Click <u>P</u>revious to return to Page 1, click <u>S</u>etup, and click the Header/Footer tab.

    b. Open the He<u>a</u>der drop-down list and choose Confidential, Northeast, Page 1. (The computer's user name may appear before "Confidential.")

    c. Click <u>C</u>ustom Header and replace Confidential with **Dunkirk Canvas Company**.

    d. Select all the text in the <u>L</u>eft Section, click the Font button, double-click Bold Italic, and click OK.

5. Choose a preset footer and modify it by following these steps:

    a. Open the <u>F</u>ooter drop-down list and choose Halfyr3.xls.

    b. Click C<u>u</u>stom Footer.

    c. In the <u>L</u>eft Section, key your name.

    d. In the <u>R</u>ight Section, click the Date button 🗓.

    e. Click OK to close the Footer dialog box and click OK again to close the Page Setup dialog box.

6. View the header and footer in Print Preview and close the Print Preview window.

7. Save the workbook as *[your initials]***13-12.xls** in your Lesson 13 folder.

8. Print the worksheet and close the workbook.

EXERCISE 13-13

Change page order and print named ranges.

1. Open the file **NESales.xls**.

2. Click the Print Preview button 🔍.

3. Page through the worksheet, then return to page 1.

4. Change the page order by following these steps:

    a. Click <u>S</u>etup and choose the Sheet tab.

◉ Exercise 13-13:
Objectives 7, 8
Required Files: NESales.xls
Solution Files: gl13-13.xls in Solutions Manual or on Solutions Disk.

        b. Click Over, Then Down, and click OK.

        c. Page through the worksheet to confirm that it prints in the correct order. (You may want to Zoom in and out.)

        d. Add the standard header with your name, the filename, and the date.

        e. Close Print Preview.

   5. Create named ranges for printing by following these steps:

        a. Select cell B1 through cell E23.

        b. Click the Name Box, key **First_Qtr**, and press ⌨Enter.

        c. To the cell range F1:I23, assign the name **Second_Qtr**, and press ⌨Ctrl + ⌨Home.

   6. Save the workbook as *[your initials]***13-13.xls** in your Lesson 13 folder.

   7. Print named ranges by following these steps:

        a. Choose Page Setup from the File menu.

        b. Click the Sheet tab.

        c. Key **First_Qtr** in the Print Area text box.

 NOTE: Print titles are already set.

        d. Click Print and click OK in the Print dialog box. The first-quarter data prints.

        e. Click the arrow to open the Name Box drop-down list and click Second_Qtr.

        f. Choose Print from the File menu.

        g. Choose Selection in the Print dialog box and click OK.

   8. Press ⌨Ctrl + ⌨Home and add a Page 1 of ? footer.

   9. Print pages 1 and 2 of the worksheet. (You have to clear the print area in the Sheet options of the Page Setup dialog box or choose File, Print Area, Clear Print Area.)

  10. Close the workbook without saving it.

A S S E S S	**Assessment Resources:**
	• Solutions Manual
	• Test Bank
	• Portfolio Builder
	• Internet Projects
	• Alternative Assessment Guide
	• Certification Procedures

For Internet projects, go to
www.glencoe.com/webprojects

Lesson Applications

EXERCISE 13-14

Modify preset headers and footers, add print titles, insert and remove page breaks, scale the worksheet, adjust margins in Print Preview, and print a named range.

Dunkirk Canvas wants to print its quarterly sales data on two pages and print its price list separately.

1. Open the file **Salesyr3.xls**.

2. Widen column A to accommodate the longest entry in column A other than the titles at the top of the worksheet. Set column A to print on each page.

3. Change the print header by moving the "Year Sales" sheet tab name to the left section and adding the date to the right section. Change the footer by deleting the page number and entering the following information in the left and right sections:

   Prepared by *[your name]*   **Filename, Page #**

4. Set the worksheet to print in landscape orientation centered horizontally on the page.

5. Make sure page breaks are displayed. Remove the page break above the Dollar Sales row and insert a page break after the Q2 column.

6. In Print Preview, adjust the left and right margins to about 0.5 inch. Adjust the width of column A on pages 2 and 3 to accommodate the titles.

7. Scale the worksheet to approximately 88% so quarters 1 and 2 fill page 1.

8. Adjust the top margin to 2 inches.

9. Name cells S16 through S22 **Prices**.

10. Press Ctrl + Home and save the workbook as *[your initials]***13-14.xls** in your Lesson 13 folder.

11. Print the range Prices.

12. Print the worksheet and close the workbook.

EXERCISE 13-15

Insert and remove page breaks, add print titles, add a custom footer, and change margins and column widths in Print Preview.

Dunkirk Canvas Company's personnel manager needs to print the employee information worksheet. The lookup data in the worksheet must be printed separately for managers' use only.

Lesson Applications:
Provide independent practice for students and may be used for assessment. Objectives are indicated for each Exercise.

● Exercise 13-14:
Objectives 1–6, 8
Required Files: Salesyr3.xls
Solution Files: gl13-14.xls in Solutions Manual or on Solutions Disk.

1 Suggest that students start by opening Print Preview and scaling the worksheet down by 5% to see how it looks.

● Exercise 13-15:
Objectives 1, 3–6
Required Files: EmpInfo.xls
Solution Files: gl13-15.xls in Solutions Manual or on Solutions Disk.

1. Open the file **EmpInfo.xls** and key the date of birth and the hire date for the last 10 employees, as shown in Figure 13-10.

FIGURE 13-10

		Date of Birth	Hire Date
Rodriguez	Marta	6/29/67	4/6/90
Ross	Sarah	4/23/72	5/19/92
Slavitt	Robert	9/17/74	1/18/98
Smythe	Susan	3/25/73	12/12/95
Torrisi	Thomas	11/3/78	3/5/99
Troisi	Stephen	3/5/78	8/12/94
Tyler	Mary	10/14/69	5/15/96
Vu	Tri	8/16/70	12/15/98
Weinstein	David	2/27/75	12/8/93
Wysocki	Mark	6/6/75	6/10/92

2. Remove the page break to the left of column G.

3. Move the page break after row 39 so it occurs between rows 36 and 37.

4. Add the worksheet title and labels in rows 1 through 4 as print titles. (*Hint:* Use the Rows To Repeat at Top option.)

5. Modify the preset footer to include the department name of Personnel on the left, the page number in the center, and the sheet name on the right. Add the standard header with your name, filename, and date.

6. Change the top margin to 1.5 inches.

7. In Print Preview, increase the width of column A to about 16 characters.

8. In Print Preview, increase the width of column B as much as possible without moving the column labeled "Wks Vactn" onto another page.

9. Save the workbook as *[your initials]***13-15.xls** in your Lesson 13 folder.

10. Print the worksheet and close the workbook.

EXERCISE 13-16

Insert page breaks in Page Break Preview mode, set print titles, change the print order of the pages, adjust the margins and column widths in Print Preview, modify preset headers and footers, and create and print a named range.

A detailed financial statement of changes in net assets for the retirement accounts of the employees of Dunkirk Canvas Company needs to be reformatted.

● Exercise 13-16:
Objectives 1, 3–8
Required Files: NetAsset.xls
Solution Files: gl13-16.xls and gl13-16.htm in
Solutions Manual or on Solutions Disk.

The completed document for this Exercise
may be used in a student's portfolio.

It needs specific page breaks and headers and footers. Each year's data should fit on one page for a total of three pages with the same print title.

1. Open the file **NetAsset.xls**.

2. Change the page orientation to landscape and examine the worksheet in Print Preview.

3. Close Print Preview and set page breaks to create three pages, one for each year's data. Use Page Break Preview mode and move the automatic page break if you need to.

 NOTE: Insert page breaks the same way in Page Break Preview mode as you would in Normal view.

4. Set columns A, B, and C and rows 1 and 2 as print titles.

5. Change the page order so the worksheet reads over, then down.

6. Adjust the column widths to make the data fill the page and to have data fit in columns.

7. Select a header that includes "Prepared by," the date, and the page number. Modify the header to identify the accounting firm, **Brown and Brown** that prepared the statement. Change the header font to Arial.

8. Create a custom footer with your name on the left, and the filename on the right. Change the footer font to Arial.

9. Lower the top margin to one inch, and horizontally center the worksheet on the page.

10. Re-center the years over the figure columns.

11. Set up a named range **CapGrowth_99** for 1999's capital growth (the column D data), so you can print only this information for clients that request it, without giving them other confidential information.

12. Press `Ctrl`+`Home` and save the workbook as *[your initials]*13-16.xls in your Lesson 13 folder.

13. Save the workbook as *[your initials]*13-16.htm in your Lesson 13 folder.

14. Print the range CapGrowth_99 and clear the Print Area, if necessary.

15. Print pages 2 and 3 of the worksheet and close the workbook without saving the changes.

EXERCISE 13-17   *Challenge Yourself*

Insert and modify page breaks in Page Break Preview mode, scale the data, adjust column widths, modify headers, and print named ranges.

 The Dunkirk Canvas Company needs to create an attractive worksheet that shows the net investment returns of the retirement accounts of its employees.

Exercise 13-17:
Objectives 1, 2, 5, 6, 8
Required Files: None
Solution Files: gl13-17.xls in Solutions Manual or on Solutions Disk.

The completed document for this Exercise may be used in a student's portfolio.

1. Sketch a design of the worksheet on paper that includes the following:

   a. An appropriate title

   b. Three entry areas designated as **Monthly Dollar Averaged**, **Single Investment**, and **Variable Monthly Investments**. These should create three sections in the worksheet.

   c. Row labels that include **Capital Growth**, **Bond Income**, **Money Market**, and **Stock Index**

   d. Column labels for each entry area for the years **1992** through **1999**.

2. Key the title and all labels in Excel. Format them attractively and increase column width where necessary.

3. Key the data in Figure 13-12 in the worksheet as percentages. Format figures attractively keeping the decimal points. (*Hint:* You can key the percentage symbol after each number and Excel automatically considers it a percentage.)

FIGURE 13-12

Monthly Dollar Averaged

	1992	1993	1994	1995	1996	1997	1998	1999
Capital Growth	67.51	94.53	52.17	-9.11	30.30	-3.82	53.45	-6.38
Bond Income	18.34	14.43	1.91	7.99	11.91	7.71	17.55	7.80
Money Market	7.88	6.43	6.16	7.14	8.87	7.81	5.84	3.43
Stock Index	4.54	8.87	-12.40	15.93	29.70	-4.48	29.98	6.92

Single Investment

	1992	1993	1994	1995	1996	1997	1998	1999
Capital Growth	67.34	94.33	52.02	9.20	30.17	3.91	53.29	6.47
Bond Income	18.23	14.32	1.81	7.88	11.79	7.60	17.43	7.69
Money Market	7.78	6.32	6.05	7.03	8.77	7.71	5.74	3.33
Stock Index	6.65	11.21	-12.46	15.82	29.57	-4.58	29.85	6.81

Variable Monthly Investments

	1992	1993	1994	1995	1996	1997	1998	1999
Capital Growth	67.09	94.04	51.79	-9.34	29.57	-4.58	29.85	-6.61
Bond Income	18.05	14.15	1.65	7.72	11.63	7.44	17.25	7.53
Money Market	7.61	6.16	5.89	6.87	8.60	7.54	5.58	3.18
Stock Index	9.87	4.52	-12.55	15.65	29.37	4.72	29.65	6.65

4. For each of the three investment categories, add a row that shows the average percentage return for each year.

This Exercise includes features from Lesson 4 (designing a worksheet and user documentation), Lesson 7, (using spell check), Lesson 8 (formatting numbers and aligning text), Lesson 9 (using borders, patterns, and colors), and Lesson 10 (using functions).

5. Change the page orientation to landscape. Insert and adjust page breaks in Page Break Preview mode so each section prints on a separate page.

6. Scale the data, adjust columns, or adjust margins so the data fills each page and each page is centered horizontally.

7. Create print titles that include the title of the worksheet and row labels, if necessary, so these print on each page.

8. Add the standard header with your name, filename, and date in Arial bold italic.

9. Add formatting to further enhance the worksheet. Align text and values appropriately. Turn off the gridlines for viewing. Center the title across the worksheet, add a shaded gold pattern to the title area, and enclose it in a thick, outline border. Add borders to the top, bottom, and sides of the data cells and row and column labels cells, and then add a thick, outline border around each of the three sections. Name the worksheet **Retirement**.

10. Create user documentation and name the sheet tab **User Information**. The sheet should contain the following: File Information (Created by, Date created, Date revised, Revised by, Contact for help); Purpose of worksheet (paragraph form); and Instructions to User (special instructions needed by user to enter data correctly). Format the documentation attractively and change column widths as necessary. Spell-check your work. Delete the extra worksheet tabs.

11. Add the standard header to the User Information sheet.

12. Save the workbook as *[your initials]***13-17.xls** in your Lesson 13 folder.

13. Create a named range for each section on the Retirement sheet and print each range separately. (Remember to clear the Print Area if you set it.)

14. Print the User Information sheet.

15. Save the workbook again, close it, and submit the worksheet pages and your sketch.

1️⃣ Students are asked to design worksheets based on description. Therefore, solutions will vary.

For Internet projects, go to
www.glencoe.com/webprojects

Unit 4 Applications

UNIT APPLICATION 4-1

Create a worksheet using the functions IF, VLOOKUP, and TODAY. Use text comments and date math in the formulas.

The owners of Dunkirk Canvas Company want to make sure their employees receive an annual performance review. They need a worksheet that shows each employee's last review date and whether he or she is due for a review.

1. Open the file **Reviews.xls**.

2. Select cells A16:C21 and name this range **T_Dates**.

3. Select cell B5. Write a formula using a VLOOKUP function that looks up the employee name in the table and returns the last review date. Use the T_Dates range name as the table_array argument in the VLOOKUP function.

4. Copy the formula from cell B5 to cells B6 through B10. Format the cells in the date format 03/14/98.

5. Select cell C5. Write a formula using an IF function that determines whether the difference between =TODAY() and the date in cell B5 is greater than or equal to 365. If the answer is true, return the text comment "Yes" to cell C5. If the answer is false, return the text comment "No" to cell C5.

6. Copy the formula from cell C5 to cells C6 through C10.

7. Add the standard header to the worksheet with your name, the filename, and the date. Change the font size in the header to 10 points.

8. Save the workbook as *[your initials]***u4-1.xls** in a new folder for Unit 4 Applications.

9. Print the worksheet.

10. Create a formula printout in landscape orientation with grids and row and column headings.

11. Close the workbook without saving.

A S S E S S	**Assessment Resources:** • Solutions Manual • Test Bank • Portfolio Builder • Alternative Assessment Guide • Certification Procedures • Projects Manual • Mid-Term and Final Exams	**Unit Applications:** Provide independent practice of the skills acquired from each lesson in the Unit.	**Project:** You can now assign Project 4 from the Projects Manual.	**Exam:** You can now assign Exam 4 from the Mid-Term and Finals booklet.	⊙ **Unit Application 4-1:** Required Files: Reviews.xls Solution Files: glu4-1.xls in Solutions Manual or on Solutions Disk	1 Since the results of the IF function depend on the current date, you may want students to change the Last Review dates starting in cell C16 so the results are more meaningful. As an alternative, students can use the DATE function with a specific date instead of TODAY. This way, all students will have the same answers. The solution shown in the Solutions Manual reflects a date of May 8, 1999.

UNIT APPLICATION 4-2

Use statistical functions COUNT, COUNTA, MIN, and MAX to analyze worksheet data. Use logical functions with multiple conditions, text comments, and nesting. Modify preset headers and footers, and adjust margins and column widths in Print Preview.

  The Dunkirk Canvas Company sent out an employee survey regarding company benefits. Surveys were returned and now the company needs to develop a worksheet to analyze the survey results.

1. Open the file **Survey.xls**.

2. Select cell F5 and key the following information in cells F5 through I10 (some cells will be left blank).

FIGURE U4-1

	F	G	H	I
5	X	X	X	X
6		X		
7		X		X
8	X	X	X	X
9		X	X	X
10		X		

3. Select cell A12 and key **Count**. Apply bold formatting to cell A12.

4. Select cell E12 and write a formula using the COUNT function that counts the number of employees needing dependent coverage.

5. Select cell F12 and write a formula using the COUNTA function that counts the number of employees with co-insurance. Copy this formula to cells G12 through I12 to count the employees needing insurance in those categories.

6. Select cell J5. Write a formula using a nested IF function and multiple conditions to determine whether Plan A, B, C, or D is appropriate for the employee. If cells G5 and H5 and I5 equal "X," then "Plan A" should be assigned; if not, create another IF statement. If cells G5 and H5 equal "X," then "Plan B" should be assigned; if not, create another IF

● **Unit Application 4-2:**
Required Files: Survey.xls
Solution Files: glu4-2.xls in Solutions Manual or on
Solutions Disk

The completed document for this
application can be used in a student's
portfolio.

statement. If cells G5 and I5 equal "X," then "Plan C" should be assigned; if not, "Plan D" should be assigned.

7. Copy the formula from cell J5 to cells J6 through J10.

8. Select cell A13 and key **Maximum**. Apply bold formatting to cell A13.

9. Select cell D13 and write a formula using the MAX function that determines the maximum life insurance policy written.

10. Select cell A14 and key **Minimum**. Apply bold formatting to cell A14.

11. Select cell D14 and write a formula using the MIN function that determines the minimum life insurance policy written.

12. Select a header that includes "Confidential," the date, and the page number. Modify the header, changing the page number to the filename. Change the font to Arial 10-point bold italic. Create a custom footer with your name in the center section. Change the font to Arial 10-point bold italic.

13. Save the workbook as *[your initials]*u4-2.xls in your Unit 4 Applications folder.

14. Print the worksheet.

15. Create a formula printout in landscape orientation with grids and row and column headings. Modify the footer, placing your name on the left, and adding Page 1 of ? on the right. Use the same font as before. Adjust the margins and column widths so the columns are wide enough to accommodate the formulas. Fit the printout on two pages.

16. Close the workbook without saving.

UNIT APPLICATION 4-3

Create a worksheet with a VLOOKUP function that uses date math to compute discounts. Include a cell comment that describes appropriate data entry.

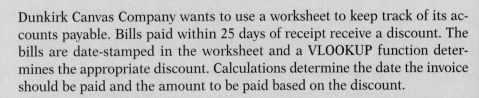

Dunkirk Canvas Company wants to use a worksheet to keep track of its accounts payable. Bills paid within 25 days of receipt receive a discount. The bills are date-stamped in the worksheet and a VLOOKUP function determines the appropriate discount. Calculations determine the date the invoice should be paid and the amount to be paid based on the discount.

1. Open the file **Payable.xls**.

2. Select cell C5. Create a cell comment that provides information about the dates to be entered in column C. Delete the default user name, key *[your initials]*: and press Enter.

3. Key the following text for the cell comment:

Type the current date. Do not use the TODAY function.

● Unit Application 4-3:
Required Files: Payable.xls
Solution Files: glu4-3.xls in Solutions Manual or on Solutions Disk

NOTE: A red triangle appears in cell C5 indicating a comment is attached to the cell.

4. Point to cell C5 and display the cell comment.

5. Select cell A5 and key the following data (as the cell comment indicates, "current date" means type today's date in the format m/d/yy).

FIGURE U4-2

	A	B	C	D	E
5	1250	Office, Inc.	*Current date*		250
6	1100	Materials, Inc.	*Current date*		575
7	1305	Regional Supply	*Current date*		990

6. Format the numbers in column E in Accounting format, with two decimal places. Left-align the numbers in column A.

7. Select cell D5. Write a formula that displays the due date for the invoice by adding 25 days to the date in cell C5. Copy the formula from cell D5 to cells D6 through D7.

8. Insert a new worksheet after the Accounts Payable worksheet, rename it from Sheet1 to **Table**, and cut and paste the lookup table in cells A22 through B26 in the Accounts Payable sheet to cells A1:B5 in the Table worksheet. Adjust the column widths appropriately. Select cells A2:B5 and name this range **T_Discount**.

9. Select cell F5 in the Accounts Payable sheet and determine the appropriate discount. Write a formula using the VLOOKUP function. (Make sure you use the range name when identifying the table_array so the formula can be copied.)

10. Copy the formula from cell F5 to cells F6 through F7.

11. Apply Percent format with no decimal places to the numbers in column F.

12. Select cell G5. Write a formula that calculates the dollar amount of the discount and subtracts it from "Amount of Invoice." The dollar amount due should be displayed in cell G5.

13. Copy the formula from cell G5 to cells G6 through G7.

14. Select cell A3. Key a formula that uses the computer clock to display the current date and time. Each time the worksheet is opened, the current date and time should be updated. Apply the date format 3/14/98 1:30 PM to the cell and left-align its contents.

15. Add the standard header to both worksheets with your name, the filename, and the date, using Arial 10-point. Add a Page 1 of ? footer to both worksheets in the same font.

16. Save the workbook as *[your initials]***u4-3.xls** in your Unit 4 Applications folder.

17. Print the entire workbook, including the comment at the end of the sheet.

18. Create a formula printout of the Accounts Payable worksheet in landscape orientation on one page with grids and row and column headings. (Make sure all formulas are visible before printing.) Do not include the Comments in this printout.

19. Close the workbook without saving.

UNIT APPLICATION 4-4

Create a worksheet using the PMT and ROUND functions for analysis of a loan repayment schedule. Add and remove a manual page break. Modify headers and footers.

Dunkirk Canvas Company needs to buy several company cars. A local bank quoted an interest rate of 7% for a $20,000 loan for three years or an interest rate of 8% for a $20,000 loan for five years. Use the PMT financial function to calculate the monthly payments and decide between the two loans.

1. Open the file **Carloan.xls**.

2. In the PMT worksheet, key the following data:

B5	**3**	D5	**5**
B6	**=B5*12**	D6	**=D5*12**
B7	**20,000**	D7	**20,000**
B8	**7%**	D8	**8%**

3. Select cell B10. Use the PMT function to determine the payment due at the end of the month.

4. Select cell B11. Use the PMT function to determine the payment due at the beginning of the month.

5. Select cell D10. Use the PMT function to determine the payment due at the end of the month.

6. Select cell D11. Use the PMT function to determine the payment due at the beginning of the month.

7. Edit the formulas in cells D10 and D11 only, adding the ROUND function so the answers are rounded to zero decimal places.

○ Unit Application 4-4:

Required Files: Carloan.xls
Solution Files: glu4-4.xls in Solutions Manual or on Solutions Disk

 The completed document for this application can be used in a student's portfolio.

8. Add the standard header to the worksheet with your name, the filename, and the date, using Arial 10-point. Add a Page 1 of ? footer in the same font. Insert a page break between columns B and C in the PMT worksheet.

9. Save the workbook as *[your initials]*u4-4.xls in your Unit 4 Applications folder.

10. Print the entire workbook.

11. Create a formula printout of the worksheet on one page with grids and row and column headings in landscape orientation. Remove the manual page break and the footer.

12. Close the workbook without saving.

UNIT APPLICATION 4-5

Create a worksheet that uses formulas with logical and statistical functions to compute operating expenses. Set print titles and print a worksheet range.

Dunkirk Canvas Company needs a worksheet to track its actual monthly operating expenses for use in budget analysis and planning. Create a worksheet sketch that includes worksheet titles, column and row headings, and a data area. There should be a column heading for expense categories, a heading for each week of the month (assume five weeks), and column headings for the total and average across the month for each expense. Under the expense heading are row labels for various company expenses (see Figure U4-3). The final row should show the totals for each week. Transfer the sketch into Excel, keying and formatting the labels.

FIGURE U4-3

Expense Categories	Week 1	Week 2
Advertising	245	*Leave blank*
Depreciation - Equipment	800	800
Lease - Building	900	900
Insurance	500	500
Office Supplies	*Leave blank*	*Leave blank*
Salaries	45,250	45,250
Travel	400	2,375
Utilities	1,350	1,450

Unit Application 4-5:

Required Files: None
Solution Files: Sample glu4-5.xls in Solutions Manual
or on Solutions Disk

 The completed document for this
application can be used in a student's
portfolio.

[1] Some students may need extra help with the
following two Applications in which there are no
numbered steps.

Total the expenses for each week with a SUM function, and use a SUM function to total expenses across the month in each category. In the Average column, calculate the average spent for the week for each expense category. Use an IF function to make sure error messages are not displayed in the AVERAGE function if there are no expenses for a category during the month. The AVERAGE function is one result of the logical_test argument. (*Hint:* Have your logical_test in the IF function test for the presence of 0 in the cell that totals the expenses across the month.)

 Add the data for Week 1 and Week 2 shown in Figure U4-3. (Leave Weeks 3 through 5 blank.) Format the headings attractively and format the numbers in number style with commas and no decimal places. Format the worksheet attractively with gridline borders and shading. Create range names for the Week 1 and Week 2 data (include the column headings).

Rename Sheet1 appropriately and rename Sheet2 **User Information**. On the User Information worksheet, create documentation that includes the following: File Information (Created by, Date created, Date revised, Revised by, Contact for help); Purpose of worksheet (paragraph form); Instructions to User (special instructions needed by user to enter data correctly). Style the documentation for easy reading.

 After completing the formulas, center the worksheets horizontally and autofit the columns to fit on one page. Add the standard header to both worksheets with your name, the filename, and the date. Save the workbook as *[your initials]*u4-5.xls in your Unit 4 Applications folder. Print the entire workbook. Set the Expense labels in column A as print titles, and print the Week 2 named range. Create a formula printout in landscape orientation with grids and row and column headings. Use a Page 1 of ? footer. Close the workbook without saving.

UNIT APPLICATION 4-6 ✓ *Making It Work for You*

Create a worksheet using IF, TODAY, text comments, and date math in the formulas. Use logical functions with multiple conditions and nesting.

 Create a bill payment schedule worksheet for personal monthly recurring expenses. List regular monthly bills, such as charge card bills, mortgage or rent payments, utility bills, insurance payments, car payments, and so on. In adjacent columns, show the date received, the due date, and amount due. Add another column that indicates whether a given bill has a late fee. Show either the amount of the late fee or just enter "Yes."

Add a "Mail By" column that computes when bills with late charges should be mailed so as to avoid the charge. Use an IF function that tests for the presence of an amount or a "Yes" in the Late Fee column. If the bill has a late charge, have the cell display the due date minus five days (roughly the

---

1 You may want students to fill in weeks 3-5 with appropriate data.

2 In this Application, student templates and worksheets will vary. A sample file is shown in the Solutions Manual and on the Solutions Disk.

Unit Application 4-6:
Required Files: None
Solution Files: Sample glu4-6.xls in Solutions Manual or on Solutions Disk

 The completed document for this application can be used in a student's portfolio.

3 This Application calls for personal financial data. Students can make up the data, model it on someone they know, or imagine their own financial situation in ten years.

number of days it may take for the postal service to deliver your payment). If the bill does not have a late charge, have a blank cell displayed instead.

Add one more column called "Comments." In this column, construct a formula that tests for bills with a late fee and if the current date is greater than the "Mail By" date. You'll want to have the formula display one of three different results. If bill has a late charge and the current date is greater than the "Mail By" date but less than the Due Date, the cell should show the message "PAY NOW!" If the current date is beyond the Due Date and the bill has a late charge, the cell should show the text "Pay late fee." If the bill does not have a late charge or the current date is before the "Mail By" date, the cell should be blank. You can construct this formula a number of different ways, but you'll need to use an IF function with a nested IF. (Hint: Use AND to test for multiple conditions in the logical tests.)

Use real or fictitious data in creating your bill payment schedule. Have at least six bills in your schedule, and have at least two bills with a late fee (create fictitious bills, if necessary). Have at least one bill show a message in the "Comments" field, adjusting the Due Date if necessary to display a message. Show the current date somewhere in your worksheet. Format the data attractively with borders, colors, and patterns.

Add the standard header including your name, the filename, and the date. Rename Sheet 1 to "Bills," and delete the remaining worksheets. Save the workbook as *[your initials]*u4-6.xls in your Unit 4 Applications folder. Print the workbook and create a standard formula printout using landscape orientation with gridlines and row and column headings. Use a Page 1 of ? footer. Close the workbook without saving.

1

In this Application, student templates and worksheets will vary. A sample file is shown in the Solutions Manual and on the Solutions Disk.

Graphics

HAND-CRAFTED
LEATHER GOODS

Charting a Running Success

Harry Hascabar's Hand-Crafted Leather Goods has been in existence for over 20 years. The company makes brief-cases, shoes, handbags, and laptop-computer cases and sells them in a five shops in the San Francisco area. But Harry Hascabar's real passion is running. He has often run in the Boston Marathon and is a nationally known sports figure.

For over a decade, the company has been quite successful making special running shoes for long-distance runners. Harry would like the company to continue moving into this market by selling sports drinks that enhance performance for long-distance runners. He's even thinking of creating a new subsidiary called "Marathon Products."

Harry wants to research all the competing sports drinks before he formulates his own. He will keep a detailed log of his distances, times, and the product he drinks before he runs. Harry will be collecting a considerable amount of detailed information, and he needs to summarize it in an attractive format to secure financing for his new company.

To present his results attractively and visually, he needs to:

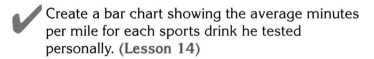
Create a bar chart showing the average minutes per mile for each sports drink he tested personally. (Lesson 14)

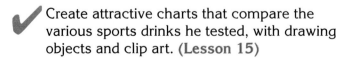
Create attractive charts that compare the various sports drinks he tested, with drawing objects and clip art. (Lesson 15)

Creating Charts

OBJECTIVES

MOUS
ACTIVITIES
In this lesson:
XL2000 **7.1**
XL2000 **7.2**
XL2000 **7.3**

See Appendix F.

After completing this lesson, you will be able to:

1. **Identify chart types and chart objects.**
2. **Use the Chart Wizard to create an embedded chart.**
3. **Size and move a chart.**
4. **Edit a chart.**
5. **Save and print a chart.**
6. **Create a chart on a chart sheet.**

 Estimated Time: 1½ hours

A chart is a visual representation of worksheet data. You link charts to worksheet data through cell references so Excel can update the data in the chart automatically when you change the data in the linked worksheet.

Objective 1

Identifying Chart Types and Chart Objects

You can create many types of charts in Excel. Once you learn the different chart types, you can match the chart to the data in the worksheet. Table 14-1 on the next page describes the types of charts available in Excel. It also indicates the charts that include 3-D effects.

PREPARE
Point out to students that the learning objectives show what they will learn in the lesson. Each heading in the lesson correlates to a learning objective.
Required files:
None

TEACH
Teaching Resources:
• Excel Classroom Presentations
• School-to-Work Strategies Manual
• Spanish Glossary
• Certification Procedures

The charts in this lesson use basic features. Design techniques vary. Charts can be placed beside, above, or below data. Provide your students with your own design techniques to enhance what is provided in this lesson.

TABLE 14-1

Chart Types in Excel

TYPE	DEFINITION
📊 Column	Column charts show variation over a period of time or demonstrate a comparison among items. (3-D effects)
📊 Bar	Bar charts illustrate comparisons among items or show individual figures at a specific time. (3-D effects)
📈 Line	Line charts show trends in data over a period of time at the same intervals, emphasizing the rate of change over time. (3-D effects)
🥧 Pie	Pie charts compare the sizes of parts of a whole. Each chart shows only one data series. (3-D effects)
📉 XY (Scatter)	XY (Scatter) charts compare trends over uneven time or measurement intervals plotted on the category axis. Scatter charts also display patterns from discrete x and y data measurements.
🏔 Area	Area charts show the relationship of parts to a whole and emphasize the magnitude of change. (3-D effects)
🍩 Doughnut	Doughnut charts compare the sizes of parts of whole. Each chart can show more than one data series.
🕸 Radar	Radar charts show changes or frequencies of data relative to a center point and to other data points. Each category has its own value axis radiating from the center point. Lines connect all values in the same series. (3-D effects)
🗺 Surface	Surface charts are useful for finding optimum combinations between two sets of data. They can show relationships between large amounts of data that would otherwise be difficult to see. (3-D effects)
🔵 Bubble	Bubble charts compare sets of three values. They are like scatter charts with the third value displayed as the size of the bubble marker. (3-D effects)
📊 Stock	Stock charts are called "high-low-close charts" and they require three series of values in this order. They are frequently used to illustrate stock prices.
🛢 Cylinder	Cylinder charts have a cylindrical shape. They lend dramatic effect to 3-D column and bar charts. (3-D effects)
🔻 Cone	Cone charts have a conical shape. They lend dramatic effect to 3-D column and bar charts. (3-D effects)
🔺 Pyramid	Pyramid charts have a pyramid shape. They lend dramatic effect to 3-D column and bar charts. (3-D effects)

1 You may want to discuss the purpose of each chart type and explain when one type would be used over another.

Each Excel chart consists of various chart objects that you can select and modify individually.

FIGURE 14-1
Excel chart objects

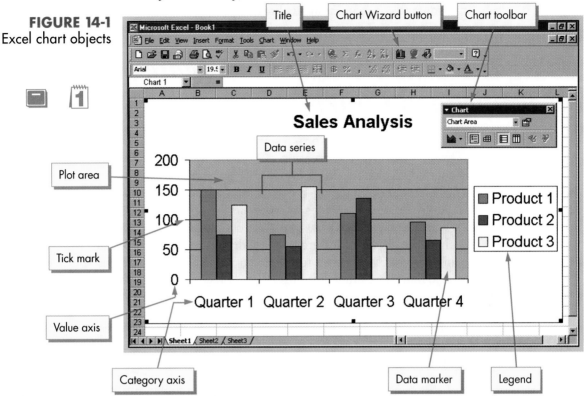

Each Excel chart object is described below:

- The *category axis* is the horizontal (or *x*) axis along the bottom of most charts; it frequently refers to time series.
- The *value axis* is the vertical (or *y*) axis against which data points are measured.
- The *plot area* is the rectangular area bounded by the two axes. It includes all axes and data points.
- A *data marker* is an object that represents individual data points. It can be a bar, area, dot, picture, or other symbol that marks a single data point or value.
- A *legend* is a guide that explains the symbols, patterns, or colors used to differentiate data series.
- A *tick mark* is a division mark along the category (x) and value (y) axes.
- A *data point* is a single piece of data.
- A *data series* is a collection of data points that are related. These values are usually found within the same column or row in the worksheet.
- The *chart title* gives the name of the chart.

Use Excel Classroom Presentation 14 to display screens from the lesson in a slide-show format.

Reinforce the various chart objects, as these objects are referred to throughout Unit 5.

The Chart toolbar is available with special charting tools. Additionally, the Chart menu replaces the Data menu in the menu bar. You use Chart menu commands to manipulate a chart.

Objective 2

Using the Chart Wizard to Create an Embedded Chart

The Chart Wizard button ▥ starts the Chart Wizard, which guides you step-by-step through the creation of a chart using selected worksheet data. The completed chart for this lesson will be *embedded* in the worksheet. You can also create a chart on a different worksheet. If you change data in one worksheet, Excel updates the chart in the other worksheet automatically.

In the case study for this unit, you learned that Harry Hascabar wants to chart the effects of different sports drinks on his running speed. Before creating the chart, you need to develop a worksheet showing the sports drinks he used and the average minutes per mile recorded for each drink.

EXERCISE 14-1 Enter the Chart Data

1. Start a new workbook and key the following data in the cells indicated.

FIGURE 14-2

	A	B
1	Drink	Average Minutes
2	HydraPunch	6.63
3	SurgeQuench	6.77
4	AllSport	5.8
5	CynoMax	5.47
6	Endrun	6.2
7	Everlast	5.99
8	Innergize	6.57

2. Modify the column widths as necessary.

3. Center the column headings and make them bold.

EXERCISE 14-2 Use the Chart Wizard

1. Select cells A1 through B8.

2. Click the Chart Wizard button on the Standard toolbar. The Chart Wizard - Step 1 of 4 dialog box opens.

FIGURE 14-3
Chart Wizard -
Step 1 of 4
dialog box

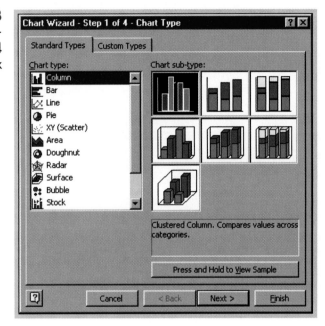

3. Click the Standard Types tab, if necessary.

> **TIP:** Many custom charts are available. Click the Custom Types tab to view the list.

EXERCISE 14-3 Choose the Chart Type

1. Under the Chart Type, click "Bar." Six chart sub-types are displayed to the right.

2. Click the various sub-types and click the Press and Hold to View Sample button to see examples of the various sub-types.

Typically data should be selected before clicking the Chart Wizard button. The Chart Wizard attempts to pick data to include in the chart if you do not select it in advance. However, the Chart Wizard - Step 2 of 4 dialog box allows you to enter a cell range, either by keying it or using the mouse to select it.

 In Excel Classroom Presentation 14.

3. When you finish viewing each sub-type, choose the first sub-type.

 NOTE: Clicking Finish in the first step of the Chart Wizard creates the chart using the Excel 2-D column default chart format.

4. Click Next. The Chart Wizard - Step 2 of 4 dialog box appears.

FIGURE 14-4
Chart Wizard -
Step 2 of 4
dialog box

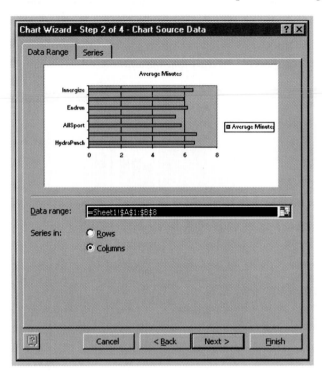

EXERCISE 14-4 Enter Additional Chart Information

In the Chart Wizard - Step 2 of 4 dialog box you specify the data that you will chart.

1. Click the Data Range tab, if necessary. A moving border surrounds the data cells in the worksheet. (Move the dialog box, if necessary.) Also notice the Data Range text box contains a formula with this cell range in it.

2. Choose the Columns option, if necessary.

3. Click the Series tab and view the information for Name, Values, and Category (X) Axis Labels. All these text boxes contain formulas with the cell addresses to plot the chart data. You can edit these formulas here.

4. Click Next. The Chart Wizard - Step 3 of 4 dialog box appears.

EXERCISE **14-5** **Edit the Title, and Add Labels and a Legend**

1. Click the Titles tab, if necessary.
2. Key **Sports Drink Comparison** in the Chart Title text box, overwriting "Average Minutes." The title appears in the sample chart.
3. Press Tab and key **Drinks** in the Category (X) Axis text box.
4. Press Tab and key **Minutes** in the Value (Y) Axis text box.
5. Click the Legend tab.
6. Make sure Show Legend is selected and choose Corner.
7. Click Next and the Chart Wizard Step - 4 of 4 dialog box opens.

FIGURE 14-5
Chart Wizard -
Step 4 of 4
dialog box

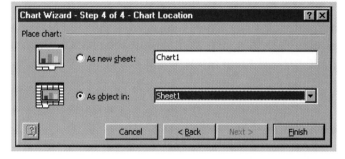

8. From the As Object In drop-down list, choose Sheet1, if necessary.

9. Click Finish. A minimized chart is displayed in the worksheet. The Chart toolbar opens and the Chart menu appears in the menu bar replacing the Data menu.

NOTE: If the point size of some data in the chart is too big, some labels will not be visible and the entire chart will not appear. You learn to adjust the font size and resize the chart in the next three Exercises.

Objective 3

Sizing and Moving a Chart

Once you create a chart, you can change its size, proportions, and position on the worksheet.

EXERCISE **14-6** **Move and Size the Chart**

1. Select the chart, if necessary, by clicking inside the chart. Small black squares, called *selection handles*, appear around the selected chart.
2. Point anywhere within the chart.

 When charts contain only one data item, a legend is not normally used. It is used here for demonstration purposes.

In Excel Classroom Presentation 14.

An embedded chart can be easily deleted if a student makes a mistake and wants to start over. Click the chart to select it (the small square selection handles appear around the chart) and press Delete.

The chart has axis labels with a point size too big for the entire chart to display properly. Students correct this in the next three Exercises.

3. Click and drag the chart with the four-headed arrow so the upper left corner is in cell A13.

4. Use the scroll bars to display the entire chart, if necessary.

5. Move the pointer over the bottom right selection handle until it changes to a double-headed arrow.

6. Using the double-headed arrow, enlarge the chart by dragging the bottom right corner to cell G31. Notice that all of the category axis labels are still not visible.

7. Click outside the chart to deactivate it. Notice that the Chart toolbar disappears and the Chart menu changes back to the Data menu.

Objective 4

Editing a Chart

After creating a chart, you may need to edit the chart font size to make labels readable. You may also want to edit the chart's contents or change the chart type to make it more attractive or easier to understand. Before modifying an embedded chart, you must activate it by clicking it. Then you can use the Chart toolbar and Chart menu to make additional modifications.

EXERCISE **14-7** **Activate the Chart and Display the Chart Toolbar**

FIGURE 14-6
Chart toolbar

1. Move the mouse pointer inside the embedded chart and click it. The chart is activated and the Chart toolbar is displayed again as well as the Chart menu. (If the Chart toolbar is not displayed automatically, right-click any toolbar displayed onscreen and choose Chart from the shortcut menu.)

TABLE 14-2 Chart Toolbar

BUTTON	NAME	DESCRIPTION
Chart Title ▾	Chart Objects	The drop-down list displays all the objects in the chart and allows you to select each of them.
🖆	Format Object (varies)	Opens the corresponding dialog box for the object you selected in the chart.
📊▾	Chart Type	Displays the different chart types available.
📇	Legend	Removes and adds a legend.
▦	Data Table	Removes or adds a table containing the data series.

continues

In Excel Classroom Presentation 14.

TABLE 14-2   Chart Toolbar   *continued*

BUTTON	NAME	DESCRIPTION
🄴	By Row	Plots a data series by rows.
🄼	By Column	Plots a data series by columns.
🄰	Angle Text Downward	Rotates text downward.
🄰	Angle Text Upward	Rotates text upward.

2. If the Chart toolbar is displayed with one row of icons instead of two, change the shape by dragging the right side of the toolbar to the left. The smaller shape makes the toolbar easier to manage.

EXERCISE 14-8 Change the Chart Font Size

You can change the font size of any data in the chart using the Formatting toolbar.

1. Look in the Chart Objects text box on the Chart toolbar to make sure "Chart Area" appears. If it doesn't, move the pointer around the white area of the chart until the Chart Area ScreenTip appears and click it.

2. From the Font Size drop-down list on the Formatting toolbar, choose 10 point. All the type in the chart is now 10 point and the labels are readable. This also enlarges the plot area.

3. Choose "Chart Title" from the Chart Objects drop-down list. (You can also click directly on the chart title.) Change the font size to 12 point in the Font drop-down list.

 NOTE: You can also use these steps to change the font, but by accessing the font drop-down list on the Formatting toolbar. This is covered in detail in the next lesson.

EXERCISE 14-9 Change the Chart Type

Viewing information arranged in a variety of chart types can provide different perspectives of your data. You can use the Chart toolbar or the Chart menu to change the chart type.

FIGURE 14-7
Drop-down list of chart types

1. Click the down arrow to the right of the Chart Type button on the Chart toolbar. Excel displays a drop-down list of chart types.

 2. Click the Area Chart button in the top left corner. The chart is displayed as an area chart.

 3. To view another perspective, re-open the drop-down list and click the Radar Chart button .

4. Choose Chart Type from the Chart menu.

5. Click the Standard Types tab, if necessary, choose the Bar chart, and click OK. The first chart type you chose is restored.

TIP: Another way to change the chart type is to right-click the activated chart and choose Chart Type from the shortcut menu.

EXERCISE 14-10 Change Chart Sub-Type

Excel offers various formats, called sub-types, for each type of chart.

1. With the chart still activated, choose Chart Type from the Chart menu.
2. Click the Standard Types tab, if necessary.
3. Choose the fourth sub-type, "Clustered bar with a 3-D visual effect" (the first sub-type in the second row).
4. Click OK. The chart is 3-D.

NOTE: When you select different chart types, some labels may disappear. You may need to edit the point size to see the label again, or you can resize the chart.

5. Press Ctrl + Z to revert to the previous chart type.

EXERCISE 14-11 Change Chart and Axis Titles

You may want to change titles, axes, or other items in your chart. You can select various chart items in an active chart by clicking the item.

---

1 Caution students about clicking the icon on the Chart Type button (which applies the chart type shown) instead of clicking the down arrow on the button (which displays the drop-down list). Students can use Undo to undo an accidental change in chart type.

 In Excel Classroom Presentation 14.

2 The drop-down list of chart types on the Chart toolbar does not allow you to choose a chart sub-type.

3 Explain that in a bar chart, the category axis is the vertical axis and the values axis is the horizontal axis. The reverse is true in a column chart.

1. Click the chart title "Sports Drink Comparison." The title is selected and "Chart Title" appears in the Name Box on the formula bar.

2. Key **Comparison for Weeks 1-5** and press Enter. The new text replaces the old title.

3. Click the category axis title "Drinks" and change it to **Sports Drinks**.

4. Click the value axis title "Minutes" and change it to **Minutes Per Mile**.

TIP: After selecting a chart text item, you can use the I-beam pointer to edit the text. Once you select a chart text item, you can use the Formatting toolbar to change its font, style, or size.

EXERCISE 14-12 Use the Legend to Display Categories

In this chart, you can remove the category labels (the sports drink names) and list them in the legend instead.

1. Select the category axis in the active chart window. (To select the axis, you can click it directly, click a tick mark, or click one of the drink names.) "Category Axis" should appear in the Name Box in the formula bar.

2. Choose Selected Axis from the Format menu.

3. Click the Patterns tab, if necessary. In the Tick Mark Labels box, click None.

FIGURE 14-8
Patterns options in
the Format Axis
dialog box

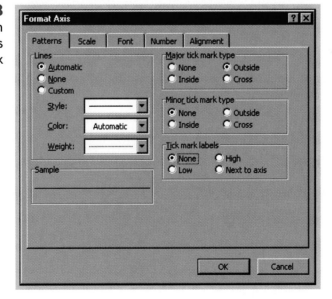

4. Click OK. The sports drink names no longer appear next to the category axis.

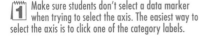 Make sure students don't select a data marker when trying to select the axis. The easiest way to select the axis is to click one of the category labels.

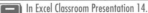 In Excel Classroom Presentation 14.

5. Click one of the blue data series bars in the chart.

6. Click the Format Data Series button 🖼 on the Chart toolbar to open the Format Data Series dialog box and click the Options tab.

NOTE: This button changes names depending on which chart element you selected.

7. Click the <u>V</u>ary Colors By Point check box to make each data point in the series a different color.

FIGURE 14-9
Options in the
Format Data Series
dialog box

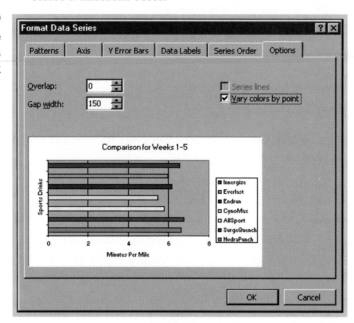

8. Click OK. The legend displays the category labels and colors corresponding to the labels used in the chart. The chart is compressed to fit the size and placement of the legend.

9. Double-click the legend to open the Format Legend dialog box.

10. Click the Placement tab and click <u>R</u>ight.

11. Click OK. Now you can see the complete chart again.

TIP: You can also resize the legend. Click the legend to activate it and resize it by dragging one of its selection handles.

EXERCISE 14-13 Add Data to a Chart

The easiest way to add data to an embedded chart is to enter it in the worksheet and extend the fill handles to include the new data.

In Excel Classroom Presentation 14.

1. In cell A9, key **PowerEase**

2. In cell B9, key **5.1**

3. Activate the chart area. (When the chart area is activated, "Chart Area" appears in the Chart Objects text box.)

4. With the cross pointer drag the fill handles in the lower right corners of cells A8 and B8 down to include the new data in row 9. (Dragging one handle moves the other one.) The new data is incorporated in the chart. (See the chart legend.)

FIGURE 14-10
Activated chart
and worksheet
chart data

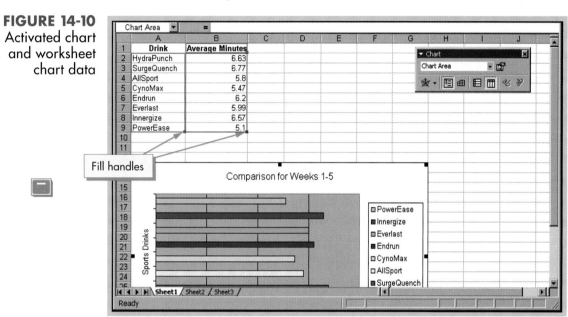

 TIP: You can also drag the fill handles up to exclude data.

☑**Objective 5**

Saving and Printing a Chart

A chart is saved each time you save the workbook in which it is embedded. Embedded charts print with the worksheet. You can preview the chart before printing to see how it looks on the worksheet. You can also print only the chart by activating it and clicking the Print button 🖨.

EXERCISE **14-14** Saving and Printing

1. Click outside the chart to deselect it.

 In Excel Classroom Presentation 14.

☑**Objective 5 Assignment:**
Exercises 14-16 and 14-17 (Skills Review) and
Exercises 14-20 and 14-22 (Lesson Applications) can
be assigned after completing Objective 5.

2. Move the data in columns A and B above the chart to columns C and D, so it is centered over the chart.

3. Adjust the widths of the columns appropriately.

4. Center the worksheet horizontally on the page.

5. Add the standard header to the worksheet.

6. Save the workbook **as *[your initials]*14-14.xls** in a new folder for Lesson 14.

7. Click the chart to activate it and click the Print button 🖨 on the Standard toolbar to print only the chart.

☑ Objective 6

Creating a Chart on a Chart Sheet

You can create a chart so it appears on a separate worksheet within a workbook. If you need to print a chart to use in a presentation, for example, creating a chart on its own worksheet is the best approach.

When you insert a chart on a worksheet, you add the chart to the active workbook. You can print the chart separately from the worksheet containing the chart data.

By default, worksheets containing charts (called "chart sheets") are named "Chart1," "Chart2," and so on, by default. You can rename them by double-clicking the tab for the chart sheet and keying a new name.

EXERCISE 14-15 **Create a Chart on a Chart Sheet**

1. Select the same data you used for the embedded chart, including the new row 9 data.

2. Choose <u>I</u>nsert, <u>C</u>hart. (You can also click the Chart Wizard button 📊.)

3. Click the Standard Types tab, if necessary, and select the Column chart type, sub-type 1.

4. Click Next three times to accept the data, labels, title, and legend default settings.

5. In the Chart Wizard - Step 4 of 4 dialog box, click As New <u>S</u>heet and keep the default sheet name, "Chart1."

6. Click <u>F</u>inish. Chart1 appears as a new sheet in the workbook. Notice that the layout of the chart defaulted to landscape. (See Figure 14-11 on the next page.)

7. Open the Page Setup dialog box and click the Chart tab. (The Chart tab replaces the Sheet tab when a chart is activated.) Notice the three chart size settings. Keep the current setting, <u>U</u>se Full Page.

The solution for this file appears in gl14-15.xls in the Solutions Manual and on the Solutions disk.

☑ **Objective 6 Assignment:**
Exercises 14-18 and 14-19 (Skills Review) and Exercises 14-21 and 14-23 (Lesson Applications) can be assigned after completing Objective 6.

FIGURE 14-11
New chart sheet

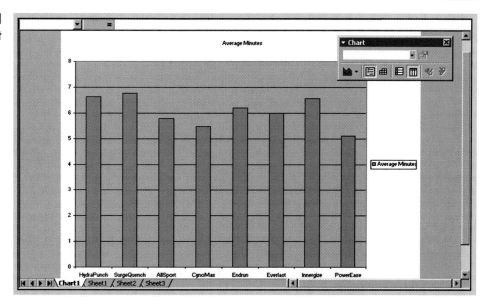

8. Insert the standard header in the chart sheet.
9. Delete the unused worksheets in the workbook.
10. Save the workbook as *[your initials]***14-15.xls** in your Lesson 14 folder.

11. Print the entire workbook and then close the workbook.

> **NOTE:** You can also use ⌷F11⌷ to insert a chart on a separate sheet. Just select the data you want to include in the chart and press ⌷F11⌷. The default 2-D column chart is inserted.

COMMAND SUMMARY

FEATURE	BUTTON	MENU	KEYBOARD
Create a chart	📊	Insert, Chart	F11

USING HELP

Microsoft Excel Help offers extensive Help on charts. For example, you can refer to Help for information on changing an embedded chart to a chart sheet and vice versa.

In Excel Classroom Presentation 14.

1 Remind students that if a chart is activated and the Print command is issued, Excel prints only the chart — not the worksheet.

2 Emphasize that students can use F11 to quickly insert a 2-D column chart on a separate sheet. Just select the data to be included in the chart and press F11.

3 Point out that the Command Summary lists a variety of ways to accomplish a particular task. Students can decide which method they prefer.

Use Help to get information on changing embedded charts to chart sheets:

1. Display the Office Assistant and click it.

2. Key **embedded charts** and click <u>S</u>earch.

3. Display the topic "Change an embedded chart to a chart sheet, and vice versa."

FIGURE 14-12
Microsoft Excel
Help window on
chart conversions

4. Review the Help window information.

5. Close the Help window and hide the Office Assistant.

Encourage students to follow the steps in "Using Help." Software companies are increasingly using their Help program — rather than printed documentation — to train users and assist in answering user questions.

In Excel Classroom Presentation 14.

TEST BANK

Concepts Review

TRUE/FALSE QUESTIONS

Each of the following statements is either true or false. Indicate your choice by circling **T** or **F**.

(T) F **1.** Charts are linked to worksheet data through cell references.

T **(F)** **2.** A tick mark represents a single piece of data.

(T) F **3.** The Chart Wizard can create an embedded chart or a chart on its own chart sheet.

T **(F)** **4.** Once a chart is created, you cannot edit its contents.

(T) F **5.** The Chart menu is displayed when a chart is activated.

T **(F)** **6.** Embedded charts do not print with the worksheet.

(T) F **7.** Before modifying an embedded chart, you must activate it.

(T) F **8.** A separate worksheet containing a chart is called a "chart sheet."

SHORT ANSWER QUESTIONS

Write the correct answer in the space provided.

1. Which type of chart shows trends in data over a period of time at the same intervals, emphasizing the rate of change over time?

Line

2. Which chart element explains the symbols, patterns, or colors used to differentiate data series?

Legend

3. What toolbar appears after a chart is activated?

Chart toolbar

4. What are the various formats for each type of chart called?

Sub-types

5. Which axis is generally the horizontal axis?

X or category

Concepts Review:
Allows students to check their understanding.

C
L
O
S
E

TEST BANK
Consider using the Test Bank to provide an additional review of lesson concepts. It may also be used as an assessment tool.

6. If you create a chart on a chart sheet in a workbook with no other chart sheets, what is the chart named by default?

Chart1

7. What is the name of the area bounded by two axes on a chart?

Plot area

8. What are the small black handles that appear around an activated chart?

Selection handles

CRITICAL THINKING

Answer these questions on a separate piece of paper. There are no right or wrong answers. Support your answers with examples from your own experience, if possible.

1. Why would a business find the charting feature of Excel advantageous? What reasons could you give your boss for creating charts?

2. On what occasion might you choose to use a line chart in a business proposal? What would be a good reason for changing from a column chart to a pie chart when presenting company stock information?

Skills Review

EXERCISE 14-16

Use the Chart Wizard to create an embedded chart, edit chart data, resize the chart, and save and print the chart.

1. Open the file **Times.xls**.

2. Use the Chart Wizard to create an embedded chart by following these steps:

    a. Select cells A3:B7.

    b. Click the Chart Wizard button 📊 on the Standard toolbar.

    c. Choose the "Column" Chart Type.

    d. Choose "Clustered column with a 3-D visual effect (the fourth subtype) and click Next.

    e. Click Next in the second Chart Wizard dialog box to confirm the range and series.

Critical Thinking Questions:
Answers will vary based on students' preferences, observations, experiences, and research.

Skills Review:
Provides guided practice for students. Objectives are indicated for each Exercise.

◉ Exercise 14-16:
Objectives 2–5
Required Files: Times.xls
Solution Files: gl14-16.xls in Solutions Manual or on Solutions Disk.

  f. In the third dialog box, click the Titles tab, if necessary, and key **Best Marathon Times** as the chart title.

  g. Click the Legend tab, and deselect Show Legend.

  h. Click Finish.

3. Edit the font size of all data to be 9 points:

  a. Select Chart Area by clicking in the white chart area. (Look in the Chart Objects text box of the Chart toolbar to be sure it is selected.)

  b. Choose 9 points from the Font size drop-down list.

4. Resize the chart by following these steps:

  a. Click the chart to display the selection handles, if necessary.

  b. Point to the bottom, center handle.

  c. Using the two-headed arrow, drag the handle down to the bottom edge of row 22. Release the mouse and check to see that all the chart data is visible. If not, resize it again.

5. Click outside the chart to deselect it.

6. Add the standard header in the worksheet.

7. Save the workbook as *[your initials]*14-16.xls in your Lesson 14 folder.

8. Print the worksheet and close the workbook.

EXERCISE 14-17

Add data to a chart, change the chart type, resize a chart, and save and print the chart.

1. Open the file **Drinks1.xls**.

2. Enter the data in Figure 14-13 in cells A9:B11:

FIGURE 14-13

	A	B
9	Exceed	5.11
10	HydraFuel	5.5
11	PurePower	6.37

3. Incorporate the new data into the embedded chart by following these steps:

  a. Click the chart to activate it.

The solution to Exercise 14-16 varies according to the choices students make concerning the size of their charts.

⊙ **Exercise 14-17:**
Objectives 3–5
Required Files: Drinks1.xls
Solution Files: gl14-17.xls in Solutions Manual or on Solutions Disk.

    b. Using the cross pointer, drag the fill handles in cells A8 and B8 down to include the three new rows of data.

   4. Change the chart type to Column by following these steps:

    a. Click the down arrow beside the Chart Type button ■▼ on the Chart toolbar.

    b. Choose the Column chart.

   5. Resize the chart so it spans from cell A13 through G33. The value labels should be clearer with more space between them.

   6. Deselect the chart.

   7. Add the standard header to the worksheet.

   8. Save the workbook as ***[your initials]*14-17.xls** in your Lesson 14 folder.

   9. Print the worksheet and close the workbook.

EXERCISE 14-18

Create a separate chart sheet, and save and print the worksheet.

   1. Open the file **Drinks2.xls**.

   2. Create a separate chart sheet by following these steps:

    a. Select cells A1:B11.

    b. Select Insert, Chart.

    c. In the first Chart Wizard dialog box, choose the Pie chart, sub-type 1, and click Next.

    d. Click Next to accept the range and series.

    e. Click the Data Labels tab in the third dialog box and choose Show Value.

    f. Click Next and choose As New Sheet. Key **Pie Chart** in the text box beside it and click Finish.

   3. Insert the standard header in the chart worksheet.

   4. Save the workbook as ***[your initials]*14-18.xls** in your Lesson 14 folder.

   5. Print the chart sheet and close the workbook.

EXERCISE 14-19

Create an embedded chart, move the chart, edit chart objects, and create a chart on a new sheet. Save and print the chart.

   1. Start a new workbook.

   2. Key the data in Figure 14-14 in cells A1:B7. Right-align the label in column B.

The solution to Exercise 14-17 varies according to the choices students make concerning the size of their charts.

Exercise 14-18:
Objectives 5, 6
Required Files: Drinks2.xls
Solution Files: gl14-18.xls in Solutions Manual or on Solutions Disk.

Exercise 14-19:
Objectives 2–6
Required Files: None
Solution Files: gl14-19.xls in Solutions Manual or on Solutions Disk.

FIGURE 14-14

	A	B
1	STATES	NUMBER OF WINS
2	UT	2
3	FL	5
4	TX	7
5	NY	3
6	IL	4
7	CA	11

3. Adjust column widths where necessary.

4. Create a bar chart on a chart sheet using the first sub-type. Make the chart include a chart title, **Harry Hascabar Wins**, and X- and Y-axis titles. Exclude the legend.

5. Change the chart title to 16-point type.

6. Create an embedded pie chart using the data for FL, TX, and CA only. Use the second sub-type, key **Warm Weather Races Won** as the chart title, place the legend on the left side of the chart, and show value data labels.

 TIP: Select cells A3:B3, A4:B4, and A7:B7 before clicking the Chart Wizard button ▣.

7. Move the chart below the data in the worksheet by following these steps:
   a. Activate the chart, if necessary.
   b. With the four-headed arrow, move the chart below the worksheet data.

8. Deselect the chart and delete unused worksheets.

9. Add the standard header to the chart sheet and the worksheet.

10. Center the worksheet with the embedded chart horizontally on the page.

11. Save the workbook as *[your initials]***14-19.xls** in your Lesson 14 folder.

12. Print the entire workbook and close it.

Assessment Resources:
• Solutions Manual
• Test Bank
• Portfolio Builder
• Internet Projects
• Alternative Assessment Guide
• Certification Procedures

ASSESS

For Internet projects, go to
www.glencoe.com/webprojects

Lesson Applications

Enter data and use the Chart Wizard to create a bar chart. Resize and move the chart. Save and print the chart.

Harry Hascabar tested eight sports drinks over an eight-week period and recorded the number of miles he ran and his running times. Enter the data and create a chart to display it.

1. Start a new workbook.

2. Key the data shown in Figure 14-15 beginning in cell A1 (making the corrections shown). Format all the times for two decimal places. Right-align the labels "MILES" and "AVERAGE," and increase column widths where necessary.

FIGURE 14-15

	A	B	C
1	hascabar's racing record		
2	Weeks 1-8		
3			
4	drink	MILES	AVERAGE
5	HydraPunch	10	7.15
6	SuperQuench	51	7.77
7	AllSport	8	6.8
8	CynoMax	12	6.45
9	Endrun	10	7.2
10	Everlast	16	6.15
11	Innergize	17	7.35
12	PowerEase	10	6.1

Lesson Applications:
Provide independent practice for students and may be used for assessment. Objectives are indicated for each Exercise.

Exercise 14-20:
Objectives 2, 3, 5
Required Files: None
Solution Files: gl14-20.xls in Solutions Manual or on Solutions Disk.

This figure contains proofreading marks. You may want to review Appendix E: "Proofreaders' Marks" with students.

3. Use the Chart Wizard to create an embedded bar chart (sub-type 1). Include a legend at the bottom, add the title **Hascabar's Racing Record**, and add the x-axis title **Sports Drink**.

4. Move the chart below the worksheet data.

5. Size the chart so all the data is visible.

6. Rename the Sheet1 tab **Bar Chart**.

7. Add the standard header and center the worksheet data and chart horizontally on the page.

8. Delete the blank worksheets in the workbook.

9. Save the workbook as *[your initials]***14-20.xls** in your Lesson 14 folder.

10. Print the worksheet and close the workbook.

EXERCISE 14-21

Create a new chart sheet, change the chart type, and edit the chart information. Save and print the chart.

Harry Hascabar ran for another eight weeks and charted his speed and distance using a column chart. He'd like a different perspective on his data by seeing it displayed in another type of chart.

1. Open the file **Wks9-16.xls**.

2. Create a Column chart as a new chart sheet. Use sub-type 3, include a legend, and add the chart title **WEEKS 9-16**

3. Use the Chart toolbar to change the chart type to 3-D Bar.

4. Change the font size of the title to 14 points.

5. Add the standard header to the chart sheet.

6. Rename the chart sheet tab to **Weeks 9-16**.

7. Save the workbook as *[your initials]***14-21.xls** in your Lesson 14 folder.

8. Print the chart sheet and close the workbook.

EXERCISE 14-22

Create an embedded chart, edit chart objects, resize and move the chart. Save and print the chart.

After competing in seven races over an eight-week period, Harry Hascabar wants to analyze how fast he ran in each state. He needs a chart that shows where he ran and his running times.

1. Open the file **Wks17-24.xls**.

1 When students center the worksheet horizontally on the page, they may find the centering is not exact. They can change the margins in Page Setup to compensate for the difference.

2 The solution to Exercise 14-20 varies according to the choices students make concerning their charts.

Exercise 14-21:
Objectives 4–6
Required Files: Wks9-16.xls
Solution Files: gl14-21.xls in Solutions Manual or on Solutions Disk.

The completed document for this Exercise may be used in a student's portfolio.

Exercise 14-22:
Objectives 2–5
Required Files: Wks17-24.xls
Solution Files: gl14-22.xls in Solutions Manual or on Solutions Disk.

2. Move the data from cells A4:A11 to B4:B11, then key the data in Figure 14-16 into cells A4:A11.

FIGURE 14-16

	A
4	STATE
5	AZ
6	TX
7	OR
8	WY
9	FL
10	CA
11	NY

3. Make the column heading in column A bold.

4. Create an embedded chart of your choice using the data in columns A and B. Include a title, axis labels, and a legend.

5. Change the chart title to **RUNNING TIME PER STATE**.

6. Delete the legend. (*Hint:* Select the legend and press [Delete].)

7. Change all axis labels to 9 points.

8. Move the chart below the worksheet data.

9. Resize the chart to make it more legible, if necessary.

10. Deselect the chart and add the standard header to the worksheet

11. Center the data and chart on the page horizontally.

12. Save the workbook as *[your initials]***14-22.xls** in your Lesson 14 folder.

13. Print the worksheet and close the workbook.

1️⃣ When students center the worksheet horizontally on the page, they may find the centering is not exact. They can change the margins in Page Setup mode to compensate for the difference.

2️⃣ The solution to Exercise 14-22 varies according to the choices students make concerning their charts.

EXERCISE 14-23 *Challenge Yourself*

Choose the appropriate chart type, create a chart as a separate sheet, and add new chart information. Save and print the chart.

 Harry Hascabar wants to see how his running times compare to three of his colleagues. Using the data for all four runners, create a chart that compares the times and miles for each runner.

1. Sketch a worksheet to include a title and the labels in Figure 14-17. Plan the type of chart you will use and roughly sketch the chart type on the plan.

FIGURE 14-17

NAME	MILES	TIME
Harry Hascabar	9.30	6.58
Jose Garcia	10.10	6.79
Mark Yingling	8.97	6.87
George Bunting	9.98	7.05

2. Start a new workbook and enter the data shown in Figure 14-17, using the alignment and formatting indicated. Also adjust column widths where necessary.

3. Create the chart as a new chart sheet, using the chart type that will best depict the information and appropriate titles for the chart and chart axes.

4. Enhance the chart using any method you learned in this lesson.

5. Rename the Chart tab, giving it an appropriate name.

6. Rename the Sheet tab, giving it an appropriate name.

7. Create user documentation on a blank worksheet and name the sheet tab **User Information**. The sheet should contain the following: File Information, (Created by, Date created, Date revised, Revised by, Contact for help); Purpose of worksheet and chart (paragraph form); and Instructions to User (special instructions needed by user to enter data correctly). Format the documentation attractively and change any column widths you think might need it. Create your own data to fill these fields and spell-check your work.

Exercise 14-23:
Objectives 4–6
Required Files: None
Solution Files: gl14-23.xls and gl14-23.htm in
Solutions Manual or on Solutions Disk.

The completed document for this Exercise
may be used in a student's portfolio.

8. Center the worksheet containing data horizontally on the page and add the standard header to all worksheets. Delete the unused worksheet.

9. Save the workbook as *[your initials]***14-23.xls** in your Lesson 14 folder, and print the entire workbook.

10. Save the workbook as *[your initials]***14-23.htm** in your Lesson 14 folder.

11. Close the workbook and submit your sketch and worksheets.

Enhancing Charts and Worksheets

OBJECTIVES

After completing this lesson, you will be able to:

1. Format chart text.
2. Enhance the legend.
3. Change data series colors and patterns.
4. Add backgrounds and borders.
5. Add and format drawing objects.
6. Size, move, and copy drawing objects.
7. Work with 3-D shapes.
8. Import clip art.

MOUS
ACTIVITIES
In this lesson:
XL2000 **7.4**
XL2000 **7.5**

See Appendix F.

 Estimated Time: 1¾ hours

To make your charts more attractive, you can enhance them by adding colors, patterns, borders, and new fonts. You can also add impact to charts and ordinary worksheet data by creating drawing objects (such as lines, arrows, or text boxes), creating 3-D shapes, or importing clip art.

Objective 1
Formatting Chart Text

Just as you can format the text in a worksheet, you can format chart text by changing its font, style, color, size, or alignment. Experiment with formatting to create charts with greater visual appeal.

PREPARE
Point out to students that the learning objectives show what they will learn in the lesson. Each heading in the lesson correlates to a learning objective.

Required files:
Sports.xls

TEACH
Teaching Resources:
• Excel Classroom Presentations
• School-to-Work Strategies Manual
• Spanish Glossary
• Certification Procedures

443

EXERCISE 15-1 Change Font, Style, and Size

1. Open the file **Sports.xls**.
2. Activate the chart by clicking it.
3. Choose Chart Window from the View menu to open a separate chart window. This way you can view the entire chart as you work on it.
4. Click the chart title, "Sports Drink Comparison." The title is selected, and "Chart Title" appears in the Name Box on the formula bar.

> **NOTE:** Each time you select a chart object, the Name Box on the formula bar displays its name. Refer to the Name Box to make sure you selected the desired object.

5. Use the Font drop-down list on the Formatting toolbar to change the font to Arial Black.
6. Right-click the value axis title, "Minutes Per Mile," to open the shortcut menu.
7. Choose Format Axis Title from the shortcut menu. Notice the various formatting options in the dialog box.

> **NOTE:** Each element of the chart has its own dialog box, which you can use to change the appearance of that element.

8. Click the Font tab, if necessary. Change the font to bold italic and click OK.
9. Click the category axis title, "Sports Drinks," to select it. Click the Italic button ⓘ on the Formatting toolbar to add italic formatting.

EXERCISE 15-2 Change Text Color

1. Double-click the chart title. The Format Chart Title dialog box opens.

> **NOTE:** Double-clicking a chart object is another way to open the dialog box to format the object. However, in this case if you double-click too slowly, the I-beam appears in the text and the dialog box does not open. If this happens, deselect the Chart Title and try again.

2. Click the Font tab, if necessary.
3. Under Color, click the down arrow to open the color palette.
4. Choose red from the third row of the palette.

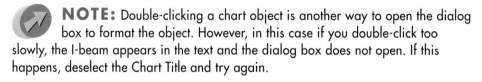

 Gridlines are turned off in the student file for this lesson so students can better see the effects of adding and manipulating drawing objects.

 You may want to tell students that an activated chart is compressed in the chart window so the category labels can appear squeezed.

 Explain that you can select the chart element and apply basic text formatting including alignment and color. In addition, a formatting dialog box that offers additional options is available for each chart element. Throughout the lesson, students practice various methods of opening this dialog box (double-clicking, right-clicking, using the Format menu, and so on).

FIGURE 15-1
Formatting the
chart title

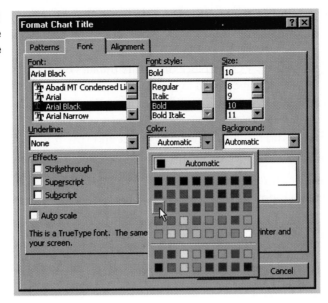

5. Change the font size to 11 points in the Size text box and click OK.

☑ Objective 2

Enhancing the Legend

A legend is a vital component of a chart. It focuses the viewer on what the chart is trying to depict. For this reason, it's important to make the legend stand out. You can customize the legend in several ways:

- Place it in a different area of the chart.
- Use colors and patterns.
- Customize the border.
- Change the font.

EXERCISE **15-3** ## Change Legend Color, Pattern, and Border

1. Double-click the legend. The Format Legend dialog box appears.

2. Click the Patterns tab, if necessary. Check the Shadow checkbox in the Border area to add a shadow to the legend.

3. Click Fill Effects to open the Fill Effects dialog box and click the Pattern tab if necessary. You use the Pattern options to choose a pattern and pattern color.

4. Click the Foreground down arrow and choose a color from the drop-down list, then click the Background down arrow and choose another color. (Avoid

---

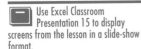
Use Excel Classroom Presentation 15 to display screens from the lesson in a slide-show format.

☑ **Objective 2 Assignment:**
Exercise 15-17 (Skills Review) can be assigned after completing Objective 2.

When charts contain only one data item, a legend is not normally used. It is used here for demonstration purposes.

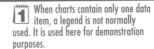
Colors are a matter of personal preference. In most cases, students are directed to select their own colors. You may need to direct the color choice for those students who are color-blind or who have difficulty differentiating between colors.

dark colors.) Notice that the foreground and background colors appear in the samples above.

 NOTE: Some black and white printers do not handle printing colors well. You may need to check your worksheet in Print Preview and adjust some colors so the worksheet and chart data are clear.

5. Choose the fourth pattern in the second row under Pattern.
6. Click OK twice. The legend now has a background color and pattern.
7. Deselect the legend, but be sure to click inside the chart area to keep the chart window open.

 NOTE: Because the legend is small, you may not be able to see the pattern in the chart window. When you enlarge the chart in Exercise 15-5, the pattern will be easier to see.

EXERCISE 15-4 Reposition the Legend

1. Double-click the legend.
2. Click the Placement tab in the Format Legend dialog box and choose Top.
3. Go back to the Font tab and change the font to Times New Roman, bold, 10 point.
4. Click OK. The legend appears at the top of the chart, below the chart title.

FIGURE 15-2
Legend with a new format and position

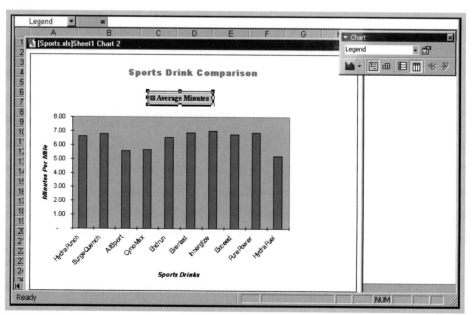

 If your class uses black and white printers, check before class to see how the printers handle colors as grayscale. You may need to advise students to reassign colors before or even after printing for worksheet and chart data to print clearly.

In Excel Classroom Presentation 15.

5. Close the chart window by clicking its Close button. Review the legend's new position and formatting.

6. If the new formatting and placement cause any labels to be missing, resize the chart. To do this, click the chart once to select it and drag one of the selection handles to increase the chart's size.

Objective 3

Changing Data Series Colors and Patterns

You can change data series colors and patterns for the entire chart or for individual data markers. When you change colors or patterns for individual markers, the legend reflects those changes by displaying the color key and data point labels.

EXERCISE **15-5** **Change Color for a Data Series**

1. Click the chart to activate it and choose Chart Window from the View menu.

2. Click a column in the chart to select the data series.

3. Choose Selected Data Series from the Format menu (or press Ctrl + 1).

 NOTE: The Format menu and Ctrl + 1 also open the dialog box to format a selected chart item.

4. Choose another color from the color palette and click OK. The columns appear in the new color.

 5. Click the Undo button to undo the color change.

6. Right-click one column in the chart and choose Format Data Series from the shortcut menu.

7. Click the Options tab.

 NOTE: The Options tab in the Format dialog box varies according to the type of chart with which you are working.

8. Click to select Vary Colors By Point and click OK. The data markers appear in different colors and the legend displays each color and label. (See Figure 15-3 on the next page.)

9. Close the chart window.

10. Resize the chart to accommodate the new legend, if necessary.

FIGURE 15-3
Legend reflecting
color changes

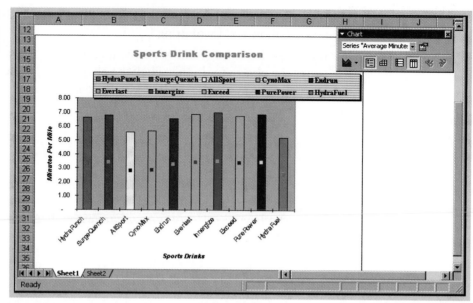

✔ Objective 4

Adding Backgrounds and Borders

To add variety to your chart, you can apply colored or patterned backgrounds and borders. Use the Format Chart Area dialog box, being careful not to make the chart look cluttered.

EXERCISE **15-6** **Add Background Color and Borders**

---

1. Activate the chart, if necessary, and open the chart window.

2. Right-click in the chart area (the white background) and choose Format Chart Area from the shortcut menu.

3. Click the Patterns tab, if necessary. Under Border, click Custom.

4. Open the <u>W</u>eight drop-down list and choose the last option (the heaviest line). See Figure 15-4 on the next page.

5. Choose a light color from the palette for the chart area and click OK. The chart area background changes to the color you choose and has a thicker border.

6. Click the Undo button 🔄 and double-click the chart area background to open the dialog box again.

7. Click F<u>i</u>ll Effects and click the Texture tab.

8. Click the first texture and click OK twice to apply the background.

9. Close the chart window.

In Excel Classroom Presentation 15.

✔**Objective 4 Assignment:**
Exercise 15-18 (Skills Review) can be assigned after completing Objective 4.

FIGURE 15-4
Formatting the
chart area

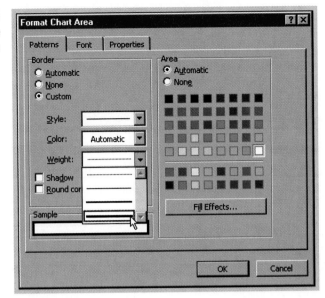

NOTE: You cannot change the color of a texture. If you want a colored background, you must select a color in the Patterns option of the Format dialog box.

Objective 5

Adding and Formatting Drawing Objects

An effective method for enhancing charts or highlighting important data is to create graphic objects with the Drawing toolbar. You can draw text boxes, arrows, rectangles, and other objects. Then you can move, size, and format these items independent of the worksheet. You can also change an object's border style, line style, fill pattern, color, or the font, font style, and font size in text boxes.

EXERCISE 15-7   **Display and Position the Drawing Toolbar**

Use the Drawing button on the Standard toolbar to display the Drawing toolbar. You can then position this toolbar anywhere you want for convenient access.

1. Click the Drawing button on the Standard toolbar. The toolbar appears in the position in which it was last located.

2. Drag the toolbar to dock it under the Formatting toolbar, if necessary.

In Excel Classroom Presentation 15.

3. Examine each menu option and button on the Drawing toolbar by pointing to it. A ScreenTip identifies the button by name.

TABLE 15-1

Drawing Toolbar

BUTTON/MENU	NAME	FUNCTION
Draw menu		Offers various ways to manipulate a drawn object.
🔘	Select Objects	Select drawn objects.
↻	Free Rotate	Rotates an object.
AutoShape menu		Offers a number of preset objects from which to choose.
\	Line	Draws a line.
↘	Arrow	Draws an arrow.
▭	Rectangle	Draws a rectangle or square.
○	Oval	Draws an oval or circle.
🔲	Text Box	Draws a text box in worksheets and charts.
📄	Insert WordArt	Inserts WordArt.
🖼	Insert Clip Art	Inserts clip art.
🪣	Fill Color	Adds a fill color to an object.
✐	Line Color	Adds a color to a line.
A	Font Color	Changes the color of words.
≡	Line Style	Offers different line styles.
▦	Dash Style	Offers different dashed lines.
⇄	Arrow Style	Offers different arrow styles.
◼	Shadow	Draws a shadow behind text boxes and most shapes.
◻	3-D	Adds a 3-D effect to objects.

EXERCISE 15-8 Add Text Boxes

You can position text boxes anywhere on a chart to provide labels or comments. Text boxes are frequently combined with arrows.

[1] This lesson introduces the most commonly used Drawing toolbar buttons for creating text boxes, arrows, ovals, and rectangles. You may also want to explain features used with multiple objects, such as Group, Ungroup, Bring to Front, and Send to Back, which are all located on the Drawing menu on the Drawing toolbar.

This Exercise demonstrates two ways to create a text box: one involving keying text directly into the formula bar and a second that uses the Drawing toolbar.

1. Activate the chart if necessary and open the chart window.

2. Position the pointer in the Formula bar. When the pointer changes to an I-beam, click the left mouse button.

3. Key **Best Tasting** and press Enter. The text box appears in the chart, surrounded by a dotted border with selection handles for sizing. You can move the text box to any position on the chart.

4. Point to the border of the text box. Use the four-headed arrow pointer to drag the text box so it's below the right side of the legend in the chart area. (You can only move it when the border is dotted, not hatched).

5. Click outside the text box in the chart window to deselect it. By default, text boxes in charts do not have borders.

6. Close the chart window.

7. Scroll to the top of the worksheet and click the Text Box button 📇 on the Drawing toolbar. The pointer changes to a crosshair (or cross).

8. Drag the crosshair pointer to draw a box that spans roughly from cell D2 through cell F3. Release the mouse button.

9. At the insertion point, key **The faster the time, the better the drink!**

10. Click outside the text box to deselect it. By default, text boxes in worksheets *do* have borders. If the box is not large enough to accommodate the text, select the box again and resize it using the selection handles.

FIGURE 15-5
Creating text boxes

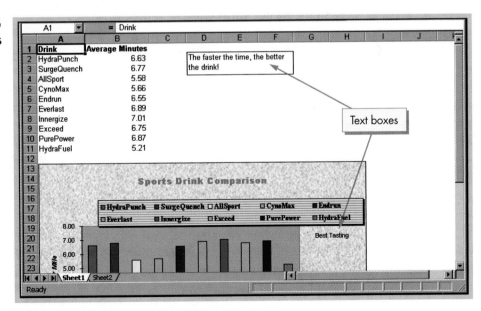

 The first method taught to create a text box is helpful because students don't have to draw the box first and then key the text. Instead, the box is sized according to the amount of text keyed.

 In Excel Classroom Presentation 15.

EXERCISE 15-9 Draw Lines, Arrows, and Shapes

Use the Drawing toolbar to create lines, arrows, rectangles, and ovals to highlight specific areas in a chart or worksheet.

Just as you created a text box, you can click the desired drawing button, position the crosshair where you want to start drawing, and drag the crosshair pointer to the desired size. When you release the mouse button, the drawing object is automatically selected and the object name appears in the Name Box on the formula bar.

 NOTE: If you click a drawing button and decide not to draw, you can press Esc to cancel the drawing process and restore the normal pointer. In addition, if you draw an object and decide you don't like it, you can delete it immediately by pressing Delete.

1. Click the Rectangle button ▢ on the Drawing toolbar.

2. Position the crosshair pointer in the upper right corner of cell B2 in the worksheet. Drag down diagonally to the left to create a rectangle around the numbers 6.63 and 6.77. Release the mouse button. The rectangle is selected, as indicated by the selection handles, and the opaque fill in the rectangle covers the numbers. (If you're not pleased with the shape of the rectangle, press Delete and try again.)

3. Click the Fill Color button drop-down arrow and select No Fill. The numbers reappear.

4. Click outside the rectangle to deselect it.

FIGURE 15-6
Drawing a
rectangle

	A	B	C	D	E	F	G	H	I	J	K
1	**Drink**	**Average Minutes**									
2	HydraPunch	6.63		The faster the time, the better							
3	SurgeQuench	6.77		the drink!							
4	AllSport	5.58									
5	CynoMax	5.66									
6	Endrun	6.55									
7	Everlast	6.89									
8	Innergize	7.01									
9	Exceed	6.75									
10	PurePower	6.87									
11	HydraFuel	5.21									

5. Click the Line button ◥.

6. To connect the rectangle with the text box, position the crosshair at the right side of the rectangle you just drew. Drag straight across to the left border of the text box and release the mouse button.

Remind students they can easily cancel a drawing process (Escape key), delete a drawing (Delete key), and undo a deletion (Undo button).

In Excel Classroom Presentation 15.

TIP: Hold down Shift to keep lines vertical, horizontal, or at a 45-degree angle; to keep ovals circular; and to keep rectangles square. You can also hold down Alt to align the corner of the object with cell gridlines.

7. Click the Select Objects button and, using the arrow pointer, point to the rectangle around the two numbers until a four-headed arrow appears behind the arrow. Click the rectangle to select it and press Delete to delete the rectangle.

NOTE: You can select objects without using the Select Objects button ; however, this feature allows you to select only objects and not cells in the worksheet. This makes it easier to select the object you want. You can also use the Select Objects button to deselect an object.

8. Use the arrow pointer to select the line and delete it. The Select Objects button remains selected until you click it again. Click it now to deselect it.

9. Click the Oval button . Position the crosshair just under the "M" in "Average Minutes." Drag down diagonally to the right until an oval surrounds numbers 6.63 and 6.77.

10. Click the Fill Color button (not the arrow beside it) to apply no fill to the oval.

NOTE: When you place the pointer on the Fill Color button and not the arrow beside it, Excel tells you what color fill is selected. You can apply that fill with the button.

11. Click the Arrow button . Position the crosshair at the left side of the text box in the worksheet. Drag to the left until the crosshair touches the right side of the oval. Release the mouse button and deselect the arrow.

FIGURE 15-7
Drawing an arrow

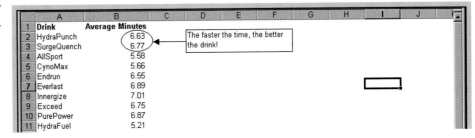

12. Scroll to the chart and activate it.

13. Draw an arrow that begins to the left of the text "Best Tasting" that points to the top of the "Exceed" column (third from the right).

Point out the Tip. Students can hold down the Shift key as they drag to create a perfectly straight line.

Selecting drawing objects takes some practice without the Select Objects button activated. Remind students to move the pointer over the object and click only when the arrow pointer is visible. In addition, they should use the Name box on the formula bar to check that they selected a drawing object and not a cell.

Remind students that when drawing arrows, the arrowhead appears at the end of the line, not at the point where they begin drawing.

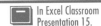 In Excel Classroom Presentation 15.

EXERCISE 15-10 Format Drawing Objects

1. Scroll to the top of the worksheet and click the oval in column B to select it. (Click the Select Objects button 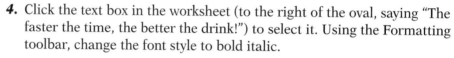 to turn it on, if it is not activated.)

2. Choose Auto**S**hape from the F**o**rmat menu to open the Format AutoShape dialog box.

 TIP: You can also open the Format AutoShape dialog box for a selected object by pressing Ctrl + 1 or double-clicking the object.

3. Click the Colors and Lines tab, if necessary. Under Line, choose a bright color from the C**o**lor drop-down list. Apply a heavier weight using the arrows beside **W**eight. (The higher the number, the heavier the weight.) Then click OK.

4. Click the text box in the worksheet (to the right of the oval, saying "The faster the time, the better the drink!") to select it. Using the Formatting toolbar, change the font style to bold italic.

5. Click the arrow beside the Font Color button  and select the color you just selected for the oval.

6. Click the Shadow button and select the first shadow in the last row. Deselect the text box to see it and click the Select Objects button to turn the selection option off.

7. In the chart, click "Best Tasting" to select it, right-click its hatched border with the selection pointer, and choose Format Text B**o**x from the shortcut menu.

8. Click the Colors and Lines tab, if necessary. Under Fill, click the arrow beside **C**olor and select black.

9. Under Line, click the arrow beside C**o**lor and select any color you want for the line. Make the line weight heavier.

10. Click the Font tab and choose Bold. Under **C**olor, choose white from the color palette and click OK. Deselect the text box and notice that the text box now has a color border with white text against a black background.

NOTE: Some of the text may disappear after the formatting. You learn to adjust text box sizes in the following Exercise.

11. Right-click the arrow in the chart and choose Format Auto**S**hape.

12. Change the line to a dashed style in the **D**ashed drop-down list and change its weight to 1.5 using the arrows beside **W**eight. Click OK.

---

1 The same methods used to open the Formatting dialog box for a chart object are used to open the Format Object dialog box for drawing objects. Students can decide which method they want to use.

2 In addition to using the Formatting toolbar to change font, font style, and font size, students familiar with keyboard shortcuts (Ctrl+B for bold, Ctrl+I for italic, and so on.) can use them after selecting a chart text object.

3 After formatting the text in the chart text box, some of the text may disappear. Students learn to resize the text box in the following Exercise.

13. Select the legend and drag it with the arrow pointer up and to the left so it is better centered under the Chart Title. Make cell A1 active.

14. Save the workbook as *[your initials]***15-10.xls** in a new folder for Lesson 15.

☑ **Objective 6**

Sizing, Moving, and Copying Objects

Drawing objects are easy to reshape, size, and move. If you need multiple copies of the same object, you can draw it once and make as many copies as you need.

EXERCISE **15-11** **Size and Move a Drawing Object**

1. Click the text box in the worksheet (not the one in the chart) to select it.

2. Position the pointer over the middle selection handle on the right side of the text box. With the double-headed arrow pointer, click and hold the mouse until the crosshair pointer appears. Drag the handle to the left so it fits the text better.

FIGURE 15-8
Resizing the
text box

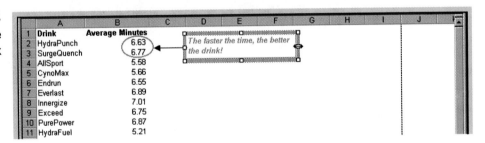

	A	B	C	D	E	F	G	H	I	J
1	**Drink**	**Average Minutes**								
2	HydraPunch	6.63		*The faster the time, the better*						
3	SurgeQuench	6.77		*the drink!*						
4	AllSport	5.58								
5	CynoMax	5.66								
6	Endrun	6.55								
7	Everlast	6.89								
8	Innergize	7.01								
9	Exceed	6.75								
10	PurePower	6.87								
11	HydraFuel	5.21								

TIP: You may want to resize the text box more than once to get the perfect fit.

3. Select the chart text box and resize it if both words ("Best" and "Tasting") are not visible.

4. Select the oval in column B. Using the white arrow pointer, drag the object down to surround the values in rows 4 and 5.

NOTE: You do not have to activate the Select Objects button 🔲 to select an object. Use the white arrow pointer to select the arrow—not the crosshair pointer, which selects cells.

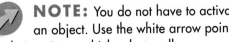

☑ **Objective 6 Assignment:**
Exercise 15-19 (Skills Review) and Exercises 15-21 and 15-22 (Lesson Applications) can be assigned after completing Objective 6.

In Excel Classroom Presentation 15.

5. Select the arrow and text box together by first selecting the arrow, then pressing and holding down Shift and clicking on the text box. Release Shift and the mouse.

6. Move the two objects down and next to the oval using the four-headed arrow.

7. Select the arrow in the chart.

8. Position the crosshair pointer over the selection handle at the tip of the arrowhead until it becomes a double-headed arrow. Drag the handle so the arrow points to the second-to-last column (the data marker for "PurePower").

FIGURE 15-9
Repositioning
the arrow

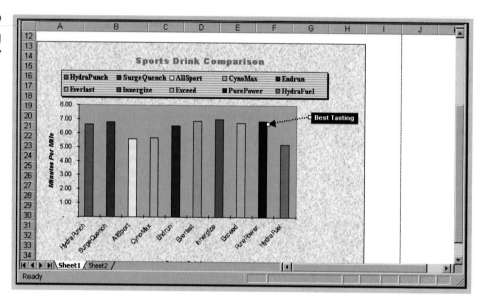

EXERCISE 15-12 Copy a Drawing Object

After selecting an object, you can Copy and Paste using the Formatting toolbar, keyboard shortcuts, the shortcut menu, or the Edit menu. You can also copy an object using drag and drop.

1. Draw an oval around the PurePower number in cell B10 of the worksheet. Use the same style and color you applied to the other oval. Reposition the object as necessary.

2. Select the text box above it. When you select the text box with the white arrow pointer, make sure the border is dotted

3. Click the Copy button 📋 to copy the text box.

 In Excel Classroom Presentation 15.

4. Select cell D10 and click the Paste button to paste the text box.

5. With the new text box still selected, click in the box and use the I-beam pointer to highlight the text in the text box. Key as replacement text **Best tasting, but poor performance!**

6. Resize the text box and reposition it to line up with the oval beside it, under the first text box.

7. Select the arrow at the top of the worksheet.

8. With the arrow pointer positioned over the arrow, hold down Ctrl until a **+** appears beside the arrow. Then drag down to move a copy of the arrow down to cell C10.

FIGURE 15-10
Copied drawing
objects

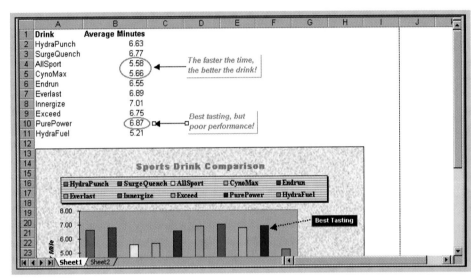

Objective 7
Working with 3-D Shapes

You can also use the Drawing toolbar to insert a variety of shapes called AutoShapes and then apply 3-D effects to add depth to these shapes. Once you create the shapes, Excel provides a full range of tools to modify them.

EXERCISE `15-13` **Create and Modify 3-D Shapes**

1. On the Drawing toolbar, click AutoShapes. Choose Basic Shapes, and then choose the Plaque shape from the submenu.

In step 3, the Select Objects button must be deactivated to select cell D10.   In Excel Classroom Presentation 15.

FIGURE 15-11
AutoShapes, Basic
Shapes category

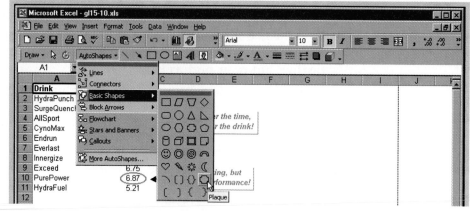

2. Using the crosshair pointer, draw the Plaque shape so it is about the height of row two and as wide as columns D and E. The shape should sit in row two.

3. With the shape selected, click the 3-D button ⬛ on the Drawing toolbar. A palette offers 20 different 3-D styles. Experiment with the different styles. Then apply 3-D Style 2.

TIP: When a basic shape is selected, a yellow diamond appears in the object.

4. Click the 3-D button ⬛ again. At the bottom of the palette, click 3-D Settings to display the 3-D Settings toolbar. You can use this toolbar to modify the depth, direction, surface, lighting, and color of the 3-D effect.

FIGURE 15-12
3-D Settings
toolbar

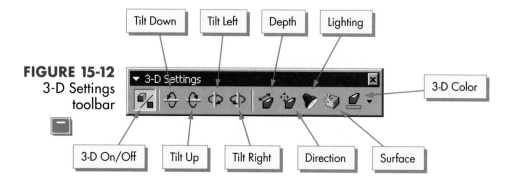

5. Click the Lighting button ▼ and change the effect so it is lit from the top (choose the second effect in the top row).

6. Click the Tilt Up button ⊕ twice, then click theTilt Down button ⊕ twice. Click the Tilt Right button ⬥ twice, then click the Tilt Left button ⬥ twice.

7. Click the down arrow on the 3-D Color button and choose Turquoise from the fourth row of the color palette. Explore some of the other options on the 3-D Settings toolbar, and then close the toolbar.

8. Click the object to select it, if necessary. Key the text **HydraFuel wins**. A text box appears within the object as you key the text.

9. Select the text in the text box and make it bold. Click the Center button to center-align the text, then use the selection handles to fit the object size to the text and make the text fit on one line.

> **NOTE:** Remember, use the double-headed arrow to resize an object and the four-headed arrow to move an object.

FIGURE 15-13
Resized 3-D shape
with text

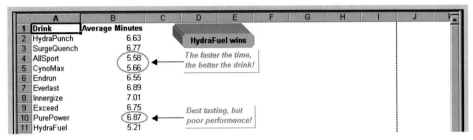

EXERCISE 15-14 Change the Position of a 3-D Shape

In addition to modifying the 3-D effect of an object, there are several ways to alter an object's position on the worksheet. For example, you can rotate the object, align it to gridlines, drag it freely on the worksheet, or move it slightly using the Nudge feature.

1. Click the object containing the HydraFuel text box to select it, if necessary. (Make sure the border is dotted and not hatched.) Click Draw on the Drawing toolbar. Point to Rotate or Flip and click Rotate Left from the submenu. This rotates the object 90 degrees to the left. Click the Undo button or choose Rotate Right from the submenu to restore the object's position.

2. Click the Free Rotate button on the Drawing menu (or choose it from the Rotate or Flip submenu). The selection handles become round rotation handles.

3. Move the rotation pointer over one of the round handles and drag up or down slightly. Click the Undo button to restore the object's position. You can use the Free Rotate tool to rotate an object to any desired degree.

 In Excel Classroom Presentation 15.

FIGURE 15-14
Rotating the
3-D shape

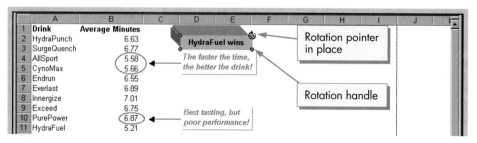

TIP: It's best to rotate objects that do not contain text.

4. Click the Free Rotate button 🔄 again or press Esc to turn off the Free Rotate tool.

5. With the object selected, use the four-headed arrow to drag the object freely to the right into the open area in rows 1-3. Place it above, and to the right of the text box containing "The faster the time, the better the drink!"

6. On the Drawing toolbar, choose D̲raw, S̲nap, To G̲rid. This turns the snap to grid feature on, which allows you to automatically align an object to the worksheet gridlines.

7. On the T̲ools menu, choose O̲ptions. In the Options dialog box, turn on grids for viewing.

8. Drag the object to the left and then to the right. Notice that the object automatically aligns with the vertical gridlines. Drag the object up and down. The object aligns with the horizontal gridlines.

9. Turn grids for viewing off.

10. Choose D̲raw, S̲nap, To G̲rid to turn snap to grid off, and drag the object back to where you had it.

NOTE: You can use the To S̲hape option on the S̲nap submenu to align an object with the vertical and horizontal edges of other objects.

11. On the Drawing toolbar, choose D̲raw, N̲udge. Float the Nudge submenu by pointing to its top gray bar and dragging it onto the worksheet. (You can float any Drawing toolbar submenu that has this gray bar.) The Nudge submenu is now an easily accessible toolbar.

FIGURE 15-15
Nudge floating
toolbar

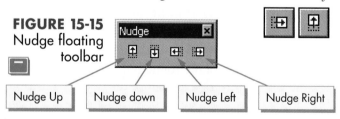

12. With the 3-D shape selected, click the Nudge Right button 🔲 several times to move the object to the right in small increments. Click the Nudge Up button 🔲 a few times to move the object slightly above where it was.

TIP: You can also use the Arrow buttons on the keyboard to nudge an object into position.

13. Nudge the 3-D shape back to the left with the Nudge Left button  and close the Nudge toolbar. Deselect the 3-D shape.

☑ **Objective 8**

Importing Clip Art

You can further enhance your worksheets by adding clip art. *Clip art* is a graphic image that is already created, which you can import into a worksheet or chart.

Some programs come with clip art collections. Microsoft Office, for example, includes images that you can use with Excel in the subfolder Microsoft Shared\Clipart folder.

EXERCISE `15-15` **Import Clip Art in a Worksheet**

---

1. Select an empty cell directly below the 3-D object.

2. Click the Insert Clip Art button on the Drawing toolbar. The Insert Clip Art dialog box opens.

3. Click the Pictures tab, if necessary, and scroll down the display of buttons until you see the Special Occasions button. Click on it or on the underlined button title below it. The Special Occasions clip art samples appear.

FIGURE 15-16
Insert ClipArt
dialog box

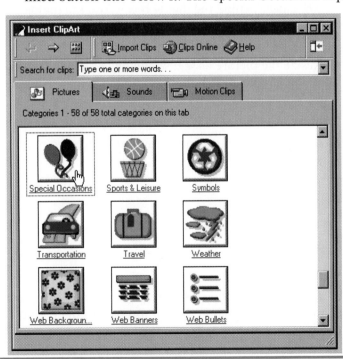

☑ **Objective 8 Assignment:**
Exercise 15-20 (Skills Review) and Exercises 15-23 and 15-24 (Lesson Applications) can be assigned after completing Objective 8.

`1` This Lesson assumes that the Microsoft Office clip art is installed on the computers in your classroom. The clip art installed is part of the "Typical" installation.

`2` After opening a clip art category, show students how to navigate in the Insert ClipArt dialog box using the Back, Forward, and All Categories buttons.

 In Excel Classroom Presentation 15.

4. Click the first picture (the man with a ribbon). Clip art buttons appear in a pop-up toolbar.

FIGURE 15-17
Insert ClipArt
dialog box with
clipart buttons

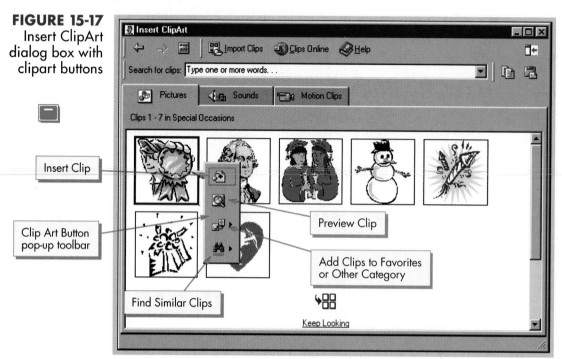

5. Click the Insert Clip button and the picture is inserted in the worksheet behind the dialog box. Close the dialog box and notice that the Picture toolbar is now open. As with any object, you can move, size, copy, or format the picture.

6. Resize the picture as you would any object, but use the bottom right sizing handle and size to 20% x 20% (see the Name Box while resizing it for dimensions).

7. Move the picture so it is centered below the 3-D shape.

8. Deselect the picture and the Picture toolbar closes.

9. Close the Drawing toolbar.

EXERCISE 15-16 Use Clip Art in a Chart

You can use clip art instead of ordinary data markers in a chart. For example, in a column chart, you can stretch a clip art image across the length of the column or stack images one on top of the other. Clip art can produce attention-getting results.

1. Select the chart. Copy it to cell A1 on Sheet2 of the workbook. (Click the Copy button 🖹, go to Sheet2, cell A1, and click the Paste button 🖹.)

2. Deselect the chart, use the Page Setup dialog box (Page tab) to change Sheet2 to landscape orientation, and return to the worksheet. Scroll over and notice that the dotted line in the worksheet indicates the next page now follows column M.

3. Make the chart wider by selecting it and dragging the middle right selection handle through column L.

4. Delete the "Best Tasting" text box, the arrow (if it copied to Sheet2), and the legend. (To delete an object, select it and press ⌐Delete⌐. However, the text box border must be dotted and not hatched to delete the entire object.)

5. Click a data marker to select the data series and choose Picture from the Insert menu.

6. From the submenu, choose From File to open the Insert Picture dialog box.

7. From the Program Files\Common Files\Microsoft Shared\Clipart\cagcat50 folder, choose **Bd00017_.wmf** and click Insert. The data columns are replaced by stretched reproductions of the clip art image.

> **NOTE:** Ask your Instructor for help if you can't find the folder with the clip art.

8. Double-click the data series to open the Format Data Series dialog box. Click the Patterns tab, if necessary, and click Fill Effects.

9. Click the Picture tab, if necessary, and select Stack. Click OK twice and the images are stacked vertically.

10. Open the chart window and select the plot area of the chart by clicking the background behind the stacked images.

> **NOTE:** When you add clip art, Excel may take longer to respond to your requests.

11. Resize the plot area so it fits in the chart better. Make sure you don't lose sight of the labels in doing so.

12. Choose Chart Options from the Chart menu and click the Gridlines tab.

13. Choose Major Gridlines for both axes and click OK

14. Change the chart colors, if you like, close the chart window, and preview the chart.

 You may need to help students locate the clip art folder on their hard drive or on a network drive. Alternatively, you can use the Insert Clip Art button rather than asking students to locate the Clip Art folder.

FIGURE 15-18
Using clip art as
data markers

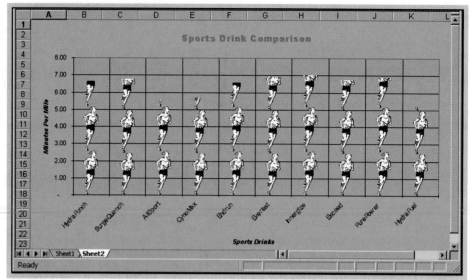

15. Deselect the chart and center the chart vertically and horizontally. Be sure the chart is not active when you use Page Setup.

16. Add the standard header to both worksheets.

17. Make cell A1 active in Sheet1.

18. Save the workbook as *[your initials]***15-16.xls** in your Lesson 15 folder.

19. Print the entire workbook and close it.

> **NOTE:** When you print the worksheet, the labels in the legend may print with white backgrounds.

USING HELP

You can enhance a worksheet with drawing objects, clip art, pictures, and special text effects. But when a worksheet has many drawing objects or imported graphics in it, scrolling and printing can be slow. Microsoft Excel Help can show you how to hide these objects to speed up scrolling or printing.

Use Help for information on displaying and hiding drawing objects and imported graphics:

1. Press F1 to activate the Office Assistant.

2. Key **hide drawing objects** and click <u>S</u>earch.

In Excel Classroom Presentation 15.

1 Charts using clip art as data markers are sometimes difficult for some printers to handle. Test printing this file before asking students to print in class. You may find the printing process to be unrealistically slow for class purposes, depending on your printer configuration. (You can recommend that students show you their finished file onscreen, and then remove the clip art and use basic data markers.)

2 Encourage students to follow the steps in "Using Help." Software companies are increasingly using their Help program—rather than printed documentation—to train users and assist in answering user questions.

3. Display the topic "Hide drawing objects."

4. Review the information on how to hide or display drawing objects or imported graphics. (When you print a worksheet with these objects hidden, they do not print.)

5. For information about graphics, click the Show button ◄▤ in the Help window.

6. Click the <u>C</u>ontents tab.

7. Click the plus sign to the left of the topic "Creating Drawings and Importing Pictures."

8. Click the subtopic "About using graphics in Microsoft Excel."

9. Click the graphic in the Help window to display the topic.

10. Explore the topics listed on the left side of the Help window by clicking them.

FIGURE 15-19
Help window
about graphics

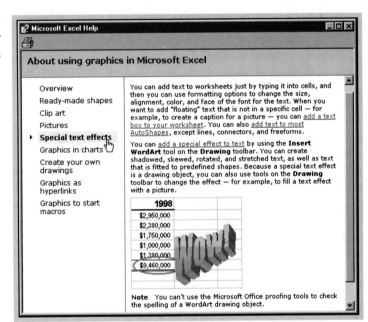

11. Close the Help window when you finish and hide the Office Assistant.

TEST BANK

Concepts Review

TRUE/FALSE QUESTIONS

Each of the following statements is either true or false. Indicate your choice by circling **T** or **F**.

Ⓣ F **1.** You use the Drawing toolbar to create an arrow in a chart.

Ⓣ F **2.** You can drag a text box to any position on a chart.

T Ⓕ **3.** You can change the font, style, and size of a chart element, but not its color.

Ⓣ F **4.** When you finish drawing an object, it is automatically selected.

T Ⓕ **5.** You cannot place legends in different positions on a chart.

Ⓣ F **6.** You use the Format Chart Area dialog box to add chart borders and backgrounds.

Ⓣ F **7.** 3-D effects can add depth to an object.

T Ⓕ **8.** You cannot use the Formatting toolbar to change text objects in a chart.

SHORT ANSWER QUESTIONS

Write the correct answer in the space provided

1. After clicking the Text Box button on the Drawing toolbar, what shape is the pointer?

Cross

2. When drawing a line or an arrow, what key can you press to ensure your line is perfectly straight?

Shift

3. What appears when you double-click the legend in an activated chart?

Format Legend dialog box

4. How do you activate a chart?

Click it once

5. Name two ways you can customize a legend.

Change placement, colors, borders, font

C L O S E

Concepts Review:
Allows students to check their understanding.

TEST BANK
Consider using the Test Bank to provide an additional review of lesson concepts. It may also be used as an assessment tool.

6. What toolbar do you use to move a 3-D object in small increments?

Nudge toolbar

7. Which shape must the mouse pointer be to select an object?

Arrow

8. Which dialog box opens when you double-click a line or shape?

Format AutoShape dialog box

CRITICAL THINKING

Answer these questions on a separate piece of paper. There are no right or wrong answers. Support your answers with examples from your own experience, if possible.

1. What are the advantages of using the methods for enhancing charts you learned in this lesson? Are there any disadvantages?

2. Give some examples of how you might use 3-D effects to enhance worksheet information.

Skills Review

EXERCISE 15-17

Format chart text and enhance the legend.

1. Open the file **MWMin1.xls**.

2. Format the chart text by following these steps:

a. Click the chart, choose Chart Window from the <u>V</u>iew menu, and double-click the chart title.

b. In the Format Chart Title dialog box, click the Font tab and choose Arial Black, italic, 14 point, single underline. Click OK.

c. Click the categories title "Drinks" to select it and click the Italic button ☐*I* on the Formatting toolbar. Repeat the process for the values title.

d. Double-click a category axis label (a drink name) and change its font color to dark blue. Repeat this formatting for the value axis labels.

Critical Thinking Questions:
Answers will vary based on students' preferences, observations, experiences, and research.

Skills Review:
Provides guided practice for students. Objectives are indicated for each Exercise.

◉ **Exercise 15-17:**
Objectives 1, 2
Required Files: MWMin1.xls
Solution Files: gl15-17.xls in Solutions Manual or on Solutions Disk.

3. Enhance the legend by following these steps:

   a. Double-click the legend.

   b. Click the Patterns tab, if necessary.

   c. Click the Sha_d_ow box.

   d. Under Area, choose a background color.

   e. Click the Placement tab and choose _B_ottom. Click OK.

4. Close the chart window and deselect the chart.

5. Look over the chart. If necessary, resize it to accommodate the legend and category labels.

6. Add the standard header and center the worksheet horizontally on the page.

> **NOTE:** When you center the worksheet horizontally, the chart shifts slightly and the data above it appears not to move. The chart is centered and the data and blank columns above the chart are centered.

7. Save the workbook as _[your initials]_**15-17.xls** in your Lesson 15 folder.

8. Print the worksheet and close the workbook.

EXERCISE 15-18

Change data series colors and add a background color and border to a chart.

1. Open the file **MWMin2.xls**.

2. Change the data series colors and pattern by following these steps:

   a. Activate the chart and open the chart window.

   b. Select the green data series (Men) by right-clicking one of the columns.

   c. Choose F_o_rmat Data Series from the shortcut menu.

   d. Click the Patterns tab, if necessary. Under Area, choose a new color from the palette.

   e. Open the Fill Effects dialog box, click the Pattern tab if necessary, and choose a pattern from the third row. Click OK twice.

   f. Repeat the preceding steps for the second data series (Women), choosing a different color and pattern.

3. Add a border and background color to the chart by following these steps:

   a. Double-click the white background area of the chart.

   b. With the Patterns tab displayed, click the Custom option under Border.

   c. Click the arrow to the right of the _W_eight box and choose a thicker line for the border.

   d. Under Area, choose a light background color from the palette.

   e. Click OK.

◉ **Exercise 15-18:**
Objectives 3, 4
Required Files: MWMin2.xls
Solution Files: gl15-18.xls in Solutions Manual or on Solutions Disk.

4. Double-click the chart title. Under Border, click Sha<u>d</u>ow and click OK.

5. Double-click the legend. Choose white from the color palette to apply a white background and click OK.

6. Close the chart window and deselect the chart.

7. Add the standard header and center the worksheet horizontally on the page.

8. Save the workbook as *[your initials]*15-18.xls in your Lesson 15 folder.

9. Print the worksheet and close the workbook.

EXERCISE 15-19

Add and format drawing objects and size, move, and copy the objects.

1. Open the file **Wks25-32.xls**.

2. Draw a text box in the worksheet by following these steps:
   a. Click the Drawing button 🔯 on the Standard toolbar to display the Drawing toolbar, if necessary.
   b. Click the Text Box button 🔲.
   c. Using the crosshair pointer, draw a box that approximately covers the cell range F5:G6.
   d. Key **Same performance, different drinks!**
   e. Resize the text box to fit the text, if necessary, then deselect the text box.

3. Draw arrows by following these steps:
   a. Click the Arrow button 🔲.
   b. Position the crosshair pointer at the left side of the text box. Drag the pointer to the right side of cell C5.

4. Format the text box by following these steps:
   a. Click the Select Objects button 🔲.
   b. Click the text box to select it.
   c. Use the Formatting toolbar to center the text, change the font to Times New Roman, and change the font style to italic.
   d. Click the Select Objects button 🔲.

5. Move the text box and arrows down by following these steps:
   a. With the text box still selected, press Shift and click the arrow to select it too.
   b. Release Shift and the mouse button.
   c. Drag the objects down one cell.
   d. Deselect both objects.

6. Copy and resize the arrow by following these steps:
   a. Select the arrow.

⊙ Exercise 15-19:
Objectives 5, 6
Required Files: Wks25-32.xls
Solution Files: gl15-19.xls in Solutions Manual or on Solutions Disk.

    b. With the selection pointer visible, hold down Ctrl until **+** appears beside the arrow.

    c. Drag a copy of the arrow down until the arrowhead is beside cell C8.

    d. With the new arrow still selected, move the pointer to the selection handle on the right side of the arrow until the double-headed arrow appears.

    e. Stretch the arrow up to the right, to the left side of the text box.

7. Draw an oval around the PowerEase numbers by following these steps:

    a. Click the Oval button ⬭.

    b. Position the crosshair in the upper left corner of cell D12. Drag down and to the left until the numbers 11 and 5.21 in row 12 are enclosed in the oval. Release the mouse button.

    c. Click the arrow beside the Fill Color button 🔲.

    d. Choose No Fill.

    e. Reposition the oval around the numbers, if necessary.

8. Format the drawing object by following these steps:

    a. Right-click the oval itself (not the inside of it) and choose Format AutoShape from the shortcut menu.

    b. Under Line, choose a thicker weight and change the line color to red. Click OK.

9. To the right of the oval, draw a text box containing the text **Impressive!** Format the text as centered and italic, Times New Roman. Resize the text box if necessary and add an arrow that points from the text box to the oval.

10. Add the standard header and center the worksheet horizontally.

11. Save the workbook as *[your initials]***15-19.xls** in your Lesson 15 folder.

12. Print the worksheet and close the workbook.

Move, size, and copy the text box, add and format a 3-D shape, and import clip art.

1. Open the file **Wks9-16.xls** and turn off gridlines for viewing (Tools, Options, View, deselect Gridlines)

2. Activate the chart window and reposition the legend at the bottom of the chart.

3. Create a text box by clicking the I-beam pointer in the Formula bar and keying **Good timing but bad tasting!** Press Enter.

The solution to Exercise 15-19 varies according to the choices students make concerning the placement and manipulation of drawing objects.

⊙ **Exercise 15-20:**
Objectives 6–8
Required Files: Wks9-16.xls
Solution Files: gl15-20.xls in Solutions Manual or on Solutions Disk.

4. Move the text box to the upper right corner of the chart window.

5. Resize the text box so the text appears on two lines.

6. Format the text box with a blue, 1.25 pt border and pale yellow fill color. (*Hint:* Use the Colors and Lines options in the Format Text Box dialog box.).

7. Copy the text box.

8. Close the chart window.

9. Select cell F9 and click the Paste button 📋 to paste the text box.

10. Edit the new text box to read **Good tasting but bad timing!** Move the text box closer to the data in column C and draw an arrow from this text box to cell C7.

11. Without activating the chart, draw an arrow from the chart text box to the top of the "PowerEase Average Mile Time" data marker.

12. Create a 3-D shape and move it by following these steps:

    a. Click A̲utoShapes on the Drawing toolbar.

    b. Choose B̲asic Shapes, and then the Cross shape from the submenu (third shape in the third row).

    c. In columns D and E with the crosshair pointer beside the worksheet column labels, draw a rectangle roughly the width of columns D and E and the height of the label row.

    d. Click the 3-D button 🔲 on the Drawing toolbar.

    e. Choose 3-D Style 7.

    f. Key **Innergize wins!** and click the Center button ≡.

    g. Click the 3-D button 🔲 and click 3̲-D Settings to open the 3-D Settings toolbar.

    h. Click the Lighting button 🔽 and choose the second lighting style in the bottom row.

    i. Close the 3-D Settings toolbar.

    j. With the 3-D shape selected, use the four-headed arrow to move the 3-D shape two to three columns over to the right.

13. Insert clip art into the worksheet by following these steps:

    a. Select a cell below the 3-D shape.

    b. Click the Insert Clip Art button 🖼.

    c. Scroll down to the Shapes button and click it or the underlined title below it.

    d. Click the first image (the compass) and click the Insert clip button 🔳.

    e. Close the Insert ClipArt dialog box.

14. Resize the picture by following these steps:

    a. With the picture selected, hold down Shift and drag the bottom right selection handle out and down until the picture is 150% x 150% (watch the Name Box as you resize it).

      b. Release the mouse button and ⟨Shift⟩ and center the picture below the 3-D shape.

      c. Deselect the picture.

15. Add the standard header in the worksheet.

16. Save the workbook as *[your initials]***15-20.xls** in your Lesson 15 folder.

17. Print the worksheet and close the workbook.

The solution to Exercise 15-20 varies according to the choices students make concerning the placement and manipulation of drawing objects, the 3-D shape, and clip art.

A S S E S S

Assessment Resources:
• Solutions Manual
• Test Bank
• Portfolio Builder
• Internet Projects
• Alternative Assessment Guide
• Certification Procedures

For Internet projects, go to
www.glencoe.com/webprojects

Lesson Applications

EXERCISE 15-21

Format chart text and add a background color and a border.

Harry Hascabar created a pie chart showing the breakdown of carbohydrates for one sports drink. Enhance the chart to make it more appealing.

1. Open the file **Pie.xls**.
2. Format the chart title font as 14-point Arial, bold, underlined.
3. Format the legend text as bold.
4. In the upper right corner of the chart, below the chart title, add a text box with the text **Percentages are approximate**
5. Format the text in the text box as 10-point Times New Roman, bold, italic.
6. Add a colored line border to the text box.
7. Add an arrow that points from the text box to the pie.
8. Add a shadow border and a light background color to the chart. (*Hint:* Use the Patterns options in the Format Chart Area dialog box to add the shadow and color.)
9. Add a standard header to the worksheet. (Make sure the chart is deselected or a header is added to the chart only.)
10. Change the left margin to 1.25 and save the workbook as *[your initials]*15-21.xls in your Lesson 15 folder.
11. Print the worksheet and save the workbook as *[your initials]*15-21.htm in your Lesson 15 folder.
12. Close the workbook.

EXERCISE 15-22

Format chart text, enhance the legend, and add a background color and border. Add and format drawing objects.

Harry Hascabar wants a separate chart sheet that uses a 3-D pie chart to show the carbohydrate breakdown of the sports drink "Endrun."

1. Open the file **Pie3.xls**.
2. Create a 3-D pie chart for Endrun as a separate chart sheet. Use subformat 2, show labels and percentages, and include a legend.

Lesson Applications:
Provide independent practice for students and may be used for assessment. Objectives are indicated for each Exercise.

◎ **Exercise 15-21:**
Objectives 1, 4–6
Required Files: Pie.xls
Solution Files: gl15-21.xls and gl15-21.htm in Solutions Manual or on Solutions Disk.

◎ **Exercise 15-22:**
Objectives 1, 2, 4–6
Required Files: Pie3.xls
Solution Files: Sample gl15-22.xls in Solutions Manual or on Solutions Disk.

TIP: Select the labels and information in rows 1 and 4 of the worksheet.

3. In the new chart sheet, format the chart title as 14-point Arial, bold, and format the legend text as 12-point Arial. (You may want to zoom in.)

4. Create an interesting pattern and border for the legend. Reposition the legend at the bottom of the chart, if it is not already there.

5. Add a border and background color to the chart.

6. Draw an oval around the label "21%" (next to "Fructose"). Use the No Fill setting and format the oval with a different line weight and color.

7. Above and to the right of "Fructose," draw a text box containing **Comparable to PurePower**. Make the line around the text box match the one around the oval.

8. Format the text in the text box as 11-point Arial Black and resize the text box to better fit the newly-sized text.

9. Move the text box close to the oval and draw an arrow from the text box to the circled chart label.

10. Add the standard header to the chart sheet.

11. Save the workbook as *[your initials]***15-22.xls** in your Lesson 15 folder.

12. Print the chart sheet and close the workbook.

EXERCISE 15-23

Format chart text, enhance the legend, and add background colors, a texture, and borders. Add and format drawing objects. Then, size, move, and copy the drawing objects. Import clip art.

Three new drinks were added to Harry Hascabar's study. Using a column chart, specify that the data series appear in rows instead of columns so the data markers for men and women are displayed as two groups.

1. Open the file **Drinks3.xls**.

2. Create a column chart as a new sheet. Include a legend at the bottom of the chart, and include the title **AVERAGE MINUTES**, but don't include axis titles.

3. Display the data series in rows. (*Hint:* Use the By Row button on the Chart toolbar.)

4. Add a background texture and a border to the chart area.

5. Add a colored pattern to the legend, make the legend text bold, and resize it to better fit all the legend text.

The solution to Exercise 15-22 varies according to how students position and manipulate drawing objects and format the legend.

◉ Exercise 15-23:
Objectives 1, 2, 4–6, 8
Required Files: Drinks3.xls
Solution Files: Sample gl15-23.xls in Solutions Manual or on Solutions Disk.

The completed document for this Exercise may be used in a student's portfolio.

6. Make the category and value axis labels bold.

7. Below the chart title, create a text box that contains the name **SuperSport** centered in it. Draw two arrows that start at the text box and point to the SuperSport data markers for men and women.

 TIP: Zoom in to approximately 75% to make the chart sheet easier to work with.

8. Format the SuperSport text box as bold with a colored border and a light fill color. Resize the text box to better fit the text if needed and adjust the arrows, if necessary.

9. Copy the chart text box and paste it to cell E14 on Sheet1. Change the new text box to read **New Drinks**. (The text box may seem to jump over a little when you paste it.)

10. Turn gridlines off for viewing and draw arrows from the New Drinks text box to the three new drinks in rows 13 through 15.

11. Import a piece of clip art above the "New Drinks" text box and size it so it fits well. Try to pick something meaningful.

12. Add the standard header to both worksheets and center Sheet1 horizontally on the page.

 13. Save the workbook as *[your initials]***15-23.xls** in your Lesson 15 folder.

14. Print the entire workbook and close it.

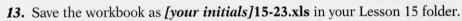

EXERCISE 15-24 *Challenge Yourself*

Format chart text, enhance the legend, change data series colors, and add background colors. Add and format drawing objects, then size and move them. Add and manipulate a 3-D shape. Import clip art.

 Harry Hascabar and three of his running buddies are always trying to beat their best marathon times. Using the best times from their last marathon, Harry wants to depict the information in two column charts—one of which uses clip art instead of regular column markers.

1. Create a sketch that includes a worksheet title and the data in Figure 15-20 on the next page. Roughly sketch where the chart will appear and the type of chart you will use (column in this case) including the title, Best Times, and the y-axis title, "Times," with a legend that includes the runners' names. There will not be x-axis labels in the embedded chart.

 The solution to Exercise 15-23 varies according to how students position and manipulate drawing objects and the clip art they choose.

Exercise 15-24:
Objectives 1–8
Required Files: None
Solution Files: Sample gl15-24.xls in Solutions Manual or on Solutions Disk.

 The completed document for this Exercise may be used in a student's portfolio.

FIGURE 15-20

	Times
Harry Hascabar	2:45
George Castle	2:38
Jerry Paglia	2:55
Sherry Raye	2:58

2. Transfer the sketch into a new workbook in Excel and key the data in Figure 5-20. Adjust column widths and add formatting.

3. Create an embedded column chart with the title **Best Times**, the y-axis title **Times**, x- and y-axis labels, and a legend. (The x-axis labels and legend are deleted or manipulated later.)

4. Size and position the chart so it extends from column A through column H and is approximately 20 rows high.

5. Format the chart title as 14-point Arial with a shadow border. Format all other text in the chart as 12-point bold, except format the value axis times as 10-point bold along with the legend text.

6. Format the chart columns with varying colors and enhance the legend.

7. Copy the chart onto Sheet2 of the workbook and delete the legend

8. On Sheet2, insert a clip art image to replace the colored data columns.

9. Change the orientation of Sheet2 to landscape.

10. Size the chart so it extends to the right margin.

11. Add a background color to the chart on Sheet2 and center the chart vertically and horizontally on the page.

12. On Sheet1, turn off grids for viewing and delete the category axis labels in the chart (the runners' names).

13. Draw an oval around the number 2:38 in the worksheet data. Change its fill to none.

14. Create a text box with an arrow pointing to the oval. The text box should read **Still in the lead with best time!**

15. Size the text box to fit the text and add a red border.

16. Create a 3-D AutoShape and add some special effects to it with the 3-D Settings toolbar. It does not have to include text. Move it to an appropriate location on the worksheet.

17. Create user documentation and name the sheet tab **User Information**. The sheet should include the following: File Information (Created by, Date created, Date revised, Revised by, Contact for help); Purpose of worksheet and charts (paragraph form); and Instructions to User (special instructions needed by user to enter data correctly). Format the documentation attractively and change any column widths you think might need it. Spell-check your work.

18. Add the standard header to all the worksheets and center Sheet1 horizontally on the page.

19. Close the Drawing toolbar and save the workbook as *[your initials]***15-24.xls** in your Lesson 15 folder.

20. Print the entire workbook and close it.

1 The solution to Exercise 15-24 varies according to the choices students make concerning the placement and manipulation of drawing objects, the 3-D shape, the clip art chosen, and formatting the legend.

For Internet projects, go to
www.glencoe.com/webprojects

Unit 5 Applications

UNIT APPLICATION 5-1

Add a border to a worksheet and create a 3-D bar chart. Format the chart text, format and resize the chart legend, and draw arrows.

After completing his experiment on sports drinks, Harry Hascabar is focusing on his leather goods business. He wants to chart the costs for each item he makes.

1. Open the file **Costs.xls**.

2. Format the first row as 10-point Arial Black, no bold.

3. Format the second row as the same font style but 9-point, no bold.

4. Insert a blank row between the worksheet title and column headings.

5. Center each column heading and resize the columns to fit the text. Format the column C heading as two lines.

6. Center the worksheet titles across columns A through E and apply light shading.

7. Place a blue border around the column headings.

8. Format cell ranges as follows:
   - Make cells A10 through A12 bold.
   - Right-align cells A5 through A12.
   - Format cells B5 through E11 in Comma style, keeping the decimal places.
   - Format cells B12 through E12 in Currency style. (Use the Format Cells dialog box.)

9. Total the costs in row 10 and column E including the Retail Price. Adjust column widths as needed.

10. Create a formula to determine the profit realized in each category.

11. Using the range A4:D9, create a 3-D bar chart with the subformat "#4" as a new sheet. Use **Mr. Hascabar's Costs** for the chart title, **Item** for the category axis title, and **Costs** for the value axis title. (Value (Z) axis in this case.) Include a legend.

12. Format the chart title as 16-point Times New Roman bold with a shadow border.

| A S S E S S | **Assessment Resources:**
• Solutions Manual • Test Bank
• Portfolio Builder
• Alternative Assessment Guide
• Certification Procedures
• Projects Manual
• Mid-Term and Final Exams | **Unit Applications:**
Provide independent practice of the skills acquired from each lesson in the Unit.
Project:
You can now assign Project 5 from the Projects Manual. | **Exam:**
You can now assign Exam 5 from the Mid-Term and Finals booklet. | **Unit Application 5-1:**
Required Files: Costs.xls
Solution Files: glu5-1.xls in Solutions Manual or on Solutions Disk |

13. Format the legend as follows:
    - Dark blue shadow border using the second weight choice
    - 9-point Arial Narrow bold
    - Bottom placement

14. Resize the legend so all text is visible, if necessary, and center it at the bottom of the page horizontally.

15. Create a text box that contains the text **Highest Cost**. Format the text box as follows:
    - Black line border using a heavy weight and bright yellow fill color
    - 11-point Arial Narrow bold

16. Resize the text box, if necessary, and place it somewhere in the open plot area between the longest bar and the top of the chart.

17. Draw arrows from the text box to the bar in each category that represents the highest cost.

18. Format the numbers along the value axis in currency style (with a dollar sign), with no decimal places. (Use the Formatting toolbar.)

19. Add the standard header to both worksheets and turn gridlines for viewing off in Sheet1.

20. Save the workbook as *[your initials]*u5-1.xls in a new folder for Unit 5.

21. Print the entire workbook and close it.

UNIT APPLICATION 5-2

Create a column chart and enhance the legend. Add, copy, and resize a text box. Change the color of the data series and draw arrows.

To plan his future inventory, Harry Hascabar wants to chart the quantity of each item sold during the past eight months.

1. Open the file **Sold.xls**.

2. Key **August** in cell A4 and fill in the months through March (A11).

3. In cell A12, key **TOTAL**. Format the cell as right-aligned and bold.

4. Calculate the total number of each item sold at the bottom of each column.

5. Create a formula in cell E4 to show how many total items were sold and copy it from E4 to E5:E12.

6. Format the data in cells B4:E12 in Comma style with no decimals.

7. Rename the Sheet1 tab as **Months**

8. Create a column chart as a new sheet using the cell range A3:D11. Use the default settings for a column chart. Use **Number of Items Sold** for

 Unit Application 5-2:
Required Files: Sold.xls
Solution Files: glu5-2.xls in Solutions Manual or on Solutions Disk

The completed document for this Application may be used in a student's portfolio.

the chart title, **Months** for the category axis title, and **Number Sold** for the value axis title. Include a legend at the bottom of the chart.

9. Make sure the legend is centered under the category axis title "Months" and that the axis title is completely visible.

10. Add a text box that contains the text **Laptop computer cases are the rage!** Move the text box to the top left corner of the plot area and format it as follows:

    ● Heavy, colored line border and light background color

    ● 12-point bold

    ● Text wraps to two lines

11. Change the data series colors to your favorite colors, making sure they complement one another.

12. Copy the text box to the top right corner of the plot area. Modify the text box as follows:

    ● Key **Highest Sales in December**

    ● 11-point bold italic text

    ● Resize text box to fit the text

13. Draw an arrow from the new text box to the "December Laptop Computer Case" column. Format the arrow to have a heavier weight and a color.

14. Rename the Chart1 tab **No. Sold**

15. Add the standard header to both worksheets, and turn off gridlines for viewing in the Months sheet.

16. Save the workbook as *[your initials]***u5-2.xls** in your Unit 5 folder.

17. Print the entire workbook and close it.

UNIT APPLICATION 5-3

Create three pie charts and add backgrounds to the charts.

  Using the sales data for items sold, Harry Hascabar wants to see a pie chart comparison for the months of September, December, and February.

1. Open the file **Pie2.xls**.

2. Change the page orientation to landscape and make the bottom margin .75 inch.

3. Using the cell ranges A3:D3 and A5:D5, create a pie chart on the same sheet as the worksheet for the month of September, as follows:

   ● Use the chart type Pie and the 3-D subformat (#2).

● Unit Application 5-3:
Required Files: Pie2.xls
Solution Files: glu5-3.xls in Solutions Manual or on Solutions Disk

The completed document for this Application may be used in a student's portfolio.

- Enter the chart title **September Sales**.
- Do not create a legend, but show values.
- Add a light background color to the chart.
- Make the chart extend from cell A14 through cell C26.

4. Create a pie chart on the same sheet for the month of December, as follows:

- Use the same chart type and subformat as the existing chart.
- Enter the chart title **December Sales**.
- Do not create a legend, but show values.
- Add a different background color to the chart.
- Make the chart extend from cell D14 through cell H26. (Change the zoom to 75% so you can see more of the worksheet.)
- Drag the December chart about one-half column to the right to separate the two charts.

5. Create another 3-D pie chart on the same sheet for February, as follows:

- Use the chart title **February Sales**.
- Do not create a legend, but show values.
- Add a different background color to the chart.
- Make the chart approximately the same size as the existing charts and center it below the two charts.

6. Preview the worksheet. If all the charts do not fit on a single page, reposition the bottom chart so it overlaps the bottom edges of the other two charts, and make the bottom chart somewhat smaller using the top selection handle, if necessary.

7. Add the standard header to the worksheet and turn gridlines off for viewing.

8. Save the workbook as *[your initials]***u5-3.xls** in your Unit 5 folder.

9. Print the worksheet and close the workbook.

UNIT APPLICATION 5-4

Create a 3-D bar chart. Edit chart objects. Create a 3-D shape and apply lighting effects to it.

Harry Hascabar's business only services the Western states. He wants to see the sales distribution by state per item, and in particular, he wants a chart of sales so can plan his marketing strategy.

1. Start a new workbook.

Unit Application 5-4:

Required Files: None
Solution Files: glu5-4.xls in Solutions Manual or on Solutions Disk

The completed document for this Application may be used in a student's portfolio.

2. Key the data shown in Figure U5-1. Widen columns as necessary

FIGURE U5-1

```
Leather Goods Distribution by State

State    Laptop       Computer Cases     Handbags

OR       315          175                205
WA       307          212                189
CA       579          343                297
AZ       437          313                278
NM       401          201                312
NV       579          234                277
UT       643          368                415

ID       247          156                217
```

3. Center the column headings along with the data under the column headings and center the title across the columns. Turn off grids for viewing and add additional formatting to make the worksheet attractive.

4. Using the data in cells A3:D11, create an embedded 3-D bar chart (sub-type #4). Key **Distribution by State** as the chart title and **Amount Sold** as the value axis title. Include a legend at the bottom of the chart.

5. Resize the chart so it ranges from cell A13 through H39.

6. Change the legend text to 9-point Times New Roman and give the legend a colored pattern.

7. Change the chart title to 12 point and the value axis title to 10 point.

8. Make all axis labels 9 point.

9. Add a shadow border and a textured background to the chart.

10. Create an octagon shape the size of cells F3:G6. (*Hint:* Choose A_utoShapes, _Basic Shapes, Octagon.)

11. Key **It's time to expand to the midwest!** in the shape and format the text as centered, 10-point Arial Narrow bold. Resize the shape, if necessary.

12. Apply 3-D Style 11 and a different lighting effect to the shape.

13. Add the standard header to the worksheet.

14. Center the worksheet horizontally on the page.

15. Preview the worksheet and resize the right side of the chart slightly if it has moved to a second page.

16. Delete the blank worksheets and save the workbook as *[your initials]*u5-4.xls in your Unit 5 folder.

17. Print the worksheet and close the workbook.

UNIT APPLICATION 5-5

Create a worksheet with drawing objects, borders, and clip art.

Harry Hascabar needs a new, professional-looking invoice for his leather goods business. He wants the invoice created in Excel and enhanced with clip art and drawing objects.

1. Create a sketch of an invoice for Harry Hascabar's Handcrafted Leather Goods. Include such typical invoice items as:
- The business name, possibly its address, phone, e-mail, etc.
- The customer's name and address
- A customer number
- An invoice number
- The date
- The product purchased
- The inventory number
- The quantity
- The unit price
- The product total
- The subtotal
- Tax
- Shipping
- Amount due

 TIP: Look at invoices you have received for other typical invoice items and for possible formatting ideas.

2. On a new worksheet, create the invoice. Use your creativity to format it with fonts, borders, colors, patterns, and drawing objects.

3. Import clip art to enhance the invoice.

4. Rename the sheet tab **Invoice**.

Unit Application 5-5:

Required Files: None
Solution: Sample file glu5-5.xls in Solutions Manual or on Solutions Disk

 The completed document for this Application may be used in a student's portfolio.

 This Application is completely freeform. Student answers vary based on design, formatting, and clip art choices.

5. Create user documentation and name the sheet tab **User Information**. The sheet should contain the following: File Information (Created by, Date created, Date revised, Revised by, Contact for help); Purpose of worksheet (paragraph form); and Instructions to User (special instructions needed by user to enter data correctly). Format the documentation attractively and change any column widths you think might need it. Spell-check your work.

6. Add the standard header to both worksheets and center the invoice on the page horizontally and vertically.

7. Delete the blank worksheets and save the workbook as *[your initials]*u5-5.xls in your Unit 5 folder.

8. Print and close the workbook, and submit your sketch, invoice, and documentation.

UNIT APPLICATION 5-6 *Making It Work for You*

Create a chart and enhance chart objects. Include drawing objects, a 3-D shape, and imported clip art.

 With your new charting skills, now is a perfect time to chart some of your personal expenses. Pick just one of your major expenses that varies month to month (this can be real or imagined) and create a worksheet with an embedded chart to track its variance. Have the data cover one full year, and in the worksheet and/or chart include drawing objects, a 3-D shape, and imported clip art. Enhance any of the chart objects and format the worksheet attractively. Delete the unused worksheets, add the standard header to the worksheet, turn gridlines off for viewing if you have not already, and save the file as *[your initial]*u5-6.xls in your Unit 5 folder. Print the worksheet and close the workbook.

Unit Application 5-6:
Required Files: None
Solution: Sample file glu5-6.xls in Solutions Manual or on Solutions Disk

This Application is completely freeform. Student answers vary based on design, formatting, and clip art choices.

Linking and Consolidating Worksheets

Electronic Company Goes High-Tech

Feestone Electronics is a nationwide distributor of business machines. Its main products are cellular phones, fax machines, copy machines, and postage meters.

Feestone has four regional offices. Each office writes its own invoices and keeps track of its own sales and inventory. The regional offices send reports to the main office each quarter. Craig Herman, the company's bookkeeper, has requested that the information be delivered as Excel files via e-mail so that he can easily consolidate the figures.

Craig has discussed this project at length with the regional managers. They're enthusiastic, but a little unsure of the process, so Craig needs to make the transition as easy as possible. He needs to receive the sales information in a specific form for the consolidation reports.

Craig needs to create the following worksheets for both the regional managers and for his own use:

✔ A product list that contains descriptions and prices of all the items sold by Feestone, and an invoice form that can be used to copy product information and calculate totals, shipping costs, and sales tax. **(Lesson 16)**

✔ A worksheet for each region that is easy to use, and a consolidation sheet for the main office. **(Lesson 17)**

Working with Multiple Worksheets

OBJECTIVES

MOUS ACTIVITIES
In this lesson:
XL2000 5.8
XL2000 5.9

See Appendix F.

After completing this lesson, you will be able to:

1. **Manage worksheets.**
2. **Open multiple workbooks.**
3. **Arrange workbook windows.**
4. **Save a workspace file.**
5. **Copy and paste between open workbooks.**

 Estimated Time: 1½ hours

As you know, Excel worksheets are contained in files called workbooks. A workbook can consist of 1 to 255 worksheets. Frequently, you may need to copy data from one worksheet to another in the same file. You may also need to work with information in multiple files. You already know how to navigate between worksheets. Now you learn how to manage worksheets and navigate between workbooks.

☑ Objective 1

Managing Worksheets

You can add and delete worksheets, change the sequence of worksheets, copy data between worksheets, edit multiple worksheets, and print a range of worksheets.

PREPARE
Point out to students that the learning objectives show what they will learn in the lesson. Each heading in the lesson correlates to a learning objective.

Required files:
Custlist.xls   Emplist.xls   Invoice.xls
Products.xls   Shipping.xls

TEACH
Teaching Resources:
• Excel Classroom Presentations
• School-to-Work Strategies Manual
• Spanish Glossary
• Certification Procedures

☑ **Objective 1 Assignment:**
Exercise 16-13 (Skills Review) can be assigned after completing Objective 1.

EXERCISE 16-1 Add and Delete Worksheets

Each new workbook opens with three worksheets named Sheet1 through Sheet3. You can add and delete worksheets using the standard menu or the sheet tab shortcut menu.

1. Open the file **Emplist.xls**. This workbook contains data on five worksheets. (Two worksheets were already added to this file.)

2. Right-click the Sheet3 worksheet tab. The sheet tab shortcut menu appears.

FIGURE 16-1
Sheet tab
shortcut menu

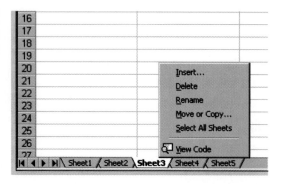

3. Choose the <u>I</u>nsert command from the shortcut menu. The Insert dialog box appears.

FIGURE 16-2
Insert dialog box

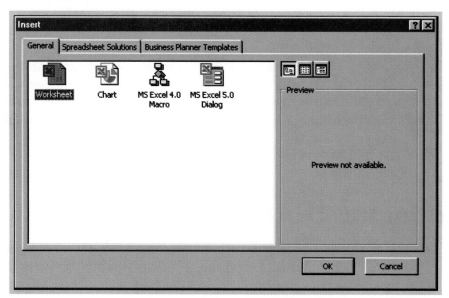

Use Excel Classroom Presentation 16 to display screens from the lesson in a slide-show format.

4. If necessary, click the General tab, click the Worksheet icon, and click OK. A new worksheet called Sheet6 is inserted to the left of Sheet3.

5. Choose Worksheet from the Insert menu. A new worksheet called Sheet7 is inserted to the left of Sheet6. Added sheets appear in front of the active sheet.

6. Right-click the Sheet7 tab. The sheet tab shortcut menu appears.

7. Click Delete. An Excel warning box appears, informing you that the selected sheets will be permanently deleted.

8. Click OK. Sheet7 is deleted.

9. With Sheet6 selected, choose Delete Sheet from the Edit menu and click OK in the warning box. Sheet6 is deleted.

10. With Sheet3 selected, press Shift + F11. Sheet8 is inserted. Notice that Excel numbers the new sheet based on the last sheet inserted.

11. Delete Sheet8 using the Sheet shortcut menu.

12. To add multiple sheets, select Sheet3, press Ctrl, and select Sheet4. Choose Insert from the shortcut menu and click OK in the Insert dialog box. Sheet9 and Sheet10 are inserted.

13. Select Sheet9, press Ctrl, and select Sheet10. Delete them using the shortcut menu the same way you deleted a single sheet.

TIP: You can make a copy of an existing worksheet by selecting the sheet to be copied, pressing Ctrl, pressing and holding the mouse button, and then dragging the icon where you want to position the copy of the worksheet. Excel gives the new sheet the same name as the original sheet with a consecutive number beginning with 2 in parentheses at the end of the name.

EXERCISE 16-2 Move a Worksheet

You can rearrange worksheets in a workbook by dragging the sheet tabs. Giving descriptive names to worksheets also helps to manage them.

1. Double-click the Sheet5 tab, key **Total Staff**, and press Enter to rename the sheet.

2. Rename sheets 1 through 4 **NE**, **NW**, **SE**, and **SW**, respectively.

Students are reminded how to rename worksheet tabs. See Lesson 4 for details, if necessary.

TIP: Using short names for worksheet tabs lets you see more tabs at one time. Be sure your worksheet names are clear. Use upper- and lowercase letters appropriately.

3. Position the mouse pointer on the tab named "Total Staff." Press and hold down the mouse button. A worksheet icon appears attached to the pointer and a black triangle indicates where the sheet will be inserted.

4. Drag to the left until the pointer is positioned on the NE tab—the first tab in the workbook—and the small triangle is in front of that tab.

5. Release the mouse button. The sheet that will contain the employee list for all four offices moves to the beginning of the workbook.

EXERCISE **Copy and Paste Data Between Worksheets**

You can use the Copy and Paste commands to build worksheets without rekeying information. For instance, you can copy the sales staff from each region into the Total Staff sheet.

1. Click the NE tab.

2. Select cells A6 through C9.

3. Click the Copy button 🔳 on the Standard toolbar. A moving border surrounds the selected range.

4. Click the "Total Staff" tab.

5. Click cell A6 and click the Paste button 🔳 on the Standard toolbar to paste the Northeast data into the Total Staff worksheet.

6. Click the NW tab and select cells A6 through C9.

7. Right-click the selected range and choose Copy from the shortcut menu.

8. Click the Total Staff tab, right-click cell A10, and click the Paste command on the shortcut menu. The data is copied to the Total Staff worksheet.

 TIP: You can press Enter instead of choosing Paste. You can also use the Copy and Paste commands on the Edit menu and the shortcut key combinations Ctrl + C and Ctrl + V.

9. Copy the names from the SE sheet to cell A14 in the Total Staff sheet and from the SW sheet to cell A18 in the Total Staff sheet. Press Ctrl + Home to return to cell A1.

FIGURE 16-3
Total Staff
worksheet after
pasting data

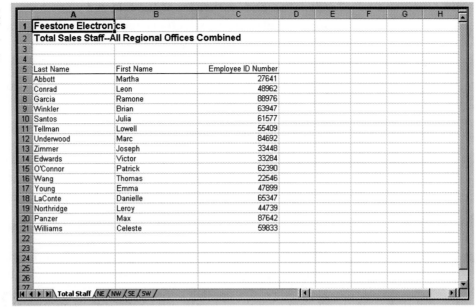

	A	B	C	D	E	F	G	H
1	Feestone Electronics							
2	Total Sales Staff--All Regional Offices Combined							
3								
4								
5	Last Name	First Name	Employee ID Number					
6	Abbott	Martha	27641					
7	Conrad	Leon	48962					
8	Garcia	Ramone	88976					
9	Winkler	Brian	63947					
10	Santos	Julia	61577					
11	Tellman	Lowell	55409					
12	Underwood	Marc	84692					
13	Zimmer	Joseph	33448					
14	Edwards	Victor	33284					
15	O'Connor	Patrick	62390					
16	Wang	Thomas	22546					
17	Young	Emma	47899					
18	LaConte	Danielle	65347					
19	Northridge	Leroy	44739					
20	Panzer	Max	87642					
21	Williams	Celeste	59833					
22								
23								
24								
25								
26								
27								

Total Staff / NE / NW / SE / SW /

EXERCISE 16-4 Edit Multiple Worksheets

You can select several worksheets and edit and format them all at once. This technique produces a uniform look. However, if you delete a row or column, it is deleted from all selected worksheets.

1. Click the Total Staff tab to active the worksheet, if necessary. Hold down Shift and click the SW tab. The five worksheets are selected. The word "[Group]" appears in the title bar.

TIP: To select nonadjacent worksheets, click the first worksheet tab, hold down Ctrl, and click the other worksheet tabs.

2. Make the column labels in row 5 bold and italic.

3. Change the label in column C to wrap to two lines (insert a line break after "Employee") and resize the column to better fit the label.

4. Delete row 4.

5. Add the standard header with your name, filename, and date, and center the worksheet horizontally on the page.

6. Right-click the Total Staff tab and choose Ungroup Sheets on the shortcut menu. Only the current sheet is selected.

In Excel Classroom Presentation 16.

7. Click the tabs for the rest of the selected worksheets to view the formatting changes, which are reflected in all selected worksheets. (Use Print Preview to see all the changes.)

 TIP: You can also click any inactive sheet in the workbook to deselect the selected sheets.

EXERCISE 16-5 Print a Range of Worksheets

You can print all the worksheets in a workbook or only selected worksheets.

1. Click the Total Staff tab to active the worksheet, if necessary, and save the workbook as *[your initials]***16-5.xls** in a new folder for Lesson 16.

2. Hold down Ctrl and click the SE tab. Only the Total Staff worksheet and the SE worksheet are selected.

3. Press Ctrl+P. The Print dialog box appears.

4. In the Print What section, make sure the Acti̲ve Sheet(s) button is selected. To print all five worksheets in the workbook, you would click E̲ntire workbook in the Print What section.

5. Click OK to print the Total Staff worksheet and the SE worksheet.

 TIP: To print selected worksheets, you can also click the Print button 🖨 on the Standard toolbar.

6. Click the NE tab to deselect the two worksheets.

7. Close the workbook without saving it.

Objective 2
Opening Multiple Workbooks

When you open a new or existing workbook, Excel opens a new workbook window. If you already have workbooks open, the new window covers the other windows, but they all remain open. As a result, you can easily move among them. You can also open multiple windows for one workbook if you need to view two different worksheets at the same time.

You can move to other windows by choosing them from the W̲indow menu or the Windows taskbar.

EXERCISE 16-6 Open Multiple Windows

1. Open the file **Invoice.xls**.

2. Choose <u>N</u>ew Window from the <u>W</u>indow menu. A new window opens over the first window. The title bar displays **Invoice.xls:2**, indicating this is a second window containing that workbook.

 NOTE: Windows of the same workbook are just images of the same file. If you edit Invoice.xls:1, your changes appear in Invoice.xls:2 simultaneously.

3. With **Invoice.xls:2** still displayed, open the file **Custlist.xls**.

4. Choose <u>W</u>indow on the menu bar. The three open workbook windows are listed at the bottom of the menu. The checkmark indicates **Custlist.xls** is the active window. Notice also that the three open workbook windows appear as buttons on the Windows taskbar at the bottom of the screen.

FIGURE 16-4
Opening multiple
workbook windows

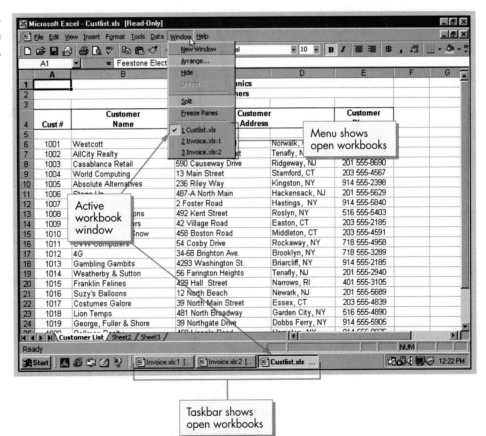

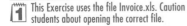 This Exercise uses the file Invoice.xls. Caution
students about opening the correct file.

 In Excel Classroom Presentation 16.

5. Choose **Invoice.xls:1** from the Window menu. The window containing the first version of **Invoice.xls** appears on top.

6. Click the **Custlist.xls** button on the taskbar to display that workbook window.

 NOTE: If buttons for open workbooks do not appear on your taskbar, use the Window menu to display a workbook.

 Objective 3

Arranging Workbook Windows

You usually work with three or fewer windows at a time. The number of windows that you can open, however, is limited only by your computer's memory.

You can arrange windows four ways: Tiled, Horizontal, Vertical, or Cascade. The best arrangement depends on the type of data and the layout of the worksheets. For example, if you are copying columns of data from one worksheet to another, use the vertical arrangement. If you are copying rows, use the horizontal arrangement.

EXERCISE **16-7** **Arrange Windows Using the Arrange Command**

1. Open the file **Shipping.xls**.

2. Choose Arrange from the Window menu. The Arrange Windows dialog box appears.

3. Click Cascade and click OK. The windows are arranged diagonally so you can see the workspace of the Shipping.xls workbook, but only the title bars and row selector buttons of the windows behind it. (See Figure 16-5 on the next page.)

4. Click the title bar of the Custlist.xls window. The workbook moves to the front of the display, like a card pulled from the bottom of the deck and placed on top. It also covers some of the other open window title bars.

5. Click the title bar of the window containing Invoice.xls:2 to activate the workbook.

6. Choose Arrange from the Window menu.

7. Click the Windows of Active Workbook check box, which arranges the windows of only the active workbook. Click Vertical, and click OK. The two windows containing Invoice.xls are arranged side by side.

8. Click the Sheet2 tab in Invoice.xls:2. The Invoice sheet is still displayed in the window containing Invoice.xls:1.

9. Choose Arrange from the Window menu.

Objective 3 Assignment:
Exercises 16-14 and 16-15 (Skills Review) can be assigned after completing Objective 3.

Students who have worked in other Windows applications may already be familiar with arranging, minimizing, maximizing, and restoring windows.

Remind students they can move any open window, including a dialog box, by dragging its title bar.

FIGURE 16-5
Cascading
windows

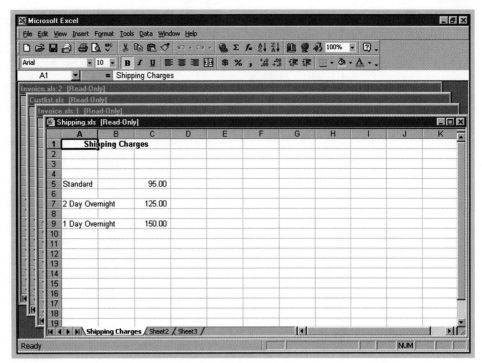

10. Clear the <u>W</u>indows of Active Workbook check box, click <u>T</u>iled, and click OK. All windows are tiled. Notice that only the active workbook displays control buttons in its title bar.

EXERCISE 16-8 Maximize, Restore, and Minimize Windows

You can expand an active workbook to its full size by double-clicking the title bar or clicking the workbook Maximize button ⬜. This button then becomes a Restore Window button ⬒. Clicking the Restore Window button ⬒ displays the workbook in its previous, arranged size. (See Figure 16-6 on the next page.)

The Minimize button _ reduces a workbook to a title bar in the lower part of the Excel window. You may need to drag windows out of the way to find and restore a minimized workbook. You also can choose a minimized workbook from the <u>W</u>indow menu to restore it.

1. Click anywhere in the Custlist.xls window to activate it.

2. Click the Maximize button ⬜. The window is displayed at full size. The Restore Window button ⬒ replaces the Maximize button ⬜. (See Figure 16-7 on the next page.)

In Excel Classroom Presentation 16.

FIGURE 16-6
Tiled windows

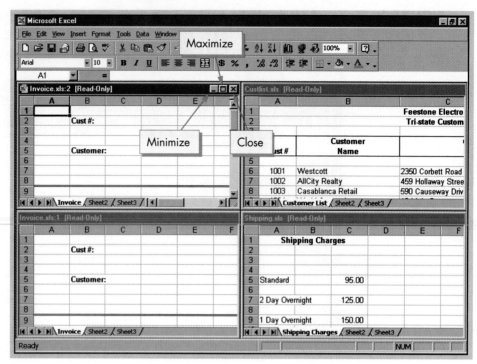

FIGURE 16-7
Maximized
window

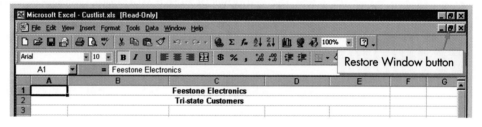

> **NOTE:** When windows are arranged, the buttons to maximize or close
> the active window are ⬜ and ❎. When a window is maximized, the
> buttons to minimize or close the active window are ⬛ and ❎.

3. Choose Window from the menu bar and choose Invoice.xls:1 from the menu.
The window containing this workbook is maximized (its previous size).

4. To restore all windows to their tiled size, click the Restore Window button
🗗 in the workbook window.

5. Click anywhere in the window containing Shipping.xls and click the
Minimize button 🗕. The worksheet changes to a title bar and moves to
the lower left corner of the Excel window behind another window.

6. Drag the window in the lower left corner over to the right. The minimized
title bar for the workbook Shipping.xls becomes visible.

 In Excel Classroom Presentation 16.

7. Minimize the window containing Custlist.xls (see step 5).

8. To restore Shipping.xls to its previous size, click the minimized workbook and choose <u>R</u>estore from the shortcut menu.

FIGURE 16-8
Restoring a
minimized
workbook

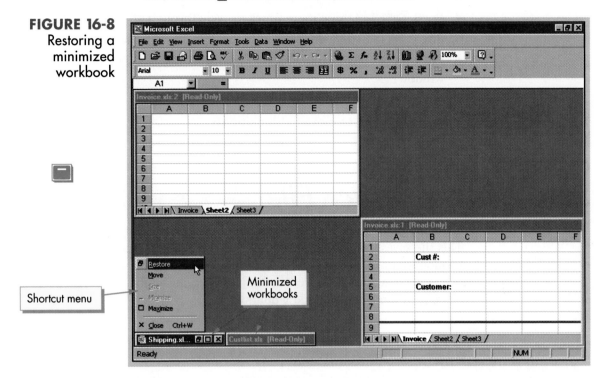

Shortcut menu

NOTE: In the active workbook, you can use the keyboard shortcuts Ctrl+F5 to restore, Ctrl+F10 to maximize, and Ctrl+W to close the window. Also minimized worksheets restore to the position before being minimized.

9. Restore the Custlist.xls window.

10. Arrange all windows horizontally. (*Hint:* Use the Arrange Windows dialog box.)

EXERCISE 16-9 Switch Between Open Windows

As you've seen, you can click a window to switch to it, use the <u>W</u>indow menu, or use the taskbar. You can also use keyboard shortcuts. Ctrl+Tab or Ctrl+F6 moves to the next open window. Shift+Ctrl+Tab or Shift+Ctrl+F6 moves to the previous open window.

1. Double-click the title bar of the Shipping.xls window. The window becomes active and is maximized to fill the screen.

 In Excel Classroom Presentation 16.

This Exercise focuses on keyboard shortcuts for switching between windows. You may want to skip this Exercise if you and your students are more comfortable using the mouse methods to switch between windows (Window menu and taskbar).

2. Choose Custlist.xls from the <u>W</u>indow menu. The Custlist.xls window moves to the front.

3. Press [Ctrl]+[Tab]. The Shipping.xls window moves to the front.

4. Press [Ctrl]+[Tab] three more times to cycle through all open windows.

5. Press [Ctrl]+[F6] four times to cycle through all of the windows.

6. Click Invoice.xls:2 on the taskbar (or use the <u>W</u>indow menu to display the window).

7. Press [Ctrl]+[W] to close the Invoice.xls:2 window.

8. Press [Ctrl]+[Tab] to move to Shipping.xls.

9. Press [Shift]+[Ctrl]+[Tab] to move back to Custlist.xls.

Objective 4

Saving a Workspace File

You can open a group of workbooks in one step by creating a workspace file. This file saves information about all open workbooks, such as their locations, window sizes, and screen positions. When you open a workspace file, Excel opens each workbook saved in the workspace. You must continue to save changes you make to the individual workbooks.

EXERCISE 16-10 Save a Group of Workbooks as a Workspace File

1. Arrange the windows horizontally.

2. Choose Save <u>W</u>orkspace from the <u>F</u>ile menu.

3. In the File <u>N</u>ame textbox, key *[your initials]***16-10.** Notice the Save As Type textbox contains Workspaces (*.xlw). Excel automatically adds the .xlw extension.

4. Locate your Lesson 16 folder, if necessary, and click <u>S</u>ave. (If prompted, do not save changes to Invoice.xls.)

5. Press and hold [Shift] and choose <u>C</u>lose All from the <u>F</u>ile menu to close all the workbooks at one time.

6. Open the workspace file *[your initials]***16-10.xlw** and all the workbooks open in the same positions and sizes in which you saved them.

☞ Objective 5

Copying and Pasting Between Workbooks

You can copy and paste between workbooks just as you can between worksheets. You use the same commands to transfer data to another workbook

☞ **Objective 5 Assignment:**

Exercise 16-16 (Skills Review) and Exercises 16-17 through 16-20 (Lesson Applications) can be assigned after completing Objective 5.

window. After you cut or copy a section to the Clipboard, switch documents, position the pointer where you want the copied data to go, and paste it.

EXERCISE 16-11 Copy and Paste Between Workbooks

1. Click in Shipping.xls and click the Minimize button ▬.

2. Choose Arrange from the Window menu, choose Vertical, and click OK. Custlist.xls and Invoice.xls are arranged vertically.

3. Right-click cell A14 in Custlist.xls and choose Copy from the shortcut menu.

4. Click anywhere in the Invoice.xls window to activate it.

5. Right-click cell D2 in Invoice.xls, choose Paste from the shortcut menu, and press Esc to clear the moving border from the source cell. Left-align the customer number in cell D2.

6. Using the same method, copy cell B14 from Custlist.xls to cell D5 in Invoice.xls.

7. Select cells C14 and D14 in Custlist.xls and click the Copy button 🗎 on the Standard toolbar. (Use the scroll bars to navigate.)

8. Activate the cell I5 in Invoice.xls and click the Paste button 🗎.

9. Move the city and state in cell J5 in Invoice.xls to cell I6 by dragging it.

10. Close Custlist.xls and open the file **Products.xls**.

11. Arrange the windows vertically.

12. Select cells A8 through E10 in Products.xls. Press Ctrl+C to copy them to the Clipboard.

13. Activate Invoice.xls, click cell B13, and press Enter.

NOTE: Pressing Enter automatically removes the moving border around the source cells.

14. In Invoice.xls, select the Unit Prices in cells F13 through F15 and drag them to cells H13 through H15.

15. Close the Products.xls workbook.

16. Restore the file Shipping.xls and arrange the windows vertically.

17. Scroll to make cell J28 visible in Invoice.xls.

18. Using the drag-and-drop method, copy the charge for standard shipping from Shipping.xls to cell J28 in Invoice.xls. (Remember to hold down Ctrl and drag the amount from one workbook to the other.)

19. Close the file Shipping.xls without saving it. Maximize the file Invoice.xls.

EXERCISE 16-12 Complete the Invoice

1. Complete the invoice by keying the data from Figure 16-9 in the cells indicated:

FIGURE 16-9

I2	20460
I3	*[today's date]*
F13	10
F14	2
F15	1

2. Key the formula **=F13*H13** in cell J13 and copy the formula down two cells.

3. Enter the SUM function in cell J26 to total the three products and in cell J29 to add the total, tax, and shipping.

4. Format the amount due in currency style and leave the two decimal places. (Use the Format Cells dialog box.)

5. Add the standard header including your name, filename, and date to the Invoice worksheet.

6. Move the data from cells I2:I3 and I5:I6 to H2:H3 and H5:H6. Delete any blank columns or rows that you feel are unnecessary and widen other columns accordingly. (*Hint:* The invoice looks best if you leave the two outside blank columns because of the outline border.)

7. Center the worksheet horizontally on the page and turn off gridlines for viewing. Add formatting that enhances the appearance of the invoice, aligning data as needed.

8. Press Ctrl + Home , delete the blank worksheets in the workbook, and save the workbook as **[your initials]16-12.xls** in your Lesson 16 folder.

9. Print the Invoice worksheet and create a formula printout in landscape orientation with grids and row and column headings. Adjust column widths to save space, being careful that all data appears on the printout. Use a Page 1 of ? footer, if necessary.

10. Close the workbook without saving it.

[1] The Invoice worksheet generated in this Exercise may contain blank columns. Students are asked to use their judgment and remove any unnecessary blank columns and to adjust other column widths to compensate for their removal. They are also asked to include additional formatting, so solution files will vary.

NOTE: If you arrange multiple workbook window(s) and then close them in that arrangement or close a minimized workbook, the next workbook you open appears in a reduced window. You may need to maximize the window to begin your work in the newly opened workbook.

COMMAND SUMMARY

FEATURE	BUTTON	MENU	KEYBOARD
Arrange windows		Window, Arrange	
Close all workbooks		Shift+File, Close	
Delete a worksheet		Edit, Delete Sheet	
Insert a worksheet		Insert, Worksheet	Shift + F11
Maximize window	⬜		Ctrl + F10
Minimize window	▬		Ctrl + F9
Open second workbook		Window, New window	
Restore a window	▣		Ctrl + F5
Switch to next window		Window, name	Ctrl + Tab or Ctrl + F6
Switch to previous window		Window, name	Shift + Ctrl + Tab or Shift + Ctrl + F6

USING HELP

Not only can you arrange workbook windows, you can also arrange minimized workbook icons.

Use Help to learn about arranging minimized workbook icons:

1. Press F1 to activate the Office Assistant.

2. Key **arrange icons** and click Search.

3. Click the topic "Arrange minimized workbook icons in the Microsoft Excel window."

4. Review the information, close the Help window, and hide the Office Assistant.

---

1 Make sure students understand that when they close a reduced or minimized window, they may need to maximize the next workbook window they open.

2 The Command Summary lists a variety of ways to accomplish a particular task. Students can decide which method they prefer to use.

3 Encourage students to follow the steps in "Using Help." Software companies are increasingly using their Help program—rather than printed documentation—to train users and assist in answering user questions.

| TEST BANK |

Concepts Review

TRUE/FALSE QUESTIONS

Each of the following statements is either true or false. Indicate your choice by circling T or F.

T **(F)** **1.** To delete a worksheet, you must first move it so it becomes the last worksheet in the workbook.

(T) F **2.** To edit multiple worksheets, you select the worksheets to be modified and then make your changes to one of the selected sheets.

T **(F)** **3.** You can print only selected sheets in a workbook, but they must be next to one another.

T **(F)** **4.** If you are copying columns of data from one workbook window to another, the best window arrangement is horizontal.

(T) F **5.** You can use the Windows taskbar to switch between open workbooks.

(T) F **6.** You can save arranged workbooks in a workspace to maintain their window arrangements and sizes.

T **(F)** **7.** After switching to an open window using the keyboard or menu commands, you must click in it to make the window active.

(T) F **8.** You can use the same techniques to copy data between workbooks as you do to copy data between worksheets.

SHORT ANSWER QUESTIONS

Write the correct answer in the space provided.

1. What indicates the position of a worksheet tab while you are moving it?

Black triangle indicator

2. Which key do you hold down while clicking worksheet tabs to select nonadjacent worksheets?

Ctrl

3. Which window arrangement displays open windows in a grid, both horizontally and vertically?

Tiled

Concepts Review:
Allows students to check their understanding.

C
L
O
S
E

| TEST BANK |
Consider using the Test Bank to provide an additional review of lesson concepts. It may also be used as an assessment tool.

4. Which window arrangement displays the open windows diagonally, showing only the title bars and row selector buttons of the nonactive windows?

Cascading

5. Which is the keyboard combination to switch to the next open workbook?

Ctrl+Tab or Ctrl+F6

6. Which command do you choose to arrange open workbooks on the screen?

Window, Arrange

7. How many workbooks can you open at the same time?

As many as your computer's memory allows

8. When two workbooks are open, which window arrangement has the same effect as the tiling option?

Vertical

CRITICAL THINKING

Answer these questions on a separate piece of paper. There are no right or wrong answers. Support your answers with examples from your own experience, if possible.

1. Excel provides several ways to arrange open workbook windows, including minimizing them. Discuss the advantage of each method. Why would you prefer one arrangement over another? Would you ever resize the windows manually? Why?

2. In Excel, you can rename worksheets and workbooks. In Windows, you can create folders to contain workbooks. Name and discuss situations in which good file management is important.

Skills Review

EXERCISE 16-13

Add and delete worksheets, rename a worksheet, move a worksheet, copy and paste data between worksheets, edit multiple worksheets, and print a range of worksheets.

 1. Open the file **Invoice2.xls**. (This workbook contains five worksheets.)

Critical Thinking Questions:
Answers will vary based on students' preferences, observations, experiences, and research.

Skills Review:
Provides guided practice for students. Objectives are indicated for each Exercise.

◉ **Exercise 16-13:**
Objective 1
Required Files: Invoice2.xls
Solution Files: gl16-13.xls in Solutions Manual or on Solutions Disk.

2. Add and delete worksheets by following these steps:

   a. Click the Shipping worksheet tab.

   b. Press ⟨Shift⟩+⟨F11⟩.

   c. Right-click the Sheet1 worksheet tab and choose Insert from the shortcut menu.

   d. If necessary, click the General tab, click the Worksheet icon, and click OK.

   e. Click the Sheet1 tab and choose Delete Sheet from the Edit menu.

   f. Click OK in the Warning box.

   g. Right-click on the Sheet2 tab, choose Delete from the shortcut menu, and click OK.

3. Rename Sheet3 as **Invoice1**, Sheet4 as **Invoice2**, and Sheet5 as **Invoice3**.

4. Drag the Invoice3 sheet to the right of the Shipping sheet.

5. Copy data from the Customer List worksheet to the Invoice3 worksheet by following these steps:

   a. Click the Customer List sheet tab.

   b. Select cells A11 and B11 and click the Copy button.

   c. Click the Invoice3 sheet.

   d. Click cell D2 and click the Paste button.

   e. Drag cell E2 to cell D5. Left-align cell D2.

   f. Copy cells C11 through D11 on the Customer List sheet to the Clipboard.

   g. Paste the contents of the Clipboard to cell I5 in the Invoice3 sheet.

   h. In the Invoice3 sheet, drag cell J5 to cell I6.

6. Copy the standard shipping charge from cell C4 in the Shipping worksheet to cell J28 in the Invoice3 sheet.

7. In the Invoice3 sheet, enter **20478** in cell I2 and enter today's date in cell I3. Left-align both cells.

8. Edit a group of worksheets by following these steps:

   a. With the sheet named Invoice3 selected, press and hold ⟨Shift⟩ and click the sheet tab of the Invoice2 worksheet.

   b. Format cell J29 in currency style and keep the two decimal places. Use the Format Cells dialog box.

   c. Widen column J to display the number.

   d. Add the standard header with your name, filename, and date.

   e. Horizontally center the worksheets on the page.

   f. Delete unnecessary blank columns or rows and widen other columns to accommodate their removal and column labels. (*Hint:* The invoice looks best if the two outside columns remain blank due to the border outline.)

   g. Turn off gridlines for viewing and add formatting to enhance the appearance of the worksheet.

[1] The Invoice worksheets generated in this Exercise may contain blank columns. Students are asked to use their judgment and remove any unnecessary blank columns and to adjust other column widths to compensate for their removal. They are also asked to include additional formatting, so solution files will vary.

h. Click the Invoice2 and Invoice1 sheet tabs to make sure columns are wide enough to accommodate their data and all formatting is uniform.

9. Click the Customer List tab to deselect the worksheets and press [Ctrl]+[Home]. Save the workbook as *[your initials]*16-13.xls in your Lesson 16 folder.

10. Select the three Invoice sheets again and choose Print from the File menu.

11. With the Active sheets option button selected, click OK.

12. Close the workbook without saving it.

EXERCISE 16-14

Open multiple workbooks, arrange workbook windows, arrange multiple windows of the same workbook, maximize a window, restore a window, and delete blank worksheets.

1. Open the following files: **Allcity.xls**, **Automatn.xls**, **Stageup.xls**, and **Westcott.xls**.

TIP: In the Open dialog box, you can [Ctrl]+click to select multiple filenames and then click Open to open them all.

2. Choose Arrange from the Window menu, click the Horizontal option button, and click OK.

3. Arrange the windows using the Cascade option.

4. Arrange multiple windows of the same workbook by following these steps:
   a. Click the Automatn.xls title bar.
   b. Choose New Window from the Window menu.
   c. With Automatn.xls:2 active, choose New Window from the Window menu again.
   d. Choose Arrange from the Window menu and check the Windows of Active Workbook check box.
   e. Click the Tiled option button and click OK.

5. Maximize a worksheet and enter data by following these steps:
   a. Click the Automatn.xls:3 window to activate it, if necessary, and click the worksheet Close button.
   b. Close the Automatn.xls:2 window.
   c. Choose Arrange from the Window menu and clear the Windows of Active Workbook check box.
   d. Make sure the Tiled option button is still selected and click OK.
   e. Click the Maximize button 🔲 in the Automatn.xls workbook.
   f. Key **Feestone Electronics** in cell A1 in 12-point bold.

⊙ Exercise 16-14:

Objectives 1–3
Required Files: Allcity.xls, Automatn.xls, Stageup.xls, Westcott.xls
Solution Files: gl16-14a.xls, gl16-14b.xls, gl16-14c.xls, gl16-14d.xls in Solutions Manual or on Solutions Disk.

   g. Click cell A2 and choose Insert, Rows on the menu bar.

   h. Key **Invoice** in cell A2 in 12-point bold.

   i. Center both titles across columns A through I.

   j. Click cell A3 and choose Insert, Rows on the menu bar.

6. Click the Restore Window button 🗗 in the workbook Automatn.xls to display the tiled arrangement.

7. Copy data between open workbooks by following these steps:

   a. Click in the Allcity.xls window to activate it, click cell A2, and insert two rows.

   b. Insert two rows above row 2 in the Stageup.xls and Westcott.xls windows.

   c. Select cells A1 and A2 in the Automatn.xls window and click the Copy button 🗎.

   d. Click in the Allcity.xls window to activate it, click cell A1, and click the Paste button 🗎.

   e. Click in the Stageup.xls window to activate it, click cell A1, and click the Paste button 🗎.

   f. Paste the contents of the Clipboard to cell A1 in Westcott.xls and press ⟨Esc⟩.

   g. Make sure the copied titles are centered across columns A through I.

8. Delete the blank worksheets in each of the workbooks and insert the standard header in the remaining worksheet in each workbook.

9. Save the workbooks and print the active worksheets by following these steps:

   a. Activate Westcott.xls, if necessary, and maximize it. Save the file as *[your initials]***16-14a.xls** in your Lesson 16 folder and click the Print button 🖨.

   b. Save Stageup.xls as *[your initials]***16-14b.xls** in your Lesson 16 folder and click the Print button 🖨.

   c. Save Allcity.xls as *[your initials]***16-14c.xls** in your Lesson 16 folder and click the Print button 🖨.

   d. Save Automatn.xls as *[your initials]***16-14d.xls** in your Lesson 16 folder and click the Print button 🖨.

10. Close all open workbooks.

EXERCISE 16-15

Switch between open workbooks and delete worksheets.

1. Open the following files: **Allcity2.xls**, **Automat2.xls**, **Stageup2.xls**, and **Westcot2.xls**.

2. Choose Allcity2.xls from the Window menu.

◉ **Exercise 16-15:**
Objectives 1–3
Required Files: Allcity2.xls, Automat2.xls, Stageup2.xls, Westcot2.xls
Solution Files: gl16-15a.xls, gl16-15b.xls, gl16-15c.xls, gl16-15d.xls in Solutions Manual or on Solutions Disk.

3. Press Ctrl+Tab as many times as necessary to make Westcot2.xls active.

4. Format cells A1 and A2 by following these steps:

   a. In the Westcot2.xls window, format cells A1 and A2 as 12-point bold and center them across columns A through I.

   b. Click Allcity2.xls on the Windows taskbar to activate it.

   c. In the Allcity2.xls window, format cells A1 and A2 as 12-point bold and center them across columns A through I.

   d. Activate the Stageup2.xls and Automat2.xls windows and format cells A1 and A2 in those workbooks.

5. Delete the blank worksheets in each workbook. Press Ctrl+F6 to move between workbooks.

6. Create the standard header for each remaining worksheet in each workbook. Press Ctrl+F6 to move between workbooks.

7. Save the workbooks, print the active worksheets, and close the workbooks by following these steps:

   a. Click Automat2.xls on the Windows taskbar.

   b. Choose Arrange from the Window menu, click the Cascade option button, and click OK.

   c. Save Automat2.xls as *[your initials]*16-15a.xls in your Lesson 16 folder, click the Print button 🖨, and click the worksheet Close button.

   d. Click in the Westcot2.xls window to activate it, save it as *[your initials]*16-15b.xls in your Lesson 16 folder, click the Print button 🖨, and click the worksheet Close button.

   e. Click in the Allcity2.xls window to activate it, save it as *[your initials]*16-15c.xls in your Lesson 16 folder, click the Print button 🖨, and close the worksheet.

   f. Click in the Stageup2.xls window to activate it, maximize the window, save the file as *[your initials]*16-15d.xls in your Lesson 16 folder, click the Print button 🖨, and close the worksheet.

EXERCISE 16-16

Arrange windows, save a workspace file, copy and paste between open workbooks, and delete blank worksheets.

1. Open the files **Allcity3.xls** and **Stageup3.xls**.

2. Arrange the windows horizontally.

3. Save a workspace file by following these steps:

   a. Choose Save Workspace from the File menu.

   b. Key *[your initials]***16-16** in the File Name textbox.

   c. Open your Lesson 16 folder, if necessary, and then click Save.

   d. Press and hold Shift, then choose Close All from the File menu. (If prompted, do not save changes to the files.)

◉ **Exercise 16-16:**
Objectives 1, 3–5
Required Files: Allcity3.xls, Stageup3.xls
Solution Files: gl16-16a.xls, gl16-16b.xls, gl16-16.xlw
in Solutions Manual or on Solutions Disk.

4. Open the workspace file *[your initials]***16-16.xlw**.

5. In the Allcity3.xls worksheet, insert a row above row 31.

6. In cell F31, key **1 year service contract**.

7. In cell H31, key **150**. Make sure it is formatted in comma style with two decimal places.

8. Click in the Stageup3.xls window to activate it.

9. Insert a row above row 31 in the Stageup3.xls worksheet.

10. Click in the Allcity3.xls window to activate it.

11. Copy data from one workbook to another by following these steps:

    a. Copy cells F31 through H31 in the Allcity3.xls worksheet.

    b. Click the Stageup3.xls window to activate it.

    c. Right-click cell F31 in Stageup3.xls.

    d. Choose Paste from the shortcut menu and press Esc.

12. Correct the formula in cell H32 in Stageup3.xls so it totals all the necessary cells to compute the amount due in the worksheet and copy the formula to Allcity3.xls.

13. Delete the blank worksheets in each workbook and create the standard header in the remaining worksheet in both workbooks.

14. Maximize Stageup3.xls, make cell A1 active, save the file as *[your initials]***16-16a.xls** in your Lesson 16 folder, click the Print button 🖨, and close the workbook.

15. Make cell A1 active in Allcity3.xls, save the file as *[your initials]***16-16b.xls** in your Lesson 16 folder, click the Print button 🖨, and close the workbook.

A S S E S S

Assessment Resources:
- Solutions Manual
- Test Bank
- Portfolio Builder
- Internet Projects
- Alternative Assessment Guide
- Certification Procedures

For Internet projects, go to
www.glencoe.com/webprojects

Lesson Applications

EXERCISE 16-17

Arrange windows, switch between windows, copy data from one worksheet to another, and format and print a group of worksheets.

Complete a customer invoice using information from several worksheets.

1. Open the file **Invoice3.xls**.
2. Open a second window of this workbook.
3. Arrange the two workbooks vertically.
4. In the Invoice sheet, complete the customer information for Electronic Discount by keying the data from Figure 16-10 and copying data from the Customer List sheet. (The address should appear in cells F5 and F6.)

FIGURE 16-10

Invoice

Cust #: (see Customer List)	**Invoice #:** 20461
	Date: (Current date)
Customer: Electronic Discount	**Address:** (see Customer List)

Product	Inventory #	Quantity	Unit Price	Total
Cellular Phone		12		0
Copier	(see Product List)	1	(see Product List)	0
				0
				0
				0
				0
				0
				0
				0
				0
				0
				0
				0
				0
		Total		0
		Tax		0
		Shipping		95.00
		Amount Due		95.00

Page 1

Lesson Applications:
Provide independent practice for students and may be used for assessment. Objectives are indicated for each Exercise.

○ **Exercise 16-17:**
Objectives 1, 3, 5
Required Files: Invoice3.xls
Solution Files: gl16-17.xls in Solutions Manual or on Solutions Disk.

5. Complete the order information by keying data from Figure 16-10 and copying data from the Product List sheet. Format the date as 3/14/98.

6. Close the second window and maximize the remaining one.

7. In cell F12, convert the formula to an IF statement that displays a blank if there is no product in B12. Otherwise, it computes the total (the existing formula). Copy this from F12 to F13 through F25 and format only the numbers in this column in Comma style with two decimal places.

8. Check the formulas to verify "Amount Due."

9. Turn off grids for viewing and check all formatting including the borders.

10. Select the Invoice and Product List sheets. Center both horizontally on the page and add the standard header to both worksheets.

11. Save the workbook as *[your initials]***16-17.xls** in your Lesson 16 folder.

12. Select the Invoice and the Product List sheets, if necessary, and print them.

13. Create a formula printout for the Invoice worksheet with grids and row and column headings. Adjust column width so the printout fits on one page.

14. Close the workbook without saving it.

EXERCISE 16-18

Open multiple workbooks, arrange windows, save a workspace file, switch between windows, copy and paste data between workbooks, maximize a window, and delete blank worksheets.

Complete a worksheet that totals product sales by copying data from several workbooks.

1. Open the following files: **Allcity.xls**, **Automatn.xls**, **Totprods.xls**, and **Westcott.xls**.

2. Tile the windows.

3. Save a workspace file named *[your initials]***16-18.xlw** in your Lesson 16 folder and close all workbooks. (If prompted, do not save changes to the files.)

4. Open the workspace file and copy the quantities from the three invoice worksheets to the appropriate cells in the Totprods.xls workbook. For instance, copy cells D13 and D14 in Allcity.xls to cells B4 and B5 in Totprods.xls.

5. Maximize the Totprods.xls window.

● Exercise 16-18:

Objectives 1–5
Required Files: Allcity.xls, Automatn.xls, Totprods.xls, Westcott.xls
Solution Files: gl16-18.xls, gl16-18.xlw in Solutions Manual or on Solutions Disk.

6. Use the AutoSum button ⟨Σ⟩ in cells E4 through E7 to sum the data in the four columns to the left of each cell. Center-align the totals.

7. Key **Total** in cell A9 and format it as bold and right-aligned.

8. Use the AutoSum button ⟨Σ⟩ to create city totals and a grand total in the Total row. Center-align these amounts.

9. Format cells B4 through E9 as 12-point type.

10. Add the standard header to the worksheet and delete the two blank worksheets in the workbook.

11. Save the workbook as *[your initials]***16-18.xls** in your Lesson 16 folder and print the worksheet.

12. Create a formula printout in landscape orientation with grids and row and column headings, and adjust column width so the printout fits on one page, if necessary.

13. Close all workbooks without saving them.

EXERCISE 16-19

Open multiple workbooks, arrange workbook windows, switch between open workbooks, copy data from one workbook to another, and delete blank worksheets.

  Feestone Electronics does not think that its analysis of total products is as useful as it could be. Create a worksheet that lists not only the quantity of each product, but also the total sales for each product.

1. Open the files **Totprod2.xls** and **Products.xls**.

2. In Totprod2.xls, copy the three rows that are below "Cell phones" and insert them below each of the other products. Each product should be followed by a blank row, a "Quantity" row, and a "Total Dollars" row.

3. Move the quantities to the correct rows.

4. Copy the unit prices from Products.xls to the first cell directly below each product name (like cell A5) in Totprod2.xls.

 TIP: Arrange windows vertically, and freeze panes in Products.xls to display column A beside column E, if necessary.

5. Format the cells containing the unit prices in Totprod2.xls as 12-point type in currency style, keeping the two decimals and applying a "$." Use the Format Cells dialog box.

⊙ **Exercise 16-19:**
Objectives 1–3, 5
Required Files: Totprod2.xls, Products.xls
Solution Files: gl16-19.xls in Solutions Manual or on
Solutions Disk.

The completed document for this Exercise may be used in a student's portfolio.

6. Maximize the Totprod2.xls window and in the "Total Dollars" rows, enter formulas to multiply the quantity of each product by its unit price.

 TIP: Use an absolute or mixed reference for the unit price.

7. Format the "Total Dollars" rows in comma style keeping the two decimals.

8. Total the values in the "Total Dollars" rows using the AutoSum function in the appropriate cells in column E.

9. Check the formula in cell E21 and edit it to sum only the dollar values in column E.

10. Format cell E21 in Currency style keeping the two decimals and add a box border. (Use the Format Cells dialog box.)

11. Create the standard header in the worksheet and delete the two blank worksheets in the workbook.

12. Save the workbook as *[your initials]***16-19.xls** in your Lesson 16 folder and print the worksheet.

13. Create a formula printout in landscape orientation with grids and row and column headings, and adjust column width so the printout fits on one page, if necessary.

14. Close all workbooks without saving them.

EXERCISE 16-20 *Challenge Yourself*

Insert a new worksheet, rename a worksheet, open a new workbook, switch between open workbooks, copy and paste data between workbooks, and delete a blank worksheet.

  In December, Feestone Electronics hires extra sales staff to help meet the increased demand for its products. The payroll for the temporary staff has to be entered and calculated separately.

1. Create a sketch of a worksheet to compute the wages due for the temporary staff. Include last names and first names in separate columns, number of hours worked, wages due, and total temporary staff wages and hours. Create an effective worksheet title and use F for formulas. You implement this worksheet later in the exercise.

2. Open the file **Emplist2.xls**.

3. Insert a new worksheet to the left of the Northeast worksheet.

◉ **Exercise 16-20:**
Objectives 1–3, 5
Required Files: Emplist2.xls
Solution Files: gl16-20a.xls, gl16-20b.xls in Solutions
Manual or on Solutions Disk.

 The completed document for this Exercise may be used in a student's portfolio.

4. Copy the worksheet title and column heads from one of the other sheets to the new worksheet. Resize the columns and rows in the new worksheet to be the same size as in the other worksheets.

5. Edit the title in row 2 to **December Temporary Sales Staff**

6. Enter the names and ID numbers shown in Figure 16-11 into the new worksheet. Use the same format as the names in the other worksheets in the workbook.

FIGURE 16-11

Last Name	First Name	Employee ID Number
Adams	Julia	90123
Bronfman	Harvey	90124
Castleman	Leonard	90125
Daly	Maureen	90126
Johns	Lisa	90127
Franks	Waldo	90128
Meth	Zena	90129
O'Reilly	Megan	90130
Petersen	Irene	90131
Wagner	Charlotte	90132

7. Rename the worksheet tab **Temp Staff**, center the worksheet horizontally on the page, and add the standard header to the worksheet.

8. Save this file as *[your initials]***16-20a.xls** in your Lesson 16 folder.

9. Open a new workbook and transfer your worksheet plan into the workbook. Format the title and labels attractively and increase column widths if necessary.

10. List each temporary staff member's last name, first name, number of hours worked, and wages due. All temporary staff are paid $10.50 per hour. Everyone except Maureen Daly and Waldo Franks worked 82 hours. Maureen Daly and Waldo Franks each worked 105 hours.

11. Calculate the wages due for each individual and format the numbers in comma style with two decimals.

12. Calculate the total wages and hours for the temporary staff.

13. Create a standard header and center the worksheet horizontally on the page.

14. Turn off grids for viewing, format the entire worksheet attractively, including text or number alignment, and name the worksheet Temp Wages.

15. Create user documentation for the worksheet that includes the following: File Information (Created by, Date created, Date revised, Revised by, Contact for help); Purpose of spreadsheet (paragraph form); and Instructions to User (special instructions needed by user to enter data correctly). Format the documentation attractively and change column widths as needed. Spell-check your work.

16. Name the worksheet User Information and create a standard header.

17. Delete the blank worksheet and save this workbook as *[your initials]*16-20b.xls in your Lesson 16 folder.

18. Print the Temp Staff worksheet in *[your initials]*16-20a.xls and the *[your initials]*16-20b.xls workbook.

19. Create a formula printout of Temp Wages in landscape orientation with grids and row and column headings.

20. Close both workbooks without saving them. Submit the plan, worksheets, and the formula printout.

Consolidating Worksheets and Exchanging Data

OBJECTIVES

After completing this lesson, you will be able to:

1. **Link multiple files through formulas.**
2. **Design worksheets for consolidation.**
3. **Create the consolidated worksheet.**

**MOUS
ACTIVITIES**
In this lesson:
XL2000 **5.10**

See Appendix F.

Estimated Time: 1¼ hours

I**n Excel, you can link worksheets and workbooks so changes in one place are reflected in another place automatically. You can also create a consolidated worksheet—one that automatically summarizes data from other sources.**

✓ Objective 1

Linking Multiple Files through Formulas

You can include ranges from other worksheets or workbooks in a formula. References to such cells are called *dynamic links* (or "hot links"). Excel keeps track of the references for you. An *external reference* points to a different workbook. An *internal reference* points to a different worksheet within the same workbook.

A *dependent worksheet* uses data from another worksheet, known as the *source worksheet*. Once a link is established, a source workbook does not have to be open.

External references begin with the filename (workbook) in brackets([ ]). The worksheet within the workbook follows the filename. This is followed by

---

PREPARE

Point out to students that the learning objectives show what they will learn in the lesson. Each heading in the lesson correlates to a learning objective.

Required Files
Average.xls Invoices.xls Secndqtr.xls

TEACH

Teaching Resources:
• Excel Classroom Presentations
• School-to-Work Strategies Manual
• Spanish Glossary
• Certification Procedures

✓ **Objective 1 Assignment:**
Exercise 15-7 (Skills Review) and Exercises 15-11 and 15-13 (Lesson Applications) can be assigned after completing Objective 1.

an exclamation point and the cell reference within the worksheet. An external reference has the following form:

[External filename]Worksheet name!Absolute cell reference

Example: [Invoices.xls]Automation!$A$1

 NOTE: The cell reference for an external reference is absolute.

Internal references begin with the worksheet name in single quotation marks. (An exclamation point separates the worksheet name from the cell reference in both the external and internal references). An internal reference has the following form:

'Internal worksheet name'!Cell reference

Example: 'Automation'!A1

EXERCISE 17-1 Use Paste Link

Feestone Electronics wants an invoice analysis that shows the average unit price for each invoice. To perform this analysis, you must first link the customer names from the "Invoices" workbook to the "Average" workbook.

1. Open the files **Average.xls** and **Invoices.xls** and arrange them horizontally.

2. In Invoices.xls, select cell C5 in the Automation worksheet and click the Copy button .

TIP: To select a cell in another window quickly, double-click it. The first click activates the window and the second click selects the cell.

3. In Average.xls, select cell A4. Choose Paste Special from the Edit menu. The Paste Special dialog box appears.

4. Click the Paste Link button. The formula bar displays the external reference to cell C5 in the Automation worksheet of Invoices.xls. (See Figure 17-1 on the next page.)

5. Press Esc to remove the moving border that surrounds cell C5.

6. In Invoices.xls, key **Westcott** in cell C5 and press Enter. Cell A4 in Average.xls is updated automatically.

7. Click the AllCity worksheet tab and copy the contents of cell C5 to the Clipboard.

FIGURE 17-1
Linking data
between
worksheets

Source worksheet

Linked data

Dependent
worksheet

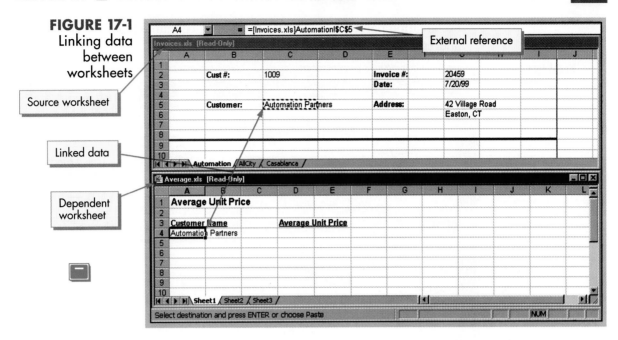

8. In Average.xls, select cell A5, choose Paste Special from the Edit menu, and click Paste Link. The contents of cell C5 in the AllCity worksheet are linked to the Average.xls workbook. Press Esc to remove the moving border.

9. Paste Link the contents of cell C5 in the Casablanca worksheet in the Invoices.xls workbook to cell A6 in the Average.xls workbook.

TIP: You can also right-click the target cell and choose Paste Special from the shortcut menu.

EXERCISE 17-2 Create a Link with Formulas

A dynamic link can refer to a single label or to a range of cells within a formula. In this exercise, you average the unit prices for each invoice and then average the invoice totals.

1. Make the Automation worksheet active in the Invoices.xls workbook.

2. In Average.xls, key **=average(** in cell D4.

3. In the Automation worksheet in the Invoices.xls workbook, select cells F13 through F15 and press Enter. Cell D4 is updated with the average unit price from the Automation invoice. Make cell D4 active. Notice that the formula contains brackets that identify the workbook name and an

Use Excel Classroom Presentation 17 to display
screens from this lesson in a slide-show format.

exclamation point that separates the worksheet name from the range address.

FIGURE 17-2
Linking worksheets
with an external
reference formula

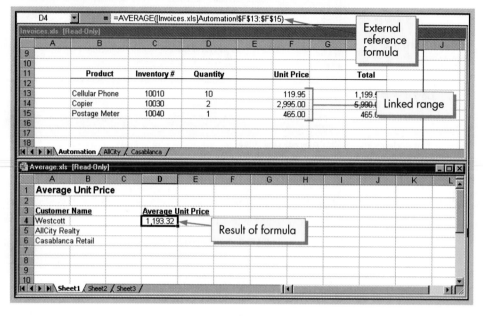

4. In Average.xls, key **=average(** in cell D5.

5. In Invoices.xls in the AllCity worksheet, select cells F13 through F14 and press Enter. Notice that the Automation worksheet becomes active again in the Invoice.xls workbook.

> **NOTE:** The worksheet that is active in the source workbook when you key the initial part of the formula becomes active again after the source cells are entered.

6. In Average.xls, use the same steps to enter the following formula in cell D6: **=AVERAGE([Invoices.xls]Casablanca!$F$13:$F$15)**

7. In Average.xls, key **Average Invoice** in cell A8. Make the text bold.

8. In Invoices.xls, open a second and third window of the workbook (choose New Window from the Window menu twice).

9. Choose Arrange from the Window menu, select the Tiled option, and click OK. The three windows containing Invoices.xls and the window containing Average.xls appear tiled on the screen.

10. In the "Invoices.xls:1" window, click the Automation tab if necessary, and scroll until you can see cell H29.

> **TIP:** To move to another worksheet, use the worksheet tab scroll buttons at the bottom left corner of the worksheet. You can also choose a worksheet from the shortcut menu by right-clicking a worksheet tab scroll button.

 In Excel Classroom Presentation 17.

11. In the "Invoices.xls:2" window, click the AllCity tab and scroll until you see cell H29.

12. In the "Invoices.xls:3" window, scroll until you see cell H29 of the Casablanca worksheet.

13. In Average.xls, key **=average(** in cell D8.

14. Double-click cell H29 in the Automation worksheet.

15. Key a comma in the formula and double-click cell H29 in the AllCity worksheet.

16. Key a comma, double-click cell H29 in the Casablanca worksheet, and press [Enter]. The formula with references to three different worksheets is complete. Change the format of this average to comma style and keep the two decimals. The result is 9,755.49.

17. Maximize the window of the Average.xls workbook. The finished Invoice Analysis contains four formulas with external references.

18. Remove any blank columns, resize other columns to fit data, make the worksheet attractive, and press [Ctrl]+[Home].

19. Create the standard header in the worksheet and delete the two blank worksheets.

20. Save the Average.xls workbook as *[your initials]***17-2.xls** in a new folder for Lesson 17 and print the worksheet.

21. Create a formula printout in landscape orientation with grids and row and column headings. Widen and reduce columns to see all the long formulas.

22. Close all workbooks. Do not save changes to Invoices.xls.

🗹 Objective 2

Designing Worksheets for Consolidation

You can design workbooks so different people working with different worksheets record data in the same way. The worksheets can then be consolidated as long as either:

- Common data items appear in the same positions.
- Worksheets have common row or column labels.

EXERCISE 17-3 Copy a Base Form with Fill Across Worksheets

In general, a source worksheet and a consolidated worksheet should resemble one another. You can use the Fill, <u>A</u>cross Worksheets command from the <u>E</u>dit menu to keep content and formats consistent.

---

1 Some answer files in this lesson contain dynamic links and depend on source files. You can use them—as they are—to check student work. To update links in these files, put their source files in the same folder.

2 The answer file gl17-2 depends on Invoices.xls, which was not saved after students updated it. If you update links upon opening the Solution file, some data may change.

🗹 **Objective 2 Assignment:**
Exercise 17-8 (Skills Review) can be assigned after completing Objective 2.

1. Open the file **Secndqtr.xls**.

2. Rename sheets 2, 3, 4, and 5 **Northwest**, **Southeast**, **Southwest**, and **Consolidated Report**, respectively.

3. Group all five sheets. (*Hint:* Activate the first sheet and ⟨Shift⟩+click the last sheet tab.)

4. Select cells A1:E12 on the Northeast sheet.

5. Choose Fill from the Edit menu and choose Across Worksheets from the submenu. The Fill Across Worksheets dialog box appears.

FIGURE 17-3
Fill Across
Worksheets
dialog box

6. Make sure the All option button is selected and click OK.

NOTE: The All button copies the contents and formatting to the cells in the destination worksheet, while the Contents button copies only the contents of selected cells and the Formats button, only the formatting.

7. Examine the worksheets to review the copied material. (Note that you can fill across any number of worksheets. For instance, if the regional worksheets were already prepared, you could fill across the Southwest and Consolidated worksheet and get the same results.)

8. Group the last four worksheets and widen column A to fit the labels. You only need to widen the column on one worksheet and all the worksheets are adjusted.

9. Format all five sheets to print centered horizontally. (Group all five worksheets to do this.)

10. Ungroup the sheets.

11. Change the title in cell A1 in the Northwest sheet to **Northwest Region** and change the name in cell A3 to **Adrian Needlehoffen**. The copied sheets still have the same data as the Northeast sheet.

12. Change the title in the Southeast sheet to **Southeast Region** and the name to **John Frisbee**.

13. Change the title in the Southwest sheet to **Southwest Region** and the name to **Jamaica Martin**.

14. Change the title in the Consolidated Report sheet to **Consolidated Report** and delete the name Holly Maplethorpe.

Creating the Consolidated Worksheet

Objective 3

A *consolidation table* summarizes the data from one or more source ranges. Placing your table in a separate worksheet—a *consolidated worksheet*—makes it easy to find. Source ranges can be on the same worksheet as the consolidation table or in different workbooks. You can also create dynamic links to ranges or cells in different worksheets or workbooks. When you consolidate the source data, you apply a summary function, such as Sum, to create the summary data.

NOTE: You can consolidate data only when common data items appear in identical positions or the worksheets have common row or column labels.

EXERCISE 17-4 Consolidate Data Using Labels

In the last Exercise, you created four regional worksheets and one worksheet for consolidating the regions. Because the row labels are all identical, you can use these worksheets to create the consolidation table. The area for the consolidation table, however, must be blank.

1. Delete the row labels and data in the Consolidated Report worksheet. (Select cells A7 through E12 and press Delete to clear the cells.)

2. Leave the cells highlighted and choose Consolidate from the Data menu. The Consolidate dialog box appears with Sum as the default function for the Consolidate command.

3. Drag the Consolidate dialog box out of the way (to the top right of the screen).

4. With the insertion point in the Reference text box, click the Northeast tab and select the row labels and the data (cells A7 to E12). Notice that the dialog box minimizes while items are selected so you can see what you are selecting.

5. Click Add in the dialog box. The absolute reference Northeast!$A$7:$E$12 is added to the All References text box. (See Figure 17-4 on the next page.)

6. Add the same range for the Northwest, Southeast, and Southwest worksheets. Excel assumes you want to select the same range as in the Northeast worksheet and surrounds it with a moving border, so all you have to do is go to the various worksheets and click Add.

7. Check the Left Column box in the Consolidate dialog box under Use Labels In and click OK. Excel consolidates the data. The Consolidate command correctly incorporated labels and data.

Objective 3 Assignment:
Exercises 17-9 and 17-10 (Skills Review) and Exercises 17-12 and 17-14 (Lesson Applications) can be assigned after completing Objective 3.

Although this Exercise uses SUM (the default function), students may see other consolidation functions in the Function drop-down list.

FIGURE 17-4
Consolidate
dialog box

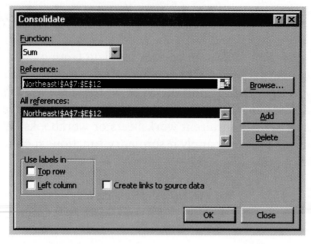

8. Click B7 in the Consolidated Report worksheet and notice that by default Excel places values—not formulas—in the consolidation table. (See data in row 12 and column E.)

> **NOTE:** The data in the consolidation table is not dynamically linked to the other worksheets. Therefore, if you change the value in cell B7 in the Northeast worksheet, the consolidation table is not updated. In the next exercise, you create dynamic links.

EXERCISE 17-5 Consolidate Data by Position and Create Dynamic Links

Because the data elements in each worksheet appear in identical locations, you can also consolidate by position. You don't have to select labels, which allows you to protect those labels later. You can also create dynamic links in the consolidation table so if you change data in one worksheet, the consolidation table is updated. The consolidation range must be blank to begin with, as before.

1. In the Consolidated Report worksheet, select cells B7 through E12. Press Delete to clear the consolidation range.

2. With the cells still highlighted, choose Consolidate from the Data menu.

3. To define a new consolidation, select each of the previous cell references in the All References text box and click Delete.

> **NOTE:** The Consolidate command uses previously defined references, so you must delete old references if your ranges change.

4. Click the Reference text box so you can select a range in a worksheet.

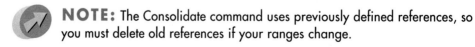

In Excel Classroom Presentation 17.

Point out that the data in the consolidation table is not dynamically linked to the other worksheets, so if data is changed in one worksheet, the consolidation table stays the same.

5. Click the Northeast tab, select cells B7 through E12, and click <u>A</u>dd in the Consolidate dialog box.

6. Add the same range for the Northwest, Southeast, and Southwest worksheets.

7. Clear the <u>L</u>eft Column check box, if necessary, and click Create Links To Source Data. Click OK. The data from the four source worksheets are summed in the destination range of the Consolidated Report worksheet.

8. Select cell B11 in the Consolidated Report sheet. When Create Links To Source Data is selected, Excel places formulas in the consolidation table. Excel also creates an outline when data is consolidated and linked to its source. Notice the Outline buttons ⊞ and ⊟ to the left of the row headings. Also notice that the row numbers have changed.

FIGURE 17-5
Consolidated data

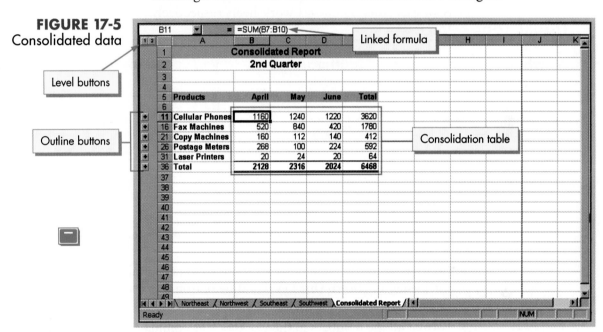

9. Click the first Outline button ⊞. Excel moves down one level and shows the makeup of the consolidated cell.

TIP: You can also click the Level 2 button ② above the Outline buttons to go to the second level of the outline. To return to the first level, click the Level 1 button ①.

10. Click cell B7 and notice that the linked address appears in the formula bar.

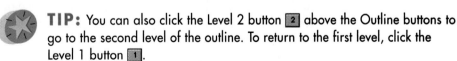

11. Click the Outline button ⊟ to move up one level. Click other Outline buttons (both ⊞ and ⊟) to see other cell makeups and linked addresses. Return to the first level for all rows when you finish.

⌐ If students consolidate with dynamic links and
the consolidation is wrong they can simply delete
the sheet and start over.

⊟ In Excel Classroom Presentation 17.

NOTE: When you create a dynamic link in a consolidation table, none of the cells you select in the various worksheets from which you are consolidating can be empty. (They can, however, contain zeros.) Ranges with empty cells are not included in the link.

EXERCISE 17-6 Update Source Data

When your source data changes, the consolidation table is updated because it is dynamically linked.

1. Key the data shown in Figure 17-6 in cells B7 to D11 of the Northwest, Southeast, and Southwest worksheets respectively.

FIGURE 17-6

Northwest		
240	300	250
140	240	300
260	160	180
340	240	250
15	20	10

Southeast		
200	300	400
210	320	450
320	450	500
180	290	390
10	20	15

Southwest		
150	250	350
400	200	300
150	250	350
250	350	400
5	10	20

2. Go to the Consolidation table and notice the new totals. Move down one level using the Down One Level outline button ⊞ to see the data that was updated. Return to the first level.

3. Format all the numbers in the workbook as comma style with no decimals. In case you group the worksheets to do this, be sure to check the numbers in the consolidation worksheet and format all the numbers there in this style.

4. Add the standard header to all worksheets. (You can group the worksheets, open Page Setup, and add the standard header. Remember to ungroup the worksheets.)

5. Save the workbook as *[your initials]*17-6.xls in your Lesson 17 folder and print the entire workbook.

6. Create a formula printout of each worksheet in landscape orientation with grids and row and column headings. You can group the worksheets and format them for the formula printouts.

7. Close the workbook without saving it.

NOTE: If you want to add, delete, or change references to data in a consolidation table that has source links, you must delete the table and outline, then reconsolidate, or you can simply delete the sheet and start over. See "Using Help" to learn more about this.

USING HELP

Once you create a consolidation table, you may need to add, delete, or change references to the data in it. The way you do this depends on whether or not the table has source links in it.

Use Help to find out more about changing data in a consolidation table:

1. Activate the Office Assistant.
2. Key **consolidation** under "What would you like to do?" and click <u>S</u>earch.
3. Click the topic "Change a data consolidation." The Microsoft Excel Help dialog box opens.

FIGURE 17-7
Help about
changing a data
consolidation

4. Go through the topics on adding, changing, deleting, and updating data. After you review each topic, click the Back button to return to the "Change a data consolidation" window.
5. Close Help when you finish and hide the Office Assistant.

Encourage students to follow the steps in "Using Help." Software companies are increasingly using their Help programs—rather than documentation—to train users and assist in answering user questions.

In Excel Classroom Presentation 17.

TEST BANK

Concepts Review

Each of the following statements is either true or false. Indicate your choice by circling **T** or **F**.

(T) F   **1.** When cells are linked, changing the value in the source cell causes the value in the dependent cell to change as well.

T (F)   **2.** You can only link dependent worksheets to other worksheets or workbooks that are currently open.

T (F)   **3.** You can only link individual cells; you cannot link cell ranges.

(T) F   **4.** You must clear the cells in a consolidation table before consolidating data.

(T) F   **5.** If you plan to consolidate worksheets, it's a good idea to plan them so common data items appear in identical locations.

T (F)   **6.** If data elements do not appear in exactly the same location on each worksheet to be consolidated, you cannot use the Data Consolidate feature, even though they have the same row labels.

(T) F   **7.** Dynamic links are references to cells in other worksheets or workbooks.

T (F)   **8.** An internal reference points to different worksheets in other files.

Write the correct answer in the space provided.

1. When cells in another workbook are referenced, what are the references called?

External references

2. In an external reference, which symbol separates the name of a worksheet from the referenced cell or cell range?

Exclamation point

3. Which command duplicates a format to several worksheets?

Fill, Across Worksheets command

CLOSE

Concepts Review:
Allows students to check their understanding.

TEST BANK
Consider using the Test Bank to provide an additional review of lesson concepts. It may also be used as an assessment tool.

4. When values from related worksheets within a workbook are consolidated in a summary worksheet, what is the summary worksheet called?

Consolidated worksheet or dependent worksheet

5. When common data items in a source worksheet do not appear in the same position as in the consolidated worksheet, how does Excel consolidate?

Using row or column labels

6. Internal references begin with the worksheet name surrounded by what characters?

Single quotation marks

7. What is a worksheet called that contains a consolidation table?

Consolidated worksheet

8. What summarizes data from one or more source ranges?

Consolidation table

CRITICAL THINKING

Answer these questions on a separate piece of paper. There are no right or wrong answers. Support your answer with examples from your own experience, if possible.

1. Would linking values be the best choice when creating a quarterly or annual report? Why or why not?

2. In what types of situations might you need to consolidate data from different workbooks?

Skills Review

EXERCISE 17-7

Link multiple files.

1. Open the files **Invoices.xls** and **Totdollr.xls** and arrange the workbooks horizontally.

2. Link the number of units of cellular phones sold on the three invoices in Invoices.xls to the Totdollr.xls workbook by following these steps:

   a. Scroll Totdollr.xls until you can see rows 4 through 7, if necessary.

Critical Thinking Questions:
Answers will vary based on students' preferences, observations, experiences, and research.

Skills Review:
Provides guided practice for students. Objectives are indicated for each Exercise.

◉ **Exercise 17-7:**
Objective 1
Required File: Invoices.xls, Totdollr.xls
Solution Files: gl17-7.xls in Solutions Manual or on Solutions Disk.

  b. Click cell D4 and click the AutoSum button Σ.

  c. Click cell D13 in the Automation worksheet in the Invoices.xls workbook and key a comma.

  d. Click the AllCity tab, click cell D14, and key a comma.

  e. Click the Casablanca tab, click cell D13, and press Enter.

3. Link the number of units of fax machines sold by following these steps:

  a. Activate cell D5 in Totdollr.xls, if necessary, and click the AutoSum button Σ.

  b. Click cell D13 in the AllCity sheet in Invoices.xls and key a comma.

  c. Click cell D14 in the Casablanca sheet and press Enter.

4. Link the number of copiers sold in cell D6 in Totdollr.xls just as you did in step 3.

5. Link the number of postage meters sold by following these steps:

  a. Click cell D15 in the Automation worksheet of Invoices.xls.

  b. Copy the cell's contents to the Clipboard.

  c. Click cell D7 in Totdollr.xls and choose Edit, Paste Special.

  d. Click Paste Link and press Esc.

6. Maximize Totdollr.xls, press Ctrl + Home, and create the standard header in the worksheet.

7. Delete unnecessary columns and resize others to accommodate column labels.

8. Delete the blank worksheets, save the Totdollr.xls workbook as *[your initials]*17-7.xls in your Lesson 17 folder.

9. Print the worksheet and create a formula printout in landscape orientation with grids and row and column headings. Adjust column width and use a Page 1 of ? footer.

10. Close all the workbooks without saving them.

EXERCISE 17-8

Copy a base form, style worksheets, and copy formulas across worksheets.

1. Open the file **Regnpay.xls**.

2. Add a fourth worksheet after the first one and rename the sheets **NE**, **NW**, **SE**, and **SW**, respectively.

3. Copy the base form on the NE sheet to the other worksheets by following these steps:

  a. Activate the NE worksheet and copy the cell range A1:F7 to the Clipboard.

  b. Click the NW tab, press and hold down Shift, and click the SW tab.

◉ Exercise 17-8:
Objective 2
Required Files: Regnpay.xls
Solution Files: gl17-8.xls in Solutions Manual or on
Solutions Disk.

    c. Activate cell A1 in the NW tab, if necessary, and paste the contents of the Clipboard to this location. Press **Esc** to clear the copied source cells in the NE worksheet.

    d. Adjust columns A and B to accommodate about 15 characters. Adjust columns C, D, and E to accommodate about 10 characters.

    e. Right-click the NW tab and choose Ungroup Sheets from the shortcut menu.

4. Change the title in cell A1 of the NW tab to **Northwest Region**

5. Change the titles in cell A1 of the SE and SW worksheets.

6. Edit the style of the worksheets by following these steps:

    a. Click the NE tab, press and hold down **Shift**, and click the SW tab.

    b. Turn off gridlines for viewing.

    c. Center the titles in cells A1 and A2 across columns A through F.

    d. Add light shading to the titles in cells A1 through F7.

    e. Make the labels in cells A6 through F7 bold and add a border below row 7.

    f. Format cells F8 through F12 in comma style with two decimal places.

    g. Set the worksheets to print centered horizontally on the page.

    h. Create the standard header in all worksheets.

7. Copy formulas across the worksheets by following these steps:

    a. With all four worksheets selected, select cells F8 through F12 in the Northeast worksheet.

    b. Choose Fill from the Edit menu and choose Across Worksheets from the submenu.

    c. Make sure the All option button is selected and click OK.

    d. Right-click the Northeast tab and choose Ungroup Sheets from the shortcut menu. Check that formulas were copied to each worksheet. (Select individual cells in each worksheet and look at the formulas in the formula bar.)

8. Save the workbook as *[your initials]***17-8.xls** in your Lesson 17 folder and print the entire workbook.

9. Create formula printouts of each worksheet in landscape orientation with grids and row and column headings. AutoFit all columns.

10. Close the workbook without saving it.

EXERCISE 17-9

Fill data across worksheets and consolidate data by location.

1. Open the workbook **Dllrsals.xls**.

2. Rename Sheet5 **Consolidated Report**

⊙ Exercise 17-9:
Objectives 2, 3
Required Files: Dllrsals.xls
Solution Files: gl17-9xls in Solutions Manual or on Solutions Disk.

3. Copy labels to the Consolidated Report worksheet by following these steps:

   a. Click the Southwest tab, press and hold down Shift, and click the Consolidated Report tab.

   b. Select cells A1 through E1 in the Southwest worksheet.

   c. Choose Fill from the Edit menu and choose Across Worksheets from the submenu.

   d. Click the Formats option button to copy only the formats in these cells and click OK.

   e. Select cells A2 through E7 and choose Edit, Fill, Across Worksheets. Click the All option button and click OK.

   f. Select cells A8 through A12 and fill across worksheets. Click the All option and click OK, if necessary.

   g. Right-click the Consolidated Report tab and choose Ungroup Sheets from the shortcut menu.

   h. Key **Feestone Electronics** in cell A1 in the consolidated report.

4. Consolidate data by position by following these steps:

   a. In the Consolidated Report worksheet, select cells B8 through E12.

   b. Choose Consolidate from the Data menu. Move the Consolidate dialog box to the upper right, if necessary.

   c. Click the Northeast tab, select cells B8 through E12, and click Add in the Consolidate dialog box.

   d. Repeat the previous step for the Northwest, Southeast, and Southwest worksheets and click OK.

   e. Resize columns A through E to accommodate the data.

5. Format the consolidated worksheet by following these steps:

   a. Turn off grids for viewing and add a single line border to the bottom of cells B11 through E11.

   b. Add a double border below cells B12 through E12 and format the totals in these cells in bold.

   c. Delete the title in cell A3.

6. Add the standard header to all the worksheets and format all worksheets to print centered horizontally on the page.

7. Save the workbook as *[your initials]***17-9.xls** in your Lesson 17 folder and print the Consolidated Report worksheet.

8. Close the workbook.

EXERCISE 17-10

Fill data across worksheets, consolidate data by labels and position, dynamically link data, and use the outline feature.

1. Open the file **Dllrsal2.xls**. (These worksheets were designed for consolidation.)

◉ Exercise 17-10:
Objectives 2, 3
Required Files: Dllrsal2.xls
Solution Files: gl17-10.xls in Solutions Manual or on Solutions Disk.

2. Group the worksheets, turn off grids for viewing, and edit the formatting. Add shading and borders and other formatting to enhance their appearance. Make all values Comma Style with two decimals.

3. Ungroup the worksheets.

4. Insert a worksheet in front of the SW worksheet.

5. Move the new worksheet after the SW worksheet and rename it **Consolidated**

6. Copy the worksheet data to the Consolidated worksheet:
   a. Group the SW and Consolidated worksheets.
   b. Select cells A1:E11 in the SW worksheet.
   c. Choose Fill from the Edit menu and choose Across Worksheets.
   d. Make sure All is selected and click OK.

7. Ungroup the worksheets and edit the title to read **Consolidated Report** in the Consolidated worksheet.

8. In the same worksheet, delete the contents of A3 and adjust the columns to fit the data.

9. Consolidate the data based on labels:
   a. Clear the cells containing data you will consolidate (A7:E11).
   b. With these cells selected, choose Consolidate from the Data menu.
   c. Click the NE tab and select cells A7:E11.
   d. Click Add and add the same cell addresses from the other three regional worksheets.
   e. Select Left column and click OK.
   f. Widen the columns to accommodate data, if necessary.

10. Consolidate the data based on position:
    a. Clear the cells containing data you will consolidate on the consolidation report (B7:E11).
    b. With these cells selected, choose Consolidate from the Data menu.
    c. Delete the references from the previous consolidation and place the cursor in the Reference text box.
    d. Click the NE tab and select cells B7:E11.
    e. Click Add and add the same cell addresses from the other three regional worksheets.
    f. Clear the Left column check box and select Create Links To Source Data and click OK.

11. Resize any columns that need it.

12. Use the Down One Level outline buttons ⊞ to go to the second level of the outline, take a look at the cells that make up the totals, and then go back up to the first level.

13. Add the standard header to every worksheet and make sure they are set up to print centered horizontally on the page.

14. Save the workbook as *[your initials]***17-10.xls** in your Lesson 17 folder and print the entire workbook.

15. Create a formula printout of the Consolidated Report in landscape orientation with grids and row and column headings. AutoFit all the columns and make sure the formulas print completely.

16. Close the workbook without saving it.

A S S E S S

Assessment Resources:
● Solutions Manual
● Test Bank
● Portfolio Builder
● Internet Projects
● Alternative Assessment Guide
● Certification Procedures

For Internet projects, go to
www.glencoe.com/webprojects

Lesson Applications

EXERCISE 17-11

Paste Link values from one workbook to another.

Feestone Electronics does not think the analysis of average unit price is as useful as it might be. Create a worksheet that calculates averages that include not only the average unit price for each invoice, but also the average quantity ordered for each item.

1. Open the file **Average2.xls.** Click Yes to re-establish the links. If necessary, use the File Not Found dialog box to locate the file, **Invoices.xls**.

2. Make the changes indicated in Figure 17-8. Leave column B blank. "Cellular Phones" should appear in column C, "Fax Machines" in column D, "Copiers" in column E, "Postage Meters" in column F, and "Average Unit Price" appears in column G.

FIGURE 17-8

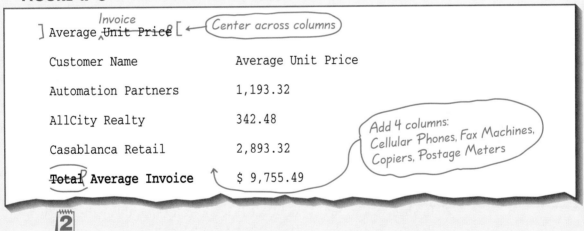

3. Format the headings in columns C through G as bold, centered with no underlines, and aligned to wrap text. Give columns B through G a width of "10."

4. Open the file **Invoices.xls**, arrange the windows horizontally, and display the Automation sheet in the Invoices.xls window.

5. Paste Link the quantity ordered of each item from column D in each invoice in the Invoices.xls workbook to columns C, D, E, and F,

---

Lesson Applications:
Provide independent practice for students and may be used for assessment. Objectives are indicated for each Exercise.

Exercise 17-11:
Objectives 1
Required Files: Average2.xls, Invoices.xls
Solution Files gl17-11.xls in Solutions Manual or on Solutions Disk.

The file Average2.xls is linked to Invoices.xls. To reestablish those links, students must find that file.

This figure contains proofreading marks. You may want to review Appendix E: "Proofreaders' Marks" with students.

respectively, in the Average Invoice worksheet. If an item was not ordered, key **0** in the cell in the Average Invoice worksheet.

6. Maximize the Average2.xls window. Make sure all quantities are right-aligned.

7. Calculate the total average quantity ordered of each item.

8. Delete the blank column B and recenter the worksheet title across the columns with data. (*Hint:* Use the Format Cells (Alignment tab) dialog box to turn off merge text under Text Control, then recenter the title.)

9. Add the standard header. Set up the worksheet to print centered horizontally on the page.

10. Delete the blank worksheets in the workbook.

11. Save the workbook as *[your initials]***17-11.xls** in your Lesson 17 folder and print the worksheet.

12. Create a formula printout in landscape orientation with grids and row and column headings. AutoFit all the columns and left-align the title so it prints completely. Use a Page 1 of ? footer.

> **NOTE:** This worksheet contains links in column A and F to the same Invoices file. The location of the file may appear different in these cells than in the cells in which you created the new links.

13. Close all workbooks without saving them.

EXERCISE 17-12

Design worksheets for consolidation and consolidate worksheets.

Feestone Electronics needs to add unit prices and dollar-value sales revenues to its regional sales reports and to produce a consolidated report.

1. Open the file **Slsreprt.xls**.

2. In sheets 1 through 4, key **Unit Price** in cell H7 and key the following unit prices in cells H8:H11. (*Hint:* Group the sheets.)

Cellular phones	**119.95**
Fax machines	**565.00**
Copy machines	**7,995.00**
Postage meters	**465.00**

3. In all four sheets, copy the labels in cells A8:A12 to cells A17:A21. Key **Revenue** in cell A14 in bold. (It is already centered across columns.)

4. In all four sheets, calculate revenues based on unit sales and unit price. (In cell C17, enter the formula **=$H8*C8** and copy this formula through cell E20.)

● Exercise 17-12:

Objectives 2, 3
Required Files: Slsreprt.xls
Solution Files: gl17-12.xls in Solutions Manual or on Solutions Disk.

5. In all four sheets, calculate totals for the "Revenue" section (columns and rows). Make the row totals bold. Add a single line border above, and a double line border below, the total row.

6. In all four sheets, format the unit prices in comma style with two decimals and the individual product revenues and revenue totals in comma style with no decimal places.

7. AutoFit column widths. Remove column B and adjust column A.

8. Change the label in row 5 to center only across columns A through E, then rename the worksheets as follows:

Sheet1	**Northeast**
Sheet2	**Northwest**
Sheet3	**Southeast**
Sheet4	**Southwest**
Sheet5	**Consolidated Report**

9. Copy the Southwest sheet to the Consolidated Report sheet, change the title to **Consolidated Report**, and delete the regional manager's name. (*Hint:* Select the entire sheet and use F<u>i</u>ll, <u>A</u>cross Worksheets.)

10. In the Consolidated Report, delete the contents of the unit sales data (cells B8:E12) and consolidate the unit sales of the four regions by position. Link to source data.

11. Adjust column widths to accommodate data, check formulas, and add formatting to create a consistent display of comma style with no decimals under the Unit Sales sections.

12. Format all sheets to print centered horizontally on the page and add the standard header.

13. Save the workbook as *[your initials]***17-12.xls** in your Lesson 17 folder and print all worksheets.

14. Create a formula printout of each worksheet in landscape orientation with grids and row and column headings. AutoFit all columns and make sure the titles print completely. (Remove column F, if necessary, to get the formula printouts each on a single page.)

15. Close the workbook without saving it.

EXERCISE 17-13

Paste Link data from one workbook to another.

  Feestone Electronics includes current prices in its product list. Recently, the vendor prices increased and the company decided to link its product list and its vendor price list, so the product list is automatically updated.

◉ Exercise 17-13:
Objectives 1
Required Files: Prodlist.xls, Vendpric.xls
Solution Files: gl17-13.xls in Solutions Manual or on
Solutions Disk.

The complete documents for this Exercise
can be used in a student's portfolio.

1. Open the files **Prodlist.xls** and **Vendpric.xls** and arrange the workbooks vertically.

2. Clear the prices in Prodlist.xls (cells B5:B8).

3. Paste Link the vendor prices in column B of Vendpric.xls to the appropriate cells in column B of Prodlist.xls.

4. Maximize Prodlist.xls and examine the newly inserted references.

5. In case someone else needs to use the worksheet, key in cell A10 **The vendor prices are linked to the workbook Vendpric.xls.**

6. Protect the worksheet from changes. No cells should be unlocked.

7. Set the worksheet to print centered horizontally on the page, add the standard header, and delete all blank worksheets.

8. Save the Prodlist.xls workbook as *[your initials]***17-13.xls** in your Lesson 17 folder and print the worksheet.

9. Create a formula printout in landscape orientation with grids and row and column headings that fits on one page. Make sure the title prints. (You have to unprotect the sheet to manipulate data.)

10. Close all open workbooks without saving.

EXERCISE 17-14 *Challenge Yourself*

Design worksheets for consolidation and consolidate worksheets.

To decide how much inventory to keep on hand this year, Feestone Electronics is analyzing the quantity of product sold in 1997 and 1998 by quarter and on an annual basis. Construct a workbook containing a 1997 worksheet, a 1998 worksheet, and a consolidated worksheet averaging the quantity of product sold by quarter and for each year.

1. Create a sketch of the three worksheets. The labels are the four quarters and the products listed in Figure 17-9 (on the next page). You may choose to use 1997 and 1998 in the worksheet titles instead of as column labels. Remember to design these for consolidation. Include Quarterly Totals as well as Yearly Totals.

2. Open a new workbook to create the three worksheets. Create two worksheets using the data in Figure 17-9.

3. Create the consolidated worksheet with links to source data and format all three worksheets using group edit. Remember to use the Average function for consolidation. The consolidation worksheet should not contain any decimal places.

4. Rename all three sheet tabs and horizontally center all the worksheets on the page.

External cell references in the answer file depend on where you place Vendpric.xls, the source workbook for this Exercise.

Exercise 17-14:
Objectives 2, 3
Required Files: None
Solution Files: gl17-14.xls in Solutions Manual or on Solutions Disk.

 The complete documents for this Exercise can be used in a student's portfolio.

FIGURE 17-9

	Qtr 1	Qtr 2	Qtr 3	Qtr 4
1997				
Cellular Phones	2,576	2,958	3,213	3,364
Fax Machines	2,287	2,189	2,608	2,367
Copy Machines	516	539	1,004	777
Postage Meters	536	589	1,323	656
Laser Printers	0	1,418	3,828	4,719
1998				
Cellular Phones	3,439	3,426	3,429	3,948
Fax Machines	2,904	1,986	2,578	3,255
Copy Machines	679	457	895	980
Postage Meters	543	498	783	486
Laser Printers	6,457	7,896	7,498	8,302

5. Create user documentation and name the sheet tab **User Information**. The sheet should include the following: File Information (Created by, Date created, Date revised, Revised by, Contact for help); Purpose of worksheet (paragraph form); and Instructions to User (special instructions needed by user to enter data correctly). Format the documentation attractively and change column widths as necessary. Spell-check your work.

[1] 6. Create the standard header in all worksheets and save the workbook as *[your initials]*17-14.xls in your Lesson 17 folder. Print the entire workbook.

7. Create a formula printout of the consolidated report in landscape orientation with grids and row and column headings. AutoFit all columns and make sure the titles print completely.

8. Close the workbook without saving it.

[1] Answers will vary based on the formatting students choose and the setup of the individual worksheets in the workbook.

For Internet projects, go to
www.glencoe.com/webprojects

Unit 6 Applications

UNIT APPLICATION 6-1

Open multiple workbooks, arrange workbooks, and create a workspace file.
Copy and paste between workbooks. Paste link between worksheets.

Feestone Electronics currently ships products through United Express. It wants to compare the costs of three other delivery companies. Since the costs might change, Feestone needs a summary worksheet linked to each company's rate card.

1. Open the files **Crntship.xls** and **Shipanls.xls**.

2. Arrange the worksheets horizontally and save the workspace as *[your initials]*u6-1.xlw in a new folder for Unit 6.

3. Close the workbooks and open the workspace file.

4. Copy the information from Crntship.xls to a new first worksheet in Shipanls.xls. Use the same formatting and positioning used in the other three worksheets and name the worksheet **United Express**. Maximize the Shipanls.xls workbook.

5. Insert a worksheet in front of the United Express sheet, name it **Analysis**, and in cell A1 key the title **Shipping Costs Analysis** in bold.

6. Starting in row 4, key the labels in bold as shown in Figure U6-1. Center the column labels.

FIGURE U6-1

	United Express	CPS Corp.	Packages R Us	Overnight Specialists
Standard				
2-Day				
Overnight				

7. Paste Link the shipping rates from each of the four delivery companies in Shipanls.xls to the proper column in the Analysis sheet.

8. In the CPS Corp. sheet, change both the 2-day and 1-day overnight rates to **125**.

A S S E S S

Assessment Resources:
• Solutions Manual • Test Bank
• Portfolio Builder
• Alternative Assessment Guide
• Certification Procedures
• Projects Manual
• Mid-Term and Final Exams

Unit Applications:
Provide independent practice of the skills acquired from each lesson in the Unit.

Project:
You can now assign Project 6 from the Projects Manual.

Exam:
You can now assign Exam 6 from the Mid-Term and Finals booklet.

Unit Application 6-1:
Required Files: Crntship.xls, Shipanls.xls
Solution File: glu6-1.xls and glu6-1.xlw in Solutions Manual or on Solutions Disk

9. Format the values in all the worksheets as Comma Style with two decimals and right-align "N/A."

10. In all worksheets in Shipanls.xls create the standard header and center the worksheets horizontally on the page.

 TIP: Select all the sheets, then choose the Page Setup command on the File menu instead of setting up each page in Print Preview.

11. Save the Shipanls.xls workbook as *[your initials]***u6-1.xls** in your Unit 6 folder.

12. Print the Analysis, United Express, and CPS Corp. worksheets.

13. Create a formula printout of the Analysis sheet in landscape orientation with grids and row and column headings. Even though there are no formulas in the worksheets, the formula printout shows the linked cell references.

14. Close both workbooks without saving them.

UNIT APPLICATION 6-2

Copy and paste between worksheets. Link workbooks.

Employees at Feestone Electronics get paid vacation, sick, and personal time. All employees get 3 personal days and 12 sick days per year. The amount of vacation time each employee receives depends on how long the person has been employed.

- Employees who have worked at Feestone for 0 to 3 years receive 1 week (5 days) paid vacation.
- Employees who have worked at least 4 years receive 2 weeks vacation.
- Employees who have worked for the company 7 years or more receive 3 weeks per year.

You need to link the employee list and hire dates to a worksheet that calculates the time off due each employee.

1. Open the files **Slryempl.xls** and **Timeoff.xls**.

2. Paste Link the Last Name, First Name, and Date Hired data from Slryempl.xls to Timeoff.xls beginning in cell A10.

3. In Timeoff.xls, copy the formula in cell D10 down to calculate the vacation time due each employee.

◉ Unit Application 6-2:
Required Files: Slryempl.xls, Timeoff.xls
Solution: File glu6-2.xls in Solutions Manual or on
Solutions Disk

4. Key the time off already used by each employee as shown in Figure U6-2 in the Timeoff.xls workbook. Key the vacation time used in column E, the sick time used in column G, and the personal time used in column I.

FIGURE U6-2

Last Name	First Name	Vacation Time Used	Sick Time Used	Personal Time Used
Abbott	Martha	3	5	0
Frisbee	John	5	1	0
Garcia	Ramone	10	9	1
LaConte	Danielle	10	12	0
Maplethorpe	Holly	5	0	3
Martin	Jamaica	5	0	0
Needlehoffen	Adrian	2	3	0
Northridge	Leroy	7	2	2
Connor	Patrick	12	0	0
Santos	Julia	5	1	0
Tellman	Lowell	5	0	3
Underwood	Marc	1	10	0
Young	Emma	15	11	1
Zimmer	Joseph	5	0	1

5. Create and copy formulas to calculate the vacation time left, sick time left, and personal time left. Remember, sick time and personal time are the same for each employee every year.

6. Insert page breaks so the worksheet prints on three pages, one for vacation time, one for sick time, and one for personal time.

7. Set up the worksheet to print in portrait orientation, centered horizontally. Have the worksheet title, employee names, and date hired print on each worksheet.

8. Create the standard header with your name, filename, and date in Arial bold, italic. Use a Page 1 of ? footer.

9. Name the worksheet **Employee Time**.

10. Save the file as *[your initials]***u6-2.xls** in your Unit 6 folder and print all three pages.

11. Create a formula printout in landscape orientation with grids and row and column headings. AutoFit all columns, and remove manual page breaks and print titles.

12. Close all workbooks without saving them.

UNIT APPLICATION 6-3

Link data between workbooks and create linked formulas.

Feestone Electronics gives bonuses to its sales managers if they exceed their sales goals for the year. Develop a new worksheet that calculates the bonuses for the managers for 1999. The goal for 1999 is a 10% increase over the 1998 total sales.

1. Open the files **Sales98.xls** and **Sales99.xls**.

2. Open a new workbook. Make the worksheet title **Feestone Electronics** in cell A1 and **1999 Bonuses** in cell A2. Key the data in Figure U6-3 into the worksheet beginning in cell A4. Tile the workbooks, if necessary.

FIGURE U6-3

Manager	Region	Goal	Actual	Difference	Bonus
H. Maplethorpe	NE				
A. Needlehoffen	NW				
J. Frisbee	SE				
J. Martin	SW				
Total					

3. In the "Goal" column, create linked formulas that multiply the regional sales in **Sales98.xls** (cell R24 in each of the regional worksheets) by 1.1.

The linked cell references vary depending on the location of Slryemp.xls.

● **Unit Application 6-3:**
Required Files: Sales98.xls, Sales99.xls
Solution Files: glu6-3.xls in Solutions Manual or on Solutions Disk

The completed document for this Application may be used in a student's portfolio.

4. In the "Actual" column, link the regional sales in **Sales99.xls** (cell R24 in each regional worksheet).

5. In the "Difference" column, subtract the Goal from the Actual.

6. If a manager meets the goal (Difference >=0), he or she receives $10,000. Use an IF function to calculate the bonuses.

7. Total the bonuses.

8. Format the worksheet attractively including the values.

9. Name the worksheet tab **Bonuses**.

10. Center the worksheet horizontally on the page and give it a standard header that includes your name, filename, and date. Create a custom footer that identifies the purpose of the bonus worksheet.

11. Delete any blank worksheets in the workbook. Save the workbook as *[your initials]*u6-3.xls in your Unit 6 folder and print the worksheet.

12. Create a formula printout in landscape orientation with grids and row and column headings. Insert the page numbers in the footer if the formula printout exceeds one page.

13. Close all files without saving them.

UNIT APPLICATION 6-4

Design worksheets for consolidation and consolidate worksheets.

Feestone Electronics needs to add unit prices and dollar-value sales revenues to its first quarter 1999 regional sales reports and to produce a consolidated report for the corporate office.

1. Open the file **RegSales.xls**.

2. In sheets 1 through 4, key **Unit Price** in cell G7 and key the following unit prices in cells G8:G11.

Cellular phones	**119.95**
Fax machines	**565.00**
Copy machines	**7,995.00**
Postage meters	**465.00**

3. In all four sheets, copy the labels in cells A8:A12 to cells A17:A21. Key **Revenue** in cell A14 in bold. ("Revenue" centers across columns because of preexisting formatting.)

4. In all four sheets, calculate revenues based on unit sales and unit price. Also calculate totals for the "Revenue" section (columns and rows).

5. Make the row totals bold and add a single line border above and a double line border below the total row.

The linked cell references in the formulas and linked cells vary depending on the location of Sales98.xls and Sales99.xls. Also, formatting in the student answer files vary.

○ Unit Application 6-4:
Required Files: RegSales.xls
Solution Files: glu6-4.xls in Solutions Manual or on Solutions Disk

The completed document for this Application may be used in a student's portfolio.

6. In all four sheets, format the unit prices in comma style with two decimals and the individual product revenues and revenue totals in comma style with no decimal places.

7. Make columns B through E just wide enough to accommodate the values.

8. Rename the worksheets as follows:

Sheet1   **NE**
Sheet2   **NW**
Sheet3   **SE**
Sheet4   **SW**
Sheet5   **Consolidated**

9. Copy the Southwest sheet to the Consolidated Report sheet, change the title to **Consolidated Report**, and delete the regional manager's name.

10. In the Consolidated Report, delete the contents of the unit sales data (cells B8:E12) and consolidate the unit sales of the four regions by creating links to source data.

11. Adjust column widths to accommodate data and check formulas.

12. Format all sheets to print centered horizontally on the page and add the standard header to each.

13. Save the workbook as *[your initials]***u6-4.xls** in your Unit 6 folder and print all worksheets.

14. Create a formula printout of each worksheet in landscape orientation with grids and row and column headings. AutoFit all columns and make sure the formulas print completely.

15. Close the workbook without saving it.

UNIT APPLICATION 6-5

Link data between worksheets and create a consolidation report.

  Feestone Electronics needs a consolidated worksheet for the sales in years 1997, 1998, and 1999. Fourth quarter data for 1999 must be projected, based on 1998 quarter 4.

1. Open the file **FeeElec.xls**.

2. In the 1999 worksheet, calculate the fourth quarter sales projections based on a 10% increase from the 1998 fourth quarter sales.

3. Add a worksheet to the workbook after the 1999 worksheet, name it **Consolidation**, and turn off grids for viewing.

4. Copy the 1999 sheet to the Consolidation worksheet and change "1999" in the title to "Consolidated Sales."

● Unit Application 6-5:
Required Files: FeeElec.xls
Solution Files: glu6-5.xls in Solutions Manual or on Solutions Disk

 The completed document for this Application may be used in a student's portfolio.

5. In the consolidated report, delete the contents of the sales data (cells B7:F11) and consolidate the sales for the three years by creating links to source data.

6. Adjust column widths as necessary.

7. Open each level of the outline and check all formulas.

8. Center all worksheets horizontally on the page. Change the page orientation to landscape.

9. Create the standard header in each worksheet and save the workbook as *[your initials]***u6-5.xls** in your Unit 6 folder.

10. Print the entire workbook.

11. Create a formula printout for the 1999 worksheet and the Consolidation report in landscape orientation with grids and row and column headings. AutoFit all columns, display all levels, and make sure the formulas print completely.

12. Close the workbook without saving it.

UNIT APPLICATION 6-6 *Making It Work for You*

Link data between worksheets and create a consolidation report.

It's time to organize your expenses and project future expense amounts. Open a new workbook and on the first worksheet record your yearly expenses from two years ago in broad categories by quarter and use a total row. On the second worksheet do the same for last year. Format both worksheets exactly the same way. On a third worksheet project your expenses for this year based on a 5% cost of living increase from last year. Add a worksheet and do the same for next year based on this year.

Consolidate the four worksheets on a consolidation worksheet based on position. After the consolidation, add a column to the consolidation worksheet that averages your expenses for the four years.

Center each worksheet horizontally on the page. Add the standard header to all the worksheets and save the workbook as *[your initials]***u6-6.xls** in your Unit 6 folder.

Print all the worksheets and create a formula printout for the worksheet for this year, the worksheet for next year, and the consolidation worksheet in landscape orientation with grids and row and column headings. AutoFit all columns and make sure the formulas print completely.

Close the workbook without saving it.

Unit Application 6-6:

Required Files: None
Solution Files: Sample file glu6-6.xls in Solutions
Manual or on Solutions Disk

[1] This Application is completely freeform. Student answers vary based on data keyed and shared workbooks created.

Portfolio Builder

List of Files Produced in the Portfolio Builder

Filename	Document
*[Your initials]*Res1.doc	Resume created using a Word Resume Template
*[Your initials]*Res2.doc	Resume created using the Word Resume Wizard
*[Your initials]*Prospects.xls	List of prospective employers
*[Your initials]*DocList.xls	List of documents to include in your Portfolio
*[Your initials]*CvrLtr.doc	Cover letter (From scratch or using Word's Letter Wizard)
*[Your initials]*AppInfo.doc	Information for use in filling out Employment Applications
10-15 additional documents	The documents listed in your Document List.

Optional Documents

Thank you letter

Contract Reference Sheet

Contract Reference Card

Portfolio Builder

OBJECTIVES
By using this Portfolio Builder, you will learn how to:

1. **Build a résumé.**
2. **Identify prospective employers.**
3. **Build a portfolio.**
4. **Target your résumé and portfolio.**
5. **Write a cover letter.**
6. **Fill out an employment application.**
7. **Prepare for a job interview.**
8. **Follow up an interview.**

Finding a job is difficult—especially today in the midst of downsizing. The number of applicants often exceeds the availability of jobs. So you need to distinguish yourself from other people interested in the same job. You need to show a prospective employer what you can do.

This *Portfolio Builder* helps you build a résumé that will tell prospective employers about your work background. It also assists you in building a "representational portfolio"—a collection of your best work that you can show as evidence of your skills. The documents in your portfolio will be geared to specific employers. Finally, the *Portfolio Builder* leads you though the job-search process: including contacting prospective employers, filling out an employment application, and following up after interviews.

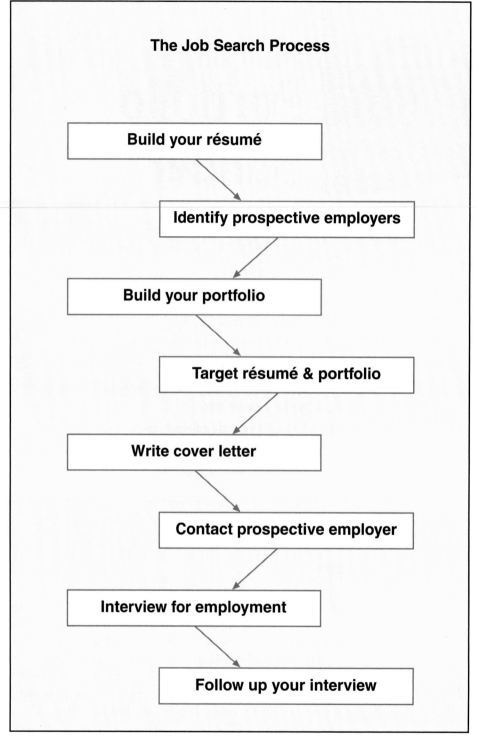

The Job Search Process

Build your résumé

Identify prospective employers

Build your portfolio

Target résumé & portfolio

Write cover letter

Contact prospective employer

Interview for employment

Follow up your interview

The *Portfolio Builder* will be helpful to you if you're planning to search for immediate employment. It is also a useful final project because it requires you to demonstrate skills you have gained from this course. Even if you're not looking for a job, it will help prepare you for an eventual job search.

Building a Résumé

A résumé is a representation of you on paper. It provides a first impression of you to a potential employer.

Building a résumé is an exercise in self-discovery. To create one, you must review your experience, identify your skills, and focus on a goal. Once you have created a résumé that states your strengths and objectives, you can begin the process of marketing yourself to prospective employers.

Although a good résumé will not guarantee a job, it is a primary tool in the job-search process.

There are three types of résumés:

- The *chronological* résumé is the traditional type of résumé. It lists your work history, starting with your most recent job. It includes a brief description of the position and your accomplishments. This is a "where you've been" type of résumé.

- The *functional* résumé highlights your skills or areas of expertise. It is a "what you can do" type of résumé.

- The *combination* résumé highlights your skill areas *and* lists the jobs you have held.

The following six pages illustrate these three kinds of résumés.

Chronological Résumé Description

Contact Information: Your name, address, and telephone number should appear at the top of the résumé. Spell out your address (do not abbreviate "Street" or "Avenue"). Include your ZIP code. Use a telephone number where you can be reached during the day or where a message can be left. Include other forms of contact, such as an e-mail address or fax number, if available. Don't use your current employer's telephone or fax number.

Job Objective: Your job objective represents the specific field or job title that you are pursuing. If you're targeting a specific job, tailor your objective to that position. Include the job type, the industry, and the geographical area in your objective (example: "Marketing position with a computer software vendor in the Chicago area"). To keep your options open, write a broader objective.

Work Experience: Describe the jobs that you have held, beginning with your most recent position. List the years of employment, company names and locations, and specific job titles. Include current and past jobs, part-time work, self-employment, volunteer work, and internships, as appropriate. The job description should focus on quantified achievements and specific skills.

Education: List the schools and training programs that you have attended. List your most recent education—school, degree or program, and date completed. Omit information about your high school if you have a college degree. Include any additional information, such as continuing education, seminars, or special course work that is related to your objective. This section can appear before **Work Experience** if you're a recent graduate, or if your education or training is your most important qualifying factor.

Additional Information: Your résumé can contain additional information that may be relevant to the job you are pursuing. For example, a section on computer proficiency can be included. You can also include **Activities**, **Professional Organizations**, or **Honors/Awards** as separate sections.

References: References are often not included on a résumé, but are provided separately if requested. Line up your references in advance, and list them on a sheet of paper. Include the name, address, telephone number, and title (if appropriate). You can ask a previous employer for a letter of recommendation, which you can then photocopy.

FIGURE P-2   Chronological résumé*

12 Juniper Drive
Any Town, State 00000
(000) 000-0000
E-mail: dmartin@xxx.xxx

Donald Martin

Objective	Seeking position as microcomputer salesperson in dynamic retail environment.

Work Experience

1996–Present   Electronics Depot   Any Town, State
Sales Associate

- Specialized in sales of computer hardware and software in busy retail outlet.
- Selected Salesperson of the Year for Midwest region.
- Established customer training program for computer sales that produced $80,000 in its first year.

1994–1996   Video Time   Any Town, State
Assistant Manager

- Managed video-rental store during most heavily-trafficked hours (evenings and weekends). Effectively handled as many as 250 customer contacts per day.
- Trained and supervised five sales assistants.
- Started "Old Time Cinema Club" that boosted sales of backlist videos by 50%.

1993–1994   Fairway Department Store   Any Town, State
Sales Assistant

- Assisted customers in busy Electronics Department.
- Handled more than $2,000 per day in cash sales.
- Completed sales training program.

Education

1997   **Fargo Technical College**   Any Town, State

- A.A., Microcomputer Systems Technology
- G.P.A. 3.93

Software/Hardware Training

- Proficiency in all Microsoft Office applications and PageMaker on both the PC and Macintosh computer.
- Can perform diagnostics on PCs and peripheral equipment, and can install/upgrade PC components such as network cards, memory chips, disk drives, and modems.

References   Available upon request.

*Created using a modified version of Word's Contemporary résumé style.

Functional Résumé Description

Contact Information: Your name, address, and telephone number should appear at the top of the résumé. Spell out your address (do not abbreviate "Street" or "Avenue"). Include your ZIP code. Use a telephone number where you can be reached during the day or where a message can be left. Include other forms of contact, such as an e-mail address or fax number, if available. Don't use your current employer's telephone or fax number.

Job Objective: Your job objective represents the specific field or job title that you are pursuing. If you're targeting a specific job, tailor your objective to that position. Include the job type, industry, and geographical area in your objective (example: "Marketing position with a computer software vendor in the Chicago area"). To keep your options open, write a broader objective.

Functional Sections: In a functional résumé, these sections provide the bulk of the information about you. Include two to four sections that describe a particular area of expertise or involvement. These areas should be directly related to the position you are pursuing. (In this résumé, the functional sections appear with the headings **Casework**, **Document Drafting**, and **Computer Skills**.) As an alternative to creating job-specific sections, create functional sections with the headings **Qualifications** and **Accomplishments**. Under these headings, list concise action statements that will catch the attention of a prospective employer.

Work Experience: A functional résumé lists your job history by date, company name and location, and title, beginning with the most recent position. Job descriptions are not included, as the résumé focuses on qualifications and skills, not work history.

Education: List the schools and training programs that you have attended. List your most recent education—school, degree or program, and date completed. Omit information about your high school if you have a college degree. Include any additional information, such as continuing education, seminars, or special course work that is related to your objective. This section can appear immediately below your **Objective** if you're a recent graduate, or if your education or training is your most important qualifying factor.

Additional Information: Your résumé can contain additional information that may be relevant to the job you are pursuing. For example, you can include sections with the following headings: **Activities**, **Professional Organizations**, **Honors/Awards**. The heading **References** may be listed at the bottom, followed by the text "Available on request" (see Chronological Résumé for more information).

FIGURE P-3   Functional résumé*

8809 Orange Terrace
Any Town, State 00000
Telephone (000) 000-0000
Fax (000) 000-0000

Lesley Brown

Objective	Paralegal position in computer or patent law
Casework	■ Researched state and federal computer and patent laws. Wrote briefs for attorneys. ■ Prepared preliminary arguments and pleadings in computer law. ■ Obtained affidavits.
Document Drafting	■ Drafted contracts under the supervision of an attorney. ■ Prepared tax returns, incorporations, patent filings, and trust agreements. ■ Prepared reports and schematic diagrams. ■ Assisted computer law specialists in preparing hardware and software patents, contracts, applications, shareholder agreements, and packaging agreements.
Computer Skills	■ Word-processing software (Word). ■ Advanced use of database software (Access) and spreadsheet software (Excel). ■ Researched on-line databases using Internet search engines.
Employment	1995–Present Collimore & Hapke, Attorneys-at-Law Any Town, State **Legal Assistant**
Education	1998 York State Technical College Any Town, State **Associate Degree, Paralegal Technology**
Activities	Legal Eagles Public Library Volunteer coordinator of weekly youth discussion group that teaches basic law principles.

*Created using a modified version of Word's Professional résumé style.

Combination Résumé Description

Contact Information: Your name, address, and telephone number should appear at the top of the résumé. Spell out your address (do not abbreviate "Street" or "Avenue"). Include your ZIP code. Use a telephone number where you can be reached during the day or where a message can be left. Include other forms of contact, such as an e-mail address or fax number, if available. Don't use your current employer's telephone or fax number.

Job Objective: Your job objective represents the specific field or job title that you are pursuing. If you're targeting a specific job, tailor your objective to that position. Include the job type, the industry, and the geographical area in your objective (example: "Marketing position with a computer software vendor in the Chicago area"). To keep your options open, write a broader objective.

Functional Sections: Include two or three sections that describe a particular area of expertise or involvement, or that summarize your qualifications and accomplishments. Use concise statements that are easy to read.

Work Experience: As in the chronological résumé, list and describe the jobs that you have held, beginning with your most recent position. Include the years of employment, the company names and locations, and the specific job titles. You can include current and past jobs, part-time work, self-employment, volunteer work, internships, and so on, as appropriate. The job description should focus on quantified achievements and specific skills. Be careful not to repeat the same information here that you have listed in the Functional Sections.

Education: List the schools and training programs that you have attended. List your most recent education—school, degree or program, and date completed. Omit information about your high school if you have a college degree. Include any additional information that might be relevant, such as continuing education, seminars, or special course work. This section can appear above **Work Experience** if you're a recent graduate, or if your education or training is your most important qualifying factor.

Additional Information: Your résumé can contain additional information that may be relevant to the job you are pursuing. For example, you can include sections with the following headings: **Activities**, **Professional Organizations**, **Honors/Awards**. The heading **References** may be listed at the bottom, followed by the text "Available on request" (see Chronological Résumé for more information).

FIGURE P-4 Combination résumé*

ANNA LUPONE
1002 LOOKOUT POINT
ANY TOWN , STATE 00000
TELEPHONE (000) 000-0000
E-MAIL 00000@AOL.COM

OBJECTIVE

Corporate Word Processing Administrative Assistant

SUMMARY OF QUALIFICATIONS

◊ Four years experience in administrative/clerical support positions.
◊ Easily establish rapport with managers, staff, and customers.
◊ Proficient at analyzing statistics and market trends to develop accurate forecasts and effective sales presentations.
◊ Excellent problem-solving, project management, decision-making, and time management skills.
◊ Proven ability to prioritize and complete multiple tasks, independently and with little supervision.
◊ Bilingual: English/Spanish.

COMPUTER SKILLS

Operating Systems:	Microsoft Windows 98
Word Processing:	Word
Graphics:	PageMaker, PowerPoint
Database and Spreadsheets:	Access, Excel
Keyboard Speed:	85 wpm

PROFESSIONAL EXPERIENCE

1994–Present   COCA COLA COMPANY   Atlanta, Georgia
Administrative Assistant
◊ Analyze sales volume and profit.
◊ Finalize and package forecasting reports for annual sales of $100 million.
◊ Monitor monthly spending and reconciliation for $8 million budget.
◊ Manage $200,000 in advertising and promotional materials.

EDUCATION

1998   Blake Business Institute   Any Town, State
A.S., Administrative Office Technology
◊ Dean's List, 4.0 GPA

REFERENCES

Available on request.

---

*Created using a modified version of Word's Elegant résumé style.

Choosing a Résumé Format

What type of résumé is right for you? Consider the following:

TABLE P-1

Choosing a Résumé Type

RÉSUMÉ TYPE	PREFERABLE IF:
Chronological	You have a history of steady work that reflects growth, and you are looking for a job in the same field or a related field.
Functional	You are new to the workforce, have gaps in your work history, or are changing careers.
Combination	You have some work history that is worth showcasing *and* want to highlight your marketable skills.

Be aware that the chronological résumé is the most traditional and conservative type of résumé. It is also the easiest to prepare. The functional and combination résumés, which use more innovative approaches, require greater thought, planning, and creativity.

Tips on Résumé Writing

When preparing your résumé, give yourself plenty of time, and keep in mind the following basics:

Content

- Everything in your résumé should support your job objective. Omit anything that doesn't.
- Be clear about what your skills are, both in your own mind and on paper. Your résumé should answer the question, "Why should I hire you?"
- Your résumé should convey the impression that you're focused. It should be targeted to a specific occupation or career field.
- Don't shortchange yourself. Emphasize any accomplishments, awards, and recognition you've received that supports your job objective.
- Mention promotions, raises, and bonuses, if appropriate, to prove your track record.
- Don't misrepresent yourself. Lying or exaggerating can only hurt—not help—you.
- Stress the positive—never include negative information about yourself. Your résumé should reflect what you *can* do, not what you can't.

Writing Style

- Strive for crisp, concise writing. Use short, easy-to-understand sentences.
- Use action words and phrases in your job and skill descriptions. For example, begin each description with words such as "Analyzed," "Administered," "Developed," "Initiated," "Organized," and so on.
- Use buzzwords and terminology that relate to the job you are pursuing.
- Proofread your résumé thoroughly for typographical, grammatical, or punctuation errors.

Appearance

- Your résumé should look professional. It should have an attractive layout, an easy-to-read format, and enough "white space" so that it is not too text-heavy.
- Use a good-quality printer to print your résumé. Avoid sending out photocopies, if possible.
- Limit your résumé to one page, unless you have substantial work experience that is relevant to your current job objective.

Getting Help

- Attend résumé and career workshops offered at your school or in your community.
- Read books about résumé writing to learn how to identify your skills, document your experience, and deal with special problems. Review résumé samples in such books.
- Ask someone whose judgment you trust to read your résumé before you send it out.

Résumé Templates and the Résumé Wizard

Word provides three résumé templates and a Résumé Wizard to help you create a résumé.

NOTE: Before using a résumé template or the Résumé Wizard, check the New dialog box in Word to see if they are available. If the templates have to be installed, use the Microsoft Office CD-ROM (Disk 1) to run the setup program. The Setup program location for these files is Microsoft Word for Windows, Wizards and Templates. You can also go to the Microsoft Office Web site (www.microsoft.com) and download wizards and templates.

EXERCISE P-1 Use a Résumé Template

The résumé templates allow you to create a chronological résumé based on one of three styles: Elegant, Contemporary, and Professional.

1. Choose <u>N</u>ew from the <u>F</u>ile menu, choose the Other Documents tab, and then double-click one of the résumé template icons.

 NOTE: To preview the template before choosing it, click the résumé template icon, and then view it in the Preview box.

FIGURE P-5
Résumé templates
in the New dialog
box

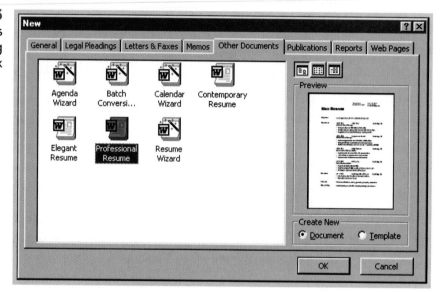

2. Replace all of the placeholder text in the document with your own information.

3. Make any formatting modifications. Save the document as *[your initials]*Res1.doc and print it.

 NOTE: Use the Résumé Wizard or résumé templates as a basis upon which to build your résumé. Modify the layout and formatting of the résumé to make it unique. Remember, you don't want your résumé to look exactly like everyone else's.

EXERCISE P-2 Use the Résumé Wizard

The Résumé Wizard guides you through the steps needed to create a chronological or functional résumé using one of the three résumé styles.

1. Choose <u>N</u>ew from the <u>F</u>ile menu, choose the Other Documents tab, and then double-click the Résumé Wizard icon. Click <u>N</u>ext to start.

2. In the Style dialog box, choose a résumé style. Click <u>N</u>ext to display the next dialog box.

FIGURE P-6
Choosing a
résumé style

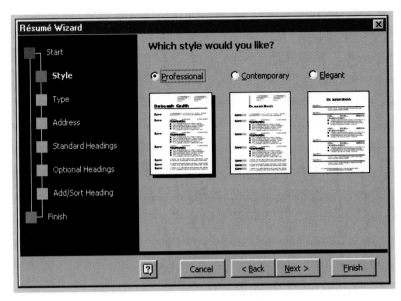

3. Choose the résumé type, and then click <u>N</u>ext.

4. Enter your name and mailing address, and then click <u>N</u>ext.

FIGURE P-7
Choosing headings
for your résumé

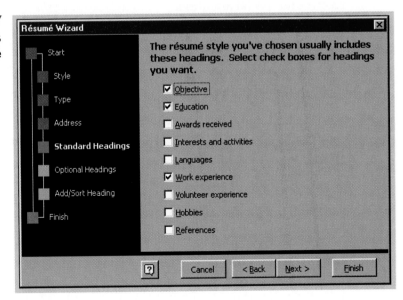

5. Choose the résumé headings you want, and then click <u>N</u>ext.

6. Choose any additional headings you desire, and then click <u>N</u>ext.

7. Add another heading or reorder your existing headings, and then click <u>N</u>ext.

8. Click <u>F</u>inish to view the résumé.

9. At the Office Assistant prompt, choose an option or click Cancel.

TIP: You can click the Office Assistant option to create a quick cover letter at this point. The letter will contain sample text for you to replace with your own information. See the section "Writing a Cover Letter" in this Portfolio Builder to learn about cover-letter basics.

10. Replace the placeholder text in the résumé with your own information.

11. Make any modifications. Save the document as *[your initials]*Res2.doc.

Identifying Prospective Employers

Now that you've prepared a résumé, it's time to think about who will view it. Your next step is to identify the companies in your area—and the people within those companies—who may be hiring people with your skills.

Always try to identify the manager in each company or organization who heads up the division, department, or group in which you hope to work. Avoid applying through a Human Resources staff member, if at all possible. In the Human Resources Department, it's easy to become just another applicant who receives no special attention.

Help Wanted Ads

Help-wanted ads can represent a useful way to research the hiring trends of a local company. Help-wanted ads are, however, less useful as a source of real employment opportunities. They should never be used as the primary focus of your job search. In fact, some experts believe that only 10 percent of all available jobs are listed in the newspaper.

Use the back issues of your local newspapers to find out whether a company has been hiring recently, what kinds of jobs have recently been advertised, and if a particular contact person was listed in the ad.

Networking

Talk to people who are in a position to provide information about job leads and the hiring process at particular companies. They can be friends, relatives, acquaintances—anyone who can put you in touch with a job contact. Try to identify the people within a company who have the power to hire you. Get the correct spelling of each person's name, official correct job title, department, company, and, if possible, a telephone number.

Company Research

An easy way to begin your company research is with the *Yellow Pages*. Use it to locate businesses in the field in which you're interested. (You may need to use the "Business-to-Business" section for some types of businesses.)

The business section of your local library contains reference books that can give you even more information about local companies. Some of the best sources are:

- *Standard & Poor's Register of Corporations, Directors, and Executives*. McGraw-Hill. (Volume 2 lists companies by location.)
- *The National Directory of Addresses and Phone Numbers*. Gale Research, Inc.
- *Million Dollar Directory*. Dun & Bradstreet.
- *Job Seeker's Guide to Private and Public Companies*. Gale Research, Inc.
- *Job Opportunities for Business and Liberal Arts Graduates*. Peterson's Guides, Inc.
- *Job Opportunities for Engineering, Science, and Computer Graduates*. Peterson's Guides, Inc.

Some of these sources are also available in easy-to-use software versions that allow you to search for particular companies based on specific criteria. Your local librarian can often provide help in locating information about specific companies as well.

Using the Internet

Many sources of company and career information are available on the Internet. Many companies operate their own Web site or home page, and some even list their job openings there. If a prospective employer is a large company, search the Internet based on the company's name. Often, promotional materials from the company (and available in a local public library) will indicate its Internet or Web site address.

Many Web search engines (such as Lycos, Excite, or Infoseek) offer career-oriented services. Search for such general keywords as "career," "employment," or "job." A targeted search using more specific keywords may produce results that prove more immediately useful to your job search.

You can also use your Internet browser to search for locations with appropriate keywords. For example, one recent search showed 600,000 matches for the keyword "career." Obviously, the more targeted your search of the Internet, the more useful it may be.

Specialized employment search engines on the Internet may prove useful. Because these services list jobs from across the nation (and around the world), they may be less useful for a local job search. A list of places to look for jobs on the Internet follows (remember that Internet options change rapidly, so this list may need to be updated and new options may be available):

- CareerPath
  Searches classified ads in U.S. newspapers
  www.careeerpath.com

- The Career Builder Network
  www.careeerbuilder.com

- CareerMosaic
  www.careermosaic.com

- E-Span Employment Database
  www.espan.com

- HotJobs
  www.hotjobs.com

- The Monster Board
  www.monster.com

EXERCISE P-3 Identify Prospective Employers

1. Identify at least five prospective employers. They may be located anywhere, but should represent the type of company for which you could imagine working.

2. For each prospective employer, obtain the name of a job contact. (This person would typically be a manager of the department, division, or group in which you would like to work.)

3. Key the list of prospective employers in a worksheet. Include the contact's name, department, company name, address, city, state, ZIP code, telephone number, and fax number. Save the worksheet as *[your initials]*Prospects.xls and then print it. You'll use this list throughout this *Portfolio Builder*.

Building Your Portfolio

Your resume *describes* your experience and your skills. Your portfolio *demonstrates* your skills. It represents the best work that you can do. It also should be work with which a prospective employer can identify—that is, documents that the employer will understand.

The first step in building your portfolio is to decide what types of documents belong in it. Use the following checklist as a starting point to create a list of possible documents for your portfolio.

TABLE P-2   **Possible Documents for Portfolio**

DOCUMENT	COMMENTS
Worksheets and Tables	Create attractive stand-alone worksheets and tables. Include charts and maps.
Invoices	Check Excel's invoice template.
Purchase Orders	Check Excel's purchase order template.
Expense Statements	Check Excel's expense statement template.
Business Planners	Check Excel's Business Planner templates, including Income Statements, Cash Flow Forecasts, and Balance Sheets.
Profit & Loss Statements	Obtain information from annual reports available at public library. Possibly include charts.
Balance Sheets	Obtain information from annual reports available at public library.
Databases	Create an Excel database. Show data filtered in multiple ways.
Letters	Create business letters with the appropriate letter formatting. Attach or embed related worksheet, chart, or map.
Memos	Create business memos with the appropriate memo formatting. Attach or embed related worksheet, chart, or map.
Reports	Include graphics, index, table of contents, footnotes or endnotes, and embedded worksheet, chart, or map.
Brochures	Check Word's brochure template. Possibly show worksheets and charts.

continues

TABLE P-2 Possible Documents for Portfolio (continued)

DOCUMENT	COMMENTS
Newsletters	Check Word's Newsletter Wizard. Include graphics, special effects, and embedded worksheet, chart, or map.
Press Releases	Check Word's press release templates. Include an attached worksheet or chart.

NOTE: If any of these Wizards or templates are not installed on your computer, you can install them by using the Microsoft Office CD-ROM (Disk 1) to run the setup program. The Setup program location for the Excel files is Microsoft Excel for Windows, Spreadsheet Templates. The Setup program location for the Word files is Microsoft Word for Windows, Wizards and Templates. You can also go to the Microsoft Office Web site (www.microsoft.com) and download wizards and templates.

EXERCISE **P-4** ## Develop a List of Documents for the Portfolio

1. Develop a list of 15 documents for inclusion in your portfolio. Use Table P-2 as a checklist, but also consider documents that you may have prepared in other courses related to your field of work. If you have work experience, list actual documents that you created. Use the following headings for your document list (see Figure P-8 on the next page):
   Number   **Type of Document**   **Description**
2. Save the list as *[your initials]***DocList.xls** and print it.
3. Finalize your document list by reviewing it with someone who is familiar with your job search area. Adjust the list as needed. Save and print it.

EXERCISE **P-5** ## Build Your Portfolio

It isn't necessary to begin every document from scratch. In fact, it may not even be a good idea. Use material from your other courses, key material from brochures and newsletters that you might receive from a professional association, or recreate sample documents from people in positions similar to the one in which you are interested.

1. Create each of the documents listed in your document list.
2. Adjust every document to give it as professional an appearance as possible. Focus on formatting. Demonstrate the skills that you learned in this course.

3. Consult the appropriate style reference for your profession to check that your formatting is acceptable.

4. Spell-check, save, and print your documents.

5. Ask someone familiar with your future profession to review your documents and then modify them as necessary.

6. Save and print your documents again.

FIGURE P-8   Sample portfolio list for student seeking accounting clerk position

No.	Type of Document	Description
1.	Invoice	For bookkeeping or accounting services
2.	Database	Client database, filtered in various ways
3.	Accounts Payable	Client's Accounts Payable statement
4.	Account Receivable	Client's Accounts Receivable statement
5.	Employee List	Records of employees including date hired, years employed (with calculations)
6.	Purchase Order	For office supplies
7.	Loan Statement	Showing principal, annual percentage rate, and so on
8.	Check Register	Showing checks, deposits, and balance
9.	Cash Flow Statement	Showing cash receipts and cash disbursements
10.	Amortization Schedule	Showing various interest rates and payment periods
11.	Income Statement	Showing cash, accruals, and net income
12.	Balance Sheet	Showing assets and liabilities
13.	Chart	Showing sales over a 12-month period, for a presentation or handout
14.	Map	Showing states shaded to reflect sales, for a presentation or handout
15.	Report	Report with accompanying worksheet, including charts and maps

Targeting Your Résumé and Portfolio

So far you've created a résumé and a portfolio of documents that reflect something about you. Now it's time to *target* a specific company and tailor your portfolio, including your résumé, to that company.

EXERCISE **P-6** **Target Your Résumé to an Employer**

---

1. From your list of five prospective employers, choose one as your target. Review the information you've gathered about the company. If you feel you don't have enough information, collect additional material. Ultimately, you should be very familiar with the company—and the position—you've targeted.

2. Review Table P-3.

TABLE P-3 **Targeting Your Résumé**

☞ TARGETING SUGGESTIONS

Objectives

☐	Change the job type to one that more closely resembles a job type available at the targeted company.
☐	Change the description of the industry or geographical area to one that more closely resembles those for the target company.

Chronological Résumé

☐	Reorder the bullets under a previous job in "Work experience" to emphasize skills that apply to the targeted position.
☐	Reorder or modify "Additional information" areas to emphasize skills that apply to the targeted position.

Functional Résumé

☐	Reorder or modify the "Functional sections" to emphasize skills that apply to the targeted position.
☐	Reorder or modify "Additional information" areas to emphasize skills that apply to the targeted position.

continues

TABLE P-3   Targeting Your Résumé   *continued*

☞   **TARGETING SUGGESTIONS**

Combination Résumé

☐	Reorder or modify the "Functional sections" to emphasize skills that apply to the targeted position.
☐	Reorder the bullets under a previous job in "Work experience" to emphasize skills that apply to the targeted position.
☐	Reorder or modify "Additional information" areas to emphasize skills that apply to the targeted position.

3. Based on the checklist shown in Table P-3, modify your résumé to increase its appeal to your targeted company.

NOTE: Modifying a résumé does not mean fabricating work experience. You can, however, increase your appeal to a specific employer by highlighting certain skills. You can also minimize potential problem areas through the design and format selected for your résumé (for example, by deciding to use a functional résumé rather than a chronological one).

4. Spell-check and save your résumé.

5. Print the final copy of your résumé on appropriate paper stock.

Choosing Paper

The most commonly used résumé papers are 20-pound bond or 50-pound off-set (both weigh the same) in a linen (textured) or laid (flat) finish. A 24-pound paper is thicker, has more texture, and is usually more expensive than 20-pound bond or 50-pound offset papers. You might consider using 24-pound Nekoosa, Classic Linen, or Becket Cambric for higher-level positions.

Let your résumé speak for itself. Don't go overboard in selecting a paper that will make your résumé stand out. Such a strategy could backfire. Don't use colored stock, for example. Neutral stock in different shades of white, gray, or beige is recommended.

If you're uncertain about paper choices, visit a stationery store, an office supplies store, a printer, or a local copy shop. Buy enough paper to use for your résumés, cover letters, and follow-up letters. Your envelopes should match the stationery. Your portfolio documents shouldn't be printed on the same stock as your résumé, however.

EXERCISE **P-7** **Target Your Portfolio to an Employer**

The job contact at your targeted company is likely to respond more favorably to your portfolio if you take the time to tailor it to the company. It shows that you made an effort to learn about your prospective employer. It may also provide more conversational opportunities in a job interview.

1. Review Table P-4.

TABLE P-4	**Targeting Your Portfolio**
☑	**TARGETING SUGGESTIONS**
☐	Use the targeted company's name in worksheet titles and its address where appropriate.
☐	Modify the contents of office documents so that they apply specifically to the targeted company.
☐	Do not change a report from one of your classes (other than to make any corrections your instructor may have recommended). It's a good idea to let the targeted company know that the report was submitted as a class assignment, especially if it relates to your chosen field.

2. Based on the checklist shown in Table P-4, modify the documents in your portfolio to increase their appeal to the targeted company.

3. Spell-check and save the portfolio documents.

4. Print the final copies of your portfolio documents. Use standard printer paper.

Writing a Cover Letter

It's been said that sending a résumé without a cover letter is like giving a gift without a card. It's incomplete and confusing, and it only decreases the value of the résumé that you've spent so much time preparing and fine-tuning.

The Cover Letter Recipient A cover letter should be addressed to the job contact at a targeted company—never to Human Resources or Personnel.

First Paragraph The first paragraph should explain what job you are applying for and why you are interested in it. Be as specific as you can. Describe how you heard about the job opening. If someone told you about the company or the job opening, mention the person's name (but make sure to get his or her permission first). Describe why the work of the department or company holds particular interest for you, but don't go overboard with superlatives or hype.

Second Paragraph Describe your credentials in the second paragraph. Don't repeat your résumé. Focus, instead, on the skills, experiences, or accomplishments that are most likely to appear relevant to the employer. If you're responding to an ad, incorporate language from the ad. If you've previously read a job description or had a discussion with the employer, try to use the language the employer used in describing the position. Mention two or three key credentials.

Third Paragraph Use the third paragraph to describe what you can do for the company. You need to show that you understand the employer's needs and that you have something to offer. In this paragraph (or as a separate paragraph), you should request a personal meeting. You could then indicate the time when it's easiest to reach you, whether the employer can contact you at work, and if you'll be following up with a phone call.

General Tips

- Your cover letter should be printed on the same paper as your résumé and should be printed in the same way.

- Do not use the letterhead of your current employer.

- Use the same typeface for both your cover letter and your résumé.

- Use the standard business letter format.

- Don't send your portfolio with your résumé and cover letter. The portfolio is generally shown in an interview, but it can be sent to a prospective employer who expresses an interest in viewing it.

FIGURE P-9 Sample cover letter

Donald Martin
12 Juniper Drive
Any Town, State 00000
(000) 000-0000

January 22, 2000

Ward T. Cleaver, Manager
The Computer Warehouse, Inc.
6 Old King's Highway
Any Town, State 00000

Dear Mr. Cleaver:

I am seeking a position as a microcomputer salesperson, and read in the *Any Town News* that The Computer Warehouse was opening a new store on Old King's Highway. I have visited The Computer Warehouse in Lincoln and was impressed with the variety of hardware and software carried by the store. The store's focus on customer service was also exceptional, both through its "Trouble-Free Technical Support" program and its wide range of software training courses.

As my enclosed résumé indicates, I specialized in the sales of computer hardware and software at the Electronics Depot on Main Street. Although the sale of computers and software constitutes only a small portion of the overall sales of the Electronics Depot, computer and software sales increased by 42 percent in the past year. Part of this increase was due to the Customer Training Program that I developed. In its first year, the program produced revenues of $80,000.

Opening a new store and training a new sales staff is a difficult prospect. With my proven background in sales and customer training, I feel I would be an asset to your sales staff and would welcome the opportunity to meet with you personally to discuss your staff needs. I will contact you in the next week to schedule an appointment at your convenience. Thank you for your consideration.

Sincerely,

Donald Martin

Enclosure

EXERCISE **P-8** Write a Cover Letter

Using your word-processor application, write a cover letter to accompany your résumé.

1. Using the standard business letter style (if necessary, check the *Gregg Reference Manual*), write a cover letter for your résumé. Use the three-paragraph format described earlier.

2. Ask someone familiar with your résumé and with jobs in your chosen field to review your letter. Make any necessary modifications.

3. Spell-check the cover letter and save it as *[your initials]***CvrLtr.doc**.

4. Print your cover letter using the same stationery as your résumé.

5. Print an envelope for your cover letter and résumé. If possible, use the same stationery for the envelope, cover letter, and résumé.

 NOTE: Some people believe that you should use a large envelope so you don't have to fold your résumé. Others recommend a standard business envelope.

TIP: You can use Word's Letter Wizard to write a cover letter for your résumé. Choose <u>N</u>ew from the <u>F</u>ile menu, choose the Letters & Faxes tab, and double-click the Letter Wizard icon. Follow the steps to create the letter. Remember to choose the page design that matches your résumé, specify whether you're using preprinted letterhead, include "Mr." or "Ms." in the recipient's name area, and include an enclosure notation. After creating the letter, you can add, remove, or change letter elements by choosing Letter Wizard from the <u>T</u>ools menu.

Filling Out an Employment Application

Some companies require that every applicant, at every level, fill out an employment application. Other companies don't even use one. Generally, however, companies do use some form of an employment application. Whether you need to fill out such a form will depend on the company's internal personnel policies.

Often applicants are asked to fill out an employment application when they arrive at the company for an interview. To minimize stress in an already stressful situation, prepare for the employment application beforehand by creating a reference sheet that contains any information that might be included in the application and isn't found on your résumé. (Of course, you should refer to your résumé in filling out your employment application. Make sure to bring an extra copy for reference.)

Tips for Employment Applications

- Be as specific as possible when describing the position that you are seeking.

- Be careful when listing a required salary. A salary that is too high may eliminate you for some acceptable jobs, while a figure that is too low might weaken your negotiating position. Sometimes it is better to leave this line blank.

- Be prepared to list dates (month and year) for the schools you have attended. Some applications may also ask for your grade-point average and your class rank.

- Be prepared to list the following information for your previous employers: address, telephone number, name and title of supervisor, start date and end date (month and year), and a description of your duties.

- If some questions are not applicable to the job you are seeking, it is usually acceptable to write "Not Applicable" next to the question.

EXERCISE **Create a Reference Sheet for an Employment Application**

1. Review the "Tips for Employment Applications." Note any information that isn't covered by your résumé.
2. Key all information that you will need to fill out an employment application. Use any format that makes sense to you.
3. Save the file as *[your initials]*AppInfo.doc and then print it.

Employment Interviews

Once you have contacted a potential employer and scheduled an appointment to meet, you'll need to prepare yourself to make a good impression in person. No matter how good your résumé or credentials may be, only the interview can, ultimately, land you the job.

The more interviews you go on, the better your interviewing skills will be.

 NOTE: If possible, avoid scheduling an interview on a Monday, which is often the most hectic day in a business environment.

Preparing Yourself

- Confirm your appointment the day before, and make sure you arrive at the interview on time.

- Become as familiar with the company as possible. Read articles about the company, if they are available, or talk to people who are, or have been, employed by the company. It's always flattering to a prospective employer when an applicant appears knowledgeable about the company in an interview.

- Approach the interview with a clear mental picture of your capabilities and your job objective. Review your résumé immediately before meeting the prospective employer. Think positively.

Presenting Yourself

- Come to the interview equipped with copies of your résumé, your references, and any recommendation letters you have gathered. Have your portfolio on hand, as well as a notepad and a pen.

- Look your best. Your attire and grooming are critical to making a good impression. Dress neatly and professionally, in a manner that is appropriate to the company you are visiting. If necessary, get help in selecting an interview outfit from someone who dresses well.

- Be yourself. Act as relaxed as you possibly can, sit in a comfortable position, and focus on the interviewer.

- Ask questions. Learn what you can about the job, the company, to whom (or to how many people) you'd report, and so on. If no job is available, or the job opening is not appropriate for you, ask for recommendations about other people in the company that you might contact.

- At the end of the interview, if you want the job, express your interest in it, and be ready to explain why the company should hire you.

Frequently Asked Interview Questions

The following are frequently asked interview questions. You may want to rehearse your answers before the interview. Never offer negative or unnecessary information to an interview question.

- Can you tell me about yourself?
- Why should I hire you?
- What are your major strengths? Weaknesses?
- What are your short-term goals? Long-term goals?
- Why do you want to leave your present job? (if employed)
- Why did you leave your previous job?
- What do you enjoy most (or least) about your current (or previous) job?
- Why do you want to work here?
- What salary do you expect to receive?

Following Up the Interview

To be successful in the interview process, you should take two important follow-up steps:

- Send a "thank you" letter.
- Keep track of your contacts.

"Thank You" Letters

Always send a "thank you" letter within 24 hours after you've interviewed with someone. It creates a positive impression, shows that you have good follow-up skills and good social skills, and reminds the person of your meeting.

The letter should be short and friendly, thanking the person for his or her time and for any information he or she may have provided. You may want to mention something that reminds the person of who you are, in case many people have interviewed for the position.

Even if you know that the interview will not lead to a specific job offer, a "thank you" letter demonstrates your professionalism.

FIGURE P-10   Sample "thank you" letter #1

Dear Ms. Jones:

Thank you for the opportunity of interviewing for the sales position. I enjoyed meeting you and appreciate the information that you shared with me.

I am very interested in the position and believe I could quickly become a productive member of your sales team.

Thanks again for the interview, and I look forward to hearing from you.

Sincerely,

FIGURE P-11   Sample "thank you" letter #2

Dear Ms. Jones:

Thank you for the interview and the information you gave me yesterday. I really appreciate your recommendation that I meet with John Doe in the Marketing Department.

I have scheduled an interview with Mr. Doe and look forward to meeting him. If this contact eventually leads to a job offer, I will be most grateful.

Thanks again for your time and help.

Sincerely,

Keeping Track of Contacts

Be organized in your job search. Keep track of everyone who has received your résumé by creating a contact log.

FIGURE P-12
Sample format for
contact log

Date Sent	Contact Name	Company	Telephone	Comments

In addition, develop a system for organizing your contacts so that you can follow up with telephone calls as appropriate. You can use a computer application of your choice or simple index cards to create the system.

If you use index cards, enter all pertinent reference information for each contact on the card. Place the cards in a box, and then sort them in the order that you want to contact the individuals. You can use tabs as date markers.

FIGURE P-13
Sample format for
contact reference
card

Company: _____

Contact Person: _____

Position:_____ Department:_____

Address:_____

Phone: _____ Fax:_____

Notes: _____

_____

_____

_____

Appendices

APPENDIX A

Lesson Applications

If you're unfamiliar with Windows, we suggest you review this Windows tutorial.

If you never used Windows before, you may need help with basic Windows actions. At appropriate points in this Tutorial, a Note will guide you to Appendix B: "Using the Mouse" or Appendix C: "Using Menus and Dialog Boxes."

Starting Windows

Individual computers may be set up differently. In most cases, however, when you turn on your computer, Windows loads and the Windows desktop appears.

The desktop contains *icons*, or symbols representing windows. If you double-click an icon, the window represented by that icon opens. Two icons are especially important:

- My Computer
  Opens a window that contains icons representing each input and output device on your printer or in your network.

- Recycle Bin
  Opens a window listing files you've deleted. Until you empty the Recycle Bin, these files can be undeleted.

 TIP: If you don't know how to use the mouse to point, click, double-click, or drag and drop, see Appendix B: "Using the Mouse."

Using the Start Menu

 The Start button on the taskbar at the bottom of the desktop is probably the most important button in Windows. Clicking displays the Start menu from which you can perform any Windows task.

1. Turn on the computer. Windows loads, and the Windows desktop appears.

 NOTE: When you start Windows, you may be prompted to log on to Windows or, if your computer is attached to a network, to log on to the network. If you are asked to key a user name and a password, ask your instructor for help.

2. Click on the Windows taskbar. The Start menu appears.

 TIP: If you don't know how to choose a command from a menu, see Appendix C: "Using Menus and Dialog Boxes."

FIGURE A-1
Windows desktop

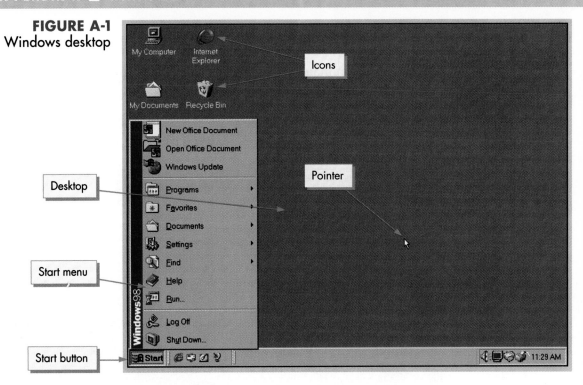

TABLE A-1   **Start Menu**

COMMAND	USE
New Office Document	Starts a new Office document of any type.
Open Office Document	Opens an existing Office document.
Windows Update	Connects to the Microsoft Web site for Windows updates.
Programs	Displays a list of programs you can start.
Favorites	Opens folders or connects you to Web sites that you designated as "favorites."
Documents	Displays a list of documents that you opened recently.
Settings	Displays a list of system components for which you can change settings.
Find	Helps you find a folder, a file, an address, a computer on a network; and helps you search the Internet.
Help	Starts Help. You can then use Help to find out how to perform a task in Windows.
Run	Starts a program or opens a folder when you type a command.
Log Off	Closes all programs, disconnects your computer from the network, and prepares your computer for someone else to use.
Shut Down	Shuts down or restarts your computer.

Using the Programs Command

The <u>P</u>rograms command is the easiest way to open a program.

1. Click 🔳 Start.

2. Point to <u>P</u>rograms. The <u>P</u>rograms submenu appears, listing the programs on your computer. Every computer has a different list of programs.

FIGURE A-2
<u>P</u>rograms submenu

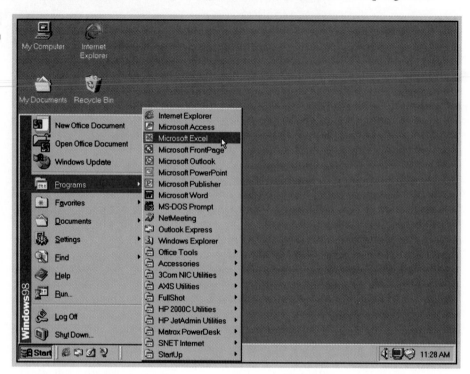

3. Point to the program you want to open and click. In a few seconds, the program loads and its first screen appears. Notice that a button for the program appears in the taskbar. Keep the program open.

NOTE: Many items on the <u>P</u>rograms menu represent names for groups of programs. These group names have an arrow ▶ across from them on the right side of the menu. When you point to the group name, a submenu appears listing programs that you can click to select.

Using the Taskbar

A major feature of Windows is that you can work with more than one program at a time. The taskbar makes it easy to switch between open programs, and between open documents within a program.

The window in which you are working is called the *active* window. The title bar for the active window is highlighted, as is its taskbar button.

1. The program you opened in the preceding procedure should still be open. (If it's not, open a program now.) Open a second program using the <u>P</u>rogram command. Notice how the second program covers the first. The window containing the second program is now active. Its title bar is highlighted and its button on the taskbar is highlighted.

2. Click the button on the taskbar for the first program you opened. The program appears again.

3. Click the button on the taskbar for the second program to switch back to it.

4. Start a new blank document in the second program. Notice that each open document has its own taskbar button so you can easily switch between documents.

FIGURE A-3
Active window

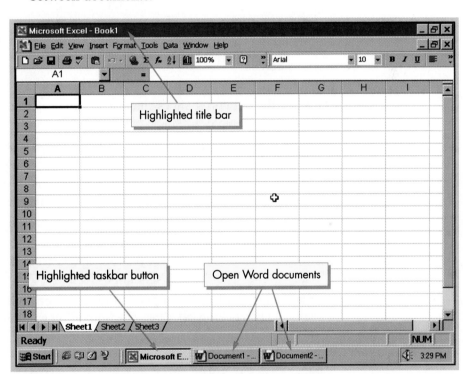

5. Practice using the taskbar to switch between program windows and document windows.

Changing the Size of Windows

In Windows it's easy to adjust the size of your windows using the pointer.

You can also use the Minimize button ▬, the Maximize button ▢, and the Restore button ⬚ to adjust the size of windows.

TABLE A-2   Sizing Buttons

NAME	BUTTON	USE
Minimize button	_	Reduces the window to a button on the taskbar.
Maximize button	□	Enlarges the window to fill the desktop.
Restore button	🗗	Returns the window to its previous size. (Appears when you maximize a window.)

1. In the open window, click 🗗 at the right side of the title bar of the window. (If □ appears instead of _, the window is already reduced. In that case, go to step 2.)

2. Move the pointer to a window border. The pointer changes to a double-headed arrow ↔.

 TIP: Sometimes the borders of a window can move off the computer screen. If you're having trouble with one border of a window, try another border.

3. When the pointer changes shape, you can drag the border to enlarge, reduce, or change the shape of the window.

4. Make the window smaller. Notice that the other open program appears behind the currently active window.

5. Click the window that was behind the first window. It now appears in front of the first window because it has become the active window.

 6. Click _ to minimize the active window to a button on the taskbar. The previous window becomes active.

7. Click the Close button ☒ at the top right corner of the window to close the window. The desktop should be clean.

8. Click a taskbar button for one of the other open windows. Close the window by clicking ☒. Close the remaining window. You have a clean desktop again.

NOTE: When one document is open within a program, the document window contains two sets of sizing buttons and two close buttons, as shown in Figure A-4. The bottom buttons are for the document, the top buttons are for the program. When two or more documents are open within a program, each document window contains one set of sizing buttons and one close button.

Using the Documents Command

You can open an existing document using the Documents command on the Start menu. This command allows you to open one of the last 15 documents previously opened on your computer.

1. On the Start menu, point to Documents. The Documents submenu appears, showing documents that were previously opened.

2. Click a document. The document opens, along with the program in which the document was written (for example, if the document were a Word document, it would open within Word). A button for the document appears on the taskbar. You can now work on the document.

FIGURE A-4
Close buttons

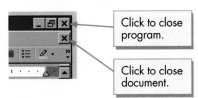

Click to close program.

Click to close document.

3. To close the document, click ⊠ on the document window. Click ⊠ to close the program window that contained the document.

Using the Settings Command

You can change the way Windows looks and works using the Settings command. Be very careful when changing settings. Don't change them unless it's really necessary.

 NOTE: Before changing any settings, talk to your instructor.

FIGURE A-5
Settings submenu

Control Panel
Printers
Taskbar & Start Menu...
Folder Options...
Active Desktop
Windows Update...

1. Open the Start menu, and point to Settings. The Settings submenu appears.

2. Click the option that relates to the settings you want to change. Close any open windows and clear your desktop.

TABLE A-3

OPTION	USE
Settings Options	
Control Panel	Displays the Control Panel, which you use to change screen colors, add or remove programs, change the date or time, and change other settings for your hardware and software.
Printers	Displays the Printers window, which you use to add, remove, and modify your printer settings.
Taskbar & Start Menu	Displays the Taskbar Properties dialog box, which you use to customize the taskbar and add and remove programs on the Start menu.
Folder Options	Displays the Folder Options dialog box, where you choose the style for your folders (classic Windows style or Web style), and select folder and file characteristics.
Active Desktop	Displays a submenu with options to view your desktop as a Web page, customize your desktop, and update Web elements you added to your desktop.
Windows Update	Connects to the Microsoft Web site for Windows updates.

Using the Find Command

If you don't know where a document or folder is, you can use the Find command to find and open it.

1. On the Start menu, point to <u>F</u>ind. The <u>F</u>ind submenu appears.

FIGURE A-6
<u>F</u>ind submenu

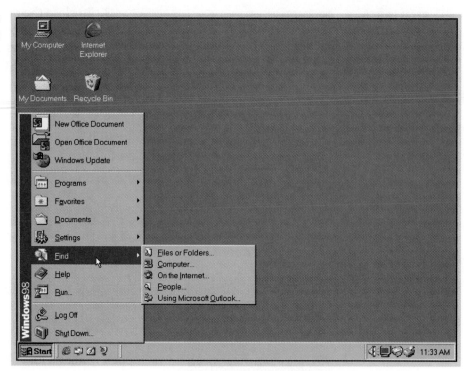

2. Click <u>F</u>iles or Folders. The Find: All Files dialog box appears.

FIGURE A-7
Find: All Files
dialog box

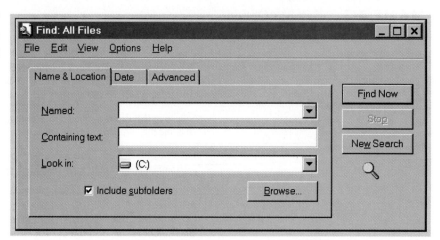

3. In the <u>N</u>amed box, key the name of the file or folder you want to find.

4. Click the arrow next to the <u>L</u>ook In box to specify where to search. (You could also click <u>B</u>rowse.)

TIP: To search files for specific text, use the Containing Text box. To narrow the search further, use the Date and Advanced tabs in the dialog box.

5. Click Find Now to start the search. Any matches for the file are shown at the bottom of the dialog box.

6. To open a file that was found, double-click the filename.

 TIP: If you set your Folder Options to Web style, you can single-click the filename, just like a hyperlink, to open the file.

7. When you finish viewing the file, close all open windows and clear your desktop.

Using the Run Command

If you know the name of the program you want to use, you can use the Run command to start it. This command is often employed to run a "setup" or "install" program that installs a new program on your computer.

1. On the Start menu, click Run. The Run dialog box appears.

FIGURE A-8
Run dialog box

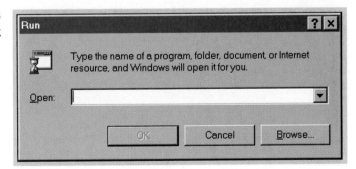

2. If you know the name of a program you want to run, key the name and click OK. The program you specified starts. Otherwise, you can click Browse to look for the program.

3. When you finish, close the program.

Displaying a Shortcut Menu

When the pointer is on an object or an area of the Windows desktop, and you click the right mouse button, a shortcut menu usually appears. This menu provides you with the commands that would be most useful in working with the object or area to which you were pointing.

FIGURE A-9
Shortcut menu for
the desktop

1. Click a blank area of the desktop with the right mouse button. A shortcut menu appears with commands that relate to the desktop, such as arranging icons, displaying properties, and so on.

2. Click outside the shortcut menu to close it.

3. Right-click the time in the bottom right corner of the taskbar. Close the shortcut menu.

4. Right-click an icon to display its shortcut menu, then close the menu.

Exiting Windows

You should always exit Windows properly before turning off your computer. You can then be sure that your work is saved and no files are damaged. To exit Windows, use the Shut Down command.

1. On the Start menu, click Shut Down. The Shut Down Windows dialog box appears.

FIGURE A-10
Shut Down
Windows
dialog box

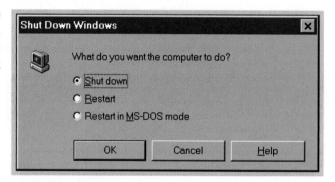

2. Choose Shut Down and click OK. Windows prompts you to save changes to any open documents. You can now turn off your computer safely.

 NOTE: Occasionally, you may need to restart your computer. One instance in which this is necessary is when you add new software.

APPENDIX B

Using the Mouse

Although you can use a keyboard with Windows, you'll probably find your-self using the mouse. Typically, you roll the mouse on a *mouse pad* (or any flat surface). A *pointer* shows your onscreen location as the mouse moves.

To select items on the computer screen using a mouse, you usually press the left mouse button. (Whenever you're told to "click" or "double-click" the mouse button, use the left mouse button. If you should use the right button, you are told to do so.)

When using a mouse, you need to become familiar with these terms.

TABLE B-1 Mouse Terms

TERM	DESCRIPTION
Point	Move the mouse until the tip of the onscreen pointer is touching an item on the computer screen.
Click	Press the mouse button and then quickly release it.
Double-click	Press and quickly release the mouse button twice.
Triple-click	Press and quickly release the mouse button three times.
Drag (or drag-and-drop)	Point to an object, hold down the mouse, and move the mouse to a new position (dragging the object to the new position). Then release the mouse button (and drop the object in the new position).

The mouse pointer changes appearance depending on where it's located and what you're doing. Table B-2 shows the most common types of pointers.

TABLE B-2 Frequently Used Mouse Pointers

POINTER NAME	POINTER	DESCRIPTION
Pointer	↖	Used to point to objects.
I-beam	I	Used when keying, inserting, and selecting text.
2-headed arrow	↘	Used to change the size of objects or windows.
4-headed arrow	✛	Used to move objects.
Hourglass	⧗	Indicates the computer is processing a command.
Hand	☝	Used in Help to display additional information.

APPENDIX C

Using Menus and Dialog Boxes

Menus

Menus throughout Windows applications use common features. To open a menu, click the menu name. An alternative method for opening a menu is to hold down [Alt] and key the underlined letter in the menu name.

Menus are adaptive—they change as you work, listing the commands you use most frequently. To see *all* the commands on a menu, expand the menu by pointing to the arrows at the bottom of the menu (or wait a few seconds and the open menu expands).

 TIP: If you open a menu by mistake, click the menu name to close it.

FIGURE C-1
Edit menu
from Excel

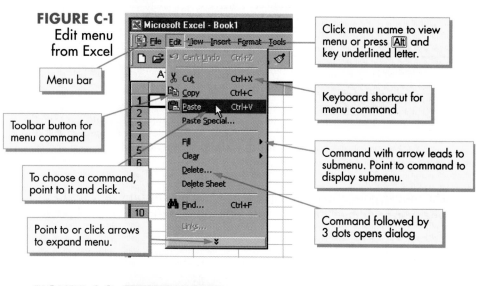

Menu bar

Toolbar button for
menu command

To choose a command,
point to it and click.

Point to or click arrows
to expand menu.

Click menu name to view
menu or press [Alt] and
key underlined letter.

Keyboard shortcut for
menu command

Command with arrow leads to
submenu. Point to command to
display submenu.

Command followed by
3 dots opens dialog

FIGURE C-2
View menu from
Word (expanded)

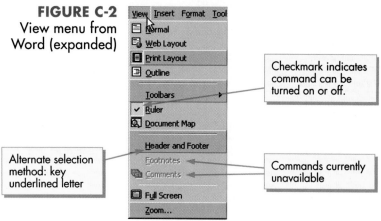

Checkmark indicates
command can be
turned on or off.

Alternate selection
method: key
underlined letter

Commands currently
unavailable

Dialog Boxes

Dialog boxes enable you to view all the current settings for a command, as well as change them. Like menus in Windows, dialog boxes share common features. The following examples show the most frequently seen features.

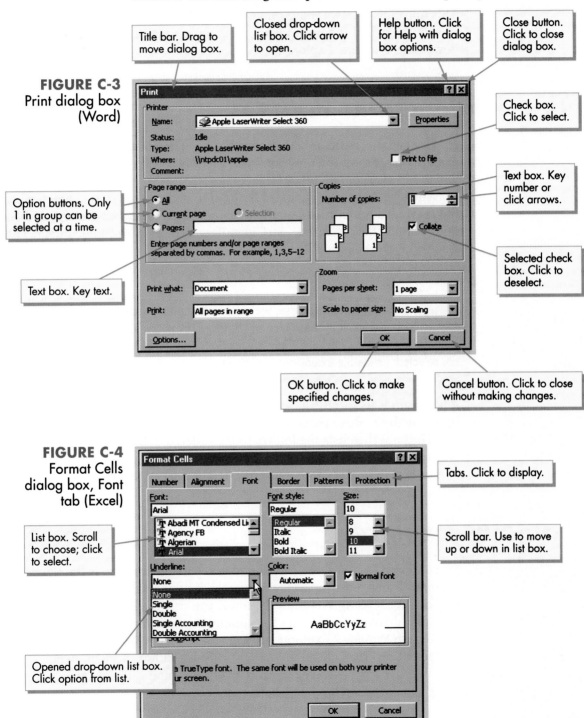

FIGURE C-3
Print dialog box
(Word)

Title bar. Drag to move dialog box.

Closed drop-down list box. Click arrow to open.

Help button. Click for Help with dialog box options.

Close button. Click to close dialog box.

Check box. Click to select.

Option buttons. Only 1 in group can be selected at a time.

Text box. Key number or click arrows.

Text box. Key text.

Selected check box. Click to deselect.

OK button. Click to make specified changes.

Cancel button. Click to close without making changes.

FIGURE C-4
Format Cells
dialog box, Font
tab (Excel)

Tabs. Click to display.

List box. Scroll to choose; click to select.

Scroll bar. Use to move up or down in list box.

Opened drop-down list box. Click option from list.

APPENDIX D

File Management

This Appendix briefly explains how information is stored in Windows. It also introduces one of the most useful tools for managing information in Windows—the Windows Explorer.

Files, Folders, and Paths

In Windows, the basic unit of storage is a *file*. The documents you create and use are files, as are the programs you use. These files are stored in *folders*, which can also contain other folders.

Windows supports filenames that can contain up to 250 characters. A filename also has a three-letter extension, which identifies the type of file. For example, the extension "doc" identifies a file as a Word document. The extension is separated from the filename by a period. For example: "Birthdays.doc."

NOTE: In this course, we assume that your machine displays file extensions. If it doesn't, open Windows Explorer, select Folder Options from the View menu, click the View tab, and make sure that the following option is *not* selected: "Hide file extensions for known file types."

A file's *path* is its specific location on your computer or network. A file's path begins with the drive letter, followed by a colon and a backslash (example: c:\). The path then lists the folders in the order you would open them. Folders are separated by backslashes. The last item in the path is the filename.

For example: c:\My Documents\Letters\Reservations.doc

Windows Explorer

One of the most useful tools in Windows for managing files is the *Windows Explorer*, which gives you a view of your computer's components as a hierarchy, or "tree." Using Windows Explorer, you can easily see the contents of each disk drive and folder on your computer or network.

To open Windows Explorer, click the Start button 🪟 Start with the right mouse button. Then click Explore on the Start button shortcut menu.

Table D-1 describes how to accomplish common file management tasks using Windows Explorer and shortcut menus.

FIGURE D-1
Windows Explorer

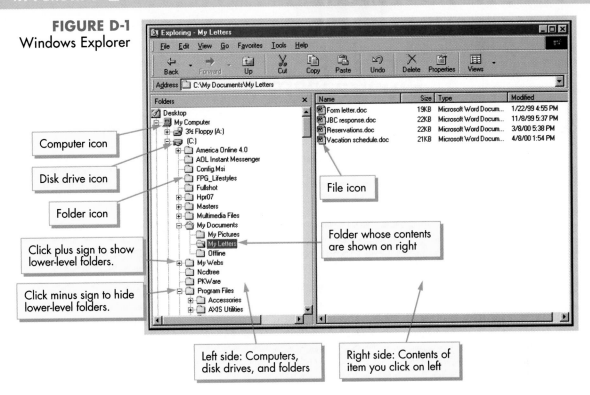

Computer icon

Disk drive icon

Folder icon

Click plus sign to show lower-level folders.

Click minus sign to hide lower-level folders.

File icon

Folder whose contents are shown on right

Left side: Computers, disk drives, and folders

Right side: Contents of item you click on left

TABLE D-1   Common File Management Tasks

TASK	HOW TO DO
Copy file or folder	Right-click file or folder to be copied and click Copy, then right-click folder in which you want to copy file and click Paste. (Alternative: Drag and drop a file from one folder to another.)
Move file or folder	Same method as above, but use Cut and Paste.
Delete a file or folder	Point to icon for file to be deleted and press Delete.
Create a new folder	Choose New from File menu, and then choose Folder. Creates new folder at current position.
Copy file to floppy disk	Point to icon for file to be copied and click right mouse button. Point to Send To and click floppy disk drive in submenu.
Edit/rename file	Point to icon for file you want to rename, press right mouse button, and click Rename.
Open file	Double-click icon for file.
Print file	Point to icon for file to be printed, click right mouse button, and click Print.

APPENDIX E

Proofreaders' Marks

PROOFREADERS' MARK		DRAFT	FINAL COPY
¶	Start a new paragraph	ridiculous! If that is so	ridiculous!
			If that is so
⌣	Delete space	to gether	together
#	Insert space	Itmay be	It may not be
⌒→	Move as shown	it is not true	it is true
∿	Transpose	beleivable	believable
		is it so	it is so
◯	Spell out	2 years ago	two years ago
		16 Elm St	16 Elm Street
∧	Insert a word	How much it?	How much is it?
⌐ OR —	Delete a word	it may not be true	it may be true
∧ OR ⅄	Insert a letter	temperture	temperature
⸖ OR ⸗	Delete a letter and close up	commitiment to buny	commitment to buy
⌐ OR —	Change a word	and if you won't	but if you can't
⋯⋯	Stet (don't delete)	I was very glad	I was very glad
/	Make letter lowercase	Federal Government	federal government
≡	Capitalize	Janet L. greyston	Janet L. Greyston
⌄	Raise above the line	in her new book*	in her new book[*]
∧	Drop below the line	H2SO4	H_2SO_4

PROOFREADERS' MARK		DRAFT	FINAL COPY
⊙	Insert a period	Mr.Henry Grenada	Mr. Henry Grenada
∧	Insert a comma	a large old house	a large, old house
∨	Insert an apostrophe	my childrens car	my children's car
∨	Insert quotation marks	he wants a loan	he wants a "loan"
=	Insert a hyphen	a first rate job	a first-rate job
		ask the coowner	ask the co-owner
—⁄M	Insert an em-dash	Here it is cash!	Here it is—cash!
—⁄N	Insert an en-dash	Pages 1 5	Pages 1–5
___	Insert underscore	an issue of Time	an issue of Time
ital	Set in italic	*ital* The New York Times	*The New York Times*
bf	Set in boldface	*bf* the Enter key	the **Enter** key
rom	Set in roman	*rom* the *most* likely	the most likely .
{ }	Insert parentheses	left today May 3	left today (May 3)
⊐	Move to the right	$38,367,000	$38,367,000
⊏	Move to the left	Anyone can win!	Anyone can win!
ss [	Single-space	*ss* ⌈I have heard ⌊he is leaving	I have heard he is leaving
ds [	Double-space	*ds* ⌈When will you ⌊have a decision?	When will you have a decision?
+1l#—	Insert 1 line space	Percent of Change +1l# 16.25	Percent of Change 16.25
−1l#→	Delete (remove) 1 line space	Northeastern −1l#→ regional sales	Northeastern regional sales

APPENDIX F
MOUS Certification

TABLE F-1 **Level 1 ("Core") MOUS Activities Related to Lessons**

CODE	ACTIVITY	LESSON
XL2000 1	**Working with cells**	
XL2000 1.1	Use Undo and Redo	3
XL2000 1.2	Clear cell content	2
XL2000 1.3	Enter text, dates, and numbers	1, 2
XL2000 1.4	Edit cell content	1, 2
XL2000 1.5	Go to a specific cell	1
XL2000 1.6	Insert and delete selected cells	3
XL2000 1.7	Cut, copy, paste, paste special and move selected cells, use the Office Clipboard	3, 5, 9
XL2000 1.8	Use Find and Replace	7
XL2000 1.9	Clear cell formats	9
XL2000 1.10	Work with series (AutoFill)	5
XL2000 1.11	Create hyperlinks	9
XL2000 2	**Working with files**	
XL2000 2.1	Use Save	1
XL2000 2.2	Use Save As (different name, location, format)	1
XL2000 2.3	Locate and open an existing workbook	1
XL2000 2.4	Create a folder	2
XL2000 2.5	Use templates to create a new workbook	9
XL2000 2.6	Save a worksheet/workbook as a Web Page	1
XL2000 2.7	Send a workbook via email	7
XL2000 2.8	Use the Office Assistant	1
XL2000 3	**Formatting Worksheets**	
XL2000 3.1	Apply font styles (typeface, size, color and styles)	9
XL2000 3.2	Apply number formats (currency, percent, dates, comma)	3, 8
XL2000 3.3	Modify size of rows and columns	8
XL2000 3.4	Modify alignment of cell content	8
XL2000 3.5	Adjust the decimal place	3, 8
XL2000 3.6	Use the Format Painter	3, 8
XL2000 3.7	Apply autoformat	9
XL2000 3.8	Apply cell borders and shading	3, 9
XL2000 3.9	Merging cells	8
XL2000 3.10	Rotate text and change indents	8
XL2000 3.11	Define, apply, and remove a style	9

TABLE F-1   Level 1 ("Core") MOUS Activities *continued*

CODE	ACTIVITY	LESSON
XL2000 4	**Page Setup and Printing**	
XL2000 4.1	Preview and print worksheets & workbooks	1, 4, 13
XL2000 4.2	Use Web Page Preview	1
XL2000 4.3	Print a selection	4
XL2000 4.4	Change page orientation and scaling	4, 13
XL2000 4.5	Set page margins and centering	4, 13
XL2000 4.6	Insert and remove a page break	13
XL2000 4.7	Set print, and clear a print area	4
XL2000 4.8	Set up headers and footers	4, 13
XL2000 4.9	Set print titles and options (gridlines, print quality, row & column headings)	4, 13
XL2000 5	**Working with worksheets & workbooks**	
XL2000 5.1	Insert and delete rows and columns	3
XL2000 5.2	Hide and unhide rows and columns	8
XL2000 5.3	Freeze and unfreeze rows and columns	4
XL2000 5.4	Change the zoom setting	4
XL2000 5.5	Move between worksheets in a workbook	1
XL2000 5.6	Check spelling	7
XL2000 5.7	Rename a worksheet	4
XL2000 5.8	Insert and Delete worksheets	16
XL2000 5.9	Move and copy worksheets	16
XL2000 5.10	Link worksheets & consolidate data using 3D References	17
XL2000 6	**Working with formulas & functions**	
XL2000 6.1	Enter a range within a formula by dragging	2
XL2000 6.2	Enter formulas in a cell and using the formula bar	2
XL2000 6.3	Revise formulas	2
XL2000 6.4	Use references (absolute and relative)	11
XL2000 6.5	Use AutoSum	2
XL2000 6.6	Use Paste Function to insert a function	10
XL2000 6.7	Use basic functions (AVERAGE, SUM, COUNT, MIN, MAX)	2, 10
XL2000 6.8	Enter functions using the formula palette	2, 10, 11
XL2000 6.9	Use date functions (NOW and DATE)	12
XL2000 6.10	Use financial functions (FV and PMT)	12
XL2000 6.11	Use logical functions (IF)	11
XL2000 7	**Using charts and objects**	
XL2000 7.1	Preview and print charts	14
XL2000 7.2	Use chart wizard to create a chart	14
XL2000 7.3	Modify charts	14
XL2000 7.4	Insert, move, and delete an object (picture)	15
XL2000 7.5	Create and modify lines and objects	15

TABLE F-2   Level 2 ("Expert") MOUS Activities* Related to Lessons

*Only selected Level 2 ("Expert") Activities covering common Office activities are included in this text.

CODE	ACTIVITY	LESSON
XL2000 E.6.1	Add and delete a named range	6
XL2000 E.6.2	Use a named range in a formula	6
XL2000 E.6.3	Use Lookup Functions (Hlookup and Vlookup)	11
XL2000 E. 7.1	Hide and display toolbars	5
XL2000 E.7.2	Customize toolbar	5
XL2000 E.10.9	Use data validation	4
XL2000 E.12.2	Apply and remove worksheet and workbook protection	4

TABLE F-3

Lessons Related to MOUS Activities

LESSON	CODES*
1 What Is Excel?	XL2000 1.5, 2.1, 2.2, 2.3, 2.6, 2.8, 4.1, 4.2, 5.5
2 Creating a Simple Worksheet	XL2000 1.2, 1.3, 1.4, 2.4, 6.1, 6.2, 6.3, 6.5, 6.7, 6.8
3 Enhancing a Simple Worksheet	XL2000 1.1, 1.3, 1.4, 1.6, 1.7, 3.2, 3.5, 3.6, 3.8, 5.1
4 Designing and Printing a Worksheet	XL2000 4.1, 4.3, 4.4, 4.5, 4.7, 4.8, 4.9, 5.3, 5.4, 5.7, E.10.9, E.12.2
5 Copying Data and Using Toolbars	XL2000 1.7, 1.10, E.7.1, E.7.2
6 Naming Ranges and Sorting	XL2000 E.6.1, E.6.2
7 Spelling, Find/Replace, and File Management	XL2000 1.8, 2.7, 5.6
8 Formatting Text and Numbers	XL2000 3.2, 3.3, 3.4, 3.5, 3.6, 3.9, 3.10, 5.2
9 Changing Fonts, Patterns, Colors, and Formats	XL2000 1.7, 1.9, 1.11, 2.5, 3.1, 3.7, 3.8, 3.11
10 Using Functions	XL2000 6.6, 6.7, 6.8
11 Advanced Formulas	XL2000 6.4, 6.8, 6.11, E.6.3
12 Working with Dates, Times, and Financial Functions	XL2000 6.9, 6.10
13 Advanced Printing	XL2000 4.1, 4.4, 4.5, 4.6, 4.8, 4.9
14 Creating Charts and Maps	XL2000 7.1, 7.2, 7.3
15 Enhancing Charts and Worksheets	XL2000 7.4, 7.5
16 Working with Multiple Worksheets	XL2000 5.8, 5.9
17 Linking and Consolidating Worksheets	XL2000 5.10

*MOUS Activity codes are abbreviated in this table.

Glossary

Active cell Cell that is current and ready to receive information. (1)

Block Group of adjacent cells (that is, cells that are next to one other). (2)

Category axis Horizontal (or x) axis along the bottom of most charts; it frequently refers to time series. (14)

Cell address Location of a cell in a worksheet. A cell address is indicated by its column letter and row number. (1)

Cell Rectangle formed by the intersection of a row and a column. Cells can contain text, numeric values, or formulas. (1)

Character string Sequence of characters in a formula or text. (7)

Clip art Ready-to-use, non-photographic, graphic images that can be imported into a worksheet or chart. (15)

Clipboard Temporary storage in the computer's memory. (3)

Consolidation table Table that summarizes the data from one or more source ranges. (17)

Consolidation worksheet Worksheet that contains a consolidation table. (17)

Constants Unchanging values used in formulas. (6)

Cut To remove cells or data in cells and placing it on the Clipboard. (3)

Data marker Object that represents individual data points. It can be a bar, area, dot, picture, or other symbol that marks a single data point or value. (14)

Data point Single piece of data on a chart. (14)

Data series Collection of data points that are related; these are usually found in the same column or row in the worksheet. (14)

Dependent worksheet Worksheet that uses data from another worksheet. (17)

Docked toolbar Toolbar that appears in a fixed position outside the work area. (5)

Dynamic link Formula reference to a different worksheet that is automatically updated when data changes. (17)

Embedded chart Chart that is part of a worksheet. (14)

External reference Reference to a cell, cell range, or defined name in another workbook. (17)

Fill handle Small box in the lower right corner of an active cell. (5)

Floating toolbar Toolbar positioned over the work area. (5)

Footer Repetitive information about a worksheet that is printed across the bottom of the page. (13)

Formulas Instructions that tell Excel how to perform calculations. (2)

Header Repetitive information about a worksheet that is printed across the top of the page. (13)

Hypertext Markup Language (HTML) File format that allows file content to be opened, viewed, edited, and printed using browser software. (1)

Internal reference Reference to a cell, cell range, or defined name in another worksheet within the same workbook. (17)

Label Text that can include any character, and cannot be included in calculations. (2)

Landscape page orientation Horizontal page orientation (11 inches by 8½ inches). (4)

Legend Guide that explains the symbols, patterns, or colors used to differentiate data series. (14)

Order of precedence Preset order in which mathematical operations in a formula are performed. (2)

Page orientation Print setting that is either 8½ inches by 11 inches (vertical page orientation, also called portrait page orientation) or 11 inches by 8½ inches (horizontal page orientation, also called landscape orientation). (4)

Panes Portions of worksheets. Panes allow you to see row and column labels as you enter data or formulas. (4)

Paste To move cells or data in cells from the Clipboard to a selected area on a worksheet. (3)

Places bar Vertical bar in the Open, Save, and Save As dialog box that contains recent or commonly used folders for easy access. (1)

Plot area Rectangular area bounded by the two axes; it includes all axes and data points. (14)

Portrait page orientation Vertical page orientation (8½ inches by 11 inches). (4)

Print area Specific range of cells you want to print. (4)

Range name Name you give a range of cells. A range name can also be given to a single cell. (6)

Range Any group of cells specified to be acted upon by a command. (2)

Relative cell reference Cell reference in a formula that adjusts to a new position when you copy it. (5)

Scaling Enlarging or reducing the view of a worksheet's contents. (13)

ScreenTip Text that identifies elements on the screen. ScreenTips are available for dialog boxes, menu commands, and button names. (1)

Selection handles Small black squares appearing around a selected object that are used to resize the object. (14)

Source range Area of the worksheet from which you copy or remove data. (5)

Source worksheet Worksheet that contains the data being used by another (dependent) worksheet. (17)

Split bar Bar that splits the screen into panes. (4)

Split boxes Gray rectangular boxes that appear in the upper right corner of the document window above the vertical scroll arrow and at the far right of the horizontal scroll bar at the bottom of the document window. Split boxes allow you to split worksheets into multiple panes. (4)

Target range New location for data that you copy or move. (5)

Test data Easy-to-calculate numbers that you enter in a worksheet to test formulas. (4)

Tick mark Division mark along the category (x) and value (y) axes. (14)

Value axis Vertical (or y) axis against which data points are measured. (14)

Value Entry that begins with a number or mathematical sign, and can be included in a calculation. (2)

Wildcard Symbol that stands for one or more letters or numbers. (7)

Workbook Excel worksheet, or group of worksheets, saved as a file. (1)

Worksheet Area in which text, numeric values, and formulas are entered. Worksheets contain a series of rows and columns. Worksheets are collected into workbooks, which can contain up to 255 worksheets. (1)

Zoom Option that changes the magnification of the display. (4)

Index

D

Photo Credits

Page 2, PhotoDisc, Inc.; Pages 5 and 9, Telegraph Color
Library/FPG; Pages 6 and 241, Buss/FPG; Pages 7 and 415,
Weber/FPG; Pages 7 and 485, Laird/FPG.